COLLEGE BOTANY

[Vol. III]

COLLEGE BOTANY

[Vol. III]

Susil Kumar Mukherjee MSc, PhD
Keeper (Retd), Central National Herbarium, BSI

New Central Book Agency (P) Ltd

Co-Published by

Bijay Publications

E-mail : bijaypublications@gmail.com

Exclusively Distributed by

Bijay Pustak Bhandar (P) Ltd

90/6A M. G. Road, Bhawani Dutta Lane, Kolkata-700007

✆ : (033) 4605-7856, 8777898576, 8274916104

E-mail : bijaypustakbhandar@gmail.com

NCBA

REGD OFFICE
8/1 Chintamoni Das Lane, Kolkata 700 009, India
email: ncbakolkata@gmail.com

OVERSEAS
NCBA (UK) Ltd, 149 Park Avenue North, Northampton, NN3 2HY, UK
email: ncbauk@yahoo.com

CORPORATE OFFICE
212 Shahpur Jat, New Delhi 110 049
email: ncbaexports@ncbapvtltd.com

BIJAY PUBLICATIONS
90/6A M. G. Road, Bhawani Dutta Lane, Kolkata-7
E-mail : bijaypublications@gmail.com

BIJAY PUSTAK BHANDAR (P) LTD
90/6A M. G. Road, Bhawani Dutta Lane, Kolkata-7
E-mail : bijaypustakbhandar@gmail.com

COLLEGE BOTANY [Vol. III] • Susil Kumar Mukherjee

First Published: 1984
Second Edition: 1990
Third Edition: 1994
Reprinted: 1997, 2000, 2004, 2006, 2010, 2012, 2015, 2016, 2023

PUBLISHER • TYPESETTER • PRINTER
New Central Book Agency (P) Ltd
8/1 Chintamoni Das Lane, Kolkata 700 009

CO-PUBLISHED BY
Bijay Publications
90/6A M G Road, Bhawani Dutta Lane, Kolkata 700007

PHOTOGRAPH
Dr S K Bhattacharyya

DIAGRAMS
Biren Das

ISBN: 978 81 7381 308 5

Price ₹ 565.00

To

Aparajita

my beloved

grand-daughter

and pupil

PREFACE TO THE FIRST EDITION

It took a long time for the 3rd volume of College Botany to see the light of the day, the 2nd volume of the book having been out in 1968. The reason was the ill-health of Prof. K. S. Das* who was to write the present volume. The idea of writing a complete text book on Botany for Indian students occurred to him and in fact it is he who chalked out a thorough and detailed plan of the whole series, particularly of volume I and approached two of our most illustrious predecessors,—Late Prof. G. P. Majumdar and Prof. I. Banerjee for their valued opinion. Their approval and kind encouragement inspired him to invite Prof. H. C. Gangulee and Prof. C. T. Dutta to join him in writing the first volume, and the joint efforts of these three experts resulted in the production of a superb treatise which created a sensation all over India, by lucidly giving the fundamental knowledge of botanical science to the students as well as to the teachers.

The 2nd volume was left to the care of Prof. Gangulee who invited Prof. A. K. Kar to join him as co-author. These two botanists of international fame spared no pains to perform the task to the entire satisfaction of all concerned and the 2nd volume of College Botany fulfilled the requirements of the students in a perfect manner.

The writer of the present volume, that completes the series 'College Botany' was eagerly waiting to see this part prepared under the authorship of Prof. K. S. Das but serious illness prevented him from taking up the work. It was arranged therefore that this volume would also be compiled jointly. That too was not possible, and the present writer did the work bit by bit. This is also a factor that delayed the production of this volume. If the students find this book useful the writer will consider himself amply rewarded.

I express my thanks to my friends Prof. K. S. Das, Prof. H. C. Gangulee and the publisher Sri J. N. Sen for encouragement, guidance and help. I am really grateful to Prof. Das for the text figures most of which were prepared from actual specimens under his supervision. My thanks are also due to Prof. S. Sen, Department of Botany, University of Calcutta, Dr. S. Chanda, Palynologist, Bose Research Institute, Calcutta, and Dr. Krishna Mitra, Palynologist, Botanical Survey of India for their help in various ways. I am also grateful to the Director, Botanical Survey of India and his staff and particularly to Sree A. R. Das for permitting me to consult the library.

New Year's Day, 1984 } AUTHOR

**Prof. K. S. Das passed away on* 3-9-83.

PREFACE TO THE SECOND EDITION

The third volume of College Botany being out of print for some time it is felt that a new edition should be published to incorporate the results of some recent researches. Accordingly, a new part has been added to this volume where the subject of Tissue Culture has been dealt with. This portion has kindly been prepared for this book by Sm. Suhita Guha, Reader in Botany, Sivanath Sastri College, Calcutta, to whom my thanks are due.

In Economic Botany 'Rubber' an important industrial product has been included. 'Santonica' the sontonin yielding plants and the 'Myrobalans' have been added to Pharmacognosy part.

Prof. Cronquist has revised his System of Classification of Angiosperms and a gist of this revised system has been incorporated in the taxonomy portion of this revised volume. A few more families have been described and up-to-date information have been supplied wherever necessary.

It is hoped that this revised volume will be useful to the teachers and students alike.

S.K.M.

CONTENTS

PART I

ANGIOSPERMS

CHAPTER I Aims and Principles of Taxonomy: Taxonomical Rank. 3—4

„ II Angiospermic Plant; Embryology in taxonomy; Palynology in taxonomy; Preparation of pollen-slide. 5—10

„ III Plant Kingdom and Origin of Angiosperm; Kingdom Plantae. 11—16

„ IV Early History and Development of Plant Taxonomy; Classification of plants; Linnaean system; Natural systems; Phylogenetic system; Sero-diagnostic system; Primitive and advance characters in Angiosperms. 17—36

„ V Herbarium; Preservation of specimens in solution; Collection of plant specimens; Preparation of herbarium sheets; Botanic Garden; Botanic Gardens in India; Botanical Survey of India; Nomenclature of Plants and History of International Botanical Congress; Rules of Nomenclature. 37—51

PART II

FAMILIES OF ANGIOSPERMS

CHAPTER VI 55—117

Monocotyledonae :

Pandanales—Typhaceae, Sparganiaceae, Pandanaceae.
Helobieae—Potamogetonaceae, Najadaceae, Alismaceae Butomaceae, Hydrocharitaceae.
Glumiflorae—Gramineae, (Poaceae), Cyperaceae.
Principes—Palmae (Aricaceae).
Spathiflorae—Araceae, Lemnaceae.
Farinosae—Commelinaceae, Eriocaulaceae, Pontederiaceae, Bromeliaceae.
Liliflorae—Juncaceae, Liliaceae, Amaryllidaceae, Iridiaceae.
Scitaminae—Musaceae, Zingiberaceae, Cannaceae, Marantaceae.
Microspermae—Burmanniaceae, Orchidaceae.

CHAPTER VII 118—278

Dicotyledonae: Archichlamydeae:

Verticillatae—Casuarinaceae.
Piperales—Piperaceae, Chloranthaceae, Saururaceae.
Salicales—Salicaceae.
Juglandales—Juglandaceae.
Fagales—Fagaceae, Betulaceae.
Urticales—Ulmaceae, Moraceae, Cannabaceae, Urticaceae.
Podostemonales—Podostemaceae.
Santalales—Santalaceae, Loranthaceae, Balanophoraceae.
Aristolochiales—Aristolochiaceae, Rafflesiaceae, Hydnoraceae.
Poligonales—Polygonaceae.

Centrospermae—Chenopodiaceae, Amaranthaceae, Nyctaginaceae, Phytolaceaceae, Aizoaceae, Portulaccaceae, Basellaceae, Caryophyllaceae.
Ranales—Nymphaeaceae, Ceratophyllaceae, Berberidaceae, Ranunculaceae, Menispermaceae, Magnoliaceae, Annonaceae, Myristicaceae, Lauraceae,
Rhoedales—Papaveraceae, Capparidaceae, Cruciferae (Apiaceae), Moringaceae.
Sarraceniales—Sarraceniaceae, Nepenthaceae, Droceraceae.
Rosales—Crassulaceae, Cephalotaceae, Saxifragaceae, Hamamelidaceae, Platanaceae, Rosaceae, Leguminosae.
Geraniales—Geraniaceae, Oxalidaceae, Tropaeolaceae, Balsaminaceae, Linaceae, Zygophyllaceae, Rutaceae, Simarubaceae, Burseraceae, Meliaceae, Malpighiaceae, Polygalaceae, Euphorbiaceae, Buxaceae.
Sapindales—Aquifoliaceae, Celastraceae, Anacardiaceae, Sapindaceae, Aceraceae, Hippocastanaceae.
Rhamnales—Rhamnaceae, Vitaceae.
Malvales—Tiliaceae, Elaeocarpaceae, Sterculiaceae, Malvaceae, Bombacaceae.
Parietales—Dilleniaceae, Ochnaceae, Theaceae, Guttiferae (Clusiaceae), Dipterocarpaceae, Tamaricaceae, Bixaceae, Violaceae, Flacourtiaceae, Passifloraceae, Caricaceae, Begoniaceae.
Opuntiales—Cactaceae.
Myrtiflarae—Lythraceae, Punicaceae, Rhizophoraceae, Combretaceae, Myrtaceae, Lecythidaceae, Melastomaceae, Hydrocaryaceae (Trapaceae), Onagraceae,
Umbelliflorae—Araliaceae, Umbelliferae (Apiaceae).

Chapter VIII 279—341

Dicotyledonae : Metachlamydeae:
Diapensiales.
Ericales—Ericaceae.
Primulales—Myrsinaceae, Primulaceae.
Plumbaginales—Plumbaginaceae.
Ebenales—Sapotaceae, Ebenaceae.
Contortae—Oleaceae, Loganiaceae, Buddlejaceae, Gentianaceae, Menyanthaceae, Apocynaceae, Asclepiadaceae.
Tubiflorae—Convolvulaceae, Boraginaceae, Verbenaceae, Labiatae (Lamiaceae), Solanaceae, Scrophulariaceae, Bignoniaceae, Orobanchaceae, Lentibulariaceae, Acanthaceae.
Rubiales—Rubiaceae, Caprifoliaceae, Valerianaceae.
Cucurbitales—Cucurbitaceae.
Campanulatae—Campanulaceae, Compositae (Asteraceae).

PART III

PHYTOGEOGRAPHY

Chapter IX Phytogeography: The Cradle of primitive Angiosperms; Migration of plants; Major Phytochoria or Phytogeographic divisions of the world's flora; Phytogeographic divisions of India; Vegetation of India; Composition of Indian flora. 345—365

PATR IV

ECONOMIC BOTANY & PHARMACOGNOSY

CHAPTER X. Useful Plants: Cereals; Fruits; Sugar yielding plants; Pulses; Fibre plants; Oil yielding plants; Beverages; Timber trees; Medicinal plants; Rubber. 369—407

" Pharmacognosy: Aims and objects; Collection and Preparation of Drugs; Organoleptic studies; Ginger; Chirata; Rauvolfia; Vasak or Adhatoda; Dita bark; Ipecac; Santonica; Myrobalan. 409—422

PART V

TISSUE CULTURE

CHAPTER PAGE

I. INTRODUCTION 425

Definition, history of tissue culture, importance of tissue culture.

II. CONDITIONS REQUIRED FOR PLANT TISSUE CULTURE 431

Aseptic conditions, aeration, equipments, nutrient medium.

III. SOME METHODS OF PLANT TISSUE CULTURE 441

IV. ROOT CULTURE 444

Previous works, methods, culture of roots of legumes, nature of cultured roots, significance.

V. SHOOT TIP CULTURE AND LEAF CULTURE 446

Shoot tip culture (early works, method, significance); culture of leaves.

VI. CULTURE OF FLOWER, OVARY, OVULE, ETC. 450

Flower culture, ovary culture, ovule culture, seed culture, nucellus culture.

VII. EMBRYO CULTURE 454

Early works, methods, factors influencing embryo culture, regeneration potentialities of different parts of an embryo, culture of embryos of root and stem parasites in absence of hosts, significance of embryo culture.

VIII. ANTHER AND POLLEN CULTURE 458

Early works, medium, factors influencing anther and pollen culture, method of anther culture, method of pollen culture, nurse culture technique, ploidy level of pollen plants, production of homozygous diploids, significance.

IX. CALLUS CULTURE 464

Early works, nutrient medium, method, carrot root culture, development of callus, nature of callus tissue, significance of callus culture.

X. ORGANOGENESIS 468

Definition, early works, factors influencing organogenesis, plantlet formation from tomato leaves.

XI. SOMATIC EMBRYOGENESIS 470

Early works, factors influencing somatic embryogenesis, methods, significance.

XII. CELL SUSPENSION CULTURE 472

Early works, method, cell suspension culture of carrot, etc.

XIII. SINGLE CELL CLONE 475

Early works, methods, significance.

XIV. ISOLATION OF PROTOPLASTS AND PROTOPLAST CULTURE 477

Early works, methods, isolation of protoplasts from leaves, isolation of protoplasts from pollen grains, protoplast culture, significance.

XV. PROTOPLAST FUSION AND SOMATIC HYBRIDIZATION 481

Early works, methods, isolation of hybrids, significance.

XVI. PLANT TUMOURS AND VIRUS ERADICATION 485

INDEX I

PART I

Angiosperms

CHAPTER I

AIMS AND PRINCIPLES OF TAXONOMY: TAXONOMICAL RANK

A *taxon* is a biological group of any rank. *Taxonomy* is, therefore, the study of grouping or classification. It provides evidences by use of which a system of classification is worked out.

Systematics is a wider term comprising identification of an individual organism, assigning a proper rank to the same and giving it a name. However, taxonomy and systematics are considered by many to denote the same thing and the terms are treated as synonymous.

The aim of taxonomy, therefore, is (a) to classify the plant Kingdom and (b) to identify and name a plant and fix its rank in a recognised system of classification. This is done by using almost entirely the external morphological characters, i.e., gross morphology. Such taxonomy is called "classical" or "orthodox" or "alpha" taxonomy to distinguish it from "experimental" taxonomy where cytological or embryological evidences are also taken into consideration. The latter is also known as "omega" taxonomy or "biosystematics" and concerns chromosome morphology, chromosome number, breeding behaviour and barriers.

Recent trend in taxonomy is to recognise character combination for taxonomical grouping. Here mathematical techniques are applied to assess similarity and disparity through diagrams and using mathematical coefficients. This is called "numerical" taxonomy.

To make use of the results of chemical analysis or tests of plant-parts and products in study of taxonomy is called *Chemotaxonomy*. This involves a study of the starch grains and raphides, study of plant-products, e.g. alkaloids, resins, etc. and serological tests.

Chemical characters, however, should not be regarded as more important than other characters. They are often affected by environmental factors such as temperature, mineral deficiencies, etc. It is possible that chemical and morphological features may have followed different evolutionary pathways. Comparative chemistry and serology are aids to establishing consanguinity, not phylogeny proper, which involves the tracing of phyletic lines back into the past.

"Many different types of information can be and should be woven into classificatory scheme and there is no obvious advantage in attaching overriding importance to any one type."

Basic unit of classification is the *species*. Each species has a combination of characters peculiar to its own. Therefore species is a group of plants having a combination of characters common to each individual in that group. Such characters are morphological, cytological, embryological, etc. Further the plants belonging to a particular species are capable of free interbreeding, and carry and express one or more gene pools.

A *genus* is a natural group of closely related species. When a species is more or less isolated the genus may often be monotypic, i.e., consisting of a single species only. Similarly a *family* is a natural group of closely related genera. Closely related families are grouped into an *order*, orders into a *class* and classes into a *division*, while the divisions are grouped under a *kingdom*. Intermediate subgroups are also recognised and intra specific categories are also known.

The International Code of Botanical Nomenclature provides a list of the groups of different ranks in the following sequence:

Plant Kingdom
Division
Class
Subclass
Order
Suborder
Family
Subfamily
Tribe
Subtribe
Genus
Subgenus
Section
Subsection
Series
Subseries
Species
Subspecies
Variety
Subvariety
Form
Subform.

In modern systems of classification of plants the above sequence is maintained.

As mentioned before, species is the basic unit of classification. Therefore, a plant must belong to a species which must be under a genus. A genus again must belong to a family, a family to an order, an order, to a class and a class to a division of the plant-kingdom. The intermediate groups may or may not exist. For instance, the family Ceratophyllaceae is not subdivided into subfamilies, tribes or subtribes as Ceratophyllum is the only genus in that family.

CHAPTER II

ANGIOSPERMIC PLANT

The seed of an angiospermic plant consists of an embryo covered by the seed-coat. The embryo has one or two cotyledons and the tigellum. One end of the tigellum is the radicle and the other end is the plumule. On germination* the radicle penetrates the soil and produces the roots, while the plumule develops into the shoot of the plant body. The shoot gradually manifests itself into the stem and branches which bear the leaves and flowers (Fig. 1). The leaves are nothing but appendages of the stem and are regarded as the lateral expansions of the stem or branches of the stem. The flowers are reproductive organs and each flower is considered to be a modified condensed branch of the stem.

The central core of the stem-root axis is called "stele" which consists of the vascular tissues and the ground tissue. The vascular tissues are composed of conducting strands called vascular bundles. A vascular bundle is again composed of xylem and phloem. In higher plants the vascular bundles form a skeleton in the plant body that differs from its plan and arrangement in different species.

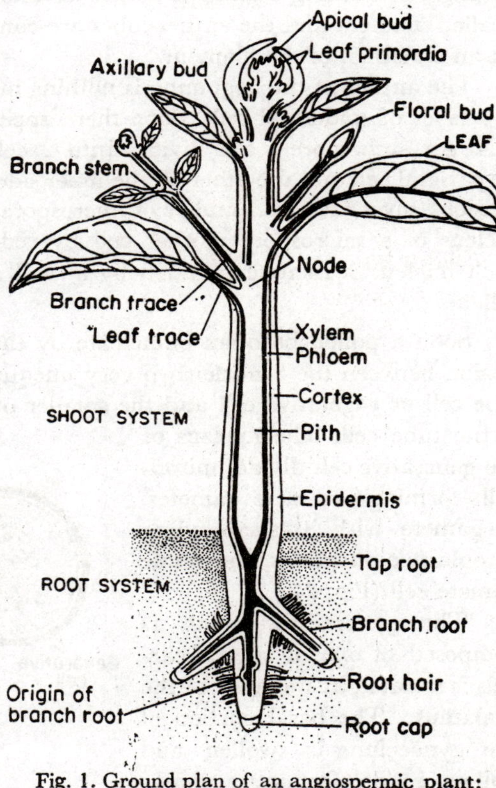

Fig. 1. Ground plan of an angiospermic plant: root, shoot, branch, leaves and buds.

The older axis is the "Mesome" which branches dichotomously, and each terminal portion of the dichotomously branching mesome is called "Telome" (cf. Telome theory in Vol. 2 of College Botany, pp. 960-962). The mesome gives rise to groups of telomes or telome-trusses. These telome-trusses or branches are in the same plane and by development of connecting tissues they fuse to form a flat structure which is the megaphyll or a leaf.

According to the Phytonic theory a shoot is made up of a series of units called "Phytons", and the growth is continued by renewed terminal budding. In the leaf-skin theory of Saunders on the other hand the shoot or the stem is regarded as composed of leaf-bases or extensions of leaf-bases. The shoot, however, is now generally regarded as one of the two basic parts of the plant, the other being the root. The leaves are regarded as ultimate parts of the shoot. There are 2 traces and one lacuna in a primitive type of node while the branches of the stem also have 2 traces and one gap. That the leaf is, like the branch, a part of the shoot is quite clear.

*For detailed morphological description of the seed and the mode of germination, see Vol. 1 of College Botany.

Flower is a specialised structure bearing the reproductive organs or the sporophylls. Flowers may be borne in the axils of leaves or may be terminal on the branches or the main axis of the shoot. A typical flower consists of the following parts:—(1) Thalamus or the axis of flower, (2) Calyx of united or free sepals, (3) Corolla of united or free petals, (4) Androecium of stamens, and (5) Gynoecium or Pistil of carpels. The stamens are nothing but micro-sporophylls and carpels are mega-sporophylls. The stamens and carpels are the reproductive organs, and are, therefore, the essential parts of a flower. A fertile stamen consists of an anther which is 2-lobed. Each anther-lobe usually has 2 pollen-sacs or pollen-chambers which are the micro-sporangia containing numerous pollens or microspores in each. The stalk of the anther is called filament and the anther-lobes are connected by a connective which is nothing but an extension of the filament.

The anther at the beginning is nothing but a mass of meristematic cells surrounded by a layer of epidermal cells. Soon there appear four longitudinal rows of archesporeal cells. An archesporeal cell divides into 2 cells of which one towards the epidermis is the parietal cell and the other on the inner side is the sporogenous cell. This, after several divisions, gives rise to a number of microspore mother cells or pollen mother cells. The nucleus of a microspore mother cell by reduction division forms 4 haploid nuclei. Each nucleus is then surrounded by a wall and is transformed into a microspore or pollen.

Soon a pollen becomes binucleate by the splitting of the nucleus. By a wall formation between the 2 nuclei two very unequal cells are formed. The larger one is the tube cell or vegetative cell and the smaller one is the generative cell that floats freely in the tube cell. The nucleus of the generative cell divides mitotically forming two male gametes. A gamete with its surrounding cytoplasmic sheath is the male gamete cell (Fig. 2).

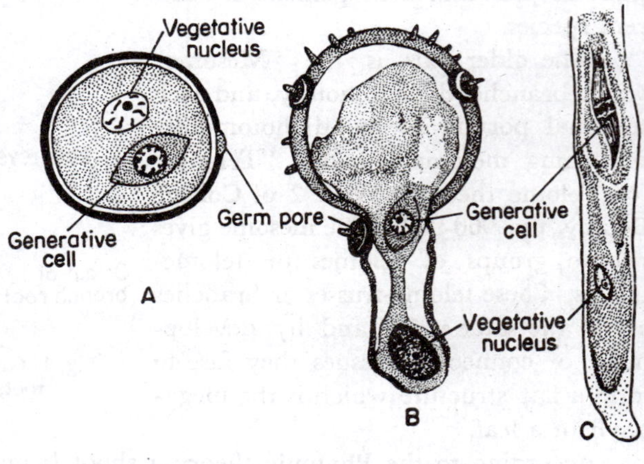

Fig. 2. Development of male gametes: A—binucleate stage; B—pollen-tube coming out through a germ-pore carrying the vegetative or tube nucleus followed by the generative cell; C—division of the generative cell within the pollen-tube to form two male gametes.

The gynoecium which is composed of one or several carpels is situated at the apex of the thalamus. The basal portion of the gynoecium is swollen and hollow inside, forming a chamber. This portion is called the ovary. The portion above the ovary is like a narrow tube and is known as the style, which is terminated by short receptive portion called the stigma where the pollens are deposited during pollination. The ovary contains the ovules, situated on a special tissue called placenta on the inner wall of the ovary or on the central axis or on the carpellary suture.

The ovule consists of 2 basic parts, viz., the nucellus, which is nothing but the megasporangium and the integuments or the 2 protective coverings. A small opening at the top of the integuments is called micropyle and the base of the nucellus is called chalaza. The ovule usually has a stalk by which it is attached to the placenta and this is known as the funicle, and the portion of attachment of the funicle with the ovule is called hilum. The megaspore mother-cell develops within the nucellus and gives rise to 4 haploid megaspore cells of which the lowermost becomes the functional megaspore and the other 3 degenerate. The functional megaspore develops into the female gametophyte or the embryo sac.

The functional megaspore or the embryo sac nucleus splits into two, which split again into four and finally the four into eight, three going to each pole and two remaining at the centre. The central pair fuse and form the fusion- or secondary-nucleus. The three nuclei at the top form the egg-apparatus consisting of 2 synergids and an egg-cell, also called ovum or oosphere. The remaining three at the base form the antipodal cells. The gametophyte formation, however, shows much more variation than the normal type described here.*

Of the 2 integuments the outer one is of cupular origin, i.e., a remnant of the cupule of the seed-ferns. The inner integument is formed according to Margaret Benson's hypothesis (1904) by the fusion of sterile megasporangia of a synangium in which only one remains fertile and that one is the ovule (Fig. 3).

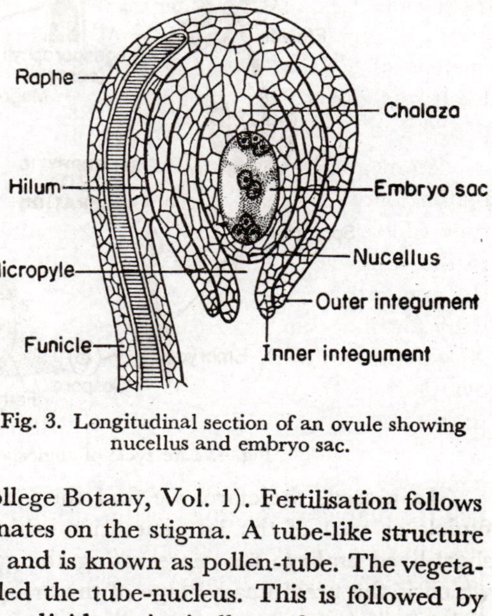

Fig. 3. Longitudinal section of an ovule showing nucellus and embryo sac.

A flower complete with androecium and gynoecium is a bisexual flower and that with only one of these two essential parts present is a unisexual flower. The basic type of angiosperm-flower is bisexual and the unisexual flowers have arisen as a result of reduction of either the androecium or gynoecium and this is evident from the presence of vestigial organs or rudiments in many unisexual flowers.

The transfer of pollens from the anther to the stigma is called pollination. The transfer is effected in various ways (cf. College Botany, Vol. 1). Fertilisation follows pollination. After pollination a pollen germinates on the stigma. A tube-like structure projects through the germ-pore of the pollen and is known as pollen-tube. The vegetative nucleus enters the tube and is now called the tube-nucleus. This is followed by the generative cell. The generative cell now divides mitotically to form two male gametes while the tube nucleus ultimately disappears. The pollen tube passes through the style to the ovule and through the micropyle to the nucellus and penetrates the embryo sac. The tip of the pollen tube dissolves and the 2 gametes are set free. One of them fuses with the egg-cell of the egg apparatus and fertilises the same. The other gamete fuses with the secondary nucleus thus causing the double fertilisation. As a result of fertilisation the oosphere or egg-cell is transformed into oospore which is a diploid cell and the secondary nucleus which is formed by the fusion of 2 haploid nuclei is changed to a triploid nucleus after being fertilised by the second male gamete. The oospore forms the embryo and the fertilised fusion nucleus after free nuclear division and cell wall formation produces the endosperm. The antipodal cells in the

* For a detailed account of the development of female gametophyte see College Botany, Vol. 1.

mean time disappear. The ovule is transformed into a seed after the full development of the embryo and formation of the endosperm.

Thus the life cycle of an angiosperm from the germination of a seed giving rise to a plant that ultimately produces fruit and seed, passes through sporophyte to gametophyte and gametophyte to sporophyte. The plant body which bears the numerous pollens or microspores lodged in the anther of stamens or microsporophylls and four megaspores within the nucellus of the ovule borne on the carpel or megasporophyll is the diploid sporophyte (Fig. 4). The pollens which carry the 2 male gametes and the embryo sac which contains the oosphere are the haploid gametophytes. The embryo formed after fertilisation is diploid and forms a part of the next sporophytic generation.

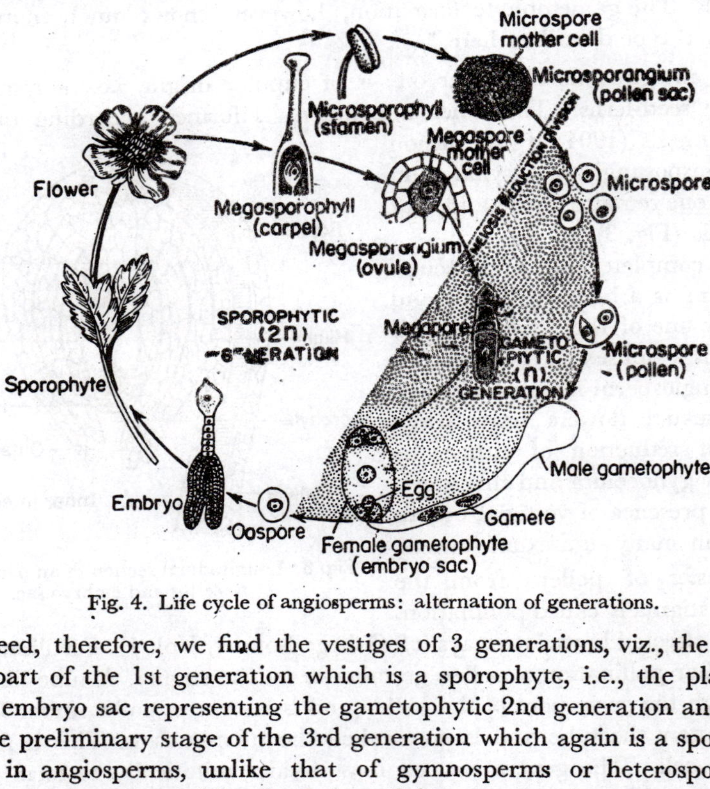

Fig. 4. Life cycle of angiosperms: alternation of generations.

In a seed, therefore, we find the vestiges of 3 generations, viz., the seed coat and funicle as part of the 1st generation which is a sporophyte, i.e., the plant body, the short-lived embryo sac representing the gametophytic 2nd generation and the embryo which is the preliminary stage of the 3rd generation which again is a sporophyte. The endosperm in angiosperms, unlike that of gymnosperms or heterosporous pteridophytes, is a new tissue formed by the fusion of the second male gamete with the secondary nucleus which again is a result of fusion of two of the eight nuclei derived from the embryo sac nucleus. Endosperm cells are, therefore, triploid in nature.

Embryology in taxonomy

Embryology is the study of the process of formation of embryo in a fertilised ovule, i.e., the study of the changes taking place in an ovule before and after the fertilisation. In other words, it is the study of (a) micro- and macro-sporogenesis in the diploid generation, (b) micro- and mega-gametophytes in the haploid generation and (c) the embryo and endosperm in the new sporophyte. As a result of such study different types of embryosac development have been noticed among the angiospermic groups, e.g., Asterad, Onagrad, Chenopodiad, Solanad, Caryophyllad and Piperad types. Some consider that such a grouping has great taxonomical significance while others are of opinion that the phylogenetic relationship apparent from the embryological studies are, however, not convincing.

Palynology in taxonomy

Study of the pollen morphology has proved of great value in the field of taxonomy. The discovery of Electron scanning and transmission microscopy, besides light microscopy, help in revealing ultra structure of the pollen grains and spores.

Pollen grains may be simple (eumonad) or composite, e.g. dyad, tetrad, polyad, etc. They may be symmetrical, i.e., bilateral or radial, or asymmetric. The shape varies from spheroidal to oval, rhomboidal, rectangular in meridional view and circular to semi-angular, angular or lobate in polar view. They may further be distinguished as apolar, polar or heteropolar. The size of pollen grains varies from 8-10 μm to 350 μm. in angiosperms.

Palynological studies are based on the detailed and critical study of (a) aperture- and (b) sporoderm-morphology. Pollen grains may be without aperture, i.e., omniaperturate, or they may be mono-, di-, tri-, tetra- or panto-(poly) aperturate. Aperture serves as weak region for pollen tube emergence or harmomegatic function. Aperture may be simple-colpate or porate, or composite-colporate or pororate. They may be proximal (as in spores of Cryptogams), distal (as in pollens of Gymnosperms and Monocotyledons) or equatorial and global which are also called ana, cata, zono or panto.

Simple apertures are present on the outer layer of exine, viz., sexine or ektexine. Composite apertures are present both on external layer of exine, i.e., sexine or ektexine and also internal layer, i.e., nexine or endexine. The apertures may be long furrows or colpa or circular pores or ora.

Pollen grains are classified and named variously on the number, position and character of apertures, e.g. trizono colpate, i.e., number of apertures three, position equatorial (zono) and character colpa-like, similarly pantocolpate, pantoporate, tetracolporate, and so on.

Sporoderm provides another important character for consideration. Sporoderm or pollen wall is made up of a very resistant substance called sporopollinin. It comprises of two layers, the outer is the ektexine (or sexine) and the inner is endexine (or nexine). The sporoderm encloses the intine and protoplasm. The spores of Pteridophytes have another external layer called penine. Both ektexine and endexine comprise more than one layer which are detectable under microscope and more so by their staining behaviour. Ektexine presents various structural and sculptural elements which help in identification, classification, etc. Endexine does not present such structure and sculpture as the ektexine but its thickness or other irregularity help in various ways.

Thus pollen morphology helps in solving many taxonomical problems at family, tribe, genus and even upto species level. It provides valuable information and together with other informations gathered from other disciplines of botany brings a reasonable solution to many disputed questions in taxonomy.

Preparation of pollen-slide

For a morphological study of the pollen it is necessary to prepare pollen-slides. The process is briefly described here. A small amount of pollen is placed on a slide. A drop of alcohol is added and allowed to evaporate partly. The oily substance exuded from the pollen is wiped out with cotton moistened in alcohol. Before the pollens dry completely a drop of methyl-green glycerine jelly is placed over it and the pollen-mass is stirred with a clean needle. It is dried by passing over a flame or on hot plate. It is then covered with a coverslip. The methyl-green stains the exine. If staining of the cell content is desired a weak eosine solution is added before applying alcohol. Character of the pollens are then studied under a microscope.

The most accepted method for preparing pollen slides is that by Erdtman known as acetolysis method. In this method a mixture of acetic anhydride and concentrated sulphuric acid is put over polliniferous material in a tube which is put in water and the water gradually heated to boiling point. The material is then transferred to an electric centrifuge and after centrifuging a few drops of water added to the sediment. The tube is thoroughly shaken until the mixture foams. The sediment is then put in a mixture of equal parts of glycerine and water. It is then centrifused again and glycerine and water added. The process is repeated several times and the liquid allowed to run off. A small quantity of the sediment is put on a slide and sealed.

CHAPTER III

PLANT KINGDOM AND ORIGIN OF ANGIOSPERMAE

The vegetative cover of the earth including plants that grow under water is estimated to comprise about 393700 species. The number of species under different major groups is roughly given below:*

Division	—	Thallophyta		... 110000 spp.
Subdiv.	—	Algae	... 20000 spp.	
Subdiv.	—	Fungi	... 90000 spp.	
Division	—	Bryophyta		... 23000 spp.
Division	—	Pteridophyta		... 10000 spp.
Division	—	Spermatophyta		... 250700 spp.
Subdiv.	—	Gymnospermae	... 700 spp.	
Subdiv.	—	Angiospermae	... 250000 spp.	

The above grouping of the plant kingdom represents the traditional classification. A recent classification based on the study of phyllogeny of plants has been proposed by Oswald Tippo and is as follows:

Kingdom Plantae

Subkingdom	Thallophyta	
Phylum	Cyanophyta	Algae
,,	Euglenophyta	Algae
,,	Chlorophyta	Algae
,,	Chryosphyta	Algae
,,	Pyrrophyta	Algae
,,	Phaeophyta	Algae
,,	Rhodophyta	Algae
Phylum	Schizomycophyta	Fungi
,,	Myxomycophyta	Fungi
,,	Eumycophyta	Fungi
Subkingdom	Embryophyta	
Phylum	Bryophyta	... Bryophytes
Class	Musci	
,,	Hepaticae	
,,	Anthocerotae	
Phylum	Tracheophyta	... Vascular plants

* Prof. V. H. Heywood (Plant Taxonomy, 1967) gives the number as 373275 approximately distributed under the following groups:

Angiosperms	287000
Gymnosperms	700
Pteridophytes	10000
Bryophytes	23000
Algae	8675
Fungi	40500
Cyanophyta	1400
Bacteria	2000

Subphyl.	Psilopsida	Pteridophytes
Class	Psilophytinae	
Order	Psilophytales	
,,	Psilotales	
Subphyl.	Lycopsida	
Class	Lycopodineae	
Subphyl.	Sphenopsida	
Class	Equisetineae	
Subphyl.	Pteropsida	
Class	Filicineae	
Class	Gymnospermae	Spermatophyta
Subclass	Cycadophytae	
Order	Cycadofilicales (Pteridospermae)	
,,	Bennettitales	
,,	Cycadales	
Subclass	Coniferophytae	
Order	Cordaitales	
,,	Ginkgoales	
,,	Coniferales	
,,	Gnetales	
Class	Angiospermae	
Subclass	Dicotyledonae	
Order	Magnoliales	
etc.	etc.	
Subclass	Monocotyledonae	

Tippo further arranges these groups of plant in a graphical form to show the relationship between them and the trend of evolution in the plant kingdom. This is reproduced below:

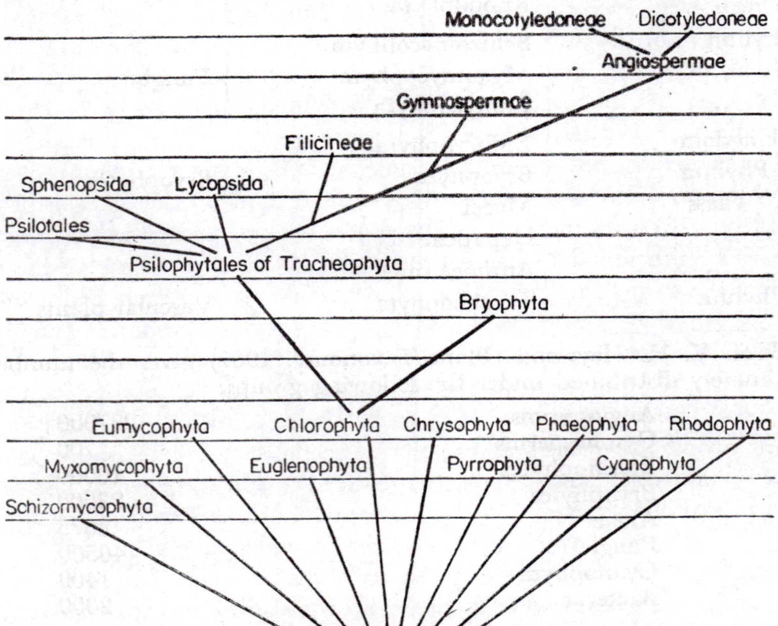

It is evident from this that Tippo considers that the Filicinae, Gymnospermae and Angiospermae were derived from a common ancestral stock. Most workers of phylogeny, however, agree that the seed-ferns (Pteridosperms) are the probable ancestors of the angiosperms. They are not the immediate ancestors but the Angiospermae is considered to have originated from, the seed-ferns through several evolutionary changes.

The Pteridosperms are a group of extinct Gymnospermae that flourished in the Carboniferous age and also occurred in the Jurassic. They had simple or branched stem and the branching was monopodial. Many species had cambium. The large pinnately compound leaves were net-veined in some species. They had micro- and megasporophylls which were compound. In some cases these were borne on the same plant. It is not unlikely that by repeated reductions the compound sporophylls developed into strobili.

The ovule of a seed-fern had a single integument like most other gymnosperms and one or more ovules were collectively subtended by a cupule. It is quite possible that in course of evolution each cupule subtended a single ovule and the cupule itself was modified into the second integument in Angiospermae.

How did then the primitive angiosperm look like? It is inferred that the hypothetical primitive angiosperm was an evergreen tree with alternate, simple, entire, stipulate, pinnately net-veined leaves. The leaves had rannunculaceous type of stomata. The nodes were unilacunar with 2 leaf-traces, or trilacunar with 3 leaf-traces. The cambium was well-developed and active but annual rings were not pronounced. Vessels were absent in the wood. The long and slender tracheids had tapering ends and numerous scalariform bordered pits as met with in the ferns. The medullary rays were uni- and multiseriate. True sieve tubes were absent in phloem and so was sclerenchyma, and probably companion cells were also absent. There was no terminal sieve-plate but the sieve-elements were elongate and overlapping with lateral sieve areas.

The flowers were rather large, solitary and terminal on the leafy branches. The perianth was not differentiated into calyx and corolla and the numerous sepals were spirally arranged. Stamens were also numerous and spirally arranged. They were large and flat with the microsporangia embedded in the blade. The pollen had one long groove and was uniaperturate. Carpels were many and free, distinctly stalked. Each carpel or carpellary leaf was folded along the midrib and the margins were just touching each other. There was a tangle of glandular hairs on the margins of a carpel and these effectively closed the carpel. There were no style and stigma but the pollen grains germinated on these hairs when captured. The ovules were borne on the inner (upper) surface of the carpellary leaf. These were anatropous and each had two integuments. Only one embryosac was produced and this was monosporic and eight-nucleate. Double fertilization occurred. Copious triploid endosperm was formed. The embryo was small at the time of ripening of the capsular fruit. The cotyledons were 2 or more in the seed. The sepals, stamens and carpels were arranged in acropetal succession so that this apocarpus ovary was superior. The flowers had no nectar, and pollination was by beetles which subsisted on the tender parts of the flower. The sepals, stamens and carpels probably had 3 leaf-traces and 3 primary veins each, from trilacunar nodes or some might have 2 leaf-traces from a unilacunar node.

Such were the characters of the most primitive taxon of angiosperm and origin of such a taxon from the seed ferns through several evolutionary changes is considered not improbable. Did such a taxon ever exist? May be yes or may be no. We have not been able to discover any concrete evidence to prove that such an ancestor of the living angiosperms ever existed. But we find that several families of angiosperms have at least a few of such primitive characters along with some specialised or advanced characters. Magnoliaceae is one of those considered as a primitive family. This is a family of trees and shrubs with alternate, usually entire, pinnately-veined, simple leaves. Young buds are enclosed by large deciduous stipules. The flowers are rather large, usually solitary and terminal and bisexual. The receptacle is elongate. The calyx and corolla are distinguishable but often very similar. The stamens are free and numerous and spirally arranged. Two pairs of linear microsporangia are deeply immersed in a laminar structure which is not differentiated into filament and connective. The sterile portion is much produced above the microsporangia. The stamens are trinerved and have 3 leaf-traces. The number of traces varies from 3-7 in some cases and rarely there is only one. The pollen is monocolpate and the sporoderm is of the type of Bennettitales, Cycads and Ginkgo.

The carpels are usually numerous, free and spirally arranged. In the 2 genera *Elmerriella* and *Manglietia* the margins of conduplicate carpels are only slightly fused and in *Michelia* they are fused only in the basal half at anthesis. The fruit is also of the most primitive type, viz. an aggregate of follicles. The seed contains copious endosperm and a small embryo. The testa in some cases is also of primitive type having a somewhat fleshy external layer.

The stem anatomy also shows primitive characters. The vessels here usually have scalariform perforations. The medullary rays are usually composed of heterogeneous elements. The nodes are multilacunar and with 6-7 leaf-traces. Palaeobotanical evidence shows that the family was widely distributed in the Late Cretaceous and in the Tertiary. The primitiveness of the family is also proved by cytological characters.

Winteraceae is another family possessing many primitive characters. This is a family of trees and shrubs with simple, entire, pinnately-veined, alternate leaves. The flowers are bisexual or unisexual. Here the calyx and corolla are well differentiated but the stamens are many and in 2-5 spiral turns. The stamens show specialisation but in ***Belliolum*** they are comparatively primitive with a long-produced connective. The carpels although in one series, are usually free. In some cases they resemble conduplicate young leaves. In some species of ***Drimys***, ***Bubbia*** and *Exospermum* the margins of a folded carpellary leaf are not at all fused. Along the margins of the inner surface there is a broad zone covered by papillose hairs. The pollens fall on the papillose hairs where they germinate and the pollen-tubes pass through the interlocking papillose hairs. The ovules are situated on either sides of the midrib or median vein away from the margin. The placentation is therefore parietal and not marginal. The flowers are insect pollinated. The fruits are aggregate of follicles or berry-like.

The stem has trilacunar nodes and the xylem is without vessels. The tracheids are long and thick walled. The medullary rays are heterogenous. The wood parenchyma is diffuse.

Degeneriaceae is another primitive family which consists of a single genus *Degeneria* with a single species *D. vitiensis*, endemic in the Fiji Islands. Here too the leaves are simple, pinnately net-veined and alternate. The flowers are solitary, supra-axillary, bisexual and spirocyclic. The calyx and corolla are quite distinct but the stamens and carpels are of very primitive nature. Stamens are many, free and spirally arranged with a few sterile ones above. The stamens are laminar. Two pairs of long microsporangia are immersed in sporophyll tissue. Pollens are monocolpate. The gynoecium consists of only one carpel or rarely 2 free carpels. The carpel is conduplicately folded; the margins are completely free and before anthesis are noticeably distant from each other. Broad lines of interlocking papillose glandular hairs on the ventral as well as dorsal surfaces of the carpels along both the margins form the so called elongate sessile stigma for receiving the pollens. The ovules are many, arranged in two rows parallel to and remote from the margins. The seed contains a small embryo and 3-4 cotyledons.

The wood is also of a primitive type having thin-walled vessel elements which are angular in outline and have scalariform perforation plates and scalariform pittings on the wall. The medullary rays are uni- or multiseriate. The nodes of the stem are pentalacunar.

Himantandraceae and Eupomatiaceae are two small families allied to Magnoliaceae and Degeneriaceae, and each consisting of only one genus, e.g. *Himantandra* and *Eupomatia*. In *Himantandra* the leaves are simple, entire, pinnately veined and alternate. There are numerous stamens in a flower, and these are laminar and spirally arranged. The microsporangia are immersed in the sporophyll tissue. The pollen is also of the primitive type. There are 6-10 conduplicate carpels spirally arranged; these are slightly connate at the base in flower but more united in fruit. The embryo is small and endosperm oily. *Eupomatia* with only 2 species also show some very primitive characters. Here also the simple leaves are entire, pinnately veined and alternate. The flowers are comparatively large, solitary and terminal. Each flower has numerous laminar stamens with 3-7 traces. There are numerous carpels spirally arranged on the concave receptacle. The carpels are united but they are slightly open and have decurrent marginal stigmatic surfaces without any style. Each carpel has several traces. The seeds of *Eupomatia* have small embryo and ruminated endorsperm.

The leaves of *Eupomatia* have 7-11 traces. The wood is also of primitive type. The vessel elements are long and slender with oblique ends; perforation bars are numerous and scalariform. The medullary rays are heterogeneous.

Annonaceae is a large family of trees, shrubs and large climbers growing in tropical and subtropical regions. Here the leaves are simple, entire, pinnately veined and alternate. There are numerous stamens in a flower spirally arranged and many free carpels. The pollens are monocolpate. The seed contains a small embryo and copious ruminate endosperm. Here the wood structure is noticeably more advanced.

Several other families also are considered as primitive by characters manifested in different parts of the plants. What do they indicate? From a study of these primitive families we can conclude that either there existed a hypothetical ancestor which had such primitive characters and which was derived from the seed-ferns or these primitive families originated from the seed-ferns by specialisation in course of evolution through the ages. So it is the Pteridosperm that gave rise to the Angiosperms as they did to different groups of Gymnosperms also.

Now we may discuss the other theories of origin of Angiosperms.

1. The Isoetes-Monocotyledon theory of Campbel: According to this theory the Monocotyledons were derived from the *Isoetes* which group bears some superficial resemblance to Monocotyledons. At present there is no supporter of this theory.

2. The Protangiosperm theory: According to this theory a group of plants existed in the Mesozoic era having bisporangiate flowers with or without a rudimentary perianth and which were animophilous. This group has been named as Protangiospermae. The embryo here had one or two cotyledons and the vascular bundles were of both types, open or closed. The protangiosperms gave rise to different lines of Angiosperms.

Engler and Prantl's system of classification is based on this theory and the Pandanales of Monocotyledonae and Amentiferae of Dicotyledonae are considered as most primitive among the angiosperms and are derived from the Protangiospermae.

3. The Gymnosperm theory: Many botanists consider that the Angiospermae arose from the Gymnospermae either from a single group or separately from different groups. Thus Wettstein thought that the primitive angiosperms were derived from the Gnetales. Markgraf, George, Manle and Fagerlind supported the Gnetalian origin of the angiosperms. Hagerup and Embergen stated that angiosperms evolved in several lines from different gymnosperm-groups. Anderson considers that the angiosperms may be hybrids of widely divergent groups of gymnosperms.

4. The Phyllospermae-Stachyospermae theory: Sahni was of the opinion that the angiosperms originated in 2 separate lines from the Pteridophytes. One group having foliar type of carpels is called Phyllospermae while the other has the carpels or megasporangia protected by sterile microsporangiophores. This theory was redefined and emended by Lam.

5. The Hemiangiosperm theory: Arber and Parkin postulated that a group of plants with cycadeoid flowers existed which gave rise to the modern flowering plants and called this hypothetical ancestor as Hemiangiospermae. Bessy, Hutchinson, Lotsy, and Hallier accepted this theory.

6. The Filicales-Cycadales and Lycopodiales-Cordaitales theory: Hagerup suggested a diphyletic origin of the angiosperms with one line extending from the Filicales through the Cycads to the Ranales and the second line from the Lycopods through the Cordaitales, Coniferales and Gnetales to such angiosperm taxa as the Centrospermae and Personatae.

CHAPTER IV

EARLY HISTORY AND DEVELOPMENT OF PLANT TAXONOMY

The early history of development of botanical science is nothing but a history of development of plant taxonomy. The herbalists and agriculturists of ancient times gathered some knowledge about plants which was passed on from generation to generation. Theophrastus (372-287 BC), the Greek philosopher-scientist, placed this knowledge of plants on a scientific footing. In his "Enquiry into Plants" he dealt with the plants at large and attempted to arrange the plants in several groups. He is, therefore, called the "Father of Botany". Pliny (Caius Plinius Secundus—23-79 AD) compiled a monumental work entitled "Historia Naturalis" where he incorporated all information about plants gathered up to that time and added much to the same collected by himself from his travels far and wide. Disocorides was a contemporary of Pliny and like him travelled a lot and gathered information about medicinal plants. He compiled his famous book "Materia Medica" where he described about six hundred species of plants mentioning their local name and giving their medicinal properties. Along with descriptions he gave sketches which increased the value of the book very much and gained much popularity among the herbalists and plant-lovers in Europe.

For a long period after this there was no contribution in the study of plants worth mentioning till Albert Magnus in the 13th century wrote his "De Vegetabilis" where the difference in the stem structure of Dicotyledons and Monocotyledons was shown and the two groups were given the terms Tunicate and Corticate. Printed books on plants were available towards the close of the 15th century and a few German herbalists carried their enquiries about plants still farther making the study of Botany quite popular. Foremost among them was Otto Brunfels who published his book "Herbarium vivae Eiconis" in three volumes (1530-1536) which was profusely illustrated with good figures. Jerome Bock (1498-1554), another German herbalist, published his "Nue Kreuterbuch" which contained accurate descriptions of about 600 species of flowering plants. In this book the author tried to trace the natural relationship of plants while classifying them into 3 major groups, viz., herbs, shrubs, and trees and also noted the original distribution of each species.

Andrea Caesalpino (1519-1603) also classified the plants on the character of their habit, viz., trees, shrubs, and herbs but also took into account the characters of ovary, fruit, and seed. He became famous for his book "De plantes" in 16 volumes, the first of which contained his principles of classification. Leonard Fuchs (1501-1566), Valerius Cordus (1515-1544), Mattias de L'Obel (1538-1616), John Gerard (1545-1612), and Charles L'Ecluse (1526-1909) were others who also advanced the cause of botanical science by their observations and contributions.

Then the Bauhin brothers came to the field. The elder brother Jean (Johna) Bauhin (1541-1631) wrote a book entitled "Historia plantarum universalis" which was published after his death. Gaspard (Casper) Bauhin, the younger brother (1560-1624), published 3 botanical treatises the third one of which, viz., "Pinax theatri Botanic" became very popular. Both the Bauhins made use of the habit-character of plants in classifying them. Gaspard Bauhin had formulated the idea of a genus and in many cases gave binary nomenclature to his plants. He also collected all names of plants published in different botanical works till his time and referred them as synonyms along with names he used as correct ones.

John Ray, an English naturalist (1628-1705), set himself seriously to the study of plants and gave much thought in proposing a system of classification of plants. He was the first to recognise 2 major taxa of flowering plants, viz., Dicotyledons and Monocotyledons. He also tried to group the plants into several families which he called "classes". He divided the plant kingdom first into 2 groups, viz., Herbae and Arbores. The Herbae were then divided into Imperfectae and Perfectae, the first of which included the Cryptogams and the second group, i.e., the Arbores included most of the flowering plants. The Perfectae were subdivided into Dicotyledonae and Monocotyledonae and under Dicotyledonae he placed 25 of his classes and 4 under Monocotyledonae. His system of classification came out in his "Historia plantarum" of which several editions were published and he revised and improved his system in the later editions.

Joseph Pitton de Tournefort was a contemporary of John Ray and tried to work out a system of classification of flowering plants. He too divided the plant kingdom first into 2 groups as trees and herbs and used the character of inflorescence and flower for subdividing the latter group. He was the first to give a clear concept of a genus although Gaspard Bauhin mentioned it in his works. Tournefort's work proved very helpful in identifying the plants up to the species.

Then came Carolus Linnaeus (1707-1778), a Swedish naturalist (also called Carl von Linne), who gave a new impetus to the study of plants. He was professor of medicine and botany in the Upsala University. He himself was an arduous collector of plants and made arrangement of collecting plant-specimens from different parts of the world by sending his students to countries far away and through missionary-men and administrators. The discovery of numerous plants from all over the world led him to think about bringing an order into the existing chaos and set himself in grouping and classifying all the plants known till his time. He proposed a system of classification which was published in his "Systema Naturae" (1735). In this system he used the character of stamens, i.e., the number and nature of stamens, to distinguish the 20 classes in which he divided the plant kingdom. He also used the number and nature of carpels to distinguish the orders, i.e., subdivisions of his classes. In addition to presenting an excellent system of classification of plants Linnaeus published many botanical works of monographic and floristic nature and also books embodying his ideas of nomenclature of plants. The "Species plantarum" the first edition of which came out in 1753 contained an enumeration of all plants known to him till that date, accompanied by brief description of each species with distribution and previous reference. In this work he consistently used binary nomenclature for every species with a generic name followed by a specific epithet. The modern taxonomists have agreed to consider the year 1753 as the starting point of nomenclature of Phanerogams, Pteridophyta, and Sphagnum. In his "Philosophia Botanica" he laid down some principles which later formed the basis of the International Code of Botanical Nomenclature. Owing to the efforts of Linnaeus the study of Botanical science entered the modern age and Linnaeus is rightly called the "Father of Modern Botany".

As in Europe, the study of plants was started by the herbalists in other countries boasting of an ancient civilisation. In India the medical men described many plants of medicinal value and classified them in various ways. Atharva Veda and Susruta Samhita were written before the Christian era. In his treatise on agriculture Parasara in 6th century classified the plants into many "ganas" or families giving clear picture of the morphology of flowers and fruits. Some of his "ganas" correspond to some families of modern taxonomists. Sarangadhara in 12th century in his "Upaban Vinoda", a book devoted to agriculture and horticulture, dealt with different aspects of plant life and had a separate chapter on the classification of plants.

Classification of plants

Linnaeus and the botanists before him tried to classify the plant kingdom using a single or a few characters chosen arbitrarily. They only thought about the convenience of following a system of classification solely to identify a particular plant. Such systems are, therefore, called artificial systems of classification. Later on plant-taxonomists conceived the idea that the plants belonged to some natural groups and they tried to designate and distinguish such groups and tried to classify the plant kingdom accordingly. Such systems are known as natural systems of classification. Such natural grouping gives the idea that the individuals under one particular group are closely related to one another although they believed in the fixity of species and simultaneous creation of all the groups by God. After the publication of the theory of Organic Evolution by Charles Darwin and Alfred Wallace the taxonomist began to think about the origin of each of the natural groups from a more primitive group, or from an individual of a more primitive group. In other words, some of the natural groups are more primitive and some are more recent or advanced and the recent groups have been derived from some comparatively primitive group. A system of classification based on the idea of organic evolution attempting to find out the relation between the different groups, i.e., to trace the phyllogeny of the groups, is called the phyllogenetic system of classification.

Fig. 5. Carolus Linnaeus

Linnaean system: artificial-sexual system (from *Systema Naturae*, ed. 10, 1759).

Linnaeus divided the plant kingdom into 24 classes depending on the number and nature of stamens. Each class was subdivided into orders according to the number and nature of stamens and carpels or on other characters of stamens. In this system the names of the classes and orders indicate the nature of androecium and gynoecium and the name given to one order under a class was often given to another order under another class and similarly name of a class was often used to designate an order under another class. This is an artificial system where very distantly related plants, i.e., plants belonging to widely distant natural groups have been placed under one order of a class. As Linnaeus made use of the morphological nature of stamens and carpels mainly to classify the plant kingdom his system is also called the sexual system. Outline of the system is given below:—

Classes	Orders
I. **Monandria** (stamen one)	Monogynia
II. **Diandria** (stamens two)	Monogynia Trigynia
III. **Triandria** (stamens three)	Monogynia Digynia Trigynia

IV. **Tetrandria** (stamens four)	Monogynia Digynia Tetragynia
V. **Pentandria** (stamens five)	Monogynia Digynia Trigynia Pentagynia
VI. **Hexandria** (stamens six)	Monogynia Digynia Trigynia Hexagynia
VII. **Heptandria** (stamens seven)	Monogynia
VIII. **Octandria** (stamens eight)	Monogynia Trigynia Tetragynia
IX. **Enneandria** (stamens nine)	Monogynia Hexagynia
X. **Decandria** (stamens ten)	Monogynia Digynia Trigynia Pentagynia Polygynia
XI. **Dodecandria** (stamens twelve)	Monogynia Trigynia
XII. **Icosandria** (stamens more than twelve, attached to the calyx)	Monogynia Digynia Pentagynia Polygynia
XIII. **Polyandria** (stamens more than twelve, attached to the receptacle)	Monogynia Tetragynia Pentagynia Polygynia
XIV. **Didynamia** (stamens didynamous)	Gymnospermia Angiospermia
XV. **Tetradynamia** (stamens tetradynamous)	Siliculosa Siliquosa
XVI. **Monadelphia** (stamens united in a bundle)	Pentandria Decandria Polyandria
XVII. **Diadelphia** (stamens united in two bundles)	Pentandria Hexandria Octandria Decandria

XVIII. **Polyadelphia** (stamens united in more than two bundles)	Pentandria Icosandria Polyandria
XIX. **Syngenesia** (stamens united by anthers)	Aequalis Superflua Frustranea Necessaria
XX. **Gynandria** (stamens adnate to ovary)	Monandria Hexandria
XXI. **Monoecia** (plants monoecious)	Monandria Diandria Triandria Tetrandria Pentandria Hexandria Heptandria Polyandria Monadelphia Syngenesia Gynandria
XXII. **Dioecia** (plants dioecious)	Monandria Diandria Triandria Tetrandria Pentandria Hexandria Enneandria Decandria Icosandria Polyandria Monadelphia
XXIII. **Polygamia** (plants polygamous)	Monoecia Dioecia Trioecia
XXIV. **Cryptogamia** (plants with hidden gamets)	Filices Musci Algae Fungi

Linnaeus's system proved to be of great help in identifying a plant and gained much popularity. Many flora-writers arranged their plants following Linnaeus's system. William Roxburgh who was the first to write a flora of India adopted the artificial system of Linnaeus in his work, viz., "*Flora indica*". Thunberg, another reputed botanist and a student of Linneaus also adopted the same system in his books. The disadvantage in using this system is that it gives no indication as to the natural or phylogenetic relationship among different taxa of plants and plants with no affinity at all are sometimes placed together in an artificially created group.

Natural systems

Bernard de Jussieu (1699-1776) who was in charge of the Royal Gardens in France tried to arrange the plants in the gardens following the system of Linnaeus and in doing so modified the system to such an extent that it became altogether a new system of classification. This, however, was not published and later his nephew Antoine Laurent de Jussieu (1748-1836) published the same in his "*Genera plantarum secundum ordines naturales deposita*" with some modifications. This was the first natural system of classification of plants where he established a hundred Natural Orders as taxa above the rank of genera giving distinguishing characters/of each. He divided the plant kingdom into 15 classes and placed the classes under 3 major heads as Acotyledonae, Monocotyledonae and Dicotyledonae. Acotyledonae consists of only one class which comprises the Cryptogams and the Naiades of the monocots, while the Monocotyledonae includes the rest of the monocots in 3 classes. Dicotyledonae comprises all of the dicotyledonous natural orders and also the Coniferae in the rest o these 11 classes.

Jussieu's system was slightly modified by Augustin Pyrame de Candolle who was Professor of Botany in Montpellier. An outline of his system of classification is given below:—

Plant Kingdom

I. Vasculares:

(Vascular plants; Cotyledons present).

Class 1. **Exogenae:**

(Vascular bundles in a ring; dicotyledons).

A. **Diplochlamydeae**

(Calyx and corolla both present)

a. **Thalamiflorae:**

(flowers polypetalous and hypogynous; 46 orders starting from Ranunculaceae).

b. **Calyciflorae:**

(flowers poly- or sympetalous and peri- or epigynous; 38 orders from Rosaceae).

c. **Corolliflorae:**

(gamopetalous and hypogynous flowers; 24 orders from Primulaceae).

B. **Monochlamydeae:**

(only calyx present; 19 orders of dicotyledons and Coniferae).

Class 2. **Endogenae:**

(vascular bundles scattered).

A. **Phanerogamae:**

(plants bearing flower; 21 orders of monocotyledons).

B. **Cryptogamae:**

(plants without flowers; 5 orders of ferns and fern-allies).

II. Cellulares:

(plants without vascular bundles; cotyledons absent).

Class 1. **Foliaceae:**

(leaves present; male and female gametes distinct; 2 orders comprising the mosses and liverworts).

Class 2. **Aphyllae:**

(leaves absent; male and female gametes not distinct; 4 orders including the algae, fungi, etc.).

Here he recognised the anatomical characters along with external morphological characters in distinguishing his divisions in the system of classification. He described 161 natural orders as against 100 of de Jussieu and the different groups or divisions in his system of classification were more natural than those of de Jussieu although he placed the Pteriydophyta in the same class Endogenae with the monocotyledons. Further he treated the Coniferae as an order in the class Exogenae along with other dicotyledonous orders. De Candolle became famous not for his system of classification but his monumental work entitled "*Prodromus systematis naturalis regni vegetabilis*", a book in 17 volumes* in which he described all the genera and species of plants discovered up to that time. The descriptions are very elaborate and are accompanied by references to previous literature and to the area of distribution of each species. He published many other books and formulated a set of rules for naming the plants. It was he who introduced the term taxonomy to designate the study of classifying and naming of plants.

Stephen Endlicher published his "*Genera Plantarum*" (1836-1840) describing 6,835 genera and arranged them in a system of his own. Here he divided the plant kingdom into 2 regions, viz., Thallophyta and Cormophyta. The Thallophyta included plants with simple structure, without stem or root or vessels and without clearly defined sex-organs, e.g., Algae, Fungi and Lichens. Cormophyta included plants with stem and roots, having vessels and clearly distinguishable sex-organs. He placed Bryophytes, Pteridophytes and seeds-plants under Cormophyta. He could not recognise the Gymnospermae as a single distinct taxon but placed the Zamiae (Cycads) with the Pteridophyta and the Coniferae with dicotyledons.

The best and most popular of the natural systems of classification is that of George Bentham and Joseph Dalton Hooker, two British Botanists, who classified the Phanerogamia and gave an account of 202 Natural Orders under that group. This was published in their great monumental work "*Genera Plantarum*" (1862-1883) where elaborate descriptions of each and every genera and of the Natural Orders were given together with names of all species under each genus, the synonyms, localities and reference to literature. Keys are also provided for easily identifying the Natural Orders and genera. This book proved to be a very useful reference book which as well as the system of classification given here became very popular in Great Britain and other countries of the world including America.

Fig. 6. J. D. Hooker

As noted above only the seed-plants were taken up here and this group was divided into 3 classes, viz., Dicotyledonae, Gymnospermae and Monocotyledonae. The dicotyledons were subdivided into 3 subclasses, viz.—Polypetalae, Gamopetalae and Mono-

* Completed by his son after his death.

chlamydeae. Each of these subclasses included more than one series. The gymnosperms included only 3 Natural Orders and were not subdivided into subclasses or series. The monocotyledons included 8 series which were not put under any subclass. The system of classification is given below in a tabular form:—

DICOTYLEDONAE

Subclass I. POLYPETALAE: Petals free.

Series i. Thalamiflorae: Flowers hypogynous.

Cohort 1 Ranales (8 N.O.)
,, 2 Parietales (9 N.O.)
,, 3 Polygalinae (4 N.O.)
,, 4 Caryophyllinae (4 N.O.)
,, 5 Guttiferales (6 N.O.)
,, 6 Malvales (3 N.O.).

Series ii. Disciflorae: Receptacle expanded into a disc; stamens inserted on the disc; ovary superior.

Cohort 7 Geraniales (11 N.O.).
,, 8 Olacales (3 N.O.)
,, 9 Celastrales (4 N.O.)
,, 10 Sapindales (3 N.O.)
Anomalous orders—2.

Series iii. Calyciflorae: Flowers perigynous, petals and stamens inserted on a cup-like receptacle, or flowers epigynous.

Cohort 11 Rosales (9 N.O.)
,, 12 Myrtales (6 N.O.)
,, 13 Passiflorales (7 N.O.)
,, 14 Ficoidales (2 N.O.)
,, 15 Umbellales (3 N.O.)

Subclass II. GAMOPETALAE: Petals united.

Series i. Inferae: Ovary inferior.

Cohort 1 Rubiales (2 N.O.)
,, 2 Asterales (4 N.O.)
,, 3 Campanulales (3 N.O.)

Series ii. Heteromerae: Ovary usually superior, carpels more than 2.

Cohort 4 Ericales (6 N.O.)
,, 5 Primulales (3 N.O.)
,, 6 Ebenales (3 N.O.)

Series iii. Bicarpellatae: Ovary usually superior, stamens alternating with corolla-lobes, carpels uaúally 2.

Cohort 7 Gentianales (6 N.O.)
,, 8 Polemoniales (5 N.O.)
,, 9 Personales (8 N.O.)
,, 10 Lamiales (4 N.O.)
Anomalous order—1.

Subclass III. MONOCHLAMYDEAE: Perianth inconspicuous or absent.

Series i. Curvembryeae: Embryo curved, ovule usually one—(7 N.O.)

Series ii. Multiovulatae: Aquaticae: Ovules numerous, aquatics—(1 N.O.)
Series iii. Multiovulatae: Terrestres: Ovules numerous, terrestrials—(3 N.O.)
Series iv. Microembryeae: Embryo very small, ovule usually one—(4 N.O.).
Series v. Daphnales: Ovary monocarpellary, ovule usually one—(5 N.O.)
Series vi. Achlamydosporeae: Ovary unilocular, ovules 1-3, seeds without testa—(3 N.O.).
Series vii. Unisexuales: Flowers unisexual, ovules 1-2—(9 N.O.).
Series viii. Anomalous orders—4.

GYMNOSPERMAE

N.O.s 3, Gnetaceae, Coniferae, Cycadaceae.

MONOCOTYLEDONAE

Series i. Microspermae: Seeds minute, numerous, exalbuminous—(3 N.O.)
Series ii. Epigynae: Ovary inferior, seeds with copious albumin—(7 N.O.)
Series iii. Coronarieae: Ovary superior, albumin in seeds plenty—(8 N.O.)
Series iv. Calycinae: Perianth sepaloid, ovary superior—(3 N.O.).
Series v. Nudiflorae: Perianth absent or reduced to scales—(5 N.O.)
Series vi. Apocarpae: Carpels free or only one carpel, ovary superior, seeds without albumin—(3 N.O.)
Series vii. Glumaceae: Flowers in spikelets, or in heads, generally subtended by imbricated scale-like bracts, perianth scale-like or glumaceous, seeds with albumin—(5 N.O.)

The system of classification of Bentham and Hooker is the best of all the natural systems. Although it is not a phylogenetic system yet the natural orders (i.e., families) having close relationship have been grouped together in most cases and in phylogenetic classifications of later workers many of such groups have been maintained. Descriptions of natural orders and genera are very elaborate and accurate, being based on actual study of the specimens by the authors. Therefore for purpose of identification of plants this system is very helpful.

As mentioned before, Bentham and Hooker's system is not a phylogenetic system and is based on the idea of fixity of species. The position of gymnosperms in this system is very unsatisfactory as it has been placed in between the dicots and monocots. Such anomaly is noted also in other cases in placing the natural orders under different series. The series Curvembryeae with natural orders Nyctaginaceae, Amaranthaceae, Chenopodiaceae, Polygonaceae, Phytolaccaceae, etc. has been placed in Monochlamydeae while Caryophyllaceae which is closely allied to the above-mentioned natural orders has been placed in series Thalamiflorae of Polypetalae. In monocotyledons inclusion of Irideae and Amaryllideae in the same series with Scitamineae and Bromeliaceae is another example of such anomaly. In the use of terminology of different rank of taxa there is no uniformity. Thus we find that under the subclasses Polypetalae and Gamopetalae of dicotyledons the natural orders are placed under cohorts which are again placed under series. But in subclass Monochlamydeae and in the monocotyledons the natural orders are placed directly under the series. In gymnosperms the 3 natural orders are not placed under any series or cohort.

A graphical representation of the outline of the system of classification by Bentham and Hooker is given below:

Phanerogamia

- Dicotyledonae
  - *Polypetalae*
    - Series 1. Thalamiflorae
    - ,, 2. Disciflorae
    - ,, 3. Calyciflorae
  - *Gamopetalae*
    - Series 1. Inferae
    - ,, 2. Heteromerae
    - ,, 3. Bicarpellatae
  - *Monochlamydeae*
    - Series 1. Curvembryeae
    - ,, 2. Multiovulatae-Aquaticae
    - ,, 3. Multiovulatae-Terrestres
    - ,, 4. Microembryeae
    - ,, 5. Daphnales
    - ,, 6. Achlamydosporae
    - ,, 7. Unisexuales
    - ,, 8. Ordines Anomali
- Gymnospermae (3 N. orders)
- Monocotyledonae
  - Series 1. Microspermae
  - ,, 2. Epigynae
  - ,, 3. Coronarieae
  - ,, 4. Calycinae
  - ,, 5. Nudiflorae
  - ,, 6. Apocarpeae
  - ,, 7. Glumaceae

Phylogenetic system

A. W. Eichler, a botanist in Vienna, proposed a new system of classification of the plant kingdom (1875) and this he later elaborated in 1883. Here he gave a more clear idea of the lower groups of plants and also separated the Gymnospermae from the Angiospermae placing them in 2 taxa of equal ranks. This system is not considered as true phylogenetic but is one that carries the idea of primitiveness and advancement in different groups in the plant kingdom. An outline of his system is given below:

A. Cryptogamae:
- I Division—Thallophyta
  - 1. Class Algae
  - 2. ,, Fungi (including Lichens)
- II Division—Bryophyta
  - 1. Class Hepaticae
  - 2. ,, Musci
- III Division—Pteridophyta
  - 1. Class Equisetineae
  - 2. ,, Lycopodineae
  - 3. ,, Filicineae

B. Phanerogamae
- I Division—Gymnospermae
- II Division—Angiospermae
  - 1. Class Monocotyleae
  - 2. ,, Dicotyleae
    - (i) Subclass Choripetalae
    - (ii) Sympetalae

Adolf Engler (Fig. 7), Professor of Botany, University of Berlin, published (1887-1899) in collaboration with Karl Prantl a monumental work entitled "Die naturlichen Pflanzenfamilien" where all the genera of plants were arranged and described systematically. In doing so they proposed a new system of classification for the whole plant kingdom. This system was based to some extent on that of Eichler but is a true phylogenetic system. In this work they tried to use the terminology for different ranks of taxa in a more scientific way. The term Natural Order was replaced by the term Family and for a taxon above the rank of families and containing several closely related families they used the term Reihe, equivalent to series or cohorts in Bentham and Hooker's system. The Reihe or orders were grouped under Classes, classes under Subdivisions and subdivisions under 13 Divisions in which they divided the Plant Kingdom or Pflanzenreich. The seed-plants, i.e., the Phanerogamia are placed in the 13th division, viz., Embryophyta Siphonogama. The classification of Phanerogamia according to Engler and Prantl is shown below:

Fig. 7. Adolf Engler

Embryophyta Siphonogama

Subdivision A. Gymnospermae
- Class 1. Cycadofilicales
- ,, 2. Cycadales
- ,, 3. Bennettitales
- ,, 4. Ginkgoales
- ,, 5. Coniferae
- ,, 6. Cordaitales
- ,, 7. Gnetales

Subdivision B. Angiospermae.
- Class 1. Monocotyledoneae
- ,, 2. Dicotyledoneae
  - Subclass 1. Archichlamydeae
  - ,, 2. Metachlamydeae.

Class MONOCOTYLEDONEAE

- Reihe 1. Pandanales
- ,, 2. Helobiae
- ,, 3. Triuridales
- ,, 4. Glumiflorae
- ,, 5. Principes
- ,, 6. Synanthae
- ,, 7. Spathiflorae
- ,, 8. Farinosae
- ,, 9. Liliflorae
- ,, 10. Scitamineae
- ,, 11. Microspermae

Class DICOTYLENDONEAE

Subclass **Archichlamydeae**

Reihe	1.	Verticillatae	Reihe	17.	Aristolochiales
"	2.	Piperales	"	18.	Balanophorales
"	3.	Hydrostachyales	"	19.	Polygonales
"	4.	Salicales	"	20.	Centrospermae
"	5.	Garryales	"	21.	Ranales
"	6.	Myricales	"	22.	Rhoedales
"	7.	Balanopsidales	"	23.	Sarraceniales
"	8.	Leitneriales	"	24.	Rosales
"	9.	Juglandales	"	25.	Pandales
"	10.	Julianiales	"	26.	Geraniales
"	11.	Batidales	"	27.	Sapindales
"	12.	Fagales	"	28.	Rhamnales
"	13.	Urticales	"	29.	Malvales
"	14.	Podostemonales	"	30.	Parietales
"	15.	Proteales	"	31.	Opuntiales
"	16.	Santalales	"	32.	Myrtiflorae

Reihe 33. Umbelliflorae

Subclass **Metachlamydeae**

Reihe	1.	Diapensiales	Reihe	5.	Ebenales	Reihe	9.	Rubiales
"	2.	Ericales	"	6.	Contortae	"	10.	Cucurbitales
"	3.	Primulales	"	7.	Tubiflorae	"	11.	Campanulatae
"	4.	Plumbaginales	"	8.	Plantaginales			

According to Engler the most primitive type of flower is without perianth; the next higher type has one whorl, then there are flowers with two whorls of perianth. Where the perianth is in two whorls, they may be distinguishable into calyx or corolla or not. The gamopetalous condition is an advancement over polypetalous condition. Indefinite number of stamens and carpels is a primitive condition, while definite number is advanced type. Superior ovary is also a primitive condition from which inferior ovary has come through perigyny. Here it is presumed that the dicots and monocots were derived separately from some extinct group of gymnosperms. Therefore considering that the Pandanales among the monocots and Amentiferous dicots nearly approach the ancestral type they are placed at the beginning of the 2 classes of Angiospermae. The Monocotyledonae is placed before Dicotyledonae in this system. The Monocotyledonae begins with Typhaceae of Pandanales and ends with Orchidaceae of Microspermae. Casuarinaceae the only family of the order Verticillatae is the first family in the Dicotyledonae and the last family is Compositae which is considered to be most highly evolved among the dicotyledonous families.

After the publication of Pflanzenfamilien Engler in collaboration with Gilg brought out a single volume book *Syllabus der Pflanzenfamilien* containing the system of classification of the plants as proposed in Pflanzenfamilien. Several editions of this book were published later by Engler and Diels with slight modifications of the system. After Engler's death Diels published the 11th edition in 1936 and Hans Melchior published the 12th revised edition of the *Syllabus* (in two volumes) in 1954-64.

Engler's system was adopted by most botanists and it replaced the Bentham and Hooker's system in many countries in Europe and America. It has been recognised by the International Botanical Congress. This is a comprehensive system for all groups of plants and is a phylogenetic system. In the case of Dicotyledons the amalgamation of Polypetalae and Monochlamydeae into one group Archichlamydeae is considered justifiable. Placing of Orchidaceae at the end of monocots and Compositae at the end of dicots is also considered proper as these 2 families are most highly evolved in their respective classes. The position of Iridaceae, Juncaceae and Amaryllidaceae shown to be closer to Liliaceae is also supported by many botanists.

This system has, however, been criticized by many. The origin of monocots is now considered to be from a primitive group of dicots and not separately from the ancestral stock that gave rise to the dicots. It is the Ranales from which the monocots have been derived, and this order is one of the most primitive among the dicotyledons and the position assigned to it in Engler's system cannot be justified. The catkin bearing families placed at the beginning of Archichlamydeae are in reality highly advanced as the simplicity of the flowers is the result of reduction and not due to primitiveness. In the case of monocotyledons also the Pandanales consists of the families which are rather recent in the evolutionary line and not at all primitive.

Richard von Wettstein, another German botanist, published a book entitled "Handbuch der systematischen Botanik" in 1901, a revised edition of which came out in 1935. Here he proposed a system which was similar to that of Engler and Prantl but differing in some cases in tracing the relationship of the orders. He divides dicotyledons into Choripetalae and Sympetalae. The Choripetalae is again subdivided into Monochlamydeae and Dialypetaleae. There are 29 orders under Choripetalae and 10 orders under Sympetalae. Unlike Engler he considers that the monocots originated from the dicots and from the order Policaripicae. Further according to him Pandanales is not an order of primitive families but is more advanced over Helobiae and Liliflorae, the two orders from which all other orders of the monocots have been derived.

Charles E. Bessey, Professor of Botany, at the University of Nebreska, U.S.A., also tried to work out the phylogeny of the seed plants, and after several suggestions in that line published in several papers, finally published his system in 1915 under the title "The Phylogenetic Taxonomy of Flowering Plants". He divided the group Anthophyta or angiosperms into Alternifoliae (Monocotyledonae) and Oppositifoliae (Dicotyledonae) and each of these 2 classes was subdivided into Strobiloideae and Cotyloideae.

The subclasses under Alternifoliae are further divided into Orders each having one or more Families under it, while the subclasses under Oppositifoliae have Super orders under them and the Super orders have the Orders and Families in descending orders.

Bessey (Fig. 8) considered that the dicotyledonous line is primitive in comparison to the monocotyledonous line and among the dicots, plants with strobiloid type of flowers are very primitive. Therefore he places the Ranales at the beginning of his system of classification as has been done by Bentham and Hooker. Magnoliaceae of the order Ranales is the most primitive family and Lactucaceae of the Asterales is the most advanced among the Dicots. He splits Compositae into several families and Lactucaceae is one of those new families. According to Bessey the Anthophyta or the angiosperms originated from the Benettitalean stock and the Alternifoliae, i.e., the Monocotyledonae was derived from the primitive group of Oppositioliae, i.e., the Dicotyledonae.

Fig. 8. Charles E. Bessey

Bessey prepared a chart to show the relationship of the orders of the Anthophyta and the chart is reproduced below:

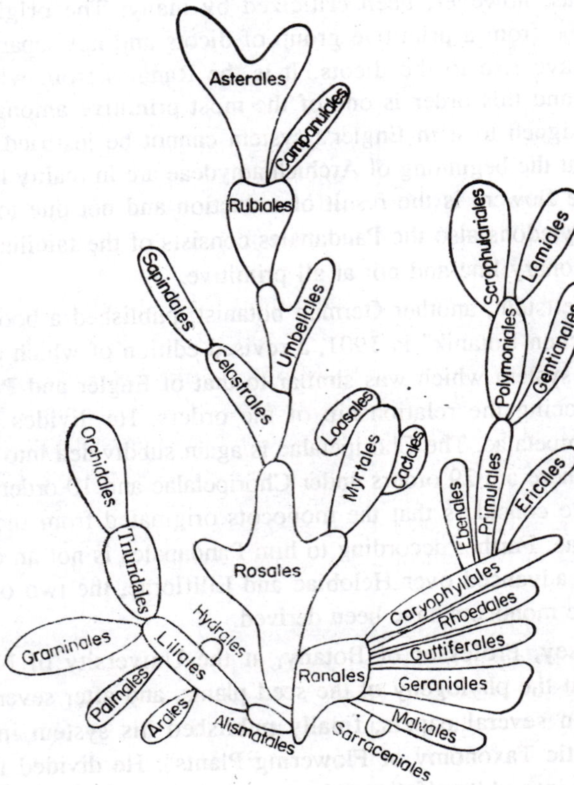

In this chart the size of the baloons and other figures is proportional to the number of species in an order.

German botanist Hans Hallier proposed another phylogenetic system in his "L'origine et le systeme phyletique des Angiospermes" (1912). Hallier considered that the angiosperms were derived from some extinct group of Cycad allied to Bennettitlaes. Like Bessey he considered the Monocotyledonae to be more advanced than the Dicotyledonae and the former group was derived from a stock which he called Proberberideae. He divided the angiosperms into 5 major groups, viz. (1) Proterogenes, (2) Anonophyles, (3) Rhodophyles, (4) Ochnigenes and (5) Monocotyledones. There are 29 orders under the Dicotyledonae and 7 orders under the Monocotyledonae. Like Bessey he considered the Ranales to be the most primitive among the dicots and the plants with amentiferous flowers to be more advanced due to reduction in floral parts. Liliflorae is the first order in his Monocotyledones. From Liliflorae he derives Helobiae Cyperales, Spadiciflorae, Enantioblastae and Ensatae on one line and Artorrhizae on another line. He splits Amaryllidaceae of earlier botanists to Agavaceae, Alstroemeriaceae and Amaryllidaceae and this treatment has met with the approval of modern workers.

Alfred Barton Rendle of British Museum of Natural History published his book "Classification of Flowering Plants" in 2 volumes in 1904 and 1925. For arranging the families he followed the Engler's system in general with slight modifications. As in Engler's system Monocotyledonae was placed before the Dicotyledonae. In the Monocotyledonae the Pandanales is the first order and the Dicotyledonae starts from Salicales. He breaks up Archichlamydeae into 2 grades, viz., Monochlamydeae and Dialypetalae while Sympetalae remains as grade 3. The Dialypetalae is more advanced over Monochlamydeae and begins with Ranales. Sympetalae originated from Dialypetalae in several lines. It has been subdivided into 2 groups, the Pentacycliae and the Tetracycliae. Tetracycliae is again divided into Superae and Inferae. In his book the descriptions of families and orders are very elaborate and in many cases the phylogeny of different groups have been nicely discussed. Even then it is considered that his system is important only from the point of convenience than from phylogenetic standpoint. As in Engler's system the Monocotyledonae ends in Orchidaceae and the Dicotyledonae terminates in the family Compositae. Like Engler he considered that monocots and dicots originated independently from a common stock.

August A. Pulle of Utrecht Botanical Museum published a system of classification of the Spermatophyta in 1938. This was a slight modification of Engler's system. According to him spermatophytes are divided into 4 subdivisions, viz., Pteridospermae, Gymnospermae, Chlamydospermae (Gnetales) and Angiospermae. The last is divided into Monocotyledoneae and Dicotyledoneae. Pulle's divisions of the extinct and living gymnosperms are considered to be natural groups by most modern workers. He also proposed some changes of position of a few angiospermic orders in the Engler's system to show their affinities.

John Hutchinson, a British Botanist working in the Royal Botanic Garden, Kew, London, published a phylogenetic system for classifying the families of angiosperms in his book "The Families of Flowering Plants". The first volume containing the dicotyledons appeared in 1926 and the second volume in 1934 and a revised edition of the 1st volume was published in 1960. He divided his Phyla-Angiospermae into 2 subphylas, viz., Dicotyledones and Monocotyledones. The dicotyledons originated according to him from an ancestral stock called Proangiospermae allied to Bennettitales. The primitive dicotyledons developed in 2 separate lines one bing predominantly woody and the other herbaceous. The primitive dicots with hermaphrodite, hypogynous flowers with numerous free and spirally arranged parts are placed in Archichlamydeae from which the Metachlamydeae is derived. In the revised system he abolished the groups Archichlamideae and Metachlamideae, and placed the woody families under division Lignosae and the herbaceous families under division Herbaceae, the 2 groups originating in 2 separate lines from the Proangiospermae.

The Monocotyledones originated according to him from the Ranales, and were subdivided by him into 3 divisions, viz., Calyciferae, Corolliferae and Glumiflorae. Here also those families are considered as primitive which have usually hermaphrodite, hypogynous flowers with numerous, free and spirally arranged parts. Such families among the monocots are almost all aquatic and therefore he concludes that the Monocotyledones were derived from primitive Dicotyledones through aquatic medium. Butomales and Alismatales are considered most primitive among the monocots from which other families of Calyciferae have been derived. Corolliferae has been derived from Butomales and Commelinales of Calyciferae. Liliales forms the basal stock of other orders of Corolliferae and also of Glumiflorae the 3rd divison of the Monocotyledones. He splits Pandanales of Engler to Pandanales and Typhales and considers the families under them to be much more recent and not at all primitive. He splits Liliaceae of the older botanists to Liliaceae, Tecophilaeaceae, Trilliaceae, Smilacaceae and Ruscaceae and transfers Draceneae to Agavaceae, Luzuriageae to Philesiaceae and Allieae to Amaryllidaceae. This treatment of the older Liliaceae meets with the approval of most modern botanists.

The system of classification of the monocots by Hutchinson (Fig. 9) appears to be more satisfactory than any other systems proposed by earlier workers on this line. Reshuffling of the orders and rearrangement of the families have gained support from anatomy and cytology. The origin of monocots from the primitive dicots is now considered a fact agreed upon by all modern taxonomists. In the case of dicots, however, dividing the group into 2 separate divisions from the beginning into Lignosae and Herbaceae seems to be arbitrary and illogical. And as a result of this many natural families had to be vivisected unnecessarily and the phylogeny was mixed up rather than simplified. Placing of Magnoliales and Ranales at the beginning of dicots and consideration of the Amentiferae as a more advanced group are the points that have been supported by other workers.

Fig. 9. John Hutchinson

Professor Oswald Tippo of Illinois University, U.S.A., proposed a system of classification in 1942 for the major taxa of the whole of the plant kingdom. Here he took into consideration the anatomical, paleobotanical and morphological characters and followed Gilbert Smith and Eames to a great extent. He divided the Plant kingdom into 2 Subkingdoms, viz., Thallophyta and Embryophyta, each having several Phyllas. In the Embryophyta there are 2 Phyllas, viz., Bryophyta and Tracheophyta. Phyllum Tracheophyta contains 4 subphyllas, viz., Psilopsida, Lycopsida, Sphenopsida and Pteropsida. Under Pteropsida there are 3 classes, viz:—Filicinae, Gymnospermae and Angiospermae. Under class Angiospermae there are 2 subclasses, viz., Dicotyledonae and Monocotyledonae. The arrangement of the orders and families of these 2 subclasses have not been shown here. (An outline of the classification of Tippo's system of classification has been given in Chapter III.)

Alfred Gunderson published a book in 1950, entitled "Families of Dicotyledons". In this book the class Dicotyledonae has been divided into 42 orders to include 242 families of which 240 are distributed under the 42 orders and 2 are placed at the end as Incertae Sedis (put apart). Magnoliales is the first order among the dicots and is followed by Ranales. The last order is Asterales containing 3 families, viz., Calyceraceae, Compositae and Chicoriaceae. He has given cytological data for the families as far as available.

In 1954 L. A. Kuprianova, a Russian Botanist, published a scheme to show the phylogeny of the class Monocotyledonae based on Palynological data. She concludes that the monocots have been derived from the Proangiospermae or Protoanthophyta along different lines directly as well as through the Polycarpicae of the dicots. The Monocotyledonae therefore is polyphyletic in origin. The families Liliaceae and Palmae are derived directly but separately from the Proangiospermae, Alismataceae and Juncaginaceae from Ranales and Araceae probably from Piperales of the Dicotyledonae. Liliaceae gave rise to Thurniaceae, Juncaceae and Cyperaceae in one line and from Amaryllidaceae to Orchidaceae in another line. Palmae gave rise to Cyclanthaceae, etc. to Graminae. Araceae gave rise to Lemnaceae, and the Helobiae group of families were derived from Alismataceae and Juncaginaceae.

The problem of classyfying the Angiospermae engaged the attention of many recent workers and the systems proposed by A. Takhtajan and also by A. Cronquist have been very popular as these are considered to be very near perfection and show the natural affinities much more clearly between different taxa of flowering plants. Armen Takhtajan is a reputed Palaeobotanist working in the Komarov Botanical Institute of Leningrad. He has also made great contributions in the field of angiosperm taxonomy and proposed a system of classification of angiosperms in 1942 based on the structural types of gynoecium and placentation. Later on he proposed another system in 1959 where he splits Ranales into Magnoliales, Illiciales, Tochodendrales, Ranales and Dilleniales. He also splits Nymphaeales into Nymphaeales and Nelumbonales. According to him Monocotyledonae was derived from Dicotyledonae along Nymphaeales through aquatic medium. Magnoliales is the most primitive order among the Dicotyledonae from which the other orders of this class originated. He further modified this system and published the same in his book entitled "Flowering plants, Origin and Dispersal" in 1969. Here he adopted new terminology for the higher taxa also according to the rules of nomenclature of plants. He, therefore, calls the Angiospermae as Magnoliophyta, the Dicotyledonae as Magnoliatae and the Monocotyledonae as Liliatae. An outline of his system may be graphically represented as shown below:

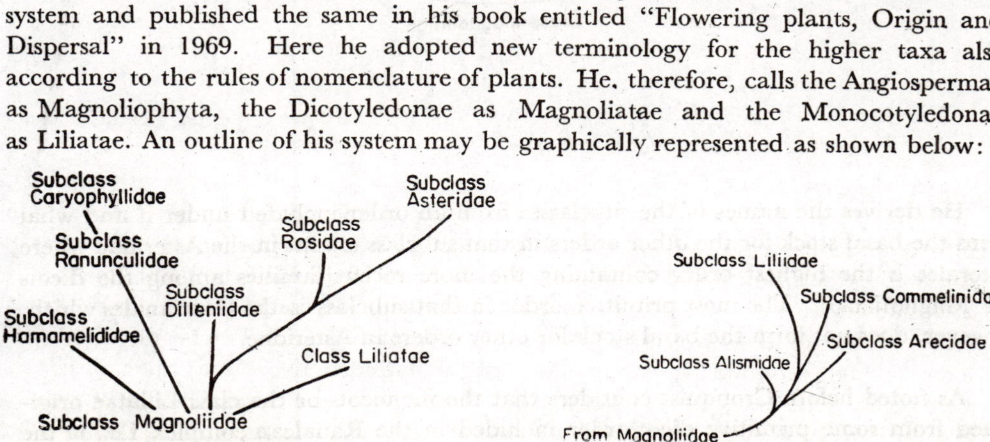

Arthur Cronquist of New York Botanic Garden drew out a scheme to show the relation of the orders of Dicotyledonae in 1957. Later on in 1965 he published a paper discussing the problem of classification of Flowering Plants where he recognised 5 complexes among the Dicotyledonae. Of these 5 complexes Ranalian complex is the most primitive and from this complex the other complexes of Dicotyledonae as well as the class Monocotyledonae have been derived. Finally he published his book, "Evolution and Classification of Flowering Plants" in 1968 where he classified the Dicots or the Magnoliatae into 6 subclasses, viz., Magnoliidae, Dilleniidae, Caryophyllidae, Hamamelidae, Rosidae and Asteridae. Magnoliidae is the most primitive subclass from which Dilleniidae, Caryophyllidae, Hamamelidae and Rosidae have been derived while Asteridae originated from Rosidae. The relationship of these six subclasses has been shown graphically by him with the help of balloon like figures, the sizes of the balloons giving an idea of the number of orders and families in each subclass. This is reproduced below:

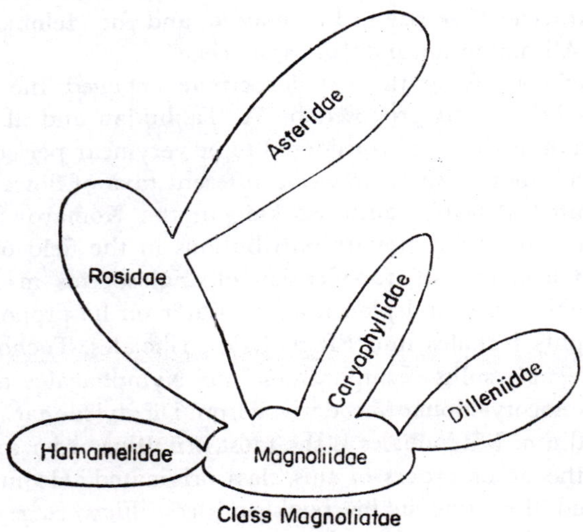

He derives the names of the subclasses from an order included under it and what forms the basal stock for the other orders in that subclass except in the Asteridae where Asterales is the highest order containing the more recent families among the dicots (or Magnoliatae). The most primitive order in that subclass is the Gentianales which, however, does not form the basal stock for other orders in Asteridae.

As noted before Cronquist considers that the monocots or the class Liliatae originated from some primitive dicot order included in the Ranalean complex, i.e., in the subclass Magnoliidae. Like Takhtajan he classifies the Liliatae into 4 subclasses, viz.,

Alismatidae, Arecidae, Liliidae and Commelinidae and represents them graphically as shown below :

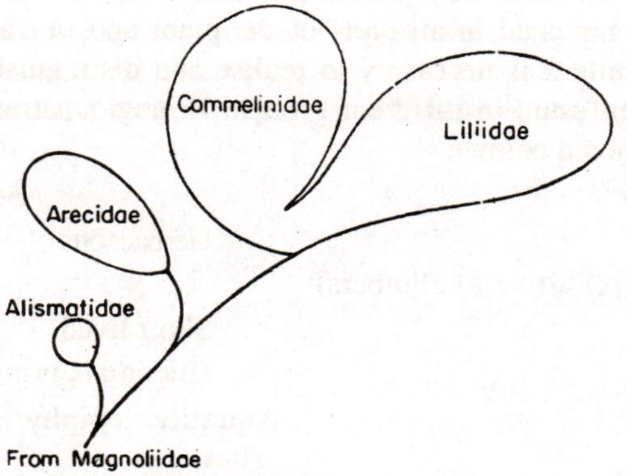

Class Liliatae

In the revised edition of his book Cronquist names the 2 classes of Angiosperms as Magnoliopsida and Liliopsida. Here he divides the Liliopsida into 5 subclasses as graphically represented below : –

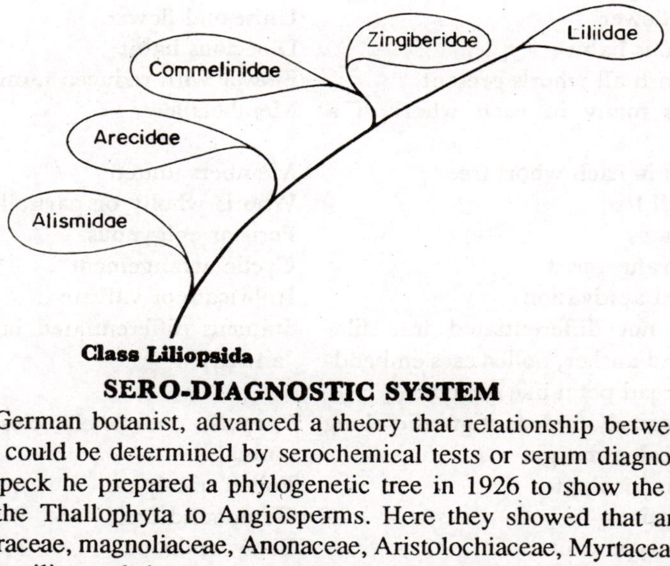

Class Liliopsida

SERO-DIAGNOSTIC SYSTEM

C. Mez, a German botanist, advanced a theory that relationship between the major groups of plants could be determined by serochemical tests or serum diagnosis. Working with H. Ziegenspeck he prepared a phylogenetic tree in 1926 to show the evolution of plant life from the Thallophyta to Angiosperms. Here they showed that among the dicots Trochodendraceae, magnoliaceae, Anonaceae, Aristolochiaceae, Myrtaceae, etc. are the most primitive families and the nomocots branched off from a stock which give rise to these primitive dicots. They consider that Compositae is at the highest position in the main line of evolution. Alismataceae, Juncaginaceae, Butomaceae, etc. occupy the basal position of the monocotyledonous branch while the grass family, Eriocaulaceae, Restionaceae, Orchidaceae and Zingiberaceae terminate the branches at the top.

This is an attempt to solve the problem of tracing the phylogeny of the plant groups from a different angle. This, however, has not gained much popularity.

Primitive and advanced characters in Angiosperms

It is presumed that the immediate ancestor of the angiosperms had a strobilus-like flower. In such a flower the thalamus was long and on this there were indefinite number of stamens (microsporophylls) and pistils (megasporophylls) spirally arranged. In habit the plants were trees with secondary growth and broad net-veined leaves. In course of evolution modifications appeared in all parts of the plant and in tracing the phyllogeny of different groups of plants it is necessary to realise and distinguish the primitive and advanced characters manifested in different groups. In angiosperms the primitive and advanced characters are noted below :

Primitive	*Advanced*
1. Woody (Trees and shrubs are primitive to climbers)	Herbaceous
2. Long lived (Perennials)	Short lived (Biennials primitive than annuals)
3. Terrestrials	Aquatics, epiphytes, saprophytes, parasites.
4. Leaves simple	Leaves compound
5. Leaves net-veined	Leaves parallel-veined
6. Stipules present	Stipules absent
7. Solitary flower	Inflorescence
8. Actionomorphic flower	Zygomorphic flower
9. Bisexual flower	Unisexual flower
10. Monoecious habit	Dioecious habit
11. Flower with all whorls present	Flower with reduced number of whorls
12. Members many in each whorl of a flower	Members few
13. Members in each whorl free	Members united
14. Whorls all free	Whorls wholly or partially united
15. Hypogynous	Peri- or epigynous
16. Spiral arrangement	Cyclic arrangement
17. Contorted aestivation	Imbricate or valvate
18. Stamens not differentiated into filament and anther, pollen sacs embedded in broad petal like structure	Stamens differentiated into filament and anthers
19. Carpels merely folded, stigmatic along the unsealed margin	Carpels, completely closed, stigma terminal
20. Pollen monocolpate	Pollen tricolpate
21. Simple fruit	Compound fruit
22. Capsular type fruit	Berry or drupe
23. Seed with copious endosperm and small embryo	Seed with scanty or no endosperm and large embryo
24. Vascular bundles in a cylinder enclosing a pith	Vascular bundles scattered
25. Cambium present and active	Cambium absent
26. Vessels absent	Vessels present
27. Chlorophyl present	Chlorophyl absent (i.e., parasites and saprophytes)
28. Evergreen	Deciduous

CHAPTER V

HERBARIUM

Herbarium is a depository of plant-specimens in dry condition. The specimens after collection are properly dried so that they retain all the essential parts necessary for identification. The specimens are then poisoned and mounted on a paper board and properly labelled. The label gives the field-data which include the name of the species to which a specimen belongs, place of collection, altitude of the place, date of collection, name of the collector and the field number. Brief ecological notes and some characters of the plant not shown in the specimens should also be noted down. The commercial name, if any of the economic plants, short notes on their uses, vernacular name, if any, are also to be noted. After labelling the specimens are then incorporated in a herbarium. Mounted specimens incorporated in a herbarium are called mounted sheets. The method of preservation is somewhat modified for the lower groups of plants.

When a collection of specimens is preserved in a herbarium, the specimens are arranged according to a system of classification of plants. For this Engler and Prantle's system has been recommended by the International Botanical Congress. Bentham and Hooker's system of classification of Angiosperms is, however, followed in many herbaria including those of the Royal Botanic Garden, Kew, London, and also the Central National Herbarium of the Botanical Survey of India. The herbarium sheets are given suitable paper covers, a genus-cover outside and within the genus-cover are the species covers. The genus-covers are of thick papers and the species-covers are of comparatively thin papers. Besides the name of the species and genus, the serial number of the particular species and genus should be noted down on the covers following a flora or monograph. The sheets with their covers are placed in special cupboards or pigeon-holed cabinets. Although the specimens were poisoned before mounting it is necessary to poison the herbarium sheets at intervals by applying poison by means of a brush or placing them inside a gas-chamber. This is to keep off the insects and to keep the sheets free from fungal infection. Naphthalene powder or dichlorobenzene is also put in the pegion-holes to serve the same purpose.

Consultation of herbarium is very essential for critical taxonomical studies. The purpose of maintaining a herbarium is to safeguard the identity of different species of plants. If an authentic specimen of a species is available the identity of that species is never confused. A large herbarium invariably shelters a number of specimens of same species collected from different localities by different collectors at different times. An examination of such a collection gives an idea of the range of distribution of a species, its phenology or the flowering or fruiting time, the range of morphological variation within the taxon and information on various other aspects.

Herbarium-specimens differ from Museum-specimens or exhibits. The former are irreplaceable while the latter can always be replaced by better ones. A herbarium-specimen may be a very poor representative of the plant but once incorporated should never be discarded. The particular poor specimen may prove to be very important and valuable to an expert.

A few important herbaria of the world with their rich collection are mentioned here:

1. Royal Botanic Garden, Kew, London ... ... 6,000,000 sheets
2. Komarov Botanical Institute, Leningrad ... 5,000,000 ,,
3. Botanic Garden, Paris ... ... 3,500,000 ,,

4. Harvard University, Massachusets	... ...	3,500,000 sheets
5. Conservatory & Botanic Gardens, Geneva	... ...	3,000,000 ,,
6. Central National Herbarium, Sibpur, Howrah	...	2,500,000 ,,

Preservation of specimens in solution

It is often necessary to preserve plant specimens in solutions. Such preserved material is easy to examine and often gives a better idea of the plant parts. Liquid preservatives are prepared according to different formulas and one commonly used is given below:

70% Alcohol	... ...	90 c.c.
Formaldehyde	... ...	9 c.c.
Glacial acetic acid	... ...	1 c.c.

If a plant specimen is preserved submerged in this solution in an airtight container it will remain in a good condition for a very long time. When the solution dries up some more of it is added so that the specimen always remains dipped in the solution. Here too the specimen is decolorised, but otherwise it remains as if in fresh condition. To preserve the colour of plant-parts alum-water serves the purpose to some extent. A solution prepared according to a formula noted below has, however, been found very useful, viz.:

50% Alcohol	... ...	90 c.c.
Formaldehyde	... ...	5 c.c.
Glycerin	... ...	2·5 c.c.
Glacial acetic acid	... ...	2·5 c.c.
Cupric chloride	... ...	20 gram
Uranium nitrite	... ...	2·5 gram

Collection of plant specimens : preparation of herbarium sheets

To understand the nature of vegetation of a particular area it is necessary to undertake field survey. While making a survey of the vegetation of the area it is not always possible to identify all plants in the field and specimens are therefore collected to be identified later. It is also necessary to keep a set of the specimens preserved for future reference and record. These specimens preserved for future reference serve as material for building a new herbarium or they are utilised to enrich an existing herbarium.

While making collection of specimens it is desirable to collect a complete plant This, however, is not possible unless it is a small herb. In other cases a small portion of the plant with the reproductive parts present should be collected. In case of Phanerogams a small twig with flowers or fruits or cones should be collected. In case of Pteridophytes usually a fertile frond is collected and where the fertile and sterile fronds are different both are to be collected. Other lower plants are usually of smaller size and are collected as a whole and sometimes a tuft of them.

For collection of plant-specimens the following equipments are necessary: 1. Pruning knife, 2. Small shovel, 3. Vasculum, 4. Plant-press, 5. A set of drying papers, 6. Field-note book, 7. Numbering tickets, 8. Pencil, and 9. Hand lens. A plant-press is made of 2, wiregauge frames of the size 45 cm × 30 cm. These are fitted with chains and bow-plates by which the frames and a bundle of specimens are tied tightly. Instead of chains leather straps may be used or the bundle may be tied with ropes. Drying papers are nothing but blotting papers but of a tough texture. When plant-specimens are placed between 2 drying papers and pressure is applied the juice coming out of the specimen is soaked by the papers and the specimen gradually gets dry. (Figs. 10 & 11)

The field-note book usually contains 100 pages. Each page is meant for one specimen. On this page the collector should note down the place of collection, the altitude of the place, date of collection, habit of the plant, colour of the flower, fragrant or not, and any other character of the plant not shown in the specimen collected and also brief ecological note, uses if any and vernacular name if any. The collector's name is also to be noted on each page. The pages of a note book are numbered and the corresponding numbers are given also to the specimens collected. So when a specimen is collected a ticket with a number is attached to it and all field notes are entered in a page of the field-book bearing the same number as shown on the ticket of the specimen. As noted before it is convenient to have 100 pages in a field-book. When a collector starts his plant collection the field notes of the first collected specimen are entered on the first page of the field-book. When 100 different specimens are collected one book is used up and for his 101st

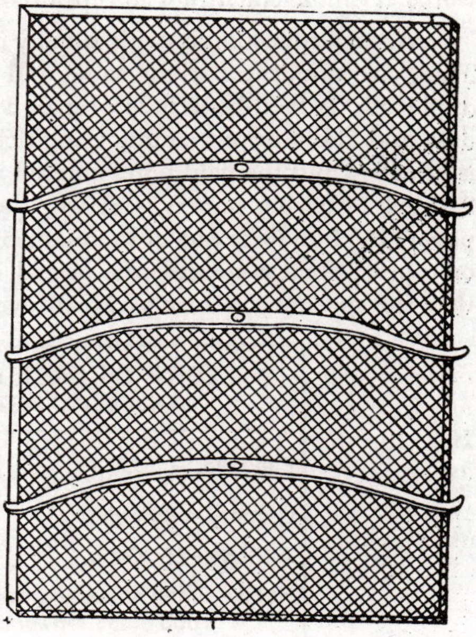

Fig. 10. Plant-press: upper frame.

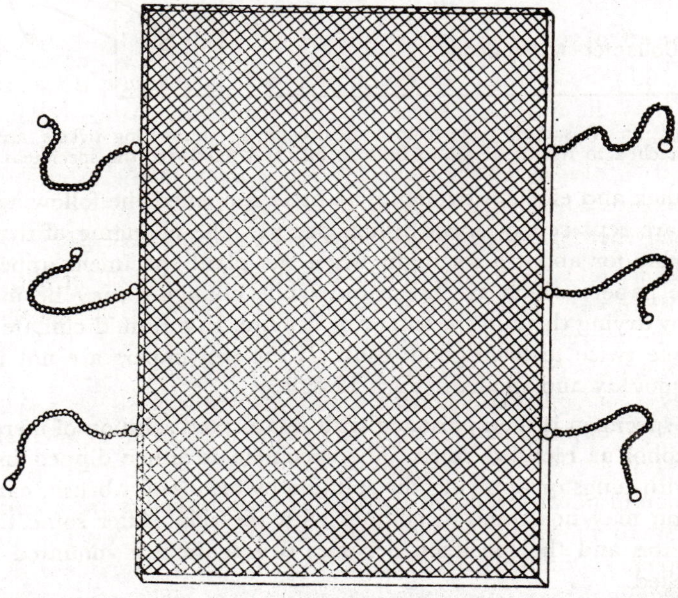

Fig. 11. Plant-press: lower frame.

specimen he must use the first page of the second book. So the 2nd book has 100 pages numbered from 101 to 200. In this way the collection number rises and it is very convenient for the purpose of reference to continue the serial number unbroken although the collector collects at different places and at different periods. In other words it is convenient not to repeat collection numbers.

When a collection is made usually more than one specimen is taken from one plant. These are duplicates of the same and have the same number given to each of these duplicates. A field-book is so prepared that it has the places for the entries of the field data and also 4 or more numbering tickets attached to one side. After the field number is attached and the field notes entered in the field-book the specimen is placed between 2 sheets of drying papers, and when a bundle is formed of such specimens in drying papers the bundle is put in the plant press and tightly tied with chains or leather straps or ropes. When a specimen is placed in between drying papers care should be taken that the specimen is nicely spread over the paper and no part overlies another part.

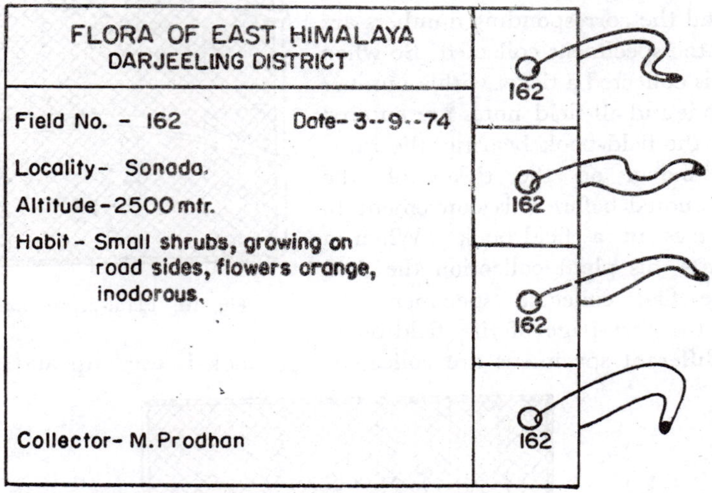

Fig. 12. A sample page from a field-book; 4 numbering tickets are attached to it; these are to be torn off and fixed to the specimens.

This ensures quick and efficient drying. The press is opened the following day and the drying papers are replaced by fresh drying papers. The changing of drying papers is repeated everyday for about a fortnight when the plant specimens appear to be perfectly dry. The papers which are taken out while changing may be used again the following day by drying them in the sun or near a fire. In a humid climate the changing of papers is done twice to have good result. If the wet papers are not taken out the specimens get mouldy and spoiled. (Figs. 12 & 13)

The dried specimen is then poisoned with a saturated solution of mercuric chloride ($HgCl_2$) in alcohol or rectified spirit. The specimen is either dipped in the solution by holding it with tongs or applying the solution by means of a brush, care being taken that the solution may not come in contact with the skin. After some time when the alcohol evaporates and the specimen becomes dry again it is mounted on a sheet of paper and labelled.

The process of mounting is described here: Mounting papers are usually rag papers; these are not very thick but are tough and hard more or less like cartridge-paper. Each sheet is usually of the size 42 cm × 29 cm. The specimen is glued to the paper and the stem or branches and the leaf-petioles are stitched. Narrow strips of adhesive linen or adhesive-coated cellophane tapes may be used instead of stitching. Some prefer to fix the specimen on the paper only by using adhesive tapes and do not use glue at all. In such cases the specimen or its parts are liable to be detached from the mounting paper with the slightest friction in handling. The glue is applied to the specimen with a brush very gently and with great care. It is then placed over the paper and the extra glue is

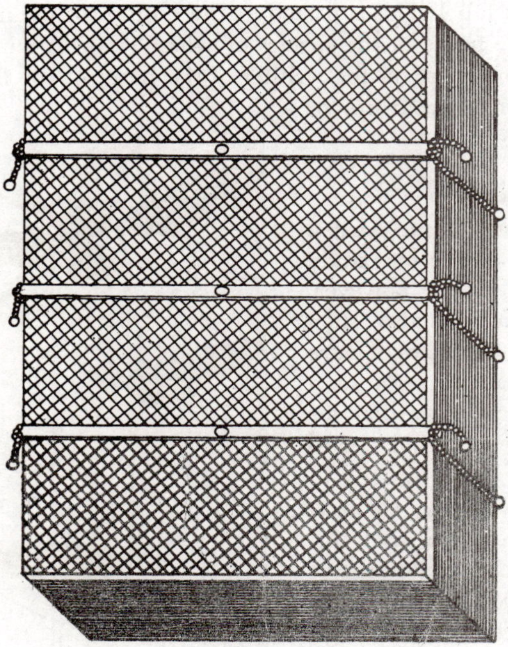

Fig. 13. A bundle of specimens with drying papers in press.

removed by means of a moistened piece of sponge. Some prefer to use a glass plate on one side of which the glue is spread generously and the specimen is placed on it. The specimen is gently pressed at several points and then lifted carefully up to be placed again on the mounting paper. When the glue dries up stitching or fixing of adhesive strips is done to complete the mounting of the specimen.

Specimens of some plants cannot be dried in the manner described above or these take very long time to dry. These are the succulents, herbs with an underground bulb, Orchids, Conifers, etc. As they do not die quickly the specimens shed their leaves. Orchids and bulbous plants continue to grow inside the press. So these require to be killed before putting them in the press. This is done by dipping them in boiling water to which a little formaldehyde may be added. Dipping them in alcohol or rectified spirit also gives the same result. They are put in the press after this treatment.

Dr. Schweinfurth while making collection in the rain forests adopted another method of drying the specimens. He took with him some deep square metal boxes with a lid on the top. After collection he placed a specimen at the centre of a large piece of paper (old newspaper or some such cheap paper) and put a few drops of a solution of alcohol and formaldehyde. Then he wrapped the specimen by drawing the corners of the paper over it which was then placed in the box. Thus when the box was filled with specimens placed one above another a little more of the solution was put in the box and the lid was tightly closed. Then by running a gum tape around the rim of the lid the box was made airtight. The specimens remained in good condition, though killed by this treatment, for a long time.

Next step is to fix a label on the mounted sheet. The label is a rectangular piece of paper generally of the size 12 cm × 10 cm on which field notes are to be entered from the field-book. The collection number of the specimen and the collector's name are also to be noted on the label. This is pasted at the bottom of the mounted sheet usually on the left corner. The name of the species of which it is a specimen is to be written now on the label. Some insist on the writing of the name of the family also. The sheet is then incorporated in a herbarium for preservation. (Fig. 14)

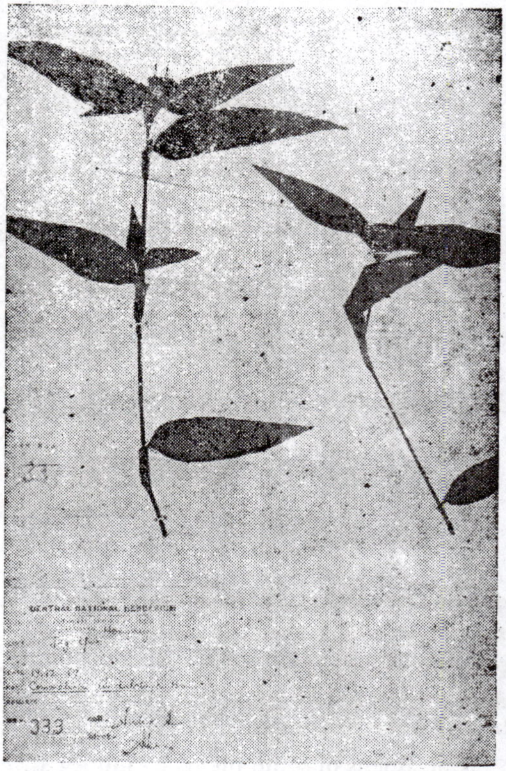

Fig. 14.

Botanic Garden

Like herbarium a botanic garden is also an important centre for study of plant taxonomy. It is, however, important from other aspects also, such as researches on other branches of pure and applied Botany and to serve as a beauty spot and pleasure garden for the enjoyment of general public. As to its scientific aspects it helps directly in the study of plant taxonomy, ecology, horticulture and agriculture and indirectly in other branches of Botany. It plays an important role in the introduction and acclimatisation of foreign plants, eradication and control of weeds, pollution and purification of air and water. For study of plant morphology, ecology and taxonomy, plants from different parts of the country as well as from foreign countries are cultivated in suitable plots within the garden in similar natural habitats often created artificially. There are conservatories for growing shade loving plants or plants of cooler or warmer countries. In temperate climates the conservatories in a botanic garden provide good opportunities for growing plants of warmer countries by controlling temperature and humidity and often reducing bright-sunlight for the shade-loving plants.

The perennial plants cultivated in a botanic garden are not planted haphazardly, but mainly arranged on a phytogeographic plan, while a separate portion is left to cultivate representatives of different families of plants following some system of classification. This portion is called students' garden. In the phytogeographic plan of arrangement the garden is divided into several plots each representing a particular country as regards to its vegetation. Foreign plants, trees, shrubs and climbers which can easily grow in the open in the prevailing climatic condition are grown in plots allotted to different countries. This gives the students some idea of the nature of vegetation of other countries of the world and also to study the morphological peculiarities of different types of plants and the ecological conditions for their growth. Separate sections are also created and kept reserved for growing special types of plants like Xerophytes, Halophytes, fresh-water aquatics, etc. Another section is kept apart for observing the behaviour of plants newly introduced from some foreign countries. This is usually called the economic section or economic garden as it is the economic or otherwise ornamental plant which is usually introduced from abroad. A nursery is always maintained in a botanic garden where seedlings are raised for planting in the garden and for distribution to other gardens and parks. Agricultural and horticultural experiments are also carried out in the nursery.

As noted before, a botanic garden has an aesthetic aspect. For that purpose decorative plants are cultivated more in a botanic garden than other type of plants, and in planting trees this aspect is always kept in view. Further, several small plots are maintained to grow flowering annuals. Beautiful lawns, paths and avenues are laid throughout the garden for the enjoyment of visitors. Small statues, bird-baths and masonry constructions are erected to decorate the garden. The pools are so arranged that they enhance the beauty of the garden. Sometimes an artificial canal is dug out inside the garden to give the idea of a streamlet. The pools and canals also serve the purpose of irrigation of the garden in addition to the cultivation of aquatic plants and for enhancing the beauty of the garden. Separate sections are set apart for laying out different styles of gardening, e.g., landscape garden, Japanese garden, Italian garden, etc. Trees and shrubs are pruned to give different shapes, sometimes of animals or birds. This art of beautifying the garden is known as Tapiary. Another art in gardening is to keep trees in dwarf condition and such trees are called Bonsai trees. These are for the enjoyment of garden-lovers as well as of general public. In large gardens a separate section is often set apart to cultivate big trees to give an impression of a forest. This is called arboretum or dendrarium.

Selection of site is also important as some places are by nature a beauty spot. Undulating areas are preferred to a flat expanse; area with a natural lake or a small streamlet passing through it possesses a natural beauty of its own and can be easily converted into an ideal garden. This, however, is not always easy, as a large area suitable for establishing a botanic garden is hard to be found. For this reason large botanic gardens have usually been established away from the cities.

Names of a few famous botanic gardens of the world are given below:

1. *Royal Botanic Garden, Kew, London:* This was a private garden of the Capel family to begin with. In 1728 it was taken over on lease by Prince Frederick, Prince of Wales. From that time it came to be known as the Royal Garden and later was given to the nation by the Royal family. It gradually developed into one of the best botanic gardens in all aspects by the efforts of the botanists and horticulturists working in the garden. It covers an area of 300 acres and has the world's largest herbarium. The garden has different sections and several large conservatories.

Sir Joseph Dalton Hooker, author of 'Flora of British India' and of many other important botanical works including "Genera Plantarum" giving a natural system of classification of flowering plants jointly with George Bentham, was once a Director of this garden, and John Hutchinson who proposed a new phylogenetic system worked in the herbarium of this garden.

2. *Royal Botanic Garden, Edinburgh:* This covers an area of 50 acres. This was at the beginning a garden of medicinal herbs established in the middle of 17th century Later it developed into a botanic garden. It has a beautiful rock garden and a herbarium with a good collection of specimens from central Asia, among other things.

3. *Botanical Garden, Berlin—Dahlem:* The Botanical Garden of Berlin had been situated in 2 other places before it was transferred to Dahlem in 1880. The area of the garden is 103 acres. Associated with it are the Botanical Museum and the Herbarium, both having rich collections. The garden is mainly geographically arranged while in one part are arranged different families according to the system of classification of Engler and Prantl. There are large conservatories, good rock-garden and several decorative pools. Prof. Adolf Engler was one of the Directors of this garden, by whose efforts the garden became one of the most important botanic gardens for the scientific arrangement and for the beautiful lay out.

4. *Bundes garden, Vienna:* This is a large garden and one of the oldest in Europe covering an area of 400 acres. It has a fine Alpine garden with varieties of cool-climate plants collected from high mountains as well as from artic region.

5. *Main Botanic Garden, Moscow:* This is the largest Botanic Garden in Europe with an area of 900 acres. It has a long line of conservatories and several tropical houses. Introduction and acclimatisation of exotic trees and shrubs is one of the main features of this garden. It has a large herbarium and good laboratory and library.

6. *Nikitisky Botanic Garden, Yalta:* This is another famous and old Botanic Garden and oldest in U.S.S.R. Established in 1812 it covers an area of 272 acres. The different sections of the garden are well arranged and the Italian garden is one of the finest with pergolas and water reservoirs. It has a good herbarium of rich collection of specimens from Southern Europe and Western and Central Asia.

7. *Indian Botanic Garden, Sibpur, Calcutta:* Established in 1787 mainly for cultivation of economic plants and timber trees. Col. Robert Kyd was the founder who was succeeded by Dr. William Boxburgh who gave the garden a botanical shape. At present it occupies an area of 273 acres. It is the oldest and largest botanic garden in Asia and has among other curious plants in cultivation; the Big Banyan tree, the largest tree in the world covering an area of about 15,000 sq. mtrs. The Central National Herbarium, the biggest herbarium in Asia is situated inside the garden.*

8. *Kebun Raya (Botanic Garden) Bogor, Java:* This is another old and famous garden being established in 1817 and covering an area of 200 acres. Among other things it has a separate section to represent a virgin rain-forest where nothing has been planted by man. It has a good herbarium and library.

9. *Missouri Botanic Garden, U.S.A.:* The garden situated in the city's suburbs covers an area of 75 acres but outside the city the Grey Summit Arboretum occupies an area of 1600 acres. It has a large dome-shaped conservatory built on geodesic principle. Collections of Orchids and succulents are excellent. It is an important centre of taxonomical work and contains a large herbarium and library.

10. *Arnold Arboretum, Boston, U.S.A.:* Starting as a small garden of the Harvard

* A more detailed account of this garden is given separately.

University it now occupies an area of 265 acres. It contains a number of green houses and a rich collection of bonsai trees, the oldest being 175 years of age.

Botanic Gardens in India

India can boast of several important and beautiful botanic gardens and among these Indian Botanic Garden, Sibpur, National Botanic Garden, Lucknow, and Lloyd Botanic Garden, Darjeeling, are well-known. Brief accounts of these three are given below:

Indian Botanic Garden : As ealry as 1786 Colonel Robert Kyd, a Military Engineer of the East Indian Company and a keen lover of gardening sent a proposal to the Directors of the Company in London that a Botanic Garden be established near Calcutta. The purpose of establishing such a garden was mainly to raise in the nursery different economic plants, such as spices, medicinal plants, timber trees, etc., and grow them in the garden and distribute seedlings of such plants among the local people for cultivation in different parts of the country. By this the people of this country would be directly benefited and the East India Company would also have some profit directly from the increase of trade and commerce. The Directors of the Company approved the proposal and asked Col. Kyd to take steps for establishing the garden, appointing him as the Hony. Superintendent. Accordingly a large plot of land was acquired on the western side of the Hooghly river and the garden was established in July 1787. The garden was named at that time as the Honble East India Company's Botanic Garden but to the Botanists of the world this came to be known as the Horto Botanico Calcuttensis. It remained under the management of the East India Company for a long time and after the Queen's Proclamation when the Indian Government of the East Indian Company went directly under the British Crown, the name of the garden was changed to Royal Botanic Garden, Sibpur. It is now called the Indian Botanic Garden and forms a section of the Botanical Survey of India.

The area of the garden is 273 acres although it had a larger area to start with. After its establishment Col. Kyd set about to arrange the garden according to his own ideas. But after six years he died and Dr. William Roxburgh who already made a name as a good botanist was appointed as Superintendent at a handsome salary. He gave the garden a botanical shape by introducing many interesting plants. He prepared and published a catalogue of the plants cultivated in the garden at that time wherein he gave botanical names to a few Indian plants which were unknown to the botanists till then. Roxburgh wrote a comprehensive flora of India and prepared a set of coloured plates of Indian plants of portfolio size which are still preserved in good condition.

Roxburgh was succeeded by Dr. Nathanial Wallich who also made great contributions for the advancement of our knowledge of the Indian flora. A herbarium was started in the Botanic Garden during his time which now functions as the Central National Herbarium. The collections of plant specimens during Wallich's time were enormous and these after identification were entered by him in a catalogue. This Wallichian Catalogue serves as a very important record of authenticated specimens from India and adjacent countries.

Sir George King became Superintendent of this garden in 1870. He rearranged the garden on a geographical plan. A portion was set aside as student's garden, where plants of different families were cultivated in different plots. Conservatories were constructed for cultivation of Orchids and shade-loving plants. Several pools were excavated for cultivation of water-lilies, lotus and other aquatic plants. The phytogeographic arrangement is still maintained with some modifications and improvements.

The centre of attraction to the visitors is the Big Banyan tree which is over 200 years old. This was a small tree when the garden was established and since then growing and extending in all directions. The leafy crown covers an area of 15,000 sq. mtr. and is resting on 1,142 proproots, the main trunk no longer existing. There are several good specimens of banyan tree in the garden other than this one of which has attained almost equal size as the Big Banyan noted above.

The garden has a good collection of palms in a separate section called the Palmetum, where are found *Hyphaene thebeica*—the African branching palm, *Corypha*—the monocarpic Talipot palm, *Elaeis guineensis*—the African Oil palm, *Caryota*—the Fish-tail palm and many other tall and dwarf species of the family. The Double-coconut—*Llodoicea maldivica* is to be found in one of the green houses.

Like Palmetum there are other sections, e.g., Bambusetum, Pandanetum and Pinetum with collections of different species of bamboos, screwpines and conifers. Of the beautiful trees mention may be made of *Amhertsia nobilis*, *Brownea*, *Monodora*, *Tabebuia*, *Lagerstroemia*, *Jacaranda* and *Cassia*. The giant water-lily of the Amazon—*Victoria amazonica* is in cultivation in several ponds with different varieties of water-lily and lotus. Among curiosities *Ficus Krishnae*, the banyan with pouch-shaped leaves, the tall unbranched Dipterocarpus, *Taxodium distichum* with flying buttress deserve mentioning.

The Indian Botanic Garden was maintained by government from the beginning as a separate entity until it was merged with the Botanical Survey of India in 1963 and formed a section of the same.

In addition to the Indian Botanic Garden the Botanical Survey of India has under it 5 experimental gardens, at (1) Barapani, Meghalaya, (2) Allahabad, (3) Pauri near Dehra Dun, (4) Mundwa near Poona and (5) Port Blair and 2 National Orchidaria at Shillong and Yercaud in Shevaroy hills.

Lloyd Botanic Garden, Darjeeling: This beautiful garden was established in 1878 on 40 acres of land donated by Mr. William Lloyd and for that reason was named after the donor. It has a good collection of Orchids and many Indian and foreign plants of the temperate region. From the beginning it served as a nursery for the introduction of many exotic ornamental shrubs for the purpose of cultivation in the hill stations of India. It has a good herbarium with representative collection of specimens from the E. Himalaya. It is financed by the state.

National Botanic Garden, Lucknow: This was the garden of the Nawabs of Oudh who had their capital at Lucknow. It was later on maintained as a pleasure-garden and afterwards converted into a botanic garden. It occupies an area of about 70 acres and is nicely decorated. It has a good herbarium with a collection of about 100,000 specimens of plants from India and adjacent countries. It is financed by the Council of Scientific and Industrial Research, New Delhi.

Garden of the Indian Agricultural Research Institute, New Delhi: This is also a nice garden occupying an area of about 60 acres. This is maintained mainly as an experimental garden of the Research Institute while carrying on other functions of a botanic garden.

Garden of the Forest Research Institute, Dehra Dun: This is a small garden with an area of over 20 acres, attached to the institute, maintained as a pleasure garden and for helping in researches carried on in the institute

There is also another large garden attached to the Bhaba Atomic Research Centre at Trombay.

Botanical Survey of India

Exploration of the plant resources of India and preparation of floristic accounts started by the middle of the 19th century by several botanists and naturalists working in different parts of the country. It was felt that co-ordination of their works was necessary and a central organisation should be created for that purpose. A scheme for the organisation of a Botanical Survey was accordingly drawn up and this having met with the approval of the Secretary of State for India in July, 1887, the Survey was formally established on the 13th February, 1890. Its functions were laid down as: (1) Exploring the vegetable resources of the then Indian Empire and (2) co-ordinating the botanical researches of the workers in different parts of India. Sir George King who was then the Superintendent of the Calcutta Gardens was made the central authority of the Botanical Survey and was designated as the Director, Botanical Survey of India. One wing of the Indian Museum, known as the Industrial Section, containing collections of economic products, art-ware and ethnology was placed under the control of the Director, who had his office in this wing.

The administrative set up was reviewed in 1936 and accordingly the posts of the Superintendent of the Botanic Garden and of the Director of the Botanical Survey of India were separated in 1937. The filling up of the post of Director after the retirement of Mr. C. C. Calder was kept in abeyance for several years.

In 1954 the Botanical Survey was reorganised and expanded, when a Chief Botanist was appointed to function as Director. Four regional circles were established under the Survey at Dehra Dun, Poona, Coimbatore and Shillong, the Headquarters having been stationed in Calcutta. A Botanical Laboratory was established at Lucknow to be transferred later to Allahabad and finally to Sibpur. The herbarium at Sibpur was taken over in 1957 and was designated as the Central National Herbarium and the Botanic Garden with its library was also transferred to the Botanical Survey of India in 1963. A regional circle was started in Allahabad and was called the Central Circle. Two more regional circles were added, one at Jodhpur, known as the Arid Zone Circle, and the other at Port Blair, the Andaman and Nicobar Circle.

At present the Headquarters of the Botanical Survey of India is located in the Indian Botanic Garden. The Headquarters Organisation consists of the following sections, viz., Ecology, Cryptogamic Botany, Plant Chemistry, Pharmacognosy, Palynology and Publications, in addition to the administrative section. The Central Botanical Laboratory consists of the Economic Botany, Plant Physiology, Biochemistry and Cytogenetic sections. The Publication section publishes two important journals devoted to plant taxonomy, e.g. the Records of the Botanical Survey of India and the Bulletin of the Botanical Survey of India and prints and circulates the Annual Report and News Letter giving the activities of the Survey. In addition to all these units in India the Survey maintains a liaison Botanist at Royal Botanic Garden, Kew, London, whose duty is to supply information on taxonomical problems to workers all over India in the Botanical Survey as well as in other institutions.

In Botanical Survey researches on almost all branches of Botany are carried on at present. And information on every aspect of plant life is furnished to research workers and interested public. Seedlings and plant-materials are also distributed to other institutions, municipalities and persons interested in gardening.

Nomenclature of Plants and History of International Botanical Congress

Linnaeus thought about adopting a system for naming the plants and in his Species Plantarum adopted the binomial system, where the name of a species had two parts, the 1st being the generic name and the 2nd the specific epithet. He published 2 books, viz., Fundamenta Botanica in 1736 and Critica Botanica in 1737 giving his ideas about taxonomy and nomenclature. Later he published another book on the subject, viz., Philosophia Botanica in 1751 amplifying his views expressed in the 2 earlier books.

In 1813 Augustin de Candolle published a book entitled "Theorie elementaire de la botanique" where among other things he laid down a set of rules on plant-nomenclature, many of them taken from Linnaeus.

In 1867 an internationl meeting was organised in Paris to discuss about framing rules for naming of plants for the guidance of all botanists. This meeting was the 1st International Botanical Congress. On this occasion Alphonse de Candolle, son of Augustin de Candolle, prepared a set of rules which he called "Lois de la nomenclature botanique" and copies of these laws were circulated to the delegates for discussion. These after slight modifications were adopted at the meetings of the congress and formed what was known as **Paris Code.**

Although the Paris Code appeared satisfactory, some botanists did not accept it in toto. Particularly in the case of transfer of a species from one genus to another the British botanists did not follow the continental botanists. Some American botanists also followed the British botanists and the rule obeyed was called the **Kew Rule**.

In America N. L. Britton and a group of botanists worked out a separate set of rules to govern the nomenclature of plants. These were passed at the meeting of the Botanical Club of the American Association for the Advancement of Science, held in 1892 in Rochester, New York. These rules formed the **Rochester Code.**

In 1900 the Continental botanists met in Paris again and discussed at length plans for a serious study of the entire nomenclatural problem. This was the 2nd International Botanical Congress and the result of the discussion was known as the **Paris Convention.** In 1905 a meeting of true international character was held in Vienna which is called the 3rd International Congress. At this session of the Congress the rules of Paris Code of 1867 were finally adopted with some modification and amplification. The American botanists following the Rochester Code refused to accept the verdict of the Vienna Congress and in 1907 prepared another set of rules which they called the **American Code.** The American Code did not, however, differ much from the Rochester Code.

The 4th International Congress was held in Brussels in 1910. Here the type concept of the Rochester Code was recognised. Otherwise it was more or less like the Vienna Code.

The Committee on nomenclature of the Botanical Society of America formulated a new Code in 1918 and called it the **Type-basis Code**, differing from the American Code in minor points. This code was never popular even in America. Afterwards botanists of different countries tried to bring harmony and accord in the subject and two conferences were held, one in London in 1924, known as the Imperial Botanical Conference and the other in Ithaca, New York in 1926 called the Ithaca Congress. After this in the 5th International Botanical Congress at Cambridge in 1930 a compromise was arrived at between the British, the continental and the American botanists and a code of nomenclature came into being that was international in nature as well as in function. It was also decided that henceforth revision or modification of rules should be done only at the meetings of the International Botanical Congress. Since then proposals about plant nomenclature are discussed at such meetings and adopted or rejected by the delegates.

After the 5th session of the International Congress, the 6th was held in Amsterdam in 1935, the 7th in Stockholm in 1950, 8th in Paris in 1955, 9th in Montreal in 1959, 10th in Edinburgh in 1964, 11th in Seattle, New York in 1969, 12th in Leningrad in 1975, 13th in Sidney in 1981 and 14th in Berlin in 1987.

Rules of Nomenclature

The rules of naming different taxa of plants are embodied in a book known as the International Code of Botanical Nomenclature. The Code has been prepared after discussion and agreement between the botanists in the International Botanical Congress held in different places since 1867 the last of which the 14th session being held in Berlin in 1987. There are 5 guiding principles in the code and 75 articles giving the rules.

The guiding principles are noted below :

1. Botanical nomenclature is independent of Zoological nomenclature.
2. Names of taxonomical groups should be governed by a rule of priority.
3. A taxon can have only one correct name.
4. All scientific names of plants should be in Latin.
5. The rules of nomenclature are retroactive.

Following are the important rules :

1. *Nomenclatural type :* The nomenclatural type is that constituent element (a specimen, or a description or a figure) of a taxon to which the name is permanently attached. This need not be the most typical or representative element but is the original material on which the description of the taxon is based.

Following kinds of types are recognised :

(a) **Holotype :** Specimen or other element designated by the author or used by him as the nomenclatural type.

(b) **Isotype :** This is a duplicate of the holotype.

(c) **Syntype :** When more than one specimen are cited by the author without mentioning which is the holotype, each specimen is designated as a Syntype.

(d) **Paratype :** Specimens cited along with the holotype are designated as Paratypes.

(e) **Lectotype :** This is a substitute of the holotype when that is lost and is to be selected from the isotypes. When no holotype was designated by the author a specimen from the original material is selected to be the Lectotype.

(f) **Neotype :** When all original materials are missing a Neotype is selected from other materials.

(g) **Topotype :** Specimen of a species collected at the same locality as the holotype.

2. *Rule of priority :* In the case of a family or a taxon below the rank of a family the earliest legitimate name should be considered as valid (or correct).

For this purpose 1st May 1753 is taken as the earliest date for all plants excepting the Fungi, some Algae, and the Musci other than the Sphagnaceae. This means the names appearing in Linnaeus's Species Plantarum are the earliest names for the purpose of consideration of the Rule of Priority, those published earlier are not to be given priority.

3. *Names of taxa:* The name of a species is a binary combination consisting of the name of the genus followed by a single specific epithet. The name of a genus is a substantive in the singular number. The specific epithet is an adjective and is of the same gender as the generic name, or is a noun in apposition to the generic name. The specific epithet must not exactly repeat the generic name.

The name of an infra-specific taxon is a combination of the name of a species and an infra-specific epithet connected by a term denoting its rank.

The name of a genus or of a taxa of higher rank is spelt with a capital initial letter. All specific and infra-specific epithets should be written with a small initial letter. Formerly it was the custom to spell the epithets with a capital initial letter where the epithets were derived from the names of persons, or were vernacular names, or were former generic names. This is not followed at present.

The name of a family is derived from the name of the genus which is the type for the family. The name of a subfamily, a tribe or a subtribe is derived from the name of the type-genus belonging to that subfamily, tribe or subtribe.

Endings of the names of taxa above the rank of genus should be in the manner noted below:

Order	—"ales" (e.g. Rosales)
Suborder	—"ineae" (e.g. Rosineae)
Family	—"aceae" (e.g. Rosaceae)
Subfamily	—"oideae" (e.g. Rosoideae)
Tribe	—"eae"
Subtribe	—"inae"

A few family-names although not complying with the above rules are treated as valid because of long usage as such. These are noted below with their alternative names:

Palmae (Arecaceae from Areca)
Gramineae (Poaceae from Poa)
Cruciferae (Brassicaceae from Brassica)
Leguminosae (Fabaceae from Faba)
Guttiferae (Clusiaceae from Clusia)
Umbelliferae (Apiaceae from Apium)
Labiatae (Lamiaceae from Lamium)
Compositae (Asteraceae from Aster).

4. *Effective and valid publication:* Any printed matter when widely circulated is regarded as effectively published. It is sufficient if the printed matter is distributed at least to the botanical institutions with libraries accessible to botanists generally.

The date of effective publication is the date on which the printed matter became available.

Valid publication of a name of new taxon is necessary to have it effectively published, to have a correct form and to be accompanied by a description or diagnosis or a reference to a previously published description.

For the name of a new taxon to be valid it is necessary that the description or the diagnosis should be in Latin. Those published earlier to 1st Jan. 1935 are considered valid even if the description or diagnosis were not in Latin. In the case of Algae the date has been fixed as 1st Jan. 1958 instead of 1st Jan. 1935. In the case of recent

Algae, the Latin description or diagnosis of a new taxon must be accompanied by an illustration or figure.

Publication of a new name of the rank of family or below on or after 1st January, 1958 is not considered valid if the type is not indicated.

The name of a taxon below the rank of a genus is not validly published unless the name of the genus or species to which it is assigned is validly published.

He who first validly published the name of a taxon is the author of that name. It is necessary to cite the name of the author after the name of the taxon.

5. *Retention of specific and infra-specific epithets:* When a species is transferred to another genus without change of rank the specific epithet must be retained. If the name of a genus is changed being illegitimate, the binary combinations for all the species under that genus should be changed also and in doing so the new generic name should be used retaining the older specific epithets.

This rule applies equally to infra-specific taxa.

A specific epithet is not illegitimate merely because it was originally published under an illegitimate generic name; it is to be taken into consideration for purpose of priority.

6. *Rejection of names:* A name is to be rejected if it is used in different senses and for that reason has become a source of error.

A name is to be rejected if it is based on a type consisting of two or more entirely discordant elements. A name is to be rejected also if it is based on a monstrosity.

7. *Splitting of a genus:* When a genus is divided into 2 or more genera the original generic name must be retained for one of the smaller genera which includes the type species of the undivided genus.

This rule applies equally to cases of division of species.

8. *Synonym and Basionym:* All names of a taxon other than the valid names are synonyms of that taxon.

When the name of a species or of an infra-specific taxon is changed the synonym of which the epithet is to be taken for the valid name, is Basionym for that taxon.

PART II

FAMILIES OF ANGIOSPERMS (MAGNOLIOPHYTA)

CHAPTER VI

MONOCOTYLEDONEAE

PANDANALES

The order according to Engler consists of 3 families, viz. Typhaceae, Sparganiaceae and Pandanaceae. The plants in these families grow in marshy habitat. They have small inconspicuous flowers which are unisexual and densely crowded in heads or spikes. Perianth is absent or rudimentary. Seeds are rich in endosperm.

According to Engler the order is a group of primitive families. The small, simple, unisexual flowers, produced in huge quantities in densely crowded inflorescences are of primitive type. Therefore in the system of classification by Engler and Prantl the order is placed in the beginning of the Monocotyledoneae and the 3 families are considered to be closely related to one another. Rendle follows Engler and states further that Sparganiaceae and Pandanaceae having the flowers crowded in heads which form a compound racemose inflorescence have a closer alliance between them than with Typhaceae. Hutchinson and most modern botanists consider that the simplicity of the flowers are due to reduction and not due to primitiveness and the 3 families are in reality more advanced among the monocots. Further the 3 families are not so closely related as to constitute a single order. He, therefore, removes Typhaceae and Sparganiaceae from Pandanales and places them in a separate order as Typhales while he treats Pandanales as a monotypic order with a single family Pandanaceae. The resemblances between Sparganiaceae and Pandanaceae as shown by Rendle are to him not of primary importance and Sparganiaceae resembles more to Typhaceae in flower-character. The splitting of Pandanales and creation of a new order, e.g. Typhales with 2 families Typhaceae and Sparganiaceae by Hutchinson have been supported by Takhtajan and also by Cronquist.

Typhaceae

Aquatic herbs growing in fresh water or in marshes, with a long creeping rhizome and erect simple shoots arising from the axils of lateral scales of the rhizome. Leaves distichous, mostly near the base; long and linear or strap-shaped, entire, obtuse at apex and sheathing at the base, rather thick and spongy; lower leaves reduced to long sheaths only. Flowers are monoecious, very small and numerous, crowded in terminal spadix, the males above and the females below, the 2 portions contiguous or remote from each other; 2 alternate deciduous bracts are present, one at the base of the female portion of the spadix and the other at the base of the male portion and a few more smaller bracts often found in between the male flowers. The axis of the spadix is more or less compressed. The female flowers are mostly borne on short cylindrical outgrowths while the male flowers are produced directly on the axis. Flowers are animophilous. Perianth is represented by very slender jointed threads or elongated spathulate scales, or these may be altogether absent. The number of stamens in a male flower is usually three but it may be less or upto 5; filaments free or united at base; anthers linear basifixed, with connective produced above; the pollen grains are often united in tetrad. Rudimentary ovary is often present in male flowers. A normal female flower has a long gynophore bearing many long simple hairs. Often these flowers are subtended by small spathulate scale-like bracts. The hairs are persistent and elongate in fruit in the dispersal of which they are very helpful. The small ovary is fusiform, unilocular, narrowed into the style with a ligulate or unilateral stigma; ovule solitary, pendulous and anatropous. Fruit is a small nutlet, ultimately splitting. The seed with a striate testa contains a fleshy or mealy endosperm and a narrow, straight, elongated embryo.

Floral formula:

$$♂—P_0A_{(1-5)}G_0$$

$$♀—P_0A_0G_1$$

This is a monotypic family containing a single genus *Typha* with about 15 species distributed in temperate and tropical countries of the world. In India *T. elephantina* Roxb. and *T. angustata* Chaub. & Bory are the 2 species growing in fresh water marshes in the plains. The long leaves of these 2 species (the Bull rush) are woven into mats and are used in thatching.

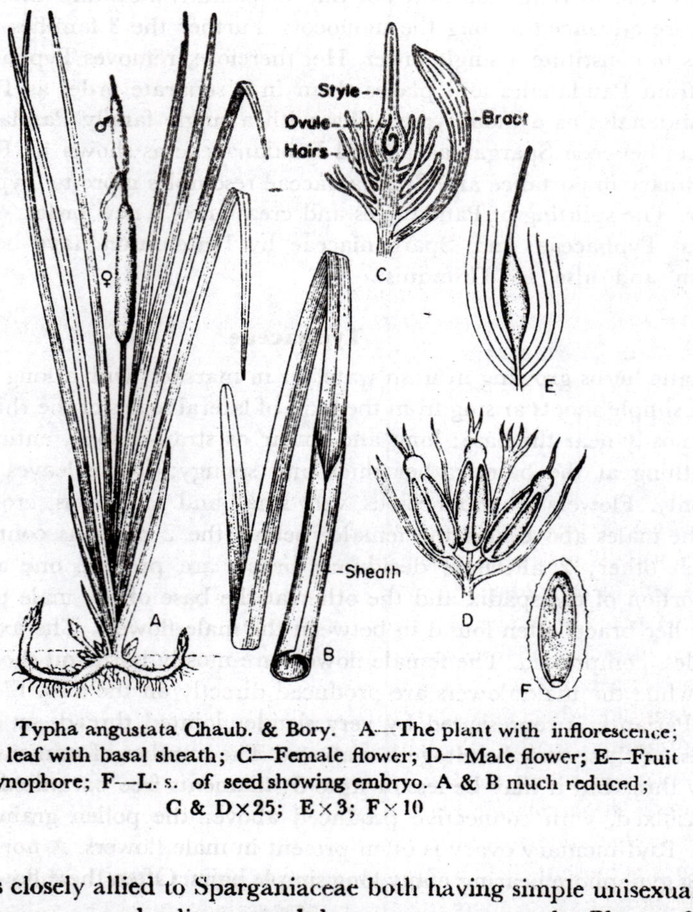

Fig. 15. Typha angustata Chaub. & Bory. A—The plant with inflorescence; B—One leaf with basal sheath; C—Female flower; D—Male flower; E—Fruit on gynophore; F—L. s. of seed showing embryo. A & B much reduced; C & D×25; E×3; F×10

Typhaceae is closely allied to Sparganiaceae both having simple unisexual flowers, superior unilocular ovary and solitary pendulous anatropous ovule. Plants of both the families grow in similar aquatic situation. Engler and Rendle consider that Typhaceae and Sparganiaceae are closely allied to each other and also to Pandanaceae which also have plants with simple unisexual flowers. The ovary is superior and unilocular and ovules are anatropous. They further consider that the 3 families are most primitive among the Monocotyledons and place them in the beginning of the Monocots under a single order Pandanales. Hutchinson and most other modern botanists are of the opinion that the simplicity of the flowers is the result of reduction and not due to primitiveness. They further split the order Pandanales of Engler to Typhales with 2 families Typhaceae and Sparganiaceae and Pandanales with the single family Pandanaceae. In Pandanaceae the dioecious plants have sporophylls usually numerous in the flowers, ovules 1–many in each carpel, oily endosperm and small embryo in the seed clearly indicate that the family is not so closely related to Typhaceae and Sparganiaceae and the removal of these 2 families from Pandanales to a separate order as Typhales by Hutchinson seems to be justified. Pandanaceae appears to resemble the Palms and Cyclanthaceae to some extent while Typhaceae has some similarity with Araceae.

Sparganiaceae

Rhizomatous aquatic herbs. Leaves alternate, linear, stiff and erect or flaccid and floating, sheathing at the base. Flowers monoecious, anemophilous, crowded in male or female globose heads forming a paniculate inflorescence, the male heads occupying the upper part and the female heads the basal part. Perianth represented by a few membranous scales. Male flowers with 3 or more stamens, free or united; anthers oblong or cuneate, basifixed, dehiscing longitudinally. Female flower with a superior 1-locular ovary; ovule solitary pendulous; style simple or forked with unilateral stigma. Fruit drupacious with a spongy exocarp and hard endocarp. Seed with a thin testa, a straight embryo and mealy endosperm.

Sparganiaceae is a unigeneric family with about 20 species but they are wide in their distribution in the temperate and frigid zones of both hemispheres. In India it is represented by *S. simplex* Huds. which is found in the Himalayas and Khasi hills at 2000 mtr. and above.

Pandanaceae

The plants of this family are shrubs or short trees, rarely root-climbers. A full grown plant usually rests on a cluster of stilt-roots which come out from the basal part of the stem as well as the older branches as the main roots and often the lower part of the stem get decayed. The leaves are long and leathery, densely whorled near the apex of the stem and branches or they are in $\frac{1}{3}$ alternate phyllotaxy; sheathing at the base and usually keeled; keel and margins spinulose.

The plants are dioecious with numerous small flowers. The male flowers are in simple or compound spadix. The lower bracts are foliacious and the upper are smaller and spathe-like and often showy. In *Freycinetia* bracts form an involucre, the inner being coloured. In *Sararanga* scale-like bracteoles are present. The male flowers usually consist of several stamens, free or united and perianthless. In *Sararanga* a short obscurely lobed perianth is present. In *Pandanus* the stamens are arranged in the form of a spike or umbel on the floral axis, or there may be a single stamen only. The anthers are basifixed, 2-locular or rarely 4-locular and split lengthwise. The numerous stamens in *Freycinetia* surround a rudimentary ovary.

The female flowers are crowded in dense globular heads or cylindrical spikes which form a cluster in *Freycinetia* due to the shortening of the axis of inflorescence. In *Sararanga* it forms a pendulous panicle. In *Pandanus* and *Freycinetia* perianth is altogether absent in pistillate flower. In *Sararanga* a ring of undulate margined perianth

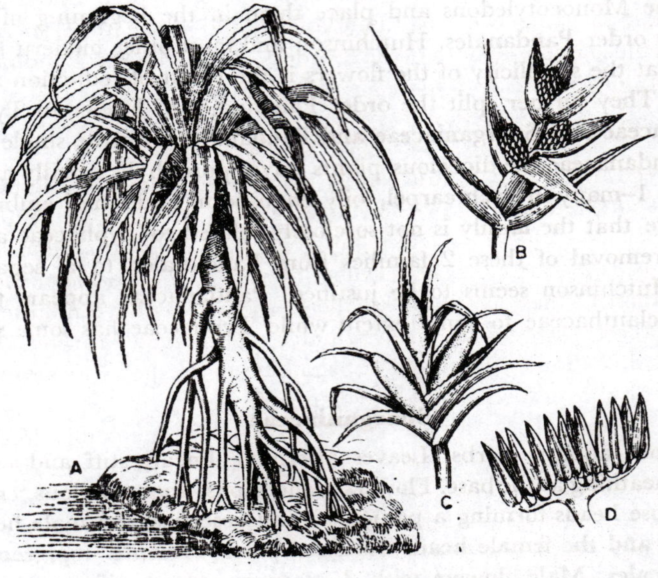

Fig. 16. Pandanus furcatus Roxb. A—One plant; B—Female inflorescence; C—Male inflorescence; D—One male flower; A, B & C reduced; D—nat size.

is present as in the male flower. The gynoecium is superior and composed of one or few coherent carpels, a large number (70-80) in *Sararanga*, each unilocular and with sessile or subsessile stigma, ovule solitary and basal or several in a row on the ventral suture, anatropous; a ring of staminodes surrounds the base of the pistil in *Freycinetia*.

The fruit is a syncarp of berries or drupes; in *Pandanus* the endocarp is hard and the mesocarp is fleshy, fibrous or woody. The seed is small and has a fleshy or oily endosperm and minute embryo.

Floral formula:

$$♂\ P_0 A_{(1-\infty)} G_0$$

$$♀\ P_0 A_0 G_{(1-\infty)}$$

The family consists of 3 genera and over 250 species distributed in the tropical and subtropical regions of the old world from the sea-shore to about 1500 mtr. in the hills in damp situations. It is represented in India by several species of Pandanus of which *P. tectorius* Sol. ex. Park (Syn. *P. fascicularis* Lam.) has sweet scented male flowers from which keora-water is manufactured.

The family Pandanaceae has been included in Pandanales by Engler along with Typhaceae and Sparganiaceae, all having perianthless, unisexual flowers and superior ovary. Pandanaceae differs from the other two in habit and being dioecious, while Typhaceae and Sparganiaceae are monoecious.

Engler as well as Rendle consider that the 3 families having simple flowers are the most primitive families among the Monocots and place the order Pandanales at the beginning of that class. Hutchinson and most other modern taxonomists believe that the simplicity is not due to primitiveness but due to reduction and the 3 families are not so closely related as to be included in a single order and therefore remove Typhaceae and Sparganiaceae from Pandanales and place them in a distinct order Typhales. Hutchinson considers that the 2 orders Typhales and Pandanales originated from Liliaceous stock in separate lines.

HELOBIEAE

In this order Engler and Prantl include the following families: Potamogetonaceae, Najadaceae, Aponogetonaceae, Scheuchzeriaceae, Alismaceae, Butomaceae and Hydrocharitaceae. The plants of these families are mainly aquatic in habit and have exalbuminous seeds. Cyclic or hemicyclic flowers and apocarpous ovary are also characters common to these families. Further many plants have minute scales associated with the leaf bases (squamulae intravaginalis). These scales are considered as appendages to the basal portion of the leaf-skin belonging to the next leaf above. Such scales, however, occur also in some Araceae and Lemnaceae.

The flowers without perianth or with free perianth segments, free stamens and apocarpus pistil indicate primitiveness. These families therefore are considered as primitive families among the Monocotyledoneae and Engler as well as Rendle place the order Helobieae just after Pandanales which according to them is the most primitive in that class. Hutchinson and most other botanists agree that these families are primitive, more primitive than the Pandanales. The family Butomaceae with several ovules on laminar placenta is considered by Hutchinson to be the most primitive and Alismaceae with many free stamens and carpels is also of same status. Therefore he places these 2 families at the beginning of this group of families as well as in the class Monocotyledoneae along with Hydrocharitaceae with laminar placentation and Scheuchzeriaceae with free floral parts. Najadaceae with unisexual and more or less simple flowers is placed at the end of this group tracing its origin from Alismataceae through Juncaginaceae and Aponogetonaceae, i.e. from bisexual flowers with many parts in each whorl to unisexual and extremely reduced flowers.

Hutchinson further breaks up the order Helobieae into 7 orders of smaller dimensions but states that these are close to one another and are a primitive group among the Monocots. In such treatment of Helobieae Hutchinson is followed by most other botanists including Takhtajan and Cronquist who put them under a subclass Alismidae (or Alismatidae). Hutchinson has no name for this group but includes them in one of his 3 divisions of the Monocots, viz., Calyciferae. The relationship of these orders as expressed by Hutchinson is shown here diagrammatically:

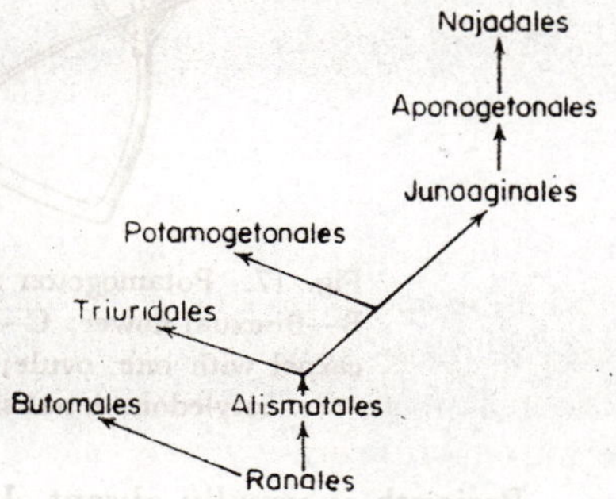

Potamogetonaceae

The plants are aquatic herbs with perennial rhizome growing in fresh water or in marshes, often marine. Leaves are submerged or floating, alternate or sometimes opposite; petiole sheathing at the base; sheath free or partially united to the petiole; floating leaves leathery, submerged leaves membranous; minute scales are present in the axils. Flowers are actinomorphic, bisexual or unisexual, in axillary pedunculate spikes; the peduncle is surrounded by a sheath at the base. Bracts are present or absent and the sheath is more like a spathe in *Zostera* where the spike is turned into a spadix. In *Ruppia* the spike is reduced to 2 flowers only and the peduncle which remain at first enclosed in the broad swollen sheaths of the uppermost foliage leaves elongates to expose the flowers. In *Posidonia* the inflorescence is a compound spike and the spike-branches are enclosed at base by the sheaths of leafy bracts. The lower flowers are bisexual and upper ones are male. In *Zostera* and *Phyllospadix* the flowers are on flattened spadices enclosed in the spathe-like sheaths of the uppermost leaves.

Phyllospadix is dioecious while *Zostera* has bisexual flowers borne on the upper surface of the membranous spadix. There are two rows of alternating stamens and carpels. Each stamen and the carpel opposite represent a single flower. On the margin of the spadix there is a row of scales which are considered as bracteoles or as prolongations of the connectives. According to some authors flowers of *Zostera* are unisexual.

Zannichellia is monoecious. Groups of 4 or fewer flowers form a cymose umbel surrounded by cup-like entire spathe. The males are long-stalked and the females are short-stalked.

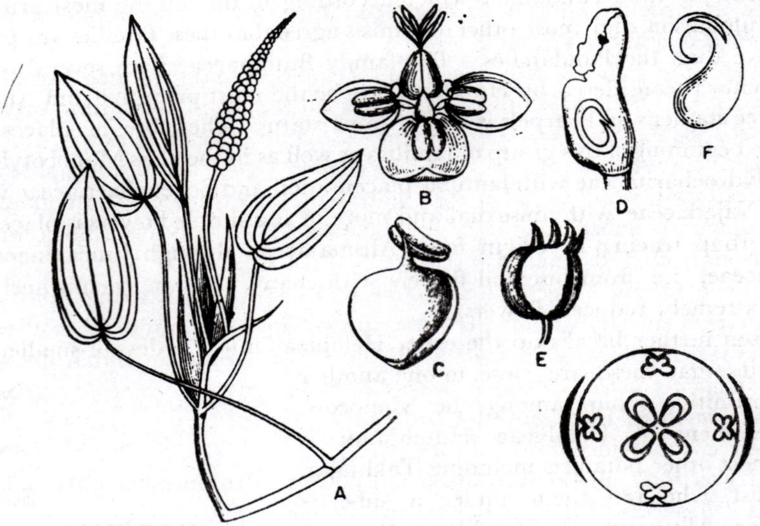

Fig. 17. Potamogeton indicus Roxb. A—A leafy shoot with a spike; B—Bisexual flower; C—A perianth segment with a sessile anther; D—A carpel with one ovule; E—Fruits; F—Embryo with hypocotyl and cotyledon. A nat size, B × 15, C × 20, D × 30, E × 20, F × 50.

Perianth is usually absent. In *Althenia* the male flowers have a short 3-toothed perianth. In *Potamogeton* the sessile anther has a tail-like projected structure at the base of the connective. This structure is considered by some as an extended part of the connective and the flower is perianthless. Others consider that it is nothing but a sepal on which the sessile anther of the stamen is situated. There being 4 stamens, the perianth is considered to consist of 4 sepals. The anther being extrose, it is very unlikely that the connective is extended at the base in the manner. This is also proved by anatomical evidence the vascular supply being separate for the stamen and the perianth segment.

A flower of *Potamogeton* may be described as consisting of a whorl of 4 sepals, 4 stamens and 4 sessile carpels. Sepals are valvate and shortly clawed. Stamens inserted on the claws of the sepals have sessile 2-locular extrorse anthers; pollens globose. Gynoecium consists of 4 free carpels, each 1-locular, sessile, superior, containing a single, campylotropous ovule, attached to the inner angle of the carpel; stigma sessile or style very short.

Kunth described the flowers of *Potamogeton* as unisexual, the male consisting of a single stamen subtended by a bract and the female with a single carpel without any bract or perianth. According to this view the so-called bisexual 4-merous flower is a cluster of 4 flowers and a part of a compound inflorescence. This has been supported by Niki (1937) and also by Uhl (1947) but is not accepted by most botanists.

The bisexual flowers of *Ruppia* consist of 2 stamens and 4 sessile carpels. Stamens have short broad filament and 2-locular reniform anther, the loculi separated by broad connective. Gynoecium consists of usually 4 carpels, sessile at first but with a long, often spirally coiled stalk at fruiting stage; style is short with peltate or umbonate stigma; ovule is solitary and pendulous in each carpel and campylotropous.

A flower of *Zostera* consists of a stamen and a carpel only. Each stamen is represented by 2 half anthers separated by a connective and lying flat on the axis of the spadix; the pollens are confervoid. Ovary has a single pendulous ovule and a lateral persistent style and a forked deciduous stigma.

In *Cymodocea* the male flower consists of 2 longitudinally jointed anthers that represent 2 stamens. The female flower has 2 free carpels, each containing a pendulous ovule; the short style terminates in 2 long, narrow stigmas. The male flower of *Zannichellia* is long pedicelled; stamen one or two. The female flower has a single short-stalked carpel with a solitary pendulous ovule; style short with a spathulate or umbonate stigma. Fruits are druplets or achenes, solitary or in clusters. The seed has a thick and tough testa and a strongly curved embryo.

The family contains 11 genera and about 120 species occurring mostly in the tropical countries of the world. None is of any importance economically. *Potamogeton* is by far the largest genus having 90 species of which 16 are found in India, the common among them being *P. indicus* Roxb., *P. natans* L. and *P. crispus* L. *Ruppia rostellata* Koch and *Zannichellia palustesis* Linn. are also Indian.

The family is subdivided into 5 tribes, viz.,

Tribe I *Zostereae:* Bisexual or unisexual flowers in compressed spike, saline.

Tribe II *Posidonieae:* Bisexual flowers in branched spike; saline.

Tribe III *Potamogetoneae:* Bisexual flower in simple cylindrical spike; in fresh and brackish water.

Tribe IV *Cymodoceae:* Unisexual flower, solitary or in cymes, pollen thread-like; saline.

Tribe V *Zannichellieae:* Unisexual flowers, solitary or in cymes, pollen globose; in fresh or brackish or salt water.

In the old system of classification of Bentham and Hooker Potamogetonaceae was not treated as a family distinct from Najadaceae. Engler established this new family to accommodate all the genera of Najadaceae excepting only the genus Najas. From the description of Potamogetonaceae as given here it is observed that the genera under this family of Engler are very variable in characters to be satisfactorily included in a single family and it is more a heterogenous group than a natural family. Hutchinson further reduced Potamogetonaceae into a family of 2 genera only and created 4 new families, viz., Posidoniaceae, Zosteraceae, Ruppiaceae and Zannichelliaceae, i.e. he raised the 5 tribes of Potamogetonaceae to distinct families and these families he distributed into several orders splitting the order Helobieae into altogether 7 orders. Such treatment of Hutchinson has met with the approval of most recent botanists including Takhtajan who kept them as distinct families and also created another family, viz., Cymodoceaceae with the single genus Cymodocea. Takhtajan, however, places all these new families in Najadales wherein are also inlcluded Aponogetonaceae, Scheuchzeriaceae and Juncaginaceae.

Najadaceae

The plants are small annual herbs, submerged in fresh or brackish water with slender much-branched stem, rooting at the nodes. Leaves numerous, subopposite or verticillate, narrow, sessile, with a sheathing base; a pair of minute scales occurring in the axil of the sheath; the margin is toothed and the teeth are spine-like outgrowths of a single or of several epidermal cells.

Plants are monoecious or rarely dioecious; the flower is situated at the base of the newly developing branches, enclosed in a cylindrical spathe. A sac-like perianth 2-lipped at the top is present in a male flower which has a single stamen; the anther is sessile or subsessile, 1-4-locular, opening by longitudinal slits; pollens spherical or oblong. The pedicel is very short at the beginning and gradually elongates pushing the flower out through the enveloping spathe. The perianth-lobes separate before the anther bursts. Pollination takes place under water.

The female flower is perianthless or there is a thin cupular perianth adhering to the carpel; ovary is of one carpel, unilocular, with 2-4 sessile or subsessile stigmas and

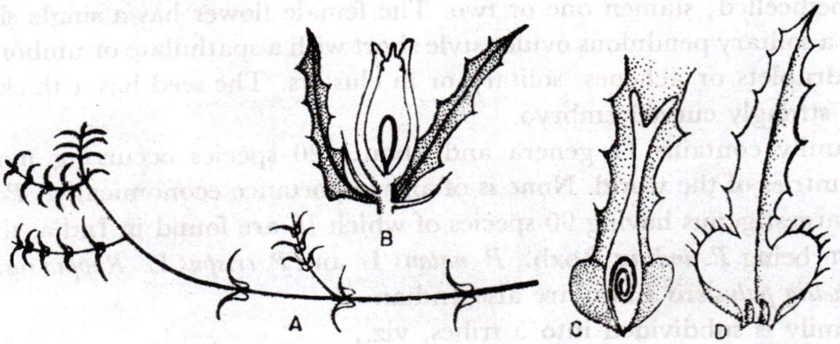

Fig. 18. *Najas minor* All. A—A portion of the plant; B—Staminate flower, C—Pistillate flower; D—Leaf with basal scales.

with a solitary, anatropous ovule, erect from the base. Fruit is an achene with a thin pericarp. Seed has a straight embryo, large hypocotyl and radicle and no endosperm; the seed-coat is often sculptured.

This is a unigeneric family with about 30 species occurring in almost all parts of the world. It is represented in India by several species, common among which are *Najas marina* Linn., *N. minor* All., *N. foveolata* A. Br., *N. graminea* Del., etc.

The flower in this family being very simple, it was considered by Engler to be a rather primitive family. Most other botanists are of opinion that the simplicity of the flower is due to reduction and not due to primitiveness and place the family at the end of the group starting from the Alismataceae through Potamogetonaceae, Zannichelliaceae, etc.

Alismaceae

(Alismataceae)

These are annual or perennial rhizomatous herbs growing in marshes or in fresh water; often stoloniferous; roots fibrous; milky juice is often present. Leaves basal, floating or erect with the petiole sheathing at the base; blade often sagittate at base; main nerves prominent and parallel. Flowers are whorled or in racemose or paniculate inflorescences, bisexual or polygamous, actinomorphic and hypogynous. The torus is large, flat or globose. Perianth is differentiated into one whorl of 3 persistent sepals and another whorl of 3 deciduous petals; rarely petals are absent. Stamens are 6 in number, sometimes more, rarely 3; anthers are 2-locular and extrorse. Carpels are few to many, free or rarely united at the base, often they are in a whorl or are spirally arranged (*Ranalisma*); style persistent. Each carpel has a solitary ovule, basal or on the inner angle, or there are several ovules in each carpel on the inner angle, i.e. marginal placenta. Seeds are curved with horse-shoe-shaped embryo and without endosperm.

The family with about 60 species are found in the tropical and temperate countries. In India *Sagittaria sinensis* Linn., *Limnophyton obtusifolium* Miq. and several species of *Alisma* are common.

Fig. 19. Alisma plantago Linn. A—Plant with inflorescence; B—Flower with parts, C—Single carpel; D—Cluster of achenes; E—L. s. of achene with seed. A × 1/8, B × 10, C × 20, D × 2, E × 5.

Alismaceae is a primitive family. This is quite evident from the floral morphology. The flowers are bisexual, hypogynous, with two whorls of free perianth segments, many free stamens and carpels. Engler includes the family in his primitive order Helobieae and Hutchinson treats it as a family of one of the 2 most primitive orders of Calyeiferae.

Due to the remarkable resemblance in floral structure of Alismaceae and Ranunculaceae many botanists hold the opinion (Hutchinson and others) that Alismaceae had its origin from Ranunculaceae. The genus *Ranalisma* which has flowers exactly like *Ranunculus* provides strong evidence in support of this theory. ***Ranalisma*** was discovered in Malaya about 50 years ago. Morphological examination of the new plant revealed that it was a monocot and belonged to the family Alismaceae and the genus was named *Ranalisma* from the close resemblance of its flower to that of ***Ranunculus***. The species was named *Ranalisma rostrata* Stapf. Later it was found out that an African plant known as *Sagittaria humilis* Kuntze should be transferred to this new genus as its characters were not considered fitting satisfactorily in *Sagittaria*. The African species after transfer to *Ranalisma* has the new name-combination as *R.* ***humile*** (Ktz.) Hutchinson. The discovery of the 2 species one at Malaya and the other at Africa proves that the genus had a wide range of distribution in the past and although comparatively recently discovered it is not at all of recent origin. It gives further support that the family Alismacea is a primitive family. The discovery of the genus ***Ranalisma*** thus has a great significance as it supports the theory of origin of the family Alismaceae from Ranunculaceae or at least from Ranales and origin of Monocotyledoneae from the primitive Dicots and most probably from the Ranales.

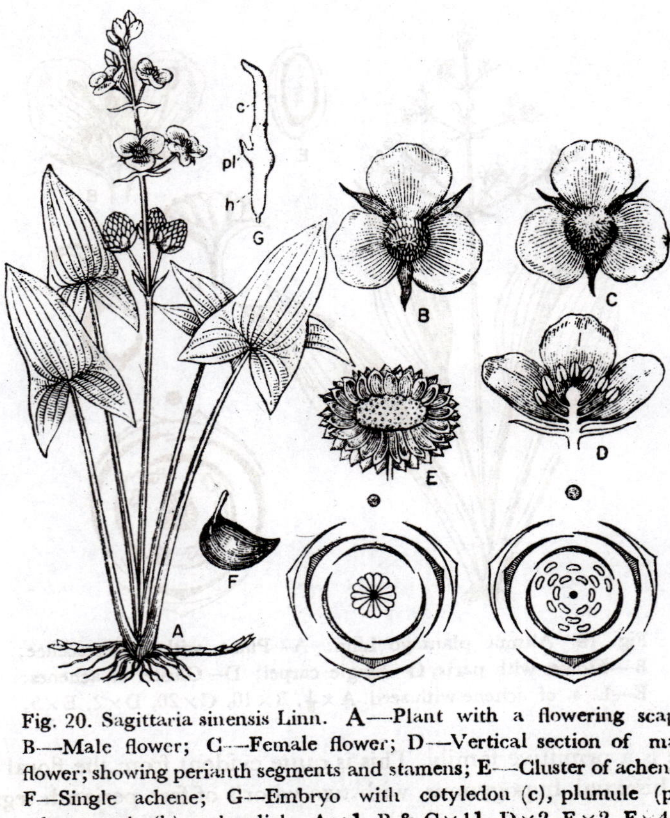

Fig. 20. Sagittaria sinensis Linn. A—Plant with a flowering scape. B—Male flower; C—Female flower; D—Vertical section of male flower; showing perianth segments and stamens; E—Cluster of achenes; F—Single achene; G—Embryo with cotyledon (c), plumule (pl), hypocotyle (h) and radicle. A $\times \frac{1}{3}$, B & C $\times 1\frac{1}{2}$, D $\times 2$, E $\times 2$, F $\times 4$.

Butomaceae

Perennial rhizomatous herbs that grow in fresh water or in swamps; milky juice is usually present. Leaves are ensiform or flat and dilated or with a distinct petiole and elliptic or orbicular blade. Flowers are bisexual solitary or umbellate. Perianth is in 2 whorls of 3 segments each; the outer sepaline or rarely coloured, imbricate and persistent; the inner segments are petal-like, usually thin and deciduous, imbricate; the inner whorl of perianth rarely absent. Stamens are 5-many on a small torus; when they are numerous the outer ones are staminodes; the filaments are free, flattened; anthers are basifixed, 2-locular, opening by lateral slits. Carpels are 6 or more, free or cohering only at the base, sometimes crowded to form a head, superior; ovules many scattered all over the inner surface of carpels, anatropous or campylotropous. Fruit is a cluster of follicles opening by the adaxial suture. Seeds are many, with a straight or horse-shoe-shaped embryo and with no endosperm.

Butomaceae was included in Alismaceae from which it has been segregated as a distinct family on account of the laminar placentation. It is very close to Alismaceae as indicated by the floral morphology and also to Hydrocharitaceae having laminar placentation. Laminar placentation having been considered as a very primitive character, Hutchinson includes Butamaceae and Hydrocharitaceae in his primitive order Butomales while Alismaceae remains in another order, viz. Alismatales, with Scheuchzeriaceae and Petrosaviaceae.

Butomaceae is a small family of 6 genera and 9 species. The genus *Butomus* stands apart from the other 5 genera in having anatropous ovules and straight embryo; here the leaves are long and narrow, not having a distinct petiole or lamina and the rhizome is without laticiferous ducts. The plants of the other genera have laticiferous ducts,

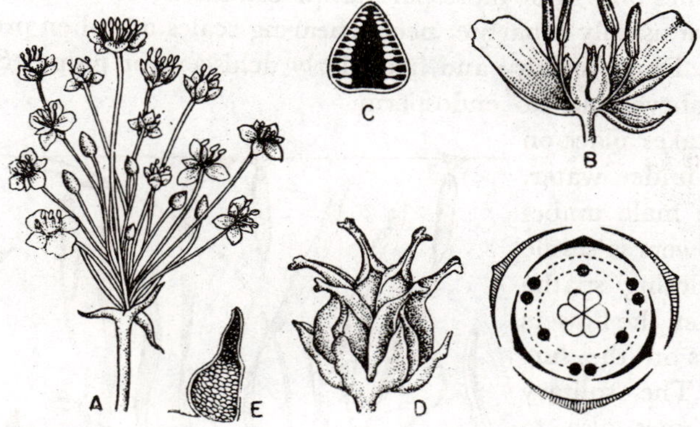

Fig. 21. Butomus umbellatus Linn. A—Umbel of flowers; B—Section of a flower to show perianth segments, stamens and carpels; C—L.s. of a carpel to show ovules on the walls (Diagrammatic); D—Cluster of follicles; E—L.s. of a follicle showing seeds. A×$\frac{1}{2}$, B×4, D & E×2.

leaves with distinct petioles and blades, campylotropous ovules and horse-shoe-shaped embryo. Pichon therefore states that these 5 genera, viz. *Ostenia*, *Hydrocleis*, *Limnocharis*, *Tenagocharis* and *Elattosis* should be transferred to Alismaceae although the placentation in the carpels is laminar. Both Takhtajan and Cronquist put these 5 genera in a separate family as Limnocharitaceae and include the 3 families Butomaceae (unigeneric), Limnocharitaceae and Alismaceae in the order **Alismales** (Alismatales) which they consider as the most primitive order among the **Monocots.**

The peculiar laminar placentation of Butomaceae, ovules scattered over the inner surface of carpels is found also in *Cabomba* of Nymphaeaceae and provides additional evidence to support the theory of origin of Monocotyledoneae from **Ranales** or rather from primitive Dicotyledonae.

Of this family *Tenagocharis lanceolatus* (Kunth) Hochst is quite common in eastern and south-western parts of this country.

Hydrocharitaceae

These are submerged or floating aquatic herbs growing in fresh water or are marine, usually stolioniferous; "turions" or vegetative buds are formed in some cases which detach from the mother plant and remaining dormant in winter grow to new plants in spring time. Leaves radical and crowded or dispersed on elongated stems and are alternate, opposite or whorled, with distinct petiole and blade or sessile and linear or strap-shaped. Umbels are few flowered, axillary, sessile or pedunculate, monoecious or dioecious, enclosed in a pair of bracts or in a spathe-like bifid bract; often flowers (usually the females) are solitary; the female peduncle is usually long and spirally coiled. Flowers actinomorphic, epigynous, unisexual, rarely bisexual (*Ottelia*). Perianth is 1-2-seriate; segments are 3 in each series or rarely 2, free to the base; the outer usually green and valvate, the inner petaloid and imbricate. The stamens are usually numerous or few or rarely 1, all free, in several trimerous whorls; the inner stamens are often sterile; anthers are 2-locular, locules parallel, opening by longitudinal slits; pollens are globose, rarely filiform (*Halophila*); rudimemtary ovary rarely present in male flower. Ovary is inferior, of 2–15 carpels, united to form a single locule, with many orthotropous or anatropous ovules on 3–6 or more parietal placentation; or the placentation may be laminar; styles are usually bipartite; nectar bearing scales are often present in the base of female flowers. Fruits are dry and irregularly dehiscent or pulpy. Seeds many with large straight embryo and no endosperm.

Pollination takes place on water surface or under water. In *Vallisneria* the male umbel with usually 3 flowers is sessile and with the enclosing spathe gets detached when the flowers mature and floats on the surface of water. The solitary female flower comes also to the surface by the elongation of the peduncle. The male flowers are carried to the female flower by water current and pollination takes place. After pollination the female flower is drawn back under water by the coiling of the peduncle and the fruit matures under water. In *Elodea* also

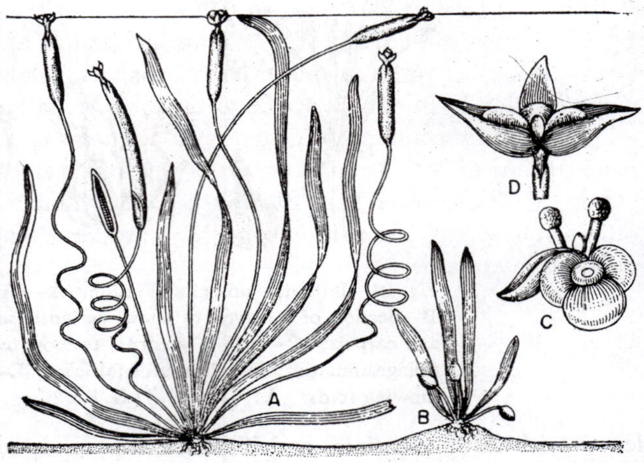

Fig. 22. Vallisneria spiralis Linn. A—Plant with female flowers and fruit; B—Plant with male flower buds; C—Male fl.; D—Female fl.—perianth segments with 3 stigmas. A & B×$\frac{1}{3}$, C & D×5.

pollination takes place on the surface of water. The flowers of *Ottelia,*, *Hydrocharis*, etc. come above water surface and are pollinated by insects.

In the order Helobieae this family is very distinct. Here more than one carpel unite to form a unilocular ovary which is inferior, unlike all other families. However, the

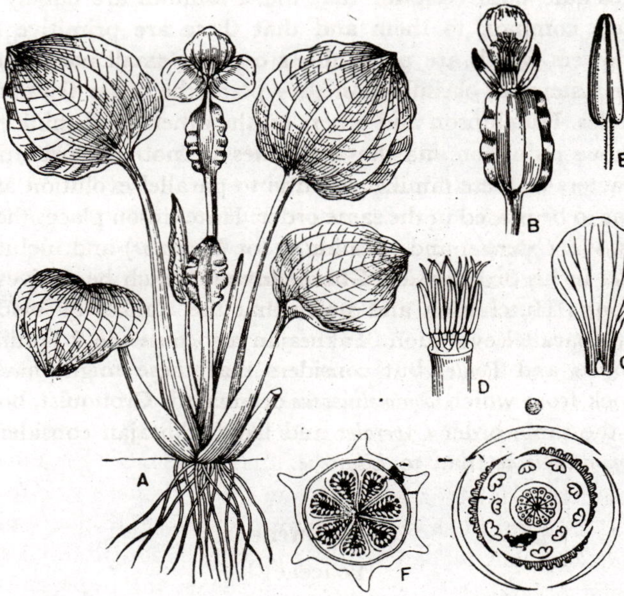

Fig. 23. Ottelia alismoides Pers. A—Plant with flower; B—flower with some perianth segments removed to show the anthers and stigmas; C—Single petal; D—Upper part of pistil with stamens and stigmas; E—Single stamen; F—T.s. of multilocular ovary with laminar placentation.

seeds in this family are devoid of endosperm and the perianth segments and stamens are free. Further the habit of the plants are similar to the other families in this order. These characters are in favour of its inclusion in Helobieae and is considered to have a closer relation to Butomaceae due to the presence of laminar placentation.

The family contains 16 genera and about 90 species occurring mostly in the tropical regions of both hemisphere. It is well-represented in India by *Hydrilla verticillata* Casp. *Ottelia alismoides* Pers, *Vallisneria spiralis* Linn., several species of *Blyxa* and by others. The plants are of no economic importance except that a few are suitable for planting in aquaria.

Floral formula:

$$\male\ P_{3+3}\ A_{3-\infty}\ G_0$$
$$\female\ P_{3+3}\ A_0\ \bar{G}_{(2-15)}$$

GLUMIFLORAE

This is the fourth order of Monocot-families in the system of classification of Engler who includes here only 2 families, viz. *Cyperaceae* and *Graminae*. The plants of these 2 families are annual or perennial herbs rarely attaining tree-size. Flowers are small, usually bisexual, hypogynous, perianthless, or perianth represented by scales or bristles, subtended or enclosed by **glumes** or special types of bracts of various shapes; stamens usually 3, rarely 6 in 2 whorls; ovary of 1–3 united carpels, unilocular and with one ovule. Fruits are dry and indehiscent. There is copious mealy endosperm in the seed. In both the families flowers are wind pollinated.

Engler and Rendle both consider that the 2 families are closely related having so many characters common to them and that these are primitive families having wind-pollinated flowers which are perianthless or have small inconspicuous perianth. Therefore in their systems of classification they place the order Glumiflorae after the 3rd order Triuridales. Hutchinson and others on the other hand think that the characters of perianth shows reduction and the 2 families are not very primitive. Further the similarity of characters in these families are due to parallel evolution and they are not so closely related as to be placed in the same order. Hutchinson places them in 2 separate monotypic orders, viz. *Cyperales* and *Graminales* (or *Glumales*) and includes the 2 orders along with *Juncales* in his 3rd division **Glumiflorae** which he derives from *Liliaceous* stock. Blaser supports Hutchinson and states that the similarity evidenced in the 2 families are due to parallel evolution. Takhtajan also puts the 2 families in 2 distinct orders, viz. *Cyperales* and *Poales* but considers that these might have been derived from the same stock from which *Commelinaceae* originated. Cronquist, however, includes the 2 families in the same order *Cyperales* and like Takhtajan considers that they are more allied to *Commelinaceae* than to *Liliaceae*.

Gramineae

(Poaceae)

Annual or perennial herbs, rarely shrubby or attaining the size of trees, e.g. the bamboos; some are biennials while some bamboos have life-cycles of 15, 30, 60 or even 120 years; stem is usually unbranched, with hollow internodes and jointed solid nodes; rarely internodes solid, e.g. *Saccharum*, *Sorghum*, *Zea*, etc. In the case of perennials the stem may be a runner or rhizomatus. The plants are often stoloniferous or may have suckers. Erect portion of the stem which bears the inflorescence is called culm (or haulm). In some species in the region just above the node protected by the leaf-sheath, there is a ring of soft meristematic tissue which becomes active when the stem is laid down upon the ground after a storm. Due to the activity of the meristem rapid growth is induced on the underside of the stem and it comes to the erect position again. The plants have fascicled or fibrous roots and also in some case adventitious roots and stilt roots.

Leaves simple, alternate and distichous, sheathed at the base, ligulate. The sheath forms the basal portion of the leaf and encircles the shoot or culm; the margin free and imbricate or united to form a tube. The sheaths are often swollen at the base and this swollen portion is called node of the sheath. The blade is usually linear and passes imperceptibly into the sheath or is constricted at the base; a distinct petiole is rarely present. Silica-deposit is found on leaves in many species rendering the margins of blade knife-sharp. The ligule is present at the junction of the sheath and the blade on the inner, i.e. the upper surface of the leaf. This is a membranous outgrowth often represented by a line of hairs. Ligule is absent in *Echinochloa*. In the Australian genus *Micraria* the arrangement of the leaves is spiral.

The inflorescence in this family is rather of a very complex type. The basic unit here is a **spikelet** which bears a few flowers or **florets** on its axis which is termed the

rachilla. The spikelets are on the axis of a spike or raceme or on the branches of a panicle. The inflorescence therefore is mostly of a compound type, i.e. a spike of spikelets, raceme of spikelets, etc. The main axis of the inflorescence is called the **rachis.** A spikelet usually has more than one flower on the rachilla which is very short. The spikelet has a series of alternating scales representing bracts and bracteoles borne in 2 opposite rows, one above the other. The 2 scales at the base are the **glumes.** Above the glumes alternating on the rachilla are several pairs of scales, the outer of each pair being the **lemma** or flowering glume and the inner scale the **palea.** Each pair encloses a flower. And a flower together with the pair of scales is termed a **floret.** The lemma is nothing but a bract subtending a flower and palea is a bracteole. The lemma is also called the lower palea or valve and the palea—the pale, upper palea or valvule. So a spikelet consists of a pair of glumes and one or more florets, and a floret consists of lemma, palea and a flower. The rachilla may terminate in a flower or it may be continued beyond the flowers.

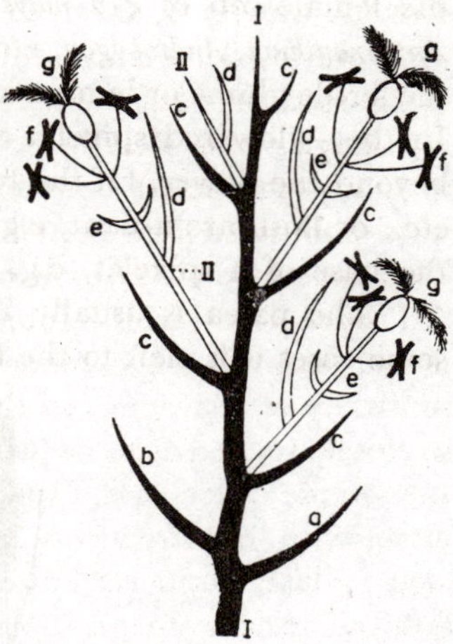

Fig. 24. Grass spikelet (diagrammatic) I—main axis; *a*—1st glume, b—2nd glume, c—lemma, d—palea, e—lodicules, f—stamens, g—ovary II—rachilla.

The general interpretation of the morphology of grass-spikelet is as given above. But some botanists consider the spikelet as nothing but a single flower. According to this view the 2 basal scales are the bracts of the flower and the lemma and palea are segments of outer perianth, i.e., the sepals, the palea representing 2 united segments, the lemma being the 3rd one. Still others think that the lemma and palea are bracts and the lodicules are bracteoles, so that the flower is naked like that in Najadaceae.

The flower may be bisexual or unisexual (monoecious or dioecious), hypogynous. Perianth is represented by 2–3 minute membranous or semi-fleshy scales which are called **lodicules.** Stamens 3 or sometimes 6, rarely less or more; anthers versatile. Ovary superior, of 3 carpels 2 of which are abortive, unilocular with one campylotropous ovule; styles 2-3 very short with long, feathery stigmas or stigmas sessile. Fruit is a caryopsis, rarely a utricle or very rarely a berry. Seed with plenty of endosperm and the shield-shaped **scutellum** lying appressed to the endosperm at the base. The radicle and the plumule are covered by sheaths known as **coleorhiza** and **coleoptile** respectively.

Opinions differ as to the real nature of cotyledon. According to Sachs scutellum and the coleoptile are the upper and lower parts of the cotyledon. Van Tieghem on the other hand stated that scutellum is the cotyledon. The coleoptile and coleorhiza are the sheaths of the plumule and radicle and are stipular in nature. Arber considered that the scutellum and coleoptile represented the single cotyledon. Avery (1930) stated that the cotyledon was represented only by the scutellum and the coleoptyle was nothing but the second leaf.

The flowers are wind-pollinated. The lodicules are hygroscopic and on absorption of moisture they swell up and push apart the palea and lemma exposing the stamens and pistil.

Floral formula : $P_{0 \text{ or } 2}\, A_{3 \text{ or } 3+3}\, G_{\underline{1}}$

Floral range: As described above the compound inflorescence may be a spike or raceme or a branched panicle, rarely forming a globose head as in some bamboos; the female cob of *Zea mays* is a spadix. Spikelet is one-flowered in *Agrostis*, *Oryza*, *Anthoxanthum*, *Andropogon*, etc. and the flower is terminal. Here the basal empty glumes, the fertile glume or lemma and the palea are on one and the same axis, i.e. the rachilla. In the 1-flowered spikelet of *Gastridium* the floret is lateral and the rachilla extends beyond the flower. Of the two empty glumes one may be absent, e.g. *Zoisia*, *Brachiaria*, etc., or both are absent, e.g. *Coleanthus*. Rarely there are more than 2 empty glumes at the base of a spikelet, e.g. *Anthoxanthum*.

The palea is usually 2-costate and more or less cleft between the 2 nerves. In some cases it is cleft to the base so that there are 2 paleas each with one midrib. The

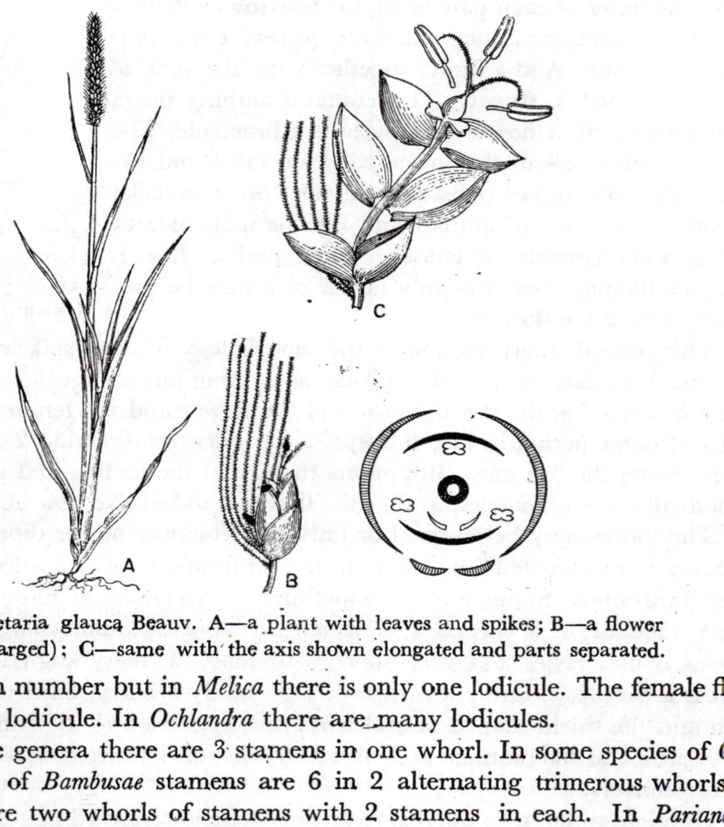

Fig. 25. Setaria glauca Beauv. A—a plant with leaves and spikes; B—a flower (much enlarged); C—same with the axis shown elongated and parts separated.

lodicules are 2–3 in number but in *Melica* there is only one lodicule. The female flower of *Zea mays* has no lodicule. In *Ochlandra* there are many lodicules.

In most of the genera there are 3 stamens in one whorl. In some species of *Oryza* and many genera of *Bambusae* stamens are 6 in 2 alternating trimerous whorls. In *Microlaena* there are two whorls of stamens with 2 stamens in each. In *Pariana* the male flower has 10-40 stamens. *Ochlandra* also has many stamens, 6–30 which are in one or several bundles, i.e. monadelphous or polyadelphous.

In most genera there are 2 styles or 2 sessile stigmas. In many bamboos 3 styles are present while in *Nardus* there is only 1 style with a simple stigma. In *Zea* the 2 simple stigmas unite to form a single silky thread-like structure.

The majority of the grasses are chasmogamous but some especially those growing in dry areas, are cleistogamous. In such cases flowers remain closed and are self-fertile. The anthers here are very small. Often chasmogamous flowers and cleistogamous flowers occur in the same inflorescences.

The grass seeds are usually very small and light and are dispersed by the wind. The lemma and palea tightly enclose the grain. Sometimes the whole spikelet drops off as a seed. In *Eragsostis, Sporobolus* and a few other genera the grains are naked. The seeds are often provided with pappus to help them to be carried away a long distance by the wind. Some seeds have the attached lemma toothed or barbed or provided with bristles and awns. These are dispersed by animals.

AFFINITY: Different interpretations of the spikelet and floret of grass give vent to different ideas as to the affinity of the family. *Gramineae* resembles *Cyperaceae* in habit. In both the families flowers are very minute and subtended by scaly bracts. They are in spikelets which form the units of a larger compound inflorescence. The two families are considered close to each other and are placed in the same order, e.g. Glumiflorae

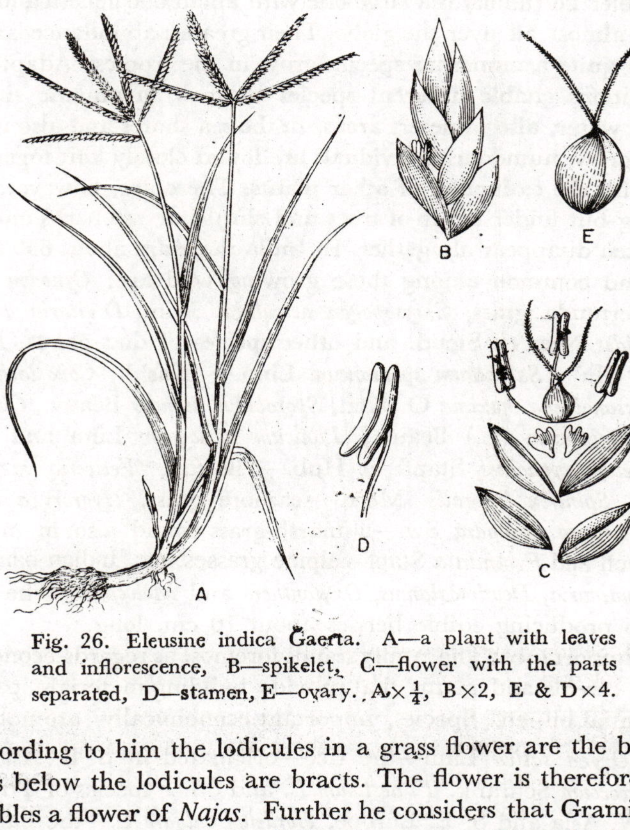

Fig. 26. Eleusine indica Gaerta. A—a plant with leaves and inflorescence, B—spikelet, C—flower with the parts separated, D—stamen, E—ovary. $A\times\frac{1}{4}$, $B\times2$, E & $D\times4$.

by Engler. According to him the lodicules in a grass flower are the bracteoles and all the other scales below the lodicules are bracts. The flower is therefore devoid of perianth and resembles a flower of *Najas*. Further he considers that Gramineae is a primitive family because it is wind-pollinated. Rendle supports Engler's views and following him includes *Gramineae* and *Cyperaceae* in one order *Glumiflorae* and places it after the order *Triuridales*.

Hutchinson and Wettstein think that *Gramineae* has been derived from *Restionaceae* of *Juncales* which again is derived from *Liliaceous* stock. Here a grass flower is considered to be a reduction from a pentacyclic flower, where the lodicules represent one of the 2 whorls of perianth, one whorl of stamens remains as a result of suppression of the other whorl and the ovary also tricarpelary but with 2 abortive carpels.

Gramineae and *Cyperaceae* have some characters common to both, but they differ considerably in other respects. Unlike *Gramineae Cyperaceae* has a triquetrous solid stem without any nodes, leaves tristichous in arrangement, with closed sheaths and without ligules, anthers basifixed, ovary of 3 united carpels, style one with tripartite stigma and the embryo embedded in endosperm. Hutchinson therefore puts the 2 families in different orders *Cyperales* and *Graminales* and places the 2 orders close to *Juncales*. Takhtajan also keeps the 2 families in distinct orders and considers *Gramineae* (Poaceae) is closer to *Restionaceae* while *Cyperaceae* is closer to *Juncaceae*. Takhatajan thinks that *Gramineae* and *Cyperaceae* have been derived from an ancestor from which *Commelinaceae* originated and not from *Liliaceous* stock. Cronquist also considers that the 2 families *Poaceae* and *Cyperaceae* originated from a Commelinaceous and not Liliaceous stock, but according to him these 2 families are sufficiently closely related to be included in one order as has been treated by Engler.

DISTRIBUTION: The family is a large one with about 650 genera and over 10000 species distributed almost all over the globe. Their greatest abundance is in the temperate region although quite a numerous species grow in the tropics. Adaptability to varied ecological conditions enable different species to grow in aquatic situation, fresh as well as brackish water, also in desert areas, in the sea shores and also in alpine regions. Wherever they grow, numerous individuals are found closely knit together to cover the ground often with the extinction of other plants. There are, however, few grasses that are shade loving but under cover of trees and shrubs or tall herbs most of the grasses thin out and often disappear altogether. In India there are about 850 species including the bamboos and common among those growing wild are: *Cynodon datcylon* Pers.—Dubgrass or Bermuda grass, *Chrysopogon aciculatus* Trin., *Digitaria sanguinales* Scop., *Eragrostis unioloides* Nees ex Steud. and other species of that genus, *Imperata cylindrica* (L.) Beauv.—"Ulu", *Saccharum spontaneum* Linn.—"Kash", *Coix lachrymajobi* Linn.—Job's tears, *Thysanolaena maxima* O. Ktz., *Sporobolus diander* Beauv., *Chloris barbata* Sw., *Dactyloctenium aegipticum* (L.) Beauv., *Panicum miliaceum* Linn and other species of *Panicum*, *Pennisetum typhoides* Stapf. et Hub.—"Bajra", *Vetiveria zizanioides* Nash,—"Khas Khas", *Spinifex littoralis* Merr.—seashore grass, *Hygroryza aristata* Nees,—a floating grass, *Leersia hexandra* Sw.—a marsh-grass found also in mangroves, *Festuca valesiaca* Schleich and *F. undata* Stapf—alpine grasses, etc. Indian bamboos are species of *Banbusa*, *Arundinaria*, *Dendrocalamus*, *Oxytanthera* and *Melocanna*. The last is the apple-fruited bamboo producing edible berries about 10 cm. long.

Economic importance: The family stands foremost as regards economic importance. It includes the cereals and plants that provide building materials, paper pulp, sugar, medicines, essential oil, etc. Species, important economically, are noted below:

Cereals: *Oryza sativa* Linn—the rice—originated in S. E. Asia; *Triticum monococcum* L., *T. dicoccum* Schrank, *T. aestivum* L. and other species of *Triticum* yield wheat originated in W. Asia and S. E. Europe, *Hordeum vulgare* L.—the barley originated in C. and W. Asia and N. Africa, *Avena sativa* L.—Oats of Europe, *Secale cereale* L.—rye of Europe and *Zea mais* Linn.—the Indian corn, originated in C. America.

Fodder: Most of the grasses are valued as cattle-food. The straw of the cereals are also used in similar manner.

Sugar: *Saccharum officinarum* L.—Sugarcane—originated in Indo-Malayan region; *Sorghum vulgare* Pers. var. *saccharatum* Koen also yields sugary juice.

Essential oil: *Cymbopogum nardus* Rendle—Citronella, *C. citratus* (DC) Stapf. and *C. flexuosus* Trin. are the Lemon grass, *C. martini* (Roxb.) Wall—Russa or Palmarosa or Geranium oil grass. *Vetiveria zizanivides* Nash. also yields a fragrant oil from the roots that are woven into mats which are hung as curtains in doors and windows in the summer months.

Paper Pulp: *Eulaliopsis binata* (Retz) Hubb.—"Sabai" grass, *Imperata cylindrica* (L.) Beauv.—"Ulu" and some bamboos are used in paper manufacturing.

Cordage: *Sacharum munja* Roxb., *S. arundinaceum* Linn. and *Imperata cylindrica* (L.) Beauv. are used for cordage.

Building Materials: Different bamboos are used for that purpose. Split-bamboos are also used to prepare baskets, tool-handles, etc. For thatching purpose *Saccharum spontaneum* Linn. and *Imperata cylindrica* (L.) Beauv. are much in demand.

Medicine: All grasses yielding essential oil have medicinal value. **Tabashir**—a siliceous substance, found in certain bamboos is considered a good tonic and astringent. *Secale cereale* Linn. is the source of **ergot** which is formed by the infection of the inflorescence by *Claviceps purpurea*.

Spikelet of Oryza

Many spikelets in a panicle. Each with 3 flowers of which the terminal one is complete and functional and the lower 2 are abortive represented by their lemma only. The 2 basal glumes are represented by a pair of opposite small swollen bodies or ridges or by very minute scales; these may often be entirely absent. Above these basal glumes

Fig. 27. Oryza sativa L. A—part of the plant with leaves and inflorescence (reduced), B—a spikelet, C—a floret, D—a grain with endosperm and scutellum. B, C & D×2.

are the lemma of the 1st and 2nd flower in the form of small scales. Above these are the lemma and palea of the fertile flower. The lemma is large and boat-shaped and often awned. The palea is more or less similar to the lemma and partially enclosed by the same. Lodicules 2 and stamens 6 in 2 whorls with capillary filaments. Styles 2, short, free, with plumose stigma; ovule solitary in unilocular ovary.

The above interpretation of *Oryza* spikelet is by Stapf and has been widely accepted. The view of earlier workers was that this spikelet is one-flowered having 4 empty glumes below the lemma. The 2 swollen bodies or the ridges are parts of the pedicell. This interpretation is not considered at present to be correct.

Spikelet of Triticum

Spikelets 2- or more flowered arranged in long spikes, solitary at each node, appressed to the cavities of the rachis which is articulated or not, upper flower male or neuter. Basal empty glumes 2, persistent. Lemma awned or awnless, usually 5-nerved. Palea ciliate on the keel. Lodicules 2, ciliate. Stamens 3. Styles very short.

Spikelet of Hordeum

Spikelets 1-flowered, 2-3-nate at each node of a long spike in the cavities of the rachis. Basal empty glumes 2, narrow and persistent. The rachilla jointed at the base of lemma and produced beyond it sometimes with an imperfect glume or lemma. Palea 2-keeled. Lodicules 2, entire, ciliate. Stamens 3 or 2. Styles very short.

Spikelets of Zea

Flowers in *Zea* are unisexual and are borne in separate inflorescences on the same plant.

Male inflorescence: This is a terminal branched panicle. The central axis bears several rows of spikelets while the branches have 2 rows of spikelets. The spikelets are paired. One of which is pedicelled and the other is sessile. Each spikelet is 2-flowered and bears 2 empty glumes at the base enclosing the spikelet. The 2 flowers are alternate, each has a green lemma and a green palea and 2 more or less fleshy lodicules. Stamens 3 in each flower with linear and pendulous anther. A rudimentary ovary is present in the centre. The upper flower matures earlier.

Famale inflorescence: This is a spadix with several rows of spikelets compactly arranged on a fleshy peduncle or cob enclosed by a number of large bracts or spathes. The spadix is axillary and more than one is borne in a plant. The spikelet is 2-flowered the lower one being sterile. There are 2 empty glumes at the base of the spikelet and the flowers have lemma, platea and lodicules like the male flowers. Ovary is unilocular with a filiform united style and long hairy stigma that comes out from the top and hangs down like a silk thread. One flower being sterile each spikelet bears only one grain and the grains are closely arranged in rows.

If the growth of the main axis of the plant is arrested at early stage, lateral shoots are produced from the base of the plant. These lateral shoots often produce terminal inflorescences which are bisexual. Male and female spikelets may be on different branches of the panicle or may be mixed up.

Subdivisions of Gramineae

Subfamily I **Pooideae:** Spikelets one to many-flowered; spikelets usually break off above the persistent basal glumes at maturity; rachilla continued above the florets. The subfamily is divided into 38 tribes.

Subfamily II **Panicoideae:** Spikelets mostly 2-flowered, rarely 1-flowered, breaking off at maturity as a whole with stalk and glumes; rachilla not continued above the florets. The subfamily is divided into 3 tribes.

Cyperaceae

Perennial grass-like herbs, rarely annuals, usually with a creeping sympodial rhizome, often tufted; stem solid, triquetrous, without nodes and usually unbranched; rarely stem hollow. *Microdracoides* is an African woody plant with forked stem, upto 3 mtr. in height. Leaves 3-ranked, usually crowded near base or alternate, sessile, eligulate, with a closed sheath and a long linear blade; very rarely the sheath is split on one side. Flowers small, bisexual or unisexual in spikelets which form a spike, spike-like cymes, panicles or dense heads; the whole inflorescence or its parts usually subtended by one or more leafy involucral bracts; each flower subtended and enclosed by a chaffy bract or glume, a second glume or bracteole is rarely present. Perianth absent or represented by scales or bristles, very rarely subpetaloid. Stamens 3, rarely

Fig. 28. Cyprus rotundus L. A—a plant with leaves and inflorescence ($\times \frac{1}{2}$); B—part of a spikelet; C—a flower; D—glume; E—fruit (much-enlarged).

6 in 2 whorls or very rarely 1; filaments slender, free, with basifixed anthers. Carpels 3 or 2, united to form a unilocular ovary with one basal anatropous ovule; ovary superior; style 1 with 3 or 2 plumose stigmas, or stigmas tooth-like. Fruit achene or nut or utricle, compressed or 3-gonous; embryo lying at the base of the seed, surrounded by mealy endosperm.

Germination of seed in *Cyperaceae* is more or less like that noticed in *Palmae* (*Arecaceae*). Here the terminal part of the cotyledon comes out of the seed while the other part remains within the seed and functions as sucker.

Floral formula: ⚥ P_0 $A_{3 \text{ or } 3+3}$ $\underline{G}_{(2-3)}$.

Floral range: Spikelets are several-flowered in most genera but in case of female flowers in *Carex* and *Diplacrum* the spikelets are one-flowered. Flowers usually bisexual but unisexual in *Carex*, *Elyna* and many genera. The secondary axis of the spikelet extends in the form of a bristle in *Uncinia* while it bears a male flower above the female in *Elyna*. Perianth is represented by bristles in *Scirpus* and many other genera while they are hair-like in *Eriophorum* and indefinite in number; in *Carex*, *Cyperus*, etc. perianth altogether absent. In *Oreobolus* there are 6 scale-like perianth segments in 2 whorls. Stamens are usually 3 but in *Rhynchospora* and some other genera these are 6 in 2 whorls; in *Hemicarpha* and *Bisboeckelera* the androecium is represented by a single stamen. Tricarpellary or bicarpellary ovary may be found in the same genus or some have only one or the other type. The flower is subtended by a bract; in the pistillate perianthless flower of *Carex* and *Kobresia* this bract completely encloses the naked ovary and is called "utricle"; in *Kobresia* the utricle is split on one side while in *Carex* it is baglike.

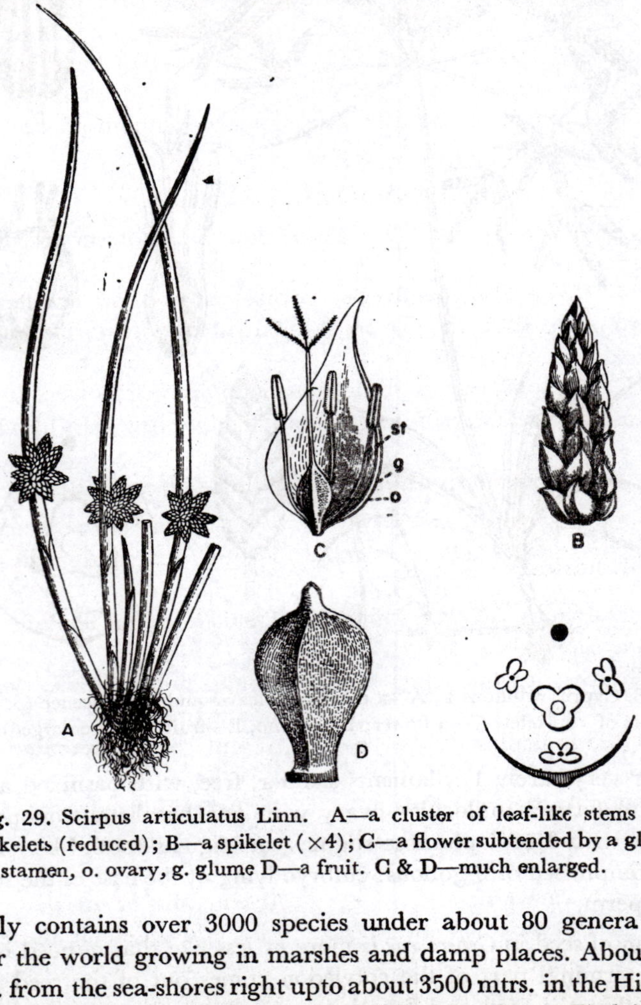

Fig. 29. Scirpus articulatus Linn. A—a cluster of leaf-like stems with spikelets (reduced); B—a spikelet (×4); C—a flower subtended by a glume, st. stamen, o. ovary, g. glume D—a fruit. C & D—much enlarged.

The family contains over 3000 species under about 80 genera and distributed almost all over the world growing in marshes and damp places. About 450 species are found in India from the sea-shores right upto about 3500 mtrs. in the Himalayas. Among the Indian species there are many species of *Cyperus*, *Carex*, *Fimbristylis*, etc. *Scirpus littoralis* Schrad is common in the mangrove forests. *Carex indica* Linn. grows on sea-beach and is a good sand-binder. *Eriophorum comosum* Wall. grows in temperate and alpine Himalayas between elevations of 2000-3500 mtrs. *Carex arenaria* Linn. occurs in deserts and is an important sand binder.

Plants of this family having economic importance are but few. *Cyperus stoloniferous* Linn. and *C. longus* Linn. yield essential oil which is also used in medicine. *Cyperus tegetum* Roxb., *C. corymbosa* Rottb. and *Juncellus inundatus* Clarke are used for manufacturing mats. *Cyperus esculentus* Linn., *Eleocharis tuberosa* Schult and *Scirpus grossus* L.f. var. *kysoor* Clarke have tuberous roots which are edible. *Cyperus rotundus* Linn., the "Mutha ghas" is used by Kavirajes to cure disentery.

Cyperus papyrus Linn. has a thick stem about 4 cm in diam. and attains a height of about 3 mtr. This is the paper-reed of the ancient Egyptians who used the long thin strips as writing papers.

AFFINITY: *Cyperaceae* and *Gramineae* were considered to be closely allied by Engler as well as Rendle and were included in the same order *Glumiflorae*. Cronquist also includes the 2 families in the order *Cyperales*. Hutchinson puts them in 2 monotypic orders, viz. *Cyperales* and *Graminales*. According to him both the families have been derived from *Juncales* but from different stocks on parallel lines. Wettstein and Takhtajan also treat them similarly. Snell and Blaser also support Hutchinson and state that the spikelets in the 2 families are not homologous.

Subdivisions of Cyperaceae

Subfamily I **Scirpoideae:** Spikelets many flowered; flowers bisexual. Tribes 2,—Scirpeae, Hypoleptreae.

Subfamily II **Rhynchosporoideae:** Spikelets one or few-flowered; flowers bisexual or the upper ones male. Tribes 4,—Rhynchosporeae, Gahmieae, Bisboeckelerieae, Sclerieae.

Subfamily III **Caricoideae:** Spikelets many flowered; flowers unisexual; male-flowers often in simple spikes; perianth absent; subtending bract is a utricle. Four genera only.

Comparison of Graminae and Cyperaceae

Gramineae	Cyperaceae
1. Stem: Cylindrical, hollow; nodes present.	Triquetrous, solid; nodes absent.
2. Leaves: Distichous, ligulate; sheath split on one side.	Tristichous, not ligulate; sheath closed.
3. Bracts: Glumes, lemma and palea; no involucral bracts.	Single floral bract, leafy involucral bracts present.
4. Perianth: 2–3 lodicules.	Absent or represented by hairs or bristles.
5. Androecium: Anthers versatile.	Anthers basifixed.
6. Gynoecium: Carpels 3 of which 2 abortive.	Carpels 3, united.
7. Fruit: Usually caryopsis.	Achene, nut or utricle.
8. Embryo: Lies outside the endosperm, coleoptile and coleorhiza present.	Lies embedded in the endosperm, no coleoptile or coleorhiza.
9. Germination: No part of the cotyledon comes out during germination.	Terminal part of the cotyledon comes out during germination.

PRINCIPES

This is the 5th order of Monocotyledonae in Engler and Prantl's system and includes only one family *Palmae*. This order is followed by another monotypic order **Synanthae** consisting of the single family *Cyclanthaceae*, the 7th order being **Spathiflorae** with two families *Araceae* and *Lemnaceae*. That these four families are close to one another is a fact recognised by almost all taxonomists. Rendle gives no account of *Cyclanthaceae* being a less important family while he includes the other 3 in one order which he terms as **Spadiciflorae.** Like Engler, Hutchinson puts the 4 families in 3 distinct orders e.g. *Palmae* in **Palmales,** *Cyclanthaceae* in **Cyclanthales** and *Araceae* and *Lemnaceae* in **Arales.** But he does not put them close to each other although he considers all the 3 orders to be derived separately from *Liliaceous* stock. According to him **Palmales** and **Cyclanthales** are nearer to **Pandanales** and **Agavales** while Arales is more related to **Typhales**. Takhtajan puts **Arecales** (Palmales), **Cyclanthales** and **Arales** in one subclass **Arecidae** where he includes **Pandanales** and **Typhales** also. Cronquist also considers the four families close to one another and distributes them in 3 different orders, viz: **Arecales** (Palmales), **Cyclanthales** and **Arales** and places them in his subclass **Arecidae** where he includes **Pandanales** also. According to him the subclass **Arecidae** is more primitive than **Liliidae** or **Commelinidae.**

Palmae

(Arecaceae)

Perennial woody plants with stout unbranched stem leafy at the top; some are very tall while a considerable number is dwarf and some are scrambling; a short horizontal rhizome is often formed which later becomes ascending and grows to an erect cylindrical stem. The primary root perishes early and a tuft of adventitious roots arise around the base of the stem. The leaves are of 2 types, palmately or pinnately compound and those with the former type of leaves are called Fan-palms and others are the Feather-palms; simple palm type of leaves also occur which are usually deeply cleft; leaves are usually very large and long-petioled, crowded only at the apex to form a dense crown; in the case of scramblers the leaves are alternately scattered over the stem; the petiole is usually woody and clasping the stem at the base and sheathing in some genera; the falling leaves leave ring-like scars on the stem or the leaf-bases remain attached to the stem and the leaves break and fall off on drying due to their own weight. Ochreate stipule is present in some cases, particularly in the scramblers and in *Korthalsia scaphigera* Mart. the ochrea form a hollow chamber where the ants take shelter.

The inflorescence is usually a large compound spadix enclosed primarily in one or more large bracts or spathes which split longitudinally and the panicle grow out exposing the flowers; the bracts are often hard and woody; the inflorescence may appear from the axil of the leaves or from the axils of fallen leaves, i.e. below the crown of leaves; rarely the inflorescence is terminal and in this case appears only when the life cycle of the plant comes to its end as in *Corypha* and *Metroxylon*; such are called *monocarpic* palms that die after producing flower and fruit once in their life time.

Flowers are unisexual very rarely bisexual and the plants are usually monoecious, rarely dioecious, e.g. *Phoenix*, *Borassus* and *Lodoicea*. The numerous small flowers are sessile and are often embedded in the fleshy axis of the spadix, spirally arranged or are distichous; the female flowers may occupy the lower portion of the spadix or its branches and males are on the upper portion or both may be mixed; in *Geonoma* flowers are in groups of three on the spike, each group having a female flower between 2 males. Flowers are regular, with 2 whorls of perianth; segments 3 in each whorl, persistent, free or connate, coriaceous, similar or the inner larger, thicker and tougher. Stamens 6 in 2 whorls, free, rarely united at the base and very rarely slightly adnate to the base of inner perianth-segments; sometimes one whorl of stamen is wanting and there are only 3 stamens, e.g. *Nypa*; or there are many stamens as in *Caryota*, *Pinanga* and a few other genera; anthers 2-locular with great quantities of powdery pollens. Ovary superior, tricarpellary, united, 3-celled or 1-celled with one ovule in each cell; rarely carpels partially or completely free; style absent or short with a trilobed or tripartite stigma; 2 of the 3 carpels often become abortive so that the fruit is one seeded. The fruit is a berry or a drupe with 1–3 seeds; the embryo very small, embedded in soft or cartilaginous or horny endosperm which is often ruminated. The fruit is often covered with imbricating scales.

The flowers are wind pollinated except in the case of a few genera, e.g. *Sabal*, *Chamaedorea*, etc. which are entomophyllous. Self pollination is prevented even in bisexual flowers as they are protandrous.

The germination of seed in this family is of a bit different type. The cotyledon elongates in the form of a tube and pushes out the radicle and hypocotyl. The tube enters the ground while the seed remains above. The radicle or the tap root gives out several branches in a very short time and then the tap root perishes. The plumule pierces the enclosing cotyledonary sheath and the first leaf emerges. The end of the cotyledon remains inside the seed forming a sucker and absorbing the food material reserved in the endosperm. The cotyledonary tube is often as long as 30 cm as has been noticed in *Hyphaene* and *Borassus*. The sucker may grow to a large size as in *Cocos nucifera* Linn. or in *Borassus*. The seedling before producing a green leaf produces 1–3 pale greenish yellow sheaths only. The green leaves that follow are at the beginning simple and narrowly lanceolate or with broader blade deeply incised from the apex. The stem elongates very slowly, increasing all the time in circumference, and as the larger leaves are produced one after another the stem takes the shape of an inverted cone due to the pressure imparted by the leaf-bases. With the production of a dense whorl of normal leaves the stem comes above the ground and grows erect to form the cylindrical trunk.

The family comprises about 217 genera and about 2500 species. They are mainly distributed in the tropical and subtropical parts of the world. *Chamaerops humilis* Linn. is the only species found wild in southern parts of Europe. On the east palms have reached the northern limit in Korea and S. Japan while in the south they have been found to grow in Australia. In the Himalayas *Trachycarpus martiana* Wendl has been found to grow at an altitude of 2000 mtr. or even at higher altitude. *Calamus floribundus* Griff., *Plectocomia himalayana* Griff. also occur at almost that height. *Nannorhops* with its single species *N. ritchieana* Wendl is found from the Western Himalaya to E. Persia through Afghanistan. On the New World palms occur as far north as California and as far south as Chili. The tall palms prefer bright sun while a few dwarf species grow well in shade under cover of large trees of the tropical forests. *Phoenix paludosa* Roxb. is a mangrove plant and form almost pure associations in open areas in the littoral forests on the banks of the creeks. *Nypa fruticans* Wurmb. is another palm of the mangrove forests. Few palms grow in arid regions. *Hyphaene thebaica* Gaertn is found in North Africa and *H. indica* Bece occurs in Gujrat of India. *Phoenix dactylifera* Linn. grows all over N. Africa and the W. Asiatic countries and brought to India by the Muslims in the 8th or 9th century. It is now cultivated in some parts of southern Europe.

Fossils of palms have been discovered in Europe as far north as 50° latitude or more. These are believed to be of Cretaceous period. This proves that the family had a wider distribution in past.

VARIATION: Variation occurs both in vegetative as well as in floral parts. There are the erect forms and the scrambling forms. The erect forms have unbranched stem except the *Hyphaene* or the Doum palm where the stem forks several times. *Phoenix sylvestris* L. and *Chrysalidocarpus lutescens* Wendl. often produce branches as a result of injury. In some genera the leaf-sheaths are long and stem clasping e.g. *Areca*, *Roystonia*,

Fig. 30. Cocos nucifera L. A—a plant with fruits and leaves; B—a spadix (much reduced); C—a part of a branch of the spadix with a male and a female flower; D.—a male flower; E—a female flower; F—a fruit; G—same with the epicarp and fibrous mesocarp removed; H.—l. s. of the fruit showing the endosperm in the seed; I—germination of the seed.

etc. while in *Phoenix*, *Borassus* and a few others the sheath is not perceptible but the leaf-base is stem-clasping. The leaves drop off leaving the scars on the trunk, but in *Phoenix* and *Elaeis* the leaves break off from the middle of the petiole and the trunk is covered from top to bottom with leaf-bases and the basal part of the petioles. Usually the palms are unarmed but quite a number of them especially the scrambling or climbing ones are armed with spines or thorns. The scrambling forms are stipulate. The ochreate stipules are in the form of long tube and often have a whip-like structure at the apex which is called "flagellum". In these palms the leaf rachis also ends in a flagellum. The flagella help in climbing. Palms are polycarpic excepting a few genera which are monocarpic, e.g. *Corypha, Metroxylon.* The species of *Arenga* behaves peculiarly at the time of flowering; a plant grows to a height of about 8 mtr. or more in course of 10-12 years. Then an inflorescence comes out on one side below the crown of leaves. Next year another spadix comes out on the opposite side a little below the

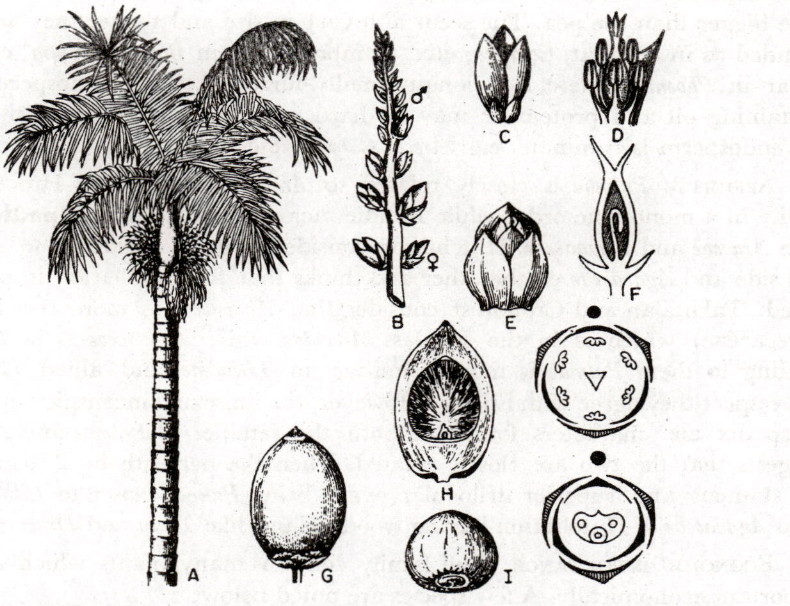

Fig. 31. Areca catechu L. A—a plant; B—a branch of the spadix with male and female flowers; C—a male flower; D—same showing the stamens; E—a female flower; F—ovary; G—a fruit; H—L.s. of same; I—the nut or the fruit with the epicarp and fibrous mesocarp removed.

first one. This is repeated until the last spadix comes out very near the ground. After the last spadix ripens its fruits the palm dies and stands for sometime like a hollow cylinder.

In this family flowers are unisexual but bisexual flowers occur in *Livistona, Licuala, Trachycarpus*, etc. In the genera *Phoenix, Borassus* and *Lodoicea* the plants are dioecious while in other genera they are monoecious.

The inflorescence is usually a branched panicle but in *Borassus* it is a simple spike. In some genera a large spathe encloses the young inflorescence and in others there are several each enclosing a branch of the panicle.

In monoecious plants female flowers are generally arranged at the basal part of the spike and the males are above them. In *Geonoma* male and female flowers are intermixed. The perianth segments are similar in both whorls and are free. In *Areca* the inner segments are much larger; in *Borassus* the inner 3 are shorter than the outer. In *Wallichia* the inner segments unite to form a 3-partite corolla. The stamens are usually 6 and free. In *Nypa* there are only 3 stamens and in *Pinanga, Caryota* and a few others there are many. In *Roscheria* and *Elaeis* they are united in a ring. Carpels are 3 and usually form a trilocular ovary, rarely they are more or less free, e.g. *Phoenix*. In *Pinanga*,

Areca, etc. the ovary is 1-celled. In *Cocos* 2 of the carpels become abortive in course of fruiting. The ovules are generally anatropous and rarely orthotropous. Fruits are berries or fibrous drupes which in the tribe *Lepidoçaryeae* are covered with imbricating scales. Some species have very large fruits, e.g. *Borassus flabelifer* Linn, *Cocos-nucifera* Linn. and *Lodoicea maldivica* (Gmel) Pers. The last looks like 2 large-sized coconuts glued together. The berries of *Euterpe*, an American genus, are on the other hand a little bigger than the pea. The seeds also vary in size and shape; they are more or less rounded as in coconut, *Corypha*, etc., compressed as in *Borassus, Nypa*, etc., oblong or linear in *Phoenix*, where it is longitudinally furrowed. The endosperm may be soft containing oil and protein or may be hard and rarely mucilaginous. In some cases the endosperm is ruminate, e.g. *Areca*, *Caryota*, etc.

AFFINITY: *Palmae* is closely related to *Araceae*. Engler and Hutchinson put the family in a monotypic order while Rendle includes this family in **Spadiciflorae** along with *Araceae* and *Lemnaceae*. Hutchinson considers it to be allied also to *Pandanaceae* on one side and *Agavaceae* on the other and thinks that from the latter it probably originated. Takhtajan and Cronquist consider that *Agavaceae* is more recent than *Palmae* (Arecaceae) which is in the subclass *Arecidae* while *Agavaceae* is in *Liliidae*. So according to them *Palmae* is more primitive to *Liliaceae* and allied families and in this respect they agree with Engler. However, the unisexual inconspicuous flowers borne in spadix are characters found in both the families of *Palmae* and *Araceae* and this suggests that the two are closely related. Then the perianth in 2 trimerous whorls, six stamens and superior trilocular ovary bring *Palmae* closer to *Liliaceae* and more so to *Agavaceae* of Hutchinson having woody plants like *Yucca* and *Dracaena*.

ECONOMIC IMPORTANCE: The family contains many plants which are very much important economically. A few species are noted below:

Cocos nucifera Linn. No other species in the vegetable kingdom is perhaps more useful than this one. It supplies food and drink from the endosperm which also yields an edible oil valued for soap-manufacture. The fibrous coat of the fruit is used for manufacture of ropes, for choir-matting and for stuffing cushions. A sugary juice is obtained by tapping the inflorescence. The shell of the fruit is used for manufacture of buttons. The trunk is used as posts in house-building and also as fuel. The stiff midribs of the leaflets are used to make brooms. The tender leaflets are woven into baskets or mats. The dry leaves and parts of the dried spadix are also used as fuel.

The genus *Cocos* have 30 species under it of which all are confined to C. America excepting *C. nucifera* L. which is widely distributed in tropical Asia.*

Metroxylon: M. rumphii Mart. and *M. sagu* Rottb. of Malaya yield sago from the starch obtained from the pith of the stems. *Mauritia flexuosa* L.f. (America) also yields sago of good quality. It may be mentioned here that sago is also manufactured from the pith of *Cycas* species and from the starch obtained from the tuberous roots of *Manihot esculenta* Crantz (Euphorbiaceae) which is now cultivated in S. India for that purpose.

Phoenix: P. dactylifera Linn. is the Date palm indigenous to Arabia and N. Africa and is found in cultivation in W. Asia and S. Europe. Cultivation of Date palm started in Arab-countries as early as 3,000 years before Christ. It was brought to India by the Muslim settlers. *P. sylvestris* Roxb. is the wild date of India and yields copious

* The genus *Cocos* is considered by some to consist of only 1 sp. *C. nucifera* L. The other species are placed under several new genera.

sugary juice by tapping from which a kind of molasses and a country liquor are prepared.

Borassus: B. flabelifer Linn. the single species of the genus also yields copious sugary sap from the peduncle when the spadix is cut down. The mesocarp of the fruit has a sweet pulp along with the fibres and is much relished. The soft endosperm of seeds of the immature fruits is also edible as well as the end part of the cotyledon that remains inside the seed as a sucker. The leaves are made into fans and the trunk is used as posts and rafters in house-building. The trunk is also hollowed to make a dug-out canoe. All parts of the tree properly dried are used as fuel. This species is considered to be indigenous to central Africa wherefrom it has come to India and growing freely.

Areca catechu L. is the Betlenut, cultivated in India and other east Asiatic countries.

Elaeis guinensis Jacq. is the African oil-palm, the fleshy mesocarp of the fruit of which yields an edible oil.

Phytelephas macrocarpa Ruiz. & Pav. is the source of vegetable ivory. It is indigenous to tropical America.

Copernicia cerifera Mart. of the Amazon region and *Ceroxylon andicola* H. & B. of the Andes yield Carnauba wax exuded from the leaves.

Calamus: Different species of the genus supply cane of good quality for chairs, baskets, walking sticks, etc. and are Indo-Malayam.

Many palms are grown in gardens as ornamentals, e.g. *Chamaerops humilis* Linn., *Raphis flabelliformis* Act., *R. humilis* Bl., *Licuala paludosa* Griff., *L. elegans* Bl., *L. grandis* Wendl., *Livistona chinensis* R. Br., *Chrysalidocarpus lutescens* Wendl., *Ch. madagascariensis* Becc., *Roystonia regia* (Kunth) Cook, *Ptychosperma macartheri* Wendl. *Pritchardia* species, etc.

Subdivisions of the family: Within the family Drude recognises 6 subfamilies which fall into 2 groups:

A. Perianth well-developed, enclosing the fertilised ovary.

I **Coryphoideae**—Spadix loosely branched; flowers scattered, not in groups, often in rows, uppermost opening first; carpels 3, free or united at first. Tribes—Phoeniceae and Sabalae.

II **Borassoideae**—Spadix simple or little branched, branches stout and cylindrical; flowers markedly diclinous-dimorphic, subtended by bracts; the males in cincinus in grooves of the branches; carpels 3, united. Tribe—Borassieae.

III **Lepidocaryoideae**—Spadix branched, often in 2-ranked manner; flowers in cincinni or 2-ranked spikes, subtended by bracts and bracteoles; carpels 3 united, covered with scales. Tribes—Mauriticae and Metroxyleae.

IV **Arecoideae**—Spadix simple or branched; flowers diclinous, usually dimorphic, when dioecious solitary and scattered on spikes with rudimentary bracts, when monoecious in cymes of 3, 2 being males and one female, or one female at top of the spike with several males below; carpels 3, united, ovary 1–3 celled.

B. Perianth rudimentary; fruits in dense heads.

V **Phytelephantoideae**—Stamens many, free; female flowers with perianth—1 genus—Phytelephas.

VI **Nypoideae**—Stamens 3, united below; female flower naked—1 genus—Nypa.

SPATHIFLORAE

This is the 7th order in the system of classification of Engler and Prantl and comprises 2 families only, viz. *Araceae* and *Lemnaceae.* These are mostly herbaceous plants having the inflorescence covered by a spathe or the spathe enclosing the individual flower. Flowers unisexual; perianth absent or much reduced; ovary superior. Seed with a fleshy testa.

Fig. 32-A. Colocasia Boryi Schott showing woody trunk.

Taxonomists agree that these two families are very closely related and that *Lemnaceae* originated from *Araceae.* They also agree that these are related to *Palmae* and to *Cyclanthaceae* also, except Bessy according to whom **Arales** had their origin from the Helobieae while the **Palmales** came from **Liliflorae.** Hutchinson and others consider that like **Palmales, Arales** is also allied to **Pandanales** which order according to Engler is most primitive among the Monocotyledonae.

Wettstein considers *Araceae* to be an advanced family derived from **Helobieae—Liliflorae** stock. According to Lotsy the **Piperales** of the Dicotyledonae is the ancestral stock from which the Palmae, Aroids and the Pandanales were derived.

Araceae

Herbs with tuberous rhizome or corm, or stem short and erect, often woody, or climbers, sometimes epiphytic; unarmed or rarely with spines or thorns; laticiferous tissues present, mostly associated with sieve tubes; where those are absent, raphides are present in the intercellular spaces; the latex is watery and acrid, or it is milky. The stem has a sympodial growth while in *Pistia* it is monopodial. The roots are adventitious; in climbing species absorbent roots and clasping roots are found. Aerial roots with velamen also occur in some species. Leaves crowded at the apex of rhizome or erect stem, or along the stem in the climbers and alternate, dstichous in *Pothos*; simple or pinnate or digitate; usually petiolate, sheathing at the base, generally net-veined but parallel-veined as in *Acorus.* In some species the leaves are very large, e.g. the simple leaves of *Alocasia indica* Schott, *Xanthosoma maximiliani* Schott, etc. or the decompound leaves of *Amorphophalus* and *Dracontium.* The leaf-blade is sagitate or ovate or even linear, attached to the petiole at the margin of the base or in some cases peltate. In *Acorus* the linear leaves are sessile.

The inflorescence is a spadix, the subtending spathe usually enclosing the spike sometimes in the primary stage only. Flowers are inconspicuous, crowded on the fleshy axis of spike, regular, hermaphrodite or unisexual and monoecious; excepting the spathe of the spadix no bract or bracteole is present. The axis of the spike may be wholly covered by flowers or the apical part is naked and is called the appendage.

Perianth absent but present in most hermaphrodite flowers in 2 trimerous or dimerous whorls; segments free or united. Stamens 6 in 2 whorls or 3 in 1 whorl and united to form a synandrium; often stamens only 2 or very rarely one only. The anthers dehisce by apical pores; the pollens are often in tetrads. Free or united staminodes may be present in female flowers. Ovary superior, one to many-locular, with few to many ovules in each cell; placentation parietal, marginal or axillary; stigma one or more; style absent. Fruit is a berry; seeds with or without endosperm.

Flowers are protogynous and entomophilous. The insects are attracted by the spathe and the appendage which are often coloured and also by the strong offensive odour emitted by some flowers. The spathe is constricted above the female flowers forming a chamber the mouth of which often closes at night; the inside of the spathe is often beset with hairs pointing downwards. The insect visiting the female flowers is thus prevented from coming out easily and pollinate the female flowers while moving inside the spathial chamber.

The family contains about 1,500 species under 115 genera growing in the warmer countries of the world with only a few in the temperate regions. Most species prefer a humid condition while some grow in marshes and *Pistia stratiotes* Linn. is an aquatic weed floating in fresh-water lakes.

ECONOMIC IMPORTANCE: The tuberous rhizome and corms of most species contain plenty of starch and these are edible after boiling. *Alocasia indica* (Roxb.) Schott. —the Man Kanda or Man Kachoo of eastern India, *Colocasia esculenta* (L.) Schott, the Kachoo, Arvi, or Ghuina, *Amorphophalus campanalatus* Blume the Ol, Suran, Zaminkanda, the Elephant's foot, etc. are much cultivated for the purpose. The leaf-blade and petiole of *Xanthosoma maximiliani* Schott. and some *Amorphophalus* and *Colocasia* are also used as vegetables. The fruiting spadix of *Monstera deliciosa* Liebm. is eaten as a fruit. Some have medicinal value, e.g. *Scindapsus*, *Rhaphidophora*, *Acorus calamus* Linn. etc. *Acorus calamus* is the sweet-flag of commerce, the rhizome of which is sweet-scented and is used in perfumery. It is the Swet Bacha of the Indian Vaidas.

Anthurium, *Caladium*, *Zantedeschia* (Arum-Lily) are cultivated as ornamental plants. Some climbers like *Monstera*, *Scindapsus* and *Rhaphidophora* are also cultivated likewise and of the last two some having variegated leaves which are very popular in Indian gardens.

FLORAL RANGE: The spadix is usually very promiment with its spathe and the appendage of the spike. In the American genus *Dracontium* and the Indo-Malayan *Amorphophallus* it is often very large, about 2 mtr. in height, and the coloured spathe which looks like a funnel is over a metre across and so in height. In most genera the spathe opens in the form of a funnel exposing the flowers; in other cases the spathe encloses the whole of the spike or only the lower part encloses the fertile part of the spike forming a chamber while the upper part is more or less a flat dorsiventral structure forming a back ground to the appendage. The spathe is green in many genera but petaloid in others; *Anthurium* has a spathe which is brilliant scarlet, *Zantedeschia* has a white spathe. The spathe is often deciduous, e.g. *Scindapsus, Rhaphidophora, Colocasia*, etc., and persistent in others, e.g. *Alocasia, Caladium, Typhonium*, etc. In *Acorus* there is no spathe but the penduncle extends on one side from the base of the axis in the form of a spathe.

The axis of the spadix is completely covered with flowers in *Acorus*, *Calla*, etc. or it is prolonged into a sterile appendage which may be coloured or green, and may be club-shaped, e.g. *Amorphophallus campanulatus* Bl., some species of *Arisaema*, etc., or it is very long, slender and thread-like as in *Sauromatum*, some *Arisaema*, etc.

Flowers are bisexual, as in *Acorus, Calla, Anthurium, Monstera*, etc. and unisexual in most other genera. Perianth usually present in bisexual flowers but absent in *Calla*,

Monstera, etc. In *Acorus* there are 6 perianth segments in 2 whorls while those are 4 in 2 whorls in *Anthurium* and *Gymnostachys*. Segments may be free as in *Acorus* or united as in *Spathiphyllum*. Stamens may be six as in *Pothos*, *Acorus*, etc. or less; in *Typhonium* there are 1–3 stamens, in *Cryptocoryne* (*Lagenandra*) 1–2 and in *Arisarum* and *Biarum* only one. Gynoecium composed of 3 carpels in most genera but there is only one carpel in *Pistia*. Ovary may be 3-celled as in *Pothos*, *Acorus*, etc., or 1-celled as in *Scindapsus*, *Lasia*, etc.; 2-locular ovary as well as ovaries with more than 3 cells also occur.

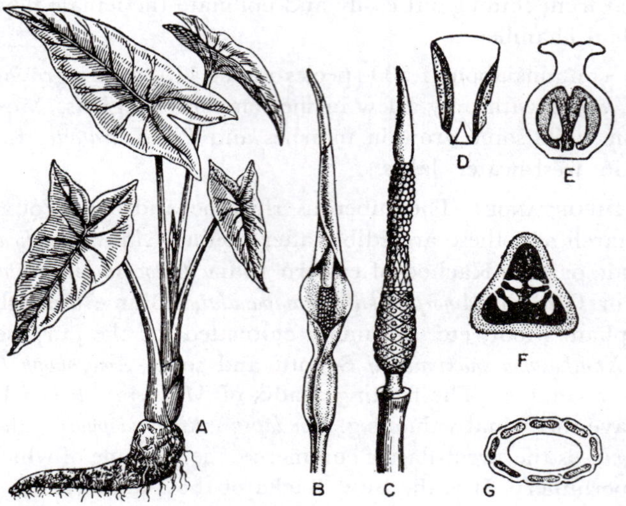

Fig. 32-B. Alocasia formicata Schott. A—whole plant ($\times\frac{1}{6}$); B. & C.—spadix with and without the spathe ($\times\frac{1}{8}$); D—anther; E—L.s. of ovary; F—T.s. of same; G—synandrium.

AFFINITY: *Araceae* appears to be closely related to *Palmae*, both the families having same type of inflorescence and inconspicuous hypogynous, regular flowers. The 2 families have been included in the same order spadiciflorae by Rendle while Engler places them in 2 distinct orders, viz. *Principes* with single family *Palmae* and *Spathiflorae* to accommodate 2 families *Araceae* and *Lemnaceae* and the 2 orders are placed close to each other in his system. Hutchinson considers that *Palmae* and *Araceae* are allied to each other both having been originated from *Liliaceous* stock in different lines. Takhtajam and Cronquist also consider that *Palmae* and *Araceae* are close to each other. *Araceae* is again closely related to *Lemnaceae* which appears to have been derived from *Araceae* through the floating genus *Pistia*.

Subdivisions of the family: Engler divided the family into 8 subfamilies, viz.

Sub. f. I **Pothoideae:** Latex and raphides absent; flowers bisexual; perianth present, *Pothos*, *Acorus*, *Anthurium*, etc.

Sub. f. II **Monsteroideae**: Latex absent, raphides present; flowers bisexual, without perianth. *Monstera*, *Scindapsus*, *Rhaphidophora*, etc.

Sub. f. III **Calloideae:** Latex present; flowers usually bisexual, perianthless. *Calla* and 3 other genera.

Sub. f. IV **Lasioideae:** Latex present, raphides present; flowers hermaphrodite or unisexual, perianth present or absent; seeds usually without endosperm. *Lasia*, *Amorphophallus*, etc.

Sub f. V **Philodendroideae:** Latex present, raphides present or absent; flowers unisexual and naked; seeds usually with endosperm; leaves parallel-nerved. *Philodendron*, *Zantedeschia*, etc.

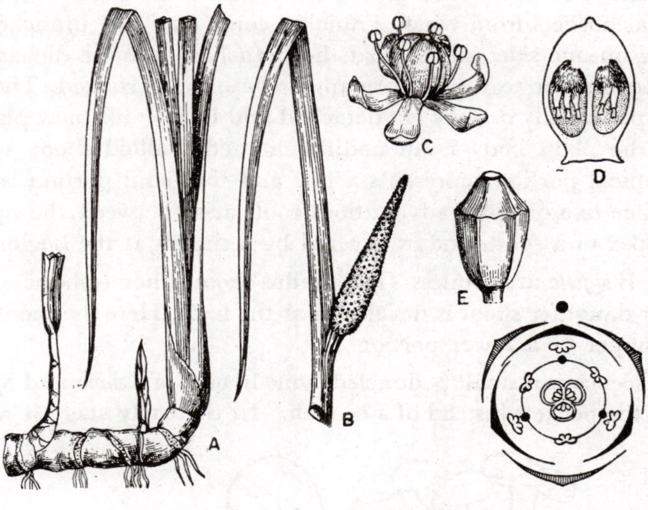

Fig. 33. Acorus calamus L. A—a part of the plant; B—the spike and the spathe-like elongated peduncle; C—a flower; D—L.s. of ovary; E—fruit.

Sub. f. VI **Colocasioideae:** Latex and raphides present; flowers unisexual and naked; seed with or without endosperm; leaves with reticulate veination, usually sagittate. *Colocasia*, *Alocasia*, *Caladium*, etc.

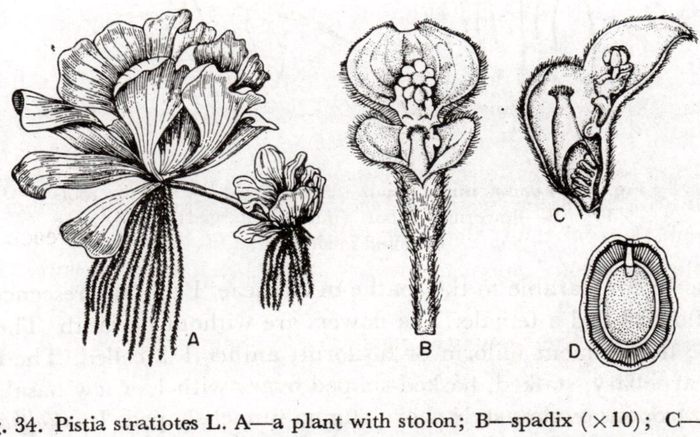

Fig. 34. Pistia stratiotes L. A—a plant with stolon; B—spadix (×10); C—L.s. of same, showing male and female flowers; D—L.s. of seed (much enlarged).

Sub. f. VII **Aroideae:** Latex present, raphides present; flowers unisexual, usually perianthless; seeds with endosperm; leaves reticulately veined. *Arum*, *Spathicarpa*, *Arisarum*, etc.

Sub. f. VIII **Pistioideae:** Floating herb; latex and raphides absent; flowers unisexual, naked; seed with endosperm. Single monotypic genus—*Pistia*.

Lemnaceae

Very small floating perennial herbs with a thalloid shoot which is dorsiventral and oblong or orbicular, or more or less hemispheric. In the former case, i.e. in *Lemna* and *Spirodela* a basal and an apical portion can be distinguished. The basal portion has 2 lateral pockets from which branches come out. The branches may develop on both sides or on one side only so that the branching may be dichasial or helicoid. The branches are similar to the main plant body and are stalked. They may remain attached to the plant body or may get detached and behave like new plants. According to Hegelmaier the plant body is an undifferentiated thalloid shoot while according to Engler the apical portion represents a leaf and the basal portion is the stem. On the ventral surface one or more adventitious roots arise between the upper and lower portions. The apex of a root remains covered by a sheath at the beginning.

Wolffia and *Wolffiela* are rootless. The thallus-shoot is hemispheric or globose and a single branch or daughter shoot is developed at the back. Here the shoot is not differentiated into an upper or a lower portion.

The inflorescence is a small peduncled cyme in case of *Lemna* and *Spirodela* coming out from one of the pockets instead of a branch. In the early stage it remains covered

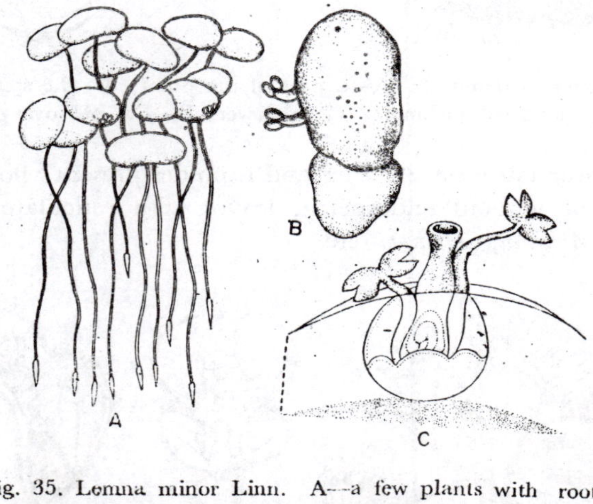

Fig. 35. Lemna minor Linn. A—a few plants with roots (×1); B—flowering shoot (much enlarged). C—Cyme enclosed in sheath.

by a minute scale comparable to the spathe in Araceae. Each inflorescence consists of a pair of male flowers and a female. The flowers are without perianth. The male with a single stamen; the filament filiform or fusiform; anther 1–2-celled. The female flower with a monocarpellary, stalked, flasked-shaped ovary with 1 or few basal, erect, orthotropous or anatropous ovules; style short, stigma funnel-shaped. In *Wolffia* and *Wolffiela* a male and a female flower develop side by side on the dorsal flat surface of the plant body. The fruit is a capsule with circumscissile dehiscence or is a utricle; the seed with an outer fleshy and an inner delicate seed-coat and scanty endosperm surrounding a large cotyledon.

The flowers are protogynous and are pollinated by insects or often by the agency of water. The pollen grains are warty and get easily stuck to the funnel-shaped stigma that secretes a sugary fluid.

The family consists of about 27 species under 4* genera occurring in fresh water pools or marshes in all tropical and temperate countries. They are of no economic importance except that they serve as food for the fish. *Wolffia arrhiza* Wimm. is the smallest among the **Angiosperms.** In tropical countries the plants flower regularly, while in temperate countries they seldom come to flower and the plants propagate by production of winter buds instead of vegetative buds. The winter buds lie dormant on the bottom of the pool or in the crevices on the sides and produce new plants at the advent of warmer period and come to the surface of water.

AFFINITY: The family is closely related to Araceae and appear to have originated from *Pistia* of which it is probably a very reduced form as evidenced by morphological, anatomical and cytological studies. Lawalree, however (1945), holds altogether a different view. According to him the presence of the minute scale in the pocket is a character common to the members of **Helobieae** as having the "squamulae intravaginalis" and states that Lemnaceae originated from that group.

FARINOSAE

Farinosae is the 8th order in the system of Engler and Prantl where they included 13 families, viz. — *Flagellariaceae, Restionaceae, Centrolepidaceae, Mayacaceae, Xyridaceae, Eriocaulaceae, Thurniaceae, Rapatiaceae, Bromeliaceae, Commelinaceae, Pontederiaceae, Cynastraceae,* and *Philydraceae*. In all these families the seeds have plenty of mealy endosperm and the ovary is superior and polycarpellary syncarpous. Flowers are usually hermaphrodite, pentacyclic and regular. Flowers are entomophillous.

These families although have some characters common to them do not appear to be closely related and although included by Engler in a single order do not form a natural group. Most other botanists distribute these families under different orders some of which are not very close. Hutchinson placed these families in as many as 7 orders, e.g. *Flagellariaceae, Mayacaceae* and *Commelinaceae* in **Commelinales,** *Restionaceae, Centrolepidaceae* and *Thurniaceae* in **Juncales,** *Xyridaceae* and *Rapatiaceae* in **Xyridales,** *Philydraceae* in **Haemodorales,** *Eriocaulaceae* and *Bromeliaceae* in distinct monotypic orders **Eriocaulales** and **Bromeliales** while *Cyanastraceae* has been merged with *Tecophilaeaceae* of **Liliales** in which order he also transfers *Pontederiaceae*. This treatment of breaking the order Farinosae and distribution of the families into 7 other orders has met with the approval of Takhtajan and Cronquist as well as of many other taxonomists. The families *Eriocaulaceae, Bromeliaceae, Xyridaceae* and *Rapatiaceae* although placed under orders other than the Commelinales by Hutchinson are placed in the same division **Calyciferae** by him close to Commelinales while *Restionaceae, Centrolepidaceae* and *Thurniaceae* are put under Juncales of **Glumiflorae** along with **Cyperales** and **Graminales** far from Commelinales.

Both Takhtajan and Cronquist maintain Cyanastraceae as a distinct family and include the same in Liliales where they place *Philydraceae* also.

According to Hutchinson Commelinales have been derived from **Butomales** and **Alismatales,** and Bromeliales, Eriocaulales and Xyridales originated from Commelinales.

---

* Some recognize 2 more genera, viz. *Pseudowolffia* and *Wolffiopsis*.

Flagellariaceae

Shrubs or undershrubs, erect or climbing. Leaves alternate, plicate or flat with several prominent nerves, with a long tubular sheath covering major part of the internode; leaf tip often prolonged into a tendril. Panicles terminal; bracts usually lanceolate. Flowers regular, hermaphrodite or dioecious, usually small. Perianth in 2 series with 3 segments in each, persistent; segments free, imbricate, scarious or somewhat petaloid. Stamens 6, filaments filiform, free or slightly adnate to the base of perianth-segments; anthers 2-celled, basifixed, introrse, dehiscing longitudinally. Ovary superior, 3-locular, with a solitary anatropous ovule on axile placentation, spreading or pendulous; style short with 3 stigmatic branches or styles 3 and distinct. Fruit small, indehiscent, a berry or a drupe; seeds with copious mealy endosperm and a small embryo situated at the end or on one side of the endosperm the position of the embryo is indicated by a disc-like callosity on the surface called as embryotega (or embryostega); embryo lenticular.

This is a small family with only 2 genera and 5 species found in the tropical Africa, India and eastward up to Australia. *Flagellaria indica* Linn. occurs in lower Bengal and different parts of S. India in damp situations. The other genus *Hanguana* (Syn. *Susum*) is found in Ceylon and Malaysia. The family is of no economic importance.

This family is included in the order Farinosae by Engler due to the mealy nature of endosperm. Hutchinson breaks up this order into 7 orders and places Fagellariaceae in Commelinales. Takhtajan as well as Cronquist considers that Fagellariaceae is closer to Restionaceae than to Commelinaceae and places Fagellariaceae under Restionales. Airy Shaw considers that the 2 genera *Flagellaria* and *Hanguana* are so distinct that these are to be treated as belonging to two separate families. He, therefore, establishes another monotypic family as **Hanguanaceae** in which he includes the genus *Hanguana* with erect robust herbs, which are stoloniferous with flowers dioecious, inner perianth segments larger, stigma sessile and broadly 3-lobed. Takhtajan supports Airy Shaw in the splitting up of the older family to 2 smaller monotypic families e.g. Flagellariaceae and Hanguanaceae.

Commelinaceae

Annual or perennial herbs, erect or occasionally twining, with jointed more or less succulent stems and often with subterranean rhizome. Calcium oxalate crystals are present in the tissues. Leaves alternate, sheathed at the base; sheaths closed membranous and often nervose. The inflorescence is of a cincinnus type or paniculate or cymose cluster, axillary or terminal, enclosed by spathe-like bracts or leaf-sheath which it sometimes perforates; rarely flowers solitary; floral bracts small, rarely foliacious and distichously imbricate. Flowers usually hermaphrodite, regular or often medianly zygomorphic, hypogynous, blue, white or pinkish. Perianth in 2 series with 3 segments in each, segments free, imbricate, rarely united; the outer sepaloid and the inner petaloid, rarely one of the 3 petals is reduced to a scale-like structure. Stamens 6 in 2 whorls, all fertile or only 3 or 2 are fertile and the rest reduced to staminodes or absent; filaments usually free, smooth or bearded with moniliform brightly coloured hairs; anthers basifixed, 2-locular; loculi parallel and usually contiguous, opening by longitudinal slits or by apical pores, connectives of various types. Ovary superior 3- or 2-locular; ovules few or solitary in each cell, orthotropous, on axile placentation; style terminal, simple with small capitate or 3-lobed stigma. Fruit a loculicidal capsule or rarely fleshy and indehiscent; seeds angular, in 2 series in each cell, mostly muricate, ridged or reticulate, with copious mealy endosperm, rarely arillate; embryo marginal or nearly so, its position indicated by an embryostega.

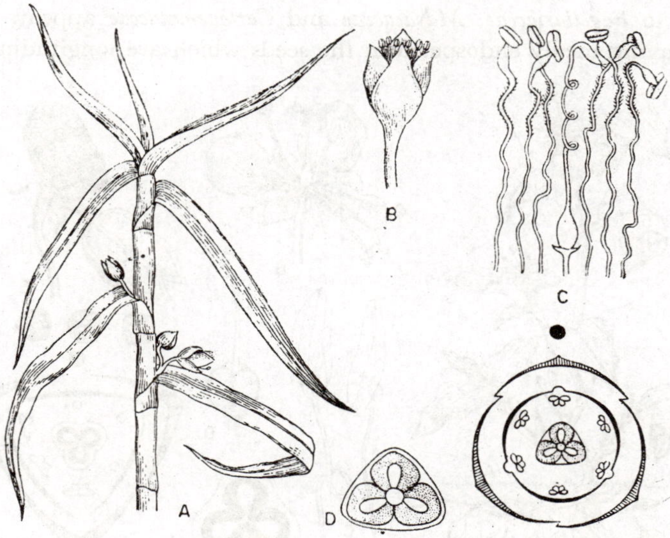

Fig. 36. Cyanotis axillaris R. & S. A—a plant with leaves and flowers; B—a flower; C—stamens and ovary; D—Cross-section of ovary.

The flowers are pollinated by insects which are attracted by the coloured petals and filaments of the stamens; self pollination has rarely been observed, while small cleistogamous flowers are produced on the subterranean branches of the rhizome of *Commelina benghalensis* Linn.

FLORAL FORMULA:

$$\oplus \text{ or } \dagger, ⚥\ P_{3+3}\ A_{3+3\ (\text{or } 3)}\ G_{\underline{(3)}}$$
$$\text{or } K_3\ C_3\ A_{3+3\ (\text{or } 3)}\ G_{\underline{(3)}}$$

The family contains about 600 species in 38 genera. These are placed under 2 subfamilies as noted below:

Sub. f. **Tradescantieae**—Flowers actinomorphic; tribes 2-Hexandreae, Triandrae.

Sub. f. **Commelineae**—Flowers zygomorphic; tribes 2, Declinatae, Inclinatae.

The family is well represented in India by several species, common among them are *Commelina benghalensis* Linn., *C. obliqua* Buch. Ham., *Murdannia nudiflorum* (R. Br.) Bruckner (Syn. *Aneilema nudiflorum* R. Br.). *Aneilema liniolatum* Kunth., *Floscopa scandens* Lour., *Cyanotis cristata* Schult. etc. *Streptolirion cordifolium* (Griff.) O. Ktz. is a climber of the temperate Himalayas. *Zebrina pendula* Schnitze. of Mexico, *Rhoeo discolor* Hance of Trop. America and *Setcreasea purpurea* Boom of Mexico are cultivated in gardens as ornamental plants. The long hairs on the stamens of *Rhoeo discolor* show protoplasmic movements when observed under microscope.

The family is included in the order **Farinosae** by Engler with other families having mealy endosperm in the seeds. Hutchinson splits Farinosae into 7 smaller orders and Commelinaceae is placed by him in **Commelinales** along with *Flagellariaceae*,

Mayacaceae and *Cartonemataceae* the last was formerly included under *Commelinaceae* but separated as a distinct family to accomodate *Cartonema* a xerophytic Australian genus. Hutchinson derives the order **Commelimales** from the 2 most primitive orders, viz. **Butomales** and **Alismatales,** i.e. from **Helobieae.** *Commelinaceae* besides being closely related to *Fagellariaceae*, *Mayacaceae* and *Cartonemataceae* appears to be close to *Pontederiaceae* having mealy endosperm in the seeds which are longitudinally ridged.

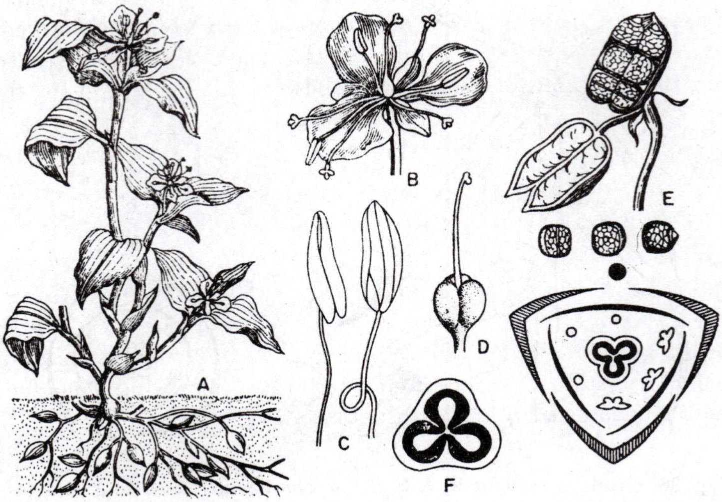

Fig. 37. Commelina benghalensis. A—a plant with leaves, aerial and underground cleistogamous flowers ($\times\frac{1}{2}$); B—one flower ($\times 1$); C—stamens; D—ovary; E—fruit and seeds; F—cross-section of ovary.

Economic importance: Besides the ornamental garden plants mentioned above there are a few species which are used medicinally. *Aneilema scapiflorum* is used as a substitute of *Curculigo orchioides* Gaert. the "Musali" or "Talmuli" of the Indian Kavirajes. The plant body of *Commelina benghalensis* Linn. and of several species of *Aneilema* and *Murdannia* are used in Leprosy and Leucoderma. The bruised plant of *Commelia nudiflora* Linn. relieves pain in burns, boils, etc. The roots of *Cyanotes* are used to expel worms in cattle and alloying fevers. The juice of the stem of *Floscopa* is used in eye sore. The leaves of *Commelina benghalensis* Linn. are taken as pot herbs and these are laxative. The juice of the leaves of this species neutralises the poisoning effect from the touch of the hairs of caterpillars.

Eriocaulaceae

(Eriocaulonaceae)

Small herbs, usually perennial, with a very short axis and a tuft of densely arranged linear grass-like radical leaves. Flowers very small crowded on a globose, monoecious or dioecious heads terminating a slender, simple, rarely branched scape, subtended by an involucre of bracts; the peduncle sheathed at the base much exceeding the leaves; the bracts of the involucre are usually prominent and the inner ones larger. Flowers unisexual sessile or shortly stalked, regular or rarely zygomorphic in the axil of a scarious, saclike, coloured or colourless bract of its own; in monoecious heads the staminate flowers are arranged in the centre and the pistillate on the periphery or flowers of both sexes are inter mixed. Perianth or perigonyum in 2 distinct whorls, segments scarious or membranous or rarely hyaline, 2–3 in each whorl, the outer segments free or united, the inner united, infundibuliform or cupular, rarely hairy at apex usually stalked, rarely inner whorl absent. Stamens alternate to and as many as outer segments, often more, inserted on the inner whorl of united segments; anther 1–2-celled, introrse, dehiscing by vertical slits; filaments slender; pistillodium often present in ♂ flowers. Ovary superior, 2–3-celled with a single orthotropus ovule in each, pendulous from the axile placentas; style 1, with 2–3 branches, each branch simple or forked; staminodes rarely present in ♀ flowers. Fruit a loculicidal capsule, 2–3-seeded; seeds with copious mealy endosperm and minute lenticular embryo situated opposite to the hilum; the horny testa is smooth or striate or hairy.

Floral formula:

♂ $P_{2+2}\ A_2$
or $P_{3+3}\ A_3$
♀ $P_{2+2}\ G_{(\underline{3})}$
or $P_{3+3}\ G_{(\underline{3})}$

The flowers are entomophyllous. When fruits mature the heads fall as a whole or the individual flowers are detached and distributed by wind, the hairy inner and wing-like outer segments help in the distribution.

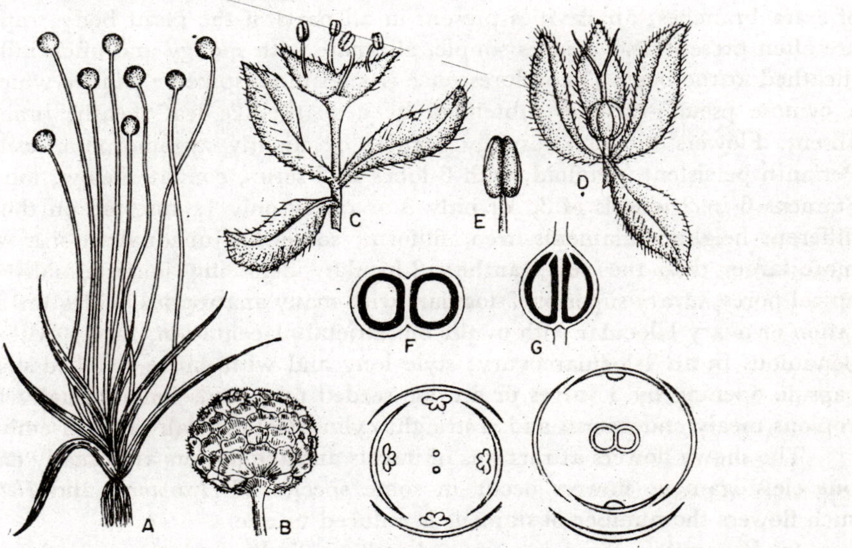

Fig. 38. Eriocaulon quniqueangulare L. A—a plant with leaves and several flowering heads (×½); B—a flower head with involucre of bracts (×2); C—male flower; D—female flower; E—stamen; F—cross section of ovary; G—L.s. of same.

The family consists of about 1150 species in 13 genera of which *Eriocaulon* contains 370 species. *Paepalanthus* is another American genus having almost equal number of species. The plants grow usually in damp situations in the warmer parts of the world. The family is represented in India by several species of *Eriocaulon* the most common among them are *E. sieboldianum* S. & Z., *E. truncatum* Buch.-Ham., *E. trilobum* Buch.-Ham., *E. quinqueangulare* Linn.

The family is subdivided into 2 subfamilies as noted below:

I **Eriocauloideae:** Inner perianth segments or petals glandular near apex on the innerside; stamens twice the number of petals.

II **Paepalanthoideae:** Glands on petals absent, petals rarely absent; stamens double the number of petals or sepals.

The family has been included in *Farinosae* by Engler on account of the mealy endosperm in the seeds. Hutchinson considers it to be a much advanced family with small unisexual flowers crowded in dense heads, reduced and united perianth-lobes and other characters, and derives the order **Eriocaulales** with the single family from **Commelinales.** Takhtajan and Cronquist also include *Eriocaulaceae* in the monotypic order **Eriocaulales** which both of them place after *Commelinales*.

The family is of little economic value. *Eriocaulon setaceum* Linn. and a few other species have medicinal value. The flower-heads if preserved before the flowers open remain as such for a long time and those of the genus *Syngonanthus* are thus preserved as ever-lasting flowers.

Pontederiaceae

Aquatic herbs, floating or rooted to the mud; rhizome with a sympodial axis, the successive branches ending in an inflorescence; plants often stoloniferous; branches often adnate to the main shoot from which they spring; sometimes the branch with the inflorescence is pushed aside and appears to spring from a leaf-sheath due to formation of extra branches; air cavities present in all parts of the plant body; raphide-crystals are often present also. Leaves simple, alternate with spongy and often inflated petiole, sheathed at the base. The inflorescence is a terminal spike or panicle which is actually a cymose pseudo-raceme, subtended by a spathe-like leaf sheath; bracts minute or absent. Flowers bisexual, usually regular or slightly zygomorphic, usually, showy. Perianth persistent, petaloid, with 6 lobes in 2 series, connate below; lobes imbricate. Stamens 6 in 2 whorls of 3, or only 3 or rarely only 1, inserted on the perianth at different heights; filaments free, filiform, somewhat unequal in size or one much more larger than the rest; anthers 2-locular, dehiscing longitudinally or rarely by apical pores. Ovary superior, 3-locular, with many anatropous ovules on axile placentation or ovary 1-locular with ovules on parietal placentation, rarely ovule solitary and pendulous in an 1-locular ovary; style long and with entire or lobed stigma. Fruit a capsule opening by 3 valves or an one seeded nut; seeds longitudinally ribbed, with copious mealy endosperm and a straight cylindrical centrally placed embryo.

The showy flowers attract lots of insects and the flowers are usually entomophilous but cleistogamous flowers occur in some species of *Hydrothrix* and *Heteranthera*. In such flowers the number of stamens is reduced to one.

In *Heteranthera* there is a central stelar cylinder and the vascular bundles are colateral. The root is polyarch in all genera. The leaf anatomy shows a reverse orientation of the pallisade cells and the xylem towards the lower surface of the leaf.

This is a small family with about 30 species under 7 genera occurring in the marshes and fresh water pools of the tropical and subtropical countries of the world. *Monochoria hastata* Solms-Laub. and *M. vaginalis* Presl. with blue flowers are common in the marshes all over India in the plains. Another exotic weed a floaing herb with beautiful pale purple flowers has become an obnoxious pest of lakes and streamlets all over India and is an introduction from tropical America, viz. *Eichhornia crassipes* (Mart.) Solms-Laub. The plants are of no economic importance.

Pontederiaceae was placed in the order **Farinosae** by Engler due to the presence of mealy endosperm in the seeds. Hutchinson places this family in his

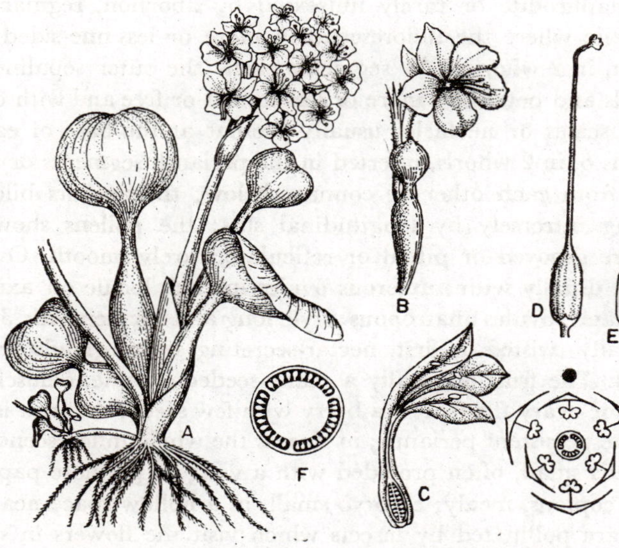

Fig. 39. Eichornia crassipes S. L. A—an entire plant, B—part of the peduncle with one flower; C—L.s. of flower; D—ovary; E.—L.s. of ovary; F—cross-section of ovary.

Liliales due to more or less similar and petaloid perianth segments in two whorls. Both Takhtajan and Cronquist support Hutchinson and included *Pontederiaceae* in **Liliales** where the families have binucleate pollens.

Bromeliaceae

Plants of this family are mostly epiphytic herbs, sometimes terrestrials, with very short stem; rarely elongated and branched, e.g. *Puya* which are erect and shrubby, *Tillandsia* hanging like lichens from forest-trees or *Pitcairnia* with climbing habit. Some terrestrials are stoloniferous and the plants propagate vegitatively, e.g. *Cryptanthus*, *Ananas*, etc. The primary root perishes early and adventitious roots develop from the nodes often piercing the leaf sheath; these roots are of 2 kinds, the absorbing roots and fixing roots. Leaves sessile, sheathed at the base, linear, channelled above, densely crowded to form a rosette on the shortened stem and with the stem-clasping sheaths represent a cup where water collects; the inside of the leaf-bases are furnished with a kind of peltate hairs which absorb water with the dissolved particles that fall there and help in the nutrition of the plant; the leaves are often fleshy or chartaceous with strongly cuticularised surface and water-storing parenchyma in the mesophyl; peculiar water-absorbing scales and hairs all over the leaves and on the whole plant body are present especially in the epiphytes that absorb atmospheric moisture while scaly hairs covering the leaf surface, reduce the rate of transpiration; the leaf-margin may be entire or spinose, the spines short or long and hook-like helping the plant to climb by fixing the hooks to the support; the leaves are often coloured.

The inflorescence is a terminal spike or panicle with bracts and bracteoles; bracts are usually brilliantly coloured and often form an involucre or a rosette; the flowering axis is often short with flowers densely crowded, or elongated with basal sterile bracts;

in some cases the flowering shoot persists for several years and produces inflorescence in each successive season; rarely flowers solitary.

Flowers hermaphrodite or rarely unisexual by abortion, regular or very rarely slightly zygomorphic where the inflorescence is more or less one-sided or pendulous; perianth persistent, in 2 whorls of 3 segments each, the outer sepaline and the inner petaline; the sepals and petals are more or less united or free and with convolute aestivation; a pair of scales or nectaries usually present at the base of each petal on the inner side. Stamens 6, in 2 whorls, inserted in the perianth segments or adnate to them at the base, free from each other or connate below; the anthers bilocular, usually, versatile, dehiscing introrsely by longitudinal slits; the pollens show characteristic markings; they are grooved or pitted or reticulate, rarely smooth. Ovary superior to inferior, 3-locular, usually with numerous ovules in each locule on axile placentation which often bifurcates; ovules anatropous; style long and slender with 3 stigmas which often remain spirally twisted at first, nectar-secreting septal glands are often present on the ovary-wall. The fruit is usually a many-seeded capsule, dehiscing septicidally, or in case of inferior ovary the fruit is a berry with few seeds; the fruit is often more or less enclosed by the persistent perianth; in *Ananas* the whole inflorescence form a succulent syncarp. Seeds small, often provided with a wing or plumose pappus-like appendage; endosperm copious, mealy; embryo small, in a hollow space near the hilum.

The flowers are pollinated by insects which visit the flowers in search of nectar and also being attracted by the bright colour of petals and bracts.

FLORAL FORMULA: ⚥ $K_3C_3A_{3+3}\,G_{(3)}$

The family consists of about 1900 species under 59 genera and almost wholly confined to the New World while *Pitcairnea feliciana* (A. Chev.) H. & M. occurs wild in W. Africa and *Ananas comosus* (L.) Merr. is cultivated in all tropical countries. Harms subdivided the family as follows—

Sub. f. I **Navioideae:** Ovary superior, ovules few; fruit a capsule seeds without wing or appendage; 1 genus—Navia.

Sub. f. II **Pitcairnioideae:** Ovary superior or half inferior, ovules many; fruit a capsule, seeds with a wing or appendage; mostly terrestrials;—12 genera, Puya, Pitcairnia, Dyckia, etc.

Sub. f. III **Tillandsioideae:** Ovary superior, rarely half inferior, ovules many; fruit a capsule, seeds with pappus-like appendage; terrestrials or epiphytes;—12 genera, Vriesia, Tillandsia (250 spp.), etc.

Sub. f. IV **Bromelioideae:** Overy inferior, ovules usually many; fruit a berry, seeds without wing or appendage; terrestrials; genera 34, Ananas, Bromelia, etc.

The genus *Navia* is now considered to be an extreme form of the Sub. f. **Pitcairnioideae** and does not form a distinct subfamily.

Engler placed *Bromeliaceae* in his **Farinosae** because of mealy endosperm in the seeds. Rendle followed Engler's treatment. Hutchinson who splitted the order Farinosae into 7 orders placed *Bromeliaceae* in a distinct monotypic order **Bromeliales** which he derives from **Commelinales.** According to him *Bromeliaceae* is related to *Commelinaceae* but is more advanced. Both Takhtajan and Cronquist place *Bromeliaceae* in a monotypic order **Bromeliales** but while Takhtajan puts **Bromeliales** and **Commelinales** very close to each other, Cronquist in his system of classification places them far apart in the same subclass **Commelinidae** considering *Bromeliaceae* to be a much advanced family over *Commelinaceae*. Smith considers that *Bromeliaceae* is more allied to *Rapataceae* both having similar type of perianth and embryo. According to him these 2 families arose from a common stock.

Economic importance: The Pine-apple—*Ananas comosus* (L.) Merr. is famous for the delicious fruit which is a syncarp formed from the whole inflorescence including the axis, bracts and floral parts. The species also yields a fine fibre from the leaves used for the manufacture of Pina cloth. The plant is widely cultivated in all tropical countries. *Neoglaziovia variegata* Mez., *Bromelia serra* Griseb. and *B. magdalenae* C. H. Weight also yield fibre. The dry plants of *Tillandsia usneoides* Linn. are used for stuffing pillows and cushions. Many plants are cultivated as garden ornamentals for their brightly coloured leaves, bracts and flowers, e.g. different species of *Billbergia, Aechmea, Vriesia, Nidularium, Puya, Pitcairnia, Tillandsia*, etc.

LILIIFLORAE

In his 9th order **Liliiflorae** Engler included 9 families, viz.—*Juncaceae, Stemonaceae, Liliaceae, Haemodoraceae, Amaryllidaceae, Velloziaceae, Taccaceae, Dioscoreaceae* and *Iridaceae*. The common characters noted here are usually perennial herbs, underground bulbs corm or rhizome present, hermaphrodite and usually regular flowers, perianth in 2 whorls, stamens usually 6 in 2 whorls, ovary tricarpellary syncarpous, ovules usually anatropous, seeds with a copious fleshy or cartillaginous endosperm. Flowers are usually entomophillous.

According to Engler as well as Rendle, **Liliiflorae** is a natural group and the order is rather recent. The petaloid perianth, syncarpous ovary and pollination by insects are advanced characters. A closer analysis of the characters of the families however indicates that it is nothing but a heterogenous assemblage and the order **Liliiflorae** of Engler has been splitted up into several orders which may or may not be very close to each other. For instance, *Juncaceae* with its inconspicuous perianth and usually grass-like habit is quite distinct from others. This family is removed from Liliiflorae by others and placed in **Juncales** which order is not very close to Liliiflorae according to many subsequent workers. *Iridaceae* appears to be a natural family but its inclusion in Liliiflorae is controversial. Both Hutchinson and Takhtajan remove *Iridaceae* from Lilliflorae (or **Liliales**) and place it in a distinct order **Iridales** which is a monotypic order according to Hutchinson while Takhtajan includes the families *Geosiridaceae, Burmanniaceae* and *Corsicaceae* along with *Iridaceae*. *Amaryllidaceae* is also removed from Liliiflorae (**Liliales**) and placed under a monotypic order **Amaryllidales** by Hutchinson while Takhtajan keeps it in **Liliales** and Cronquist takes a bold step to merge *Amaryllidaceae* with *Liliaceae*. Hutchinson puts *Haemodoraceae*, *Velloziaceae* and *Taccaceae* in **Haemodorales** and *Dioscoreaceae* and *Stemonaceae* (*Roxburghiaceae*) in **Dioscoreales.** These five families however are retained in Liliales both by Takhtajan and Cronquist. The limitations of the families *Liliaceae* and *Amaryllidaceae* have also been regarded to be different. These have been splitted to create smaller families to give them a more natural and compact shape. Hutchinson in his order **Liliales** includes six families, viz. *Liliaceae, Tecophilaeaceae, Trilliaceae, Smilacaceae, Ruscaceae* and *Pontederiaceae* of which excepting *Pontederiaceae* all were subfamilies or tribes of the older *Liliaceae*. This splitting up of *Liliaceae* as well as of *Amaryllidaceae* by Hutchinson has been supported to some extent by most recent workers including Takhtajan who raises the tribe *Alliaeae* to a distinct family, viz. *Alliaceae*.

Liliiflorae (or Liliales) is considered by some to have originated from **Commeli-**

nales, i.e. from **Farinosae** while others think it had its origin from **Alismatales,** i.e. from **Helobieae.** According to Takhtajan as well as Cronquist Liliales and Commelinales belong to two distinct subclasses, viz. **Liliidae** and **Commelinidae** and these 2 subclasses originated from a common stock similar to **Alismatidae,** i.e. both Liliales and Commelinales originated separately from the Helobial group.

Liliiflorae (or Liliales) is considered by most authors as the basal stock from which many other orders of the Monocotyledons had their origin by further elaboration in flowers or by reduction.

Juncaceae

Annual or perennial herbs, rarely undershrubs of marshy places with creeping sympodial rhizomes and hairy roots; rarely plants tall and Yucca-like, e.g. *Prionium.* Stem usually angled, with a soft pith. Leaves usually in a basal tuft, linear, filiform or cylindric or flat and dorsiventral, sheathing at the base; rarely sometimes reduced to sheath only.

The inflorescence is various; usually the small flowers are aggregated in condensed head-like cymes or it is a panicle of racemes or corymbs or false umbeles; rarely flowers solitary; bracts and bracteoles present. Flowers regular, bisexual or often unisexual and dioecious, hypogynous. Perianth in two or one whorl of 3 members in each; segments glumaceous with scarious or coriaceous margins, free and imbricate; rarely perianth petaloid. Stamens 6 in two whorls, inserted on the base of perianth segments; filaments triquetrous, slender; anthers basifixed, introrse, opening by longitudinal slits; pollen in tetrads. Ovary superior, trilocular with axile placentation or unilocular with parietal placentation; ovules many or few, rarely one and basal; style with 3 plumose stigmas which are often twisted to the right; often styles 3. Fruit a loculicidal capsule with small and often appendaged seeds; embryo straight, endosperm mealy.

Flowers are anemophyllous, some with coloured perianth are however pollinated by insects. The floral formula in case of ⚥ flowers is $P_{3+3} A_{3+3 \text{ (or } 3+0)} G_{(\underline{3})}$.

The family contains a little over 300 species in 8 genera occurring in cool damp places in temperate countries with a few even in antartic region. In India the family is represented by several species of *Juncus* and a few of *Luzula* at high elevations of the Himalayas and hills of eastern India. *J. bufonius* Linn. and *J. prismatocarpus* R. Br. come down to the plains of Bihar and Bengal.

Only a few plants of this family are of economic importance. Fibres obtained from *Juncus textilis* Buchen. and species of *Marsippospermum* and *Prionium* are used in weaving mats, making hats, chair-seats and cushions. Some species of *Luzula* have medicinal properties.

Juncaceae has been included in the order **Liliiflorae** by Engler because of the general plan of the flower having 6 perianth segments in 2 whorls, 6 stamens in 2 whorls and superior trilocular ovary. But the nature of the perianth appears to be a strong character to remove this family from Liliiflorae and place it in a distinct order **Juncales** with *Thurniaceae* and also with *Restionaceae* and *Centrolepidaceae* according to Hutchinson. Hutchinson derives Juncales from Liliales but states that it has closer affinities with **Cyperales** and **Graminales** and includes these three orders in Division **Glumiflorae.** Both Takhtajan and Cronquist agree to include *Juncaceae* and *Thurmiaceae* in Juncales which order according to them has been derived from a stock that gave rise to **Commelinales** rather than Liliales. They also think that *Juncaceae* is closely allied to *Cyperaceae.*

Liliaceae

Generally perennial herbs with an underground rhizome or bulb or corm; the rhizome is sympodial; sometimes shrubby, often climbing or arborescent; branches often modified into cladodes. Leaves radical or cauline, sessile and sheathed at the base or petiolate, linear or lanceolate or ovate, leathery or very thick or soft and fleshy; often leaves are converted into scales subtending the cladodes; veins obscure in thick leaves, otherwise prominent.

Racemes simple or branched, often condensed into an umbel, each flower subtended by a bract; or flowers solitary. Flowers hermaphrodite, very rarely unisexual, hypogynous rarely perigynous, regular or rarely zygomorphic. Perianth in 2 whorls of 3 segments each; segments usually all similar and petaloid or rarely the outer sepaloid, free and imbricate, rarely connate below. Stamens 6, opposite perianth segments; filaments free or rarely connate; anthers dehiscing longitudinally or by apical pores; rarely stamens fewer. Ovary superior or semi-inferior, trilocular or rarely 2, 4 or 5-locular; ovules usually many in 2 rows on axile placentation, anatropous. Fruit usually a capsule, loculicidal or septicidal, rarely fruit is a berry; seed with fleshy or hard endosperm. Polyembryony has been observed in certain cases.

Flowers are pollinated by insects attracted by brightly coloured perianth, nectar and odour.

The usual floral formula is as follows: $\oplus$ ⚥ $P_{3+3}\ A_{3+3}\ G_{\underline{(3)}}$

The family is a large one with about 2500 species under 250 genera distributed almost all over the world. The plants show a great range of variations in vegetative as well as floral parts. The underground stem may be a bulb as in *Lilium*, *Tulipa*, a corm as in *Colchicum* and rhizome as in *Gloriosa*. The majority of the plants are herbs but a few genera like *Gloriosa*, *Asparagus*, etc. are climbers, and shrubby plants often attaining the size of trees, e.g. *Dracaena*, *Cordyline*, etc. In the last group forming the subfamily *Dracaenoideae* secondary growth in stem occurs by the formation of successive concentric rings of vascular bundles in the ground tissue. In some genera the branches are modified into cladodes arising from the axil of scale-leaves, broad and leaf-like as in *Ruscus*, needle-like as in *Asparagus*. Leaves are clustered on top of the bulbs or enclosing them or scattered over stem and branches or whorled near the apices; soft and fleshy or thick and leathery or thin and papery; linear or with a distinct lamina and petiole. The inflorescence terminates a leafless scape or on leafy stem and branches or may be axillary; it is of racemose type, simple or paniculate, often forming a false or true umbel; solitary flowers occur also in many genera. In *Ruscus* the clusters of flowers arise from the surface of the cladodes or from the margins. Flowers are bisexual in most genera but unisexual in *Ruscus*, *Smilax*, etc. Perianth segments are usually all similar or the outer calyx-like and different from those of the inner whorl. Stamens are free but rarely

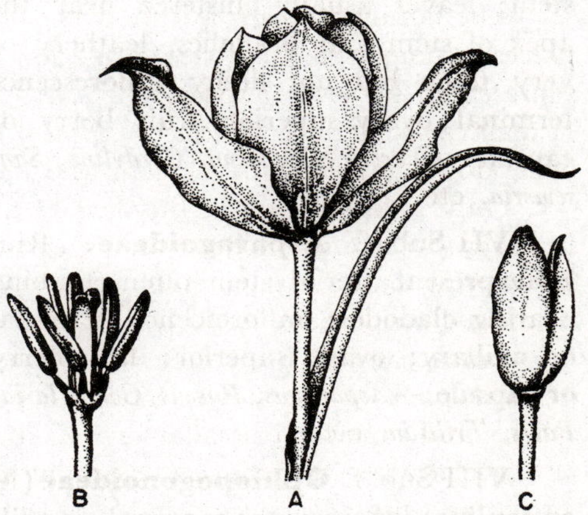

Fig. 40. Tulipa hoogiana Fed. A—flower and a part of the leaf; B—flower without the perianth; C—fruit. (all × $\frac{1}{2}$).

united in a column as in *Ruscus*, *Heterosmilax*, *Tricyritis*, etc., free from the perianth or adnate to it; connective rarely prolonged; dehiscence of anthers by longitudinal slits or by apical pores. Ovary is usually superior but semi-inferior ovary is found in the subfamilies *Ophiopogonoideae* (*Mondoideae*) and *Aletroideae*; ovary is syncarpous but carpels are almost free to the base in *Petrosavia* and *Protolirion*. Fruit is a capsule but in many genera it is a berry.

Petrosavia is saprophytic while *Protolirion* is a root-parasite.

The family is subdivided into 11 subfamilies by Krause following the treatment of Engler as given below:

I Sub. f. **Melanthioideae:** Rhizome or bulb present; leaves radical or cauline; inflorescence terminal; ovary superior; fruit a capsule:—*Tofieldia*, *Gloriosa*, *Colchicum*, etc.

II Sub. f. **Asphodeloideae:** Rhizome with radical leaves or with aerial leafy stem; inflorescence terminal; ovary superior; fruit a capsule or berry:—*Asphodelus*, *Chlorophytum*, *Anthericum*, etc.

III Sub. f. **Herrerioideae:** Twiner with underground tuber; leaves tufted; ovary superior; fruit capsular:—*Herreria* (single genus).

IV Sub. f. **Allioideae:** Short rhizome or bulb; inflorescence on leafless scape, an umbellate cyme enclosed by a pair of membranous spathes; ovary superior; fruit capsular:—*Allium*, *Gagea*, *Gilliesia*, etc.

V Sub. f. **Lilioideae:** Bulbous plants; inflorescence racemose, terminal; leaves radical or cauline; ovary superior; fruit capsular:—*Lilium*, *Tulipa*, *Scilla*, *Urginea*, *Hyacinthus*, etc.

VI Sub. f. **Dracaenoideae:** Erect stem; leaves usually clustered near the apex of stem and branches, leathery or very thick but not fleshy; inflorescence terminal; ovary superior; fruit berry or capsule:—*Yucca*, *Dracaena*, *Cordyline*, *Sansevieria*, etc.

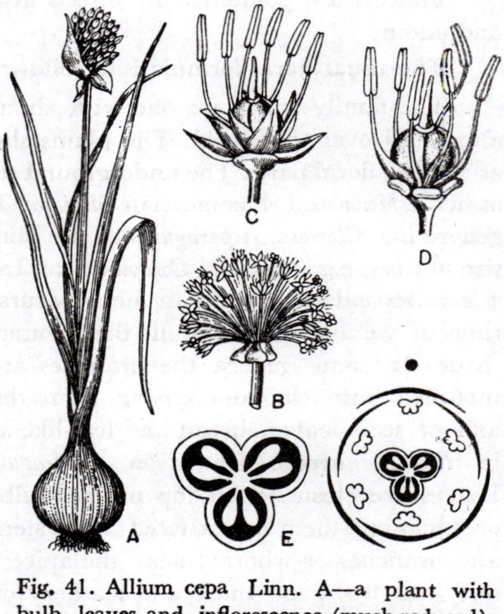

Fig. 41. Allium cepa Linn. A—a plant with bulb, leaves and inflorescence (much reduced); B—the umbel ($\times\frac{1}{3}$); C—a flower ($\times 2$); D—same with the perianth removed; E—Cross section of ovary.

VII Sub. f. **Asparagoideae:** Rhizome present; aerial stem often climbing bearing cladodes; inflorescence terminal or axillary; ovary superior; fruit berry or capsule:—*Asparagus*, *Ruscus*, *Convallaria*, *Paris*, *Trillium*, etc.

VIII Sub. f. **Ophiopogonoideae (Mondoideae):** Rhizome short; leaves radical or cauline; inflorescence terminal or axillary; ovary semi-inferior; ovules only 2 in each cell; fruit capsule or berry:—*Ophiopogon* (*Mondo*), *Peliosanthes*, etc.

IX Sub. f. **Aletroideae:** Rhizome short; leaves radical, lanceolate; inflorescence terminal; perianth segments connate; ovary semi-inferior; fruit a capsule; *Aletris* etc.

X Sub. f. **Luzuriagoideae:** Shrubs or undershrubs, often scandent; inflorescence terminal; ovary superior; fruit berry; *Lapageria*, *Luzuriaga* etc.

XI Sub. f. **Smilacoideae:** Climbing or scandent shrubs from a rhizome; leaves cauline, net-veined, flowers small dioecious in axillary umbels; ovary superior; fruit a berry: *Smilax, Heterosmilax, Rhipogonum*, etc.

The large family contains many ornamental plants as well as those important medicinally or otherwise. Garden ornamentals are species of *Lilium, Tulipa, Gloriosa, Fritillaria, Agapanthus, Hayacinthus, Yucca, Dracaena, Cordyline*, etc. Among those having medicinal value *Aloe vera* L., *Veratrum album* L., *Asparagus racemosus* Willd. *Smilax sarsa-parila* L., *Smilax macrophyla* Roxb., *Convalaria majalis* Linn. may be mentioned. *Phormium tenax* Forst., *Yucca filamentosa* Linn. and a few others yield fibres from the leaves. The rhizome of *Gloriosa* and bulbs of *Urginea* and *Scilla* are poisonous. As food-plants *Allium cepa* L. the onion, *A. satium* L. the garlic and *A. porrum* Linn. the leek are well known. Fresh young shoots of *Asparagus officinalis* Linn. and *A. adscendens* Roxb. are taken as vegetables. *Lapageria rosea* Ruiz & Pav. of Chili yields edible berries.

The family **Liliaceae** as understood by the older taxonomists including Engler and Krause is a large family as described above. The great diversity of characters noticed in the different groups within the family indicates however that such a taxon cannot be a natural one. Hutchinson therefore tried to give *Liliaceae* a more homogenous shape by removing 4 subfamilies, e.g. Allioideae, Dracaenoideae, Luzuriagoideae and Smilacoideae, 5 tribes, e.g. Petrosavieae, Dasypogoneae, Lomandreae, Calectaesieae and Parideae and 2 subtribes, e.g. Odontostomineae and Ruscineae from this family. This reduction in size however made rather slight alteration in the overall character of the family, only in the nature of the inflorescence which Hutchinson said might be of various types but never an umbel. Hutchinson changed the name of the order as **Liliales** wherein he included besides Liliaceae *Tecophilaeaceae, Trilliaceae, Smilacaceae, Ruscaceae* and *Pontederiaceae*. According to Hutchinson most of the petaloid families of Monocots have been derived from Liliaceae. Such treatment of the family Liliaceae by Hutchinson has been supported by most modern workers like Anderson (1940), Maia (1941), Cheadle (1942) and Takhtajan (1969). Cronquist while defining the family according to the older broad sense felt it necessary to merge *Amaryllidaceae* with Liliaceae although he maintains *Agavaceae* and *Smilacaceae* as distinct families. The ancestral stock of **Liliaceae** or the order **Liliales** has according to Hutchinson affinities with **Commelinales** and **Butomales,** while Takhtajan and Cronquist consider that Liliales has been derived from **Alismatales** or the subclass **Alismatideae.**

The amended description of Liliaceae and of Tecophilaeaceae, Trilliaceae, Ruscaceae and Smilacaceae are given below—

Liliaceae: Herbs, mostly perennial or rarely soft wooded shrubs; roots from a rhizome, corm or bulb, sometimes tuberous; stem erect or climbing, leafy or scapose. Flowers bisexual or rarely unisexual, actinomorphic or slightly zygomorphic, in an inflorescence which is never an umbel. Perianth mostly corolla-like, with or without a tube; segments or lobes 6, rarely 4 or more, mostly in 2 distinct but similar series, imbricate or the outer valvate. Stamens usually 6 (rarely 3, or upto 12), hypogynous or adnate to and always opposite to the perianth-segments; filaments free or variously connate; anthers 2 locular, opening by slits lengthwise or rarely by apical pores. Ovary superior or very rarely more or less adnate to the base of the perianth-tube and then semi-inferior, mostly 3-locular with axile placentas or rarely 1-locular with parietal placentas; style entire or divided, rarely styles free. Ovules usually numerous and mostly 2-seriate in each locule, rarely solitary. Fruit a loculicidal or septicidal capsule or a fleshy berry. Seeds with copious endosperm and straight or curved embryo.

Tecophilaeaceae: Herbs with fibrous tunicated corms or thick flattened orbicular tubers. Leaves radical or towards the base of the flowering stem, linear or ovate-orbicular and cordate. Flowers bisexual, actinomorphic in simple racemes separately from the tuber or corm or paniculate, bracts large or small and membranous. Perianth with or without a short tube, limbs 6, spreading or reflexed, subequal, imbricate. Stamens 6, perfect or 3 reduced to staminodes, inserted at the throat of the perianth; anthers 2-locular, often connivent, *connective often produced at both ends, the base then swollen or spur-like*, loculi opening by terminal pores, rarely by slits to the base and introrse. Ovary more or less semi-inferior, 3-locular; style subulate or filiform. Ovules numerous, axile, 2-seriate in each loculus. Fruit a loculicidal capsule. Seeds numerous with a large embryo and fleshy endosperm.

Hutchinson merges Cyanastraceae of Engler with Tecophilaeaceae while both Takhtajan and Cronquist treats Cyanastraceae as a distinct family.

Trilliaceae: Small herbs with a simple erect stem from a short, thick or creeping rhizome. A few short leaf sheaths at base of stem and a pair of opposite leaves or a whorl of 3 or more leaves at the top of the stem; lamina distinctly nerved and reticulate between the nerves. Flowers one or more, terminal, sessile or pedicellate, variously coloured or sometimes greenish, bisexual, actinomorphic. Perianth deciduous or persistent; segments free, subequal or very different in two series; in the latter case the outer often broader and calyx-like, the inner petaloid, linear or filiform. Stamens as many as the perianth segments, hypogynous or at the base of the segments and opposite to them; filaments filiform or slightly flattened, free; anthers 2-locular, basifixed, opening at the sides by slits lengthwise; connective sometimes produced at the apex. Ovary superior sessile one locular with parietal placentas, or 3-locular or more locular with axile placentas. Style or style-branches 3-5; ovules numerous. Fruit a berry or a fleshy capsule at length loculicidally dehiscent. Seeds with hard or fleshy endosperm and a small embryo.

Ruscaceae: Stem woody, erect or climbing. Leaves reduced to small scarious scales bearing in their axils the cladodes which are sometimes acute and spinescent at apex and bear on either surfaces or on their margins the small flowers in fascicles, or the flowers are in short terminal racemes. The flowers are bisexual or dioecious. Perianth segments 6, free or partly connate, in the latter case with a fleshy corona inside. Stamens 6 or 3, the filaments connate into a column; anthers sessile extrorse, in the female flowers represented by an antherless tube. Rudimentary ovary sometimes present in male flowers. Ovary 3- or 1-locular; ovules 2 in each loculus, collateral, orthotropous or hemianatropous. Fruit a globose berry. Seeds solitary and globose, or two and flat on one side; embryo cylindrical, 2-4 times shorter than the endosperm.

Takhtajan transfers *Asparagus* to this family which he names as **Asparagaceae.**

Smilacaceae: Shrubs, climbing or straggling, often with tendril-like petioles and prickly stem and branches; rhizome often stout. Leaves alternate or opposite mostly leathery, 3-nerved, reticulately veined between the nerves. Flowers dioecious or rarely bisexual, small, arranged in axillary umbels, racemes or spikes. Perianth segments 6, equal or subequal free or rarely united into a dentate tube. Stamens 6, rarely more or fewer, filaments free or united into a column; anthers apparently 1-locular, by the confluence of the cells, introrse. No rudimentary ovary in male flowers. Ovary superior, sessile, 3-locular; ovules 1-2 in each loculus, pendulous, orthotropous or half-anatropous, staminodes present in female flowers. Fruit a berry with 1-3 seeds; embryo small in hard endosperm.

Pontederiaceae: This is included in Liliales by Hutchinson as well as by Takhtajan and Cronquist. Description of this family has been given with other families of Farinosae in which order it was placed by Engler.

Amaryllidaceae

Generally herbs from perennial bulbs, rarely shrubby or arborescent from a rhizomatous root stock. Leaves radical or distichous or spirally scattered on the aerial stem or in dense whorls forming a rosette; linear or lanceolate, thick, fleshy or stiff or grasslike and plicate. Flowers on a distinct leafless scape, solitary or forming an umbellate monochasial cyme enclosed by a pair of united spathelike bracts or many bracts; the inflorescence is often recemose, spicate or paniculate, of great size. Flowers hermaphrodite, regular or medianly zygomorphic, usually epigynous. Perianth in 2 whorls of 3 segments in each; segments all similar united to form a tube, rarely free; lobes imbricate or valvate; a corona often develops at the throat of the corolla-tube. Stamens 6 in 2 whorls, epipetalous; filaments often have stipule-like outgrowths on each side near base or the filaments have a basal cup, funnel-shaped or tubular; anthers introrse, dehiscing longitudinally or by terminal slits. Ovary inferior or rarely semi-inferior, trilocular or 1-locular with many ovules in each cell in 2 series on axile placentas or ovules few. Fruit a loculicidal capsule, sometimes splitting irregularly, or a berry. Seeds compressed or not with a small straight embryo in copious fleshy endosperm.

The above description of the family Amaryllidaceae is *sensu lato* as understood by Engler and other botanists. According to them the family consists of about 1000 species under 86 genera distributed mostly in the tropical and sub-tropical regions of the world with a few in the temperate countries, usually in dry situations.

The family exhibits great variations in vegetative as well as floral characters. Plants are bulbous or rhizomatous; the latter group may be acaulescent or with short aerial stem or may be woody and branched. Leaves crowded, radical or at the end of the stem and branches or scattered along the stem; thick and fleshy or leathery or papery and often plicate. The inflorescence is an umbellate monochasial cyme on a distinct leafless scape or it may be a raceme terminating a leafy stem or a huge panicle as in *Agave*. The flower often develops a petaloid corona or para-corolla while in some cases petaloid stipule like outgrowths are formed and these often cohere in the shape of a staminal cup. Stamens are 6 in the flowers of most genera but in some species the number may be 12 or more. The ovary is trilocular but in *Leontochir* and *Calostemma* it is unilocular. It is always inferior but in *Tribonanthes* it is superior. Fruit is usually a berry but capsule with leathery or woody pericarp also occurs.

The flowers are pollinated by insects which are attracted by the bright colour, the fragrance or by the nectar. Self pollination also occurs where cross pollination fails. Flowers are often replaced by viviparous bulbils e.g. *Agave*, *Fourcroya*. The usual floral formula is—$\oplus$ ⚥ P_{3+3}, A_{3+3}, $G_{(\overline{3})}$.

Many plants of this family have showy flowers and are cultivated as ornamentals. All species of *Narcissus* (including *N. pseudonarcissus* Linn.—the Daffodil) *Haemanthus coccineus* Linn., *Crinum latifolium* Thunb., *Zephyranthes rosea* (Spr.) Lindl., *Hymenocallis andreana* Nichols., *Pancratium triflorum* Roxb., *Leucojam*, *Amaryllis*, etc. belong to the subfamily Amaryllidoideae. These have underground bulbs and flowers on leafless scapes. Many species of *Alstromeria* have beautiful red or yellow flowers and are cultivated. *Agave sisalana* Pers. the Sisal hemp and other species of *Agave* as well as different species of *Fourcroya* are cultivated in tropical countries for fibre obtained from the long thick leaves. The peduncle of the huge panicle yields a copious

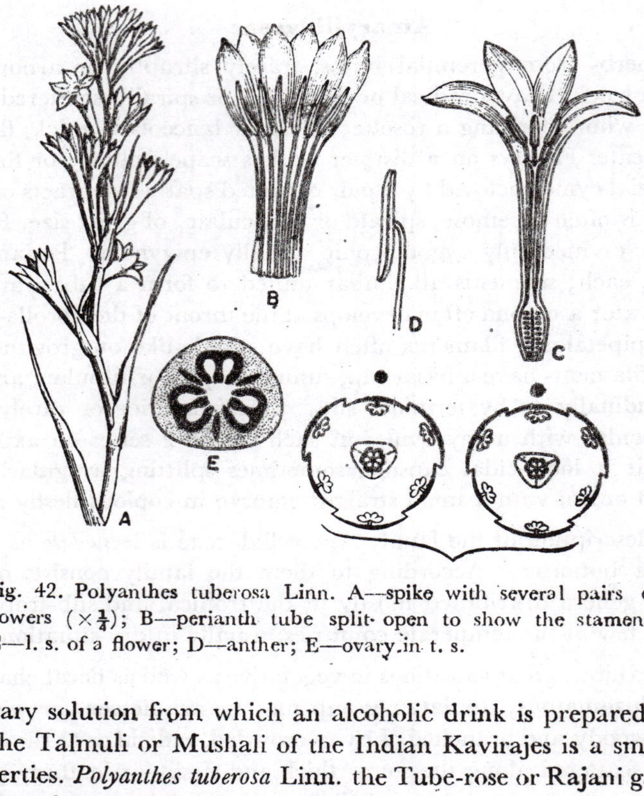

Fig. 42. Polyanthes tuberosa Linn. A—spike with several pairs of flowers (×¼); B—perianth tube split open to show the stamens; C—l. s. of a flower; D—anther; E—ovary in t. s.

quantity of sugary solution from which an alcoholic drink is prepared. *Curculigo orchioides* Gaertn—the Talmuli or Mushali of the Indian Kavirajes is a small herb having medicinal properties. *Polyanthes tuberosa* Linn. the Tube-rose or Rajani gandha has white fragrant flowers and are cultivated in Indian gardens.

The family is subdivided into 4 subfamilies, e.g. :—

1. **Amaryllidoideae:** Herbs with underground bulbs; flowers on leafless scape, solitary or in false umbel with an involucre of two or more spathe-like bracts; *Amaryllis*, *Crinum*, *Narcissus*, *Pancratium*, *Hippeastrum*, etc.

2. **Agavoideae:** Rhizomatous plants, acaulescent or arborescent, with thick fleshy leaves in dense whorls and terminal racemose inflorescence often paniculate; *Agave*, *Fourcroya*, *Doryanthes*, etc. Some of these live to a great age and are known as "Century plants".

3. **Alstroemerioideae:** Rhizomatous plants with long leafy aerial stem ending in an inflorescence; *Alstroemeria*, *Bomarea*, etc.

4. **Hypoxidoideae:** Rhizomatous herbs with plicate leaves and spicate or racemose terminal inflorescence; *Hypoxis*, *Curculigo*, *Monileria*.

Most authors place *Amaryllidaceae* very close to *Liliaceae* and recently Cronquist merges *Amaryllidaceae* with *Liliaceae.* Rendle extends the scope of *Amaryllidaceae* by merging *Velloziaceae* with the same. This treatment of Rendle does not meet with the approval of others. Hutchinson redefines the family *Amaryllidaceae* wherein he includes only the subfamily Amaryllidoideae of Engler's family and transfers to this family 3 tribes Allieae, Agapantheae and Gilliesieae which were included in *Liliaceae* as described by the Englerian school. He raises the subfamilies Agavoideae, Alstroe merioideae and Hypoxioideae to the rank of distinct families. Takhtajan supports Hutchinson in such treatments but keeps the tribe Allieae distinct from both and places the same in a family of its own, viz. *Alliaceae.* Hutchinson who puts more importance on the nature of inflorescence describes *Amaryllidaceae* as noted below:—

Herbacious plants with perennial underground bulb or rhizome, leaves radical, linear, terete or flat, sessile or petioled, sheathing at the base; inflorescence on a scape, cymose, umbelliform or globose and compact, rarely flowers solitary; flowers regular, rarely zygomorphic, usually very showy; perianth petaloid, in 2 whorls of 3 similar segments each; stamens 6 in 2 whorls, opposite to perianth segments, anthers introrse, versatile, often some are staminodes, a conspicuous corona is usually present between the perianth and the androecium; ovary inferior, rarely half-inferior, 3-locular or 1-locular, ovules ∞, anatropous on axile placentation; fruit a loculicidal capsule or berry, seed with fleshy endosperm and straight embryo.

The descriptions of the other 3 newly created families of Hutchinson are given below:

Agavaceae: Rootstock a rhizome, stem short or well-developed. Leaves usually crowded at the base of the stem or near the apex, linear, often thick or fleshy, entire or with prickly teeth on the margin. Flowers hermaphrodite, polygamous or dioecious, actinomorphic or slightly zygomorphic, racemose or paniculate, sometimes in a large thyrsus, the branches subtended by bracts. Perianth-tube short or rather long, lobes or segments unequal to subequal; stamens 6, inserted at the base of the lobes or tube, filaments filiform or thickened towards the base, free; anthers introrse, linear, usually dorsifixed, 2-celled, opening lengthwise by slits, ovary superior or inferior, 3-celled with axile placentation, style slender, ovules numerous to solitary in each cell, superposed in 2 series, anatropous. Fruit a localicidal capsule or berry. Seeds numerous or solitary, compressed, with fleshy endosperm surrounding the small embryo.

The following genera are included in this family by Hutchinson, e.g. *Agave*, *Fourcroya*, *Sansevieria*, *Dracaena*, *Cordyline*, *Phormivum*, *Yucca* and *Polyanthes*.

Alstroemeriaceae: Rootstock a rhizome with fibrous roots, sometimes bearing tubers; stem erect, ascending or climbing, leafy. Leaves alternate crowded or scattered, entire, the petiole usually twisted and reversing the surfaces. Flowers in a terminal cluster or irregular raceme, rarely solitary, showy, bisexual, more or less actinomorphic but often one segment of the perianth different from the others. Perianth segments free to the base, inserted on an epigynous annulus, in two series often narrowed to the base, or spathulate. Stamens 6, inserted on an annulus at the base of the segments; filaments free, anthers introrse, oblong or ovoid, basifixed, opening lengthwise. Ovary inferior, 3-locular with axile placentation or one locular with parietal placentas; style filiform shortly 3-lobed. Ovules numerous in each loculus or on each placenta, anatropous. Fruit a capsule, more or less truncate, locucidally 3-valved, crowned by the persisting epigynous annulus or by the persistent perianth-segments. Seeds numerous with a small embryo in copious endosperm.

About 100 species under 3 genera are restricted to Central and S. America. Different species of *Alstroemeria* are cultivated in tropical countries for the showy flowers.

Iridaceae

Plants are generally herbs with an underground corm or rhizome, rarely bulbous; rarely plants are under-shrubs. Leaves equitant and sheathing at the base, radical or cauline, mostly narrow and ensiform; the cauline leaves are usually distichous. Inflorescence terminal, cymose or racemose or paniculate, or flowers solitary; sometimes a few axillary flowers develop subsequent to the terminal flower; each flower is subtended by a spathe and a two-keeled bracteole is often present. Flowers hermaphrodite, regular or medianly zygomorphic. Perianth petaloid, of 2 whorls of 3 members in each, united in a tube, sometimes the 2 whorls differ in structure. Stamens 3, representing the outer whorl of the androecium; filaments free or partially connate, inserted on the outer perianth segments; anthers extrorse. Ovary inferior, trilocular with axile placentation or unilocular with parietal placentation; ovules many in each cell; styles 3 or style-branches 3, often petaloid, simple or bifid. Fruit a loculicidal capsule; seed with a small embryo enclosed in hard or fleshy endosperm.

The characters of the family is more or less quite distinct. The flowers vary only in some unimportant characters except that in the tribe **Ixieae** they are often medianly zygomorphic while usually they are regular. Leaves are equitant and in 2 rows in most of the genera while in *Crocus* and a few others they are linear or filiform and in several rows. The floral formula is,— ☿ P_{3+3} A_3 $G_{(\overline{3})}$. Three genera are shrubby with much branched stem. The secondary growth is due to the formation of a meristematic ring in the pericycle producing new vascular bundles and an outer secondary cortex.

The family with over 1000 species in about 60 genera is widely distributed in temperate and tropical parts of the world. In India a few *Iris* grow in the Himalayas and Assam and *Crocus sativus* Linn. is cultivated in Kashmir, the broad flat stigmas of which yields the saffron of commerce. Species of *Gladiolus* are cultivated in the hills for the beautiful flowers. *Belamcanda chinensis* (L.) Leman—Dosh-bi-chandi (Beng.) and *Cipura paludosa* Aubl are cultivated in the plains.

The family is subdivided into 3 tribes by Diels as noted below:—

1. **Sisyrhinchieae:** Spathes terminal or lateral, stalked, rarely sessile; flowers solitary or more often several, developed centrifugally round a central one, mostly petioled; style-branches alternating with stamens; *Crocus*, *Sisyrhinchiun*, *Romulea*, etc.

2. **Ixieae:** Spathes lateral, sessile, 1-flowered; fls. often zygomorphic; *Ixia*, *Gladiolus*, *Freesia*, etc.

Fig. 43. *Gladiolus tristis* Linn. A—Inflorescence ($\times \frac{1}{4}$). B—Flower showing the floral parts ($\times \frac{1}{2}$); C—Same in vertical section.

3. **Irideae:** Flowers numerous in terminal or lateral spathes, usually regular; style-branches opposite the stamens: *Iris, Maraea, Tigridia,* etc.

Iridacea is close to *Liliaceae* and *Amaryllidaceae.* It is included in the **Liliflorae** by Engler while Hutchinson places it in a monotypic order **Iridales** and traces its origin from **Liliales.** Takhtajan also places it in **Iridales** wherein he includes the families *Geosiridaceae, Burmanniaceae* and *Corsicaceae.* He includes **Iridales** in subclass **Liliidae.** Cronquist does not differ from Takhtajan in this respect. The family is considered advanced over *Liliaceae* and *Amaryllidaceae* having only one whorl of stamens.

SCITAMINAE

The four families comprising this order, *Musaceae, Zingiberaceae Marantaceae* and *Cannaceae,* form a natural and homogenous group. Here the plants are usually herbaceous with a subterranean rhizome and occasionally aerial stem; leaves large, slightly asymmetric, with a long petiole and well-developed sheath; flowers usually hermaphrodite, zygomorphic, with 2 trimerous whorls of perianth; androecium represented by 2 whorls of perfect stamens or with some staminodes; ovary inferior, generally trilocular; seeds with plenty of perisperm and scanty or no endosperm. The flowers are pollinated by birds or insects.

Scitamineae is considered to be an order of closely related advanced families. The irregular flowers, the epigynous condition, pollination by insects and birds are characters that indicate advancement. In the older classification of Bentham and Hooker Scitaminae was considered to be a single Natural Order (equivalent of a family) and was placed under the second series **Epigynae.** Engler while tracing the line of advancement raised it to the rank of an order with 4 families of which *Musaceae* was considered to be most primitive from which the other 3 families were derived by reduction. The name of the order has been changed to **Zingiberales** by Hutchinson who splitted the family *Musaceae* into 3 families *Musaceae, Strelitziaceae* and *Lowiaceae,* raising the 3 subfamilies into the ranks of distinct families. Hutchinson derived **Zingiberales** from **Commelinales** through **Bromeliales** and included it in his Division **Calyciferae** due to the presence of a distinct herbacious calyx. Cronquist supports Hutchinson and states that **Zingiberales** has been derived from a stock giving rise to **Commelinales.** He places Zingiberales in his Subclass **Commelinidae.**

Takhtajan traces the origin of **Zingiberales** from **Liliaceous** stock and places it in the Subclass **Liliidae.** He splits *Strelitziaceae* further into 2 families, viz. *Strelitziaceae* and *Heliconiaceae* and splits *Zingiberaceae* into *Costaceae* and *Zingiberaceae.* In his order **Zingiberales** he therefore has 8 families, viz. *Musaceae, Strelitziaceae, Heliconiaceae, Lowiaceae, Costaceae, Zingiberaceae, Cannaceae* and *Marantaceae* instead of 6 of Hutchinson.

Musaceae

Large herbs with a perennial rhizome, rarely trees with a woody unbranched trunk. Leaves large, 2-ranked or spirally arranged, pinnately veined and with a blunt apex, having a long broad sheath and a stout, channelled petiole. Inflorescence terminal or axillary, a cymose panicle or a cincinnus. The flower clusters are subtended by green or coloured spathes which are often caducous. Flowers zygomorphic, hermaphrodite or unisexual, epigynous and often showy. Perianth-segments 6 in 2 whorls, similar or distinguished into two series, free or coherent, imbricate, greenish or coloured. Fertile stamens five, rarely six or the sixth one is a staminode, in 2 whorls, free; anthers

2-celled, linear. Ovary inferior, trilocular; ovules many on axile placentation, anatropous, rarely ovule solitary in each cell and basal; style simple; stigma capitate or lobed; nectar-secreting glands often present on the septa. Fruit a berry or capsule; seeds usually with hard testa, with copious or scanty endosperm or with perisperm only and straight embryo; endosperm or perisperm mealy; sucker disc-or cup-shaped.

Musa has a pseudostem which may be as tall as 4 mtr and is composed merely of the long, stiff and spongy leaf-sheaths rolled round one another. The leaves are spirally arranged on the underground large conical rhizome and the blades are crowded in a whorl at the top of the pseudostem; the petiole is long, stout and spongy. At flowering time the aerial stem pushes through the centre of the leaf sheaths bearing one or 2 smaller leaves and terminating in a compound spadix which stands erect or bends down. The large caducous coloured bracts are also spirally arranged like the leaves.

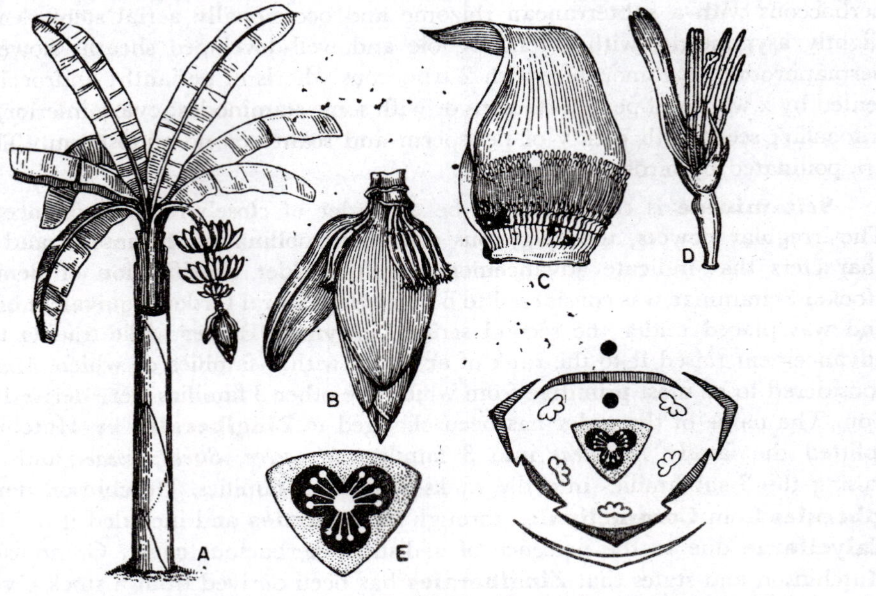

Fig. 44. Musa paradisiaca Linn. A—The plant with pseudostem, leaves and inflorescence (much reduced). B—Apical part of the inflorescence with spathes and flowers. C—A spathe subtending a bunch of flowers (reduced). D—A flower (slightly reduced). E—T. s. of ovary (×3).

Ravenala and some species of *Strelitzia* have a woody palm-like trunk. In other cases a few long-petioled leaves arise from an underground rhizome. The leaves are in 2 rows in *Ravenala* and other genera. In *Ravenala* there are several cincinnus inflorescence which are axillary, each subtended by a spathe. In *Strelitzia* there is only one cincinnus with a large spathe. In *Helicoina* the spadix is terminal with several bracts arranged in 2 rows. Each bract subtends a cincinnus. In *Musa* the sepals and 2 lateral petals are united near the base, while the median petal is free and much smaller. In *Ravenala* sepals and petals are free and equal, the median petal is slightly smaller. In *Strelitzia* the sepals are free, while the 2 lateral petals are united to form a broad winged, arrow-shaped structure. The other petal is short and broad. In *Heliconia* the median petal is free and very small while the sepals and other 2 petals are more or less coherent. There are 6 perfect stamens in *Ravenala*. In other genera 5 stamens are fertile, the sixth is absent or reduced to staminode, often petaloid. In *Heliconia* a single basal ovule is present in each cell while in other genera there are many ovules on axile placentation.

The genus *Lowia* of the subfamily *Lowioideae* has an axillary peduncle rising from the rhizome. Flowers few or solitary not subtended by a spathe but bracteate. The calyx is cup-shaped and 3-lobed. The lateral petals are smaller while the median petal forms a large coloured lip and alters its position due to resupination. Stamens are five with 2-celled anthers without any staminode; pollens granular. Ovules numerous in each cell of ovary; stigma deeply 3-lobed and the lobes are laciniate, seeds with 3-lobed aril.

The family is subdivided into 3 subfamilies, viz:—

I. **Musoideae:** Leaves spirally arranged; spadix terminal.

II. **Strelitzioideae:** Leaves distichous; spadix cincinnus type, axillary.

III. **Lowioideae:** Leaves distichous; cyme one- or few-flowered on axillary peduncle.

The 3 subfamilies have been raised to the rank of distinct families by Hutchinson as *Musaceae*, *Strelitziaceae* and *Lowiaceae*, included in the order **Zinziberales.** This treatment of Hutchinson is supported by all subsequent botanists.

The family includes 6 genera and a little over 100 species in the tropical countries with a few in S. Africa and Madagascar. The edible bananas that are available in India fall into 2 species, viz. *Musa acuminata* Colla which includes the varieties Basrai or Kabuli (Dwarf Cavendish), Harichal or Singapuri (Giant Cavendish) and Lal Kela or Red Banana, and *Musa* × *paradisiaca* Linn. which includes Champa or Mysore, Martaban, Kanthali or Silk and Kanchkela or Bluggoe; *Musa acuminata* is a good species while the other one is a natural hybrid. *Musa textilis* Linn. of the Philippines yields good fibre known as the Manila hemp. Several species of Musa are cultivated as ornamental plants. Species of *Ravenala*, *Heliconia* and *Strelitzia* are also cultivated as garden ornamentals. *R. madagascariensis* Gmel. is the Traveller's tree. *Heliconia* and *Strelitzia* have beautiful large flowers.

Zingiberaceae

Annual or perennial aromatic herbs with underground rhizome and with or without aerial stems; rhizome creeping or horizontal or tuberous. Leaves radical or cauline, alternate or opposite, usually distichous, with a sheathing petiole, ligulate; midrib prominent; secondary veins parallel or reticulate. Flowers hermaphrodite in racemes or spikes, axillary or terminal, often on a distinct scape, rarely corymbose, strongly zygomorphic, subtended by one or more bracts or spathes. Sepals 3. Petals 3, united below in a tube. Androecium of 2 whorls of stamen and staminodes; only one stamen of the inner whorl is fertile, other 2 of the same whorl and all 3 of the outerwhorl are modified into large petaloid staminodes; the filament of the perfect stamen is broad and grooved; anther 2-locular. Ovary inferior, 3-celled; ovules many on axile placentation; style passing through the groove of fertile stamen, undivided or 2-lipped or dentate; ovary rarely 1-celled with parietal or basal placentas. A pair of epigynous glands are present that secrete nectar. In *Costus* there are septal glands instead of epigynous glands. Fruit fleshy and indehiscent or loculicidally 3-valved capsule. Seeds round or angular, mostly covered with large divided aril; perisperm copious with scanty endosperm and straight embryo.

The flowers are pollinated by insects which are attracted by the showy flowers and the nectar. In *Globba* the inflorescence bears in the axils of lower bracts small bulbils instead of flowers; these fall to the ground and grow into new plants.

The family includes 47 genera and over 1100 species. These are found in tropical countries of the world but the majority are Indo-Malayan. A few grow as far north as Japan and one in Australia. The family is subdivided into 2 subfamilies, viz:—

I. Subf. **Zingiberoideae:** All parts aromatic, leaves in 2 rows, nectaries present.

II. Subf. **Costoideoe:** The rhizome only is aromatic, leaves spiral, nectaries replaced by septal glands.

The family is closely related to Musaceae in habit, in zygomorphic flowers and inferior ovary. It is, however, considered to be more advanced due to reduction in the androecium. Both Takhtajan and Cronquist raise the subfamily *Costoideoe* to the rank of distinct family viz.—*Costaceae*.

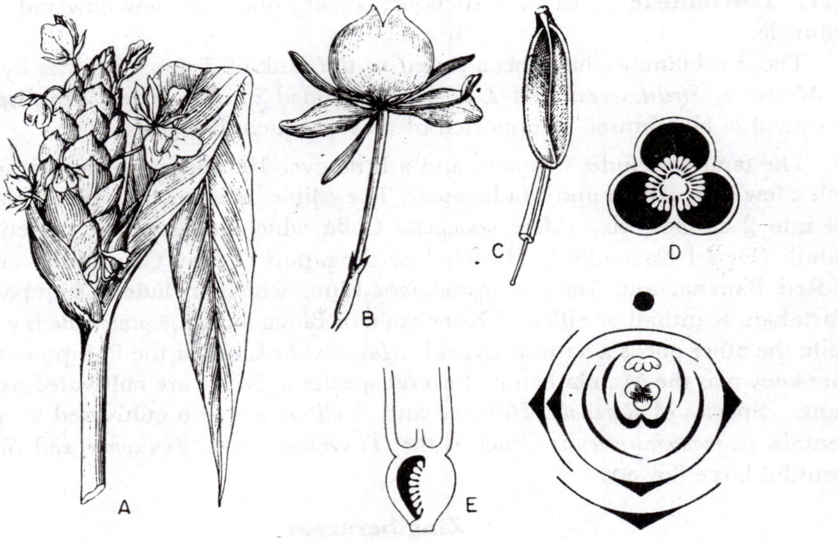

Fig. 45. A—Flowering spike of Hedychium coronarium Koen ($\times\frac{1}{4}$). B—A flower ($\times\frac{1}{2}$). C—Anther and the style placed on the groove of the anther and filament. D—Cross section of ovary. E—Vertical section of same.

The family is very important for the economic plants it includes. Many have medicinal properties while others produce spices and condiments. *Zingiber officinale* Rosc., is the ginger; *Z. zerumbet* Smith is also used as spice. *Curcuma domestica* Wall. is the turmeric (Haldi), *C. angustifolia* Roxb. is the East Indian Arrow-root, the rhizomatous tuber of which yields starch like that of *Maranta arundinacea* Linn. the true Arrow-root. *C. amada* Roxb. is used to flavour chutnies. *C. zedoaria* Rosc. yields starch and is called the Shati food of Bangladesh. *Alpinia allughas* Rosc. and *A. galanga* Sw. are medicinal. *Amomum subulatum* Roxb. is the Bara Elachi, while *A. aromaticum* Roxb. is Morung Elachi. *Elettaria cardamomum* Linn. is the cardamon or Chhoti Elachi. *Costus speciosus* Smith is the Mahabari Bach, the rhizome of which has medicinal properties.

Many are cultivated in the gardens for the beauty of the flowers and different species of *Hedychium* are favourites. *H. coronarium* Koenig is the Dulal Champa having large faint yellow very fragrant flowers. *H. coccinium* Buch.-Ham. has a long spike of bright red flowers growing in the hills of East India. *Kaempferia rotunda* L. and *K. linearis* Wall. are called Bhuin Champa. *Mantisia saltatoria* Sims. the Dancing Girl has a lax inflorescence the flowers of which are almost always moving by the lightest touch of wind.

Cannaceae

Tall herbs with a perennial rhizome. Leaves large, alternate, pinnately veined, with prominent midrib and sheathing petiole. Flowers hermaphrodite, zygomorphic bracteate, in terminal spike or panicle. Sepals free, often scarious, imbricate. Petals united below in a tube, brightly coloured and subequal, adnate to the staminal column, imbricate. The androecium consists of a petaloid stamen with half anther on the margin and 5 petaloid staminodes of which 3 outer imbricate, 2 inner more or less

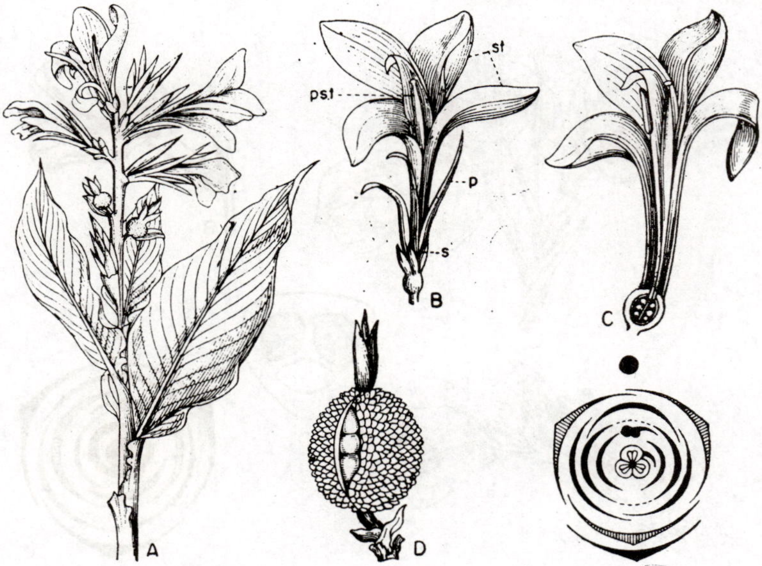

Fig. 46. Canna indica Linn. A—Upper part of the stem with leaves and inflorescence ($\times \frac{1}{4}$). B—A flower ($\times \frac{1}{2}$) showing sepals (s.); petals (p), staminodia (st.) and pistil (pst). C—A flower splitted to show the ovary-chamber. D—Fruit ($\times 1$).

connate. Ovary inferior, 3-locular, with 2 series of anatropous ovules in each chamber on axile placentas; style petaloid, stigma oblique. Fruit a capsule, with a fibrous, warty or weakly spinose pericarp; seeds many, rounded, with copious hard perisperm and a straight embryo.

Cannaceae is a monotypic family with about 50 species, mainly in tropical America. *Canna indica* Linn. with many varieties are grown in gardens while one with small scarlet flower is found wild in eastern India. *C. orientalis* Rosc. is another species much cultivated in Indian gardens. Many species contain large quantities of starch in the rhizome and *Canna edulis* K.G. is cultivated for that purpose.

The family is closely related to *Zingiberaceae* from which it differs in not having a ligule and the fertile stamen having 1-locular anther.

Marantaceae

Perennial herbs with a sympodial rhizome, often stoloniferous; aerial shoots often branching. Leaves distichous or spiral, with an open sheath, a terete and often winged petiole and a blade which is oblique at base; a pulvinus is present at the apex of the petiole. Spikes or rarely panicle terminal or on distinct scape, bracteate; flowers hermaphrodite, zygomorphic and epigynous. Calyx of 3 sepals. Petals 3, united below in a tube with 3 unequal lobes. Outer whorl of stamens entirely supressed or only 2 or 1 is present modified as staminode; the posterior stamen of the inner whorl bears only a unilocular anther on one side; the lateral stamens are modified to petaloid staminodes one of which is hooded and encloses the style and stigma while the other is broad and flat. Ovary 3-celled with only one basal ovule in each chamber; style stout, often involute or dilated at the apex; rarely ovary 1-celled. Fruit fleshy or a loculicidal capsule; seeds often arillate, with copious perisperm surrounding the curved or folded embryo.

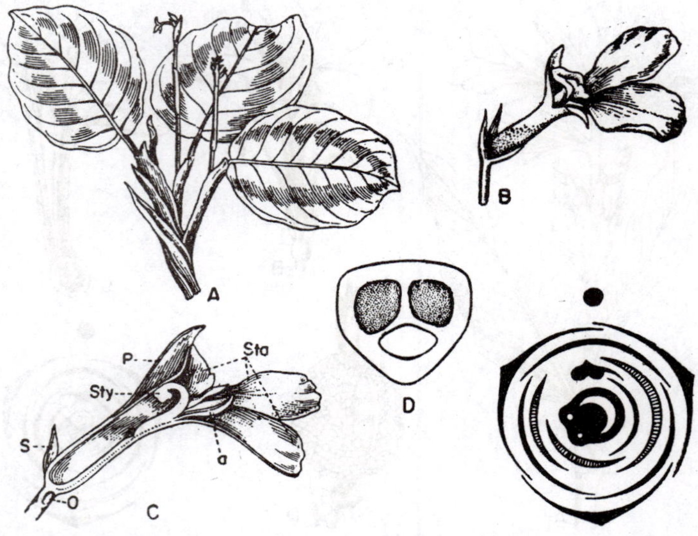

Fig. 47. Maranta bicolor Ker-Gawl. A—Flowering branch ($\times\frac{1}{6}$). B—One flower ($\times$1). C—Vertical section of the same.—s. sepal, p. petal, sta. staminodia, a, anther, sty. style with stigma. D—Cross section of ovary.

Septal glands secrete nectar that collects in the lower part of the tube. Insects visit the flowers in search of nectar and pollinate them.

The family contains 27 genera and about 300 species mostly in tropical America. *Maranta arundinacea* L. is the Arrow-root, indigenous to West Indies but is now cultivated in many tropical countries. *Donax arundiastrum* Low. of eastern India and Malaya is the Mukta-pati or Shital-pati plant, the strips of the polished bark of which are woven into mats. A few others are cultivated in gardens as ornamental plants.

The family is closely related to the other families of **Scitaminae** and particularly to *Cannaceae* from which it differs in having solitary ovule in the ovary-chambers, involute or dilated style and curved or folded embryo. It is considered to be most advanced in this group having only 1 fertile stamen with half anther and solitary ovule in the cells of the ovary which again is frequently 1-celled.

K. Schumann subdivides the family into 2 tribes, viz:—
Tribe I, **Phrynieae:** Ovary trilocular.
Tribe II, **Maranteae:** Ovary unilocular.

Comparison of the Characters of the families of Scitaminae

Musaceae	Zingiberaceae	Cannaceae	Marantaceae
Leaves large with long petioles and prominent sheath, ligule or pulvinus absent.	Leaves large or small, petiole and sheath not very long, ligule present.	Leaves large, petiole and sheath not very long, no ligule or pulvinous.	Leaves large or small, petiole and sheath small pulvinous present.
Spathe usually conspicuous.	Bracteate.	Bracteate.	Bracteate, spathe often present.
Inflorescence a spadix or cincinnus.	Racemes or spikes.	Spikes or panicles.	Spikes or panicles.
Perianth segments 6 in 2 whorls variously united.	6 in 2 whorls of 3 sepals and 3 united petals.	6 in 2 whorls of 3 sepals and 3 united petals.	6 in 2 whorls of 3 sepals and 3 united petals.
Fertile stamens 6 or 5 and one staminode, or only 5 fertile stamens; anther 2 locular.	Only the median stamen of the inner whorl is fertile, other 2 of the same whorl and 2 of the outer whorl modified to petaloid staminodes, 3rd of the outer whorl suppressed; anther bilocular.	Only the median stamen of inner whorl fertile, all other modified to staminodes; anther 1-locular.	Only the median stamen of inner whorl fertile, others modified to staminodes, one or two of the outer may be present as staminodes; anther 1-locular.
Ovary inferior, 3-locular with many ovules on axile placentas, or solitary and basal.	Ovary inferior, 1- or 3-locular, ovules many, placentation axile or parietal.	Ovary inferior, 3-locular, ovules many on axile placentas.	Ovary inferior, 3- or 1-locular, ovule solitary basal.
Embryo straight.	Embryo straight.	Embryo straight.	Embryo curved or folded.

MICROSPERMAE

This the 11th and last order of Monocotyledoneae, contains only 2 families, viz., **Burmanniaceae** and **Orchidaceae.** *Burmanniaceae* has flowers which are generally actinomorphic, and the seeds have endosperm. In *Orchidaceae* the flowers are usually zygomorphic and the seeds have no endosperm. The two families are placed close to each other under one order for the reason that in both families the seeds are minute, the testa is thin, membranous and extended, and the embryo is undifferentiated.

Hutchinson places these two families in two different orders, viz. (i) **Burmanniales** which contains besides **Burmanniaceae, Thismiaceae** and **Corsicaceae,** and (ii) **Orchidales** with one family **Orchidaceae.** According to him both these orders have originated from **Liliales** through **Haemadorales.** Takhtajan also considers that the two families are not so close as to be included in a single order. He thinks that **Burmanniaceae** is allied to **Iridaceae** and places **Burmanniaceae** in **Iridales** while **Orchidaceae** remains in the monotypic order **Orchidales.** Cronquist however does not agree to this treatment of Hutchinson and Takhtajan but includes *Burmanniaceae* and *Orchidaceae* in his **Orchidales** which also embraces two other families, e.g. *Goesiridaceae* and *Corsicaceae*. He places **Orchidales** in the subclass **Liliidae** after the order **Liliales.**

Burmanniaceae

Saprophytic herbs with a small slender stem and under ground rhizome or tubers; the rhizome is associated with endotrophic mycorrhiza. Leaves small scale-like or linear and green. Inflorescence is terminal and scorpioid cyme. Flowers small, bisexual, usually actinomorphic, rarely medianly zygomorphic, epigynous. Perianth in 2 whorls of 3 segments in each, all petaloid and united in a cup or tube, persistent. Stamens 6 in 2 whorls, adnate to the perianth tube, often the outer whorl absent; filaments very short or absent and then the anthers are sessile; connective appendaged or winged or very broad; anthers bilocular, dehiscing transversely or longitudinally. Ovary inferior, 3- or 1-locular, ovules numerous, minute, on axile or parietal placenta; style short with 3 stigmatic lobes. Fruit a capsule; seeds many, minute, with an undifferentiated embryo and scanty endosperm; testa thin and membranous.

The family contains a little over a 100 species under 20 genera found in most tropical countries. The family is represented in India by a few species of *Burmannia*.

The family is considered to be allied to *Orchidaceae* in having minute seeds, undifferentiated embryo and epigynous flowers and is placed in the order **Orchidales** by Engler and also by Cronquist. Hutchinson places *Burmanniaceae* in a different order **Burmanniales** where he includes besides *Burmanniaceae* two other families, viz. *Thismiaceae* and *Corsicaceae*. Takhtajan places *Burmanniaceae* in **Iridales** along with *Iridaceae*, *Geosiridaceae* and *Corsicaceae* with which families he considers *Burmanniaceae* is more allied than with *Orchidaceae*.

Orchidaceae

Perennial herbs, terrestrials or epiphytes, rarely saprophytes. The stem is monopodial or sympodial; in case of sympodial growth the successive annual shoots may or may not end in an inflorescence. The terrestrials usually have a rhizome. The internodes in many are thick and form a pseudobulb, and in some cases a fleshy tuber is formed at the base of the growing shoot.

In the case of epiphytes there are 3 types of roots: (1) the clinging roots which are negatively heliotropic, fasten the plant to its support, the network of such roots form a mass which act as a reservoir for humus; (ii) the absorbing roots which are negatively geotropic penetrate into the network of clinging roots and absorb moisture; (iii) the true aerial roots which hang down in long festoons have a layer of dead spongy cells below the epidermis known as *velamen*.

The roots of saprophytic orchids are associated with endotrophic or endophytic mycorrhiza. *Didymoplexis* and *Gastrodia* are Indian examples. *Neottia nidus-avis* is a peculiar saphrophytic orchid where the roots comming out from the rhizome from a birds-nest like mass. *Corallorhiza* has a rhizome which bifurcates repeatedly and a number of lobular branchlets lie closely crowded together forming a coral-like body.

Leaves are usually thick and fleshy, sessile or petioled, in some terrestrial orchids the leaves are thinner and plicate; often with closed sheath; whorled on top of pseudobulb or distichous along the short stem.

The inflorescence is a spike or raceme, sometimes a panicle, rarely flower solitary. Flowers hermaphrodite, strongly medianly zygomorphic, epigynous, usually showy and colourful, with a complicated morphology. The perianth in 2 whorls, segments all petaloid, either free or variously united, imbricate or subvalvate, usually differentiated into calyx and corolla. The median or posterior sepal and petal are unlike the laterals. This petal called labellum, is larger and by the twisting of the ovary through 180° it comes to the anterior side (resupination). The labellum is produced into a sac or spur-like structure containing within it nectar secreting glands. Rarely the labellum is formed of the median sepal; often lateral sepals unite to form a sac-like structure known as mentum or chin. The filaments of stamens and the style of the ovary unite and form a column (which according to some is nothing but a prolongation of the floral axis). In majority of the genera the column bears one anther and 2 fertile stigmas (which sometimes unite) and a special structure called the rostellum representing the third stigma. The

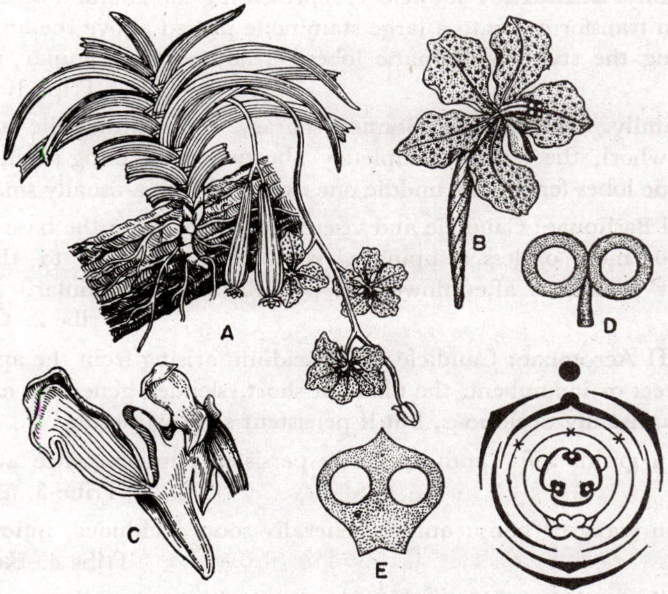

Fig. 48. Vandatesselata G. Don. A—Plant with roots, leaves, and inflorescence (×¼). B—Flower (×1). C—Flower with sepals and petals removed; showing the labellum with spur and column. D—Pollinium. E—Anther.

single anther is that of the anterior stamen of the outer whorl. The other 2 of this whorl and the entire inner whorl are absent. The anther is bilocular and each cell contains a pollinium where the pollens are tied together by fine threads which unite at the base forming a caudicle. In the other group there are 2 anthers and a simple stigma. These anthers are of 2 stamens of the inner whorl. There is a large staminode representing the outer whorl of the androecium. The pollens are in tetrads in a sticky fluid; rarely pollens granular. The stigma is not sticky. Ovary inferior, of 3 united carpels, 1-celled with ovules on 3 double rowed parietal placentas. The fruit is a capsule with a large number of minute and light seeds. The seed is enclosed in a membrane and contains no endosperm; embryo is an undifferentiated mass of cells. The seeds are dispersed by wind.

In many orchid flowers the arrangement is very complicated; the labellum may be spurred, there may be one axial protuberance bearing the labellum and sepals. The column may also show great variety in structure. The various complexities in flowers are adaptations for insect-pollination.

This is a large family with over 2,000 genera and 18,000 species mostly found in damp tropical and temperate regions of the world. The flowers are very showy and many species are cultivated. Few are fragrant and *Vanilla planifolia* is important for the essential oil. A few are used medicinally.

As regards the structure of the androecium and gynoecium of flowers the family is divisible into 2 clear groups, one having 2 stamens and the other with one stamen. The following is an outline of the classification of the family by Schlechter: —

I. Subfamily. **Diandrae:** Stamens 2, representing the lateral 2 of the inner whorl, a third stamen transformed into a large staminode placed above the anthers and more or less covering the style; 3 stigmatic lobes fertile; pollen granular, not united into masses. Tribe 1. **Cypripedieae**

II. Subfamily. **Monandrae:** Stamen solitary, representing the abaxial member of the outer whorl, the lateral completely abortive or forming small staminodes; 2 lateral stigmatic lobes fertile, the middle one extended into a usually small rostellum:

Division I Basitonae: Caudicle and viscidium arising from the base of the pollinia; anther erect or more or less resupinate, very closely adnate to the broad-based column, never deciduous after flowering; pollinia always granular.
Tribe 2. **Ophrydoideae.**

Division II Acrotonae: Caudicle and viscidium arising from the apex of the pollinia; anther erect or incumbent, the filament short, slender generally narrowly jointed to the column, usually deciduous, but if persistent soon withering:

(a) Pollen grains soft; anther mostly persistent; inflorescence always terminal.
Tribe 3. **Polychondreae**

(b) Pollen waxy or bony; anther generally soon deciduous; inflorescence terminal or lateral. Tribe 4. **Kerosphaereae.**

The family *Orchidaceae* is considered to be the most advanced and highest evolved among the **Moncotyledonae.** The most diverse and complex development of flowers and reduction in the number of stamens, the resupinate epigynous ovary, reduction in stigmatic lobes and formation of the rostellum, absence of endosperm in the seeds and undifferentiated embryo all point towards great advancement in the course of evolution. The habit of the plants, all herbs with a large number of epiphytes and a few saprophytes also support this view.

Most authors agree that the family originated from Liliaceous stock. According to Hutchinson it has been derived from Liliaceae through *Hypoxidaceae* and *Apostaciaceae* the latter included in *Orchidaceae* by earlier authors. Takhtajan and Cronquist also consider that *Orchidaceae* although does not have close affinity with *Liliaceae* has been derived from this family through others with epigynous flowers. Another line of parallel evolution is traced from *Musaceae* through *Lowiaceae* which has resupinate epigynous ovary and a distinct labellum.

About 700 species are found in India and two zones rich in Orchids can be demarcated, viz. (1) the eastern zone comprising E. Himalaya and the hilly area of eastern India and (2) the south-western zone comprising Western Ghats and Nilgiri hills. Species of *Paphiopedilium*, *Dendrobium*, *Cymbidium*, *Coelogyne*, etc. are among others having large beautiful flowers and are much cultivated. *Cattleya*-flowers are most beautiful among Orchids and are to be found in almost all Indian nurseries but this is an American genus.

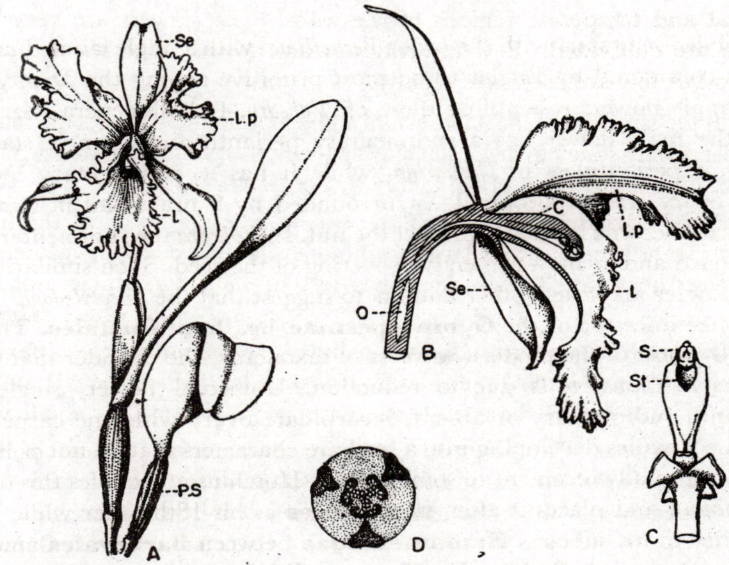

Fig. 49. Cattleya lueddemanniana Reichb. f. A—Plant with leaves and a flower ($\times \frac{1}{4}$). B—L. s. of a flower showing sepal (Se.), petal (P), labelum (L), column (C) and ovary (O). C—Column shown separately—s.—stigma, st.—style.

The description of the family as given here is as understood by the modern authors. **Orchidaceae** of the older authors included a few genera which have more or less regular flowers having 2-3 stamens. These are now placed in a distinct family **Apostaciaceae,** *Apostasia* being an Indian example.

CHAPTER VII

DICOTYLEDONAE

(Magnoliatae)

Archichlamydeae

VERTICILLATAE

The Dicotyledonae start with the order *Verticillatae* with a single family *Casuarinaceae*. This family is considered by Engler to be most primitive among the Dicotyledons on account of simple flowers resembling those of *Ephedra*. In both genera, viz., *Casuarina* and *Ephedra* the male flower has a rudimentary perianth and a single stamen. The female flower is perianthless in *Casuarina* while it has a rudimentary perianth in *Ephedra*. The ovary (megasporophyll) is surrounded by 2 bracteoles in *Casuarina* and these on maturity become hard and protect the nut. In *Ephedra* the rudimentary perianth also becomes hard and forms a protective covering of the seed. Such similarity in floral structure led Engler and a few other authors to suggest that the *Dicotyledonae* originated from *Ephedra*-like ancestor of the **Gymnospermae**, i.e., from **Gnetales.** This opinion is not shared by most of the modern workers of taxonomy who consider that the simplicity of flowers in *Casuarina* is due to reduction. Unisexual flower, single terminal stamen, perianth rudimentary or absent, bicarpillate ovary with one carpel abortive, only one of the 2 ovules developing into a seed are characters that do not point towards primitiveness but to advancement to some degree. Hutchinson includes this order in his division **Lignosae** and places it after **Juglandales** as his 18th order while Takhtajan places this order in his subclass **Hamamelididae** between **Barbeyales** and **Fagales.** Cronquist also traces its affinity with **Hamamelidales** and includes it in subclass **Hamamelidae.** Moseley on the anatomical study of many species of *Casuarina* traces the origin of the family from **Hamamelidaceae** and considers that the simplicity of the flowers is the result of reduction in course of evolution and not due to primitiveness. It is to be noted that most authors consider the order **Casuarinales** to be a monotypic order consisting of the single family **Casuarinaceae.**

Casuarinaceae

Perennial shrubs or trees, evergreen, with jointed stem and branches and a whorl of slender branches at each joints or nodes; branchlets grooved, green in colour and resemble the pine-needles to some extent; branches and branchlets usually drooping. Leaves scale-like, whorled at each node, united at the base forming toothed sheath round the axis. Flowers unisexual, very small and inconspicuous, in catkin-like inflorescences at the end of the branchlets; the male flowers are in several whorls on the catkin-like spike, each whorl in a sheath formed by the union of bracts; each flower is surrounded by a pair of bracteoles; the pistillate or female flowers are borne in a small capitate spike, each flower in the axil of a bract and subtended by a pair of bracteoles which enlarge and form a hard covering of the fruit. The male flower has a rudimentary perianth represented by an anterior and a posterior scale often one or both being absent and a single stamen; filament slender and anther bilobed; lobes dehiscing longitudinally. Female flower is without a perianth; carpels 2 of which the posterior one is abortive with the result that ovary is unilocular; style short with 2 long filamentous stigmas; ovules 2, ascending orthotropous, only one maturing into a seed. The mature carpel forms a winged nut; enclosed by the enlarged hardened bracteoles; seed without endosperm; cotyledons large. The nuts are aggregated into a dry cone-like structure and form a multiple fruit.

The plants are monoecious; the male catkins are at the end of the branches and the female heads a little below. Flowers are wind-pollinated; the pollen grains are in tetrads and all develop pollen tube.

The leaves being very small and scale-like, the work of photosynthesis is carried on by the green branchlets; the pallisade cells are arranged in the ridges of these branchlets below the sclerenchymatous hypodermis; the stomata are sunken and situated in the furrows. The branches have two rows of vascular bundles, the outer or the cortical bundles are the leaf-traces; the inner bundles form a continuous ring with narrow medulary rays. The xylem-vessels usually have simple perforations.

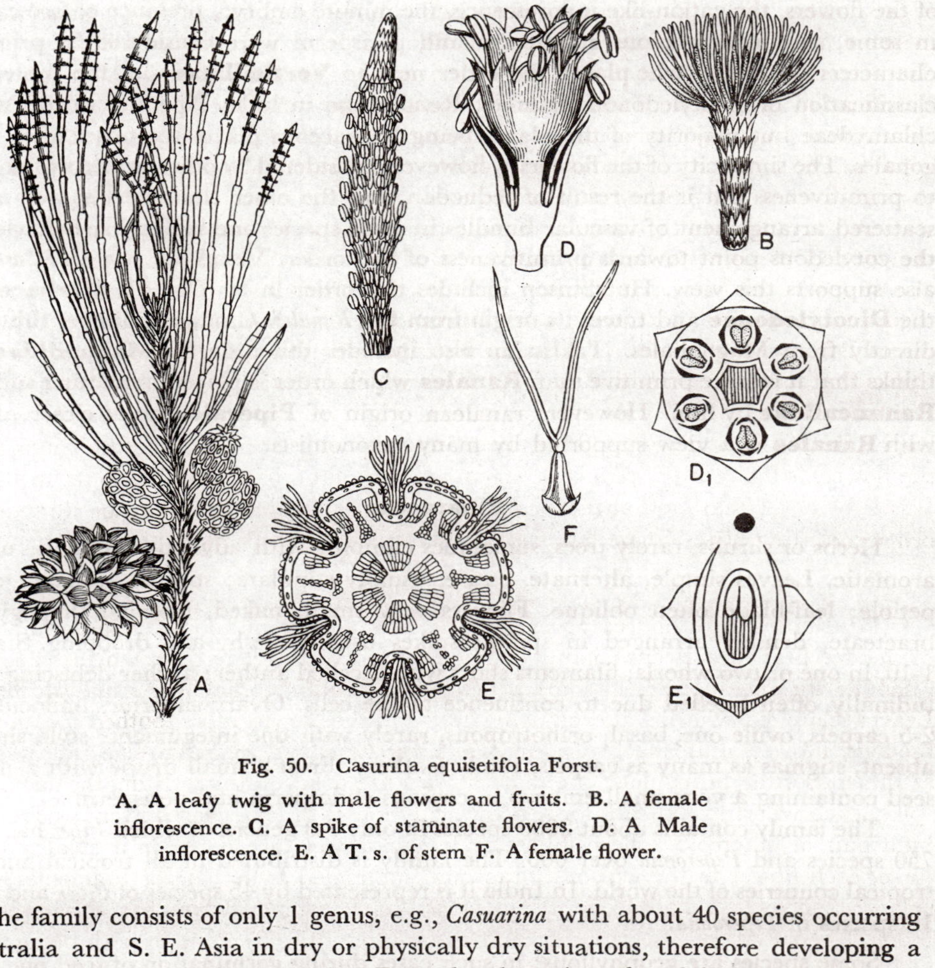

Fig. 50. Casurina equisetifolia Forst.

A. A leafy twig with male flowers and fruits. B. A female inflorescence. C. A spike of staminate flowers. D. A Male inflorescence. E. A T. s. of stem F. A female flower.

The family consists of only 1 genus, e.g., *Casuarina* with about 40 species occurring in Australia and S. E. Asia in dry or physically dry situations, therefore developing a xerophytic habit *Casuarina equisetifolia* Forst. has been introduced into India and trees are often planted on road sides and parks. They grow well on sea-shores and are much planted to check the advance of the sea. It is a quick-growing tree; the timber is hard but not suitable for planking. The wood yields good fuel.

As regards the affinity of the family the discussion under the order may be seen.

PIPERALES

This is the second order of subclass **Archichlamydeae** of Engler and consists of four families, e.g. *Saururaceae*, *Piperaceae*, *Chloranthaceae* and *Lacistemonaceae*. Plants of these families are usually herbaceous with simple leaves. Flowers are small and inconspicuous, usually bisexual perianthless, often associated with bracts, in spikes or racemes. Ovules are orthotropous and the seeds have a minute embryo and plenty of endosperm and perisperm. The vascular bundles in some cases have scattered arrangement. One of the cotyledons functions as sucker.

That this order is primitive is agreed upon by almost all workers. The simplicity of the flowers, the catkin-like inflorescence, the minute embryo, presence of free carpels in some, seed with copious endosperm and perisperm were considered as primitive characters by Engler who placed the order next to **Verticillatae** in the system of classification of dicotyledonous families. Rendle also includes Piperales in his Monochlamydeae but majority of the plants being harbaceous places the order after Polygonales. The simplicity of the flowers is, however, considered by other workers as not due to primitiveness but is the result of reduction. But the other characters as well as the scattered arrangement of vascular bundles in some species and sucker-like behaviour of the cotyledons point towards primitiveness of this order. Vessel-less wood of *Sarcandra* also supports this view. Hutchinson includes this order in his Div. II, **Herbaceae** of the **Dicotyledonae** and traces its origin from the *Ranales*. Cronquist derives this order directly from Magnoliales. Takhtajan also includes this order in **Magnoliidae** and thinks that it is more primitive than **Ranales** which order is placed in another subclass, **Ranunculidae** by him. However, ranalean origin of **Piperales** or a closer affinity with **Ranales** is a view supported by many taxonomists.

Piperaceae

Herbs or shrubs, rarely trees, sometimes climbing with adventitious roots, usually aromatic. Leaves simple, alternate, entire, usually stipulate; stipules adnate to the petiole; leaf-blade often oblique. Flowers very small, naked, bisexual, hypogynous, bracteate, densely arranged in spikes; spikes usually fleshy and drooping. Stamens 1-10, in one or two whorls; filaments short with 2-celled anther; anther dehiscing longitudinally, often 1-celled due to confluence of the cells. Ovary superior, unilocular, of 2-5 carpels, ovule one, basal, orthotropous, rarely with one integument; style short or absent, stigmas as many as carpels, rarely feathery. Fruit a small drupe with a minute seed containing a very small embryo in copious endosperm and perisperm.

The family contains about 2000 species in only 7-8 genera of which *Piper* has about 750 species and *Peperomia* over 600. The family is distributed in all tropical and subtropical countries of the world. In India it is represented by 45 species of *Piper* and about 10 species of *Peperomia*.

Some species are geophyllous; in such cases during germination of seed one of the cotyledons remains inside and functions as sucker while the other is borne on the elongated hypocotyl developing into the green cotyledonary leaf. Such a geophyllous species—*Peperomia umbilicata* Ruiz. & Pav. has an underground, short, thick stem resembling a rhizome or tuber. In some genera the vascular bundles are scattered in the ground tissue like that of a monocotyledonous plant. In *Piper nigrum* L. there are 2 rings of vascular bundles, the outer ultimately forming a continuous ring while the inner remains distinct.

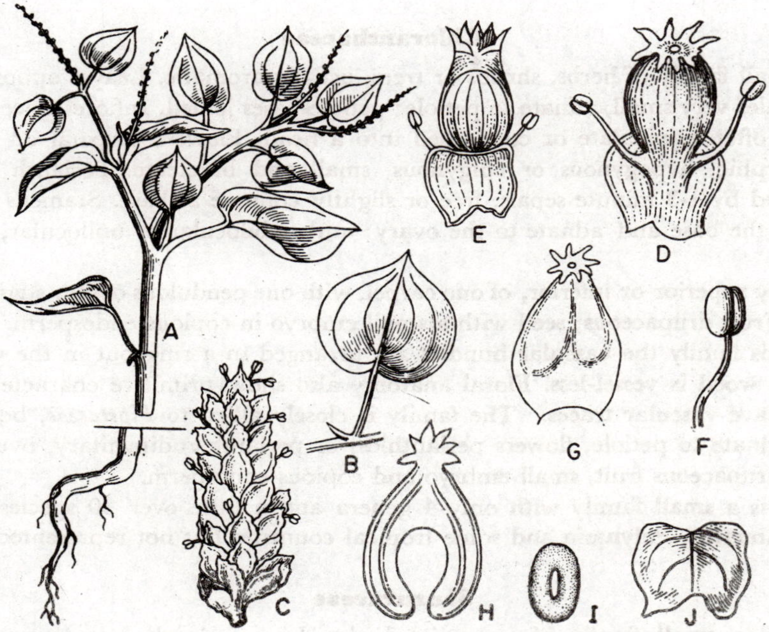

Fig. 51. Peperomia pellucida Kunth.

A. A leafy twig with spikes. B. One of a pair of leaves. C. A portion of the spike with flowers (×6). D & E A flower subtended by a bract (×10). F. Stamen. G. Ovary. H. L. S. of same, I. Seed.

The family is economically important for the genus *Piper*, many species of which have medicinal properties or are used as spices. *Piper nigrum* L. is the Black-pepper, cultivated in India and Malaya. *Piper longum* L. is used medicinally and grows wild in India and Malaya and is also cultivated. *Piper betle* L.f. is the betle-vine, the leaves of which are chewed in the tropical Asiatic countries. *Piper Chaba* Hunt. *Piper Cubebe* L.f. are also important for their medicinal properties.

The family is closely allied to **Chloranthaceae** which has very small flowers, perianth absent or rudimentary, drupaceous fruit, embryo minute in copious endosperm. The two families are placed in one order **Piperales** by Engler as well as by Hutchinson who includes this order in his **Herbaceae** and traces its origin from **Ranales.**

On account of the scattered arrangement of vascular bundles in some members and sucker-like behaviour of one of the cotyledons some taxonomists like Hill and others suggest that the Monocotyledons have originated from *Piperaceae*. From palynological study Kuprianova comes to the conclusion that one group of Monocot families, i.e., *Palmae*, *Araceae* and *Lemnaceae* has been derived from **Piperales.** The inflorescence of *Araceae* bears some resemblance to that of *Piperaceae* but this, however, is superficial.

Some taxonomists prefer to split the family into two, e.g., **Piperaceae** and **Peperomiaceae.** According to them Peperomiaceae have the following characters:—

Succulent herbs or subshrubs; exstipulate leaves; flowers hermaphrodite, in spikes, with succulent bracts; perianth absent; stamens 2, lateral, anthers finally confluent; ovary superior, monocarpellary, with one basal orthotropous ovule, stigma pilose; perisperm mealy.

Chloranthaceae

A small family of herbs, shrubs or trees, usually aromatic. Leaves opposite, stipulate; stipules very small, adnate to petiole; petiole-bases joined. Inflorescence is a spike or cyme, often paniculate or condensed into a head. Flowers bisexual or unisexual, actinomorphic, hypogynous or epigynous, small and bracteate. Perianth absent or represented by 1-3 minute sepals, free or slightly connate at base. Stamens 1-3, often united at the base and adnate to the ovary; anther bilocular or unilocular, dehiscing laterally.

Ovary superior or inferior, of one carpel, with one pendulous ovule; stigma sessile, 2-lobed. Fruit drupaceous; seed with a small embryo in copious endosperm.

In this family the vascular bundles are arranged in a ring but in the genus *Sarcandra* the wood is vessel-less. Floral anatomy also shows primitive character, e.g., the stamens have vascular traces. The family is closely allied to *Piperaceae*, both having stipules adnate to petiole, flowers perianthless or perianth rudimentary, ovules orthotropous, drupaceous fruit, small embryo and copious endosperm.

This is a small family with only 4 genera and a little over 30 species found in tropical America, Polynasia and some tropical countries but not represented in India.

Saururaceae

This is a small family of perennial herbs. Leaves simple, alternate, stipulate; stipules adnate to petiole; upper leaves often coloured. Flowers small, hermaphrodite, regular, in spikes or racemes; an involucre of bracts is often present. Perianth absent, stamens 3, 6 or 8, free or adnate to the ovary; anthers extrorse or introrse. Ovary superior or inferior, of 3-4 free or united carpels; when apocarpous with 3-4 orthotropous ovules in each carpel, when syncarpous with 6-8 or only 1 ovule in each cell on parietal placentation. Fruit of 1-4 dehiscent cocci or in case of syncarpous ovary indehiscent or dehiscing apically, sometimes glochidiate. Seed with scanty endosperm and plenty of mealy perisperm and a small embryo.

The small family of 7 species under 5 genera is distributed in E. Asia and N. America. It is represented in India by a single species of a creeping herb, viz. *Houttuynia cordata* Thunb.

SALICALES

The order **Salicales** consists of a single family **Salicaceae.** These are a primitive group of plants according to Engler who places the order in **Archichlamydeae** after **Hydrostachyales.** Rendle, however, places this order at the beginning of his **Monochlamydeae**, the plants being predominantly woody. The perianthless flowers borne in catkins help them to be classed as primite families. Eichler considered that the flowers of **Salicaceae** were derived from an ancestor having bisexual perianthed flowers as a result of reduction and the family should be classed among the more advanced of the woody families. Hutchinson also considers it to be fairly advanced and most probably derived from **Hamamelidaceae**-like ancestor. He, therefore, places it after

Hamamelidales in the division **Lignosae.** Both Takhtajan and Cronquist consider **Salicaceae** to be far removed from **Hamamelidaceae** and include the monotypic order **Salicales** in the subclass **Dilleniidae.** Many authors, however, are of opinion that **Salicaceae** is closely related to **Juglandaceae** having unisexual flowers in catkins, reduced perianth represented in the form of scales or glands bicarpellary ovary and chalazogamy during fertilisation.

Salicaceae

Trees or shrubs, usually deciduous; branching of 2 types, the normal leaf-bearing branches and dwarf shoots emerging from the axils of previous years leaves bearing scale leaves or foliage leaves or both and terminating in a catkin. Foliage leaves are simple, alternate and stipulate; stipules early deciduous. Catkins erect or pendulous, bracteate; bracts alternately or spirally arranged on the axis of the catkins. Flowers usually unisexual and dioecious each subtended by a hairy bract and a nectariferous glandular, cupular or variously shaped disc; perianth absent. Stamens 2-many; filaments long, free or united at base. Carpels 2, transversely placed, united to form a unilocular ovary; rarely carpels 4; stigma lateral or anteroposterior, usually sessile; ovules many on parietal placentas, anatropous, with only the outer integument or rarely with a short inner integument. Fruit a capsule dehiscing by 2 valves; seeds very small, comose, with thin testa; embryo straight with scanty or no endosperm.

The catkins fall as a whole, the males after flowering and the females after the fruits burst. Flowers are entomophylous in erect catkins and animophylous when the catkin is pendulous. The glandular or cupular disc represents the vestige of a perianth. Phellogen is usually formed in the epidermis of the shoot and one or more closed rings of xylem and phloem are present at the distal end of the petiole.

The family comprises about 350 species in only 3 genera, e.g., *Salix* with 300 species distributed in N. Temperate zone in both the worlds, and in the hills of tropical Asia. *Populus* is confined to N. Temperate zone only and *Choisenia* in Korea. Fossil records of Tertiary period show a more northernly distribution. In India the family is represented by species of *Salix* in the Himalayas and Khasi and Naga Hills while *Salix tetrasperma* Roxb. occurs in the terai region of the Himalayas and in Chota Nagpur.

The wood of *Salix* is light and durable and much used for the manufacture of cricket-bats and such other articles. It is suitable for making good charcoal. The young twigs of some species are woven into baskets.

JUGLANDALES

In the 9th order **Juglandales** of Engler only one family **is included**, viz., *Juglandaceae*. Here also the flowers are perianthless or with inconspicuous perianth, in catkins or spikes, with many free stamens in the males. Engler, therefore, considered the family *Juglandaceae* as a primitive family and includes the order in his **Archichlamydeae**. Rendle allots 3rd position to **Juglandales** in his system **and includes** *Myricaceae* also in that order along with *Juglandaceae*. *Myricaceae* is **the single family under Myricales** the 6th order in Engler's system conisdering *Myricaceae* **as more primitive** to *Juglandaceae*. In Hutchinson's system **Juglandales** consists of 3 **families**, viz., *Rhoipteleaceae*, *Juglandaceae* and *Picrodendraceae*. It is the 17th order **under** the division **Lignosae** while **Myricales** with one family *Myricaceae* is the 14th order. Takhtajan includes *Rhoipteleaceae* and *Juglandaceae* under **Juglandales** and places the order just after **Myricales** with one family *Myricaceae.* Both these orders are placed in the Subclass **Hamamelididae** by Takhtajan. Cronquist also puts these 2 orders in subclass **Hamamelidae** and considers that both of them are derived from **Hamamelidales.**

Juglandaceae

Trees or large shrubs often deciduous. Leaves imparipinnately compound, alternate or rarely opposite, exstipulate. Flowers unisexual and monoecious in various types of catkins or spikes bearing either exclusively male or female flower, erect or pendulous, simple or branched and paniculate; bracts and bracteoles present; each flower is subtended by a bract and associated with 2 bracteoles; in a female flower bracts and bracteoles are free or adnate to the ovary. Perianth of one whorl with 4 or fewer segments; in female flowers perianth segments are scale-like, unequal in size, adnate to ovary; rarely perianth altogether absent. Stamens 2—many, filaments short, anthers basifixed, cells parallel. Ovary of 2-3 united carpels, unilocular, inferior, with one orthotropous basal ovule; integument one only; fertilisation is chalazogamic. Fruit a drupe or nut, usually covered by the macrescent bracts and bracteoles, often winged; pericarp fleshy, endocarp hard, sometimes dehiscent with inflexed inner walls. Seed with a large embryo and without endosperm; cotyledons deeply bilobed or subfoliaceous and contorted.

Plants contain watery juice or resins which are often secreted through peltate glands on leaf-surface. Some plants also contain tanin. In the stem vessels are in groups or not. These are mostly with tyloses and with simple and scalariform perforations. Fibres are with bordered pits.

It is a comparatively small family with not more than 60 species in 6 genera chiefly found in the north temperate zone and in the hills of tropical countries. In E. Himalaya and Khasi hills *Juglans regia* Linn. and a few species of *Engelhardtia* occur. *Juglans regia* Linn. and *J. nigra* Linn. yield the Walnuts and *Carya pecan* Engl. et Graeb produce the pecan nuts. Valuable timber is obtained from different species.

Juglandaceae appears to have some resemblance to *Myricaceae*, *Fagaceae*, *Betulaceae* and *Julianiaceae* and these 5 families are placed by Engler in 4 closely allied orders, e.g., **Myricales, Juglandales, Julianiales** and **Fagales.** Due to the simplicity of the flowers which are borne in catkins these families are considered as primitive both by Engler and Rendle, but by others who think that the simplicity of the flowers resulted from reduction, regard them as fairly advanced. They appear to have some relation with *Hamamelidaceae* from which these might have been ultimately derived.

FAGALES

In the 12th order **Fagales** Engler includes 2 families, e.g. *Fagaceae* and *Betulaceae.* Although classed among the primitive families Engler considered this order to be advaneed over **Myricales** and **Juglandales.** Rendle supports Engler in this respect. Hutchinson also regards **Fagales** as a primitive group of plants but he places **Fagales** before **Juglandales.** Takhtajan has the 2 families, *Fagaceae* and *Betulaceae*, under 2 monotypic orders, **Fagales** and **Betulales,** both of which he includes in his subclass **Hamamelididae** before **Myricales** and **Juglandales.** Cronquist includes **Fagales** in the subclass **Hamamelidae** considering that it has originated directly from **Hamamelidales.**

The plants of these 2 families are trees or shrubs with stipulate leaves. Flowers, unisexual and borne usually in catkins. Perianth scale-like or absent. Ovary inferior. Seed without endosperm. Flowers are wind-pollinated. Because of woody habit, catkin inflorescence, pollination by wind and rudimentary perianth or perianth absent the order was conisdered to be primitive by Engler and Rendle, but other taxonomists consider that the families included in this order having unisexual flowers with inferior ovary and seeds devoid of endosperm are more or less advanced. The simplicity of the flowers is considered by them to be the result of reduction. They, therefore, place the order **Fagales** among orders which are more advanced than many of the primitive orders.

Fagaceae

Trees or rarely shrubs, deciduous or evergreen; subepidermal cork usually develops; tanin is often contained in the cells. Leaves simple, alternate, stipulate; stipules scaly, deciduous, protecting the vegetative bud. Flowers unisexual, solitaryey disposed or in clusters along the catkins or in small spikate heads, rarely solitary; the flower culsters on the catkins are usually in cymes forming often a dischasium. Each flower or a flower cluster is in the axil of a bract and surrounded by an involucre of bracteoles which in female flowers enlarge and form the so called cupule of the fruit. Perianth in one whorl, segments scale-like 4-7 in males and 6 or rarely 4 in females. Stamens 4—many, free; filaments filiform, anthers bilobed, dehiscing by vertical slits. Ovary inferior, tricarpellary syncarpous, 3-celled with 2 pendulous ovules in each cell; styles 3, free to the base; ovules anatropous, with 2 integuments. Nuts 1-3 enclosed at base by the cupule. Seed with a large embryo and no endosperm.

Plants are monoecious except in *Nothofagus* which has dioecious plants. Bisexual flowers are rarely found. Usually male flowers occur at the upper part of the caktin while the females occupy the lower portion. In some species of *Castanea* male and female flowers occur in separate catkins in the same plant. The cupule varies in structure in different genera; in *Castanea* it is spinous, in *Fagus* four bristly segments represent the cupule, in others it is cup-shaped enclosing the basal portion of the nut. A cupule may have only one nut or 2 or 3. According to Prantle the cupule is an outgrowth of the axis of the flower and Celakovsky considers it to be an outgrowth of the thalamus; most others think it to be an involucre of bracteoles.

Cork is found in all species developed subepidermally but is more deep seated in *Nothofagus*. The vessels have simple and scalariform pits and are arranged singly. The flowers are wind pollinated but in *Castanea* they are entomophillous.

The family consists of about 900 species in 8 genera and occurs in the N. Temperate zone, in the hills of the Mediterranean region and of the Asiatic countries. It is found in the Himalayas and in the Khasi hills where several species of *Quercus*, *Pasania* and *Castanea* are found. Many species of *Quercus* are the oaks yielding very good quality of timber suitable for ship-building. Species of other genera also yield good timber. *Quercus suber* Linn. of the Mediterranean region yields bottle-cork.

Fagaceae is closely related to **Betulaceae** and both are placed under one order by most workers. Hutchinson and most others consider that the family has been derived from **Hamamelidaceae.** This is supported from anatomical evidence also.

Betulaceae

Trees and shrubs, usually deciduous, resin secreting glands present in young branches. Leaves simple, alternate, stipulate; stipules deciduous. Flowers small, unisexual, in distinct male and female catkins on the same plant; bracts and bracteoles present; the catkins bear dense clusters of 3 or 2 flowers in cymes each subtended by a bract; the lateral flowers are provided with bracteoles, in the central flower usually the bracteoles are lacking; the bracts and bracteoles often unite to form a protective covering of the fruit. Perianth present or absent, often scale-like, 2 or 4 or more, persistent. Stamens 4, opposite to perianth-lobes, often stamens only 2, or more than 4, splitted from above with one anther lobe on each splitted filament; anthers extrorse dehiscing longitudinally. The ovary inferior, bilocular, with one pendulous ovule in each cell; styles 2 persistent; stigma clavate; ovule anatropous, with one integument; only one ovule in an ovary matures to a seed, the other becomes abortive. Fruit a small nut, shortly winged or not, subtended or enclosed by the united bract and bracteoles forming a cover-scale or a cupule, the cover-scales detach from the axis or are woody and remain attached to the axis so the entire fruiting catkin resembles a small cone. Seed with a straight embryo and no endosperm; cotyledons large, containing oily substance.

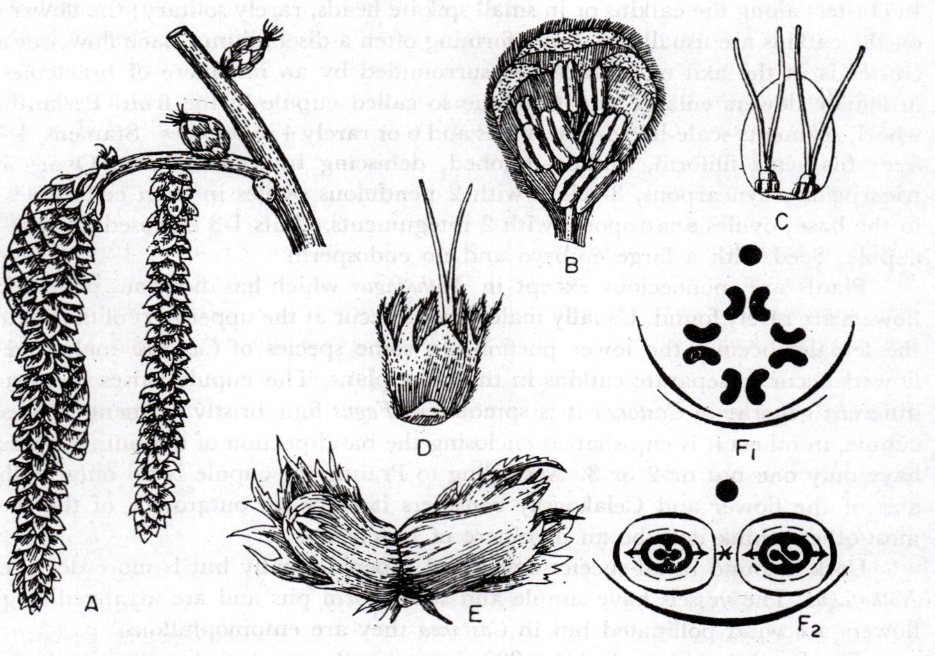

Fig. 52. Coryllus avellana Linn. A. Branch with male and female catkins; B. Male flower with bracts and bracteoles; C. A dichasium of female flowers; D. Young fruit with cupule; E. Mature fruit.

The family comprises a little over 100 species in 6 genera, distributed in the N. Temperate region and in hills of tropical countries. Several species of *Betula* and *Alnus* occur in the Himalayas and Khasi and Naga Hills. Some species yield valuable timber; the wood is good for charcoal. *Corylus avellana* Linn. produces the Hazel-nut and *C. tabulosa* Linn. and *C. colurna* Linn. also yield edible nuts. The bark of *Betula* contains tanin and is used to tan leather; the spring sap of some species of this genus is sweet and is often used for manufacturing a liquor. The bark of *Betula utilis* D. Don comes off in very thin paper like strips and at one time used as paper in India, particularly in Nepal where it is known as "Bhurjapatra".

Betulaceae is closely allied to *Fagaceae* and both the families are supposed to have originated from *Hamamelidaceae* or from a stock allied to *Hamamelidaceae*. The family is subdivided into 2 tribes, viz., Betuleae and Coryleae which are treated as 2 distinct families by Hutchnison as *Betulaceae* and *Corylaceae*.

URTICALES

In the system of classification by Engler and Prantl this order is placed next to **Fagales** and consists of 3 families, viz., *Ulmaceae*, *Moraceae* and *Urticaceae*. The common characters noticed in these 3 families are : simple stipulate leaves, generally unisexual flowers, perianth inconspicuous, usually in one whorl, stamens as many as perianth segments and opposite to them, ovary superior, usually unilocular with one ovule.

That these families are closely allied to one another and the order **Urticales** forms a natural taxon is the opinion of almost all taxonomists. In the older classification of Bentham and Hooker these families were considered to constitute a single N.O., i.e., a family. Engler splitted them into 3 distinct families to be included under the order **Urticales** and because the perianth is rudimentary placed it among the primitive orders. Rendle also considers the order as a primitive one and names it as **Urticae-florae.** Rendle further splits *Moraceae* into *Moraceae* and *Cannabinaceae*. According to Hutchinson the unisexual inconspicuous flowers indicate advancement and not primitiveness and therefore he considers the families to be fairly recent. He includes the order in his **Lignosae** and places it after the orders **Fagales, Juglandales** and **Casuarinales.** He further divides *Moraceae* and establishes 2 more distinct families, viz., *Eucommiaceae* and *Barbeyaceae* so that according to him **Urticales** consists of 6 families, viz., *Urticaceae*, *Ulmaceae*, *Moraceae*, *Cannabinaceae*, *Barbeyaceae* and *Eucommiaceae*.

Urticales is related to **Juglandales** and **Fagales** and has been derived from **Hamamelidales.** Takhtajan and Cronquist both place the order in the subclass **Hamamelideae.** They recognise *Barbeyaceae* and *Eucommiaceae* as distinct families but do not include them in **Urticales.**

Ulmaceae

Trees or shrubs, often with mucilage, evergreen or deciduous. Leaves simple, stipulate, distichous, often with asymmetrical blades; stipules caducuous. Flowers minute, unisexual or rarely polygamous, solitary or in cymose clusters. Perianth in one whorl, sepaloid, persistent, with 4-5 members or sometimes upto 9, free or connate, imbricate, rarely valvate. Stamens as many as perianth segments and opposite to them, rarely, fewer; filaments erect; anther bilocular, dehiscing longitudinally. Ovary bicarpellate, unilocular, rarely 2-locular; styles 2, divergent, stigmatic on their inner surfaces; ovule solitary in each chamber, pendulous from near the top. Fruit a samara or drupe, rarely 2-seeded; seed with a straight or curved embryo and with no endosperm or with scanty endosperm; cotyledons rarely unequal.

This is a small family with about 150 species in 15 genera distributed in the temperate as well as tropical regions. Although a comparatively small family it shows a wide range of variations. *Ulmus* -the Elms and *Holoptelea* are deciduous, while others are evergreen. Unisexual flowers generally occur but bisexual flowers also occur in some genera along with unisexual flowers. Leaves are penninerved or with 3-7 prominent veins from the base as the *Celtis* and *Trema*. Ovary is usually sessile but stipitate in *Holoptelea*. *Celtis* has a curved embryo while others have straight embryo. The fruit of *Ulmus*, *Holoptelea* etc. is a samara while in *Celtis*, *Trema* and others it is a drupe.

The timber obtained from the Elms is good. *Planera abelica* Gemel (=*Zelkova cretica* Spach.) has fragrant wood which is known as False Sandal wood. Wood of *Trema* and others make good charcoal. In India the family is represented by a few species of *Ulmus*, *Holoptelea*, *Celtis* and *Trema*.

Ulmaceae is closely related to the other 2 families of the order, viz., *Moraceae* and *Urticaceae*. Hutchinson splits *Ulmaceae* into *Ulmaceae* and *Barbeyaceae* with a single species and this is maintained as a distinct family by the recent workers.

Moraceae

Trees or shrubs, rarely climbing and very rarely herbs, with milky latex. Leaves simple, alternate, stipulate; stipules usually large and covering the leaf bud, caducous; often cystoliths are present in leaf epidermis. Flowers unisexual in monoecious or dioecious, mainly cymose head like inflorescences or condensed spikes, bracts often present. Perianth sepaloid, usually 4 in 2 whorls, rarely 2 or 1, persistent, very small. Stamens as many as sepals and opposite to them, or only 2 stamens or rarely 1; filaments straight or incurved in bud; anthers usually versatile. Carpels 2; ovary superior, one chambered or two-chambered, one chamber with a pendulous ovule and the other empty; styles 2 or rarely 1, short, with a bifid stigma; ovule curved. Fruit a drupe or a multiple of achenes or berries. Seeds with usually curved embryo and with fleshy endosperm, or endosperm absent.

In this family the flower-structure as well as the inflorescence shows great variations in different genera. *Broussonetia* is dioecious, the male spikes are borne in plants which never produce the female flowers which are in globose heads on different trees. *Morus* may be monoecious or dioecious. *Streblus* is usually dioecious; the males in spikes which may be elongated or condensed into a head while the female flowers are solitary or 2-4 together. *Cannabis* (now included under **Cannabinaceae**) is dioecious; the male flowers in paniculate cymes and the females in short racemes. In *Ficus* the peduncle enlarges in the form of a vessel enclosing the male and female flowers as well as some sterile female flowers known as the gall-flowers. This type of inflorescence is called **hypanthodium.** Another special type of inflorescence is found in *Dorstenia* where peduncles of several cymes unite to form a flat saucer-shape structure with both type of flowers in the central portion.

Stamen solitary in *Artocarpus* and usually so in *Ficus*; in most genera the number is 4 while in *Cannabis* there are 5 sepals and 5 stamens. Filaments of stamens inflexed in bud in *Streblus*, *Morus*, *Broussonetia*, etc. but erect in *Balanostreblus*, *Artocarpus*, *Ficus*, *Cudrania*, etc. Fruits are simple achenes in *Streblus*, *Conocephalus*, *Taxotrophis* etc. but multiple or aggregate fruit occurs in many genera. In *Ficus* the whole hypanthodium matures into a fruit. In *Artocarpus* the whole female inflorescence including the club-shaped receptacle turns into a fruit which is a **sorosis.** Usually the seeds have 2 equal cotyledons but in few genera, e.g. *Phyllochlamys*, *Streblus*, *Artocarpus*, etc. one cotyledon is much larger than the other.

Flowers are entomophyllous. In *Ficus* where the flowers are enclosed within the hypanthodium, these are pollinated by the insect *Blastophaga* which enters the hypanthodium through an opening at the apex. The insect lays eggs in the ovary of gall

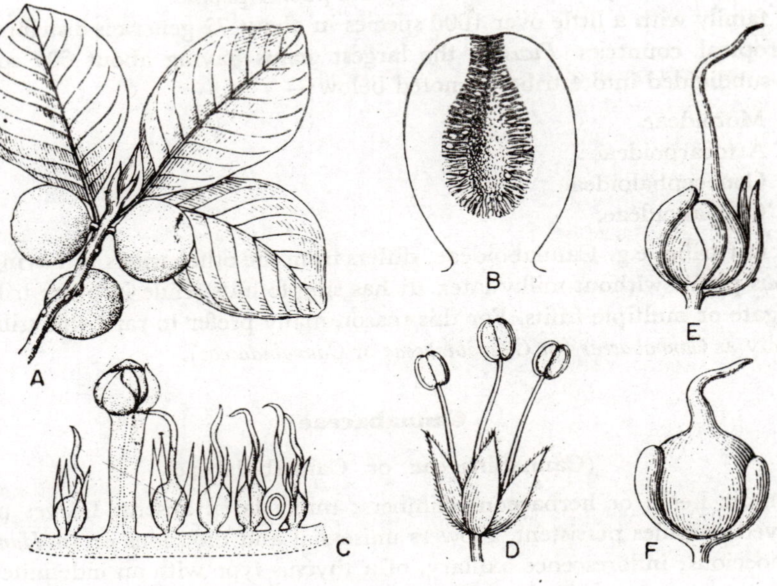

Fig. 53. Ficus benghalensis Linn.

A—Branch with leaves and fruits. B—L. s. of hypanthodium. C—A part of the hypanthodium. D—Male flower. E—Female flower. F—Gall flower.

flowers where the style is much shorter than that in the normal female flowers. The fertile female flowers have long style with papillose stigma. The insect while moving inside the hypanthodium collects pollen from the stamens of the male flowers and the papillose stigma of the female flowers catches them from the body of the insect.

Many species of this family are economically important. *Ficus carica* Linn. produces the edible fig and is cultivated in the Mediterranean region and W. Asia. *Ficus glomerata* Roxb. (=*F. racemosa* Linn.) is Jagnya Dumur or Gular which is cooked as vegetable and taken raw when ripe. *F. hispida* L. f. is also used as vegetable and is called Dumur in Bengal. *Ficus elastica* Roxb. of eastern India yields a latex suitable for manufacturing rubber. *F. benghalensis* Linn. is the Banyan tree and *F. religiosa* Linn. is the Aswattha or Pipal tree usually planted in villages as shade trees. *Artocarpus heterophyllus* Lam (Syn. *A.* integrifolia L. f.) is the Jack fruit and *A. incisa* Linn. is the Bread fruit-tree. *A. lakoocha* Roxb. is the Dehu or Deo phal, the ripe fruit of which is also edible. The timber of most *Artocarpus* and particularly of *A. heterophyllus* and *A. Chaplasha* Roxb. is very valuable. *Morus* is a small genus different species of which are cultivated to feed silk worms with their leaves. *Morus nigra* Linn., *M. alba* Linn. and *M. australis* Poir produce delicious fruits. The timber obtained from the species that attain tree-size is hard and is used in many ways. *Brosimum galactodendron* H. B. & K. of Venezuela yields copius latex which is sweet and nutritious and taken as milk. The tree is known by the name "Cow-tree". *Streblus asper* Lour a short tree grows wild in tropical Asiatic countreis the leaves of which are very rough and are used to polish ivory; the branches are much used as tooth brushes, the latex being good for the gum. The fibre obtained from the bark of *Broussonetia papyrifera* Vent, is woven into a coarse cloth and also used to manufacture paper and cardboard. *Antiaris toxicaria* Lesch.—the Upas tree, the latex of which is used as arrow-poison, has a bark which is the Balkal or a coarse type of cloth worn by the poorer people.

The family with a little over 1000 species in about 72 genera is distributed mainly in the tropical countries. *Ficus* is the largest genus having about 600 species. The family is subdivided into 4 tribes as noted below:—

I. Moroideae.
II. Artocarpoideae.
III. Conocephaloideae.
IV. Cannaboideae.

The last tribe, e.g. Cannaboideae, differs from the other tribes in having aromatic herbaceous plants without milky latex. It has simple nuts while in other tribes there is an aggregate or multiple fruits. For this reason many prefer to raise this tribe to a distinct family as *Cannabaceae* (or *Cannabinaceae* or *Cannabidaceae*).

Cannabaceae

(Cannabinaceae or Cannabidaceae)

Aromatic herbs or herbaceous climbers; milky latex absent. Leaves palmate or palminerved; stipules persistent. Flowers unisexual and dioecious or in *Humulus* some time monoecious; inflorescence axillary, of a thyrsus type with an indefinite main axis

Fig. 54. Cannabis sativa Linn.

A—A branch with leaves and female flowers (×1).
B—Male flower. C—Female flower. D—L. s. of seed.

and cymose clusters; the ♂ loosely many-flowered while the ♀ dense and few-flowered; bracts and bracteoles present. Perianth in male flower 5-lobed, cup-like in female flower surrounding the base of the ovary. Stamens 5, opposite to the perianth lobes. Ovary superior, unilocular with one pendulous ovule; styles 2 with brush-like stigma. Fruit a nut; seed with scanty fleshy endosperm and curved embryo.

The family contains 2 genera and 3 species occurring in temperate and subtropical regions of the old world and are cultivated. *Cannabis sativa* Linn. is the Hemp, useful for its long and strong bast fibres. This plant is however more reputed for the narcotic resin it yields which is used in the preparation of an intoxicating drink known as *Hashish* or *Bhang* or *Siddhi*. The female inflorescence with the resin is smoked and is called *Ganja*. The bracts and bracteoles of *Humulus lupulus* Linn. bear numerous resinous glands which are aromatic and sedative and the floral-heads are used to flavour beer.

Urticaceae

Herbs or shrubs, rarely climbers; watery sap present; many with stigning hairs. Leaves simple, alternate or opposite, stipulate; cystoliths often present in leaf-epidermis. Flowers very small, unisexual monoecious or dioecious rarely polygamous in cymose clusters on short axillary shoots, often crowded in heads, rarely catkin-like. Perianth of 4 sepaloid segments, rarely 5, in 2 whorls; free in male flowers, more or less connate and persistent in female flowers. Stamens as many as perianth segments and opposite to them; filaments inflexed in bud but spring elastically outwards when flowers open discharging the pollens in clouds; anthers bilocular, opening by longitudinal slits. Ovary

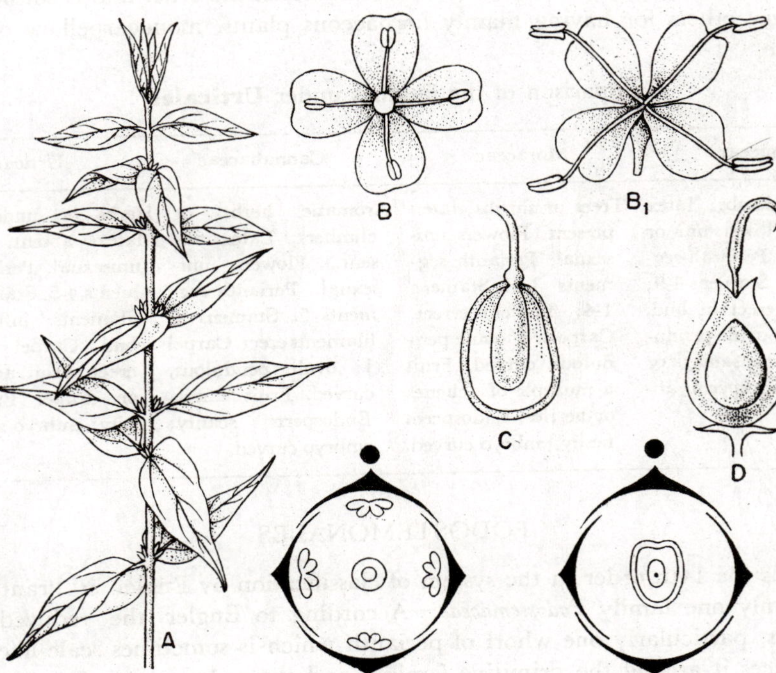

Fig. 55. Pouzolzia indica Gaud.

A—A branch with leaves and flowers (×1). B & B_1—Male flower (×10).
C—L. s. of fruit with seed (×10). D—Female flower (×10).

superior, of one carpel, 1-celled, with one erect, orthotropous ovule; style ends in a plumose stigma; rarely ovary inferior. Fruit an achene or drupe; seed with oily endosperm and straight embryo.

The family includes many species possessing stinging hairs—the stinging nettles, e.g. *Fleurya interrupta* Gaud., species of *Urtica*, *Girardinia*, *Laportea*, etc. *Laportea crenulata* Gaud. is the Devil- or Fever-nettle of the Terai-region of the Himalayas, the slight touch of which brings severe irritation and pain all over the body often resulting in fever. These nettles have hairs of which the apex is knob-like. The apex breaks very easily on coming into contact with animal body and the poisonous acid-sap contained in the hair is ejected and falls on the skin of the animal and produces irritation.

The plants of the family are more or less uniform in characters although some variations are noticed. In *Parietaria* bisexual flowers occur along with unisexual flowers. Here the inflorescence is often a biparous cyme. In *Forskohlea* perianth is absent or much reduced. In this genus the male flowers have only one stamen. The peculiar feature in the family is the elastic nature of the stamens which throw off the pollens in the form of cloudy mass by their sudden movement.

The family consists of 42 genera and about 600 species occurring in tropical and temperate countries. It is represented in India by several species of *Girardinia*, *Elatostemma*, *Pouzolzia*, etc. *Boehmaria nevea* Hook. & Arn. grows in N. Bengal and is cultivated in eastern India and China for its fibre which is known as Rhea or Ramie-fibre. Otherwise the family is not of much economic importance.

The family is closely related to the other families of the order and is considered advanced over others for having mainly herbaceous plants, monocarpellary ovary and basal ovule.

Comparison of the families under **Urticales**

Ulmaceae	Moraceae	Cannabaceae	Urticaceae
Trees or shrubs; latex absent. Flowers uni- or bisexual. Perianth-segments 4-9. Stamens 4-9; filaments erect in bud. Carpels 2; ovule pendulous. Fruit a samara or drupe. Endosperm absent.	Trees or shrubs; latex present. Flowers unisexual. Perianth segments 1-4. Stamens 1-4; filaments errect. Carpels 2 ovule pendulous, curved. Fruit a multiple of achenes or berries. Endosperm fleshy, embryo curved.	Aromatic herbs or climbers; Latex absent. Flowers unisexual. Perianth segments 5. Stamens 5, filaments erect. Carpel 1; ovule pendulous, curved. Fruit a nut. Endosperm scanty; embryo curved.	Herbs or undershrubs; latex absent. Flowers unisexual. Perianth segments 4-5. Stamens 4-5; filaments inflexed in bud. Carpel 1; ovule erect. Fruit an achene or drupe. Endosperm oily; embryo straight.

PODOSTEMONALES

This is the 14th order in the system of classification by Engler & Prantle and it includes only one family *Podostemaceae*. According to Engler the reduced type of floral parts, particularly one whorl of perianth which is sometimes scale-like or often absent places it among the primitive families and the order is therefore placed after **Utricales** in his system. Hutchinson includes *Hydrostachyaceae* also in this order while according to Engler *Hydrostachyaceae* is much more primitive than *Podostemaceae* and is under the 2nd order **Hydrostachyales** in his system. Rendle includes both the families

Podostemaceae and *Hydrostachyaceae* in his order **Rosales** along with *Crassulaceae*, *Saxifragaceae* and others. Hutchinson places the order **Podostemales** near **Saxifragales** after **Sarraceniales.** That *Podostemaceae* is allied to *Rosaceae*, *Saxifragaceae*, *Crassulaceae* group is a fact agreed upon by many workers including Takhtajan and Cronquist. Both Takhtajan and Cronquist consider however that the 2 families *Podostemaceae* and *Hydrostachyaceae* are not at all close to each other but *Hydrostachyaceae* should be included in **Scrophulariales** far removed from *Podostemaceae*.

Podostemaceae

(Podostemonaceae)

Submerged aquatic plants growing on rocky substratum under running water; the vegetative body is a flat and dorsiventral structure, thallus like in appearance or filamentous, sometimes slender and threadlike. Leaves very small and scaly or moss-like, often linear or subulate, rarely broader and dissected. Flowers solitary and terminal on short secondary shoots or many in cymose inflorescence; very small and bisexual; bracts and in case of solitary flowers a spathe is often present; pedicels usually long and slender. Perianth of 3-5 segments in one whorl; segments free or more or less united; sometimes perianth-segments are many and scale-like or may be altogether absent and in such cases a membranous structure encloses the flower-bud. Stamens many, in one or more whorls, free or the filaments united, often forming a tubular sheath; anthers introrse, dehiscing longitudinally by lateral slits; pollens in diads or tetrads. Ovary superior, of 3-2 carpels, 3-1-celled; styles as many as carpels, stigma fimbriate; ovules many, anatropous, on axile or in unicellular ovary on free central placentas. Fruit a capsule with many minute seeds which have a mucilaginous covering, thick cotyledons and no endosperm.

The seed on germination gives rise to a very short primary axis but no primary root. From the primary axis rises the creeping thalloid or filamentous body endogenously. This flat thalloid body is more root-like than stem, having a root-cap at the tip and branching endogenously or exogenously. It also produces the **haptera** or the fixing organs exogenously from the surface tissue. The branches or the secondary shoots produce leaves and bear the flowers.

Anatomy of the vegetative body shows that the vascular bundles are closed and collateral and usually scattered. The xylem is very much reduced but the phloem is well developed with large sieve tubes.

The plants of this family show a considerable range of variation in vegetative as well as floral characters. In some *Podostemon* the vegetative body is thread-like and in *Dicraea* it is flat and dorsiventral. In *Mourera* the main body is like a creeping rhizome bearing rather large leaves with a distinct petiole and much dissected lamina; the petiole sheathing at the base which remains attached to the shoot while the blade falls away. *Hydrobryum* has an exogenously developed main body which is flat and much-branched and is not root-like in character. In this case the secondary shoots are also exogenously developed and bear densely close small leaves giving the plant a moss-like appearance. The root-like body performs the work of photosynthesis. In some *Dicraea* there are short floating roots in addition to the hapteras.

Flowers of *Dicraea* are sessile while in *Tristicha* and others they are pedicelled. Spathela is present in the flowers of *Dicraea*, *Mourera*, *Podostemon*, etc. In *Lacis monadelpha*

Bong. there are many stamens the filaments of which unite to form a tubular sheath round the ovary.

The embryo-sac development is of bisporic 4-nucleate type. In the final stage there is one synergid, an egg-cell and 2-closely lying antipodal cells. Some of the nucellus cells break down forming a cavity which contains some free nuclei. This cavity is known as pseudoembryosac and is a peculiar structure.

The family with 43 genera and about 150 species is distributed over the tropical and temperate regions of the world. It is represented in India by several species of *Podostemon, Dicraea, Terniola* and *Hydrobryum.*

Podostemaceae is allied to *Crassulaceae, Saxifragaceae* and *Rosaceae* as shown by Rendle, Hutchinson, Takhtajan and Cronquist. P. Maheshwari proved from embryological study that *Podostemaceae* and *Crassulaceae* are closely related. The family *Hydrostachyaceae* which is placed in the same order with *Podostemaceae* by Rendle and Hutchinson is not at all closely related according to the opinion of most authors.

SANTALALES

In the 16th order **Santalales** Engler includes 7 families, viz. *Olacaceae Opiliaceae, Octoknemataceae, Grubbiaceae, Santalaceae, Myzodendraceae* and *Loranthaceae.* The order was sub-divided into 2 suborders, viz. **Santalineae** with 6 families *Olacaceae, Opiliaceae Octoknemataceae Santalaceae, Grubbiaceae* and *Myzodendraceae* while the 7th family *Loranthacea* was placed in the 2nd suborder **Loranthineae.** Later on Engler included *Balanophoraceae* also in this order and placed the family under a 3rd suborder **Balanophorineae.** The above families have the following characters common to them, e.g. flowers, usually unisexual and regular; perianth segments small, in one whorl; stamens as many as perianth-segments and adnate to them; carpels 2-3, united to form a unilocular ovary; ovules few, pendulous; seed with endosperm and straight embryo.

The order **Santalales** with the above named 8 families appears to be a natural taxon and the families appear to be closely related to each other. Most of them are parasites or hemiparasites. Reduction of ovule to archesporial tissue is noticed in some cases in all these families. Hutchinson splits Engler's **Santalales** into **Olacales** and **Santalales** but place them adjacent to each other. Takhtajan transfers *Grubbiaceae* to **Ericales** which is under subclass **Dilleniidae** while **Santalales** with the rest seven families and six others is under subclass **Rosidae** in his system of classification. Cronquist places all these families under **Santalales** and also 3 more families, viz. *Medusandraceae, Dipentodontaceae* and *Cynomoriaceae.* He combines *Octoknemataceae* with *Olacaceae.* Hutchinson following Bessey places **Olacales** and **Santalales** just after **Celastrales** considering them very close to each other. Takhtajan also considers that **Santalales** is close to **Celastrales** both having originated from Rosaceous ancestor. Cronquist supports this view and states that **Santalales** arose directly from **Rosales.** Engler considered this order to be one of the earlier group among the **Dicotyledonae** and Rendle thought it to be more so. But Bessy, Hutchinson and others consider **Santalales** to be fairly advanced in course of evolution.

Santalaceae

Herbs or shrubs, or small trees; hemiparasites. Leaves simple, opposite or alternate, exstipulate, entire. Inflorescence various, often flowers solitary and axillary

Flowers bisexual or rarely unisexual, actinomorphic. Perianth of one whorl, sepaloid or petaloid; segments 3-6, usually 4-5, valvate. Stamens as many as perianth segments and opposite and adnate to them; filaments short; anthers 2-celled ultimately 1-celled, and opening by vertical slits. Nectar secreting disc is often present. Carpels 3-5, rarely 2, united to form a unilocular ovary; ovary inferior or semi-inferior or superior; ovules usually 3 but only one is fertile, pendulous from the upper part of the central placenta, orthotropous or anatropous, with 1 integument only. Fruit a drupe or an achene. Seeds without testa and with fleshy endosperm and straight embryo.

Plants are semiparasites on the trees or on roots. Flowers are bisexual or unisexual and monoecious; but *Osyris pyrularia* is dioecious. In the pentamerous flowers of *Leptomeria* the ovary is five-locular at base becoming unilocular above. In *Anthobolus*, *Exocarpus*, etc. ovule is solitary and basal. In *Exocarpus* the ovule shows no differentiation from nucellus and embryo sac, and the pollen chamber resembles that of **Gymnosperms** and therefore treated as a **Gymnosperm** by many. Floral formula of a bisexual flower *may* be shown like this:—$P_{(4-5)}$ $A_{(4-5)}$ $G_{(3-5)}$.

A peculiar bent tube-like structure is formed by the elongation of the embryo sac at the chalazal region. This is called *chalazal caecum* which encloses the antipodal cells. It is a kind of haustoria in the embryo sac.

The family consists of 26 genera and about 600 species occurring in the temperate and tropical countries of the world. Only a few species are found in India, the Sandal wood tree—*Santalum album* Linn. growing in S. India while the rest are Himalayan. The Sandal wood tree is cultivated in India and Malaya while species of *Buckleya* and *Pyrularia* are cultivated as ornamental plants.

The family is closely related to the other families of the order **Santalales,** viz., *Olacaceae*, *Opiliaceae*, *Octonemataceae*, *Grubbiaceae*, *Myzodendraceae*, *Loranthaceae* and *Balanophoraceae*. *Santalaceae* appears to be more allied to *Loranthaceae* both having mucilaginous seeds and chalazal caecum in the embryo sac among other common characters.

Loranthaceae

Hemiparasitic herbs or shrubs with sympodial stem, attached to the branches of trees by means of haustoria; the growth of the stem is often dichasial, e.g. *Viscum*. Leaves persistent, simple, coriaceous, exstipulate, entire, opposite or rarely alternate; sometimes leaves reduced to opposite scales which are united. Inflorescence axillary, usually a biparous cyme which may be of a mixed type, or flower solitary. Flower regular or almost so, bisexual or unisexual, monoecious or dioecious, epigynous; bracts present, often adnate to the pedicel. Perianth in 2 whorls with 2-3 segments in each whorl, all similar and petaloid or sepaloid, or in one whorl with 6 segments; segments free or connate in a tube arising from the rim or ring-like outgrowth of a cup-shaped receptacle. The inner members are valvate, the outer valvate or imbricate. Stamens as many as perianth segments, opposite and adnate to them; anthers, bithecal or unithecal, or transversely multithecal, dehiscing longitudinally, or by transverse slits or by apical pores. Carpels 3-4, united to form a unilocular ovary; ovary inferior, with an indistinctly differentiated chamber; ovules several, indistinct on a large central placenta and only 1-3 attaining maturity. Fruit a pseudocarp or drupaceous, 1-3 seeded; seed mucilagenous, without testa, with a large straight embryo and fleshy endosperm.

The ring-like outgrowth of the receptacle is found in the tribe *Loranthoideae* where the perianth is uniseriate. This is called '*calyculus*'. Some authors consider that the calyculus is the remnant of the calyx while others think it to be the part of the receptacle. The embryo sac development is like that in *Santalaceae*; it grows to an elongated structure at the base containing the antipodals and forms the chalazal caecum. The plants are parasites on the branches of the hosts but the Australian genus *Nuytsia* consists of erect trees. The seeds in this genus have 3 cotyledons. A few species are leafless and the work of photosynthesis is performed by the green stem, e.g., *Viscum articulatum* Burm. f. and species of *Arceuthobium*. *Arceuthobium minutissimum* Hk. f. parasitising on *Pinus excelsa* Wall. is the smallest plant among the **Dicotyledonae.** This is found in West Himalaya. The ovary of the flower in this family remains apparently solid at first but later on a chamber is formed. In *Lysiana* the ovary is 4-celled.

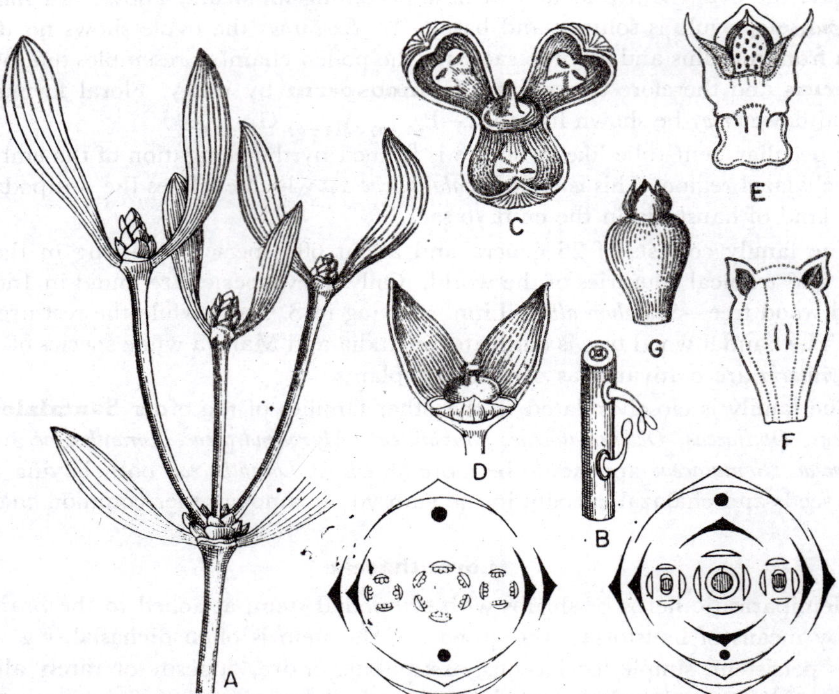

Fig. 56. Viscum album Linn.
A—Flowering branch with flower and fruit (×1). B—Germination of seed on host. C—Male flower. D—Female flower. E—L. s. of male flower of V. orientale. F & G—Female flower of V. orientale in L. s. and entire. Diagrams of male and female inflorescences.

The family consists of over 1100 species under 30 genera and are distributed in the tropical as well as temperate countries of the world. The family is of no economic importance. *Viscum album* Linn. is Misletoe much used for decoration in European countries during Christmas time when most other plants are leafless. *Viscum articulatum* Burm. f., *V. monoicum* Roxb., *V. orientale* Willd., several species of *Dendroptho*, *Scurrula*, etc. are found in India.

Balanophoraceae

Small leafless total parasites on roots of other plants; the plant-body consists of a tuber-like underground rhizome; scale leaves seldom present. The inflorescence is a dense-flowered spike often a more or less globose head; the spike is formed within the rhizome and ultimately comes up breaking through the rhizome; the cylindrical axis or the peduncle is covered by sheathing bracts; the inflorescence is a panicle in the genus *Sarcophyte*. Flowers unisexual, actinomorphic, monoecious or dioecious. The staminate flowers with one whorl of perianth; segments 3-4, valvate. Stamens as many as perianth segments and opposite to them; anthers 2-8-chambered, opening by pores or slits. Pistillate flowers with or without perianth. Carpels 1-3; ovary unilocular, inferior; styles 1-2; ovules 1-3, without integument, sometimes reduced to embryo sac and often united with ovary wall. In *Balanophora* and some other genera the gynoecium is merely a slender emergence. There is a single archesporial cell without a proper placenta. The fruit is a nut with one seed containing oily endosperm and a small undifferentiated embryo.

The family is closely related to the other families of the order *Santalales*. Reduction in the development of the gynoecium to some extent is noticed in all these families and extreme condition is attained in the family *Balanophoraceae*.

The family with about 120 species under 18 genera occurs in the tropical countries of the world. A few species of *Balanophora* are found in India in the forests and savannah formations. *Rhopalochnemis phalloides* Jungh of E. Himalaya and Assam has a tuberous root stock as big as a man's head. The family is of no economic importance.

ARISTOLOCHIALES

Three families, viz., *Aristolochiaceae*, *Rafflesiaceae* and *Hydnoraceae* were included in this order by Engler. The common characters between them are perianth in one whorl, ovary inferior, ovules numerous and usually many stamens, small embryo and copious endosperm in the seed.

Engler included this order in his subclass **Archichlamydeae** due to the presence of haplochlamydious perianth and placed this order after **Santalales.** Rendle supported Engler and placed the order in his **Monochlamydeae** after **Santalales.** He also followed Engler and included the above 3 families in this order. Hutchinson places the order **Aristolochiales** in his Division **Herbaceae** after **Berberidales** considering that **Aristolochiales** has been derived from *Berberidaceae*. Takhtajan splits the **Aristolochiales** of Engler into 2 orders **Aristolochiales** and **Rafflesiales** but place them one after another in his system of classification and considers that both the orders were derived from **Magnoliales.** Cronquist also keeps **Aristochiales** and **Rafflesiales** as 2 distinct orders and expresses the opinion that they are not at all close. *Aristolochiaceae* the single family in the order has pollen which is monoaperturate. This type of pollen is found in **Magnoliales** and other orders in the subclass **Magnoliidae.** The seed in *Aristolochiaceae* resembles to those in **Magnoliidae** and further ethereal oil-glands are found in *Ariostolochiaceae* and in **Magnoliales.** The wood-anatomy in *Aristolochiaceae* is also of Ranalian type. The genus *Saruma* of *Aristolochiaceae* has free carpels and the fruit is a cluster of follicles. Cronquist therefore includes **Aristolochiales** in the subclass **Magnoliidae** and states that **Aristolochiales** probably originated from **Magnoliales.**

In **Rafflesiales** Cronquist has a 3rd family *Mitrastemonaceae* besides *Rafflesiaceae* and *Hydnoraceae*. About the relationship of this order Cronquist says that this is not very clear. The pollen in **Rafflesiales** is similar to that in *Balanophoraceae* both being triaperturate. He therefore includes **Rafflesiales** in the subclass **Rosidae** close to **Santalales.**

Aristolochiaceae

Herbs or shrubs, climbing or creeping, rarely attaining tree-size; usually more or less foetid. Leaves simple, alternate, exstipulate, with ethereal oil-glands. Flowers solitary or in cymose clusters or racemes or spikes, terminal or axillary; bisexual, zygomorphic or actinomorphic, epigynous, bracteate or not. Perianth usually in one whorl, petaloid, tubular, 3-lobed or with an oblique mouth; tube contracted in the middle, inflated below and dilated at the mouth; lobes valvate. Stamens 6, often much more, very rarely 5, in one or more whorls, free or adnate to the style; filaments short and thick or the anthers sessile; anthers erect with parallel cells dehiscing longitudinally and dorsally; pollen uniaperturate. Carpels 6 or 4, united to form a syncarpous ovary; ovary inferior, with cells as many as carpels; style columnar; stigma lobed; ovules anatropous, usually many on axile or parietal placentas. Fruit a septicidal capsule or a berry; seeds with copious fleshy endosperm and minute embryo.

Flowers are insect pollinated. In *Aristolochia* the jug-shaped perianth keeps the insect captive for sometime. The narrow middle portion of the perianth tube is beset with stiff hairs which point downwards. These prevent the insect to climb up and run away. After sometime the hairs wither and drop down and the insect is freed from captivity. While inside the perianth-tube the insect moves about in the basal inflated portion of the perianth and gets itself dusted with pollens which it carries on its body and when visiting another flower pollinates the stigma. The mouth of the perianth tube is of various shape and with peculiar colouring and attracts the insects which it traps for pollination.

In *Asarum* the flower is actinomorphic and there is an inner whorl of scale-like perianth which represents the corolla. In *Saruma* the petals and the carpels are free and the fruit is a cluster of follicles: Species of the genus *Apama* are small trees.

The family contains 8 genera and about 600 species and are found in temperate and tropical region of northern hemisphere. In India it is represented by several species of *Aristolochia*, e.g. *A. indica* Linn., *A. acuminata* Lam., *A. saccata* Wall, *A. Roxburghiana* Klotz, etc. and *Apama Wallichii* R. Br. The family is of no economic importance but a few are cultivated in gardens as ornamental plants and also as curiosities due to the shape of the flowers, e.g. *Aristolochia grandiflora* Sw.—the Pelican flower, *A. drurior* Hill—the Dutchman's pipe.

The family was included in **Aristolochiales** along with **Rafflesiaceae** and **Hydnoraceae** by Engler, Rendle and others but modern taxonomists think that these 3 families are not closely related and not to be included in the same order. It is considered that *Aristolochiaceae* has been derived from **Magnoliales** or **Ranales** and its relationship might be with *Berberidaceae* or *Lardizabalaceae*. Anatomical characters also show some similarities between *Aristolochia* and *Berberis*.

Rafflesiaceae

(Cytinaceae)

Leafless root—rarely stem-parasites with a mycelium-like body; the vegetative body consisting of network of filiform cellular structure remains within the host plant. The flowers come out through the intercellular space of the root of the host and are solitary; unisexual, monoecious or dioecious, epigynous, actinomorphic and with one whorl of perianth. Perianth sepaloid or petaloid, with 4-6 segments which are free or basally connate. A disc is often present in the centre. Stamens many in the male flower and the sessile anthers are inserted on the lower side of the disc; anthers bursting by apical pores or by longitudinal slits, pollen often viscuous. Ovary inferior or semi-inferior, 1-locular or apparently many-locular due to the placentas reaching almost the centre of the cell; stigma discoid or lobate or stigmas many on top of ovary; ovules many on parietal placentas or pendulous from the apex of ovary-chamber; integument one only. Fruit a berry, often dehiscing irregularly; seed with an undifferentiated embryo surrounded by one layer of oily endosperm cells.

The family consists of 8 genera and about 50 species widely distributed in the tropical region. The flowers in this family are usually large and particularly in *Rafflesia* they attain a great size. In *R. Arnoldi* R. Br. the flower is not less than a metre across. The family is represented in India by a single species, viz. *Sapria himalayana* Griff.

Hydnoraceae

Leafless root parasites with a rhizome. The rhizome bears large fleshy solitary flowers that come above ground. Flowers bisexual, epigynous, with one whorl of perianth. Perianth segments 3-4, thick and fleshy, united below in a tube. Stamens in *Hydnora* as many as perianth-lobes with a large number of pollen sacs. In *Prosopanche* stamens 3, united to form a covering over the stigma and 3 staminodes. Ovary inferior, unilocular; ovules many, orthotropous, on parietal placentation; integument 1 or absent. Fruit baccate with minute seeds; endosperm copious.

This is a small family with 20 species under 2 genera, viz., *Hydnora* in Africa and *Prosopanche* in Argentina.

Hydnoraceae is closely related to *Rafflesiaceae*. It is not economically important.

POLYGONALES

This order consists of only one family, viz., Polygonaceae and is placed next to **Aristolichiales** by Engler. In Engler and Prantls's system as well as in Rundle's system it is followed by the order **Centrospermae,** i.e., **Caryophyllales** of other taxonomists. Hutchinson includes **Polygonales** in his subclass **Herbaceae** and places it after **Caryophyllales.** Besides *Polygonaceae* he includes *Illecebraceae* in **Polygonales.** Takahtajan places this order under subclass **Caryophyllidae** next to **Caryophyllales.** Cronquist agrees to this treatment and traces its origin from **Caryophyllales.**

Polygonaceae

Plants are herbaceous or shrubby, rarely climbing plants or trees are met with; stem usually with swollen nodes. Leaves simple, alternate, entire, stipulate; stipules ochreate. Inflorescence is usually a raceme often forming a panicle, rarely the inflorescence is cymose or the flowers are in clusters. Flowers usually bisexual, regular, usually with 2 whorls of perianth, hypogynous or perigynous; bracts and bracteoles usually present. Perianth members 3 or 2 in each whorl or rarely 5 and more or less spirally arranged, persistent, free and imbricate or connate; usually sepaloid and similar or rarely with distinct calyx and corolla. Stamens 6-9 or less, in 2 whorls or in

1 whorl due to the suppression of the inner whorl, each of the outer whorl of stamens often doubles itself; stamens free or united; nectaries often present. Carpels 2-3, uniting to form a syncarpous, superior, 1-celled ovary with a single basal orthotropous ovule; ovary biconvex or triangular; styles 2-3, free; stigma capitate or fringed. Fruit a trigonous or ovoid nutlet enclosed by the persistent and often-enlarged perianth; seed with copious starchy endosperm and a laterally placed straight or curved embryo; endosperm often ruminate.

The plants of this family show great variation in vegetative as well as floristic characters. Most plants are herbs or shrubs but *Coccoloba* are trees; *Antigonon leptopus* Endl. and a few species of Polygonum are climbers or twiners. In *Antigonon* the upper branches of the panicle are bare of flowers and act as tendrils. *Muehlenbeckia platycados* Meissn is a shrub having stem and branches transformed into flat phylloclades bearing small leaves. Ochreate stipules are present in many genera but absent in *Erigonum*, *Antigonon* etc.

Flowers are bisexual but in *Triplaris* and some species of *Rumex* these are unisexual. Usually the flowers are trimerous but dimerous in *Oxyria* and *Rumex*. Doubling of the

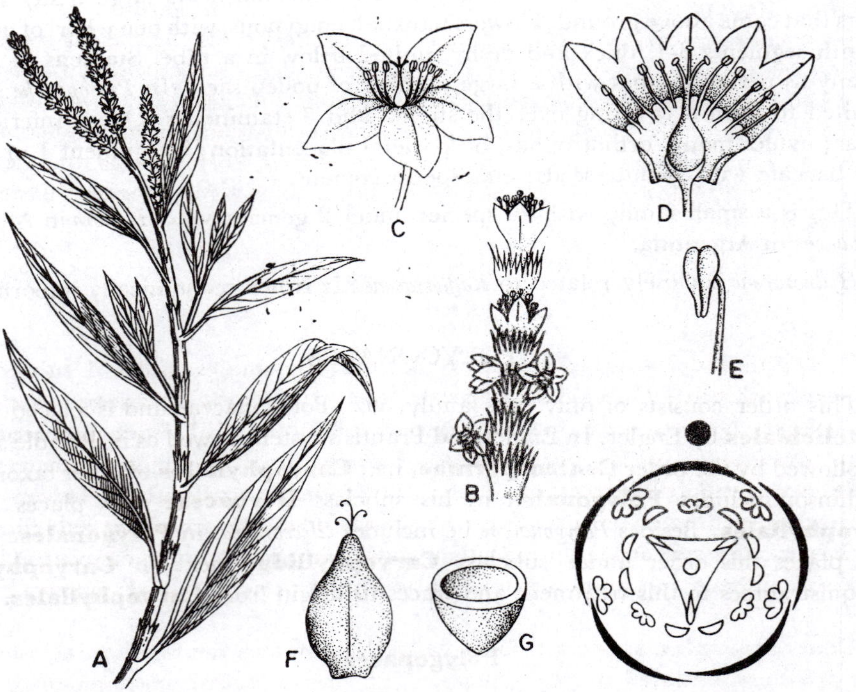

Fig. 57. Polygonum orientale Linn. A—A leafy twig with terminal raceme ($\times \frac{1}{8}$). B—Portion of spike; C—Flower with one whorl of perianth, stamens and ovary ($\times$ 15). D—Same with perianth split open. E—Stamen. F—Ovary. G—L. s. of same.

outer whorl of stamens takes place in many species while partial or complete suppression of stamens of the inner whorl is also noticed. Perianth is in 2 whorls but in *Koenigia* the inner whorl is absent. *Fagopyrum* has dimorphic flowers with long stamens and short styles and short stamens and long styles. Endosperm is ruminate in the seeds of *Coccoloba*, *Muehlenbeckia*, etc. but usually it is not ruminate in other genera.

Pollination is usually done by insects that come in search of nectar and also by wind where the stigma is brush-like.

The family consists of about 40 genera and about 750 species occurring mostly in the temperate region of Northern Hemisphere while a quite fair number occurs also in the tropical countries and some reaching north as far as the Arctic regions. In India many species of *Polygonum* are found in the plains, e.g., *P. orientale* Linn., *P. barbatum* Linn., *P. plebeium* R. Br. etc. and P. molle D. Don., *P. chinensis*, *P. runcinatum* Buch. Ham. etc. are in the hills. *Fagopyrum*, *Rumex*, *Rheum*, *Calligonum* are other genera having Indian species. *Antigonon leptopus* Endl. is commonly cultivated in gardens for its pink or white flowers.

Plants of economic importance in this family are few. *Rheum* species are the Rhubarb, the long succulent petioles of which are taken as vegetables. *R. emodi* Wall. of the Himalayas, *R. officinalis* Baill, *R. rhaponticum* Linn. of Europe, *R. palmatum* of Central Asia have medicinal properties. *Rumex vesicarius* Linn. is cultivated in India for the acid leaves which are used as pot-herbs. *Coccoloba uvifera* Linn. produces edible fruits. Besides *Antigonon*, *Muchlenbeckia platyclados* Meiss. is cultivated in gardens as a curiosity. *Fagopyrum esculentum* Moench. is the Buck-wheat cultivated for the starchy seeds.

Polygonaceae is allied to the families *Amaranthaceae*, *Chenopodiaceae*, *Caryophyllaceae*, etc. of **Caryophyllales** or **Centrospermae.** Hutchinson considers that Polygonaceae and the families under **Caryophyllales** were derived from a common ancestor which originated from **Ranales.** Most taxonomists agree that **Polygonales** and **Caryophyllales** are closely related and Bessey and Hallier included Polygonaceae under Caryophyllales.

CENTROSPERMAE

(Caryophyllales)

The 20th order **Centrospermae** includes 10 families under 4 suborders, viz. (i) **Chenopodiinae**—*Chenopodiaceae Amaranthaceae*, (ii) **Phytolaccineae**—*Nyctaginaceae*, *Phytolaccaceae*, *Gyrostemonaceae*, *Achatocarpaceae*, *Aizoaceae*, (iii) **Portulacineae**—*Portulacaceae*, *Basellaceae*, (iv) **Caryophyllinae**—*Caryophyllaceae*. Common characters in these families are—usually herbaceous plants; leaves simple, exstipulate; flowers bisexual or unisexual, pentamerous; perianth of 2 whorls or of one whorl by reduction; ovary superior, usually syncarpous, unilocular; ovules campylotropous on central placenta and with 2 integuments and long funicle; perisperm present in seed; embryo curved or coiled.

Centrospermae appears to be a natural taxon and the families included in this order are closely related to one another. The embryological development is similar; ovules campylotropous or amphitropous with 2 integuments, the inner being longer than the outer with space between them on the chalazal end and large nucellus; the curved embryo is peripheral and surrounds the perisperm. Almost all taxonomists therefore agree that the families included in **Centrospermae** by Engler constitute a natural group and have originated from a common ancestor. The families *Achatocarpaceae* and *Gyrostemonaceae* are merged by many with *Phytolaccaceae*.

Phytolaccaceae is considered as the most primitive among these families and from this the other families originated. Rendle shows the connections between the families diagrammatically in the following manner:—

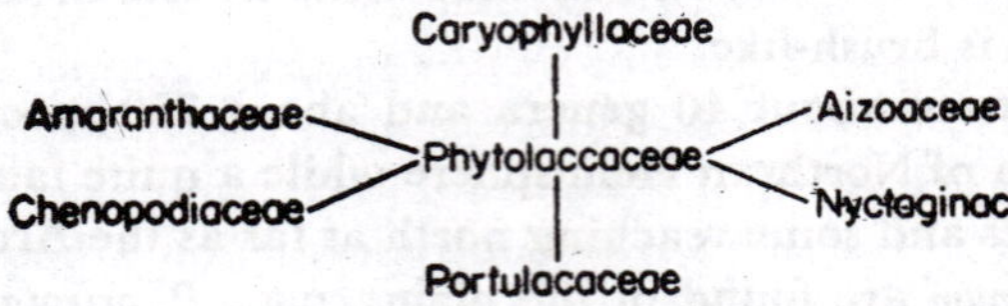

Cronquist who includes *Cactaceae* and *Didiriaceae* also in this order supports Rendle in tracing this relationship among the families of **Caryophyllales (Centrospermae).** According to him *Amaranthaceae* has been derived from *Phytolaccaceae* through *Chenopodiaceae* which like all the other families have been derived directly from *Phytolaccaceae.* The relationship is shown by Cronquist in the following diagram:—

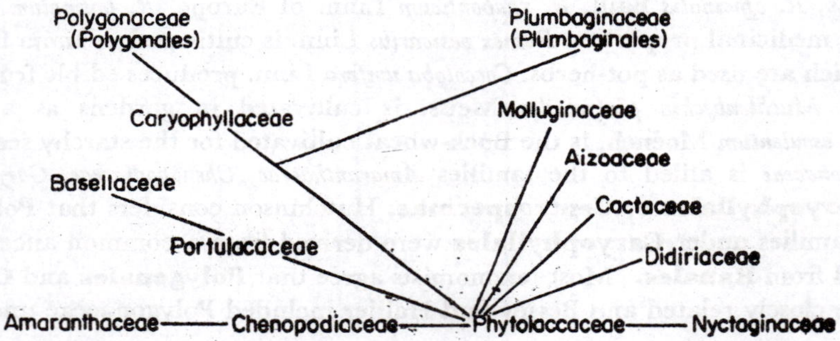

Cronquist splits *Aizoaceae* to *Aizoaceae* and *Molluginaceae.* He considers **Polygonales** with the single family *Polygonaceae* has been derived from *Caryophyllaceae* and **Plumbaginales** with single family *Plumbaginaceae* originated from a stock intermediate between *Caryophyllaceae* and *Phytolaccaceae.*

The relation was shown in a different way by Pax and Hoffmann in Pflanzenfamilien. This is given below—

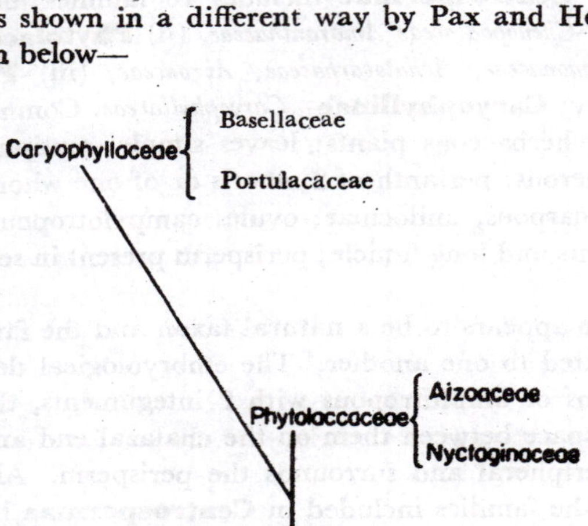

According to them *Chenopodiaceae* with the closely associated *Amaranthaceae* represents the origin of the group.

Hutchinson splits the order into 2, viz., **Caryophyllales** and **Chenopodiales.** According to him *Chenopodiaceae*, *Amaranthaceae*, *Phytolaccaceae*, *Gyrostemonaceae*, and *Basellaceae* together with *Barbeuiacede*, *Agdestidaceae*, *Petiveriaceae*, *Cynocrambaceae* and *Batidaceae* consistuting Chenopodiales are more advanced families and originated from **Caryophyllales** while the families included under **Caryophyllales** as well as the family *Polygonaceae* were derived from **Ranales.** He therefore places **Polygonales** with *Polygonaceae* and *Illecebraceae* between **Caryophyllales** and **Chenopodiales.** Further he brings *Nyctaginaceae* in **Thymelaeales** under **Lignosae.**

Hallier, Bessey, Takhtajan and many others also consider that **Caryophyllales** has originated directly from the **Ranales.** Takhtajan includes quite a number of families in his **Caryophyllales.** He says *Phytolaccaceae* is the most primitive among these families and is more closely related to the **Ranales** than other families of the order. In *Phytolaccaceae* the pollen is tricolpate, granular on the central part of the membrane of the furrow and the extine is thin as are met with in the **Ranales.** The bent embryo and the polycambial structure of the stem of many families in **Caryophyllales** bring them closer to *Menispermaceae* of the Ranales. Apocarpus gynoecium in some members of *Phytolaccaceae* and presence of perisperm also show a relationship between the **Ranales** and **Caryophyllales.**

Chenopodiaceae

Annual or perennial herbs or shrubs, very rarely trees, often with swollen nodes, glabrous or "mealy" (covered with small hairs with a large terminal cell that readily falls off). Leaves simple, exstipulate, often thick and fleshy, glabrous or "mealy", alternate or rarely opposite, entire or variously lobed. Inflorescence is a mixed panicle, small cymes arranged in racemes or spikes or often a thyrsus. Flowers small and inconspicuous, bisexual or unisexual, usually regular, bracteate and bracteolate or without bracts and bracteoles. Perianth of 5 or less segments in one whorl, sepaloid, persistent, free or connate. Stamens as many as perianth segments and opposite to them; anthers 2-celled; pollens spherical and with numerous spores; filaments often connate at base; often stamens less; rarely a whorl of staminodes also present. Ovary superior, rarely inferior, of 3-2 carpels, syncarpous, unilocular; ovule one, basal; style usually one, rarely 2 or 3 and free; stigma capitate or 2-3-lobed. Fruit a nut or a utricle usually enclosed by the persistent perianth, rarely dehiscing transversely. Seed with powdery perisperm and curved or coiled embryo.

Floral formula of the usual type of flowers is: $\oplus$ ⚥ $P_{(5)}\ A_{(5)}\ G_{(\underline{2-3})}$ but deviation from the type occurs. In *Halocnemum*, *Alexandra* and *Crorispermum* flowers are irregular, the perianth segments being of different shape and size. *Artiplex*, *Spinacea*, *Sarcobatus*, *Garrya* etc. have unisexual flowers. The female flower of *Artiplex* have no perianth but have 2 bracteoles which enlarge and completely cover the fruit. Some authors consider these as 2 perianth segments and not bracteoles. In male flowers of *Sarcobatus maximiliani* Nees perianth is wanting and a single perianth segment is present in *Monolepis* where there is only one stamen.

Some plants are succulents and the jointed stems are almost leafless. In *Salicornia* the leaves are very small, sheath-like and connate. These are often terete e.g. *Suaeda*, linear-lanceolate in *Kochia*. *Kochia indica* Linn. is a tall erect annual up to 2 mtr. high, *Chenopodium album* Linn. also is tall and erect while *Haloxylon ammodendron* Bunge of the Central Asian steppes is a small tree attaining 6-7 mtrs. in height.

Anomalous secondary growth is a characteristic feature in the family. Secondary cambium develops in the pericycle or rarely in phloem and due to its activity concentric zones of scattered collateral vascular bundles are formed.

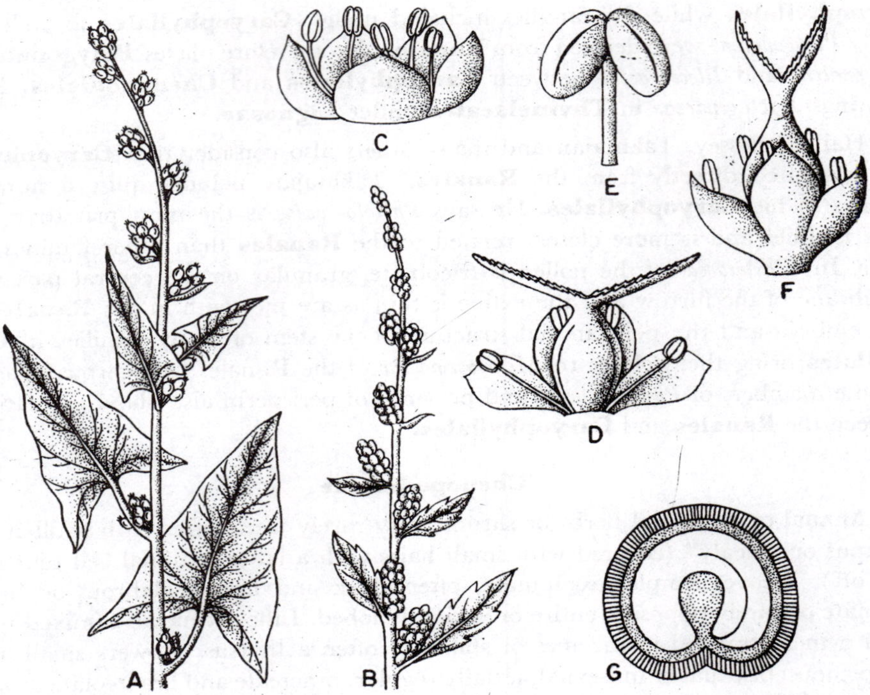

Fig. 58. Chenopodium album Linn. A—Flowering shoot with clusters of flowers. B—Same with different type of leaves. C—Male flower. D—Bisexual flower. E—Stamen. F—Female flower. G—T. s. of seed with embryo (C, D, E, F, G much enlarged).

The family consists of about 105 genera and 1,500 species, distributed almost all over the globe especially on saline tracts. Most of them are halophytes or xerophytes. The mealy hairs of many species have the capacity of storing water. In *Artiplex* the dense coat of hairs store enough water in the rains to prevent desiccation in the prolonged dry season. In India a few species are met with in the Sundriban forests, viz. *Suaeda maritima* Dumort, *Arthrocnemum indicum* Moq., *Salicornia brachiata* Roxb. etc. *Chenopodium album* Linn. and *Ch. ambrosioides* Linn. are common almost all over the country and the former is often cultivated. *Suaeda fruticosa* (*L*) Forsk. *Atriplex crassifolia* C. A. Mey, *Salicornia herbacea* Linn. grow in saline and arid regions of N. India. *Acroglochin chenopodioides* Schrad. and *Chenopodium botrys* Linn. occur in the Himalayas above 2000 mtrs.

Of those species of the family economically important *Beta vulgaris* Linn. the Beet root is cultivated on a large scale in temperate countries for manufacture of sugar. It is also cultivated in other countries for the tuberlike taproot which is used as vegetable or in salad. *Chenopodium anthelminticum* Linn. yields "Oil of Chenopod" having medicinal value. *Ch.. quino* Linn. of the hills of Peru produces starchy seeds used as a substitute of rice. The tender parts of *Chenopodium album* Linn., *Spinacea oleraceae* Linn. and a few others are used as pot-herbs. The Palang or Palki is a variety of *Beta vulgaris*

Linn. *Kochia scoparia* Schr. and *K. trichophylla* Voss. are cultivated in gardens as ornamental plants.

Among other families of the order Centrospermae this family is closely allied to *Amaranthaceae* and *Phytolaccaceae*.

Amaranthaceae

Predominantly annual or perennial herbs, rarely shrubs, either erect or scandent. Leaves simple, exstipulate, alternate or opposite, usually entire. Inflorescence is a dense simple or branched spike or raceme, sometimes a dichasial cluster. Flowers small, regular, hermaphrodite or rarely unisexual or polygamous, with a scarious bract and a pair of persistent bracteoles; the anatomy of the bracteoles show that these are nothing but the metamorphosed lateral flowers of a biparous cyme. Perianth of single whorl, segments 3-5, free or connate at base, imbricate, persistent, dry and membranous, scarious or sepaline, often coloured. Stamens usually 5, opposite to

Fig. 59. Achyranthes aspera Linn. A—Branch with leaves and flowering spikes ($\times\frac{1}{2}$). B—Flower with bracteoles ($\times 4$). C—Same showing stamens and pistil. D—Androecium with stamens and alternating fimbriate scales. E—Ovary. F—Fruit.

perianth segments, free or united partially or completely into a tube, often with fringed or lobed outgrowths between 2 filaments; anthers 4-celled or 2-celled, dehiscing by vertical slits; often staminodes are present. Ovary of 2-3 carpels, syncarpous, unilocular, superior; ovule solitary, basal, campylotropous, rarely ovules several; styles 1-3; stigmas various. Fruit a nutlet or utricle, rarely a capsule dehiscing irregularly or transversely by a lid, enclosed by persistent perianth and bracteoles; very rarely the fruit is a drupe or a berry. Seed with a shining or rough testa, small and lenticular, with a horse-shoe shaped or annular embryo surrounding copious mealy endosperm.

Deeringia amaranthoides (Lamk.) Merrill is a climbing shrub with long branches hanging from the supporting trees. Branching is often trichotomous, e.g. *Pupalia, Psilotrichum.* Leaves often coloured or mottled. Spines rarely present in leaf-axils; bracts and bracteoles often spinescent at the tip. Sometimes the lateral flowers in a cluster are abortive and are replaced by spiny outgrowths. These persist in fruit and help in distribution by animals, e.g. *Achyranthes.*

Anomalous secondary growth occurs similar to *Chenopodiaceae* in the formation of collateral vascular bundles from cambium in the pericycle. The fascicular cambium is functionless in the scattered vascular bundles.

The family consists of about 800 species in 72 genera distributed mainly in tropical countries of the world. It is represented in India by several species of *Amaranthus, Achyranthus aspera* Linn. *Aerva lanata* Juss., *Pupalia atropurpurea* Moq. etc. *Celosia cristata* Linn. the Cock's Comb and *Gomphrena globosa* Linn. the Globe Amaranth are garden favourites, and *Alternanthera versicolor* Regel is planted as a border plant in flowerbeds. *Achyranthes aspera* Linn. is reputed to have medicinal value and much used by Indian Vaidyas. *Amaranthus tricolor* Linn. and its varieties are much used as pot herbs and the tall herb *A. caudatus* Linn. is also used in the same manner and the seeds are eaten as substitute of rice.

Amaranthaceae is allied to the other families of **Centrospermae** and particularly to *Chenopodiaceae* from which it differs in having flowers very densely arranged in the inflorescence, bracts and bracteoles scarious, perianth membranous and shining and filaments of stamens usually connate.

Nyctaginaceae

Perennial herbs or shrubs often scandent, rarely attaining great size. Leaves simple, exstipulate, opposite or rarely alternate, often one of the opposite pair smaller than the other. Inflorescence is usually a panicle of biparous cymes often becoming uniparous in the upper part due to suppression of branches on one side; bracts usually forming an involucre. Flowers hermaphrodite, rarely unisexual, actinomorphic, with one whorl of perianth. Perianth segments 4-5, usually petaloid, connate, infundibuliform or tubular; lobes imbricate or contorted; the base of the perianth tube is persistent while the upper part withers and gets detached. Stamens 2-20, more often 5-8; filaments unequal. Ovary monocarpellary, unilocular, superior, with one basal campylotropous ovule; style usually long. Fruit an achene enclosed by the persistent perianth-base—the anthocarp. Seed with a thin testa, with perisperm and curved embryo; cotyledons broad, foliacious and unequal.

Bougainvillea are lianes; here 3 flowers are found in a cluster each subtended by a coloured bract of the involucre, the terminal flower is wanting. *Pisonia spp.* are shrubs or trees, the bracts of the involucre here are reduced to small teeth; the seeds have straight embryo. In *Mirabilis* the 5-partite involucre is sepaloid and subtends one or more flowers. In *Neea* the fruit is a pseudo-drupe, the persistent portion of the perianth becoming fleshy.

Abnormal secondary growth in the stem is also met with in this family and the vascular bundles are scattered. Calcium oxalate crystals are found in the cells in almost all parts of the plants.

The family contains about 30 genera and about 300 species confined to the warmer parts of the world the majority being tropical American. Only a few are economically important. *Neea theifera* Oerst. of Brazil is used as a substitute of tea. *Boerhaavia repens* Linn. the "Punarnaba" of the Indian Kabirajas is reputed to have medicinal properties. *Mirabilis jalapa* Linn. the Four-o-clock plant and *Bongainvillea spectabilis* Willd. are much cultivated in gardens as ornamental plants.

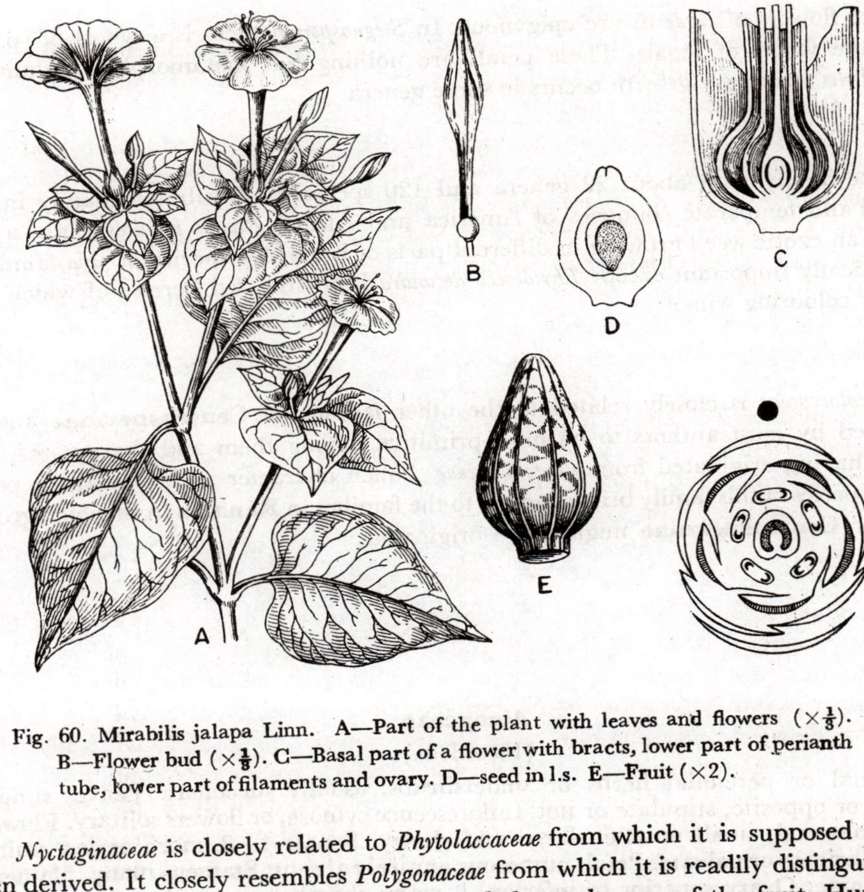

Fig. 60. Mirabilis jalapa Linn. A—Part of the plant with leaves and flowers ($\times\frac{1}{3}$). B—Flower bud ($\times\frac{1}{3}$). C—Basal part of a flower with bracts, lower part of perianth tube, lower part of filaments and ovary. D—seed in l.s. E—Fruit ($\times 2$).

Nyctaginaceae is closely related to *Phytolaccaceae* from which it is supposed to have been derived. It closely resembles *Polygonaceae* from which it is readily distinguished by the involucre of bracts, unilocular ovary and the anthocarp of the fruit. Hutchinson removes *Nyctaginaceae* from **Centrospermae** and assigns it a position after *Thymeleaceae* in **Thymeleales** under **Lignosae** but this treatment has not been approved by other workers.

Phytolaccaceae

Mostly herbs or shrubs, often climbing rarely trees. Leaves simple, alternate, exstipulate or with minute stipules. Inflorescence is a raceme or spike, usually terminal but often appearing axillary due to the vigorous growth of a branch from the base of the inflorescence; rarely the inflorescence is cymose. Flowers small, bisexual or rarely unisexual, regular, with one whorl of perianth. Perianth segments 4-5, connate or free, imbricate, sepaline or coloured. Stamens as many as perianth segments and opposite or alternate to them, filaments free or connate near base; often stamens more and in 2 whorls, rarely only 3; sometimes *chorisis* or splitting of stamens occurs and the number is much increased. Carpels one or several, free or syncarpous; ovary superior, uni- or multilocular, with one basal ovule in each cell; styles free. Fruit various, a nut or utricle, capsule or berry or drupe or often a schizocarp; seed with a curved peripheral embryo surrounding the powdery perisperm.

The flowers of *Agdestis* are epigynous. In *Stegnosperma* there is a whorl of petals above the whorl of sepals. These petals are nothing but metamorphosed stamens. Anomalous secondary growth occurs in some genera.

The family with about 22 genera and 120 species is distributed mainly in the tropical and temperate countries of America and Africa. *Rivina humiles* Linn. a tall herb is an exotic weed growing in different parts of India. No species of this family is economically important except *Phytolacca decandra* Linn. the red berries of which are used for colouring wine.

Phytolaccaceae is closely related to the other families of **Centrospermae** and is considered by most authors to be most primitive among them and the rest of the families having originated from *Phytolaccaceae*. Pollen character and apocarpous pistil in some species of this family brings it close to the families in **Ranales** from which group the order **Centrospermae** might have originated.

Aizoaceae

(Ficoideae)

Annual or perennial herbs or undershrubs, usually succulent. Leaves simple, alternate or opposite, stipulate or not. Inflorescence cymose, or flowers solitary. Flowers regular, bisexual, small or often large and showy. Sepals 4—8, more or less united below, imbricate or valvate. Petals numerous or rarely absent. Stamens many, filaments often connate. Ovary superior or inferior, 1-many chambered; ovules many in each chamber, axile or parietal; stigma 1-many. Fruit capsule, berry or nut. Seeds many; embryo curved, surrounding a mealy endosperm.

Some plants have succulent roots or caudices. Large watery cells rich in sugar cover the xerophytic plants. Calcium oxalate crystals are often present in epidermal cells. In some plants, e.g. *Lithos* species the leaves are somewhat hemispheric in shape and look like pebbles. These grow in rocky areas and resemble small stones scattered on the rocks. In some cases only one pair of leaves appear in a year.

The petals are staminodial in origin. The capsule are often hygroscopic the valves opening when wetted.

In *Mesembryanthemum* the ovary behaves peculiarly. The ovules are borne on axile placentas at first but subsequently the placentation becomes parietal.

Aizoaceae is a large family containing over 2,000 species, majority of which are found on the sandy tracts of S. Africa and a few in Europe, America, S. E. Asia and the South Seas. Common Indian species are: *Trianthema portulacastrum* Linn., *Mollugo spergula* Linn., *Sesuvium portulacastrum* Linn., etc.

The family is closely related to Phytolaccaceae, Portulacaceae, Chenopodiaceae and Caryophyllacae, and is considered to have been derived from Phytolaccaceae.

Many species of Aizoaceae are cultivated as ornamental plants, otherwise the family is of little economic importance. *Tetragonia expansa* Murr.—the New Zealand spinach is cultivated as potherb. *Trianthema portulacastrum* is also used as a potherb and is said to have medicinal value.

Portulaccaceae

Succulent herbs or undershrubs; calcium oxalate crystals present in the cells. Leaves simple, opposite or alternate, usually stipulate; stipules scarious or bristle-like, often stipules absent (*Claytonia*). Flowers may be solitary but usually in racemose or

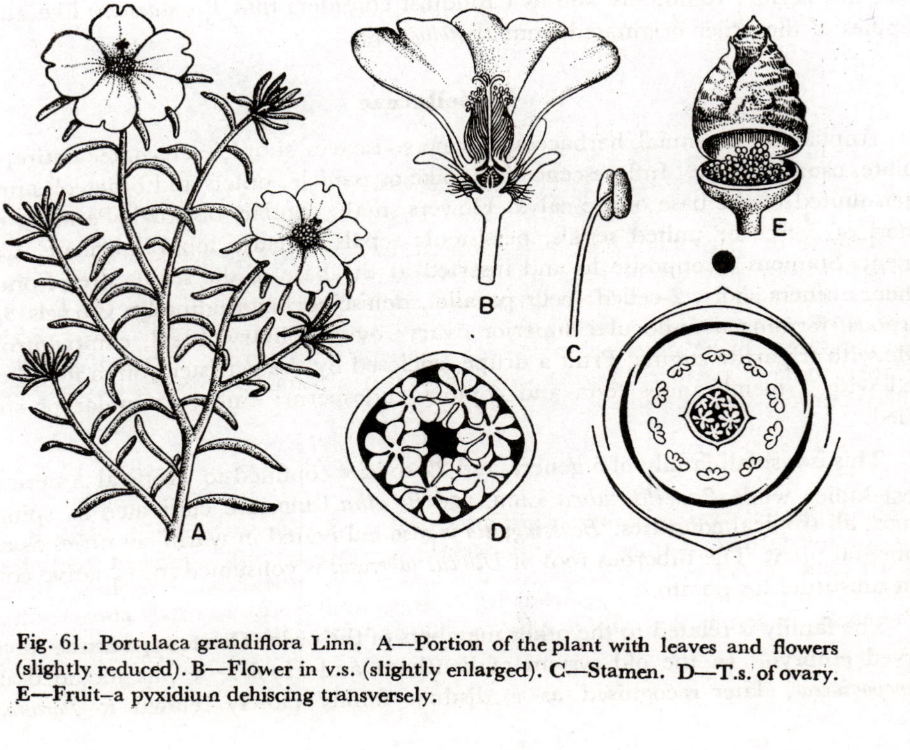

Fig. 61. Portulaca grandiflora Linn. A—Portion of the plant with leaves and flowers (slightly reduced). B—Flower in v.s. (slightly enlarged). C—Stamen. D—T.s. of ovary. E—Fruit–a pyxidiuın dehiscing transversely.

cymose inflorescence, regular and hermaphrodite, hypogynous or slightly perigynous, with 2 whorls of perianth. Sepals 2, anteroposterior, imbricate. Petals 4-6, rarely 2 or 3, distinct or connate below. Stamens as many as petals and adnate to them at base, rarely stamens 3, sometimes double the number of petals as a result of splitting; anthers 2-celled, introrse, dehiscing longitudinally. Carpels 2-5, syncarpous; ovary superior or semi-inferior, unilocular; ovules 2-∞ on free central placenta, campylotropous; funicle long and slender; styles 2-5. Fruit a capsule, dehiscing circumscissilely or by 2-5 apical valves; rarely fruit is a nut. Seed compressed, with a much curved embryo surrounding a mealy perisperm.

There is difference of opinion as regards the morphology of the perianth. According to some authors the perianth is uniseriate and the outer whorl is nothing but an involucre of bracts and not calyx and the apparent corolla is a perigone composed of sepals. Pax & Hoffmann and Warming are among others who are the supporters of this view.

Floral formula of a typical flower may be shown as:—$\oplus$ ⚥ $K_2C_{4-6}\ A_{4-6}\ G_{\underline{(2-5)}}$.

The family comprises 19 genera and 500 species found in tropical and temperate countries but more in America and S. Africa. *Portulaca oleracea* Linn. and *P. quadrifolia* Linn. are common weeds all over India in the plains. The former is often used as a pot herb. *P. grandiflora* Linn. is much cultivated in gardens for the showy flowers. Species of *Talinum* and *Calandrina* are also cultivated as ornamental plants. No other species is of any economic importance.

The family is allied to the other families of **Centrospermae** but more so to *Baselaceae*. It is allied to *Caryophyllaceae* and according to Pax and Hoffmann was derived from this family. Rendle as well as Cronquist considers that *Portulacaceae* like all other families of the order originated from *Phytolaccaceae*.

Basellaceae

Annual or perennial herbaceous twiners. Leaves simple, alternate, entire, exstipulate, usually fleshy. Inflorescence is a spike or panicle, bracts and bracteoles present, often united to the base of the calyx. Flowers small, regular, bisexual. Perianth of one whorl of 5 free or united sepals, persistent; sepals or calyx lobes imbricate. Corolla absent. Stamens 5, opposite to and inserted at the base of the sepals, free from each other; anthers short, 2-celled; cells parallel, dehiscing longitudinally. Carpels 3, syncarpous, forming a unilocular superior ovary; ovule solitary, basal, campylotropous; style with tripartite stigma. Fruit a drupe, enclosed by the persistent often fleshy calyx; seed with a membranous testa and copious endosperm; embryo annular or spirally rolled.

This is a small family of 5 genera and 22 species confined to Tropical America and West Indies while *Basella rubra* Linn. and *B. alba* Linn. are cultivated as spinach in almost all tropical countries. *Boussingultia* is also cultivated in warm countries as an ornamental plant. The tuberous root of *Ullucus tuberosus* is consumed in its native country as a substitute for potato.

The family is related to the other members of the order **Centrospermae** having a curved embryo. In the old system of Bentham and Hooker it was included under *Chenopodiaceae*, later recognised as a distinct family closely related to *Portulacaceae* originating either from *Caryophyllaceae* or from *Phytolaccaceae*. Hutchinson, however, places *Basellaceae* under his **Chenopodiales** while *Portulacaceae* is included in his **Caryophyllales.**

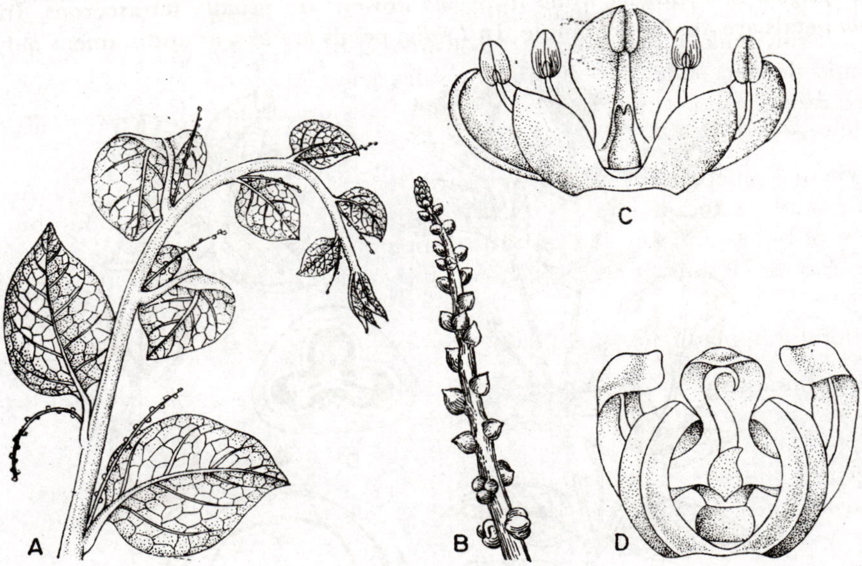

Fig. 62. Basella rubra Linn. A—Leafy branch with spikes (×¼). B—Portion of spike with flowers (×½). C—Male flower. D—Female flower. (C & D much enlarged).

Caryophyllaceae

Generally herbaceous plants or undershrubs; branching is of biparous cymose type; nodes often swollen. Leaves simple, opposite and decussate, rarely alternate; stipules often present, scarious or membranous; usually one leaf of a pair develops earlier and has a more vigorous bud in the axil giving rise to a branch while the axillary bud of the other leaf does not develop into a branch; the close scale-like leaves of *Pycnophyllum* gives the plant a "Lycopodium"—like appearance. Inflorescence is generally a biparous cyme the ultimate branches of which pass into scorpioid cymes; flowers are rarely solitary (*Githago*); bracts present subtending the branches of the inflorescence. Flowers actinomorphic, hermaphrodite or unisexual by reduction, hypogynous or perigynous, 5-merous or 4-merous. Perianth in 2 whorls with distinct calyx and corolla, rarely corolla absent. Sepals persistent, free or connate, imbricate, often scarious. Petals free often clawed, valvate; the receptacle between corolla and androecium is often elongated. Stamens in 2 whorls, 4-5 in each whorl, often fewer; staminodes sometimes present; anthers 2-celled, dehiscing longitudinally; disc annular or a whorl of glands, or often elongated in the form of a gynophore; nectaries present at the base of outer stamens or concealed at the base of calyx tube. Carpels 2-5, united to form a syncarpous superior ovary; ovary often stipitate, unilocular or multilocular below; styles free or united below; ovules curved, 1-many on basal or central placenta. The fruit is a nut or achene, or capsule opening by apical valves or teeth as many as or double the number of carpels; rarely the fruit is a berry; seed with a curved embryo and mealy endosperm; rarely embryo is straight.

Floral formula of a typical flower is $\oplus$ ⚥ $K_5C_5A_{5+5}G_{(5)}$, where there are 2 whorls of perianth, 2 whorls of stamens and the pistil, and 5 members in each whorl; instead of 5 there may be 4 members in each whorl, i.e. flowers may be pentamerous as in *Spergula* or *Cerastium* while in *Sagina* flowers are usually tetramerous. In *Sagina apetala* petals are absent or minute. In *Lyallia* petals are absent and stamens only 3. In

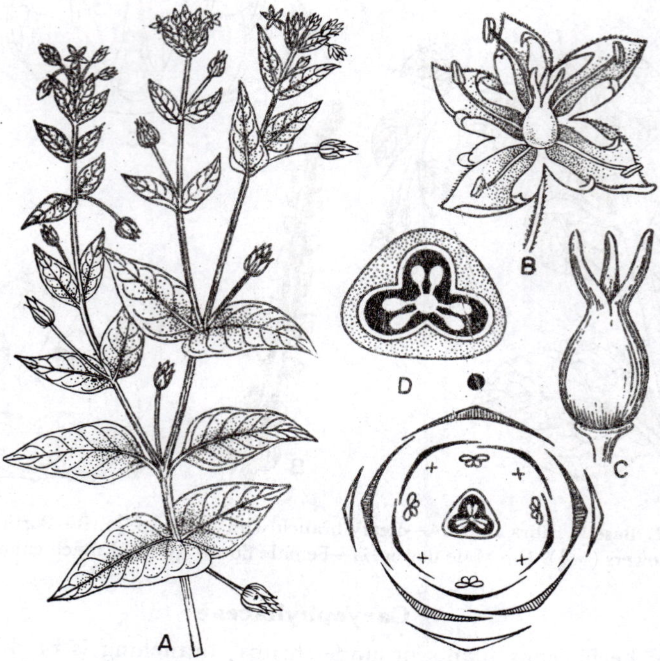

Fig. 63. Stellaria media Linn. A—Part of the plant with leaves and flowers (×½). B—flowers showing 2-partite petals (×5). C—Ovary (×6). D—T. s. of same.

Drymaria, *Polycarpon* and *Polycarpaea* stamens are in one whorl, 5 or less. Sepals are free in the subfamily **Alsinoideae** but united in a tube in **Caryophylloideae.** In this subfamily usually a corona is present. In *Pteranthus* the lateral flowers of a cluster of 3 are more or less abortive. Fruit is generally capsular but a nut in *Paronychia*, *Herniaria*, etc. and a berry in *Cucubalus*. Embryo is curved in all the genera but straight in *Dianthus*.

Where there are 2 whorls of stamens present obdiplostemonous condition is noticed. But this obdiplostemony is not true but apparent as has been proved by the study of floral anatomy. It is the result of pushing out of the inner stamens towards outside. Anomalous secondary growth occurs in a few genera of this family in the formation of more than one ring of vascular bundles. The nature of stomata is very characteristic in this family. Each stoma has two subsidiary cells with transverse common wall, i.e. the common wall is at right angles to the guard cell. This type of stomata is the diacyclic type, also known as the Caryophyllaceous type.

The family consists of about 70 genera and about 1,750 species and are found to grow in almost all parts of the world but more in the Mediterranean region where there are several endermic genera. In India there are several species in the plains as well as in the hills. *Polycarpon loeflingiae* Benth. & Hook. f., *Stellaria media Linn.*, *Saponaria vaccaria* Linn. *Polycarpaea corymbosa* Lamk. are quite common in the plains while *Spergula arvensis* Linn., *Drymaria diandra* Bl. etc. in the hills. Several species of *Arenaria* occur in the Himalayas and a few in the alpine region which form a dense cushion. *Lyallia* is found above 3000 mtr. altitude.

Most plants of this family are of no economic importance except a few species of *Saponaria* which contain saponin in the roots. Some genera have beautiful flowers and

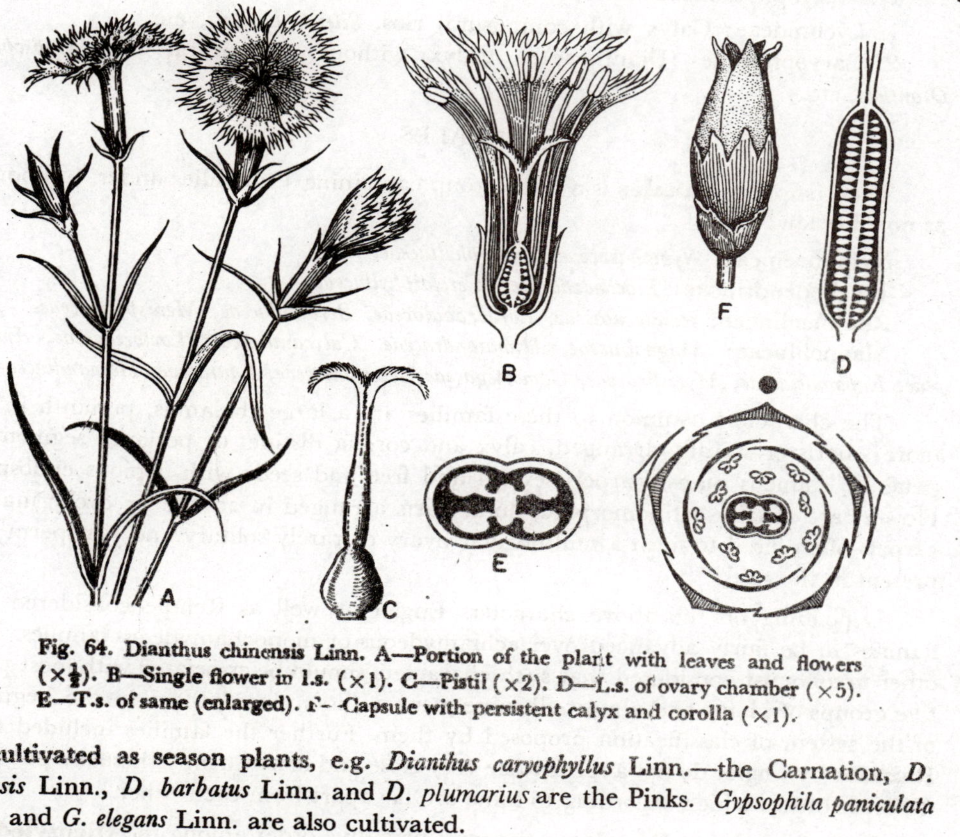

Fig. 64. Dianthus chinensis Linn. A—Portion of the plant with leaves and flowers (×½). B—Single flower in l.s. (×1). C—Pistil (×2). D—L.s. of ovary chamber (×5). E—T.s. of same (enlarged). F—Capsule with persistent calyx and corolla (×1).

are cultivated as season plants, e.g. *Dianthus caryophyllus* Linn.—the Carnation, *D. chinensis* Linn., *D. barbatus* Linn. and *D. plumarius* are the Pinks. *Gypsophila paniculata* Linn. and *G. elegans* Linn. are also cultivated.

The family is related to the other families of the order **Centrospermae** all having curved embryo and perisperm in the seeds. Eichler considered that *Caryophyllaceae* originated from *Phytolaccaceae* and this view is supported by Pax, Wettstein and Rendle. Wernham expressed the opinion that this family was derived from a Ranalian stock and most authors agree to this view. Hutchinson splits this family into *Caryophyllaceae* and *Illecebraceae* and places the latter with *Polygonaceae* in **Polygonales** but this treatment has not met with the approval of others.

The family is subdivided by Pax into 2 tribes and 8 subtribes as shown below:

I. Alsinoideae: Flowers polysepalous, often perigynous.

(a) Fruit capsule—

1. Alsineae: Styles free to the base, leaves exstipulate. *Stellaria*, *Cerastium Sagina*, *Arenaria*, etc.

2. Sperguleae: Styles free to the base, leaves stipulate, *Spergula, Spergularia etc.*
3. Polycarpeae: Style united near base, *Drymaria, Polycarpon,* etc.

(b) Fruit achene or nut–

4. Pornychieae: Flowers all alike, leaves stipulate *Corrigiola, Pornychia, Illecebrum, Hermiaria,* etc.
5. Sclerantheae: Flowers all alike, leaves exstipulate *Scleranthus,* etc.
6. Pterantheae: Flowers in clusters of 3, the 2 laterals ± abortive, *Pteranthus.*

II. Caryophylloideae (Silenoideae): Flowers gamosepalous, hypogynous.

1. Lychnideae: Calyx with commisural ribs, *Silene, Lychnis,* etc.
2. Caryophylleae (Diantheae): Calyx without commisural ribs, *Gypsophila, Dianthus,* etc.

RANALES

The 21st order **Ranales** is a large group containing 19 families under 4 suborders as noted below:

Nymphaeineae: *Nymphaeaceae, Ceratophyllaceae.*

Trochodendrineae: *Trochodendraceae Cercidiphyllaceae.*

Ranunculineae: *Ranunculaceae, Lardizabalaceae, Berberidaceae, Menispermaceae.*

Magnoliineae: *Magnoliaceae, Himatandraceae, Calycanthaceae, Lactoridaceae, Annonaceae, Eupomatiaceae, Myristicaceae, Gomortegaceae, Monimiaceae, Lauraceae, Hernandiaceae.*

The characters common to these families are a large thalamus, perianth in 2 or more whorls or spirally arranged, calyx and corolla distinct or perianth segments all petaloid, stamens many, carpels several and free and seeds with copious endosperm. Flowers are usually actinomorphic, floral parts arranged in acyclic or cyclic manner, carpels often fused to form a multilocular ovary or rarely solitary and perisperm often present in the seed.

Depending on the above characters Engler as well as Rendle considered these families to be fairly advanced over achlamydeous or monochamydeous families. Later other taxonomist considered that such characters should be associated with most primitive groups of plants and almost all subsequent authors placed them in the beginning of the system of classification proposed by them. Further the families included under **Ranales** by Engler do not appear to be very close and consequently these are put under different orders which according to some are far apart from each other.

Bessey stated that **Ranales** is the most primitive order among the **Dicotyledonae** and placed the order at the beginning of this group. He merged **Piperales** and **Dillaneales** with **Ranales.** Hutchinson redistributes the families of **Ranales** of Engler mainly under 5 distinct orders, 3 of which, viz. **Magnoliales, Annonales** and **Laurales** are predominantly trees and placed at the beginning of his Division **Lignosae** while the other 2, viz. **Ranales** and **Berberidales** are herbs, shrubs or lianes and placed at the beginning of the Division **Herbaceae.** Takhtajan also distributes these families under several orders, viz. **Magnoliales, Laurales, Nymphaeales, Illicales, Nelumbonales, Ranunculales, Trochodendrales, Cercidiphyllales** and Paeoniales and of these orders the first 3 are included in subclass **Magnoliidae, Illicales, Nelumbonales**, and **Ranunculales** in subclass **Ranunculidae, Trochodendrales** and **Cercidiphyllales** in subclass **Hamamelididae** and **Paeoniales** in subclass **Dilleniidae.** According to Takhtajan all the families under **Ranales** of Engler are not closely related and some are very primitive while a few are fairly advanced. He changes the name of the order **Ranales** to **Ranunculales.**

Cronquist splits **Ranales** of Engler into 4 orders, viz. **Magnoliales, Nymphaeales** and **Ranunculales** which are under subclass **Magnoliidae** and **Trochodendrales** which is in subclass **Hamamelidae.** Further he transfers **Cercidiphyllaceae** to **Hamamelidales.** According to him **Ranunculales** and **Nymphaeales** are derived from **Magnoliales.** He states that **Magnoliales** is a heterogenous group of relic families. All of the most primitive angiosperm-characters are to be found in the families included in this order. These families might have originated from a remote common ancestor or stock and no family gave rise to any other family within the order. The order **Ranunculales** which originated from **Magnoliales** are closely allied to *Illiciaceae* and *Schisandraceae* which were formerly included under *Magnoliaceae*. The family *Ranunculaceae* might be ancestral to all the other families of the order *Ranunculales*.

The primitive characters noticed in different families of **Ranales** of Engler are the following:—(1) Woody habit in many families; (2) Xylem made up of tracheids in *Trochdendraceae*, *Winteraceae*, *Amborella*, *Tetracentron*, etc.; (3) Simple secondary phloem without fibres in *Calycanthaceae*, *Eupomatiaceae*, *Lardizabalaceae* and *Austrobaileyaceae*, the last one having no companion cell in the phloem—a gymnospermic feature; (4) Unilacunar nodes in *Illiciaceae*, *Schizandraceae* and others; (5) Monocolpate pollens in most families; (6) Perianth segments free in most families and spirally arranged on a long receptacle; (7) Many free stamens, with laminar filaments and wall-less microsporangia, embedded in the laminar filament; (8) Carpels free, often folded but unsealed, e.g. *Drimys* and *Degeneria* with a decurrent stigma; (9) Laminar placentation found in *Nymphaeaceae* and *Lardizabalaceae*; (10) Anatropous ovule usually in all families; (11) Pollination by beetles in certain cases; (12) Small embryo often undifferentiated in ripe fruit. All these primitive characters are not found in any single family but every one of the families possesses several of such very primitive characters.

Nymphaeaceae

Annual or perennial aquatic herbs, often rhizomatous. Leaves floating or submerged, rarely raised above water-surface, simple or deeply incised, peltate or cordate, usually long petioled; petiole with many air spaces. Flowers solitary usually on a long scape, regular, bisexual, hypogynous or peri- or epigynous, spirocyclic or rarely cyclic, usually large and showy. Perianth usually differentiated into calyx and corolla, with a gradual transition from sepals to petals and petals to stamens; sepals 3-6, petals 3-many; perianth segments often adnate to torous. Stamens 3-6 or numerous, free; filaments petaloid; anther lobes remote. Carpels 3-many, fused to form a multilocular ovary or free and often sunk in an enlarged spongy thalamus; ovary superior or inferior or semi-inferior; ovules 1-many, parietal. Fruit a spongy berry or a follicle or an aggregate of achenes. Seeds often arillate, with endosperm and perisperm; embryo straight with fleshy cotyledons.

Calcium oxalate crystals are present in cells of some genera and stellate hairs are found in the air spaces. Laticiferous vessels also occur. The vascular bundles are closed and scattered like the Monocotyledons. The xylem is very reduced and with little lignified elements. The stomata are of ranunculaceous type and are found on the upper surface.

The stamens in *Nymphaea* and *Victoria* are laminar, flat and broad and without distinction between anthers and filament; the anthers are provided with sterile apicular appendages. The anther cells are deeply sunk in the lamina. The transitional forms between stamens and petals are very clear. The petals and stamens are arranged in a spiral manner. Such conditions prove the primitiveness of *Nymphaea* and allied genera. In *Euryale* and *Barclaya* anther and filament are well-differentiated and there is no sterile appendage.

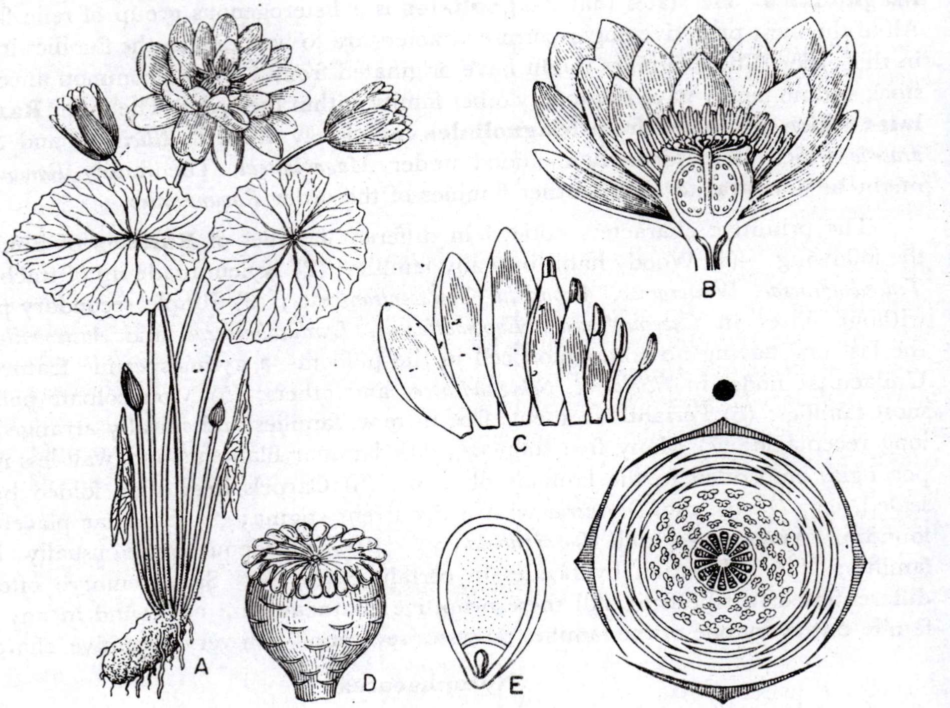

Fig. 65. Nymphaea stellata Willd. A—Plant with rhizome, leaves and flowers (reduced). B—Flower in vertical section (×½). C—Transition of petals to stamens. D—Syncarpous ovary sunk in the torus showing scars of attachment of perianth segments. E—L.s. of seed.

In *Cabomba* and *Brasenia* the flowers are trimerous and the floral parts are arranged in a cyclic manner. Calyx and corolla are quite distinct; stamens 6 or more, carpels 3-6, free, hypogynous. *Nelumbo* has a spirocyclic arrangement of the parts and the petals gradually pass into stamens. Carpels are free and sunk in a spongy elongated obconic thalamus, raised above the perianth and androecium. In *Nymphaea* and *Euryale* there are many carpels arranged in a ring and fused together; the ovary is inferior in *Euryale* but semi-inferior in *Nymphaea*.

Depending on the floral characters the family is subdivided into 3 sub-families, viz.—

1. Cabomboideae: *Cabomba, Brasenia.*
2. Nelumboideae: *Nelumbo.*
3. Nymphaeoideae: *Nymphaea, Nuphar, Victoria, Euryale* and *Barclaya.*

The family with 8 genera and about 80 species are distributed in the temperate and tropical parts of the world. *Nelumbo nucifera* Gaertn is the lotus flower of India and other parts of Asia, occurring also in Egypt. *Euryale ferox* Salisb. is found in eastern parts of India and in China. *Brasenia schreberi* Gmel. is found in Assam. *Nymphaea* comparatively a large genus is distributed in many countries and several species are found in India, e.g. *N. stellata Willd., N. nouchali* Burm.f.

V. regia Lindl. of the amazon-country is cultivated in India and many other tropical countries for the large flowers and very large orbicular leaves more than a mtr. across.

The family is of little economic importance. The seeds of *Euryale ferox* and of several species of *Nymphaea* are edible. A few are considered to have medicinal value.

Nymphaeaceae as described above is not considered to be a single family by many taxonomists of the present day. Hutchinson splits the family into **Nymphaeaceae** and **Cabombaceae** both of which he includes in **Ranales** and Cronquist splits it into *Nymphaeaceae* and *Nelumbonaceae* and places them in a new order **Nymphaeales** along with *Ceratophyllaceae*. Takhtajan also keeps **Nymphaeales** as a distinct order and splits the family *Nymphaeaceae* (sensu lato) into *Nymphaeaceae, Cabombaceae, Barclayaceae* and *Nelumbonaceae*, the first three families being included in **Nymphaeales** along with *Ceratophyllaceae* and the 4th family in a new monotypic order **Nelumbonales.** Takhtajan keeps **Nymphaeales** in the subclass **Magnoliidae** and **Nelumbonales** in the subclass **Ranunculidae.** This means that according to Takhtajan the genera included under the family Nymphaeaceae as understood by Engler are not at all related to each other but are so different in their characters that they should be placed in different families and orders and even in different subclasses of the Dicotyledonae.

Ceratophyllaceae

Submerged fresh-water aquatic rootless herbs with slender stem and branches, the lower end of the stem is often embedded in mud and the branches modified into rhizoids. Leaves whorled, linear and bifurcate, sessile; lobes filiform, acuminate, minutely toothed, brittle; whorls much crowded near the apex of branches; stipules absent. Flowers usually solitary at each node, rarely 1 or more lateral abortive flowers are present indicating the presence of a reduced inflorescence; monoecious, male and female flowers at different nodes, rarely at the same node. Flowers minute, sessile, with one whorl of perianth. Perianth segments 10-16, narrow, subvalvate, 2-fid, sepaloid, often called involucre of bracts. Stamens 10-20, spirally arranged on a convex receptacle; filaments very short, anthers extrorese, 2-celled, cells deeply embedded, connective extending at the apex or cuspidate; pollen large nearly smooth, thin-walled, acolpate. The pistillate flower with a single carpel; ovary superior, sessile, 1-celled with 1 pendulous orthotropous ovule; style subulate, stigmatic on one side. Fruit a small ovoid or ellipsoid nutlet, slightly compressed, terminated by the persistent style, spurred on either side, sometimes narrowly winged; seed with scanty endosperm or endosperm absent; embryo large, straight; cotyledons thick.

The tips of branches often become much thickened and break off and fall to the mud where they lie till the end of winter when they germinate and grow to new plants. The vascular bundles have reduced xylem and phloem and mechanical cells are lacking. The single ovule is the result of reduction from many or a laminar type of placenta is evidenced from the vascular supply to the ovule.

The plants of the family are herbaceous, the flowers are unisexual, carpel and ovule reduced to one. The family thus possesses some advanced characters. But the spirocyclic, flower stamens numerous and free, anther cells long and deeply embedded in the tissue of the microsporophyll, elongated connective, placentation modified laminar type and somewhat decurrent stigma are characters that indicate that the family is a primitive one and is allied to *Nymphaeaceae*.

It is a small family with a single genus and 3 species, cosmopolitan in its distribution in fresh water lakes. *Ceratophyllum demersum* Linn. is common in lakes all over India and is often cultivated to feed the carps and protecting the spawns. The plant has no other use.

Berberidaceae

Shrubs or small trees or rhizomatous herbs; the wood is yellow. Leaves simple or pinnate, alternate, often crowded near apex. Inflorescence is racemose or cymose, often umbellate; rarely flowers solitary. Flowers bisexual, actinomorphic, trimerous or bimerous. Sepals 3, free, caducous; petals in one or more whorls of 3 segments each, free; the inner whorls are usually nectaries. The stamens are 6-18, free, in two or more whorls of 3 members in each; the outer stamens are antipetalous; anthers introrse, opening by valves. Ovary of 1 carpel, superior; ovules many or few on ventral suture; style very short; stigma subsessile, large and disc-like. Fruit a berry, rarely capsule or achene; seed with copious endosperm and small embryo.

In *Berberis* 2 types of branches develop, the long branches have thorns which are the modified leaves in the axil of which the short branches come out with simple leaves and the racemes. The terminal flower of the raceme is often pentamerous. *Mahonia* has imparipinnate leaves crowded near the apex of the branches. Flowers are dimerous in *Epimedium*, and have the petals spurred. In this genus the fruit is a capsule. *Podophyllum* has a sympodial rhizome bearing usually 2 large more or less orbicular leaves and a single flower. In the flower of *Achlys* there is no perianth.

From a study of flower anatomy Eames states that the gynoecium in *Berberidaceae* is made up of 2-3 united carpels of which one is functional while the others are abortive. The carpels are obliquely and spirally arranged. In many genera the vascular bundles are scattered and in other genera they are in a ring but wide apart with broad medullary rays.

The stomata in *Berberidaceae* is Ranunculaceous type and the seed germination is similar in *Berberidaceae* and *Ranunculaceae*. Some genera in *Ranunculaceae* have rhizome like that of *Podophyllum* of *Berberidaceae*. Many free stamens, superior ovary, small embryo are other characters by which a relationship is established between *Berberidaceae* and *Ranunculaceae*. Affinity with *Lauraceae* is also close as is evidenced by the valvular dehiscence of the anthers.

The family consists of 12 genera and about 400 species distributed mainly in the temperate regions. It is represented in India by several species of *Berberis* in the hills and a few *Mahonia* and *Podophyllum*. A few species of *Berberis*, e.g. *B. lycium* Royle, *B. vulgaris* Linn. etc. have medicinal value. The rhizome of *Podophyllum* yields a resin and an alkaloid—berberine used in medicine. An yellow dye is obtained from the wood of *Berberis* and *Mahonia* used by Buddhist monks to colour their garments.

Ranunculaceae

Annual or perennial herbs, often shrubs or climbers, a few are aquatics; the perennials have rhizomes or tuberous roots, the rhizome is sympodial; acrid juice is present in some cases. Leaves radical or cauline, usually alternate, simple or pinnately or palmately compound or decompound, entire or variously sected, pinnately or palmately nerved, petiole usually sheathed at the base, exstipulate; in climbing plants petioles and petiolules often coiling round the support. Flowers in cymose or racemose inflorescences or solitary, axillary or terminal, hermaphrodite, very rarely unisexual, usually regular, hypogynous, usually with a prominent convex receptacle and spiral, spirocyclic or cyclic arrangement of parts. Perianth of one or two whorls, similar or differentiated into calyx and corolla. Sepals 5, free, caducous, petaloid, often a few produced into spurs, rarely sepals absent. Petals 5 or more, often spurred. Stamens usually numerous, free, spirally arranged; anthers extrorse, dehiscing by longitudinal slits. Nectaries usually present, formed by the modified outer whorl of stamens or by the modified petals. Carpels many, free, superior, each with one or more, erect or pendulous ovules on ventral suture; styles long or short, with simple stigma; often carpels coherent to form a compound and multilocular ovary with free styles; ovules anatropous, when many usually in 1-3 series. Fruit an etaerio of follicles or achenes with persistent styles, rarely capsular or berry. Seeds with a small embryo and copious oily endosperm.

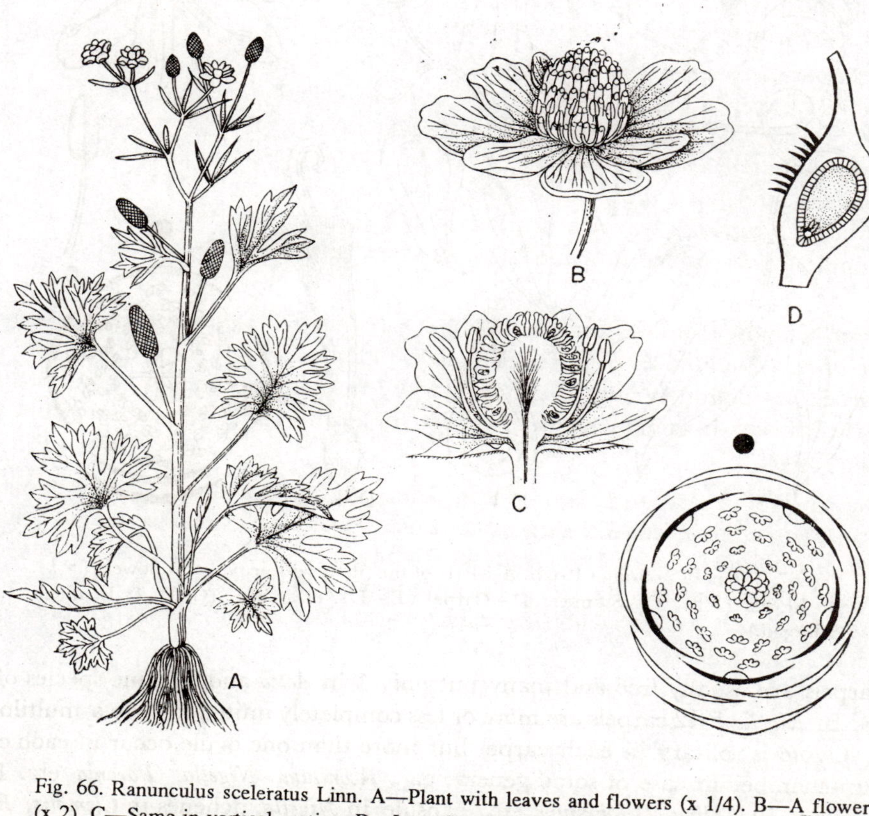

Fig. 66. Ranunculus sceleratus Linn. A—Plant with leaves and flowers (x 1/4). B—A flower (x 2). C—Same in vertical section. D—L.s. of a seed with embryo and endosperm.

Floral formula in the case of *Ranunculus* is as follows:— $\oplus$ ⚥ K_5 C_5 A_∞ G_∞.

Species of *Paeonia* are tall shrubs while *Clematis, Naravelia* and *Atragene* are climbing shrubs. In the former the petioles and petiolules coil round the support while in the latter the leaf-rachis ends in a tendril. Leaves of *Thalictrum* are decompound and large. Much variation is noticed in the floral parts. Usually the flowers are regular, but *Delphinium, Aconitum,* etc. have zygomorphic flowers. Flowers are bisexual as a rule but unisexual in *Thalictrum*. An involucre of 3 bracts occurs in *Anemone, Nigella, Eranthis* etc. Sepals are often petaloid and are called tepals, e.g. *Anemore, Caltha,* etc. Petals may be absent as in *Clematis, Isopyrum,* etc. In *Caltha* and *Helleborus* sepals and petals are spirally arranged but in most cases they are in whorls, the stamens and the carpels are, however, generally arranged spirally. The posterior sepal and the petals in *Delphinium* are spurred. The petals in *Aquilegia* are spurred and store honey. The outer stamens in most cases are modified into nectaries and in some cases it is the petals that turn into honey-leaves.

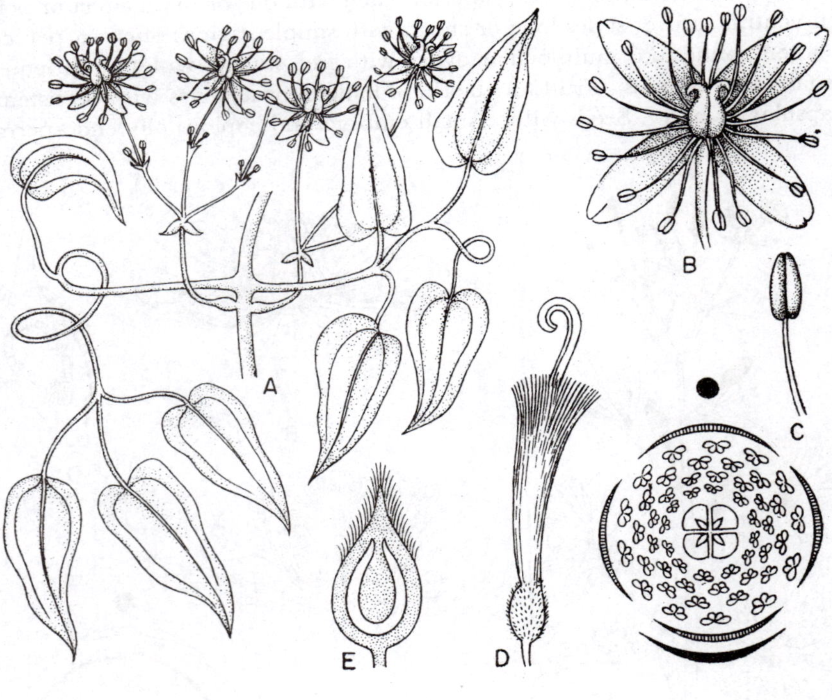

Fig. 67. Clematis gouriana Roxb. A—Part of the plant with leaves and flowers ($\times\frac{1}{2}$). B—Flower ($\times$2). C—Stamen. D—Carpel. E—L.s. of a seed. (C. D. & E. much enlarged.)

The carpels are usually free and many but only 1 in *Actea* and in some species of *Delphinum*. In *Nigella* 5-12 carpels are more or less completely united to form a multilocular ovary. Ovule is solitary in each carpel but more than one ovule occur in each carpel or ovary-chamber in case of some genera, e.g. *Aconitum, Nigella, Paeonia* etc. Fruits are follicular in *Caltha, Delphinium,* etc., capsule in *Nigella*, achenes in *Clematis, Ranunculus,* etc. and berry in *Actea.*

The germination is epigeal. The cotyledons have stalks which in some genera are united in a tube. The plumule pierces the tubes laterally as in Monocotyledons. In *Clematis* the germination is hypogeal. In *Ranunculus ficaria* and in *Eranthis* two cotyledons are united to form a single cotyledon.

In most herbaceous species in the family the vascular bundles are closed with 'V' shaped xylem. The bundles are scattered or in more than one ring. These characters, viz. tubular sheath of the cotyledons, union of 2 cotyledons, sheathed leaf-bases, closed vascular bundles, scattered arrangement of vascular bundles,, copious endosperm and small embryo in the seed indicate that the Monocotyledons might have originated from Ranunculaceae.

The family is a fairly large one having about 1500 species (2000 according to Cronquist) in 35 genera. These are mostly found in the temperate parts of the world and in India many species are found to grow in the Himalayas, e.g. *Aconitum*, *Delphinium*, *Thalictrum*, *Anemone*, *Caltha*, etc. while a few *Clematis*, *Naravelia zeylanica* DC, *Ranunculus sclerotus* Linn. etc. grow in the plains. *Nigella sativa* Linn. is cultivated for the seeds.

Some species have acrid juice often strong enough to cause blister on the skin and some have poisonous alkaloids. Few are medicinal, e.g. *Aconitum napellus* Linn., *Anemone pulsatilla* Linn. *Delphinium staphisagria* Linn. (Stavesacree seeds), *Cimicifuga racemosa* Nutt. (Black snake root), *Hydrastis canadens* Linn. (Hydrastic rhizome), etc. Cumin seeds are obtained from *Nigella sativa* Linn. used as a condiment. Many species of *Delphinium*, *Clematis*, *Anemone*, *Aquilegia*, *Paeonia* etc. have beautiful flowers and are cultivated as garden annuals.

Ranunculaceae is one of the primitive families according to Hutchinson and most other botanists including Takhtajan and Cronquist although Engler, Rendle and a few others consider it to be fairly advanced. Spiral arrangement of floral parts, numerous free stamens and carpels and presence of copious endosperm indicate that the family is not of recent origin. Xylem vessels with simple pits also support this view. The stomata are without subsidiary cells and are known as Ranunculaceous type of stomata. The pollen is uniarperturate and this fact also points to its primitiveness.

Many workers in taxonomy consider the family *Ranunculaceae* to be a natural group. Rendle subdivides the family into 3 tribes as noted below:—

Helleboreae: Ovules arranged in 2 rows along the ventral suture of carpels; fruit a cluster of follicles or rarely a berry.

Anemoneae: Solitary ovule at the base of ventral suture of carpels; fruit a cluster of achene.

Paeonieae: Ovules as in Helleboreae; a fleshy disc present around the carpels; the outer integument is much larger; follicles with fleshy walls.

The tribe Paeonieae is segregated by Hutchinson and others as a separate family **Paeoniaceae.** Hutchinson also raises the tribe Helleboreae to the rank of a family e.g. **Helleboraceae** but most others prefer to retain it under Ranunculaceae. The genus *Hydrastis* having flowers without petals and without nectaries is an anomalous genus and is placed under *Berberidaceae* (or *Podophyllaceae*) by many taxonomists. Takhtajan places it under a new family **Hydrastiaceae** close to *Ranunculaceae*.

Paeoniaceae as a distinct family has the following characters:—Herbs or rarely undershrubs with a stout perennial rootstock or tubers; stem-base covered with scale like sheaths. Leaves alternate, petiolate, twice ternate, segments pinnately nerved. Flowers solitary or panicled, hermaphrodite, slightly irregular, usually large and showy. Sepals 5, free, subfoliaceous, unequal, persistent, imbricate. Petals usually 5, or sometimes 6-10, orbicular, subequal, imbricate. Stamens numerous, free, centrifugal and spirally arranged; anthers 2-locular, extrorse, opening by slits lengthwise. A fleshy disc surrounds the carpels sometimes almost enclosing them. Carpels 5 or fewer, free, fleshy, arcuate-divergent; stigma sessile, thick, falcate, 3-lipped. Fruit a cluster of divergent follicles, dehiscing by the adaxial suture; seeds globōse, arillate, shining; aril umbonate; endosperm fleshy copious; embryo small.

Hutchinson includes Paeoniaceae in his **Ranales** but Takhtajan and Cronquist consider this family closer to *Dilleniaceae* than to *Ranunculaceae* and remove it from **Ranales** (the name changed to Ranunculales).

Menispermaceae

Usually woody twiners, rarely erect shrubs. Leaves alternate, simple or rarely 3-foliolate, exstipulate, rarely palmately lobed, usually palmi-veined. Inflorescence a raceme or cyme or panicle. Flowers minute, unisexual and dioecious generally actinomorphic, cyclic and 2-3-merous. Sepals and petals each in 2 whorls, usually 3 in each whorl, sometimes 2, very rarely 1; petals usually smaller than sepals; sepals and petals free, imbricate. Male flowers usually with 6 stamens, often 3 and opposite to petals or rarely many, free or variously connate; anthers 2-celled or falsely 4-celled dehiscing longitudinally or transvesely; rudimentary pistils rarely present. Female flowers with 3-6 free carpels, often carpels more, rarely 2 or 1; ovary superior, ovules 2 in each carpellary chamber, anatropous, one is abortive; placentation parietal; style very short or absent; stigma capitate or discoid, entire or bilobed; a gynophore is often present; staminodes often present. Fruit is an aggregate of drupes or achenes; seeds with or without fleshy endosperm and curved embryo.

The floral formulas may be represented in the following manner:

1. ♂ $\oplus$ K_{3+3} C_{3+3} A_{3+3}
2. ♀ $\oplus$ K_{3+3} C_{3+3} $G_{\underline{3}}$

The flower, however, varies much in this family in different genera. As a rule the flowers are actinomorphic but *Cissampelos* has zygomorphic flowers. The family is characterised by dioecious plants but monoecious condition is found in *Albertia* and in some species of *Cissampelos*. The number of sepals may be as many as 36, e.g. in *Scidotonia*, they may be only 4 (2+2), e.g. male flower of *Cissampelos pariera* Linn., and only 1 in the female flower of the same; *Pycnarrhena* also has 4 sepals. Petals 4 (2+2) in the staminate flowers of *Cissampelos pariera* but only 1 in the pistillate flower. Female flower of *Scidotonia* has no petal. In *Anamirta* petals absent in both types of flowers. *Antiaxis* has 2 petals. In *Cissampelos* the petals of male flowers are connate. Filaments of stamens are usually free but monadelphous in many genera, e.g. *Parabaena*, *Anamirta*, *Stephania*, etc. In *Rhiziocarya* there are 5 stamens in 2 whorls, the outer 2 are free while the inner 3 are united into a column. Anthers 2-celled but 1-celled in *Antitaxis*; dehiscence is longitudinal but transverse in many genera. Usually the carpels are 3 but 6 in *Haematocarpus*, 9-12 in *Tiliacora*, 3-6 in *Cocculus*, solitary in *Cissampelos*, *Stephania* and *Cyclea*. Gynophore present in *Anamirta*. Style is 3-6 partite in *Stephania*, 3-fid or 3-toothed in *Cissampelos* but simple in other genera. Flowers usually trimerous but in *Cissampelos* the staminate flower is dimerous while the pistillate flower is unimerous. In *Cyclea* also the pistillate flower is unimerous. In *Pycnarrhena calocarpa* (Kurz) Diels the flower is dimerous. Further, dioecious or monoecious, all genera have unisexual flowers but *Cocculus carolinus* DC. and *Abuta rufescens* Aubl. in cultivated condition produce bisexual flowers instead of female flowers.

Plants are twining shrubs but *Pycnarrhena calocarpa* is erect. *Stephania oynantha* is an epiphyte.

Anatomy of the stem shows unusual secondary thickening. Meristematic layers are formed outside the original ring of vascular bundles. These meristematic cells produce new vascular bundles while the original cambium ceases to grow. Secondary phloem formation is poor and interxylary phloem is mostly present. Vessels usually large and solitary with simple perforations. Wood parenchyma is apotracheal.

The family consists of about 400 species under 70 genera. They are mostly found in the tropical countries. In India it is represented by *Cissampelos pareira* Linn., *Stephania japonica* (Thunb.) Miers (Beng. Nimukha), *Tinospora cordifolia* (Willd.) Miers (Beng. Gulancha), *Cocculus hirsutus* (Linn.) Diels (Beng. Huyer), etc. In Europe and N. America fossil specimens were discovered from Tertiary beds. This indicates wider distribution of the family in the past.

The family is of little economic importance. *Tinospora cordifolia* is used as a febrifuge and a few others have medicinal value.

Menispermaceae is a natural taxon. It appears to be more closely related to *Lardizabalaceac* than to the other families of the order **Ranales.** The apocarpous gynoecium marks it as one of the primitive families although in some other characters it appears to be fairly advanced. Hutchinson placed the family in the order **Berberidales** while Takhtajan as well as Cronquist places it in **Ranunculales** wherein both *Lardizabalaceae* and *Menispermaceae* are included.

Magnoliaceae

Trees and shrubs, usually evergreen. Leaves simple, alternate, stipulate; stipules deciduous, large and forming bud-scales, free or adnate to the petiole. Flowers solitary, usually large and showy, actinomorphic, bisexual, rarely polygamous, very rarely unisexual, usually spirocyclic, with an elongated or convex receptacle. Perianth segments many, differentiated into calyx and corolla or all petaloid, spirally arranged on the receptacle or in whorls, imbricate. Stamens numerous, free, spirally arranged; filaments showing a transition from laminar type to terete filaments and proper anthers; anther lobes 2, introrse, dehiscing longitudinally. Carpels numerous free spirally arranged on elongated or convex receptacle; ovary superior; ovules 2 or more in each carpel, anatropous, parietal on the ventral suture; rarely carpels are united. Fruit an aggregate of follicles or berries or samaras. Seeds suspended by a long slender funiculus; endosperm copious, oily; embryo small; testa bright coloured.

Although predominantly erect plants, trees or shrubs, climbing plants or scandents are also met with, e.g. *Schizandra* and *Kadsura*. Sheath-like stipules cover the vegetative bud in most genera but in *Drimys, Schizandra, Illicium,* etc. stipules are absent. Bisexual flowers occur in most of the genera but flowers are unisexual in *Kmeria, Drimys, Schizandra,* etc. Carpels are usually free, but in *Pachylarnax* and *Zygogynum* they are fused and in *Talauma* they do so in fruiting. Fruits are mostly follicles but *Schizandra* has an etaerio of berries, and samaras in *Liriodendron* and *Euptelea*. The floral formula for

the family may be expressed as:—⊕ ⚥ $P_{(9-\infty)}$ A_{∞} G_{∞} or

⊕ ⚥ K_{3+} $C_{(6-\infty)}$ A_{∞} G_{∞}.

The family consists of 12 genera and 230 species with a peculiar distribution with an eastern centre comprising the Indo-Malayan region, S. China, Japan and Australia to the south and western centre in N. E. United States and southwards to Brazil and W. Indies. It is absent in Africa and Europe. But fossil remains were discovered in Tertiary deposits in the Artic Circle, Greenland, Europe and Central N. America.

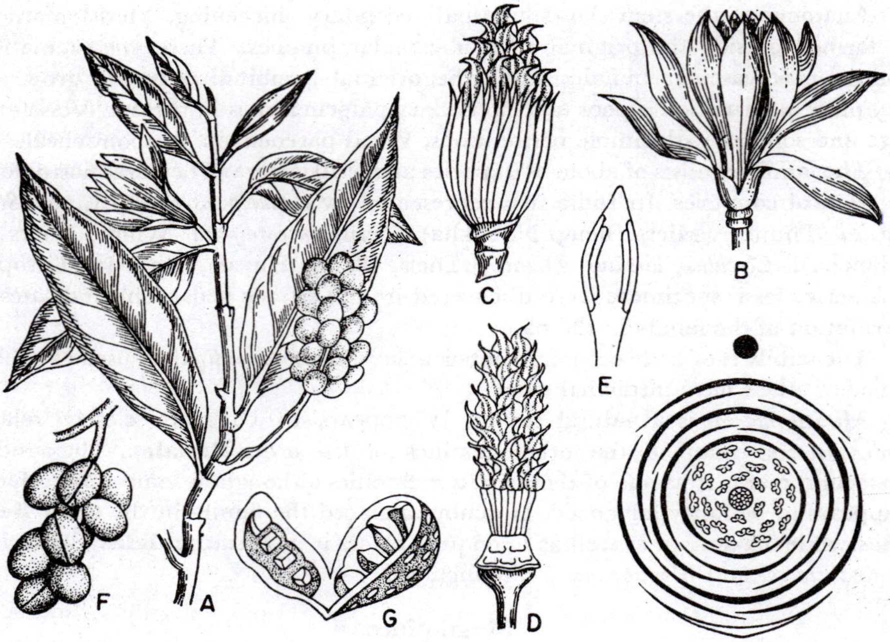

Fig. 68. Michelia champaca Linn. A—Branch with leaves and fruits ($\times\frac{1}{3}$); B—Flower ($\times\frac{1}{3}$); C—Flower with perianth segments removed ($\times 1$); D—Carpels ($\times 1$); E—Stamen showing broad filament, long anther lobes and protruded connective; F—Aggregate fruit ($\times\frac{1}{3}$); G—Split follicle.

This suggests a wider distribution in past and it is surmised that during the ice-ages the family migrated southwards and the present distribution of the family is the result of that migration. In India the family is represented by several genera, e.g., *Magnolia*, *Michelia*, *Manglietia*, *Schisandra*, *Talauma* and *Kadsura*. *Michelia champaca* Linn. is much cultivated in the plains for its fragrant beautiful flowers. *Magnolia Campbelli* Hkf. & Th of the East Himalayas is a deciduous tree with large white or pink flowers. *Magnolia grandiflora* Linn. an American species is also cultivated in India in the plains as well as in the hills at low altitude. *Liriodendron tulipifera* Linn.—the Tulip tree of America is also cultivated.

A few species are economically important. *Liriodendron tulipifera*, a tall tree reaching about 70 mtr. in height, is a good timber-tree. Some species of *Michelia*, *Magnolia*, *Manglietia*, *Talauma*, *Pachylarnax* also yield good timber. *Illicium verum* Hk.f. of S. China is the Star-Anise. An essential oil is obtained from the flowers of *Michelia champaca*.

The wood possesses vessels which have scalariform perforations with many bars, bordered at the ends or at the middle or completely. Vessels are very long, narrow, thin walled, polygonal in outline and with highly inclined perforation plates. Some genera have vessel-less wood, e.g. *Drimys*, *Exospermum*, *Trochodendron*, etc. Stamens usually have 3 traces, often 5 or 7 although rarely 1 trace also occurs. The marginal placentation of the carpels appears to be a modified laminar plancentation. The stomata have guard-cells accompanied by subsidiary cells parallel to the pore.

Magnoliaceae appears to be closely related to *Annonaceae* both of which are included in **Ranales** by Engler and also by Rendle. Both of them consider that the families included in this group are fairly advanced having a well-defined perianth. But according to subsequent authors these are very primitive having polymerous flowers. *Magnoliaceae* is one of the most primitive families among the **Dicotyledonae** as is evident from floral as well as anatomical characters. Hutchinson, Takhtajan and Cronquist place *Magnoliaceae* in a distinct order **Magnoliales,** the first order among the Dicotyledons. The elongated floral axis bearing many perianth segments usually spirally arranged, the numerous stamens and carpels, also often acyclic in arrangement, indicate a primitive flower. To have copious endosperm in the seed is also a primitive character. The scalariform pitting of the vessels resembles the xylem of the Mesozoic **Cycadeoideae.** The vessel-less wood in some genera, being characteristic of the Gymnosperms, also points to primitiveness.

Hutchinson splits the older *Mangoliaceae* into 6 families, viz. Magnoliaceae, Winteraceae, Illiciaceae, Schisandraceae, Eupteleaceae and Tetracentraceae based principally on the morphology of the flowers. The cytological findings of Whitaker also support the separation of these families from *Magnoliaceae* sensustricto. Some also prefer to seggregate *Degeneriaceae* as a family distinct from *Winteraceae*. The distribution of these families, however, throws some doubt as to the validity of such treatment establishing so many smaller families.

Annonaceae

Trees or shrubs, often scandant or lianas. Leaves simple, exstipulate, entire, alternate. Flowers cauliflorous, i.e., produced on the older woody part of the branches, solitary or often fascicled; regular and spirocyclic, usually bisexual. Perianth in 3 whorls, each with 3 segments; the outermost whorl is sepal-like with much smaller segments than the inner whorls, valvate, free or connate below; the inner whorls with petal-like segments, similar in the same whorl, often differing in size in different whorls; valvate or imbricate, free. The receptacle is convex or conical on which numerous stamens and carpels are borne. The stamens are spirally arranged; filaments short, thick; anthers long, extrorse, with a prominent truncate connective. Gynoecium superior, of many free carpels, spirally arranged on the receptacle, each carpel with 1-many basal or marginal ovules, stipitate; style short or absent; stigma simple. Fruit an etaerio of drupes or berries, rarely follicles, sometimes fused to form a composite fruit. Seeds often arillate, with a small embryo and copious ruminated endosperm.

Floral formula:— $\oplus$ ⚥ $K_3 C_{3-6} A_\infty \underline{G_\infty}$

The structure of the flower is more or less uniform in the family. On rare cases deviation from the general type is noticed. The Malayan genus *Stelechocharpus* is dioecious. In the African genus *Monodora* the petals being slightly unequal, the flowers are irregular. In this genus carpels are united to form a unilocular ovary with parietal placentation. In *Xylopia* the anthers are transversely septate. *Anaxogorea* has follicular fruits.

The family with about 80 genera and 880 species is distributed in the tropical countries of the world. In India the family is well represented by several species of which *Polyalthia longifolia* (Sonner) Thaw.—the Debdaru, *Artabotrys hexapetala* Bhandari —the Kanthali Champa, *Desmos dunalii* (Hk.f. & Th.) Saff., *Cananga odorata* (Lamk.)

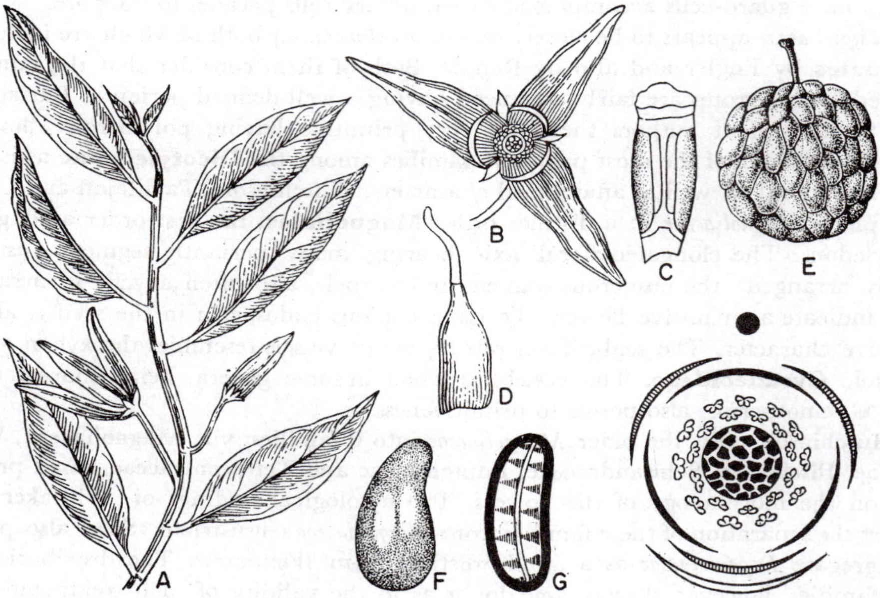

Fig. 69. Annona squamosa Linn. A—Branch with leaves and flowers (×½); B—A flower (×1); C—Stamens; D—one carpel; E—Fruit (×¼); F—Seed; G—Same in l.s. (C & D much enlarged, F & G—slightly enlarged.

Hk.f. & Th., *Goniothalamus cardiopetalus* Hk.f. & Th., *Miliusa indica* Leschen., *M. tomentosa* (Roxb.) Sinclair, *Alphonsea lutea* Hk.f. & Th., *Uvaria hamiltonii* Hk.f. & Th. are quite common among the indigenous species. *Annona squamosa* Linn. the Custard Apple (Beng. Ata), *A. reticulate* Linn.—the Bullock's heart (Beng. Nona) both native of Trop. America are widely cultivated for the edible fruits.

A few species are economically important. Besides the 2 species of *Annona* mentioned above, *A. cherimolia* Mill. and *A. muricata* Linn. have edible fruits. The fruits of *Asimina triloba* Dun. are also edible. *Polyalthia longifolia*, *Bocagea laurifolia* Bth. & Hk.f., *B. virgata* Bth. & Hk.f. and *Duguetia qutarensis* Bth. yield timber. Cananga oil or Macassar oil is obtained from *Cananga odorata* (Lamk.) Hk.f. & Th.

The family is allied to *Magnoliaceae* having free floral parts, numerous stamens and carpels and the gynoecium superior. Along with *Magnoliaceae* it is included in **Ranales** by Engler and Rendle. Wettstein placed it in his **Polycarpicae** with *Magnoliaceae*, *Ranunculaceae*, etc. Above authors considered these families to be fairly advanced but the floral characters do not indicate advancement but primitiveness and these families are now considered so by all recent workers. Hutchinson includes *Annonaceae* in a new order **Annonales** along with *Eupomatiaceae* and places this order next to **Magnoliales.** Eames, Takhtajan and Cronquist keep *Annonaceae* in **Magnoliales**.

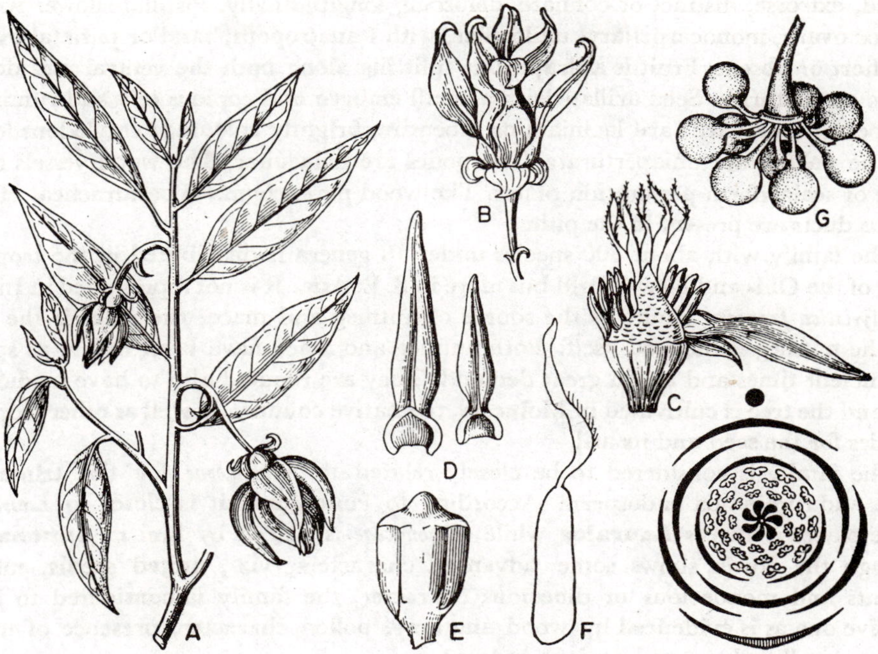

Fig. 70. Artabotrys hexapetalus (L.f) Bhandari. A—Branch with leaves and flowers ($\times\frac{1}{3}$); B—One flower ($\times\frac{1}{2}$); C—Stamens and carpels spirally arranged on a conical receptacle; D—Petals, outer longer, inner shorter; E—subsessile stamens; F—Carpel with flat style; G—Cluster of berries ($\times\frac{1}{6}$).

The family is subivided into 2 subfamilies and 4 tribes as noted below:—

I. **Annonoideae**—Carpels free, spirally arranged.

(i) *Uvarieae:* Leaves distichous; petals imbricate (rarely valvate)—Uvaria, Unona, etc.

(ii) *Annoneae:* Leaves distichous; petals valvate (rarely imbricate)—Annona, Desmos, Polyalthia, etc.

(iii) *Tetramerantheae:* Leaves spirally arranged; sepals imbricate (stigma 3-lobed). —1 genus-Tetrameranthus.

II. **Monodoroideae**—Carpels united into a unilocular ovary, cyclic arrangement.

(iv) *Monodoreae:* Placentation parietal,—2 genera, Monodora and Isoloma.

The family resembles the **Monocotyledonae** by its typically trimerous flowers and a small embryo in copious endosperm.

Myristicaceae

Evergreen trees or shrubs, usually aromatic; the inner bark often exuding reddish sap. Leaves alternate, simple, entire, often with pellucid dots, exstipulate. Flowers unisexual, in monoecious or dioecious plants, in racemose, corymbose, fascicled or in globose heads, actinomorphic and hypogynous. Perianth uniseriate, gamosepalous, tubular or campanulate, 3-lobed; lobes imbricate. Staminate flower with 3-30 stamens, monadelphous, the staminal column sometimes spread out in the form of a disc; anthers

2-celled, extrorse, distinct or connate, dehiscing longitudinally. Pistillate flower with a superior ovary, monocarpellary, unilocular, with 1 anatropous, basal or parietal ovule; style short or absent. Fruit is a drupe but splitting along both the ventral and dorsal sutures on maturity. Seed arillate with a small embryo and copious oily and ruminate endosperm; testa hard; aril laciniate or subentire, brightly coloured; cotyledons leafy.

The pollens are uniaperturate. The nodes are trilacunar. The wood vessels have simple or scalariform perforation plates. The wood parenchyma is paratracheal. Taniniferous ducts are present in the pith.

The family with about 300 species under 18 genera is distributed in the tropical region of the Old- and New-World but more in S. E. Asia. It is not represented in India.

Myristica fragrans Houtt. is the source of nutmeg and mace; the mace is the aril while the nutmeg is the seed itself. Both nutmeg and mace have been in use as spices from ancient times and are in great demand. They are reputed also to have medicinal value and the tree is cultivated in Moluccas, the native country, as well as other tropical countries for the seed and its aril.

The family is considered to be closely related to *Annonaceae* for the trimerous flowers and ruminated endosperm. According to Hutchinson it is closer to *Lauraceae* and he places it in his **Laurales** while *Annonaceae* is placed by him in **Annonales.** Although the flower shows some advanced characters, viz., united sepals, united filaments and monoecious or dioecious character, the family is considered to be a primitive one as is evidenced by wood anatomy, pollen character, presence of many stamens, small embryo and copious endosperm.

Lauraceae

Trees and shrubs, usually with aromatic bark and foliage; rarely parasitic twining herbs. Leaves simple, alternate, rarely opposite, usually entire, penninerved rarely with 3 prominent nerves from the base, coriaceous, glandular punctate, exstipulate. Inflorescence is a raceme, spike or umbel, often a panicle, axillary or subterminal. Flowers bisexual, rarely unisexual and the plants dioecious, actinomorphic, trimerous, small and inconspicuous. Perianth in 2 whorls of 3 similar segments in each, greenish, yellowish or white; segments connate near the base, imbricate, usually persistent. The androecium consists of 4 trimerous whorls; stamens adnate to perianth tube; the innermost whorl or the inner 2 whorls reduced to staminodes; rarely there are only 2 whorls, the outer of fertile stamens and inner of staminodes; filaments are usually free from each other; anthers basifixed, 2- or 4-celled, introrse, but those of the 3rd whorl when fertile extrorse, dehiscing by valvular flaps opening upwards; the filaments of the 3rd whorl usually bearing a pair of glandular protuberances at the base; the valves are superposed when the anther is 4-celled. Ovary superior, 1-celled, with a solitary anatropous ovule pendulous from the wall of the ovary; style 1, stigma entire or 2-3-lobed. Fruit a drupe or berry, usually surrounded at the base by the persistent and often enlarged perianth tube; the receptacle is often elongated. Seed with a large straight embryo and no endosperm; cotyledons large and fleshy.

The floral formula may be represented as: $\oplus$ ⚥ $P_{3+3}\ A_{3+3+3+3}s\ G_{\underline{1}}$. The ovary is monocarpellary but the often trilobed stigma suggests that originally carpels were 3 of which 2 became abortive. All plants are erect and with a woody perennial habit. Only exception is the genus *Cassytha* the species of which are herbaceous twiners. Further the species of *Cassytha* are total parasites with scale-like leaves or leaves altogether absent. In *Sassafras* the leaves are lobed; in other genera the leaves are entire. Flowers are hermaphrodite but in *Laurus* they are unisexual. *Actinodaphne* and *Litsaea* also have unisexual flowers and are dioecious. Anthers 2- celled in *Cassytha, Cryptocarya, Beilschmedia* etc. but 4-celled in *Cinnamomum, Phoebe, Litsaea* etc. The cells are parallel but in *Nectandra* the the 4 cells are arranged in an arc.

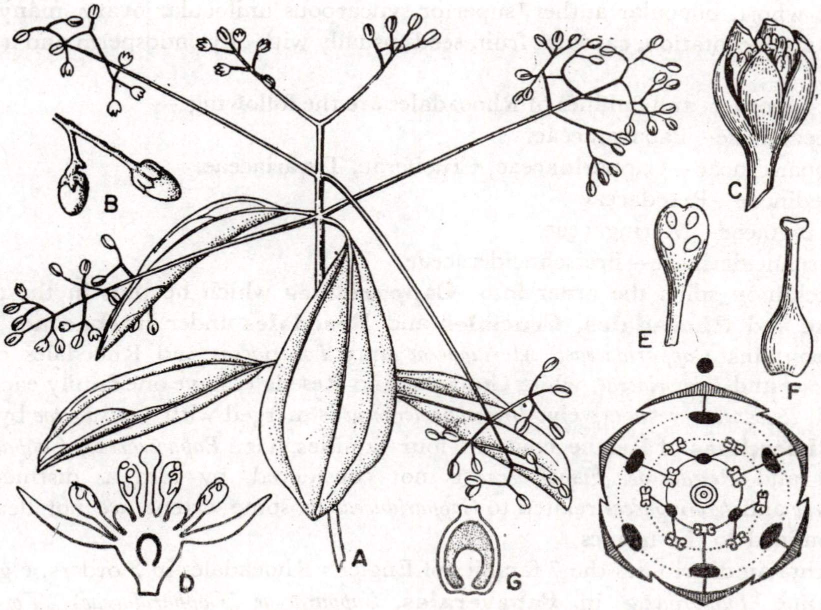

Fig. 71. Cinnamomun tamala F. Nees. A—Branch with leaves and panicle ($\times\frac{1}{4}$); B—Buds ($\times$1); C—Flower ($\times$2); D—Same in v.s.; E—Stamen showing 4 anther cells embedded in the tissue of the filament; F—Ovary; G—L.s. of seed.

The family contains about 1,100 species in 45 genera. They are found mostly in E. Asia, some extending northwards to Japan and a few are Australian. In the New World, species of this family are found in Chili and Brazil in south and up to Canada in the north. A few species occur in Africa while *Laurus nobilis* Linn. is found in Mediterranean region and in W. Asia. It is well represented in India by several species of *Cinnamomum, Litsaea, Lindera, Beilschmedia* etc.

A few species are economically important of which *Cinnamomum camphora* Linn. is well known as the source of natural camphor. *C. zeylanicum* Breyn. of India and Sri Lanka yields the cinnamon bark. *C. tamala* Nees & Eber. is the Tamala-tree of Sanskrit literature. The leaves of this tree as well as those of *C. zeylanicum* and a few other species of the genus are used as spice and are known as Tejpatra. *Persea americana* Mill. produces the Avocado pear. *Sassafras albidum* Nees is an important medicinal plant. Many species yield good timber which is not attacked by insects and boxes prepared from the planks are used to keep costly clothings. The wood of *Sassafras* and *Cinnamomum* are scented.

Pax divided the family into 2 tribes:—

Perseoideae: anthers 4-celled, dehiscing by 4 valves.

Lauroideae: anthers 2-celled, dehiscing by 2-valves.

The family is related to *Annonaceae* and *Myristicaceae* having trimerous flower and many stamens. It is also related to *Magnoliaceae* where the receptacle enlarges in fruit.

RHOEADALES

In this order are included 7 families under 5 suborders. Characters common to them are: mostly herbs with simple alternate exstipulate leaves, usually regular bisexual hypogynous flowers, free sepals, caducous free petals in 2 whorls, stamens free in more than one whorl, bilocular anther, superior syncarpous unilocular ovary, many ovules on parietal placentation, capsular fruit, seeds usually with oily endosperm and a curved embryo.

The suborder and families of Rhoeadales are the following:—

Rhoeadineae—Papaveraceae.

Capparidineae—Capparidaceae, Cruciferae, Tovariaceae.

Resedineae—Resedaceae

Moringineae—Moringaceae

Bretschneiderineae—Bretschneideraceae.

Hutchinson splits the order into **Capparidales** which he puts in the division **Lignosae** and **Rhoeadales, Cruciales** and **Resedales** under **Herbaecae.** Capparidales contains *Capparidaceae*, *Moringaceae* and *Tovariaceae* and Rhoedales contains *Papaveraceae* and *Fumariaceae*, while Cruciales and Resedales have one family each *Cruciferae* and *Resedaceae* respectively. *Bretschneideraceae* is merged with *Sapindaceae* by Huchinson. **Rhoeadales** of Rendle contains four families, viz. *Papaveraceae*, *Capparidaceae*, *Cruciferae* and *Resedaceae*. *Fumariaceae* is not considered by him as distinct while *Tovariaceae* and *Moringaceae* related to *Capparidaceae* to some extent are not dealt with being confined to the tropics.

Takhtajan distributes the 7 families of Engler's Rhoeadales in 3 orders, e.g. *Papaveraceae* and *Fumariaceae* in **Papaverales,** *Capparaceae* (*Capparidaceae*), *Tovariaceae*, *Moringaceae*, *Resedaceae*.and *Brassicaceae* (Cruciferae) in **Capparales** and *Bretschneideraceae* in **Sapindales** distinct from *Sapindaceae*. Like Hutchinson Cronquist merges *Bretschneideraceae* with *Sapindaceae* while the other families are distributed under Papaverales and Capparales.

Rhoeadales of Engler does not appear to be a natural taxon. *Fumariaceae* although having zygomorphic flowers was not recognised as a separate family. Hutchinson and other authors treating *Famariaceae* as distinct from *Papaveraceae* have mentioned about the close affinity between the two. Inclusion of *Bretschneideraceae* in Rhoedales has not been supported by any subsequent workers. *Cruciferae*, *Resedaceae* and *Capparidaceae* although placed in 3 distinct orders by Hutchinson appear to tbe close enough to be included in a single order but *Papaveraceae* deserves to be removed to a separate order where *Fumariaceae* should also be placed. *Tovariaceae*, a monotypic family, is related to *Capparidaceae* and is placed in **Capparidales** by Hutchinson and other workers.

Papaveraceae

Predominantly herbs with milky or coloured latex. Leaves alternate, simple, entire or lobed, often much dissected, exstipulate; rarely crowded at base. Flowers solitary or in racemes or cymes; bisexual, usualy regular, hypogynous 2- or 3-merous. Sepals 2 or 3, free, caducous, imbricate. Petals 4 or 6 in 2 whorls, imbricate, crumpled in bud, deciduous. Stamens numerous, in more than one alternating whorl, 2-3 in each whorl or in multiples of 2 or 3; anthers bilocular, dehiscing longitudinally. Carpels 2-many, syncarpous, forming a unilocular superior ovary; ovules many on parietal placentas which are usually protruding inside and often meeting at the centre so that the ovary becomes multilocular, sometimes falsely bilocular by a septum joining the 2 opposite placentas; stigmas as many as carpels, radiating from the centre and forming a lobed structure, persistent, style present or not. Fruit usually a capsule, opening by apical pores or valves, rarely fruit indehiscent. Seeds small, globose or somewhat kidney-shaped with oily endosperm and small embryo.

Although generally herbaceous a few are climbers or scandent shrubs, e.g. *Adlumia*, *Dactylocapnos*, etc. *Hypecoum procumbens* Linn. is a creeper. *Bocconia arborea* S. Wats. is a short tree. Leaves are simple, but *Dactylocapnos* and some *Corydalis* have compound or decompound leaves. In *Chelidonium* the small flowers are in umbels; in *Macleya* the inflorescence is paniculate. In *Eschscholtzia* the 2 sepals are coherent and form a calyptra which falls off as the petals grow. In the subfamily **Fumarioideae** the flowers are transversely zygomorphic; one or both of the 2 petals of the outer whorl are saccate or

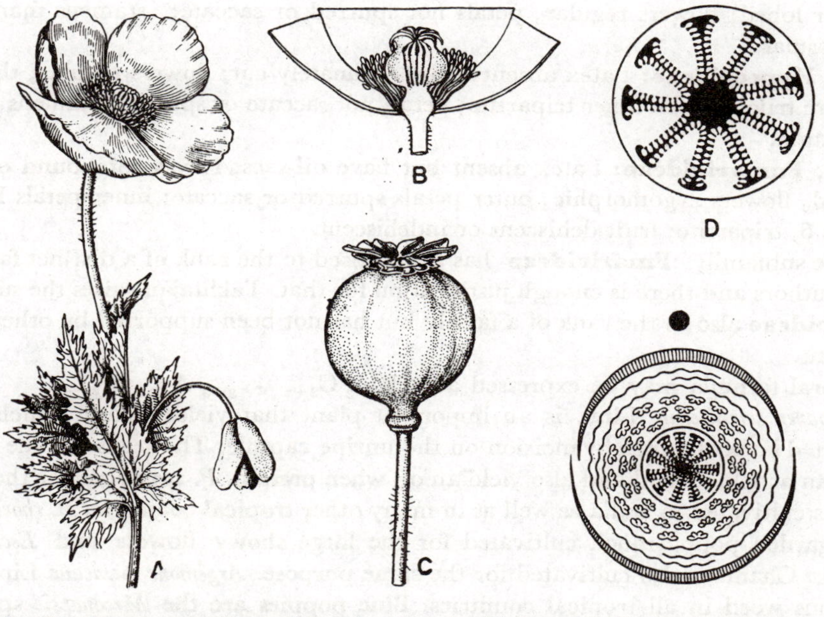

Fig. 72. Papaver somniferum Linn. A—Branch with flower (×½); B—Androecium and gynoecium; C—Fruit with macrescent umbrella like stigma; D—T.s. of ovary.

spurred, the inner petals form a hood over the stamens. Outer stamens have bithecal anthers while the inner have monothecal anthers. In *Bocconia* and *Macleya* corolla is absent. The ovary is unilocular or it is multilocular when the placentas meet in the centre. In *Glaucium* the ovary becomes 2-chambered due to the formation of a replum uniting the 2 opposite placentas. *Platystemon* has a partially syncarpous multilocular ovary of many carpels united laterally in the lower portion, the styles remaining free. *Bocconia* has a unilocular ovary with a solitary basal ovule. Fruits are capsular and open by valves or pores near the apex or dehiscing longitudinally from apex downwards as in *Glaucium* or from base upwards as in *Chelidonium*. In *Hypecoum* the pod like fruit develops transverse septa between the seeds and breaks up into several one-seeded parts when ripe. The seeds are arillate in *Bocconia*. In some species of *Corydalis* the embryo germinates with one cotyledon only.

The flowers are insect-pollinated. In *Hypecoum procumbens* L. the inner surface of petals have pockets where the pollens fall when the stigmas are still immature. When an insect enters the flower the pockets open as the insect presses against them and dust the body of the insect with pollens. The flower is protandrous in this case but is protogynous in other cases. Self-pollination also sometimes occurs.

In this family the stomatal guard cells are usually not accompanied with subsidiary cells. Vessels have simple perforations and simple pits in wood parenchyma. Latex tubes or vessels are present in almost all parts of the plant body; these are thin-walled, articulate and closed.

The family with about 700 species in 35 genera is distributed in the temperate and subtemperate countries of the northern hemisphere. It is subdivided into 3 sub-families as given below:—

I. **Papaveroideae:** Milky or coloured or watery latex present; leaves simple, entire or lobed; flowers regular; petals not spurred or saccate; stamens many, free, fruit capsular.

II. **Hypecoideae:** Latex absent; leaves pinnately cut; flowers regular; the outer petals are trilobed, the inner tripartite; petals not saccate or spurred; stamens 4; fruit a lomentum.

III. **Fumarioideae:** Latex absent but have oil-sacs; leaves compound or much dissected; flowers zygomorphic; outer petals spurred or saccate; inner petals hooded; stamens 6, tripartite; fruit dehiscent or indehiscent.

The subfamily **Fmarioideae** has been raised to the rank of a distinct family by many authors and there is enough justification for that. Takhtajan raises the subfamily **Hypecoideae** also to the rank of a family but has not been supported by others in his treatment.

Floral formula may be expressed as $⚥ K_{2-3}\ C_{2+2 \text{ or } 3+3}\ A_{\infty}\ G_{\underline{(2-\infty)}}$.

Papaver somniferum Linn. is an important plant that yields opium which is the coagulated latex obtained by incision on the unripe capsule. The seeds are the "Postadana" an article of food and also yield an oil when pressed. *P. somniferum* or the opium poppy is cultivated in India as well as in many other tropical countries. *P. rhoeas* Linn. is the garden poppy much cultivated for the large showy flowers and *Eschcholtzia californica* Cham. is also cultivated for the same purpose. *Argèmone mexicana* Linn. is an obnoxious weed in all tropical countries. Blue poppies are the *Meconopsis* species of the Himalayas and China and are often cultivated. *Dactylocapnos thalictrifolia* Wall. and many species of *Corydalis* occur also in the Himalayas.

Papaveraceae is allied to *Capparidaceae* and *Cruciferae* to some extent having dimerous flowers, superior, unilocular, syncarpous ovary, ovules many on parietal placentas, etc. The sessile stigmas and the projecting placentas resemble the family *Nymphaeaceae* to some extent and particularly the genus *Platystemon* with its trimerous flower and semi-free carpels resembles *Cabomba* of *Nymphaeaceae* (or *Cabombaceae* if treated as a distinct family). The genus Corydalis resembles the **Monocotyledonae** also to some extent having only one cotyledon functioning at the time of germination.

The characters of **Fumariaceae** when treated, as a separate family are given below in brief:

Herbs, climbers or scandent shrubs with repeatedly pinnate leaves; latex absent. Racemes subteneded by bracts. Flowers generally transversely zygomorphic. Sepals 2, caducous; petals 4 in 2 whorls, more or less connate, one or both of the outer whorl saccate or spurred, the inner petals hooded. Stamens 6 in 2 series more or less coherent in

2 bundles; each stamen is branched into 3 near the upper end, the middle branch is bithecal and the lateral branches are monothecal; one bundle of the stamens has a spur projecting into the spur of the petal. Nectar glands often present at the base of the androecium. Carpels 2; ovary syncarpous, unilocular, superior; ovules 2-many on parietal placentas; stigma entire or bilobed on a slender style. Fruit a capsule, dehiscing transversely, or a nut. Seeds with a very small embryo and fleshy endosperm; cotyleledons 2 or 1.

Fumariaceae consists of about 425 species in 19 genera mostly in the temperate countries. *Fumaria indica* Pugsl. occurs in the plains of India. *Dactylocapnos* and *Corydalis* are found in the Himalayas.

Capparidaceae

(Capparaceae)

Herbs or shrubs, often scandent or climbing, rarely trees; latex absent. Leaves alternate, simple or palmately compound, stipulate or exstipuate. Inflorescence racemose, or flowers solitary; bracteate. Flowers bisexual, hypogynous, actinomorphic or zygomorphic, usually tetramerous; androgynophore or gynophore usually present; lateral outgrowth of the axis also often seen in the form of swelling or disc or tubular structure below or above corolla. Sepals 4, in 2 whorls, free or rarely more or less united, valvate or imbricate. Petals 4, rarely more, free, imbricate; rarely petals absent. Stamens numerous or 8 or 6 or only 4 and alternate to the petals, free, sometimes on an androphore; filaments long; often some stamens reduced to petaloid staminodes; stamens never tetradynamous. Carpels 2, sometimes 4; ovary syncarpous, unilocular, usually on a gynophore; ovules many, campylotropous, on parietal placentation; style

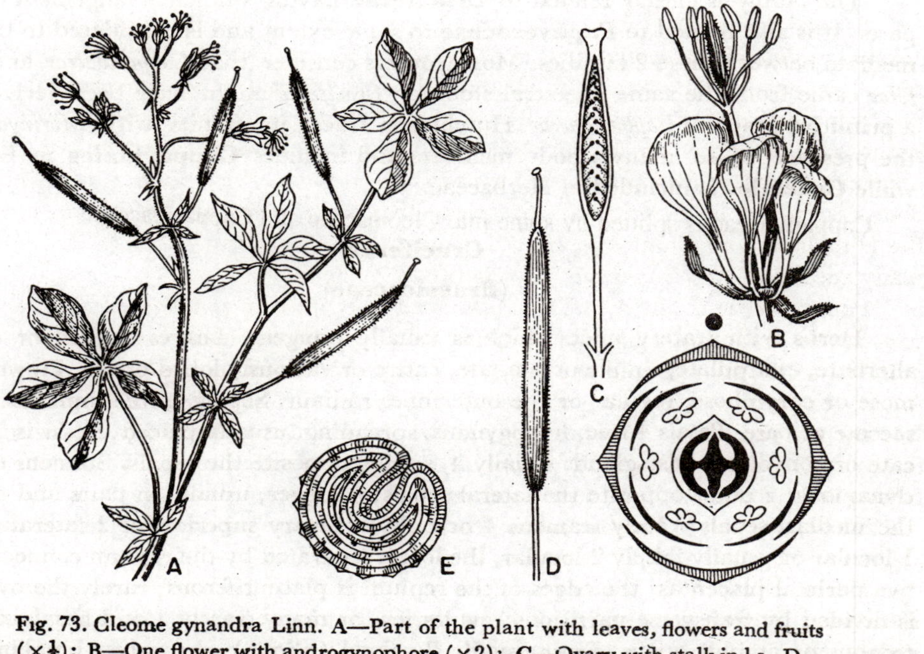

Fig. 73. Cleome gynandra Linn. A—Part of the plant with leaves, flowers and fruits (×½); B—One flower with androgynophore (×2); C—Ovary with stalk in l.s. D—Fruit (×½); E—Seed in l.s.

short or absent, stigma depressed or capitate. Fruit a siliqua, capsule, berry or samara, rarely a nut. Seed kidney-shaped, exalbuminous; embryo large, variously folded.

Flowers are bisexual but unisexual flowers are produced in *Podandrogyne*. Actinomorphic flower is found in almost all genera but there are exceptions. The zygomorphy results due to unequal development of sepals and petals. In some species of *Capparis* the posterior sepals form a hood like structure. In *Pteropetalum* the posterior petal is much larger than the anterior. Sepals and petals are united in *Emblingia* where the calyx is 4-lobed and the petals are also united and the posterior petals form a large hood protecting the stamens. In some genera petals are absent.

Anomalus secondary thickening is observed in a few genera where the original cambium ring is replaced by new cambium rings that add secondary phloem and xylem. Some genera being xerophytic heavy cuticularisation of epidermis takes place having sunken stomata. Large amount of mechanical tissue and stone cells also develope. The plants have thorns or spines and small leaves and are provided with trichomes.

Floral formula is shown below:—

$$⚥\ K_{(2+2)}C_4A_{4+\infty}G_{(2)}$$

The family contains about 700 species in 46 genera and is distributed in all tropical and subtropical countries; some are inhabiting the deserts of Africa and the steppes of Australia. In India it is represented by several species in the plains belonging to the genera *Cleome*, *Polanisia*, *Gynandropsis*, *Capparis*, *Crataeva*, etc. *Crataeva nurvala* Buch.-Ham. is the Barun tree, the bark of which has antiseptic properties. The flower buds of *Capparis spinosa* L. are the "Capers" used in flavouring food. *Clcome viscosa* Linn. and *Cleome gynandra* Linn. have medicinal properties.

The family is closely related to **Cruciferae** having similar arrangement of floral parts. It is also related to **Papaveraceae** to some extent and is considered to be intermediate between these 2 families. Most workers consider that *Capparidaceae* and *Cruciferae* came from the same ancestral stock or *Cruciferae* might have been derived from a primitive group of *Capparidaceae*. Hutchinson traces its affinity with *Moringaceae* for the presence of so many woody members and includes **Capparidales** in Lignosae while **Cruciales** is included in Herbaceae.

Capparidaceae is splitted by some into Cleomaceae and Capparidaceae.

Cruciferae

(Brassicaceae)

Herbs with watery juice which is usually pungent. Leaves radical or cauline, alternate, exstipulate, simple or pinnate, entire or variously lobed or cut. Flowers racemose or corymbose, regular or the outer ones radiant. Sepals 4, free, imbricate, often saccate at base. Petals 4 free, hypogynous, spreading, usually placed crosswise, imbricate or convolute. Disc-glands usually 4, sessile, opposite the sepals. Stamens 6, tetradynamous; 2 outer opposite the lateral sepals; 4 longer, usually in pairs and opposite the median sepals; rarely stamens 4 or only 2. Ovary superior, of 2 lateral carpels, 1-locular or usually falsely 2-locular, the loculi separated by the replum connecting the two parietal placentas; the edges of the replum is placentiferous; rarely the ovary cell is divided by transverse partitions; ovules few or many, rarely 1 and basal, campylotropous or amphitropous. Fruit usually 2-valved (siliqua), the valves breaking away from the replum, or indehiscent. Stigma generally commisural, i.e. placed immediately above the placentas. Seeds without endosperm, with large cotyledons and folded embryo.

The commissure in the pistil is regarded by some as the true carpel bearing the placentae, so that the pistil consists of 2 pairs of carpels, a lateral barren pair and a median fertile pair. The lateral pair forms the valves of the fruit which separate at maturity and the median pair forms the replum.

Range of floral structure: Plants of this family have regular flowers as a rule, but in *Iberis* and *Teesdalia* the flower becomes zygomorphic with 2 outer petals enlarged. Petals are sometimes absent or almost so in some species of *Coronopus*, *Lepidium* or *Rorippa* as well as in *Capsella* where the petals are sometimes modified into stamens. Lateral stamens are generally absent in some *Cardamine* while in *Lepidium* and *Coronopus* only 2 median stamens are present. In *Megacarpaea* there are as many as 16 stamens.

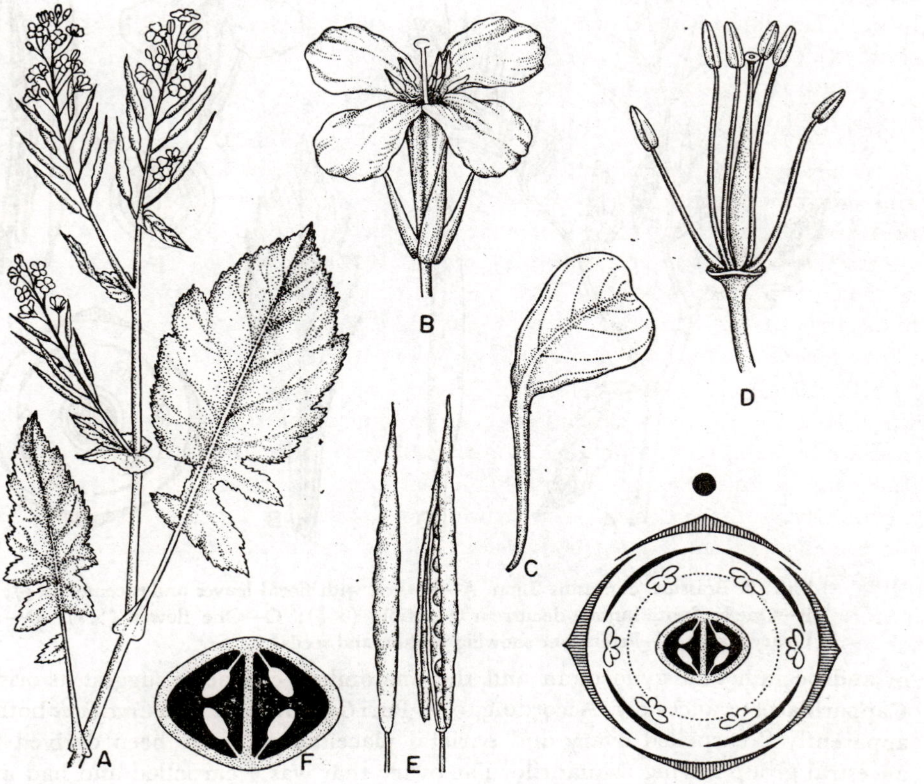

Fig. 74. Brassica nigra Koch. A—Part of the plant with leaves and flowers ($\times\frac{1}{4}$); B—Flower (slightly enlarged); C—One petal; D—Tetradynamous stamens and ovary; E—Fruit F—T.s. of ovary; ($\times\frac{1}{2}$).

Four or more carpels are found in *Tetrapoma* and *Holargidium*. *Lepidium sativum* Linn. has a tricarpellary ovary. Many genera produce abnormal flowers with ovaries composed of carpels more than 2 in number.

Puri concludes that the present bilocular type of ovary with parietal placentation has resulted from a 4-loculed ancestral type with axile placentation. Eames and Wilson (1930) hold that the modern Cruciferous ovary has been derived from 4 carpels, 2 fertile ones in the inner whorl and 2 sterile ones representing an outer whorl and that the replum is formed by the fused walls of the 2 fertile carpels with their ovules now in the locules of the sterile carpels.

That the family is closely related to *Papaveraceae* and *Capparidaceae* there is little disagreement. It is placed along with 2 above families in the **Rhoedales** of Engler where are included *Resedaceae* and *Moringaceae*. The common characters are bisexual hypogynous flowers, typically cyclic perianth and androceium, syncarpous ovary, parietal placentation and usually capsular fruits.

Hutchinson following Bentham and Hooker states that the family has been derived from Papaveraceous ancestors. But other authers hold that the morphological characters

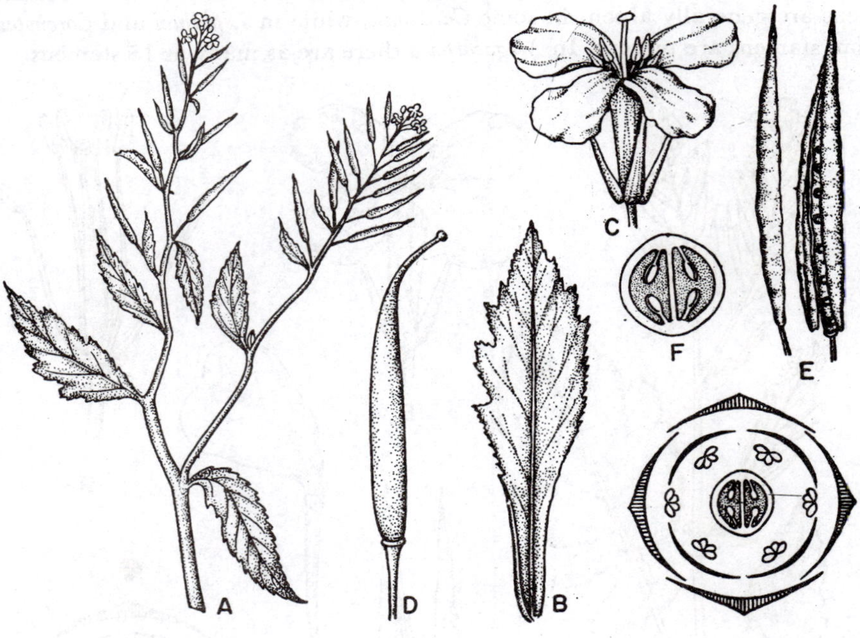

Fig. 75. Brassica campestris Linn. A—Branch with floral leaves and racemes ($\times\frac{1}{4}$); B—One leaf with lamina decurrent to petiole ($\times\frac{1}{8}$); C—One flower ($\times1$); D—Ovary ($\times3$); E—Fruits, one showing replum and seeds.

of androecium and gynoecium and the anatomical character suggest its origin from Capparidaceous ancestors. According to V. Puri *Capparidaceae* and *Cruciferae* both having apparently 2 carpelled ovary and parietal placentation, have been derived from an ancestral group having a quadrilocular ovary that was 4 carpelled and had axile placentation.

This is a large family with about 2500 species in 350 genera growing in the cooler parts of both hemispheres with their chief development in the northern hemisphere and especially in the Mediterranean region. Pomel classified the family into 3 groups on the basis of cotyledons as noted below:

A. Platylobeae: Cotyledons flat, radicle accumbent or incumbent.

B. Orthoploceae: Cotyledons longitudinally folded, radicle in the channel formed by the cotyledons.

C. Pleuroploceae: Cotyledons rolled or transversely folded.

The family includes a number of plants economicaly important. Seeds of *Brassica nigra* Coch; *B. campestris* Linn, *B. juncea* Czern. & Coss. etc. yield the Mustard oil. *Brassica oleracea* Linn. var. *botrytis* Linn. is the Cauliflower. *B. oleracea* Linn. var *capitata* Linn. is the Cabbage, *B. oleracea* Linn. var *gongylodes* Linn. is the Knolkhol and *B. oleracea* Linn, var *gemmifera* DC is the Brussels sprout. *Brassica rapa* Linn is the Turnip and *Raphanus sativus* Linn, is the Radish. Many are cultivated as ornamental plants, viz.: *Iberis* (Candy-tuft), *Matthiola* (Stocks), *Cheiranthus* (Wall-flower), etc.

Moringaceae

A monotypic family of soft wooded trees with gummy juice; deciduous. Leaves compound, simple pinnate or bi- or tripinnate, leaflets opposite, entire; stipules reduced to glands or absent; pulvinus distinct. Panicles cymose, axillary; flowers zygomorphic, hermaphrodite, perigynous. Sepals 5, imbricate, inserted on the margin of cupular hypanthodium. Petals 5, free, unequal, inserted on the hypanthodium; the upper pair smaller than the lateral, the lowest (the anterior) largest. Stamens inserted on a disc, 10-12, free and declinate, 5 fertile alternating with 5-7 staminodes; filaments unequal in length, anthers of fertile stamens versatile, monothecal, dehiscing longitudinally. Ovary peri- or hypogynous, of 3 carpels, syncarpous, unilocular, stipitate, often curved and hairy; ovules many, anatropous, biseriate on 3 parietal placentas; style slender, tubular with a truncate or club-shaped stigma. Fruit an elongated 3-valved capsule, 3-6-angled, corky and pitted inside; seeds many in the depressions of the valves, winged or not, without endosperm and with oily cotyledons, embryo straight.

The single genus *Moringa* with 8 species occurs in Africa and Asia. *M. oleifera* Lam. is cultivated all over India in the plains and in other tropical countries for the fruits, flowers and young leaves which are used as vegetables. The seeds yield an oil which is used in lubricating fine machinery, e.g. watches, etc. The soft wood is used for fuel and is useless for any other purpose.

The family was placed in **Rhoeadales** by Engler because of its syncarpous ovary, many ovules on parietal placentation, capsular fruits and oily seeds. The monothecal anther and straight embryo are characters that speak against its inclusion in an order containing *Papaveraceae*. The stipitate ovary has some resemblance to the gynophore of *Capparidaceae* where the flowers are often slightly irregular. Moringaceae is therefore placed in **Capparidales** (or Capparales) by Hutchinson, Takhtajan and Cronquist.

SARRACENIALES

The order includes 3 families of insectivorous plants, viz:—*Sarraceniaceae*, *Nepenthaceae* and *Droseraceae*. In these families the leaves are modified variously to form traps for capturing small insects. Flowers are actinomorphic, bisexual or unisexual, hypogynous. Perianth in 2 whorls, with 4-5 segments in each. Stamens as many as petals or more, often numerous, with free or connate filaments. Ovary of 3-5 carpels, syncarpous, unilocular or 3-5-celled, superior; ovules numerous. Seeds minute; endosperm present.

That the 3 families are related to one another and should be included in a single order is supported by Harmes, Macfarlane, Diels and recently by Cronquist. Although we find in the family *Droseraceae* the leaves are differently modified for the purpose of insect-catching Mark-graf has shown that the leaves in all the three families are homologous. This order is placed next to **Rhoeadales** and is considered to have probably been derived from **Ranales.** *Sarraceniaceae* resembles *Nymphaeaceae* and *Papaveraceae* to some extent. K. Stern also considers that **Sarraceniales** is a natural taxon and *Nepenthaceae* although having unisexual flower bears strong affinity to *Droseraceae* both having similar pollen tetrads.

According to Hutchinson *Sarraceniaceae* and *Droseraceae* are close to each other but *Nepenthaceae* is not at all related to them. He therefore removed *Nepenthaceae* from **Sarraceniales** and placed it under **Aristolochiales** while **Saraceniales** with the other two families was placed after **Saxifragales.**

Takhtajan also splits **Sarraceniales** into 2 orders but in a different way. He places *Nepenthaceae* and *Droseraceae* under a new order **Nepenthales** which is included in his subclass **Rosidae,** while **Sarraceniales** with one family *Sarraceniaceae* is included in the subclass **Ranunculidae.**

Sarraceniaceae

Perrenial herbs of marshy places. Leaves radical, rosulate, tubular, usually with a small terminal lamina and retrorsely hairy within, often winged. Flowers solitary on a central scape or racemose, actinomorphic, bisexual, hypogynous, usually spirocyclic and pentamerous. Sepals 5 or rarely upto 9, free, imbricate, persistent, often petaloid. Petals 5, free, or absent. Stamens numerous, free, anthers 2-celled, dehiscing longitudinally. Ovary superior, of 3-5 united carpels, 3-5-locular, usually 3-5-lobed, with numerous ovules on axile placentation; style lobed at the apex or expanded like an umbrella over the stamens; stigmas situated beneath the tips of the lobes; ovules anatropous. Fruit a loculicidal capsule; seeds minute, with small embryo and soft fleshy endosperm; testa membranous and winged.

The leaves are modified to form pitchers, or ascidium. The upper part of the pitcher is prolonged into a lid or operculum. According to some the pitcher is the petiole and the lid is the leaf-lamina. Baillon considers the pitcher to be the modified lamina and the lid is nothing but an apical outgrowth of the lamina. This view is generally accepted. The pitcher has a velvety smooth slippery zone inside near the mouth. Then there is the glandular zone and last is the absorptive zone bearing reflexed hairs and filled with fluid rich in proteolytic enzyme. The body of the captured insect is digested by the fluild and absorbed by the glands on the pitcher wall. In *Sarracenia* the pitcher bulges out from a narrow base and has a more or less deltoid lid which is often brightly coloured and possesses nectar secreting glands. In *Darlingtonia* the pitcher is about a metre long gradually widening upwards and has a lid which is forked like a fish-tail.

The family contains 14 species only under 3 genera which are restricted in their distribution to eastern N. America. It is related to the other two families of the order and probably originated with the other two families from the **Ranales.** Hutchinson considers that *Sarraceniaceae* and *Droceraceae* are close together and originated from **Saxifragales** while *Nepenthaceae* is not closely related with these two families and originated from **Ranales.**

Nepenthaceae

Herbaceous or shrubby plants, often climbing by means of tendrilar leaf-apex. Leaves alternate, simple, subsessile or sessile, with a linear or lanceolate blade and a prolonged apex forming a tendril; the tendril usually terminates in a cylindrical or urceolate pitcher or ascidium with a lid or operculum; stipules absent. Plants are dioecious; flowers borne in axillary racemes or panicles, actinomorphic, hypogynous.

Perianth in 2 whorls, segments 2 in each whorl arranged crosswise, all similar and sepaloid, free, rarely perianth members 3 or 5-6; imbricate, glandular inside and hairy outside. Stamens 4-24, monadelphous in a column; anthers distinct, 2-celled, dehiscing longitudinally, extrorse; pollens in tetrads. Ovary spuperior, 4-carpelled and 4-chambered; rarely 3-carpelled and 3-chambered; ovules many, anatropous, on axile placentation; style small and stout or absent, stigma discoid. Fruit an elongated loculicidal capsule; seeds many, filiform, ascending and imbricate; embryo straight embedded in a thin layer of fleshy endosperm.

The pitcher has a recurved fluted rim and a lid which is often brightly coloured and variously margined; nectar is secreted on the rim, at the mouth of the pitcher and often at base of the lid. The pitcher contains a fluid with a proteolytic enzyme secreted by the glands lining the lower portion of wall. The insects falling into the pitcher gets drowned in the fluid and is digested, the soluble proteid being ultimately absorbed by the walls of the pitcher.

The family contains only 1 genus with over 60 species (according to some 2 genera *Nepenthes* and *Anurosperma*) distributed in the eastern tropical zone from Madagascar to New Caledonia and occurring more in Malaysia. In India *N. khasiana* Linn. is found to grow in and around Shillong in Meghalaya.

The family is closely related to *Sarraceniaceae* and *Droseraceae* and has been placed in the order **Sarreceniales** along with these 2 families by most authors. Takhtajan considers that *Nepenthaceae* is allied to *Droseraceae* but is not at all related to *Sarraceniaceae*. According to Hutchinson *Nepenthaceae* is allied to *Aristolochiaceae* and therefore includes *Nepenthaceae* in **Aristolociales** while *Sarraceniaceae* and *Droseraceae* are placed in **Sarraceniales** having probable affinity with **Saxifragales.**

The family is of no economic importance but plants are often cultivated as curiosities.

Droseraceae

Annual or perennial herbs or undershrubs, often with perennial rhizome, inhabiting marshy places. Leaves alternate, rarely whorled near the base forming a rosette, usually covered with viscid glands or tentacles for catching small insects; often circinate in bud; membranous stipules often present. The inflorescence is a spike or a raceme or sometimes a cincinnus, or flowers may be solitary. Flowers bisexual, actinomorphic, hypogynous, pentamerous or tetramerous. Sepals 4-5, connate near base, imbricate, persistent. Petals usually 5, free, convolute. Stamens 5-10 or more, in one or more pentamerous whorls, free or rarely connate below; anthers extrorse, 2-celled, cells often divergent and with broad connective, dehiscing longitudinally; the pollens are in tetrads. Ovary superior or half-inferior, 3-5-carpelled, syncarpous, unilocular with numerous anatropous ovules on 3-5 parietal placentas; rarely ovules few on basally free central placenta; styles 3-5, usually free, often forked or branched with capitate stigmas; very rarely the ovary 3-5-chambered with axile placentation. Fruit a loculicidal capsule; seeds numerous with straight embryo and granular endosperm.

The leaves have 2 kinds of glands, the stalked glands that always secrete a sticky fluid and the sessile glands which secrete a digestive ferment only when stimulated by a nitrogenous matter. *Drosera* and *Drosophyllum* have such stalked glands or tentacles. They attract the small insects and keep them attached to the leaves by means of the viscid substances. They are capable of movement or curvature and bend down over the body of the captured insect from all sides to hold it tightly. The digestive fluid secreted by the sessile glands absorb the decomposed body of the insect. *Aldrovanda* and *Dionaea* have different mechanism for capturing their prey. The leaf has a broad lamina on a distinct petiole. The lamina is divided into two halves which can fold and close along the midrib on slight stimulus and trap an insect alighting on the

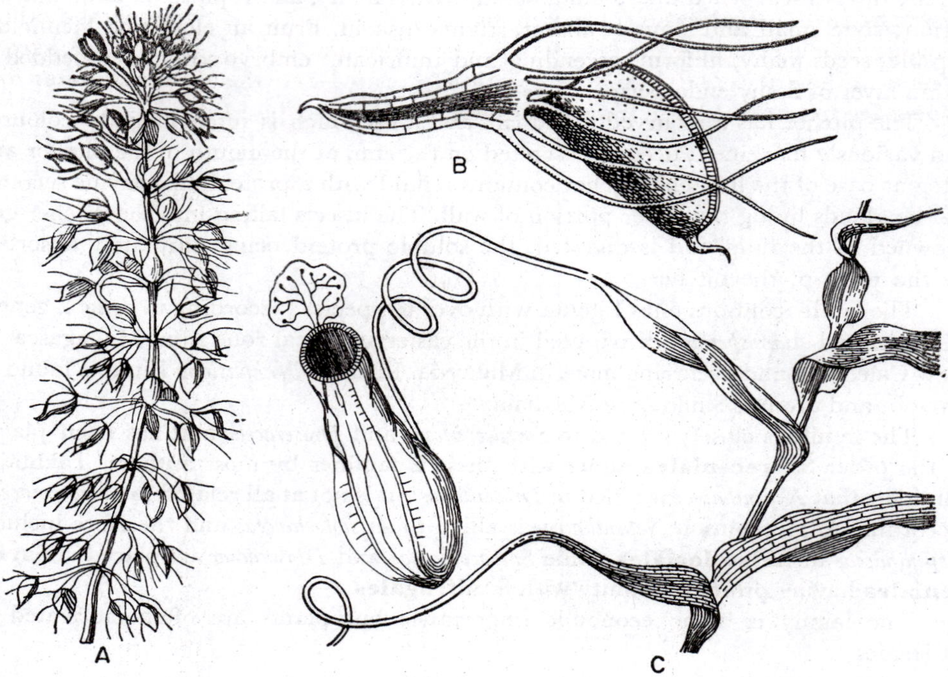

Fig. 76. A—Aldrovanda vesiculosa Linn. part of the plant with whorls of leaves (×1); B—one leaf of same with closed blade (much enlarged); C—Pitcher plant (Nepenthes) with one pitcher (reduced).

surface of the lamina. The digestive fluid secreted by the glands on the surface of lamina gradually absorb the decomposed body.

Dionaea is a small herb with a rosette of basal leaves. It has a perennial rhizome. *Aldrovanda* is a rootless submerged herb with slender stem and branches and a whorl of leaves at each node. *Drosophyllum* has a short woody stem which is often branched. The long narrow leaves are crowded at the apical part of stem and branches and the persistent leaf bases of the older leaves cover the lower part of the stem.

Drosophyllum and *Dionaea* have primary root, but in most *Drosera* species primary root is absent and protocorm like structure develops from the hypocotyl bearing filiform rhizoid-like structure.

The family consists of 4 genera only of which *Drosera* has 84 species distributed over wide areas in the 2 hemispheres having quite a number in Australia. Other 3 genera are monotypic. *Drosophyllum* is N. American, *Dionaea* is confined to western Mediterranean region while *Aldrovanda* occurs in Europe, Asia and Australia. Several species of *Drosera* occur in India, e.g. *D. indica L.*, *D. burmannii* Vahl., *D. peltata* Sm. etc. *Aldrovanda vesiculosa L.* which has a very wide distribution is found in Dacca. It was reported from Calcutta about a century ago but is no longer found.

The leaves of *Drosera* yield a violet dye.

As to the affinity of the family different opinions have been expressed. Engler, Rendle and others consider the 3 families *Sarraceniaceae*, *Nepenthaceae* and *Droseraceae* closely related and place them in a single order next to **Rhoedales.** Cronquist also considers that the 3 families are allied to one another. Diels, Wettstein, and few other placed *Droseraceae* in the **Parietales** for having parietal placentation. Hutchinson and others following Lindley consider the family to be close to *Saxifragaceae*. It is, however, agreed by most authors that the 3 families are closely related and that **Sarraceniales** like **Rhoedales** has been derived from **Ranales.**

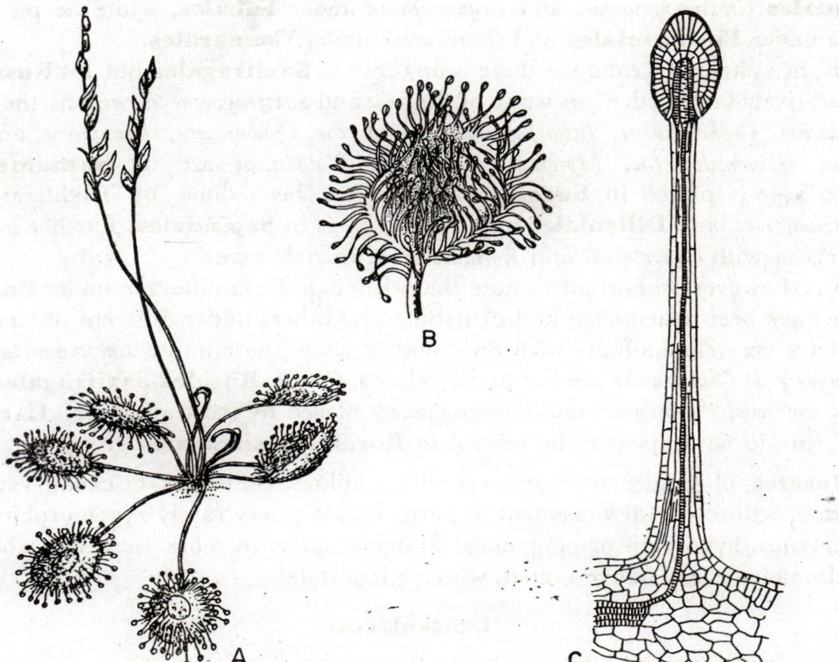

Fig. 77. Drosera burmannii Vahl. A—Plant with leaves and flowering shoot (×1); B—One leaf-blade (×3); C—One tentacle (much enlarged).

ROSALES

In Engler and Prantl's system **Sarraceniales** is followed by Rosales whichis a very large group consisting of 17 families in 2 sub-orders, viz. **Saxifragineae** and **Rosineae.** Later in the revised system *Podostemonaceae* and *Hydrostachyaceae* were also placed in this order under another suborder **Podostemonineae.** In **Saxifragineae** Engler included the following families, viz. *Crassulaceae*, *Cephalotaceae*, *Saxifragaceae*, *Pittosporaceae*, *Byblidaceae*, *Brunelliaceae*, *Cunoniaceae*, *Myrothamnaceae*, *Bruniaceae*, *Hamamelidaceae*, *Roridulaceae* and *Eucommiaceae*. In *Rosineae* were included only 5 families, viz., *Platanaceae*, *Crossosomataceae*, *Rosaceae*, *Connaraceae* and *Leguminosae*.

All subsequent workers (except Rendle) hold the opinion that Engler's **Rosales** is a heterogenous assemblage of distantly related families. Different workers, therefore, arrange the families under several smaller orders which are again placed in different subclasses or groups higher than orders. Hutchinson distributes them in 8 orders, viz. **Saxifragles** with *Saxifragaceae, Crassulaceae* and *Cephalotaceae*, **Pittosporales** with *Pittosporaceae* and *Byblidaceae*, **Cunoniales** with *Cunoniaceae*, **Hamamelidales** with *Hamamelidaceae, Myrothamnaceae, Bruniaceae* and *Platanaceae*, **Rosales** with *Rosaceae*, **Leguminales** with *Leguminoceae*, **Dilleniales** with *Dilleniaceae, Brunelliaceae, Crossosomataceae* and *Connaraceae* and **Urticales** with *Eucommiaceae*. He merges *Roridulacea* with *Byblidaceae*.

Takhtajan includes only *Rosaceae* (sensu latro of Engler) in his **Rosales.** He has under his **Saxifragales** the following families, viz. *Crassulaceae, Cephalotaceae, Saxifragaceae, Pittosporaceae, Byblidaceae, Brunelliaceae, Cunoniaceae, Bruniaceae* and *Roridulaceae.* Under **Hamamelidales** he has *Myrothananaceae, Hamamelidaceae* and *Platanaceae*, under **Dilleniales** *Crossosomataceae*, and *Leguminoseae* under **Fabales,** while he puts *Eucommiaceae* under **Eucommiales** and *Connaraceae* under **Connarales.**

In the system of Cronquist there is no order as **Saxifragales** but his **Rosales** is a comparatively large order consisting of *Rosaceae* and *Saxifragaceae* as well as the families *Crassulaceae, Cephalotaceae, Pittosporaceae, Byblidaceae, Cunoniaceae, Bruniaceae* and *Leguminosae. Hamamelidaceae, Myrothamnaceae* and *Platanaceae* are in **Hamamelidales.** *Eucommiaceae* is placed in **Eucommiales** as has been done by Takhtajan, while *Crossosomataecae* is in **Dilleniales** and *Connaraceae* is in **Sapindales.** Further he merges *Brunelliaceae* with *Cunoniaceae* and *Roridulaceae* with *Byblidaceae.*

It is, however, important to note that although the families put under **Rosales** by Engler have been rearranged and distributed by others under different orders some of them have very close affinity with one another while the families *Eucommiaceae, Crossosomataceae* and *Connaraceae* are not at all related to the **Rosales-Saxifragales** group. *Myrothamnaceae, Platanaceae* and *Hamamelidaceae* placed by most authors in **Hamamelidales** also do not appear to be related to **Rosales-Saxifragales** group.

Rosales of Engler is characterized as follows:—Flowers bisexual, very rarely unisexual, with cyclic arrangement of parts, regular, very rarely zygomorphic, usually pentamerous, hypo-peri- or epigynous. Stamens many in more than one whorl, free. Carpels many or few, free or united, with distinct styles.

Crassulaceae

Succulent perennial herbs or shrubs. Leaves simple or compound, opposite, alternate or whorled, exstipulate, more or less thick and fleshy. Inflorescence a dichasial or monochasial cyme or panicle, rarely raceme or spike. Flowers bisexual, rarely unisexual, actinomorphic, usually hypogynous, 4-5-merous. Sepals 4-5, usually free, valvate, persistent. Petals as many as sepals, free or united in a tube, imbricate. Stamens as many as petals or twice as many as petals in 2 whorls; filaments free, inserted on a swollen or cup-like disc; anther bilocular, introrse, dihescing longitudinally. Ovary superior or rarely semi-inferior, with free or almost free carpels, usually as many as petals or more, rarely carpels 3, styles free with small stigmas; each carpel is provided with a nectar secreting scale; ovules many in each carpel on marginal placentas. Fruit a cluster of follicles. Seeds small, with straight embryo and scanty fleshy endosperm or endosperm absent.

The floral formula is $K_n C_n A_{n+n} G_n$ where "n" is usually valued as 4-5 but in some cases several and rarely upto 30. The genus *Rhodiola* has unisexual flowers in dioecious plants. The leaves are provided with hydathodes and often impregnated with silica. In some cases the leaves are cylindrical or subulate. Adventitious buds develop on leaf-margin by which vegetative reproduction takes place. The leaves have sunken stomata.

Water storage tissues are present both in leaves and stem. Xylem cylinder is usually continuous. The secondary vessels are with simple pits and reticulate thickenings. Perforations are simple.

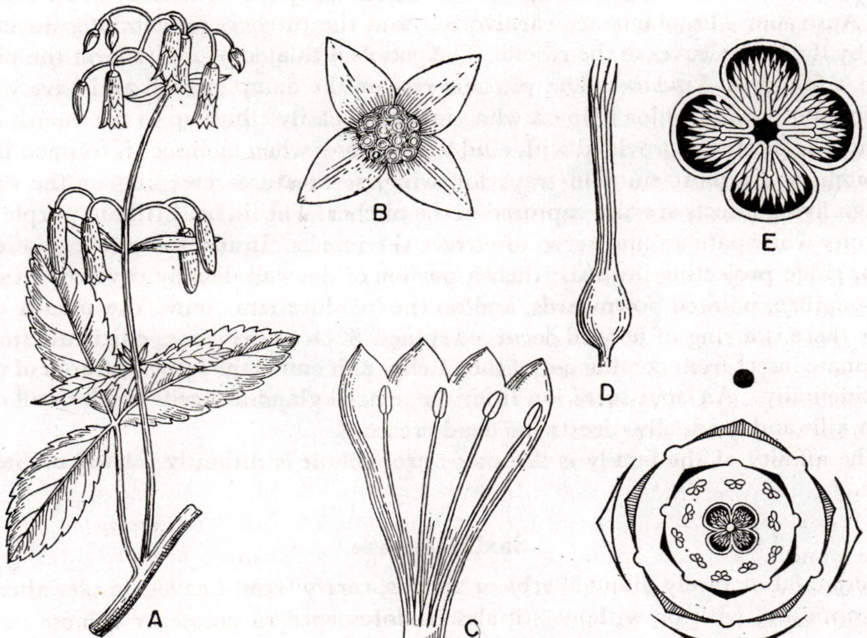

Fig. 78. Kalanchoe pinnata Pers. A—Portion of the plant with leaves and flower: $(\times\frac{1}{4})$; B. Front view of a flower; C—Corolla and stamens; D—Ovary; E—T.s. of ovary.

The family consists of about 1,300 species in 29 genera distributed in comparatively drier parts of the world but absent in Australia. In India several species of *Sedum* occur in the Himalayas and *Kalanchoe pinnata* (Lam.) Pers. and *K. laciniata* Adams are common in the plains. Plants of this family have no economic importance but a few are cultivated as garden ornamentals.

The family is very much allied to *Saxifragaceae* having 2 whorls of stamens, bisexual flowers, fleshy endosperm, etc. It is also related to *Rosaceae* to some extent. It is, therefore, included in **Rosales** or **Saxifragales** by most authors subsequent to Engler.

Cephalotaceae

Perrnnial herbs with short under-ground rhizomes. Leaves radical, crowded in a rosette round the erect flowering scape; these are of 2 kinds, the lower leaves bearing pitchers like those of *Nepenthes*, the upper leaves simple, with normal elliptic blades, entire, nerveless. The inflorescence is a thyrsus—a raceme of cymules, bracteate at the base. Flowers small hermaphrodite regular and perigynous. Calyx gamosepalous, campanulate, coloured, persistent; lobes 6, valvate, hooded. Corolla absent. Stamens 12, inserted on the margin of a setose glandular disc at the top of the calyx; filaments free, 6 longer than the others; anthers 2-locular, dehiscing longitudinally; connective swollen at the top and glandular. Carpels 6, free, or more or less united, hairy, in a single whorl, each 1-locular and with 1, rarely 2 basal erect ovules. Ovary superior. Style short, recurved, subulate with simple stigma. Fruit a cluster of follicles surrounded by the accrescent calyx, shortly stipitate and densely hairy, 1-seeded. Seeds with fleshy endosperm and small straight embryo.

The small family with a single species *Cephalotus follicularis* Lab. is restricted to S. W. Australia. The plants are carnivorous and the pitchers for catching insects are borne by the lower leaves of the rosette. The petiole is dilated at top to form the pitcher like that found in *Nepenthes*. The pitchers rest on the damp ground and have winged ridges on the outside which help crawling insects to easily climb up to the mouth of the pitcher. The pitcher is provided with a lid which closes when an insect is trapped inside. The pitchers are most suitable traps for wingless creatures creeping on the ground although flying insects are also captured in the pitcher. The lid has brilliant purple veins and pretty white patches and serve to attract the insects. Inside the pitcher there is a circular ridge projecting inwards; then a portion of the wall densely covered with little sharp papillae, pointed downwards, and on the involute rim round the mouth of the pitcher there is a ring of hooked decurved spines. Such contrivances efficiently stop the unfortunate insect from coming out of the pitcher as it enters the same in search of nectar or accidentally. An acid secretion from the special glandular cells on the wall of the pitcher kills and gradually digests the dead creature.

The affinity of the family is disputed; probably it is distantly related to Saxifragaceae.

Saxifragaceae

Perennial or rarely annual herbs or shrubs, rarely trees. Leaves simple, alternate, rarely opposite, with or without stipules. Inflorescence racemose or cymose or of a complex type, flowers usually bisexual, regular, usually 5, numerous with cyclic arrangement; receptacle flat or cupular or tubular so that the flower is hypo-, peri-, or even epigynous; bracts often present. Sepals 4-5, free or united at base and adnate to the receptacular cup forming a hypanthodium, imbricate or valvate. Petals as many as sepals, usually free, rarely united or absent, imbricate or valvate, inserted on the hypanthodium. Stamens usually double the number of petals and in 2 whorls, often as many as petals and in 1 whorl, free, inserted on the hypanthodium; anthers bithecal, with longitudinal dehiscence. Ovary superior, semi-inferior or inferior; carpels 2-5, united below with free styles; cells as many as carpels with rows of anatropous ovules on axile placentation; ovary is often 1-celled or rarely carpels may be free; often the ovary is obliquely placed. Fruit a capsule or berry. Endosperm, fleshy, copious, surrounding a small embryo.

Flowers are insect-pollinated and are protrandrous or protogynous. The typical floral formula is $K_5\ C_5\ A_{5+5}\ G_{(\underline{2})}$.

Plants are usually herbs but shrubs and trees are also found, e.g. *Hydrangea*, *Philadelphus*, *Escallonia*, etc. Leaves are simple but in *Bauera* 3-foliolate leaves are produced. *Saxifraga*, *Astilbe*, *Parnassia*, etc. have alternate leaves but *Hydrangea*, *Deutzia* etc. have opposite leaves. Inflorescence may be a raceme or spike, or a cyme, often paniculate. *Chrysosplenium* has a biparous cyme. In *Hydrangea* it is an umbel-like spreading panicle of biparous and uniparous cymes. Zygomorphic flowers are found in some *Saxifraga*, and in *Hydrangea* the peripheral barren flowers are so. Unisexual flowers are found in some *Ribes* and *Astilbe*. *Ribes alpinum L.* is dioecious. Petals are absent in *Chrysosplenium*. In *Parnassia* the inner whorl of stamens are sterile and modified into palmately lobed staminodes. Ovary may be superior, semi-inferior or inferior even in the same genus, e.g. *Saxifraga*. In *Ribes, Bauera*, etc. ovary is 1-locular, while 2-5-locular ovary are found in others.

The family consisting of about 1,200 species in 80 genera occur usually in the cooler parts of the globe; many are alpine and some occur in the artic region. Some are xerophytic and a few are even hygrophilous. In India the family is represented in the Himalayas by *Hydrangea, Astilbe, Ribes, Parnassia, Deutzia, Saxifraga* etc. *Vahlia viscosa* Roxb. and *V. oldenlandioides* Roxb. occur in the plains of eastern India.

Currants are different species of *Ribes* and *R. grossularia L.* is the Goose-berry. *Dichroa febrifuga* Hk.f. of E. Himalaya is reputed to have medicinal properties, *Philadelphus coronarius L.* with fragrant flowers and *Hydrangea hortensis* are cultivated as ornamental plants. Otherwise the family is not of much economic value.

The family is subdivided into several sub-families by Engler as given below:—

I. *Saxifragoideae:* Herbs with alternate, exstipulate leaves; flowers hypo-, peri-, or epigynous; sepals and petals 5 or 4; carpels usually 2, rarely more. *Saxifraga, Astilbe, Parnassia*, etc.

II. *Francoideae:* Herbs with radical leaves; flowers tetramerous with 4-celled ovary. *Francoa, Tellima.*

III. *Hydrangeoideae:* Shrubs or trees with opposite leaves; flowers usually epigynous; sepals 5, petals 5, ovary 3-5-celled. *Hydrangaea, Deutzia, Philadelphus.*

IV. *Pterostemonoideae:* Shrubs, leaves stipulate; flowers epigynous, 5-merous; stamens 10, ovary of 5 carpels, 5-celled. *Pterostemon.*

V. *Escallonioideae:* Shrubs or trees, leaves gland-dotted, exstipulate; flowers hypo-, peri- or epigynous; stamens as many as petals, carpels 2-5. *Escallonia, Itea.*

VI. *Ribesioideae:* Shrubs, leaves exstipulate; flowers epigynous; ovary 1-celled; placentation parietal; fruit berry. *Ribes.*

VII. *Baueroideae:* Shrubs, leaves 3-foliolately compound; flowers perigynous; ovary 1-celled with parietal placentation. *Bauera.*

Saxifragaceae is related to *Crassulaceae* having usually 5-merous flowers and stamens in 2 whorls. In *Crassulaceae* endosperm when present is fleshy as in *Saxifragaceae*. This family is also allied to *Rosaceae* to some extent.

Variations in the floral structure prompted many authors to split the family into several smaller families, e.g. *Saxifragaceae* (sensu stricto), *Eremosynaceae, Vahliaceae, Francoaceae, Parnasiaceae, Petrostemonaceae, Philadelphaceae Hydrangeaceae, Grossulariaceae* and *Escalloniaceae*. According to Takhtajan these are more or less closely related and are all included in his **Saxifragales** along with some other families while Hutchinson puts first five families in **Saxifragales** and the other five families in **Cunoniales.** The two orders are not close to each other and **Cunoniales** is one of the primitive orders among the **Lignosae** while **Saxifragales** is in the **Herbaceae** and is considered fairly advanced.

Cronquist does not recognise so many small families but has separated only *Hydrangeaceae* and *Grossulariaceae* from *Saxifragaceae*. His *Hydrangiaceae* includes *Petrostemonaceae* and *Philadelphaceae* and *Grossulariaceae* includes *Escalloniaceae*.

Hamamelidaceae

Trees and shrubs; bark containing a bitter and acrid juice. Leaves simple, alternate, stipulate; stipules caducous. Inflorescence is a capitulum or spike. Flowers bisexual or polygamous or unisexual and monoecious or dioecious, actinomorphic or very rarely zygomorphic, perigynous or epigynous, rarely hypogynous, usually tetramerous. Calyx of 4, rarely 5 sepals united at base in the form of a cup or tube; segments imbricate. Petals 4 or rarely 5, inserted on the calyx tube, free, usually valvate, linear and circinate in bud, often petals absent. Stamens usually 8-10 in 2 whorls, the inner whorl often sterile, often stamens in one whorl and few or many; anthers bithecal, dehiscing longitudinally or by valves; connective prolonged to a horny tip. Ovary inferior, semi-inferior or superior, of 2 united carpels, 2-locular, styles free, usually recurved, persistent; ovules many or few in each cell, pendulous from axile placentation, anatropous. Fruit a loculicidal or septicidal capsule, 2-beaked, bursting at top, with leathery or woody exocarp and bony endocarp, usually with 1 seed in each chamber. Seed with or without endosperm and a large straight embryo.

Plants are evergreen but deciduous trees are also found, e.g. *Hamamelis*, *Parrottia*, etc. Leaves are pinnately veined and with glandular toothed margin while *Liquidambar* has palmately lobed leaves. *Liquidambar* and *Altingia* have unisexual flowers; the males are in dense spikes, the female flowers crowded in globose heads with rudimentary calyx and few staminodes. Here the flowers are epigynous and the floral heads often subtended by coloured bracts. *Distylium*, *Hamamelis*, etc. have hypogynous flowers.

This is a small family with about 100 species in 27 genera of which 14 are monotypic. Most of them are confined to Western and Central Asia while a few are found in distant countries so that the family has a wide range of distribution from N. America to Australia. It is represented in Africa and Madagascar and also in S. Europe. In the Himalayas *Exbucklandia populnea* R.W.Br., *Corylops himalayana* Griff., *Altingia excelsa* Noronha and some species of *Liquidamber* are good timber trees.

Liquidambar orientalis Mill. of W. Asia and *L. styraciflua* Linn. of N. America are the source of storax—a fragrant balsam. *Exbucklandia populnea* R.W.Br., *Altingia excelsa* Griff. and some species of *Liquidamber* are good timber trees.

The family appears to be closely allied to *Myrothamnaceae* and *Platanaceae*. The 3 families are placed under **Hamamelidales** by Hutchinson along with five other families. According to him **Rosales** and **Hamamelidales** are not very close but both are derived from same ancestral stock. Tippo states that from **Hamamelidales** orders like **Casuarinales, Fagales, Urticales** and **Juglandales** originated. This view is supported by Cronquist according to whom **Trochodendrales, Eucommiales, Leitneriales** and **Myricales** are also derived from **Hammelidales.** Takhtajan also considers these orders close to each other and includes them in his subclass **Hamamelididae** along with **Cercidiphyllales, Eupteleales, Didymelales, Barbeyales** and **Balanophorales.**

The family is subdivided into 5 subfamilies as follows:—

I. **Disanthoideae:** Capitula of 2 different flowers; petals long, narrow; ovules up to 6 in each locule.

II. **Hamamelidoideae:** Flowers bisexual, rarely unisexual, usually superior, petals long, narrow; ovules 1-2 in each locule.

III. **Rhodoleioideae:** Capitula axillary, pendulous, surrounded by many imbricating bracts; woody capsule; endosperm copious.

IV **Exbucklandioideae:** Capitula polygamo-monoecious; leaves palmiveined, simple or 3-lobed.

V. **Liquidambaroideae:** Flowers unisexual and monoecious, males without perianth, females with rudimentary perianth; leaves glandular serrate or palmately lobed; ovules many in each cell.

The subfamilies *Rhodoleioideae* and *Liquidambaroideae* are raised to the rank of families by some workers as **Rhodoleiaceae** and **Altingiaceae.** Fossils of *Liquidambar* and *Parrotia* were discovered in upper oligocene belt; *Hamamelis* was found in chalk-belt.

Platanaceae

Large deciduous trees, bark exfoliating in large flakes leaving a smooth trunk. Leaves simple, alternate, usually palmately lobed and palmately nerved, dentate, stipulate; stipules membranous, caducous, usually large and conspicuous and sheathing; the petiole is dilated at base enclosing the axlliary bud. Inflorescence of globose heads or capitula several in a pendulous peduncle; each head wholly male or wholly female; bracts linear or scale-like. Perianth absent. Stamens in male flowers many, each subtended by a minute scale; anthers subsessile, oblong or obpyramidal with expanded peltate connective, bilocular, dehiscing longitudinally; pistillode often present in ♂ flowers. Ovary of a single carpel, 1-locular with 1 or rarely 2 pendulous orthotropous ovules; stigma unilateral on an elongated linear style; staminodes often present in female flowers. Fruit a globose head of ± turbinate achenes or caryopsis with persistent styles, surrounded by tufts of long bristle-like pappus or hairs, each with a single linear seed. Embryo straight and narrow; endosperm scanty.

The family consisting of a single genus with 10 species has a scattered distribution, from Tropical America, S. E. Mediterrnean region and W. Asia and in Indo-China. W. Asiatic species *Platanus orientalis* Linn was introduced into India and was naturalised in Kashmir. This is a large tree often with a girth of 12 mtr. or more and lives to a great age. The timber obtained is used for manufacture of furniture although it is of a rather inferior quality. It is mainly planted as a shade tree or avenue tree.

The family is related to *Hamamelidaceae* through the genus *Altingia* or to *Altingiaceae* when considered as a distinct family having unisexual capitula, anthers with prominent connective and ovary with persistent style. It is placed in the suborder **Rosineae** of **Rosales** by Engler while **Hamamelidaceae** is placed in the suborder **Saxifragineae.** Most of the subsequent workers including Hutchinson, Takhtajan and Cronquist recognise the close affinity of *Platanaceae* with *Hamamelidaceae* and place the family in **Hamamelidales,** an order distinct from **Saxifragales** or **Rosales.**

Rosaceae

This is a large family of herbs, shrubs and trees; herbs may be erect or prostrate with runners; shrubs erect or scandent or climbing. Leaves simple or pinnately, rarely palmately compound, usually stipulate, mostly alternate. Inflorescence is a raceme or panicle, sometimes cymes, rarely solitary. Flowers actinomorphic, very rarely zygomorphic, usually bisexual, perigynous or hypogynous, rarely epigynous. Receptacle large, flat or cupular. Sepals usually 5, connate and adnate to the receptacle, lobes imbricate or valvate. Petals 5 or more, free, inserted on the receptacular cup or hypanthium. Stamens many or sometimes 5 or 10; anthers 2-locular, dehiscing laterally; filaments in different whorls differing in length. A cushion-shaped or ring-like nectar secreting disc is present between the stamens and carpels. Carpel 1 or more, often many, free or syncarpous in the cup-shaped receptacle forming a superior or semi-inferior or sometimes inferior ovary; ovule 1-few in each carpel, pendulous or ascending; styles free in case of syncarpous ovary. Fruit a drupe or berry or pseudocarp or an aggregate of achenes or berries. Seed with a small straight embryo and usually no endosperm.

The family with about 2,000 species in about 100 genera is distributed mainly in the N. temperate regions of the globe. It is well represented in India, especially in the Himalayas where a large number of *Rubus* species occur, besides species of *Rosa*, *Cotoneaster*, *Pyrus*, *Prunus*, *Eriobotrya*, *Spiraea*, *Potentilla*, *etc.*

Much diversity of forms, vegetative as well as floral, is noticed in this large family. There are trailing or creeping herbs like *Fragaria*, erect herbs like *Agrimonia*, some *Potentilla*, erect shrubs like *Spiraea*, some *Rosa*, scrambling like most *Rubus* and a few *Rosa* species, trees like *Pyrus*, *Prunus*, *Eriobotrya*, etc. Leaves simple in *Prunus*, *Quillaja*, *Eriobotrya*, etc., pinnate as in *Rosa*, *Pyrus*, etc., digitate as in *Fragaria* and *Rubus*. Stipules usually present but absent in *Spiraea*; caducus in *Prunus* and adnate in many genera. Flowers bisexual but polygamous in *Poterium*.

Fig. 79.
Eriobotrya japonica Lindl. A. Part of a branch with leaves and inflorescence (× 1/4); B. One flower (× 2).

Regular flower in all genera but in the subfamily **Chrysobalanoideae** the flowers are zygomorphic. In *Potentilla* a whorl of epicalyx is present. The receptacle shows much variation in shape and may be more or less flat or concave of varying depth, and in **Chrysobalanoideae** forms a tube; a convex receptacle is found in *Fragaria*. The character of the receptacle forms the basis of the subdivisions of the family. Stamens are usually many but in *Alchemilla arvensis* Scop there is only one stamen while in *Couepia* (**Chrysobalanoideae**) there are as many as 300; stamens are free but rarely monadelphous, e.g. *Acioa*. Carpels many or few, rarely 1 as in *Prunus* and *Acioa*, usually free, but connate and adnate to the receptacular cup as in **Pomoideae** and **Neuradoideae**; in **Pomoideae** the united carpels form an inferior ovary; in other cases the gynoecium is superior or semi-inferior. Style is usually terminal but lateral in *Fragaria* and basal in *Acioa* and *Alchemilla*. The style is often persistent, becoming feather-like in *Dryas*. The nature of fruit also varies from a cluster of achenes or follicles or berries to a pome or a drupe.

The typical floral formula would be: $K_{(5)}\ C_5\ A_\infty\ G_{1-\infty}$ or $G_{(\infty)}$

The family is important not only for the ornamental plants cultivated in the gardens but also for many species yielding edible fruits. Roses of the gardens are different species of *Rosa* with hundreds of hoticultural varieties. The famous essence Oto is obtained from *R. damascena* Mill. much cultivated in Bulgaria, in Iran and in Gazipur in India. The cherries are different species of *Prunus*, much cultivated in Japan for showy flowers. Many species of *Spiraea*, some *Pocntillla*, a few *Rubus* are also cultivated for the same purpose.

Famous fruit trees are: the apple—*Malus sylvestris* Mill., the pear—*Pyrus commumis* Linn., the plum—*Prunus domestica* Linn., the peach—*Prunus persica* (L.) Batsch., the apricot—*Prunus armeniaca* Linn., the almond—*Prunus dulcis* L. the strawberry—*Fragaria vesca* Linn., the raspberry—*Rubus caesius* Linn., the loquat—*Eriobotrya japonica* Lindl., the quince—*Cydonia oblonga* Mill. etc.

A few have medicinal value. The petals of *Rosa centifolia* L. boiled in sugary solution is called Gulcand and is used as a rejuvenating tonic. *Quillaja saponaria* L. is the soap-bark tree, the bark of which contains saponin and is used for cleaning textiles.

The family is divided into 6 subfamilies by Focke in Pflanzenfamilien as given below:

I. **Spiraeoideae.** Stipules usually absent; receptacle flat or slightly concave; stamens 10-∞, carpels 12-1 (usually 5) in a central whorl, ovules 2 or more in each; fruit a cluster of follicles.

II. **Pomoideae (Pyroideae).** Stipules present; receptacle deeply cup-shaped; stamens many; carpels 5-2, syncarpous and completely adnate to the inner wall of the receptacular cup forming an inferior ovary; ovules 2 in each locule; fruit a pseudocarp or pome, seed 1 in each chamber.

III. **Rosoideae.** Stipules adnate to petiole; receptacle a deep cup or convex and swollen, rarely flat; stamens ∞ ; carpels many, free on the flat or convex receptacle or at the bottom of the cup-shaped torus, ovules 2 or 1 in each carpel; fruit a cluster of 1-seeded drupelets or achenes, the drupelets may fuse to form a pseudocarp or berry; seed 1 in each chamber.

IV. **Neuradoideae.** Stipules minute or absent; receptacle cup-shaped; stamens 5+5, filaments long; carpels 3-10, horizontal and verticillate, ± connate and adnate to the receptacular cup which enlarges and forms a dry covering in fruit, ovules 1-2 in each carpel, pendulous; seed 1 in each mature carpel.

V. **Prunoideae.** Stipules small, often caducous; receptacle cup-shaped; stamens 10, 20 or more on the rim of the cupular receptacle; carpel 1, rarely up to 5, at the centre of the receptacular cup forming a superior ovary, ovules 2, pendulous in each carpel; fruit a one seeded drupe.

VI. **Chrysobalanoideae.** Stipules present; flowers usually zygomorphic; receptacle saccate or spurred on posterior side; stamens 10, pushed to the anterior side and often monadelphous; carpel solitary, free from the receptacle and superior, ovules 2, erect, style gynobasic or lateral, often carpels 2 and united; fruit a drupe.

The last subfamily, i.e. Chrysobalanoideae is raised to the rank of a distinct family by most authors as **Chrysobalanaceae.** Heywood who recognises Chrysobalanaceae as a distinct family arranges the rest of the 5 subfamilies in 2 groups depending on the basic chromosome numbers as noted below:

Group I—basic chromosome nos. 7, 8, 9, Subf. 1 Sipraeoideae, Subf. 2 Rosoideae, Subf. 3 Neuradoideae, Subf. 4 Prunoideae.

Group II—basic chromosome no. 17, Subf. 5 Maloideae.

The subfamily Neuradoideae is also recognised by some as deserving distinct family status but most authors are in favour of retaining same under Rosaceae. Hutchinson, however, treats the family Rosaceae in a broad sense and divides the family into 20 tribes, viz. (1) Quillajeae, (2) Spiraeeae, (3) Neillieae, (4) Gillenieae, (5) Neuradeae, (6) Osmaronieae, (7) Pruneae, (8) Chrysobalaneae, (9) Ulmarieae, (10) Rubieae, (11) Holodisceae, (12) Rodotypeae, (13) Kerrieae, (14) Potentillae, (15) Dryadeae, (16) Poterieae, (17) Cercocarpeae, (18) Adenostomateae, (19) Roseae and (20) Pomeae.

The characteristic anatomical features are the presence of tracheids and fibre-tracheids with bordered pits, solitary vessels small as well as large, with simple perforations, often ring porous alternate intervascular pitting and apotracheal diffuse wood parenchyma. The solitary vessels, trachleds and fibre-tracheids indicate that the family is primitive to some extent. This is supported by the morphological characters of flat or convex receptacle in sone genera, many free stamens and free carpels. Fossil records also show that Rosaceae is one of the most ancient families among the Dicotyledons.

Engler included several families in his **Rosales** along with Rosaceae, e.g., Crassulaceae, Cephalotaceae, Saxifragaceae, Pittosporaceae, Brunelliaceae, Cunoniaceae, Myrothamnaceae, Bruniaceae, Hamamelidaceae, Eucomiaceae, Platanaceae, Crossosomataceae, Connaraceae and Leguminosae. But **Rosales** of others contains only few families and the order is considered to have given rise to many other orders of Dicotyledons.

Rosaceae is allied to **Saxifragaceae.** According to Hutchinson it is derived from the same stock as **Dilleniaceae.** It is also related to **Leguminosae,** the flowers of Prunoideae and Chrysobalanoideae having monocarpellary pistil and in Chrysobalanoideae the flowers being zygomorphic.

Chrysobalanaceae as a distinct family may be described briefly in the following manner: Trees and shrubs. Leaves simple, alternate, stipulate, entire. Flowers bisexual or unisexual, usually zygomorphic. Receptacle very deep, prolonged to a tubular structure, in racemose inflorescence. Calyx of 5 sepals, ±unequal or calcarate at base. Petals 5, often unequal, shortly unguiculate, inserted at the mouth of calyx, rarely corolla absent. Stamens 2-many (300 in *Couepia*), filaments filiform pushed to anterior side, often monadelphus, anthers introrse. Ovary superior or semi-inferior, of 3 carpels but only one carpel develops; ovules 2, basal, erect; style lateral or gynobasic. Fruit a drupe with bony endocarp, rarely a crustaceous berry. Seeds with fleshy cotyledons and without endosperm.

Leguminosae

Herbs, shrubs or trees, sometimes climbers and lianas; trees are evergreen or rarely deciduous. Leaves simple or pinnately or digitately compound; alternate or opposite, stipulate; a pulvinus is often present at the base of the petiole or petiolules. Inflorescence racemose, often paniculate, rarely in globose heads or solitary. Flowers zygomorphic or actinomorphic, bisexual, hypogynous, rarely perigynous. Sepals 5, rarely less, usually connate at base, imbricate or rarely valvate; the odd sepal is anterior. Petals 5, rarely less, usually free, unequal or equal, imbricate or rarely valvate. Stamens 10, often many, rarely less than 10, free or monadelphous or diadelphous, filaments equal or unequal; anthers dehiscing by longitudinal slits or by apical pores; pollens are often in tetrads. Ovary superior or rarely semi-inferior, monocarpellary with posterior ventral suture, lateral at first but ultimately terminal; ovules on marginal placentation; funicle rather prominent; style usually bent; stigma simple. Fruit usually a legume, the valves diverticating on maturity and usually twisting; or fruit is a lomentum or fleshy. Seed usually with shining testa, variously coloured or often mottled; cotyledons plano-convex; endosperm absent or in a very thin layer.

The large family is divided into 3 clear subfamilies, viz. Mimoseae, Caesalpineae and Papilionaceae, the characters of which are given below:

Mimosae (or Mimosoideae): Predominantly trees; bark exuding a gum. Leaves are usually bipinnate, sensitive or possessing sleep-movement character; in some *Acacia* modified into phyllodes; stipules usually represented by a pair of thorns. Flowers in compact globose capitula or in spikes, often paniculate, regular, hypogynous or perigynous, usually 4-merous. Calyx gamosepalous. Corolla gamopetalous; aestivation valvate; corolla often absent. Stamens equal or double the number of petals or numerous, free or monadelphous, often adnate to the corolla; filaments much longer than corolla and often coloured; pollens in tetrads. Fruit a follicle or lomentum or nut. Seeds flat or compressed; embryo straight.

About 2,800 species in 38 genera; mainly tropical and subtropical; largest genus *Acacia* consists of about 750 species many of which are Australian.

Caesalpineae (or Caesalpinioideae): Trees and shrubs. Leaves paripinnate or bipinnate, rarely simple and bilobed. Inflorescence is usually a raceme rarely corymb or flowers solitary. Flowers slightly zygomorphic, hypogynous or perigynous, 5-merous. Calyx gamosepalous or sepals free, imbricate, usually 5, rarely less. Corolla of 5 petals, imbricate in ascending order, the odd 5th posterior petal is innermost in bud enclosed by the lateral pair which are again enclosed by the 2 lowest anterior petals. Stamens 10, free, rarely united below, often a few reduced to staminodes, filamens often unequal, anthers dehiscing lengthwise or by apical pores, rarely stamens less than 10 or very rarely 11-12. Ovary superior or semi-inferior, often stipitate, straight or curved. Fruits dehiscent or indehiscent, with or without transverse septa. Embryo straight.

About 3,000 species in 180 genera, mainly in tropical and subtropical countries. *Cassia* containes about 400 species.

Fig. 80. Mimosa pudica Linn. A—Spiny twig with leaves and flower-heads; B—One flower; C—One cluster of pods. (A & C slightly reduced; B much enlarged).

Papilionaceae (Papilionoideae or Papilionatae): Mostly herbs, shrubs also common, trees and climbers frequent. Leaves pinnate, rarely digitate or ternate, sometimes simple. Inflorescence is a raceme or spike or capitulum, rarely an umbel. Flower strongly zygomorphic, 5-merous, hypogynous. Calyx gamosepalous and persistent. Petals 5, very unequal and papilionaceous; the posterior is the largest covering the others in the bud, the laterals more or less lanceolate and slightly curved, covering the anterior pair in between them, the anterior petals usually asymmetrical in shape and more or less united to form a boat-shaped structure; the posterior petal is called the standard petal or vexillum, the laterals are called wings and the united anterior pair is the keel, the aestivation is vexillary i.e., imbricate in descending order; all petals have a claw at the base. Stamens 10, diadelphous, 9+1 or 5+5; where 9 are united the free stamen is posterior; often the posterior stamen is sterile or altogether wanting and there are 9 monadelphous stamens. Ovary or the style only is curved. Fruit a pod or lomentum or nut, very rarely a drupe. Seeds curved with a curved embryo : endosperm absent.

Species about 10,000 in about 500 genera distributed all over the globe excepting artic region. The largest genus Astragalus contains about 2,000 species. The subfamily

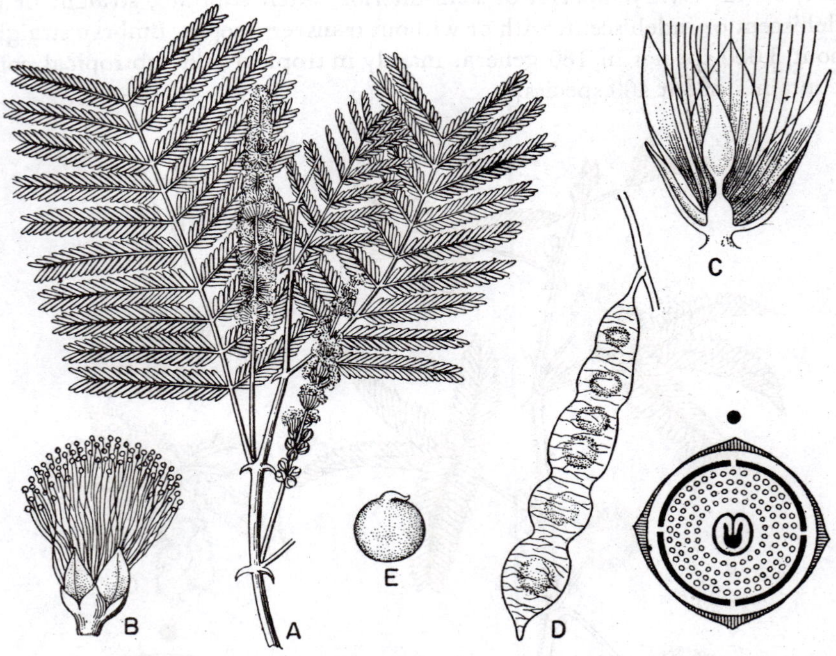

Fig. 81. Acacia suma Buch.-Ham. A—Leafytwig with spikes; B—One flower; C—Same with a part of calyx, corolla and androecium removed to show the ovary; D—Pod; E. Seed. (From J. N. Mitra).

being very large, variation is noticed in vegetative as well as floral parts. In *Carmichaelia australis* R. Br. and *Bossiaea rufa* R. Br. the branches are flat while the leaves are scale-like or without a blade. The 3 leaflets in *Desmodium motorium* (Houtt.) Merr. are very unequal, the laterals very small and show a peculiar movement with rise of temperature as the day advances. In some genera e.g., *Genista*, *Ononis*, etc. the compound leaves are unifoliate. The persistent calyx of *Anthyllis* is membranous and bladder-like and encloses the nut and falls with it; the calyx helps in the dispersal of the fruit by wind. *Trifolium* has a globose inflorescence and gamopetalous corolla. In *Sophora* and *Ormosia* stamens are free. The legume in *Astragalus* is incompletely 2-locular due to the formation of a septum by the incurved dorsal suture. *Dipteryx* and *Andira* have drupaceous fruit.

Fruits are geocarpic in *Arachis hypogaea* L., *Trifolium subterraneum* L. *Vicia amphicarpa* Doroth. etc. where the stalk of the ovary elongates after flowering and pushes the young fruit into the earth and the fruit ripens underground. The embryo in the seeds of *Cicer* and *Arachis* is almost straight.

Typical floral formula:

Mimosae: $\oplus$ ⚥ $K_{(4-5)}\ C_{4-5}\ A_{\infty \text{ or } 10 \text{ or } 4}\ G_{\underline{1}}$

Caesalpineae: † ⚥ $K_{5 \text{ or } (5)}\ C_5\ A_{10}\ G_{\underline{1}}$

Papilionaceae: † ⚥ $K_{(5)}\ C_{1+2+(2)}\ A_{(9)+1 \text{ or } (5)+(5)}\ G_{\underline{1}}$

The flowers are especially adapted for cross pollination by insects in the family Leguminosae. In *Papilionaceae* the structure of the flower, the coloured petals and presence of nectar in many are factors that are well suited to attract the insects. In *Caesalpineae* the same factors are responsible while in some cases the long coloured filaments make the flowers more attractive. In *Mimosae* the flowers being crowded in the inflorescence and having long exserted coloured filaments produce the same effect.

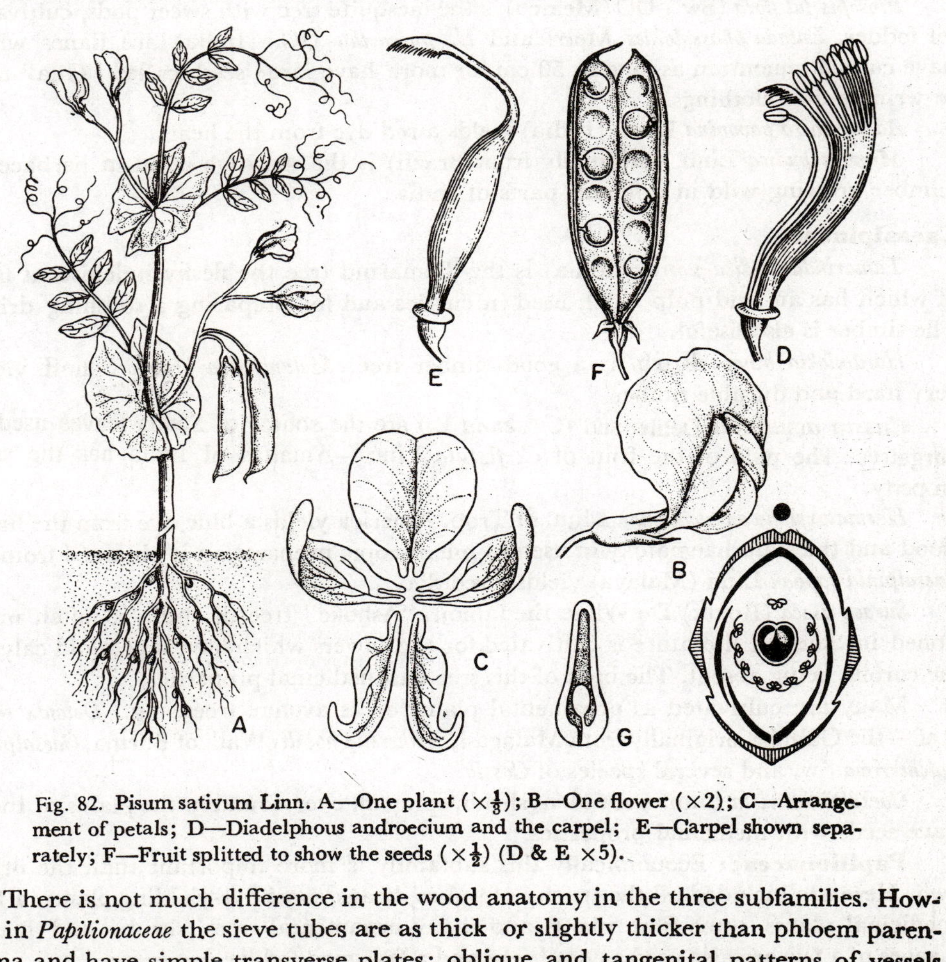

Fig. 82. Pisum sativum Linn. A—One plant ($\times\frac{1}{3}$); B—One flower ($\times 2$); C—Arrangement of petals; D—Diadelphous androecium and the carpel; E—Carpel shown separately; F—Fruit splitted to show the seeds ($\times\frac{1}{2}$) (D & E $\times 5$).

There is not much difference in the wood anatomy in the three subfamilies. However in *Papilionaceae* the sieve tubes are as thick or slightly thicker than phloem parenchyma and have simple transverse plates; oblique and tangenital patterns of vessels are distinct; fibres are rarely septate, anomalous secondary growth occurs in the stem of twiners. In *Caesalpiniaceae* the sieve tubes are much thicker and shorter and have inclined plates; vessels occasionally oblique or tangential; fibres commonly septate. In *Mimosae* the sieve tubes are very long and narrow; oblique and tangential patterns of vessels are not at all distinct; fibres commonly septate.

The large family includes many species which are economically important. A few are named below:

Mimosae—

Acacia catechu Willd.—Catechu, Kattha, (India) used for colouring khaki clothes and taken with betel leaves. *Acacia mearusii* De Wild., *A. pycnantha* Benth. and *A. dealbata* Link (Australian)—source of Wattle bark. *Acacia stenocarpa* Hochst (Ethiopia) and *A. senegal* (L) Willd. (Tropics) yield gum arabic.

Acacia melanoxylon R. Br., *A. visco* Lour. ex. Gris. *Albizzia procera* Benth. *A. lebbek* Benth. (India), *Xylia dolabriformis* (Burm.) Benth. supply useful timber. *Acacia nilotica* (L.) Willd. ex. Del. (India) is the Babul-tree, the timber of which is very hard and is used in various ways.

Prosopis juliflora (Sw.) DC (Mexico) is the mesquite tree with sweet pods, cultivated for fodder. *Entada phaseoloides* Merr. and *E. pursaetha* DC. (India) are lianes which have curved lomentum as long as 50 cm. or more have large seeds called "Gila" used to wrinkle fine clothings.

Adenanthera pavonina Linn. (India) yields a red dye from the heart

Mimosa pudica Linn. (originally from Brazil) is the sensitive plant, a herbaceous climber growing wild in different parts of India.

Caesalpineae—

Tamarindus indica Linn. (India) is the Tamarind tree the fleshy indehiscent fruit of which has an acid pulp much used in curries and for preparing a soothing drink. The timber is also useful.

Hardwickia binata Roxb. is a good timber tree. *Melanoxylon brauna* Schoff. yields very hard and durable timber.

Cassia acutifolia Delile and (*C. senna* L.) are the source of Senna-leaves used as purgative. The pulp of the fruit of *C. fistula* Linn.—Amaltas of India has the same property.

Haematoxylon campechianum Linn. of Trop. America yields a blue dye from the heart wood and the stain haematoxylin used in microscopic preparation is obtained from it. *Caesalpinia sappan* Linn (Malaya) yields a red dye.

Saraca asoca (Roxb.) De Wilde the famous "Ashoke" tree of India so often mentioned in Sanskrit literature is cultivated for the flowers which have a petaloid calyx⁻, the corolla being absent. The bark of this tree has medicinal properties.

Many are cultivated as ornamental plants or as avenue trees, e.g., *Delonix regia* Raf —the Gulmor, originally from Malagasi, *Amherstia nobilis* Wall. of Burma, *Caesalpinia pulcherrima* Sw, and several species of *Cassia*.

Caesalpinia crista Linn. a scandent shrub, spiny all over, found in the plains of India have seeds with medicinal properties.

Papilionaceae: Economically this subfamily is more important than the other two. Here are included all the species of pulses, beans, some dye-yielding plants, a few medicinal plants, some fibre plants and many ornamental trees, shrubs and herbs. Leaves of a few are also used as pot-herbs and a few good fodder.

Pulses:—*Pisum sativum* Linn—the pea, *Cicer arietinum* Linn—the gram, *Cajanus cajan* (L.) Millsp. the Arhar, *Vigna mungo* (Linn.) Hepper, the Urud or Mashkelai, *V. radiata* (L.) Wilc. the Mung dal, *Lens culinaris* Medic. the lentil, *Lathyrus sativus* L. the grass pea, etc. *Phaseolus vulgaris* Linn. is the French bean, *Vicia faba* L. the broad bean, *Dolichos lablab* Linn. the lablab bean, *Canavalia ensiformis* (L.) DC. the Jack bean, *Phaseolus lunatus* Linn. the Lima bean, *Glycine max* (L.) Merr. the Soya bean, etc. *Indigsfera tinctoria Linn.* and a few other species of *Indigofera* give a blue dye while *Genista tinctoria* Linn. yields yellow dye. *Pterocarpus santalinus* Linn. is the red Sandalwood. *Trigonella foenum-graecum* Linn. the Methi, *Glycyrrhiza glabra* Linn., and *Psoralea corylifolia* L. are important medicinal plants. *Crotalaria juncea* Linn.—the Sunn-hemp yields a strong bast fibre. *Dalbergia sisoo* Roxb. and *Pterocarpus marsupium* Roxb. and a few other species of these two genera yield good timber. *Abrus precatorius* Linn., the Gunja, has small scarlet seeds with a black spot which are used as weights by the goldsmiths; the seeds are strongly poisonous, while the root can be used as a substitute for the root of *Glycyrrhiza glabra*. *Derris elliptica* Benth. has poisonous roots from which "Rotenone", an insectiside is obtained.

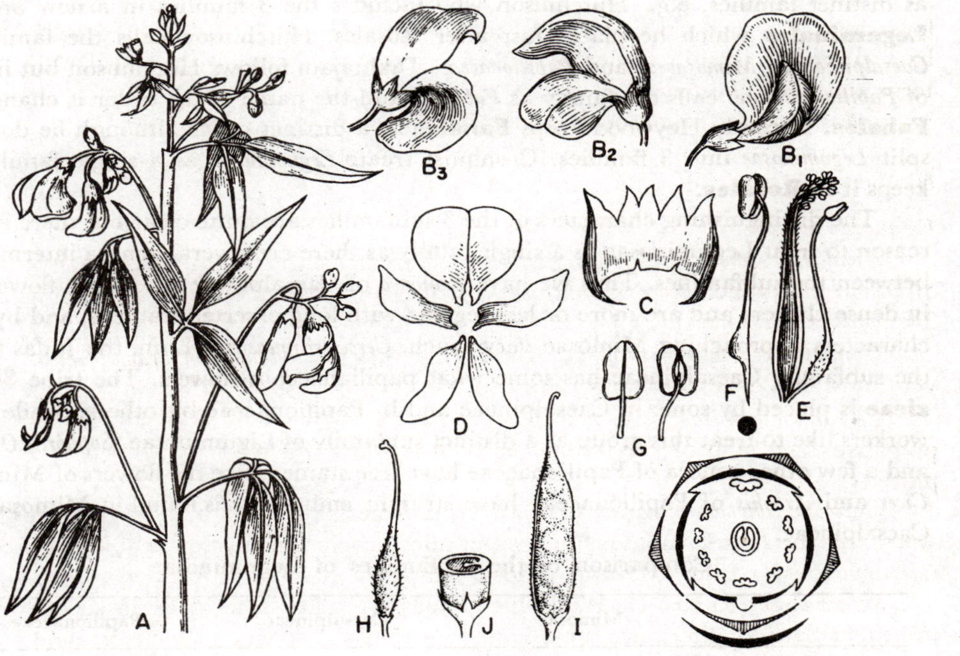

Fig. 83. Cajanus cajan (L.) Millsp. A—Portion of the plant with leaves and flowers; B—Flower:—different views; C—Calyx shown separately; D—Arrangement of petals; E—Nine stamens in one bundle and the pistil; F—The 10th vexillary free stamen; G—Anther: front and back view; H—Pistil; I—Fruit; J—Same transversely cut.

Pachyrhizus angulatus Rich. a climber has tuberous roots which are sweet and edible. *Lathyrus macrorrhizus* Wimm. also has tuberous roots and used similarly. *Pueraria mirifica* A. Shaw is the rejuvenating plant of Thailand, the tuberous root of which contains a oestrogenic substance. *Pueraria tuberosa* DC. of India has root tubers also having medicinal properties. *P. thunbergiana* Benth. is the Kudzu-vine a valuable fodder plant, the root tubers of which yield starch.

Arachis hypogea L. is the ground nut, that sends its fruits below the soil after flowering. This is much cultivated for the seeds which are edible and yield an edible oil.

Aeschynomene aspera L. and *A. indica* L. have spongy wood used for manufacturing solar hats, toys etc. and as bottle corks.

Many species have large and showy flowers and are often cultivated. *Butea monosperma* O. Ktz. and *B. superba* Roxb. are the Palas and Lata Palas respectively. *Erythrina variegata* Linn. and other species of the genus are the "Mandar" of Sanskrit literature. *Sesbania grandiflora* Pers. has large white or pink flowers. *Milletia ovalifolia* Kurz. has beautiful mavue flowers in drooping racemes. *Gliricidia maculata* H. B. K. is common in gardens cultivated for white or pink flowers in short racemes. *Crotalaria sericea* Retz. a shrub with simple leaves and golden yellow flowers is a common garden plant. *Lathyrus odoratus* Linn. is the Sweet pea, a garden annual.

Leguminosae is closely related to Rosaceae. Both the families are considered to have been derived from a common ancestor. *Chrysobalanus* and allied genera approach very near to the subfamily *Caesalpiniaceae*. Floral anatomy reveals that there are 5 traces in the carpels of Mimosae as noted in Rosaceae. Many authors treat the 3 subfamilies as distinct families, e.g. Hutchinson who includes the 3 families in a new order as **Leguminales** which he places just after Rosales. Hutchinson calls the families as *Caesalpiniaceae*, *Mimosaceae* and *Papilionaceae*. Takhtajam follows Hutchinson but instead of *Papilionaceae* he calls the family as *Fabaceae* and the name of the order is changed to **Fabales.** Recently Heywood keeps **Fabales** as a distinct order although he does not split *Leguminosae* into 3 families. Cronquist treats *Leguminosae* as a single family and keeps it in **Rosales.**

The distinguishing characters of the 3 subfamilies are quite clear but there is good reason to treat Leguminosae as a single family as there are several genera intermediate between the subfamilies. Thus we have *Brownea* of Caesalpineae where the flowers are in dense clusters and are more or less regular with long exserted stamens, and by such characters approaching Mimosae very much. *Cercis siliquastrum* Linn. the Judas tree of the subfamily Caesalpineae has some what papilianaceous flowers. The tribe **Swartzieae** is placed by some in Caesalpineae and in Papilionaceae by others; while some workers like to treat this group as a distinct subfamily of Liguminosae. *Sophora*, *Ormosia* and a few other genera of Papilionaceae have free stamens like the flowers of Mimosae. *Cicer* and *Arachis* of Papilionaceae have straight embryo as is found in Mimosae and Caesalpineae.

Comparison of the subfamilies of Leguminosae

	Mimosae	Caesalpineae	Papilionaceae
1. Habit	Predominantly trees.	Trees or shrubs rarely other type.	Herbs predominating, other type also common.
2. Leaves	Bipinnate, rarely other type.	Usually paripinnate.	Usually imparipinnate.
3. Flowers	Regular, usually 4-merous.	Slightly irregular, petals subequal, posterior innermost.	Strongly zyomorphic, petals very unequal, posterior biggest and outermost.
4. Aestivation	Valvate.	Imbricate.	Vexillary.
5. Stamens	Usually ∞, free or monadelphous.	Usually 10, free	(9)+1, or (5)+(5) or (10).

GERANIALES

This is also a large order having 22 families included in it and subdivided into 6 suborders as named below:

S.O. 1. **Geraniineae**—Oxalidaceae, Geraniaceae, Tropaeolaceae, Linaceae, Humiriaceae, Erythroxylaceae, Zygophyllaceae, Cneoraceae, Rutaceae, Simarubaceae, Burseraceae, Méliaceae, Akariaceae.

S.O. 2. **Malpighineae**—Malpighiaceae, Trigoniaceae, Vochysiaceae.

S.O. 3. **Polygalineae**—Tremandraceae, Polygalaceae.

S.O. 4. **Dichapetalineae**—Dichapetalaceae.

S.O. 5. **Tricoccae**—Euphorbiaceae, Daphniphyllaceae.

S.O. 6. **Callitrichineae**—Callitrichaceae.

This order does not appear to be a natural group although the families under respective suborders are related to each other to some extent. *Callitrichaceae* with a fruit of 4 druplets ultimately separating resembles *Boraginaceae* and *Labiatae* (*Lamiaceae*) to some extent and is placed in **Lamiales** by Tahktajan as well as by Cronquist. *Euphorbiaceae* and *Daphniphyllaceae* have unisexual apetalous flowers and therefore inclusion of **Tricoccae** in **Geraniales** does not appear justifyable. Of the families included under S.O. **Geraniineae** *Oxalidaceae*, *Geraniaceae* and *Tropaeolaceae* are closely allied as is evidenced from floral morphology. These are predominantly herbaceous. Cytological evidence also shows the relationship. Both Takhtajan and Cronquist include these 3 families in **Geraniales** in which order *Linaceae*, *Humiriaceae*, *Erythroxylaceae*, *Malpighiaceae* and *Zygophyllaceae* are also placed by Takhtajan. *Humiriaceae*, *Erythroxylaceae*, and *Linaceae* are placed by Cronquist in **Linales** which is very close to **Geraniales.** The S.O. **Polygalineae** of Engler is raised to the rank of a distinct order **Polygalales** both by Takhatajan and Cronquist. *Burseraceae*, *Simarubaceae*, *Cneoraceae*, *Rutaceae* and *Meliaceae* are included in **Rutales** by Takhtajan and in **Sapindales** by Cronquist where in he includes *Zygophyllaceae* and *Akariaceae* also. These families included under 4 orders by Takhtajan, viz., Rutales, Sapindales, Geraniales and Polygalales and by Cronquist in Sapindales, Geraniales, Linales and Polygalales, are close to each other and so the orders containing these families are arranged one after another. It is considered that Geraniales, Polygalales and Linales have been derived from Sapindales—Rutales stock.

The 22 families of Geraniales of Engler were distributed under several orders by Hutchinson in a very different way. Under **Lignosae** he put *Rutaceae*, *Simarubaceae* and *Burseraceae* under **Rutales**, *Meliaceae* under **Meliales,** *Akariaceae* under **Sapindales,** *Cneoraceae* in **Celastrales,** *Dichapetalaceae* under **Rosales,** *Daphniphyllaceae* under **Hamamelidales**, *Euphorbiaceae* in **Euphorbiales,** *Humiriaceae*, *Zygophyllaceae*, *Malpighiaceae*, *Linaceae* and *Erythroxylaceae* in **Malpighiales,** and *Polygalaceae*, *Trigoniaceae* and *Vochysiaceae* under **Polygalales,** while under **Herbaceae** he placed *Oxalidaceae*, *Geraniaceae* and *Tropaeolaceae* in **Geraniales** and *Callitrichaceae* under **Lythrales.** In his arrangement **Rutales, Meliales** and **Sapindales** come closer to each other while the other orders are far removed.

Rendle included 6 of the above families in **Geraniales,** viz. *Geraniaceae*, *Oxalidaceae*, *Tropaeolaceae*, *Linaceae*, *Zygophyllaceae* and *Malpighiaceae*. He placed *Euphorbiaceae* and *Callitrichaceae* in **Tricocce** and *Rutaceae*, *Simarubaceae*, *Burseraceae* and *Meliaceae* in **Rutales.** According to him the affinity of *Polygalaceae* is not clear and places it at the end of **Sapindales** but does not include the family in that order.

Following Takhtajan and Cronquist Heywood assigns a position of *Callitrichaceae* in **Lamiales.** He does not recognise Rutales distinct from Sapindales and Linales distinct from Geraniales. Like Cronquist he puts *Dichapetalaceae* in **Celastrales.**

The common characters of these 22 families included in *Geraniales* of Engler are noted below:

Usually herbaceous, sometimes woody; leaves exstipulate, usually alternate; flowers usually bisexual and regular, pentamerous, hypogynous, usually dichlamydeous; stamens obdiplostemonous, filaments often united in a tube; carpels 3-5, syncarpous, ovules pendulous with ventral raphe; seeds usually without endosperm. Obdiplostemonous condition of the androecium and ovules with ventral raphe appear to be the important common characters depending on which these families are placed under a single Order.

Geraniaceae

Annual herbs or undershrubs, rarely shrubs. Leaves simple, palmately lobed or incised or compound, stipulate, alternate or rarely opposite. The inflorescence is a few-flowered scorpioid cyme or many-flowered cymes clustered in the form of an umbel; or flowers may be solitary. Flowers bisexual, actinomorphic, rarely zygomorphic, hypogynous. Sepals 5, rarely 4 or 8, free or rarely connate, more or less imbricate; in zygomorphic flowers the posterior sepal is spurred. Petals as many as sepals, imbricate, rarely twisted; nectar glands alternating with petals. Stamens 10 in 2 whorls, obdiplostemonous, often 15, rarely less than 10, 9 or 7 or even only 2; filaments united at base, rarely completely free, rarely few stamens are reduced to staminodes; anthers pendulous, bithecal, with small connectives. Carpels 2-5, rarely 8; ovary syncarpous with as many cells as there are carpels, superior; style one with as many stigmatic branches as there are cells in the ovary; stigmas ligulate; ovules 2 in each cell, pendulous, superposed, campylotropous, with upwardly directed micropyle and ventral raphe, rarely ovules many or solitary in each cell; placentation axile. Fruit a capsule, dehiscing into as many parts as there are carpels and roll up or become spirally twisted along the beak-like style, i.e. divided into mericarps. Seed without or with scanty endosperm and a curved embryo, the cotyledons folded.

In some cases there is a rhizome at the base or the base is tuber-like. *Dirachma socotrana* Balf. f. is a shrub. The small leaves in *Sarcocaulon* are metamorphosed into spines. *Geranium Wallichianum* D. Don and *Pelargonium zonale* L'Her. have large stipules. The leaves in this family are glandular hairy, the glands containing fragrant volatile oil. The stomata are ranunculaceous type. The flowers of *Vivania* have 4 sepals and the fruit dehisces loculicidally. In *Biebersteinia* the 5 carpels are free below united above in a single style; fruits are 5 small nuts.

The typical floral formula is as given here: ⚥ $K_5\ C_5\ A_{5+5}\ G_{(\underline{5})}$.

The peculiar anatomical feature is the continuous ring-like pericycle of schlerenchymatous cells, several layers thick. The vascular bundles are in alternating smaller and larger groups. Perforations are simple or often scalariform, and intervascular pitting is alternate. In secondary xylem secondary rays are lacking. In some *Geranium* species the pericycle lies above phloem.

The family with about 750 species under 11 genera is distributed in the temperate and tropical countries while a few are alpine. Some are xerophytes and occur in the steppes. *Sarcocaulon* is found in S. African deserts. Several species of *Geranium* are found in the Himalayas and hills of E. India. *Pelargonium zonale* L. and a few other species of the genera are cultivated in the cooler parts of the country for the beautiful flowers. An essence known as *Geranium-oil* is obtained not from any species of *Geranium* but from *Pelargonium graveolens* L. Her., *P. odoratissimus* Ait., *P. capitatum* Ait. and *P. rodule* L. Her.

Geraniaceae is closely related to *Oxalidaceae* and *Tropaeolaceae*. The floral characters as well as the wood anatomy in the 3 families are very similar. Cytological evidence also proves that they are close to each other. Older workers like De Candole, Bentham and Hooker, did not distinguish *Oxalidaceae* and *Tropaeolaceae* from *Geraniaceae*. Engler splitted the large family into 4 distinct families e.g. *Geraniaceae*, *Oxalidaceae*, *Tropaeolaceae* and *Balsaminaceae*. The first three be placed in the order **Geraniales** while *Balsaminaceae* was placed by him in the order **Sapindales.** Later workers recognising the closer affinity of *Balsaminaceae* to the other 3 families transferred *Balsaminaceae* to **Geraniales** from which many other families included in that by Engler have been removed by them. According to Cronquist **Geraniales** with these 4 families and *Limnanthaceae* has been derived from **Sapindales.**

Oxalidaceae

Perennial herbs with underground rhizomes, bulbs or corms, rarely short trees. Leaves radical or cauline, whorled or alternate, pinnately or palmately compound, rarely simple, exstipulate or stipulate. Flowers in cymes or cymose umbels, or solitary, axillary or terminal, regular, bisexual, hypogynous, pentamerous. Sepals 5, imbricate, rarely twisted; petals 5, twisted. Stamens 10 in 2 whorls, obdiplostemonous, i.e. the outer antipetalous, inner antisepalous, often stamens 15 in 3 whorls, united at the base; anthers bithecal, dehiscing longitudinally, connective small. Ovary superior, 5-locular and 5-lobed, styles 5, stigmas capitate; ovules 1-many in each cell; rarely ovary 3-locular and 3-lobed with only one style. Fruit a loculicidal capsule dehiscing elastically or the fruit is a berry. Seeds with straight embryo and fleshy endosperm, sometimes arillate; aril springs off elastically with the seed.

Although predominantly herbaceous the family includes 2 genera of trees, viz. *Averrhoa* and *Connaropsis*. The leaves of most species show sleep movement and in *Biophytum* these are sensitive to touch. Calcium oxalate crystals are present in the cells of the green tissues. The petiole is modified into a flat phyllode in some cases. In *Lepidobotrys* and *Hypseocharis* the overy is tricarpellary and 3-locular with a single style. Fruits of *Averrhoa* are berries.

The vascular anatomy shows that the vessels are arranged in 4 or more cells; intravascular pitting is alternate and large; perforations are simple. Fibres are septate with simple pits. The pericycle is a continuous ring and is made up of sclerenchymatous cells, several layers thick.

The family consists of about 900 species in 8 genera of which *Oxalis* alone has about 800 species. The plants of the family are distributed in the tropical and temperate regions, the majority occurring in S. America. In India we have *Oxalis corniculata* Linn., *Averrhoa carambola* Linn., *Biophytum sensitivum* DC. etc. The plants are not of much economic importance. The berries of *Averrhoa carambola* (Kamrak or Kamranga) is acidic with a pleasant flavour and is eaten raw or cooked. A few species of *Oxalis* are cultivated for the small beautiful flowers and a few have medicinal value. *O. tetraphylla* Cav. as well as a few others have tuberous roots which are edible.

Oxalidaceae is closely allied to **Geraniaceae** in which it was formerly included and later treated as a distinct family by **Engler. The structure of the flower, the fruit and the vascular anatomy are more or less similar in both the families. The**

Fig. 84. **Averrhoa carambola Linn. A. Leafy twig with axillary racemes** ($\times \frac{1}{2}$); B. One flower ($\times 2$); C One stamen; D. Ovary; E. T.'s of ovary.

2 families are placed side by side in the same order by all workers of Angiosperem taxonomy. The 2 genera of trees, viz. *Averrhoa* and *Connaropis* are now placed by some in a distinct family **Averrhoaceae.**

Tropaeolaceae

Herbs usually with soft prostrate stem, often climbing with the help of long petioles. Leaves alternate, simple more or less lobed, peltate, exstipulate. Flowers solitary, axillary, bisexual, zygomorphic, hypogynous. Sepals 5, usually coloured, the posterior is prolonged into a spur. Petals 5, free, clawed, the posterior pair near the mouth of the spur are slightly smaller and situated a little above the anterior three which are larger and fringed on the margin. Stamens 8 in 2 whorls. Carpels 3; ovary syncarpous, 3-locular, 3-lobed, superior; ovule anatropous, 1 in each cell, pendulous; style solitary with 3-fid stigma. Fruit a 3-seeded schizocarp separating into 3 one-seeded drupelets. Seeds without endosperm and thick cotyledons which are often slightly coalescent; embryo straight.

Floral formula: † K_5 C_5 A_{4+4} $G_{(3)}$

The family consists of about 90 species in 2 genera occurring in the hilly areas of America. *Tropaeolum majus* Linn. is much cultivated for the large beautiful flowers. The plants have an acrid taste like that of a *Nasturtium* plant (Cruciferae), that is why it is called **Garden-Nasturtium.** The leaves of this plant are used to make sandwitches; T-tuberosum Linn, a Peruvian plant has edible tuberous roots. The family is closely allied to *Geraniaceae, Oxalidaceae* and *Balsaminaceae*, the four being formerly included in a single family *Geraniaceae* by earlier workers.

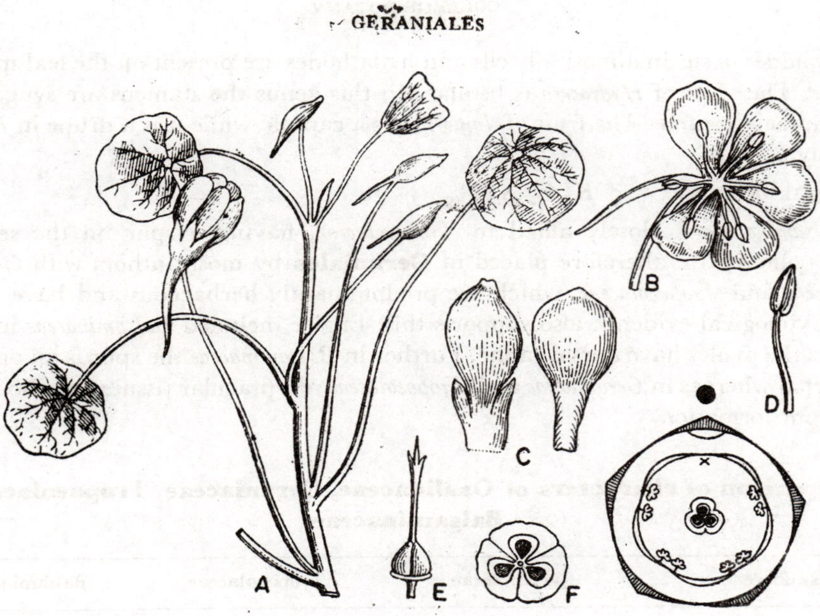

Fig. 85. Tropaeolum majus Linn. A. Portion of the plant with leaves and flowers ($\times\frac{1}{2}$); B. One flower ($\times 1$); C. Perianth segments ($\times 1$). D. One stamen; E. Ovary; F. T.s. of ovary.

Balsaminaceae

Herbaceous annuals with brittle translucent stems with watery juice and swollen nodes. Leaves simple, alternate, opposite or whorled, exstipulate, often with stipulary glands at the base of the petioles. Flowers solitary and axillary or in lax axillary cymes or panicles with slender peduncles and pedicels, bisexual, strongly zygomorphic, hypogynous and pentamerous. Sepals petaloid, imbricate; the posterior the largest and prolonged into a nectariferous spur; the 2 anterior ones much smaller and sometimes altogether suppressed and the lateral sepals come to anterior position. Of the 5 petals the posterior petals are united to the laterals, so that apparently there are 3 petals; the anterior one is the largest and cover the other petals in bud. Stamens 5, filaments short and broad, anthers bilocular, introrse, both filaments and anthers unite to form a hood over the gynoecium; ultimately the anthers break at the base and are carried up by the growing gynoecum. Disc absent. Ovary superior, of 5 united carpels, 5-celled, with a 5-toothed sessile stigma; ovules many, pendulous on axile placentation and one seriate in each cell, or ovules 2-3 in each cell. Fruit a loculicidal capsule, bursting on maturity to a slight touch or pressure ejecting the seeds to a considerable distance while a central column of the capsule persists, or the fruit is a drupe with a bony 5-celled stone. Seeds with a straight embryo and without endosperm.

The family consists of only 2-genera of which *Impatiens* has over 500 species. *Hydrocera* is a monotypic genus occurring in Bengal. *Impatients* has most of the species growing in tropical mountains of Asia and Africa, and a few in N. Asia, Europe, N. America and S. Africa. Species of *Impatiens* grow in damp situations while *Hydrocera* is an aquatic with floating stems. *I. noli-tangere* Hook. and *I. parviflora* Royle are found in Europe. *I. balsamina* Linn. is cultivated in almost all countries. *I. fulva* Nutt. an American plant has been naturalised in many parts of Europe. In India about 230 species are found to grow wild in the hills at lower elevations.

Raphides occur in almost all cells and hydathodes are present on the leaf margin of *Impatiens.* The stem of *Hydrocera* is fistular. In this genus the stamens are syngeneseous and the petals are free. The fruit of *Impatiens* is a capsule while it is a drupe in *Hydrocera* with only 5 seeds.

Floral formula: † ⚥ K_5 C_5 A_5 $G_{(5)}$.

Balsaminaceae is closely allied to *Tropaeolaceae*, having a spur on the sepal and similar pollens. It is therefore placed in **Geraniales** by most authors with *Geraniaceae* *Oxalidaceae* and *Tropacolaceae*, which are predominantly herbaceous and have capsular fruits. Cytological evidence also supports this. Engler included *Balsaminaceae* in **Sapindales** as the ovules have dorsal raphe. Further in *Balsaminaceae* the spur is an outgrowth of the sepal whereas in *Geraniaceae* and *Tropaeolaceae* receptacular tissues are also involved in the spur formation.

Comparison of characters of Oxalidaceae, Geraniaceae, Tropaeolaceae & Balsaminaceae

Oxalidaceae	Geraniaceae	Tropaeolaceae	Balsaminaceae
Predominantly herbs, often shrubs or trees.	Herbs, rarely shrubs	Herbs	Herbs
Leaves palmately or pinnately compound, stipulate or not.	Leaves simple or compound, stipulate.	Leaves, simple, peltate exstipulate.	Leaves simple, exstipulate.
Flowers regular	Flowers regular or zygomorphic.	Zygomorphic	Zygomorphic
Calyx not spurred.	Calyx with or without a spur.	Calyx spurred	Calyx spurred.
Stamens in 2-3 whorls.	Stamens in 2-3 whorls.	Stamens in 2 whorls.	Stamens in 1 whorl.
Styles usually free.	Styles united.	Styles united.	Style 0, stigma sessile.
Raphe ventral	Raphe ventral	Raphe ventral	Raphe dorsal
Elastically dehiscing capsule or berry.	Capsule dehiscing into 3-5-mericarps.	Capsule dehiscing into 3 fleshy schizocarps.	Elastically dehiscing capsule.
Endosperm fleshy.	Endosperm scanty or 0.	Endosperm 0.	Endosperm 0.

Linaceae

Annual or perennial herbs, undershrubs or shrubs, rarely climbing, very rarely trees. Leaves simple, sessile, alternate or opposite, ex-stipulate or with small stipules, which are often caducous. Inflorescence is a dichasial cyme, or a raceme or spike, often a cymose umbel, or flowers slolitary. Flowers actinomorphic, bisexual, hypogynous. Sepals 5, free or more or less connate, imbricate or valvate, usually persistent, rarely caducous. Petals 5, twisted in bud, clawed, with pocket-like slits or ligulate. Stamens as many as petals or twice, thrice or 4-times as many; filaments broader near the base, united in a tube below, with nectar-glands outside; anthers bithecal, introrse, dehiscing by lateral slits; connective acute at apex; rarely some stamens are reduced to staminodes; often an extra or inter-staminal disc is present, free or adnate to the staminal tube. Carpels 5 or 3, united to form a 5 -or 3-celled ovary, or the cells double that number due to a partition formed by the intrusion of the ovary wall; the partition is often incomplete, ovary superior; styles free, as many as carpels; ovules 2 in each cell or one if the partition wall is complete, anatropous, pendulous; funicle long; raphe ventral; an obturator is often present at the micropyle. Fruit a septicidal capsule, dehiscing into 2-valved cocci. Seeds often arillate or with an winged appendage; testa shining; endosperm scanty, fleshy; embryo straight or slightly curved.

Stipules are represented by glands in some species of *Linum* and *Hesperolinon*. *Hugonia* and *Durandea* are climbers, climbing by hooked branchlets and peduncles. Branching is dichotomous in *Radiola*, the flowers of which are tetramerous. In *Hesperolinon congestum* Small and in a few species of *Linum* the calyx is caducous. Carpels are 2 in *Nectaropetalum* forming an 1-celled ovary with only 1 ovule.

The anatomical feature is more or less similar to *Geraniaceae*. The pericycle is a continuous ring of schlerenchyma often having fibres which are long and pointed. The xylem vessels are solitary, large, with simple or often scalariform perforations. Bordered pits are found on the walls of the fibres.

Fig. 86. Linum usitatissimum Linn.

Floral formula: $\oplus$ ⚥ $K_5\ C_5\ A_{5 \text{ or } 10}\ G_{(\underline{2-5})}$.

The family with about 300 species in 13 genera is found in the tropical countries while a few occur also in the temperate regions. *Reinwardtia cicanoba* Hara occurs in the hills of India in temperate zone while *R. indica* Dum grows in the plains as well as in the hills at lower elevations. *Linum usitatissimum* L. is cultivated in India as well as in other countries for the seeds which yield an oil much used in paints and varnish. A fine quality of fibre is also obtained from this plant which is woven into the linen cloth. This is a tall variety much cultivated in Russia and other European countries. It is the Tisi or Masina plant of India. Species of African genus *Hugonia* have edible fruits. *Ctenolophon parvifolium* Oliv. is a good timber tree. Root of *Hugonia mystax* Linn. is a cure for snake bite.

Linaceae closely resembles *Geraniaceae* in floral as well as anatomical characters. It is also allied to *Humiriaceae* and *Erythroxylaceae* and the 3 families are placed in a distinct order **Linales** by Cronquist. It comes closer to **Polygalaceae** as regards the anatomical structure of the stem is concerned. It resembles *Zygophyllaceae* to some extent having regular and hypogynous flowers, obdiplostemonous androecium and anatropous ovules with ventral raphe. Bessey considers that *Linaceae* is related to *Malvaceae* as it is to *Geraniaceae*.

Zygophyllaceae

Herbs or shrubs, rarely trees; branches often articulate. Leaves pinnate or 2-foliolate, rarely simple, opposite or alternate, leaflets entire; simple leaves entire or multifid; stipulate, stipules often spinescent. Inflorescence is cymose, terminal or axillary, often flowers solitary and axillary. Flowers hermaphrodite, actinomorphic, rarely zygomorphic, hypogynous, often with a pair of small bracts. Sepals 5 or 4, free or rarely connate below, imbricate, or valvate, rarely open in bud. Petals 5 or 4, free, imbricate or contorted, rarely valvate; rarely petals absent. Disc often present, convex or depressed, rarely annular, eglandular. Stamens in one, two or three whorls, 5 or 4 in each, obdiplostemonous; filaments often unequal, with scaly appendages at base, those of the outer whorl often adnate to the petals; anthers introrse, bilocular, dehiscing by lateral slits. Carpels 5 or 4, united to form a 5-4-chambered syncarpous ovary; ovary superior, often stipitate, lobed or angled; the locules often partically transversely septate; style terminal, often slightly gynobasic, with ridges and furrows, stigmatic on the angles or with simple capitate stigma, or with 5 stigmatic branches; ovules 1-many in each cell, ascending or pendulous from an axile placenta, with ventral raphe. Fruit a capsule or a schizocarp breaking into 2-10 spiny cocci, very rarely berry-like. Seeds pendulous; endosperm absent or scanty, fleshy or horny; embryo straight or curved.

Guiacum of tropical America and *Balanites* of W. Asia are trees. The rest are mostly dwarf shrubs. *Neoleuderitzia* has unisexual flowers. Flowers in *Militanthus* and *Seetzenia* are apetalous. Diverse types of pollens are met with in this family. *Kalstroemia* has the gynoecium with 8-12 carpels. *Peganum** has a baccate fruit; *Nitraria* and *Balanites* have drupaceous fruits; the rest have capsules or schizocarps. The fruiting carpels of *Tribulus* are septate.

The family consisting of about 25 genera and 200 species is found in the warmer parts of the world especially in arid zone. *Balanites aegyptiaca* Del. grows in India and extends westwards to North Africa. It is the **Ingudi Briksha or Hingul** which yields an oil from the seeds. *Peganum harmala* Linn. and *Tribulus terrestris* L. have also the same distribution; the former yields a red dye and the latter called "Gokshur" in Sanskrit is a reputed medicinal plant. The wood of *Guiacum officinale* L. is the Lignum—vitae which gives the resin called *gum-guiacum* reputed to have medicinal value. The wood of *G. officinale* and *G. sanctum* Linn. as well as of *Bulnesia arborea* Eng. and *B. sarmientis* Lor. is very hard and heavy and the timber is valuable.

The peculier anatomical feature in this family is that the wood elements is in stories which vary from 8-17 per mm. Fusiform parenchymatous cells predominate and tracheids are present. Vessels are solitary with simple perforations. Fibres are bordered pitted.

The family is closely related to *Rutaceae*. The genus *Peganum* is intermediate between the two families and by some it is placed under *Rutaceae*. Hutchinson includes *Zygophyllaceae* in **Malpighiales** which is far removed from **Rutales.** The relationship of *Zygophyllaceae* with *Malpighiaceae* has been recognised also by Takhtajan who includes both these families in **Geraniales.** Cronquist places *Zygophyllaceae* in **Sapindales** where in he includes *Rutaceae*. The family *Zygophyllaceae* resembles *Euphorbiaceae* to some extent: the fruit is often a schizocarpic capsule in both families.

---

* *Peganum* is included by some in *Rutaceae*.

Rutaceae

Shrubs or trees, usually armed; rarely herbs. Leaves usually compound, alternate or opposite, exstipulate, pellucid gland-dotted. Inflorescence racemose or cymose, or the flowers solitary. Flowers actinomorphic rarely zygomorphic, bisexual, very rarely unisexual, hypogynous. Sepals 5 or 4, free or connate, imbricate. Petals 5 or 4, free, rarely connate, imbricate or rarely valvate. Stamens as many as petals or double the number, often many; filaments usually free, obdiplostemonous, often polyadelphous; anthers bilocular introrse. An annular disc or a gynophore is present above the androecium. Carpels 4-5, united to form a 4-5-locular superior ovary; sometimes the carpels are loosely united or free at the base with a united style; ovary is usually more or less deeply grooved and the style is short often somewhat gynobasic; stigma capitate; carpels often less than 4 and rarely up to 12; ovules 1-2 in each cell with ventral raphe on axile placentation, often ovules more than 2. Fruit a hesperidium or amphisarca, or capsule; seeds with or without endosperm and often polyembryonic.

The armed species have thorns which are metamorphosed branches or have spines which are modified leaves. Simple leaves are found in *Calodendron*, *Diosma*, *Adenandra* etc. Leaves of *Citrus* are unifolilate compound (it is simple according to some authors). Leaves of *Aegle* and *Triphasia* are trifoliate, in *Murraya* they are pinnate, bipinnate in *Ruta* and tripinnate in *Boenninghousenia*. Flowers are tetramerous in *Achronychia*, *Boenninghausenia* and a few other genera, and trimerous flowers are found in *Triphasia*

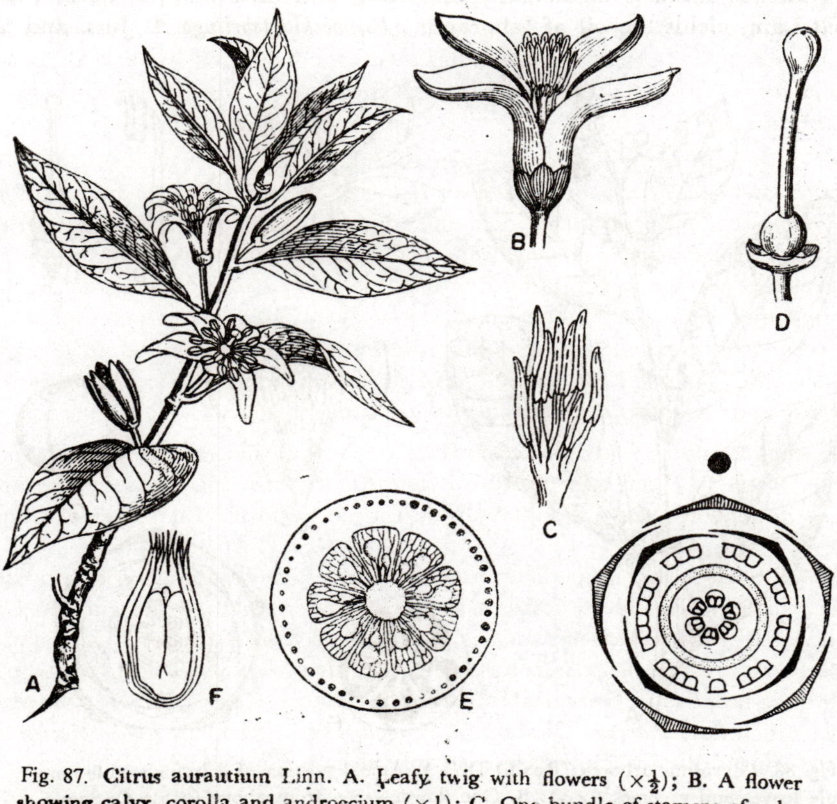

Fig. 87. Citrus aurautium Linn. A. Leafy twig with flowers ($\times\frac{1}{2}$); B. A flower showing calyx, corolla and androecium ($\times$1); C. One bundle of stamens of polyadelphous androecium; D. Ovary on disc. E. T.s. of fruit ($\times$1); F.L.s. of seed.

and *Lunasia*, while pentamerous flowers are found in most genera. Unisexual flowers occur in *Toddalia*, *Xanthoxylum* and *Empeleurum*. The flowers of *Dictamnus*, *Galipea* and *Alnicida* are zygomorphic. Petals are free but in *Correa*, *Ticorea*, *Galipea*, etc. corolla is gamopetalous. Stamens are polyadelphous in the family but in some *Atalantia* stamens are monadelphous. Diplostemonous androecium is met with in *Fagara*. *Teclea* and *Empleurum* have monocarpellary ovary. Carpels are entirely free in *Xanthoxylum*, *Choisya*, *Evodia*, *Correa*, etc. Fruit is capsular or drupaceous or berry-like. In *Spathelia* it is a winged drupe. In *Chloroxylon* the seeds are winged. The fruit of *Aegle* is an amphisarca while that of *Citrus* is a hesperidium.

Floral formula is generally expressed as, ⊕ ⚥ $K_5C_5A_{5+5}\ G_{(\underline{5})}$.

The stem anatomy shows the presence of isolated strands of sclerenchymatous fibres in the pericycle which in some cases unite to form a continuous ring. Vessels are in multiples and usually small; perforations simple; xylem parenchyma usually surrounding the vessels. Pits are simple or indistinctly bordered.

The family with about 1200 species in 120 genera is distributed in the tropical and subtemperate parts of the world, and quite a few of them are xerophytic. It is well represented in India by about 70 species, e.g. many species of *Citrus*, *Aegle marmelos* Cor. *Murraya paniculata* Jack and *M. Koeningii* Spr. *Glycosmis arborea* (Roxb.) DC., *Atalantia monophylla* Corr.. etc. are common in the plains, while *Skimmia lauriola* Hook. f., *Boenninghousenia albiflora* Reichb. f., species of *Fagara* are found in the hills.

Ruta graveoleus Linn. is medicinally important and used as a pot herb. *Pilocarpus pennatifolius* Lam. vields the oil of Jaborandi. *Esenbeckia febrifuga* A. Juss. and *Tiwrea*

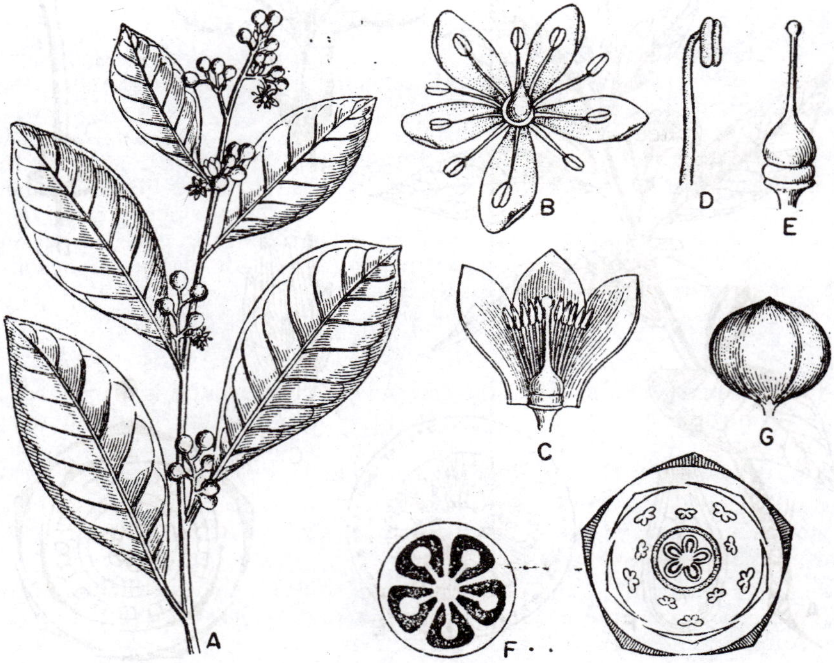

Fig. 88. Glycosmis arborea (Roxb.) DC. A. Apical portion of a branch with simple leaves and racemes (×½); B. One flower—seen from above (×5); C. Same, side-view; D. One stamen; E. Ovary on disc., F.T.s. 2 of ovary; G. Berry (×1).

febrifuga St. Hill. both Brazilian, are used as substitutes of **Cinchona,** *Aeagle marmelos* Corr. is the Bael tree, famous for its large delicious fruits which also have medicinal properties. The trifoliate leaves are much wanted in religious ceremonies by the Hindoos, *Limonia acidissima* Linn. has similar fruit which is acid to taste and is used in chutneis. *Chloroxylon swietenia* DC. is a good timber tree. *Murraya Koenigii* Spr. is the curry-leaf tree the leaves of which are used to flavour curries. *M. paniculata* Jack is a garden plant commonly cultivated for its beautiful foliage and white fragrant flowers. The large Indo-Malayan genus *Citrus* has several species with edible fruits of which the following are well known:—(i) *C. reticulata* Blanco, the Santara of Nagpur, the Kamala of E. India, the Mandarin orange or the Loose skinned orange much cultivated for the delicious fruits, (2) *C. sinensis* (L.) Osbeck, the Musambi orange, the Tight-skinned orange, (2) *C. paradisi* Macf.,—the Grape Fruit, (3) *C. maxima* (Burm.) Merrill, the Batabi Nimbu of E. India, (4) *C. limettioides* Tanaka, Mithanimbu or Sherbati nimbu, *C. aurantifolia* Swingle, the Kagzi and the Pati nimbu, etc. The juice of these fruits is very tasteful and rich in vitamin contents. The oranges are used to prepare marmalade and the fruit-rind as well as the fruits of some species are used as pickles and chutney.

The family is closely related to *Simarubaceae*, *Burseraceae* and *Meliaceae*, all of them being predominantly woody, having oil glands and a disc between the androecium and gynoecium. Wettstein considers it also allied to *Terebinthaceae* and includes it in his **Terebinthales** along with *Simarubaceae*, *Burseraceae* and *Meliaceae* while Hallier also includes *Rutaceae* in his order **Teribinthenae** and considers that the family has been derived from the *Ranalian* stock probably from *Lardizabalaceae* through *Capparidaceae*.

Simarubaceae

Trees or shrubs with a bitter principle in the bark. Leaves pinnate, alternate, exstipulate; rarely leaves simple. Flowers in raceme or in cymose panicles; regular, usually unisexual in dioecious plants, or rarely bisexual, hypogynous. Sepals 3—5, rarely more, free or united, valvate or imbricate. Petals as many as sepals, free or united, valvate or imbricate; rarely petals absent. Stamens as many as or double the number of petals in 2 series; filaments with a scale at the base; anthers bilocular, dehiscing laterally. Carpels usually 4—5, completely united to form a syncarpous ovary or united only by the styles and stigmas, superior; ovule solitary in each carpel on marginal placenta. Fruit a samara or a schizocarp or a capsule, or rarely drupaceous; seed with scanty or no endosperm; cotyledons thick.

The family consists of about 200 species under 30 genera and is distributed in the tropical and subtropical countries of the world while a few are found in temperate regions. It is represented in India by 13 species, common among them are: *Ailanthus excelsa* Roxb., *A. integrifolia* Lamb., *Balanites aegyptiaca* (L.) Del. etc.

The family is allied to Rutaceae from which it differs in the absence of oil glands and presence of a scale at the base of a filament, the genus *Balanites* is segregated as a distinct family Balanitaceae by some authors.

A few species belonging to this family are important for their medicinal properties, viz., *Quassia amara* Linn., *Brucea antidysenterica* Linn., *Picrasma excelsa* (Pl.) Lindl., *Simaruba amara* Aubl. and *Samadera indica* J. Gaertn.

***Ailanthus excelsa* and a few other species of the genus yield soft and light timber and also have medicinal properties. *Balanites aegygtiaca* is the Hingul or Ingudi Briksha of Sanskrit literature, the seeds of which yield an oil.**

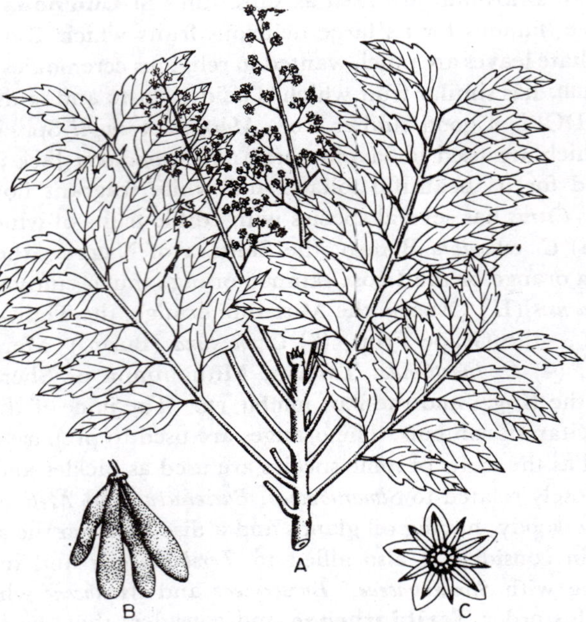

Fig. 89. Ailanthus excelsa Roxb. A. Part of the branch with leaves and inflorescence (× 4); B. A cluster of samaras (× 1/2); C. Male Flower (× 2).

Burseraceae

Deciduous trees or shrubs. Leaves gland-dotted, exstipulate, alternate, pinnately compound. Inflorescence racemose or paniculate or rarely flowers solitary. Flowers actinomorphic, uni- or bisexual, hypogynous. Sepals 3—5, free or united at base, valvate or imbricate. Petals 3—5, free, valvate or imbricate, rarely petals absent. A cupular or annular disc is present. Stamens as many as or double the number of petals; anthers bilocular, introrse. Ovary superior, syncarpous, 2—5-locular; ovules 1—2 with ventral raphe, anatropous, on axile placentas. Fruit a drupe with 1—5 stones, or a capsule. Seed with a straight or curved embryo and without endosperm.

Schizogenous or lysigenous resin canals are present in the phloem. Mucilage cells occur in the upper surface of epidermis of leaves. A few genera are polygamodioecious. viz., *Garuga*, *Commiphora*, *Crepidospermum*, etc. Corolla is gamopetalous in *Hedwigia*. *Amyris* has monocarpellary pistil.

The family consists of 16 genera having about 600 species most of them occurring in tropical America. Common Indian plants of Burseraceae are *Boswellia serrata* Roxb., *Bursera serrata* Coleb, *Garuga pinnata* Roxb. *Commiphora wightii* (Arn.) Bhandari etc.

Burscraceae is much allied to Rutaceae from which it differs in having resin ducts in the cortex. It is also close to Simarubaceae and Meliaceae and the four families are placed in the same order by most authors. This family resembles Euphorbiaceae to some extent having ovules with ventral raphe.

The family is economically important, many species yielding fragrant resin which is burnt as frank-incense. *Boswellia thurifera* Roxb. ex Flem. yields East Indian Olibanum. *Dacryodes hexandra* Griseb is the source of elemi while Manila elemi is obtained from *Canarium commune* Linn. *Commiphora wightii* yields guggul—the Indian olibanum. Guggul is also obtained from *Boswellia serrata* Roxb.—the Saloi tree of Peninsular India. The soft wood of this trees is used as paper pulp of news print. The inner bark of *B. papyrifera* separates in sheets and is used as paper. The balsam of *Amyris toxicofera* Linn. is poisonous.

Meliaceae

Trees or shrubs, deciduous or evergreen. Leaves pinnate, alternate, exstipulate. Panicles cymose, axillary. Flowers bisexual rarely unisexual, actinomorphic, hypogynous. Calyx of 4-5 free sepals, imbricate, rarely valvate; often sepals connate at base. Petals 4-5, rarely fewer or more, free or united, imbricate, rarely valvate. Stamens 8-10, monadelphous. rarely free; anthers 2-celled, dehiscing longitudinally. A disc is usually present between the androecium and gynoecium. Carpels 2-5; ovary syncarpous, superior, 2-5-celled; ovules 1-2 in each cell, rarely more, anatropous with ventral raphe, on axile placentation; style short, stigma capitate, discoid or lobed; Fruit a berry or drupe or a capsule; seeds often winged, with or without endosperm, rarely arillate.

Melia & Toona are deciduous. Most other genera also remain leafless for a very short period. *Appanamixis* is evergreen. Leaves are pinnate in most genera but twice or thrice pinnate in *Melia;* leaflets few or many, rarely 3 or only 1. In *Appanamixis* the flowers are polygamo- dioecious and the females are in spikes or racemes. In this genus flowers are 3-merous with 6 monadelphous stamens and 3-locular ovary. Free stamens are found in *Toona* and in some other genera. In most of the genera ovules are 2 or 1 in each cell of the ovary but in *Soymida, Swietenia* and *Toona* ovules are many and the fruits are many seeded. Seeds are winged in *Toona, Soymida, Swietenia, Khaya,* etc. while *Azadirachta, Melia, Carapa* ,etc. have wingless seeds. The seeds in *Appanamixis* are arillate.

Xylocarpus has a very large globose capsule the 4 coriaceous valves of which open opposite the obliteratdd dissepiments.

The Californian species *Guarea ropalocarpa* has leaves which behave like short branches. These are 30-40 cm. long and have several leaflets which gradually unfold. The lowest leaflets remain in the rachis for 2-3 years when apex of the rachis continues to grow. When the uppermost leaflets develop many of the lower leaflets drop off. One leaf thus remains in the tree for 10-12 years.

Stem-anatomy shows that the pericycle is composed of distinct crescent-shaped fibres which are often close to each other forming a continuous ring. Vessels are in multiples of 2-3 and the perforations are simple. There is paratracheal wood parenchyma.

Meliaceae is a tropical family, with about 800 species under 50 genera. *Swietenia* a genus of timber yielding species is tropical American. *Cedrela* is distributed in the Old as well as the New World. In India the family is well represented. Some are suitable for comparatively dry situations while *Appanamixis, Walsura* etc. prefer more or less humid soil and *Xylocarpus* is a typically mangrove genus.

The family comprises a good number of excellent timber trees. *Swietenia mahagoni* Jacq. the true Mahogany and *S. macrophylla* King—the Honduras Mahogany are American. *Khaya senigalensis* A. Juss is the African Mahogany and is equally good. *Chloroxylon swietenia* DC. is the Indian Satin wood.*Chickrassia tabularis* A.Juss of E. India and Burma is the Chikrasi, a tall timber tree. *Cedrela odorata* Linn. a valuable timber tree also yields the cedar-oil used in microscopy. *Azadirachta indica* A. Juss. is the Neem tree or Margosa tree the juice of which has antiseptic properties. Margosa oil obtained from the seeds is used for burning as well as in medicine. The pulp of the fruit of *Melia azedarach* is poisonous and a decoetion of the leaves is used as an insecticide. *Soymida febrifuga* A. Juss a timber tree is also medicinally important. The flowers of *Chickrassia* yield a red dye.

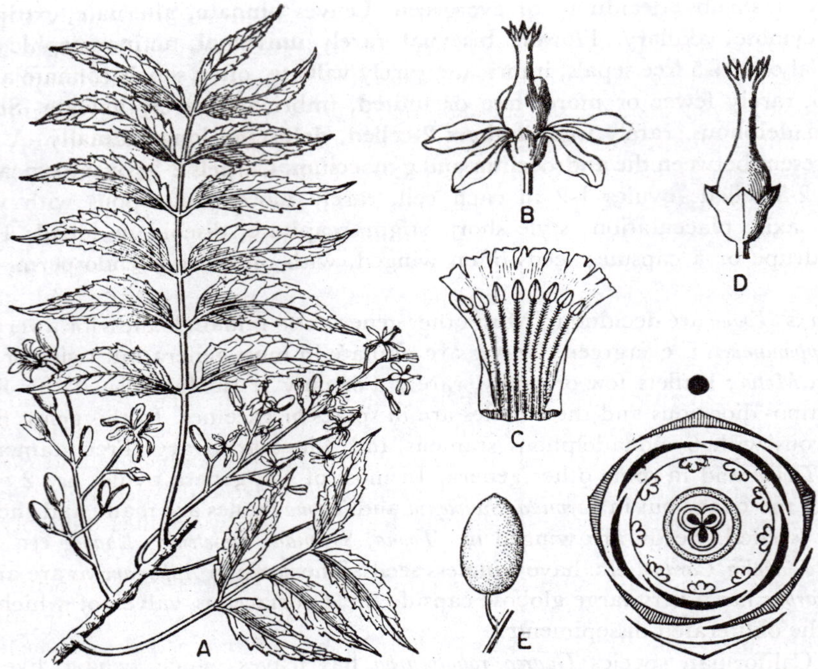

Fig. 90. Azadirachta indica Juss. A. Leafy twig with panicles ($\times\frac{1}{2}$); B. Flower ($\times 3$); C. Staminal tube with anthers at the throat; D. Flower with petals removed to show the ovary; E. Fruit (slightly reduced).

Meliaceae is related to *Rutaceae* on one side and to *Burseraceae* and *Simarubaceae* on the other. It is included in the **Geraniales** by Engler for the character of the ovule which has a ventral raphe. Bessey also included it in *Geraniales* and considered that it originated from the **Malvales,** due to the presence of monadelphous stamens. Hallier considered that *Meliaceae* was derived from *Rutaceae* and he included *Meliaceae* in his *Terebinthales*. Hutchinson places *Meliaceae* in an order of its own viz. **Meliales** which he places next to **Rutales.** Takhtajan includes *Meliaceae* in **Rutales** where *Burseraceae* and *Simarubaceae* are also included. In his system of arrangement **Rutales** is followed by **Sapindales. Cronquist** has *Meliaceae* in **Sapindales** where in are included *Burseraceae*, *Simarubaceae*, *Rutaceae*, *Zygophyllaceae* along with *Sapindaceae* and other allied families.

Malpighiaceae

Trees or shrubs, often scandent or lianes, often densely hairy; hairs unicellular and usually branched; in some species stinging hairs are present. Leaves glandular below or on petiole, opposite or alternate, often whorled, simple, stipulate; stipules deciduous, usually small, rarely large and opposite the leaves. Inflorescence is a simple raceme or a panicle. Flowers bisexual or polygamous, actinomorphic or obliquely zygomorphic, hypogynous or perigynous, pentamerous; torus pyramidal or flat or slightly depressed; pedicels jointed at base and bracteolate. Sepals 5, free or connate at base, imbricate or rarely valvate, persistent, each or at least one is provided with a large gland at the base on the outer side. Petals 5, free, clawed, usually convolute in bud and imbricate. Disc small; stamens 10 in 2 whorls obdiplostemonous, often some reduced to staminodes; filaments connate at base in a ring or short tube; anthers bilocular, introrse, with a thick connective produced at apex. Carpels 2-5, usually 3, wholly or partly coherent, often keeled; cells as many as carpels; ovary obliquely placed. Ovule solitary in each chamber, pendulous from a long funicle, with a ventral raphe; placentation axile; styles distinct; stigma capitate. Fruit a schizocarp breaking into one-seeded mericarps which are winged or nut-like, rarely fruit is drupaceous. Seeds without endosperm and with a large embryo; cotyledons usually convolute, thick or leaf-like, often unequal; rarely the seed has more than one embryo.

Anomalous secondary growth occurs in most of the climbing genera, with several vascular strands without forming a ring. Vessels are in multiples of 2-3 with alternate intervascular pitting; perforations simple; wood parenchyma paratracheal. Fibres are simple pitted.

Floral formula: ⚥ $K_5C_5A_{(5+5)}$ $G_{(3)}$.

Camarea a Brazilian genus has low growing shrubs with small leaves and large swollen leaves; they are xerophytic. In this genus the flowers have free carpels as are found in *Gaudichaudiana*, *Jamesia*, *Aspicarpa* and *Schwannia*. In *Acmantherea* and *Pterandra* anther loculi are winged. In *Lasiocarpus* stigmas are 2-lobed and twisted. In *Stigmatophyllon* (*Stigmaphyllon*) stigmas are broad and leaf like. *Brathypteris* has one cotyledon aborted in the seed.

The family consists of about 800 species under 60 genera the majority being tropical American. *Hiptage benghalensis* Kurz (Syn. *H. madablota* Gaertn) is the Madhabika or Madhabilata planted in gardens for the fragrant flowers. *Aspidopteris rotundifolia* A. Juss is found in eastern parts of India. *Malpighia glabra* is much cultivated in garden as an ornamental perennial. The fruits of this species are eaten in West Indies where it is indigenous. The leaves and shoots of *Banisteria caapi* Spruce yields a hallucinatory drug.

Malpighiaceae has been included in **Geraniales** by Engler as well as by Rendle who puts this family and *Zygophyllaceae* side by side. These 2 families are also placed in one order by Hutchinson, e.g. **Malpighiales** which according to him is a comparatively primitive order in **Lignosae** while **Geraniales** is an advanced order in the **Herbaceae.** According to him **Malpighiales** has been derived from **Tiliales.** Takhtajan includes *Malpighiaceae* in **Geraniales** where he includes *Zygophyllaceae* among other families. Cronquist and Heywood include *Malpighiaceae* in **Polygalales** and consider it to be associated with *Trigoniaceae* and *Tremandraceae* and also close to *Humiriaceae* and *Zygophyllaceae*. That *Malpighiaceae* and *Zygophyllaceae* are closely allied is the opinion of most taxonomists. One genus *Nitraria* is intermediate between the two families and are included by some in *Zygophyllaceae* while in *Malpighiaceae* by others while Takhtajan places it in a family of its own, e.g. *Nitrariaceae* which he places between *Malpighiaceae* and *Zygophyllaceae* in the order **Geraniales.**

The family *Malpighiaceae* is subdivided into 2 tribes by Niedenza as noted below:

I **Pyramidotorae**—Receptacle pyramidal; mericarps winged.

II **Planitorae**—Receptacle flat or concave, mericarps not winged.

Polygalaceae

Herbs, shrubs, rarely short-sized trees; few are lianes. Leaves simple, opposite or alternate, or often whorled; exstipulate or often scale-like stipules present or stipules represented by glands or spines. Inflorescence is an axillary or terminal raceme or spike or panicle, rarely flowers solitary. Flowers strongly medianly zygomorphic, bisexual and hypogynous, subtended by a bract and a pair of bracteoles. Sepals 5, free, unequal, imbricate and persistent; the 2 laterals are much larger and petaloid and usually project on each side like wings; rarely sepals united. Petals 5, usually connate at base; the anterior median petal is largest, boat shaped, lobed, fimbriated or with a crest at the apex and is termed the keel; the 2 lateral petals are often rudimentary or altogether suppressed; the petals are often adnate to the staminal tube; the margin of the petals are usually oblique or irregular. Stamens 8, all united in a tube split on the back and united to the keel near the base, anthers 1-2-locular, opening by apical pores; pollen grains are ellipsoidal with a coarse pitting at the poles and longitudinal bands broken in the middle by an equatorial ring; floral anatomy reveals that originally there were 10 stamens in two 5-merous whorls and the median member of each whorl became suppressed; sometimes the reduction was carried on more in some genera so that there remained only 7, 4 or 3 stamens. Ovary superior, of 2 united carpels, bilocular, with 1 anatropous ovule in each locule, pendulous from axile plancentation; style short, sometimes broadened upwards with an elbow-bend at the apex, rarely with a lateral or apical projection; stigma oblique; sometimes carpels are 3. Fruit usually a capsule, rarely nut, samara or drupe. Seed caranculate, with fleshy endosperm, rarely endosperm absent, the carancle functions as elaiosome; embryo straight.

In this family majority of the plants are shrubs or undershrubs or herbs. *Xanthophyllum* has trees while *Securidaca* is mainly lianes. Some species of *Salomonia* are parasitic on roots. *Epirrhizanthes* has 2 species in Malaya which are saprophytes. The flowers of *Carpolobia* have 5 united petals and only 5 stamens. In this genus as well as in *Trigoniastrum* the ovary is tricarpellary and trilocular. *Xanthophyllum* has a monocarpellary unilocular ovary; here of the 8 stamens 2 are free, other six united in a tube.

Floral formula † ⚥ $K_5\ C_5\ A_8\ G_{(\underline{2})}$.

Wood anatomy shows the presence of large vessels which are usually isolated; intervascular pitting alternate; perforations simple; wood parenchyma paratracheal; rays uniseriate, heterogenous, and with bordered pitted fibres.

The family consists of about 700 species in 10 genera; the genus *Polygala* containing more than 500 species of which 23 are Indian. The family is distributed all over the tropical and temperate zones but absent in New Zealand and Polynesia. In addition to 23 *Polygala* species *Salonionia*, *Securidaca* and *Xanthophyllum* are also found in Eastern India.

The family is not of much economic importance. *Polygala senega* Linn. an American plant has emetic, purgative and diuretic properties and is a reputed antidote against snake-poison. *P. crotalarioides* Buch.-Ham. of the Himalayas has the same properties. *Xanthophyllum flavescens* Roxb. is a good timber tree. *Polygala venenosa* is a very poisonous plant. *P. tinctoria* and *Krameria triandra* are used in dyeing.

Polygalaceae has been included in **Geraniales** by Eugler in the suborder *Polygalinae* with *Tremandaceae*. Engler places the genus *Krameria* in *Caesalpinioideae* of *Leguminosae* suggesting that *Polygalaceae* might have been derived from a stock ancestral to *Leguminosae*. *Krameria* is placed in a distinct family by Hutchinson who includes *Polygalaceae* and *Krameriaceae* in **Polygalales** after **Violales.** Rendle places *Polygalaceae* after **Sapindales** as a family of anomalous affinity. Takhtajan also keeps *Krameriaceae* as distinct from *Polygalaceae* and includes both these families in **Polygalales** along with *Trigoniaceae*, *Vochysiaceae* and *Tremandraceae* and places **Polygalales** next to **Geraniales.** According to Cronquist **Polygales** should include *Malpighiaceae* also along with

Trigonaceae, *Vochysiaceae* and *Tremandaceae* and he does not separate *Krameria* from *Polygalaceae*. Heywood agrees with Takhtajan in his treatment of the order *Polygalales*.

Euphorbiaceae

Herbs, shrubs or trees, rarely climbing or creeping; milky latex often present Leaves usually simple, alternate or opposite, stipulate or not; leaves rarely reduced to scales or spines. Inflorescence various, a simple raceme or spike, cymose panicle or head like cluster or a cyathium—a special type of inflorescence with one female flower surrounded by many male flowers; bracts and bracteoles often present and often glandular. Flowers unisexual in monoecious and dioecious plants, usually small and inconspicuous, perianthless or with perianth, actinomorphic or very rarely zygomorphic. Perianth when present usually consisting of calyx only; rarely calyx and corolla both present, usually pentamerous, imbricate or valvate. Disc present or absent and often represented by glands. Stamens few to very many, free or monadelphous or polyadelphous, often stamen only one in a male flower; anthers 2-celled opening lengthwise, transversely or by apical pores. Female flower with a superior ovary; carpels usually 3, syncarpous; ovary sessile or stipitate, usually 3-celled with 1-2 pendulous ovules; ovules anatropous, with ventral raphe, on axile placentation beneath a prominent "obturator" or placental outgrowth; styles as many as carpels, free or united below, each often 2-lobed and then with stigmas double the number of styles. Fruit a schizocarpic capsule (*regma*), sometimes berry or drupaceous, or nut-like.

The large family has a wide range of variation in vegetative as well as in floral parts. There are trees, shrubs or herbs but few are climbing. *Putranjiva*, *Bischofia*,* *Trewia*, *Aleurites*, etc. are trees. Most of them are evergren but *Trewia* is deciduous as are *Antidesma** *ghaesembilla* Gaertn., *Croton oblongifolius* Roxb. etc. *Tragia*, *Cnesmone*, etc. are climbers or twiners. *Tragia* is hispid with stinging hairs. Some species of *Euphorbia* are marked xerophytes and have a Cactus-like appearance. They have fleshly stem, cylindric or angular, with thick succulent leaves or small scaly leaves or are leafless, thorny or unarmed. In some species of *Phyllanthus* the branches are modified into flat leaf-like cladodes and the true leaves are rudimentary. *Phyllanthus flutians* Muell-Arg. of Brazil is the only submerged aquatic plant belonging to this family. Leaves are simple but species of *Hevea* and *Bischofia javanica* Bl. have trifoliate leaves.

Cyathium is a special type of inflorescence. This has a calyx-like involucre bearing large glands near the rim. A solitary female flower with only a naked tricarpellary ovary terminates a slender peduncle surrounded by a number of male flowers. The male flowers are like the female flower perianthless and each is represented by a single stamen. All the flowers are pedicelled and are subtended by a thin scaly bracteole. The pedicel of the female flower is much longer than those of the males and brings the flower out of the involucral cup. The glands on the margin of the involucre are nectar-secreting. Rarely perianth is present in the form of minute scales. The involucre is urn-shaped and regular in *Euphorbia* but irregular and with a posterior appendage in *Pedilanthes*.

In the genus *Monotaxis* the cup-shaped involucre is replaced by a whorl of scale-like bracts and the solitary central pistillate flower is surrounded by staminate flowers.

*** Transferred to a unigeneric family Bischofiaceae.**

* *Antidesma* is placed by some in Stilaginaceae.

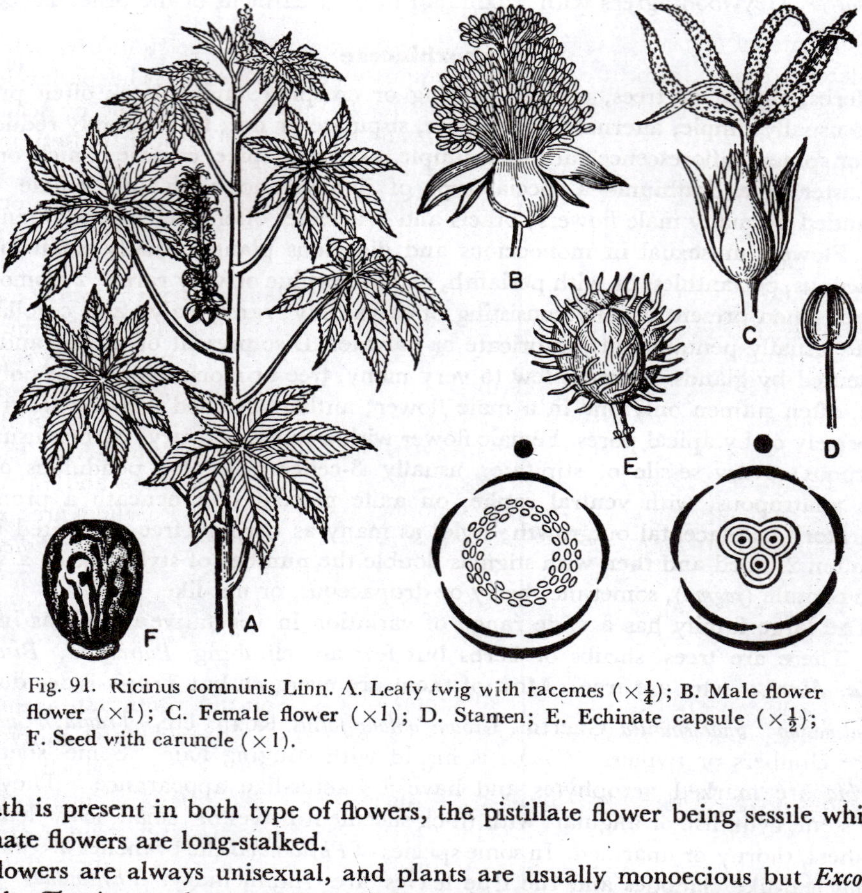

Fig. 91. Ricinus comnunis Linn. A. Leafy twig with racemes ($\times\frac{1}{4}$); B. Male flower flower ($\times 1$); C. Female flower ($\times 1$); D. Stamen; E. Echinate capsule ($\times\frac{1}{2}$); F. Seed with caruncle ($\times 1$).

Perianth is present in both type of flowers, the pistillate flower being sessile while the staminate flowers are long-stalked.

Flowers are always unisexual, and plants are usually monoecious but *Excoecaria*, *Suregada*, *Trewia*, etc. have species which are dioecious. Corolla is usually absent but in *Jatropha*, *Aleurites*, *Croton*, etc. the flowers are dichlamydeous with a distinct corolla. The number of stamens vary from 1 to many. In *Euphorbia*, *Pedilanthus*, etc. the male flower has a single stamen. In *Breynia*, *Phyllanthus*, etc. there are 3 stamens, monadelphous, forming a central column. In *Baccauria* stamens are free. In *Manihot*, *Jatropha*, *Chrozophora*, etc. stamens are in more than 1 whorl. In *Trewia*, *Mallotus* etc. numerous free stamens are crowded on a flat or convex receptacle. In *Homonoia* and *Ricinus* the filaments of stamens are repeatedly branched. According to Pijl the so called male flower of Ricinus is in reality an inflorescence, a condensed panicle, consisting of numerous male flowers each of which is reduced to a single stamen only. This view has been supported by Eames.

In most genera carpels are 3; *Mercurialis* usually has a bicarpellate bilocular ovary while in *Antidesma*, *Drypetes* and a few other genera the ovary is unilocular by abortion. *Hura* has a multicarpellate multilocular ovary, the number of carpels being as many as 15. In *Glochidion* the number of carpels vary from 2-15. Styles free or connate near base in most cases but in *Endospermum* they are completely united forming a flat spreading disc. Fruits are schizocarpic capsule in most cases; in *Putranjiva*, *Emblica*, *Aleurites* and a few other genera they are drupes while in *Bischofia* the fruit is a berry.

Floral formula for Eupharbiaceae may be expressed as:—

♂ P_{3-5} $A_{1-\infty}G_0$ and ♀ P_{3-5} A_0 $G_{(3)}$ or more.

Anatomical characters also vary in different genera. In the stem pericycle occurs as isolated strands of fibres or as a continuous mechanical ring. The pericycle fibres occur in groups in some genera and also singly. Vessels have simple or scalariform perforations or both. Wood parenchyma occur as scattered cells, in uniseriate bands or apotracheal cells. Fibres are thick-walled and simple-pitted and often septate. Intraxylary phloem is present in the stem of some genera. Cambiform tissue occurs as isolated patches or as continuous sheath. Latex vessels are segmented or unsegmented and branched.

The family consists of about 300 genera and over 6000 species, the genus *Euphorbia* having about 2000 species. Throughout tropical and temperate zones of both the hemispheres the family is distributed. Many are xerophytes and are found in arid regions of Africa, W. Asia and Australia, and almost all the members of the group **Stenolobeae** are Australian. Tropical America is very rich in plants of this family and in Brazil is found the only aquatic submerged plant. viz. *Phyllanthas flutians* Muell-Arg. *Excoecaria agallocha* Linn. is a halophyte occurring in the littoral forest of India and E. Asia. In India the family is represented by about 500 species most common of them are: *Jatropha curcas* Linn., *J. gossypifolia* Linn., *Chrozophora rottleri* Juss & Spr., *Acalypha indica* Linn. *Ricinus communis* Linn., *Targia involucrata* Linn. (Stinging Nettle), *Putranjiva roxburghii* Wall., *Trewia nudifora* Linn., *Euphorbia neriifolia* Linn., *E. antiquorum* Linn., *E. pilulifera* Linn., *E. dracunculoides* Lamk., *Emblica officinalis* Gaertn., *Phyllanthus fraternus Web., P. simplex* Retz., etc.

The family contains a number of useful plants. The most important is the Pararubber plant of Brazil *Hevea brasiliensis* (H. B. K.) Muell-Arg. which is cultivated in India, Ceylon, Malaya and many other countries. *Manihot glaziovii* Muell-Arg. also indigenous to S. America yields ceara-rubber and is cultivated in many tropical countries. *Manihot escuenta* Crantz. yields Cassava or Tapioca starch from the tuberous roots. *Ricinus communis* Linn. yields castor oil from the seeds used as a lubricating agent, as purgative and also for burning. *Aleurites moluccana* Willd. is the source of Tung oil much used in paints and varnish and for manufacture of oil-cloth. *Sapium sebiferum* Roxb. is the Chinese Tallow tree found wild in many parts of India, yields an oil used in soap-manufacture, and a black or purple dye is obtained from the leaves. *Mallotus philippinensis* Muell-Arg. yields a red dye from the gnandular hairs. Oil obtained from the seeds of *Jatropha curcas* Linn. and *Croton tiglium* Linn. are strong purgative. Fruit of *Emblica officinalis* Gaertn. is pickled and is much used in Kabiraji and Unani medicine. Species of the African genus *Ricinodendron* are good timber trees and are known as African Oaks. The latex of many species are poisonous and that of *Toxicodendron* species of S. Africa are strongly so.

The family was included in *Geraniales* by Engler particularly on the character of ovule which has a ventral raphe. It resembles *Geraniaceae* and allied families in the character of the fruit. It has much in common with *Sterculiaceae*, e.g. the monadelphous or polyadelphous stamens, presence of androphore and gynophore in some cases. Presence of schizocarpic capsule and carunculate seeds in some members of Sterculiaceae speaks also of the close relation between the two families. Rendle placed *Euphorbiaceae* under a small order **Tricoccae** in between **Malvales** and **Geraniales** recognising

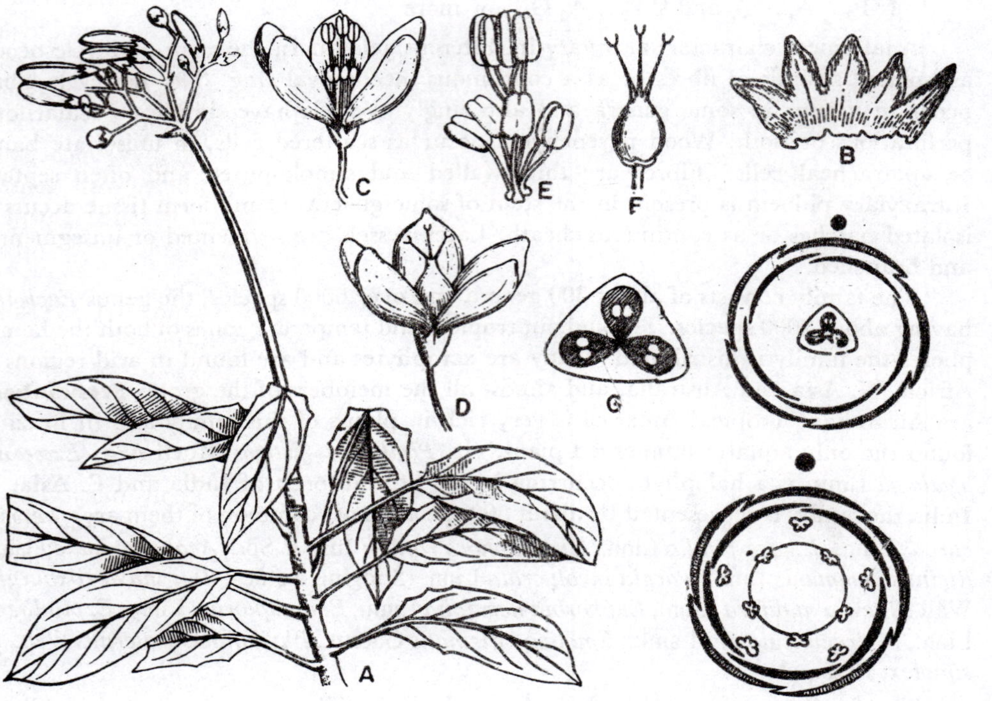

Fig. 92. Jatropha hastata Jack A. Leafy twig with flowers ($\times\frac{1}{2}$); B. Calyx split open; C. Male flower; D. Female flower; E. Androecium ($\times3$); F. Gynoecium ($\times2$); G.T.s. of ovary.

the affinity of the order with **Mavales** and **Geraniales**-Hutchinson places **Euphorbiales** with single family *Euphorbiaceae* nearer to **Tiliales, Malvales** and **Malpighiales** in his Lignosae while **Geraniales** is a much advanced order in Herbaceae. Takhtajan also recognises the affinity of *Euphorbiaceae* with *Sterculiaceae* and in his system of arrangement places **Euphorbiales** just after **Malvales** in the subclass **Dilleniidae** while **Geraniales** is included in subclass **Rosidae.** Cronquist considers that *Euphorbiales* is closer to **Sapindales** as well as to **Geraniales, Linales** and **Polygalales** all having been derived from *Rosaceous* stock while **Malvales** has been derived from **Dilleniales** through **Theales** and not much close to **Euphorbiales.**

The family has been divided by Pax in the following manner:

Group A. PLATYLOBAE: Cotyledons much broader than radicle.

Sub f. I **Phyllanthoideae:** Ovules 2 in each cell; latex absent.

Tribe 1. *Phyllantheae*—Calyx of ♂ fl. imbricate.

Tribe 2. *Brideleae*—Calyx of ♂ fl. valvate.

Sub f. II **Euphorbioideae:** (Ctotonoideae) Ovule 1 in each cell; latex present.

Tribe 1. *Crotoneae*—Stamens bent inwards in bud.

Tribe 2. *Acalypheae*—Stamens erect in bud; fls. usually apetalous; ♂ calyx valvate; infl. a raceme, spike or panicle.

Tribe 3. *Jatropheae*—Stamens erect in bud; petals present, ♂ calyx imbricate; infl. a dichasial thyrsus.

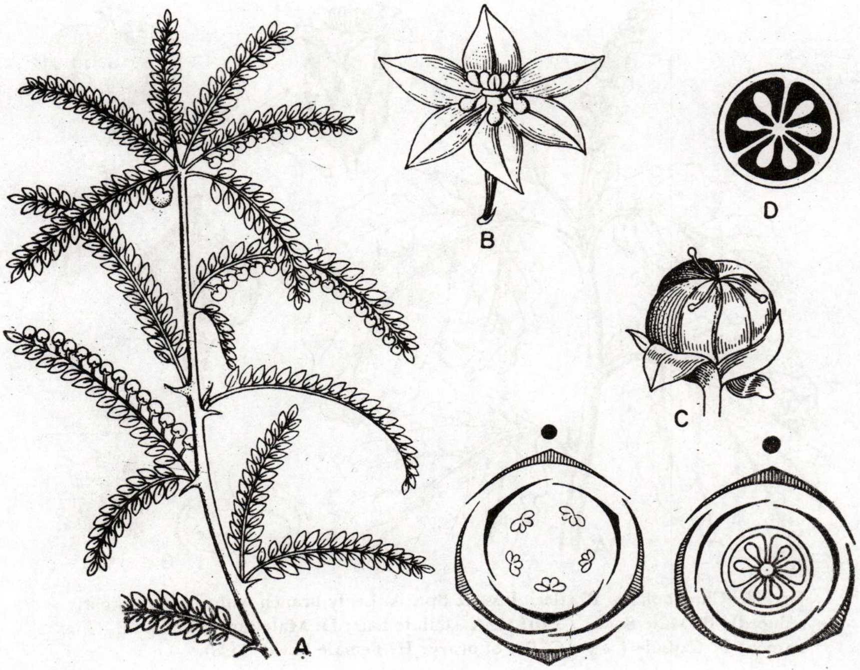

Fig. 93. Phyllanthus fraternus Web. A. Portion of the plant with several leafy branches with flowers and fruits (×½); B. Male flower (×2); C. Fruit; D.T.s. of ovary.

Tribe 4. *Adrianeae*—Stamens erect in bud; ♂ calyx imbricate; infl. terminal spike or raceme; petals absent.

Tribe 5. *Clutieae*—Stamens erect in bud; sepals imbricate; petals present in ♂ fls.; infl. cymose or fls. in clusters.

Tribe 6. *Gelonieae*—Stamens erect in bud; petals absent; ♂ sepals imbricate; infl. leaf-opposed.

Tribe 7. *Hippomaneae*—Stamens erect in bud; petals absent; inflorescence spicate.

Tribe 8. *Euphorbieae*—Inflorescence a cyatheum.

Group B. STENOLOBAE: Cotyledons as broad as radicle.

Sub f. I **Porantheroideae:** Ovules 2 per locule; latex absent.

Sub f. II **Ricinocarpoideae:** Ovule 1 per locule; latex present.

Radcliff-Smith (Heywood's Fl. Pl. of the World) divides the family into following 8 tribes :—*Phyllantheae*, *Bridelieae*, *Crotoneae*, *Acalypheae*, *Ricineae*, *Jatropheae*, *Suregadeae* and *Euphorbieae*. Recent workers are in favour of slightly altering the conscription of the family *Euphorbiaceae* so that the following genera are now excluded from this family, viz., *Androstachys*, *Antidesma*, *Bischofia*, *Centroplacus*, *Galcerea*, *Hymenocardia*, *Microdesmis*, *Pera* and *Upaca*. In the old classification of Bentham and Hooker the family *Buxaceae* was included in *Euphorbiaceae* but Engler separated it as distinct on account of the ovules having a dorsal raphe.

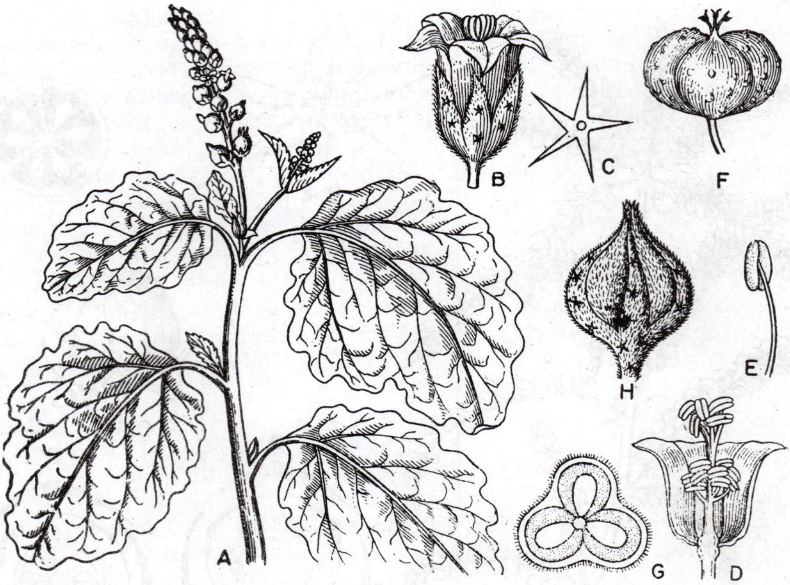

Fig. 94. Chrozophora Rottleri Juss. & Spr. A. Leafy branch with raceme (slightly reduced); B. Male flower (×6); C. A. stellate hair; D. Male flower in l.s.; E. One stamen; F. Capsule (×½); G.T.s. of ovary; H. Female flower (×8).

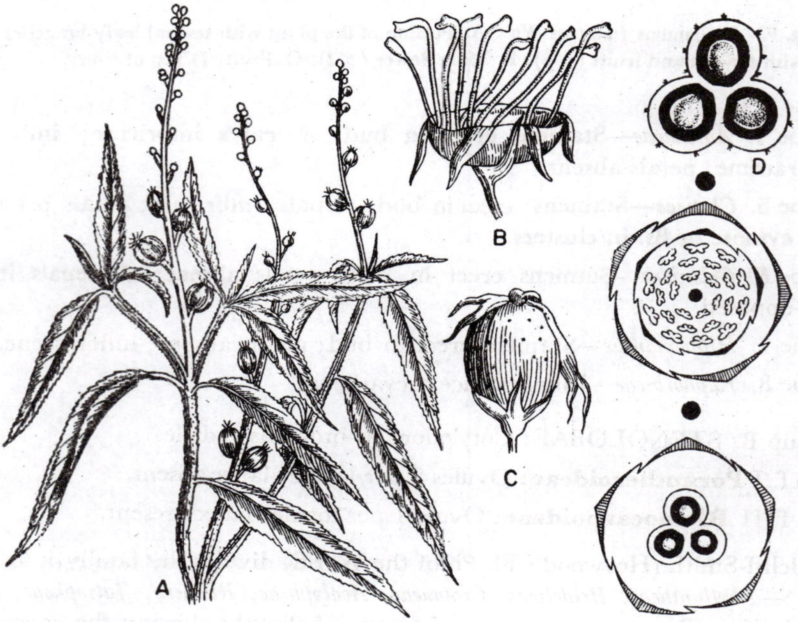

Fig. 95. Croton Bonplandianum Bail. A. Leafy branch with racemes (×½); B. Male flower (×6); C. Female flower (×6); D.T.s. of ovary.

Buxaceae

Evergreen shrubs or trees, very rarely herbaceous (*Pachysandra*). **Leaves coriaceous,** opposite or alternate, simple, exstipulate. Inflorescence spikate, elongated or head-like. Flowers unisexual, in monoecious or dioecious plants, rarely flowers bisexual; actinomorphic, with or without perianth; female flowers often solitary or in lax racemes. Male flowers with one whorl of calycine perianth; sepals usually 4, connate at base. Stamens 4–6, rarely more; anther bilocular, dehiscing by valves or longitudinal slits. Pistillode often present. Female flowers larger than males with one or two whorls of perianth, or without perianth. Ovary tricarpellary syncarpous, superior, trilocular, with 2 ovules in each locule; ovules anatropous with dorsal raphe; carpels often 2 or 4; styles as many as carpels, each often bifurcate. Fruit capsular or berry-like. Seeds black and shining, endospermic, usually caruncula te; embryo straight.

Buxaceae is a comparatively small family consisting of about 100 species under 6 genera but widely distributed in the tropical parts of both the worlds and extending to temperate region. *Buxus wallichiana* Bail. and *Sarcococca pruniformis* Lindl. are Himalayan species.

Buxaceae is closely allied to Euphorbiaceae where it was formerly included. Engler treated this as a distinct family due to the presence of dorsal raphe and absence of milky sap. He included the new family in **Sapindales** while Euphorbiaceae was placed by him in Geraniales. Subsequent authors support Engler in segregating Buxaceae as a distinct family but they recognise the close relationship of Buxaceae with Euphorbiaceae and consequently place the two families in the same order **Euphorbiales.**

Buxus semprevirens Linn. is an ornamental hedge plant. It is a small tree the wood of which is good for engraving and carving. Otherwise, the family is not economically important.

SAPINDALES

The order **Sapindales** consists of 23 families included under 12 sub-orders as noted below:

1. Buxineae—Buxaceae.
2. Empetrineae—Empetraceae.
3. Coriarineae—Coriariaceae.
4. Limnanthineae—Limnanthaceae.
5. Anacardineae—Anacardiaceae.
6. Celastrineae—Cyrillaceae, Pentaphylacaceae, Corynocarpaceae, Aquifoliaceae, Celastraceae, Hippocrateaceae, Salvadoraceae, Stackhousiaceae, Staphyliaceae.
7. Icacinineae—Icacinaceae.
8. Sapindineae—Aextoxiaceae, Aceraceae, Hippocastanaceae, Sapindaceae.
9. Sabineae—Sabiaceae.
10. Melianthineae—Melianthaceae.
11. Didiereineae—Didiereaceae.
12. Balsamininеae—Balsaminaceae.

In these families the plants are usually shrubs or trees with bisexual or unisexual flowers which are usually regular and hypogynous with a tendency to perigyny; a hypogynous disc is usually present; stamens many, diplostemonous; ovules pendulous with a dorsal raphe. The two characters, viz. diplostemonous androecium and dorsal raphe of the ovules distinguish the families of this order from those of **Geraniales.** It is to be noted however that the type family Sapindaceae has ovule with ventral raphe.

Placing of these 23 families under one order does not seem to be proper, because their relationship is considered to be distant and their origin is from different ancestral stocks. *Anacardiaceae*, *Sapindaceae*, *Aceraceae*, *Hippocastanaceae*, *Burseraceae*, *Cneoraceae*, *Julianiaceae*, *Meliaceae*, *Rutaceae*, *Melianthaceae* and *Simarubaceae* appear to be very closely related and are placed in orders which are arranged one after another in different systems. Thus we find *Anacardiaceae*, *Sapindaceae*, *Aceraceae*, *Hippocastanaceae*, *Melianthaceae* and *Julianiaceae* are placed by Hutchinson in his **Sapindales,** *Burseraceae*, *Simarubaceae* and *Rutaceae* in **Rutales** and *Meliaceae* in **Meliales,** and the 3 orders are arranged close to each other. Takhtajan places *Anacardiaceae*, *Burseraceae*, *Cneoraceae*, *Julianiaceae*, *Meliaceae*, *Rutaceae* and *Simarubaceae* in his **Rutales** and *Sapindaceae*, *Aceraceae*, *Hippocastanaceae* and *Melianthaceae* in **Sapindales** which follows **Rutales.** Cronquist includes *Anacardiaceae*, *Sapindaceae*, *Aceraceae*, *Hippocastanaceae* and *Melianthaceae* in *Sapindales* and also *Rutaceae*, *Meliaceae*, *Burseraceae*, *Simarubaceae*, *Cneoraceae* and *Julianiaceae* in the same order. Engler placed *Cneoraceae*, *Rutaceae*, *Simarubaceae* *Burseraceae* and *Meliaceae* in **Geraniales** and *Anacardiaceae*, *Sapindaceae*, *Hippocastanaceae*, *Aceraceae* and *Melianthaceae* in **Sapindales.** and these 2 orders are placed side by side in his system. Therefore the close relationship of these 11 families has been recognised by Engler and most subsequent authors. But placing *Rutaceae*, *Meliaceae*, etc. with *Geraniaceae* and allied families in a single order **Geraniales** and inclusion of *Anacardiaceae, Sapindaceae*, etc. in another order along with families like *Aquifoliaceae*, *Celastraceae*, *Stackhousiaceae* and *Icacinaceae* which should go to **Celastrales** according to Takhtajan and Cronquist, cannot be justified.

Buxaceae was segregated as a distinct family from *Euphorbiaceae* and is included by Engler in **Sapindales** only on the basis of the character of having dorsal raphe of the ovules. *Buxaceae* as a distinct family is maintained by all subsequent workers but most of them are in favour of keeping it close to *Euphorbiaceae* in the order **Euphorbiales.** *Didiereaceae* is placed in **Caryophyllales** by Takhtajan and Cronquist, and in **Sapindales** by Hutchinson. *Empetraceae* is placed in **Ericales** by Takhtajan and Cronquist but in **Celastrales** by Hutchinson. *Pentaphylacaceae* is placed in **Theales** by Hutchinson and Takhtajan while Cronquist treats the family as a part of *Theaceae.* It is therefore clear that Engler's **Sapindales** is, like his order **Geraniales** an unnatural group of families of which a few are allied to each other while others are distantly related or not related at all.

Anacardiaceae

Trees or shrubs, rarely woody vines, containing resin-passages with plenty of gum and acrid juice. Leaves simple or pinnate, alternate, rarely, opposite exstipulate. Inflorescence an axillary or terminal cymose panicle; flowers small and numerous, bisexual or polygamous, actinomorphic and hypogynous. Sepals 3-7, but usually 5, free or more or less connate, imbricate; petals 3-7, free or rarely connate, imbricate, sometimes absent; a cupular extrastaminal or intrastaminal disc is usually present. Stamens double the number of petals or 10 or more in 2 whorls, free, arising from the rim of the disc. Carpels 1-5, united to form a unilocular or multilocular superior ovary, having a solitary ovule in only one of the ovary-chambers; rarely carpels free; styles 1-5, lateral or terminal and widely separated; ovule anatropous, pendulous or ascending, with dorsal raphe. Fruit usually a drupe, rarely nut. Seeds without endosperm, with thick and fleshy cotyledons and curved embryo.

Some plants of this family are notoriously allergenic to man. The juice is pungent in most cases and very poisonous in some, e.g. *Rhus* species, particularly *R. toxicodendron* Linn. and *R. venenata* DC., the juice of which when applied to the skin causes erysipelas. Most species are evergreen while *Spondias*, *Lannea*, etc. are deciduous. Leaves are ternate in *Ozoroa* and in some species of *Rhus*, but simple or pinnate leaves are found in most of the genera; leaves are alternate but in *Bouea* they are opposite. *Cotynus coggygria* Scop (*Rhus cotinus* Linn.) grows long hairs on the sterile part of the fruiting panicle which gets detached from the tree and is carried far by the wind.

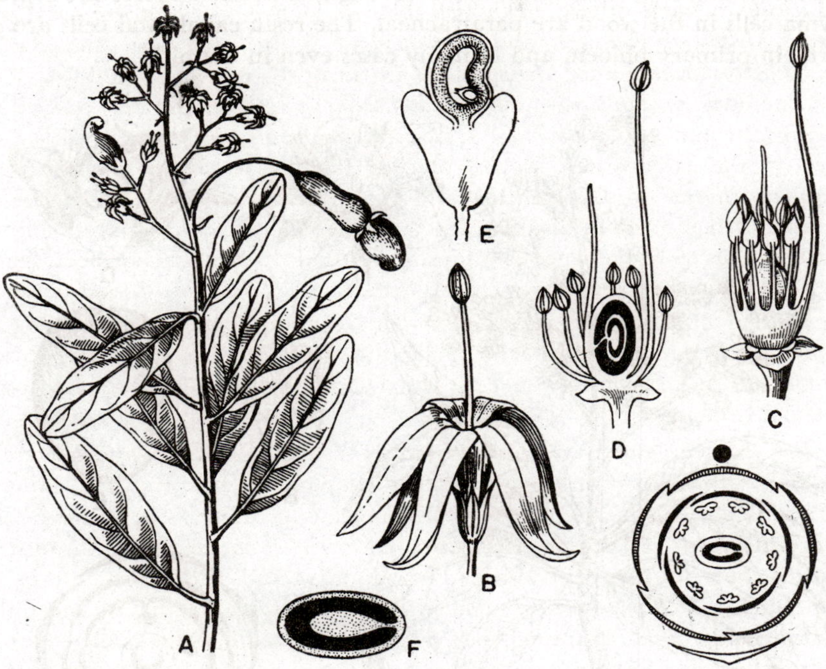

Fig. 96. Anacardium occidentale Linn. A. Leafy branch with terminal panicle (much reduced); B. One flower showing calyx, corolla and the longest stamen; C. Same with the corolla removed, showing stamens of unequal length and ovary; D. Same in l.s. to show lateral style; E. Young fruit with carpophore. (B, C & D ×4).

The floral axis is a short convex receptacle with hypogynous perianth and androecium with nectaries; it is often extended in the form of a disc which is cupular or cushion-like and intrastaminal as in *Rhus*, or thick and extrastaminal as in *Mangifera*, or elongated to form a gynophore as in *Melanorrhoea*. *Pistacia* has one whorl of perianth which is sepaloid in staminate flowers and in pistillate flowers small and scarious. Calyx deciduous in *Semecarpus*, and persistent in *Rhus*, *Lannea*, etc., Petals are accrescent in *Suritonia* and remain attached to the fruit. In *Anacardium* there are 8-10 stamens of which some are fertile and some sterile, and one fertile stamen is much longer than the rest. In *Mangifera* there are 1 fertile and 4 sterile stamens. In *Mangifera* and *Anacardium* ovary is monocarpellary; in *Buchanania* there are 5 free carpels only one however, has an ovule. *Drimycarpus* has inferior ovary. Styles are united or free and usually terminal but in *Mangifera* and *Anacardium* it is lateral. in *Lannea* the 4 free styles are perisistent. Ovary when polycarpellary and syncarpous is usually 1-celled but 4-5-celled in *Spondias*.

Fruit is an one-seeded drupe in most genera but in *Spondias* there are 4-5 seeds inside the stone. The fruit is a nut in *Anacardium* and is situated on a pyriform fleshy mass derived from the accrescent disc and top of pedicel. In *Semecarpus* similar fleshy mass is formed from the accrescent disc and calyx-base but the fruit is a drupe.

The typical floral formula for the family is: ⊕ ⚥ $K_5C_5A_{10}G_{\underline{(1-4)}}$.

In *Anacardiaceae* the stem anatomy shows that the pericycle is made up of arc-shaped isolated strands of fibres, rarely of continuous sclerenchymatous ring. Vessels are with simple perforation plates and intervascular pitting is alternate. Fibres are septate and parenchyma cells in the wood are paratracheal. The resin canals and cells are present in all parts, in primary phloem and in many cases even in the pith.

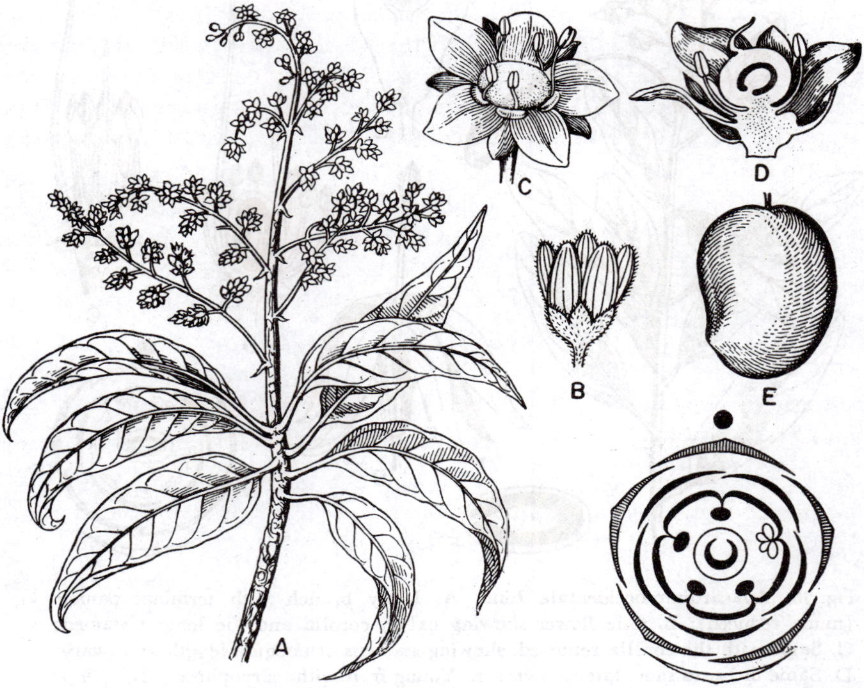

Fig. 97. Mangifera indica Linn.—A. Leafy twig with terminal panicle ($\times\frac{1}{8}$); B. One flower ($\times$ 3); C. Male flower; D. Hermaphrodite flower; E. Fruit (C & D. much enlarged; E. reduced).

The family contains about 600 species under 77 genera distributed in the tropical and subtropical regions of the world. It is represented in India by 65 species of which *Mangifera indica* Linn. is best known. *Rhus* a genus with 120 species and widely spread over the subtropical and temperate regions of the world from America to Japan has several species in the Himalayas at lower altitudes. *Buchanania*, *Semecarpus*, *Holigarna Swintonia*, *Lannea* etc. are other genera common in the plains. *Rhus punjabensis* Stew. and *Pistacia integerrima* Stew. grow in the W. Himalayas up to an elevatoion of 2500 mtr. while, *Rhus khasiana* Hook. grows in the Khasi hills.

Many species of this family are of economic importance. *Mangifera indica* Linn. produces the delicious Mango-fruits and for this reason is cultivated on a large scale all over India and other tropical countries. *Anacardium occidentale* Linn. is the Cashew nut tree, original of Brazil, now cultivated in India and other tropical countries; the fleshy pedicel of the ripe fruit is also edible. The pericarp of the nut yields an oil which is very poisonous. *Pistacia vera* Linn. of W. Asia and Mediterranean region is also much cultivated for the seeds which are the Pistaceo nuts of commerce. Seeds of *Buchanania lanzan* Spr. the Piyal tree are also used similarly as a substitute of pistaceo nut and are called Chiranjee. Fruits of *Spondias pinnata* (L. f.) Kurz is the Amara or Hog-plum of India while *S. purpurea* Linn. and *S. mombin* L. are Hog-plums of Brazil and W. Indies. Kafir plum is the fruit of *Harpehyllum caffrum* Bernh. of S. Africa. *Pistacia lentiscus* Linn. yields a mastic resin while *P. terebinthes* L. yields turpentine. *Semecarpus anacardium* L. f. the Marking-nut tree, (Hindi-Bhilwa, Bhela) exudes a juice from the ripe fruit that stains cotton a permanent black. Resinous juice of *Rhus styphina* Linn., *R. glabra* L., *R. coriaria* Linn. etc. is used for tanning. *R. vernicifera* DC. of Japan yields lacquer. *R. succedanea* Linn. yields Japanese wax when the berries are crushed. *R. toxicodendron* Linn., and *R. venenata* DC. are very poisonous. Galls formed on *Rhus khasiana* Hook. f. and *Pistacia integerrima* Stew. called Karkatashringi or Kakra shinga are used by Hakims and Kabirajes in India. Timbers obtained from *Mangifera indica* Linn., *Swintonia floribunda* Griff. etc. are valuable.

Almost all workers on phylogeny of Angiosperm trace the affinity of *Anacardiaceae* with *Sapindaceae* and place *Anacardiaceae* in **Sapindales.** It is however closely related to *Aceraceae, Hippocastanaceae, Sapindaceae, Simarubaceae, Meliaceae, Cneoraceae, Burseraceae* and *Rutaceae* and more so to the last two families possessing special type of resin ducts.

The family is divided into 5 tribes as noted below:

I. **Mangiferae:** Leaves simple; carpels 1-6. *Mangifera*, *Buchanania*.

II. **Spondieae:** Leaves pinnately compound; carpels 4-5, ovules as many as carpeles; *Spondias*, etc.

III. **Rhoideae:** Leaves usually pinnate; carpels 4-5, ovary free from floral axis, ovule only one; *Rhus*, *Pistacia*, etc.

IV. **Semecarpeae:** Leaves simple; ovary is adnate to and sunken in the thalamus *Semecarpus*, etc.

V. **Dobineae:** Leaves pinnate; perianth absent; carpel only one: *Dobinea*, *Compylopetalum*, etc.

Many modern taxonomists raise the tribe *Dobineae* to a distinct family *Podoaceae* and the genus *Pistacia* to a family of its own as *Pistaciaceae*.

Aquifoliaceae

Trees or shrubs, evergreen or deciduous, leaves simple, alternate, exstipulate or with minute stipulates, coriaceous or chartaceous. Inflorescence axillary, cymose, very rarely flowers solitary. Flowers small and inconspicuous, bisexual or often unisexual, hypogynous. Sepals 3 – 6, usually united at the base, imbricate, persistent. Petals 4 – 5, or more, free or united at the base, imbricate or valvate. Stamens equal to the number of petals or more; filaments often adnate to the petals; anthers bilocular, dehiscing longitudinally. Disc absent. Ovary superior, 4- or more-celled; ovules 1 – 2 in each cell, pendulous, anatropous; style short or absent; stigma lobed. Fruit a drupe, usually of 4 pyrenes. Seeds with copious fleshy endosperm and small straight embryo with superior radicle.

In the genus *Nemopanthus* 2 types of shoots occur, viz., long shoots and short shoots. In this genus petals are completely free. In *Byronia* stamens and carpels are much more in number than petals. Species of *Ilex* have typical tetrameroses flowers and unisexual in some cases. *I. aquifolium* Linn. is dioecious.

The family contains 4 genera of which *Ilex* consists of about 400 species. Others have only few each. These are distributed in the temperate and subtropical parts of the world. In India, the family is represented by 17 species of *Ilex*, common among them are *I. insignis* Hook. f., *I. dipyrina* Wall., *I. malabarica* Bedd. etc.

Aquifoliaceae is allied to Celastraceae having flowers often tetramerous and the endosperm fleshy. The family is splitted into two by some workers as Aquifoliaceae and **Phellinaceae.** This includes only one genus *Phellie* having exstipulate leaves, flowers in spikes and petals valvate.

Ilex aquifolium Linn, is the Holly, the leafy twigs of which are much in demand for Christmas decoration. Many south American species of *Ilex* contain caffein and *I. paraguensis* St. Hill is the Yerba mate, the leaves of which are used as substitute for tea. Otherwise the family is not of much importance economically.

Celastraceae

Trees or shrubs, rarely lianas. Leaves simple, alternate or opposite, often stipulate; stipules small and caducous. Inflorescence a cyme or cymose panicle, axillary or terminal. Flowers very small, usually bisexual actinomorphic, hypogynous, or more or less perigynous. Calyx 4—5-lobed, often persistent, lobes imbricate, often free very near to the base. Corolla of 4—5 free petals, imbricate or rarely valvate. A well developed flat or cupular disc is always present. Stamens as many as and alternate to the petals, rarely double that number, inserted below or upon the disc or on its margin; anthers bithecal, dehiscing longitudinally. Ovary superior or semi-inferior, of 2—5 united carpels, 2—5 celled; style short, stigma lobed or capitate; ovules 2 in each cell, erect anatropous. Fruit a berry or a capsule or dry and indehiscent; seeds arillate with fleshy endosperm; aril coloured.

The disc secretes nectar. In some species a few flowers are functionally male while others remain perfect, the plants thus becoming polygamous. The aril of seeds in some genera are of micropylar origin.

The family with about 475 species under 45 genera are found in tropical and temperate countries of the world. It is well represented in India, more in the hills while a few occur also in the plains. Common Indian plants are: *Euonymus indicus* Heyne, *E. crenulatus* W. &. A. , *Microtropis ramiflora* Wt., *Lophopetalum wightianum* Arn., *Celastrus paniculata* Willd., *Gymnospoia wallichiana* Spreng., etc.

Cellastraceae is allied to Aquifoliaceae, Stachousiaceae and Icacinaceae, having ovules with dorsal raphe, presence of a prominent disc, usually one whorl of stamens and fleshy endosperm. It is also related to Empetraceae and Salvadoraceae to some extent.

A few plants of the family are important having medicinal properties. *Euonymus europaeus* Linn. have seeds which are purgative and emetic. *Catha edulis* Forsk have leaves with stimulant properties. The seeds of *Celastrus paniculata* Willd. cure rheumatism.

Sapindaceae

Trees or shrubs, sometimes tendril-climbers; the tendrils being the flowerless branches of the inflorescence. Leaves alternate, usually pinnately compound, rarely ternate and very rarely simple; exstipulate or in climbing species often stipulate; stipules when present small and usually deciduous. Inflorescence is usually a cymose panicle or a thyrsus. Flowers small, regular or obliquely zygomorphic, bisexual or unisexual or polygamous, pentamerous or rarely tetramerous, hypogynous. Calyx usually of 5 free sepals or in regular flowers sepals 4 due to union of 3rd and 5th sepals; sepals imbricate. Corolla usually of 5 petals but 4 in actinomorphic flowers as a result of suppression; petals free, imbricate, usually with a scale-like or hairy appendage at base. Stamens 8 or 10 in 2 whorls, free, often eccentric. An extrastaminal disc is usually present; the disc is unilateral or annular, often represented by glands. Ovary tricarpellary syncarpous, 3-locular, superior, lobed or not; style terminal; ovules 1-2 in each loculus, ascending with ventral raphe. Fruit dry or fleshy; dry fruit may be a capsule or nut and fleshy fruit a drupe or berry. Seeds usually arillate, without endosperm and with curved embryo.

Cardiospermum is a herbaceous climber but *Serjania*, *Paullinia*, etc. are lianas; they climb by tendrils which are metamorphosed sterile branches of the inflorescence coiled like watch-spring. *Sapindus*, *Aphania*, *Litchi*, etc. have actinomorphic flowers, while, *Erioglossum*, *Cardiospermum*, etc. have zyogomorphic flowers with eccentric androecium. In many cases the apparent bisexual flowers are functionally female having stamens with anthers that do not open and pollens do not germinate. *Schleichera*, *Dodonae* a etc. have flowers apetalous. Stamens are usually 8, but in *Turpinia* there are 5 stamens and *Deinbollia* has numerous stamens.

Anomalous condition is observed in the stems of woody climbers as well as of some erect genera where groups of fibro-vascular structures are distributed outside the

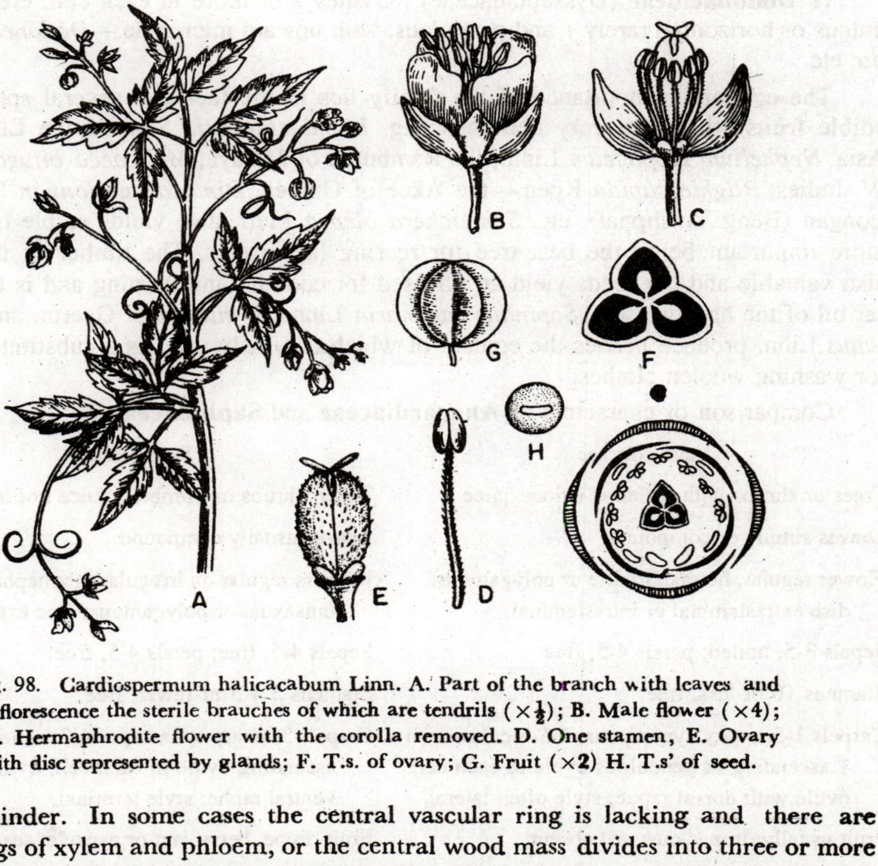

Fig. 98. Cardiospermum halicacabum Linn. A. Part of the branch with leaves and inflorescence the sterile brauches of which are tendrils ($\times\frac{1}{2}$); B. Male flower ($\times 4$); C. Hermaphrodite flower with the corolla removed. D. One stamen, E. Ovary with disc represented by glands; F. T.s. of ovary; G. Fruit ($\times 2$) H. T.s' of seed.

central cylinder. In some cases the central vascular ring is lacking and there are several rings of xylem and phloem, or the central wood mass divides into three or more portions which grow in thickness separately. Vessels are small, perforations simple and intervascular pitting alternate. Xylem parenchyma is usually paratracheal. Pericycle forms a continuous ring of fibres.

The floral formula for a hermaphrodite flower is— φ $K_5 C_5$ or $_0$ A_{8-10} $G_{(3)}$.

Sapindaceae with about 900 species under 92 genera is distributed in almost all tropical countries of the world.

The family is allied to *Anacardiaceae, Aceraceae* and *Hippocastanaceae*, **the last 2 families being formerly included in *Sapindaceae*. It is also related to *Simarubaceae, Burseraceae, Cneoraceae, Fulianaceae, Meliaceae* and *Rutaceae* to some extent. it resembles the family *Euphobiaceae* having ovule usually 1 in each cell, ventral raphe, tricarpellary** ovary, arillate seeds and often unisexual flowers.

The family is divided into 2 subfamilies :

I Sapindoideae : (Eusapindaceae) Ovule solitary in each cell, erect or ascending, with downward micropyle.

(i) Nomophyllae—Leaves usually imparipinnate, disc oblique,—*Serjania, Erioglossum,* etc.

(ii) Anomophyllae—Leaves usually paripinnate, disc annular—*Sapindus, Schleichera,* etc.

II Dodonaeideae (Dyssapindaceae) : Ovules 2 or more in each cell, erect or pendulous or horizontal, rarely 1 and pendulous, with upward micropyle.—*Dodonea, Harpullia,* etc.

The economic importance of the family lies in the fact that several species yield edible fruits which are very delicious, e.g. *Litchi chinensis* Sonner. the Litchi of E. Asia, *Nephelium lappaceum* Linn., the Rambutan of Malaya, *Melicocca bijuga* Linn., of W. Indies, *Blighia sapida* Koen.—the Akee of Guinea, *Dimocarpus longan* Lam—the Longan (Beng. Anshphal), etc. *Schleichera oleosa* Merr. also yields edible fruit but is more important being the best tree for rearing lac insects. The timber of this tree is also valuable and the seeds yield an oil used for cooking and burning and is the macassar oil of the hair dressers. *Sapindus saponaria* Linn., *S. mukorossi* Gaertn. and *S. trifoliatus* Linn. produce berries the epicarp of which is widely used as a substitute for soap for washing woolen clothes.

Comparison of characters of **Anacardiaceae** and **Sapindaceae.**

Anacardiaceae	Sapindaceae
Trees or shrubs with resinous irritant juice.	Trees, shrubs or climbers; juice not irritant.
Leaves simple or compound.	Leaves usually compound.
Flower regular, hermaphrodite or polygamous; disc extrastaminal or intrastaminal.	Flowers regular on irregular, hermaphrodite or unisexual or polygamous; disc extrastaminal
Sepals 3-5, united; perals 4-5, free.	Sepals 4-5, free; petals 4-5, free.
Stamens 10 or less, free.	Stamens 5 + 5 or fewer, free.
Carpels 1-5, ovary syncarpous, 1-5-locular, with 1 ascending or pendulous ovule in each cell, ovule with dorsal raphe; style often lateral.	Carpels 3, ovary synacarpous, 3- celled with 1 ascending ovule in each cell, ovule with ventral raphe; style terminal.
Fruit usually drupacious; aril absent.	Fruit drupe, berry, nut or capsule, seeds ariallate.

Aceraceae

Trees or shrubs, deciduous. Leaves opposite, simple, palmiveined, entire or lobed, or leaves compound, exstipulate. Inflorescence is a raceme, rarely corymbose or fasciculate. Flowers small, regular, polygamous or diocious or only hermaphrodite, dich-

lamydious hypo- or perigynous, 5-4-merous. Sepals 4-5, free or connate at base, imbricate. Petals 4-5, free, imbricate, sometimes absent. Extrastaminal disc is usually present, annular or lobed, or reduced to teeth. Stamens 8 in 2 whorls, rarely 10, very rarely less than 8, hypogynous or perigynous or rarely inserted on the margin of the disc; anthers bilocular, introrse, dehiscing longitudinally; rudimentary gynoecium usually present in male flowers. Ovary usually superior, bicarpellary syncarpous, bilocular, laterally compressed; ovules 2 in each locule orthotropous or anatropous, superposed or colateral on axile placentation, with dorsal raphe; styles 2, free or united below. Fruit a schizocarp of 2 winged nut-like fruitlets separating into 2 samaras when ripe. Seed solitary in each fruitlet, exalbuminous and with curved embryo and thin folded or rolled rarely flat cotyledons.

Most species have simple leaves, lobed or not; some species of *Acer* and *Dipteronia* have 3-foliolate or 5-foliolate leaves. The racemes have the male flowers in the lower portion and bisexual flowers in the apical portion. Flowers are apetalous in *Acer grandidentatum* DC. and *A. carpinifolium* Linn. In *A. rubrum* Linn. stamens are in one whorl. In some species of *Acer* carpels are more than 2. Sometimes the seeds have more than 2 cotyledons.

The wood anatomy shows the vessels to be small, with spiral thickenings and simple perforations. Wood parenchyma is absent or almost so; fibres are short and simple pitted and medullary rays are homogeneous.

The flowers are entomophilous or anemophilous. The floral formula may be expressed as:

$$⚥ \oplus K_5\ C_5\ A_{4+4}\ G_{(2)}$$

or $$♂ \oplus K_5\ C_5\ A_{4+4}$$

or $$♀ \oplus K_5\ C_5\ G_{(2)}$$

The family consists of about 200 species under 3 genera distributed mainly in the temperate regions of the northern hemisphere. It is represented in India by 15 species of *Acer* occurring in the Himalayas and Khasi hills. Fossil remains of *Acer* were discovered belonging to the Tertiary period.

The family is economically important for the fact that a few species yield good timber and that of the sycamore tree—*Acer pseudoplatanus* Linn. is hard and durable. *A. saccharum* Marsh and *A. nigrum* Michx. are the Sugar-maples reputed for yield of a sweet sap. Many species of *Acer* are cultivated as avenue trees and as garden-ornamentals.

The family is closely related to *Sapindaceae* and *Hippocastanaceae* and also to *Anacardiaceae* and *Simarubaceae* to some extent. It is allied also to *Burseraceae*, *Cneoraceae*, *Julianiaceae*, *Meliaceae*, *Rutaceae* on one side and *Hamamelidaceae* and *Altingiaceae* on the other.

Hippocastanaceae

Deciduous trees with large winter buds covered with resinous scale-leaves. Leaves with a long petiole and a palmately compound blade, opposite, exstipulate, hairy when young. Inflorescence is a thyrsus type of panicle, terminal. Flowers polygamous, obliquely zygomorphic; male flowers in the upper part of the inflorescence and the bisexual flowers in the lower part. Sepals 5 united, lobes valvate. Petals 5 or 4, free, imbricate. Stamens 8-5; inserted on a disc; anthers introrse; disc is often one-sided. A rudimentary ovary present in male flowers. Bisexual flower with a superior, tricarpellary syncarpous, 3-locular ovary; ovules 2 in each loculus, superposed, upper with dorsal raphe and lower with ventral raphe; style one. Fruit 3-valved leathery capsule often spiny, usually with one seed. Seeds exalbuminous, with united cotyledons and the radicle lying in a fold of the testa.

The small family consists of 2 genera and 15 species occurring in the north temperate regions as well as in Mexico and S. America. *Aesculus indica* Hook-occurs in the W. Himalayas while *A. assamica* Griff. grows in E. Himalayas and Naga Hills and comes down to the plains of northern Bengal.

The family is not of much economic importance. It is very close to *Sapindaceae* in which it was previously included.

RHAMNALES

Sapindales is followed by a small order **Rhamnales** consisting of only 2 families, viz., *Rhamnaceae* and *Vitaceae.* Most authors agree that these 2 families are very close to each other and therefore form a natural taxon. Takhtajan and Cronquist split *Vitaceae* into 2 distinct families, viz. *Vitaceae* and *Leeaceae* and both of them keep these 2 families in **Rhamnales** so that in their systems of arrangement this order consists of 3 families instead of 2. Hutchinson includes *Heteropyxidaceae* and *Elaeagnaceae* in his **Rhamnales** along with *Rhamnaceae* and *Vitaceae.*

The common characters of the 2 families *Rhamnaceae* and *Vitaceae* are the following: erect or climbing shrubs or trees; flowers small, regular, bisexual or rarely unisexual; calyx entire or lobed; stamens in one whorl, antipetalous; intrastaminal disc well-developed; ovules ascending.

Most authors agree that the order **Rhamnales** is closely allied to **Celastrales.** Rendle put the 2 orders close to each other and considered that these 2 had a common origin from **Rutales**-like diplostemonous ancestor. Takhtajan includes the 2 orders **Celastrales** and **Rhamnales** in his subclass **Rosidae** and Cronquist also does the same and traces the origin of these 2 orders from **Rosales.** Bessey includes *Rhamnaceae* and *Vitaceae* in his **Calastrales** placing them just before *Celastraceae.* Wettstein also considered **Calastrales** and **Rhamnales** close to each other and in his arrangement of the *Dicotylodonous* orders placed **Celastrales** just before **Rhamnales.**

Rhamnaceae

Trees or shrubs, often armed with spines, or climbers, climbing by hooks or tendrils or twining stems, rarely herbs. Leaves simple, stipulate, alternate or rarely opposite. Inflorescence an axillary cyme or cymose panicle or corymb. Flowers hermaphrodite, rarely unisexual regular, peri- or epigynous, usually minute. Calyx 4-5-lobed; lobes valvate, usually internally ridged. Petals 4-5, free, inserted on the calyx-tube forming a hypanthium, usually clawed and hooded, rarely petals absent. Stamens as many as petals and opposite to and enclosed by them; inserted on the hypanthium or on the margin of an intrastaminal disc. Carpels 2-4, syncarpous, forming a 2-4-celled, peri- or epigynous ovary; ovule 1, rarely 2 in each cell, basal, anatropous, with dorsal raphe; style 1 or 2, short; stigma simple or bilobed; rarely ovary 1-celled. Fruit a capsule or berry or samaroid; seeds with fleshy endosperm or rarely without endosperm and large straight embryo.

The spines in *Zizyphus* are stipulary in nature. *Colletia* and *Condalia* have thorns which are modified branches. *Colletia spinosa* Lam. has thorny shoots with small caducous leaves although at seedling stage it bears normal foliage leaves. *Gouania*, *Helinus* and *Reissekia* are tendril-climbers, the tendrils being metamorphosed branches. *Ventilago* is a large twiner. Leaves palminerved in *Zizyphus* but pinninerved in other genera. In *Microrhamnus* and in a few species of *Rhamnus* flowers are solitary and axillary. In *Gouania* flowers are polygamous. *Rhamnus cathartica* Linn. is dioecious. *Hovenia dulcis* Thunb. has fleshy peduncle. Flowers of *Berchemia scandens* Trel. are hypogynous and have no hypanthium. Apetalous flowers occur in some species of *Colletia*. In *Paliurus* the base of the style develops into a large broad rim like that of a hat. Fruit is a capsule in *Phylica, Pomaderris*, etc. a juicy drupe in *Rhamnus, Zizyphus* etc. while *Gouania* and *Ventilago* have samaroid fruits.

The stomata are of Ranunculaceous or Rubiaceous type. Secretary cells containing tannin and mucilage occur in primary cortex. Vessels have simple perforations and intervascular pitting is alternate. Wood parenchyma is paratracheal. In *Zizyphus* the stem has continuous sclerenchymatous pericycle while in others the pericycle is made up of isolated strands of fibres.

The family consists of about 550 species under 45 genera occurring in the tropical and temperate parts of the world. *Rhamnus* and *Zizyphus* are widely distributed; the former occurs in America, Europe and extra tropical Asia while the latter, although mainly Indomalayan, is found in Africa and spreads eastwards to Australia. *Colletia* is found in S. America and *Pomaderris* is an Australian genus. In India 53 species occur in the plains as well as in the hills, e.g. *Rhamnus virgata* Roxb. *R. nepalensis* Wall. ex. M. Laws., *Ventilago maderaspatana* Gaertn., *Zizyphus mauritiana* Lam., *Z. oenoplia* Mill, *Gouania leptostachya* DC., etc.

Several species of the family are economically important. Jujubes are the drupes of *Zizyphus mauritiana* Lam. (Baer of India, Beng. Kool.), *Z. jujuba* Mill., *Z. vulgaris* Lam., etc. *Z. mauritiana* Lam. is cultivated in India and Western Asiatic countries and also grows wild. It is also used for rearing lac insects. *Rhamus purshiana* DC. of N. America yields the Cascara sagarda bark—a purgative, while the bark of *R. chlorophora* Dcne. yields a green dye. Root-bark of *Ventilago maderaspatana* Gaertn. yields red dye. Dye is also obtained from the fruits of *R. infectoria* Linn. *Frangula alnus* Mill. is the Dogwood, the charcoal obtained from which is much valued for making gun-powder. The bark of this species is also used as purgative. *Zizyphus mauritiana* Lam. yields wood also suitable for making gun-powder. *Maeosopis emini* Eng. of E. Africa yields good timber. Leaves of *Ceanothus americanus* Linn. and *Sageretia theezans* Brong. are used as substitute of tea.

The family Rhamnaceae is very close to Vitaceae (and also to Leeaceae when it is treated as a distinct family) and the two families constitute the order **Rhamnales** which forms a natural taxon. Rhamnaceae is also allied to Celastraceae to some extent and the orders **Celastrales** and **Rhamnales** are placed close to each other by most taxonomists.

Vitaceae

Extensive climbers with leaf-opposed tendrils, rarely erect shrubs or small trees; nodes often swollen or jointed. Leaves alternate, the lower often being opposite, simple or pinnately or palmately compound, pellucid punctate, with petiolar stipules or exstipulate, usually distichous. Inflorescence is a leaf-opposed cymose panicle, often very large with numerous minute flowers or corymbose and terminal; bracteoles present. Flowers usually hypogynous, actinomorphic, bisexual or unisexual in polygamo-monoecious or polygamo-dioecious plants, 5-4-merous. Calyx gamosepalous, cupular, entire or shortly 5-4 toothed. Petals 5-4, minute, valvate, free or connate, caducous, flat or with hooded incurved apex; often corolla obsolete. Intrastaminal disc prominent, annular or lobed or glandular. Stamens as many as petals and opposite to them, free or connate at base inserted below the disc; anthers distinct or connate, dehiscing

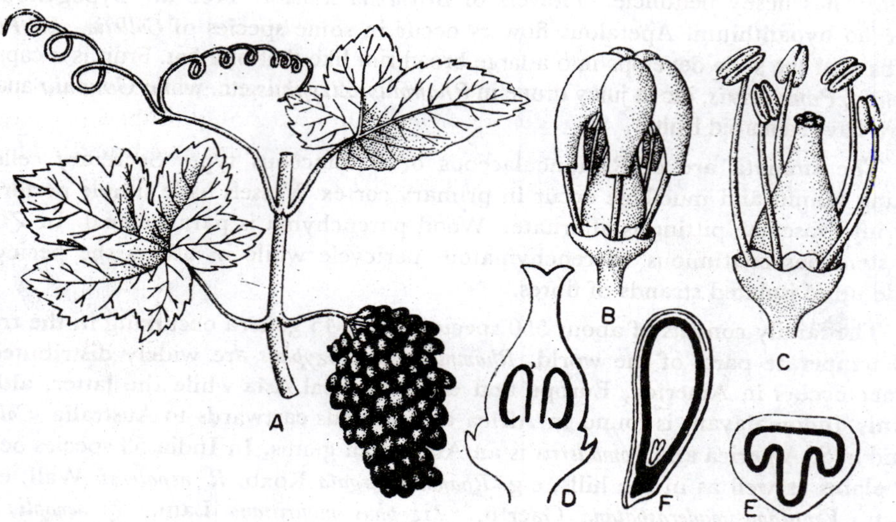

Fig. 99. **Vitis vinifera Linn.—A. Part of a branch with leaves, leaf opposed tendril and a bunch of fruits (×½); B. A flower showing the caducous petals; C. Same without petals showing stamens and ovary; D. L. s. of ovary showing ovules; E. Seed in t.s.; F. Same in l.s.**

longitudinally. Ovary superior, 2-8-carpelled and 2-8-celled; ovules 1-2 in each cell on axile placentation, anatropous, ascending with ventral raphe. Style, short, stigma discoid or capitate. Fruit a berry. Seed with hard testa, copious ruminate endosperm and small straight embryo.

Most genera are vines; *Carameriana* is a tree while *Leea* has trees, shrubs and erect herbs. The tendrils are leaf-opposed and are interpreted by Eichler as the metamorphosed apical part of the sympodial stem. The inflorescence replaces the tendril. In *Cissus quadrangularis* Linn. the internodes are 4-angled and succulent. The peduncle in *Pterisanthes* is flat and ribbon-like. In *Vitis* petals are free near base and united by the apices and falling off early as a cap. The filaments of stamens in *Leea* are united to form a 5-lobed tube.

The tendril in *Vitis* is negatively phototropic and thus forces its way into crevices of the support running away from the light. The ends of the tendrilar branches expand to form ball like structures which become sticky and mucilaginous and as a result the tendril adheres firmly to the support. The leaves have globular and shinning stalked emergences known as 'pearl glands'. These bear the stomata which are of ranunculaceous type. Most of the cells contain raphide crystals and mucilage cells are also common.

The disc sometimes functions as nectaries to attract the insects which pollinate the flowers. The floral formula of a hermaphrodite flower may be expressed as:

$$\oplus ⚥ K_{4-5}\ C_{4-5}\ A_{4-5}\ G_{(2-6)}.$$

The family comprises 11 genera and about 750 species. The plants are found in the tropical regions of the Old- and New-World. Some are xerophytic succulent plants occurring in the drier parts of Africa and S. America. There are about 70 species in India mostly growing in the plains, e.g. *Ampelocissus latifolia* Planch., *Cissus repens* Lam., *C. adnata* Roxb., *C. quadrangularis* Linn., *Cayratia pedata* (Wall.) Gagnep., *Leea macrophylla* Roxb., *Vitis vinifera* Linn. etc.

Stem anatomy shows that the vessels are large in all genera except *Leea*; perforations are simple or scalariform. A more or less continuous ring of fibres constitute the pericyle with a few isolated strands. Medullary rays are long and broad and parenchyma paratracheal. Abnormal secondary growth occurs in *Cissus* and *Tetrastigma*.

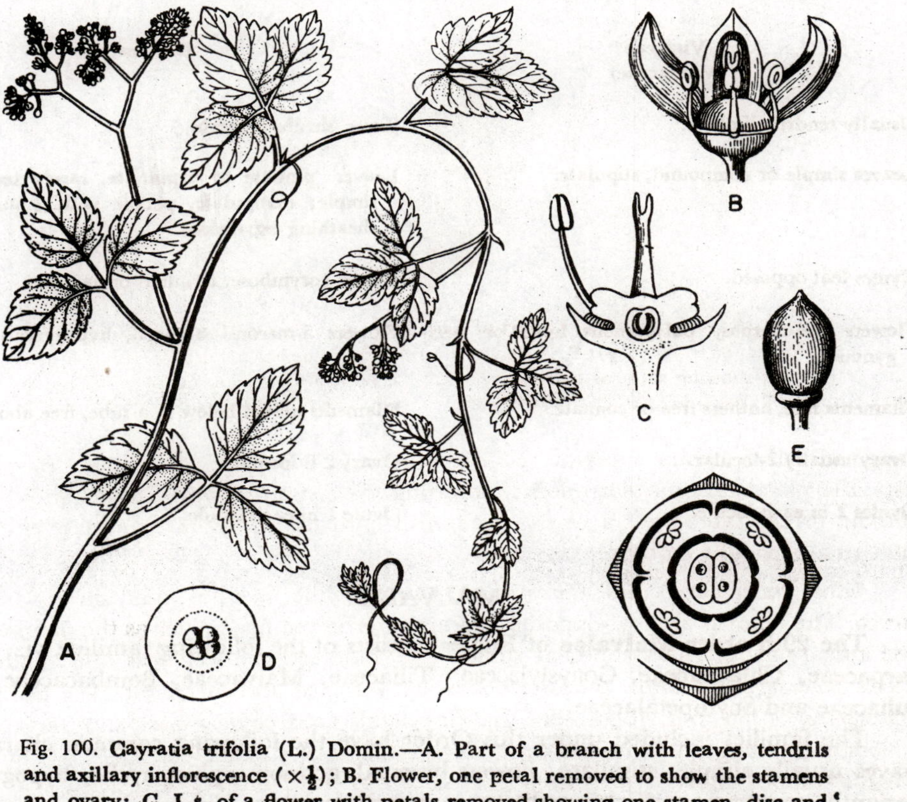

Fig. 100. Cayratia trifolia (L.) Domin.—A. Part of a branch with leaves, tendrils and axillary inflorescence (×½); B. Flower, one petal removed to show the stamens and ovary; C. L.s. of a flower with petals removed showing one stamen, disc and ovary-chamber; D. T.s. of ovary: E. Fruit (×1).

The family gains importance from the grape-vine,—*Vitis vinifera* Linn. with its innumerable varieties, originally of W. Asia and Mediterranean region now cultivated in almost all countries of the world. Raisins and currants are dried fruits of different varieties of this species. *V. labrusca* Linn. and *V. aestivalis* Michx of N. America produce edible berries inferior to grapes. A few others have medicinal properties.

The family is closely allied to *Rhamnaceae* and together with that family constitute the order *Rhamnales* which is a natural taxon according to most taxonomists. Some recent workers are in favour of segregating the genus *Leea* from *Vitaceae* and placing it in a distinct family of its own, viz. **Leeaceae.**

The family *Leeaceae* may be briefly described as having following characters: Erect shrubs or herbs or small trees. Leaves alternate, simple or pinnate, often bi- or tripinnately compound; petiole dilated at base to form 2 sheathing expansions or auricles, exstipulate. Cymes corymbose, leaf opposed or terminal. Flowers 5-merous, hypogynous. Stamens outside the annular disc united in a 5-lobed tube with 5 free filaments arising between the lobes; anthers free and exserted from or connate and included in the tube. Ovary on the disc, 3-6 locular with a solitary ovule in each locule. Fruit a berry, depressed at the apex. Seed with hard testa and minute basal embryo and cartilaginous endosperm.

Comparison of *Vitaceae* and *Leeaceae* when treated as 2 distinct families:

Vitaceae (Vitidaceae)	Leeaceae
Usually tendril-climbers.	Trees, shrubs or herbs.
Leaves simple or compound, stipulate.	Leaves pinnate to tripinnate, rarely ternate, or simple; exstipulate, petiole with 2 auricles or sheathing expansions.
Cymes leaf opposed.	Cymes corymbose, terminal or axillary.
Flowers 5-4-merous, polygamous, hypo- or perigynous.	Flowers 5-merous, bisexual, hypogynous.
Filaments free, anthers free or connate.	Filaments united below in a tube, free above.
Ovary usually 2-locular.	Ovary 2-6 locular.
Ovules 2 in each locule.	Ovule 1 in each locule.

MALVALES

The 29th order **Malvales** of Engler consists of the following families, viz. Elaeocarpaceae, Chlaenaceae, Gonystylaceae, Tiliaceae, Malvaceae, Bombacaceae, Sterculiaceae and Scytopetalaceae.

The families included under this Order have the following common characters: leaves usually simple, stipulate; flowers bisexual, actinomorphic, cyclic, hypogynous; perianth pentamerous; calyx valvate; stamens numerous, monadelphous, polyadelphous or free with tendency of union at the base, ovary polycarpellary syncarpous, with axile placentation; ovules anatropous.

Bentham and Hooker in Genera Plantarum included 3 Natural Orders in his Cohort **Malvales** viz. : *Malvaceae*, *Sterculiaceae* and *Tiliaceae*. Engler adopted Eichler's concept and treated the Order **Malvales** as consisting of 4 suborders viz. : Elaeocarpineae, Chlaeneae, Malvineae and Scytopetalineae. *Malvaceae* of Bentham and Hooker was plitted into *Malvaceae* and *Bombacaceae* while *Tiliaceae* was splitted into *Tiliaceae* and *Elaeocarpaceae*. Most phylogenists follow Eichler's concept. Hutchinson however restricted **Malvales** to include only *Malvaceae* and placed *Tiliaceae*, *Bombacaceae* and *Sterculiaceae* in a new order **Tiliales.** He did not distinguish *Elaeocarpaceae* as a separate family from the *Tiliaceae*. The family *Chlaenaceae* (or *Sarcolaenaceae*) is considered by some to be more closely related to *Theales* than to **Malvales.**

Malvales appear to be releated to **Guttiferales,** both having regular, hypogynous, pentamerous flowers with androecium having a tendency to unite in groups. The order appears to be related also to **Euphorbiales** in having branched multicellular hairs and fruits splitting into cocci.

Tiliaceae

Trees and shrubs, rarely herbs; bark usually mucilaginous and with strong fibres. Leaves alternate rarely opposite, simple, often lobed; stipules usually caducous rarely absent. Flowers regular, bisexual, rarely unisexual, cymose and axillary, rarely solitary. Sepals 3-5, valvate, free or connate, caducous. Petals as many as sepals, imbricate, contorted or valvate, often petals absent. Stamens usually many, free or slightly connate at base forming 5-10 bundles, often a few reduced to staminodes, a gynandrophore is sometimes present; anthers 2-celled, opening by lateral slits, introrse. A glandular disc is usually present. Ovary superior, 2-many celled; ovules 1-many in each cell

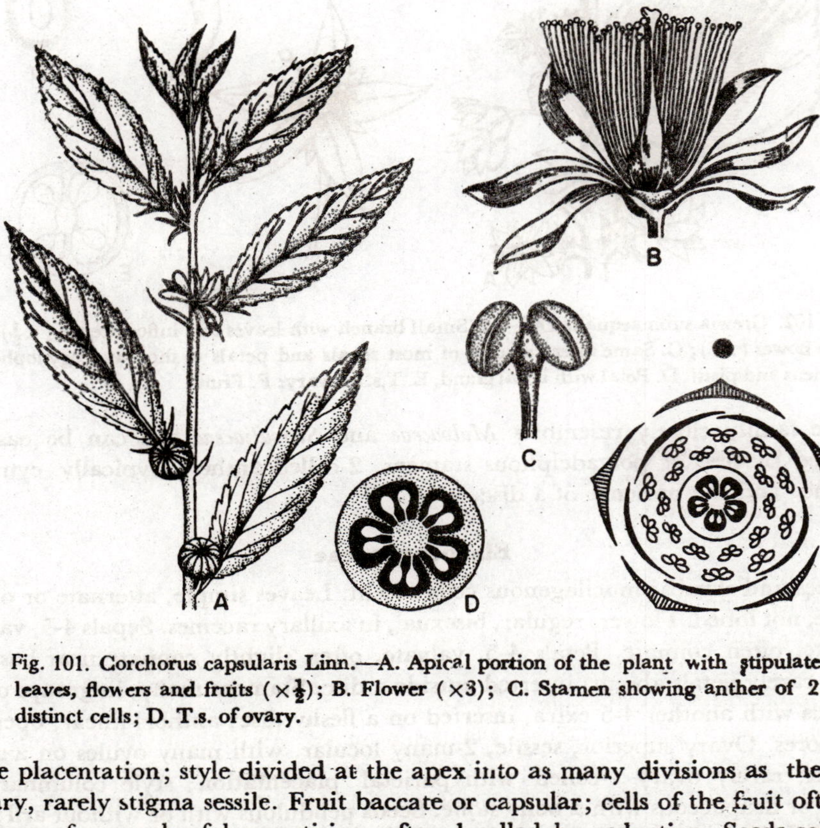

Fig. 101. Corchorus capsularis Linn.—A. Apical portion of the plant with stipulate leaves, flowers and fruits ($\times\frac{1}{2}$); B. Flower ($\times3$); C. Stamen showing anther of 2 distinct cells; D. T.s. of ovary.

on axile placentation; style divided at the apex into as many divisions as the cells of the ovary, rarely stigma sessile. Fruit baccate or capsular; cells of the fruit often more than those of ovary by false partision, often 1-celled by reduction. Seeds solitary or many; embryo straight, usually with leafy cotyledons, endosperm usually copious.

The family consists of about 400 species under 41 genera mainly in tropical countries. Most important plants of this family are *Corchorus capsularis* Linn. and *C. olitorius* Linn. the bast fibres of which yield the jute of commerce. *Grewia* is a large genus with about 100 species, of which 33 are found in India. *G. subinaequalis* DC. is cultivated for the berries which are called "Phalsa". The Linden tree of Europe is *Tilia europia* Linn. *Muntingia calabura* Linn. a small spreading tree of the West Indies is planted in gardens for its beautiful foliage and white flowers. *Berria cordifolia* (Willd.) Burr. is a timber tree of S. India and is planted as an avenue tree in towns and cities.

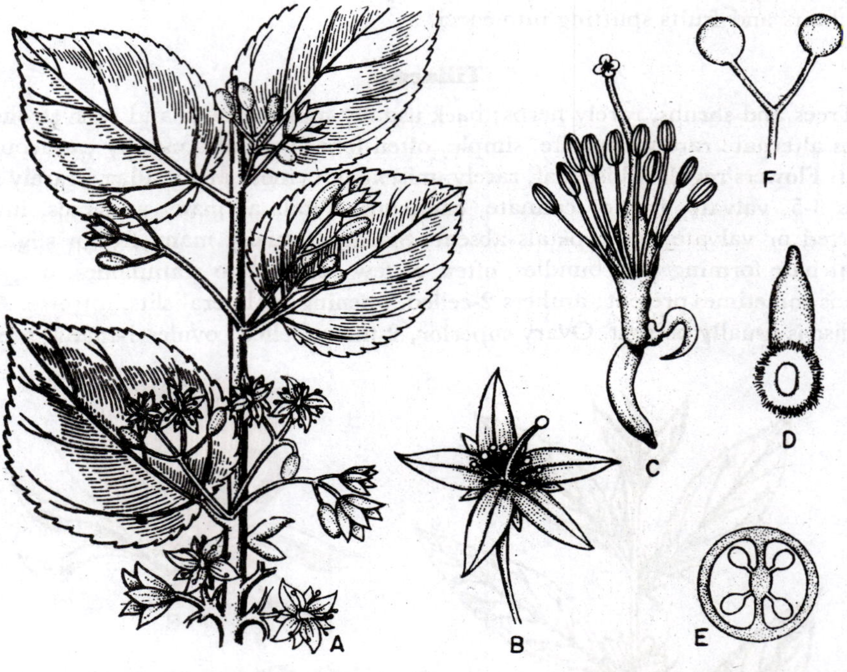

Fig. 102. Grewia subinaequalis DC.—A. Small branch with leaves and inflorescence ($\times\frac{1}{8}$); B. One flower ($\times 1$); C. Same after removal of most sepals and petals to show androgynophore, stamens and pistil. D. Petal with basal gland, E. T.s. of ovary; F. Fruit.

The family closely resembles *Malvaceae* and *Sterculiaceae* but can be easily distinguished by free or polyadelphous stamens, 2-celled anthers, typically cymose inflorescence and the presence of a disc.

Elaeocarpaceae

Trees and shrubs; mucilagenous cells absent. Leaves simple, alternate or opposite, stipulate, not lobed. Flowers regular, bisexual, in axillary racemes. Sepals 4-5, valvate or imbricate, often connate. Petals 4-5, valvate, often slightly connate near base, often fringed; rarely petals absent; inserted outside a disc. Stamens many, in groups opposite the petals with another 4-5 extra, inserted on a fleshy disc; anthers linear, opening by apical pores. Ovary superior, sessile, 2-many locular, with many ovules on axile placentation; rarely ovary 1-celled with parietal placentation; style columnar. Fruit capsular or drupaceous with a bony stone. Seeds pendulous with or without aril; endosperm small, fleshy; cotyledons flat.

The family consists of 12 genera and about 350 species occurring in tropical and subtropical countries of the world. Over 200 species are included in the genus *Elaeocarpus* which is well represented in India and are good timber trees. *E. ganitrus* Roxb. is the Rudraksha, the stones of the fruits of which are used as beads by the mendicants, and *E. serratus* Linn. of N. Bengal is the Jalpai or Indian Olive.

The family was included in Tiliaceae but later separated and raised to the rank of a distinct family differing from *Tiliaceae* by sepals not being caducous, absence of epicalyx, petals valvate and pendulous ovules. Hutchinson followed the old concept and treated both as a single family *Tiliaceae*.

Sterculiaceae

Trees, shrubs or herbs, sometime lianes. Leaves alternate, simple and entire or rarely palmately lobed; very rarely digitately compound; stipules caducous; often stellately hairy. Inflorescence various, often cauliflorous. Flowers bisexual, rarely unisexual, actinomorphic or rarely zygomorphic, pentamerous, hypogynous. Perianth often uniseriate; sepals 3-5 connate near base, lobes valvate; petals 5, often very small,

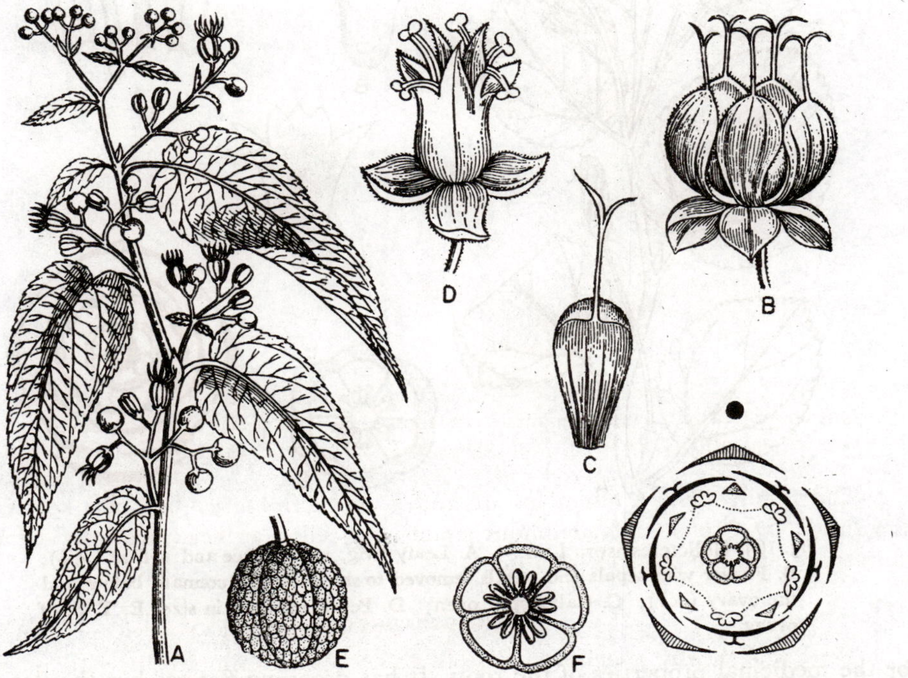

Fig. 103. Guazuma ulmifolia Lamk.—A. Leafy twig with inflorescences ($\times\frac{1}{2}$); B. One flower with sepals and appendaged petals ($\times4$); C. One petal; D. One flower with petals removed showing staminal tube; E. Fruit ($\times1$); F. T.s. of ovary.

sometimes absent, adnate to the base of androecium or not, contorted in bud. Stamens 5 or 10 or more, united to form a tube, often antisepalous; staminodes present, alternating with the fertile stamens which are antipetalous; the staminodes are said to represent the outer whorl of the androecium; very rarely stamens are free; the anthers are 2-celled, parallel or divergent. Ovary superior, 4-5-carpelled and 4-5-celled, rarely 10-12-celled; androgynophore usually present; ovules 2-many in each chamber, ascending or horizontal on axile placentation, anatropous; styles as many as carpels, free or connate. Fruit indehiscent or capsular, sometimes separating into cocci; seeds with fleshy endosperm and flat, often folded cotyledons.

The family comprises about 50 genera and about 750 species occurring in the tropical and subtropical countries. *Theobroma cacao* Linn., the Cocoa or the Chocolate tree of trop. Am. belongs to this family. It produces large fruits from cauliflorous flowers, each containing many seeds, and cocoa is the powder of the roasted seeds. The tree is now widely cultivated in S. India and Ceylon. *Cola acuminata* Linn. yields thein and theobromine from the seeds. *Abroma augusta* of N. E. India is cultivated in many places

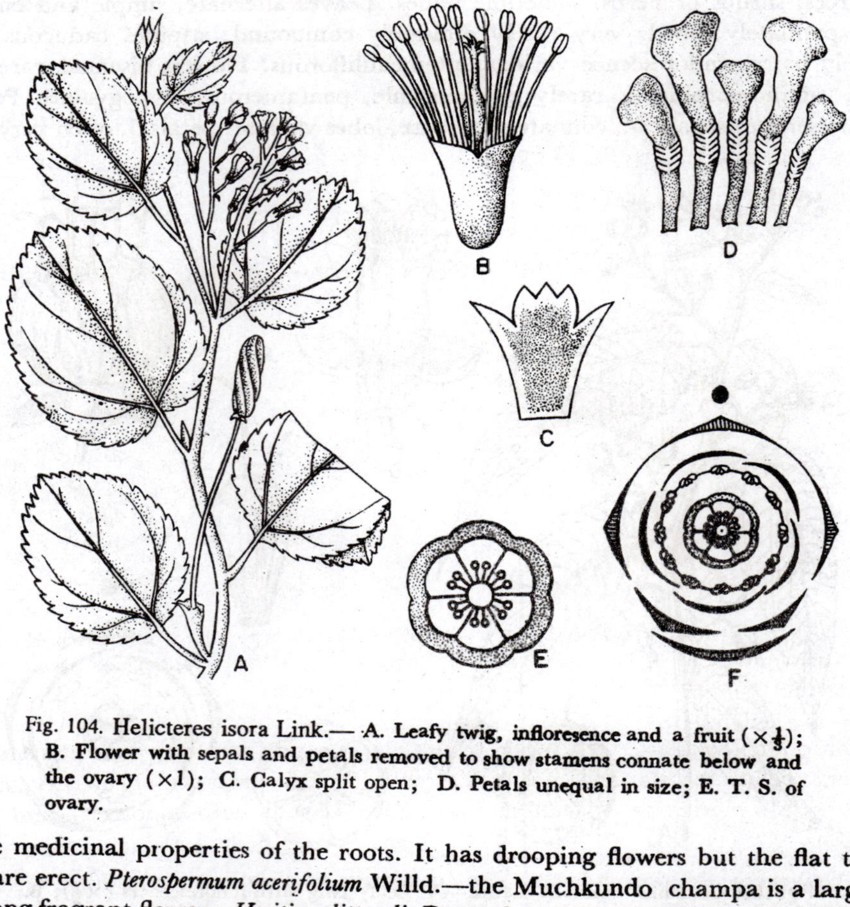

Fig. 104. Helicteres isora Link.— **A. Leafy twig, infloresence and a fruit** ($\times\frac{1}{3}$); **B. Flower with sepals and petals removed to show stamens connate below and the ovary** (×1); **C. Calyx split open; D. Petals unequal in size; E. T. S. of ovary.**

for the medicinal properties of the roots. It has drooping flowers but the flat topped fruits are erect. *Pterospermum acerifolium* Willd.—the Muchkundo champa is a large tree with long fragrant flowers. *Heritiera littoralis* Dryand. and *H. fomes* Bush. are the Sundari trees from which the name Sunderban has come for the littoral forests in the southern part of Bengal. *Guazuma ulmifolia* Lamk., *Helicteris isora* Link., *Kleinhovia hospita* Linn. and *Dombeya Mastersii* Hk.f. are other common trees.

As a member of the Order **Malvales** it has much in common with *Malvaceae* from which it differs by the absence of epicalyx, 2-celled anthers, an outer whorl of staminodes and usually stalked ovary.

Malvaceae

Herbs, shrubs, or small trees; bark fibrous; mucilage present; often stellately hairy or lepidote. Leaves alternate, palmately lobed or not, palmately veined, with free lateral, often caducous stipules. Flowers solitary or in various types of inflorescence, axillary or terminal; epicalyx (bracteoles) usually present. Sepals 3-5, more or less united, valvate. Petals 5, twisted in bud or often imbricate, free from each other, usually adnate at base to the staminal column. Stamens indefinite, hypogynous, united below in the form of a tube, free near the apex; anthers reniform, 1-celled; transversely attached to the filament, pollen grains characteristically spiny. Ovary superior, usually

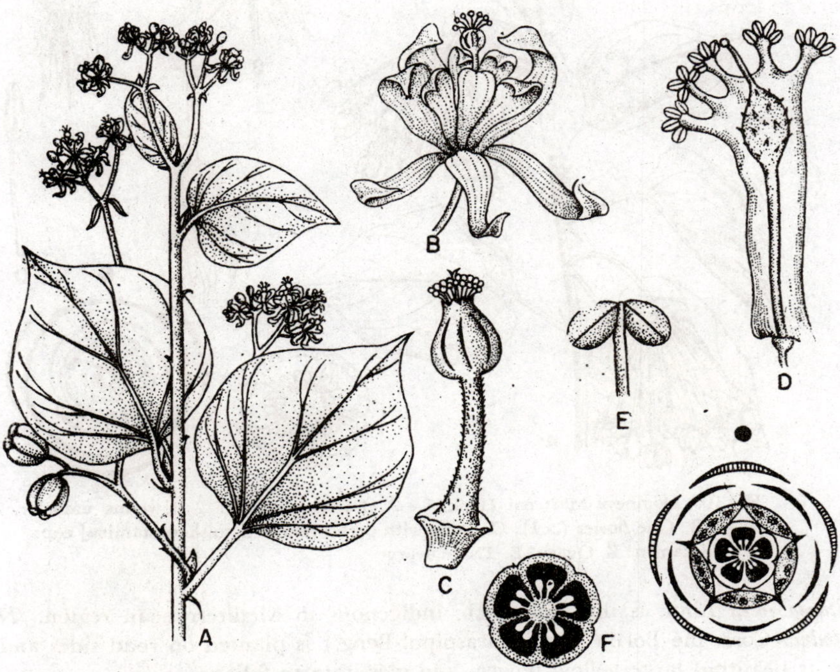

Fig. 105. Kleinhovia hospita Linn.—A. Short branch with leaves inflorescences and fruits ($\times\frac{1}{3}$); B. One flower ($\times 2$); C. Staminal tube; D. Same split open to show ovary on gynophore; E. Divergent anthers; F. T.s. of ovary.

5-locular, often 2-locular, rarely more; ovules many, rarely only 1 on axile placentation; style enclosed in the staminal column, branched near the apex. Fruit dry, carpels separating into mericarps, or fruit capsular. Seeds usually with endosperm and folded cotyledons.

The flowers are protandrous. The immature stigmas remain hidden inside the staminal tube at first and after the dehiscence of the anthers the filaments bend down and the mature stigmas appear in the centre and spread out.

The family *Malvaceae* is a fairly large family with about 1500 species under 82 genera distributed mostly in the tropical countries of the world. It consists of many economically important plants and many ornamentals. Species of *Gossypium* has the seeds hairy, the hairs being fine and elongated form the cotton fibre of commerce. *G. arboreum* Linn., *G. barbadense* Linn. and *G. herbaceum* Linn. are cultivated in India for cotton. *Hibiscus cannabinus* Linn. yields a fibre from the bark similar to Jute-fibre. *Abelmoschus esculentus* Moench. is cultivated for its fruit viz. the Lady's Finger used as vegatable. *Hibiscus subdariffa* Linn. is the Roselle, the fleshy calyx of which is used in making pickles and chutney. *H. rosa-sinensis* Linn., *H. schizopetalus* (Mast.) Hook. f., *H. mutabilis* Linn. and H. *syriacus* Linn. are cultivated shrubs with showy large flowers.

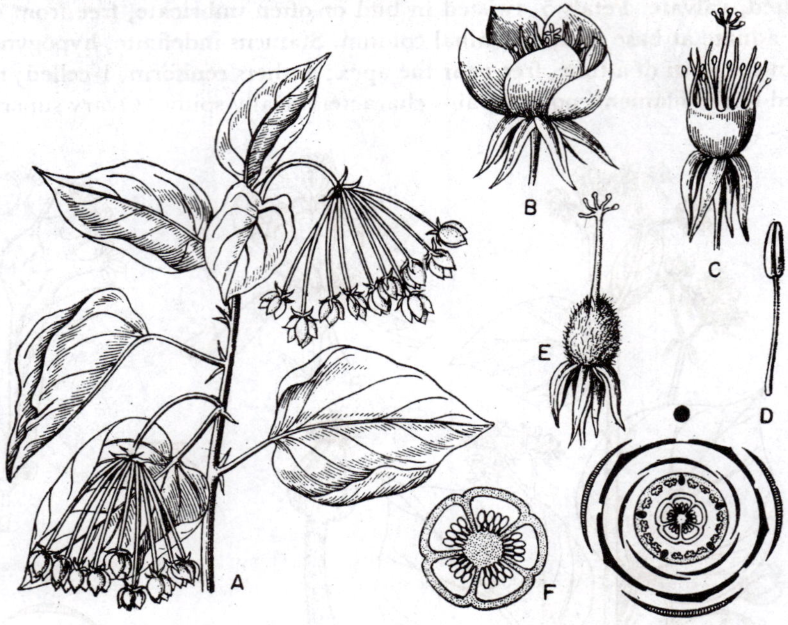

Fig. 106. Dombeya Mastersii Hook. f.—A. Leafy twig with 2 flowering umbels (×½); B. One flower (×1); C. Same with petals removed to show staminal cup; D. One stamen; E. Ovary; E. T.s. of ovary.

Althaea rosea Linn. is the Hollyhock, indigenous to Mediterranean region. *Thespesia populnia* Corr. the Portia Tree (Paraspipul-Beng.) is planted on road sides and parks for its beautiful large yellow flowers and glossy green foliage.

Floral range : The epicalyx or the bracteoles vary in number and position in different tribes and genera; they are completely free from each other or are more or less united; rarely these are absent e.g. *Sida, Abutilon*. The median sepal is posterior in most cases and is anterior in cases of few genera. Although the number of carpels in most genera are 5 there are only 1 or 2 in *Plagianthus*, while 8-10 in *Malvastrum*, 15-20 in *Malva* and numerous in *Malope trifida* Linn. where they are arranged vertically on an elongated thalamus; style branches as many as carpels or in *Urena, Pavonia, Malachra* etc. twice as many. Fruit of *Malvaviscus* is a berry; in other genera it is a schizocarp or capsule.

The family is divided into 4 tribes :

A. Carpels in vertical rows : –

I Malopeae — Malope, Kitabelia, etc.

B. Carpels in one plane;

II Malveae — Fruit a schizocarp; styles as many as carpels : Abutilon, etc.

III Ureneae — Fruit a schizocarp; styles twice as many as carpels : Urena, etc.

IV Hibiscae — Fruit a capsule : Hibiscus, Gossypium, etc.

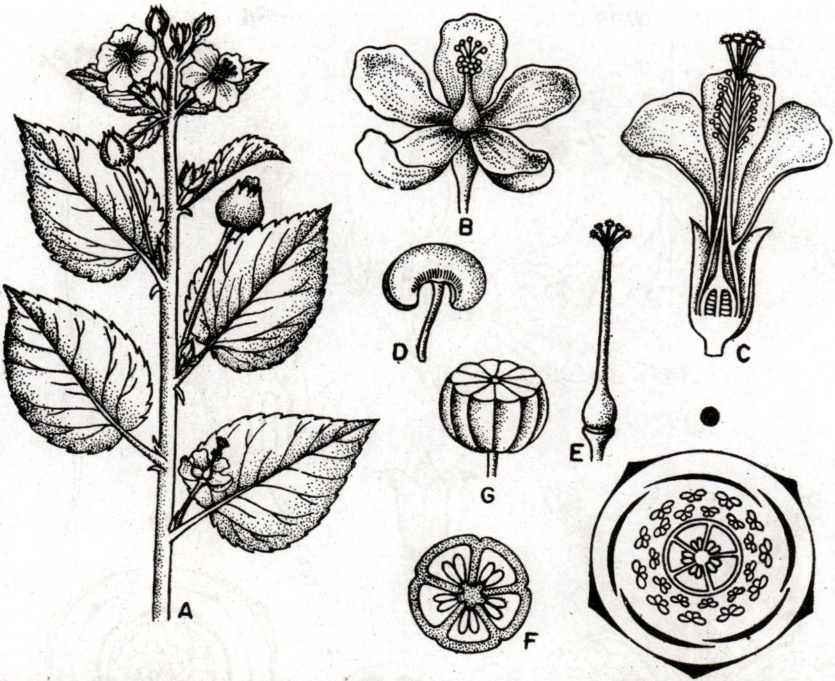

Fig. 107. **Sida cordifolia L.—A. Apical portion of the shoot with leaves and flowers (×½); B. Flower (×2); C. Same in vertical section showing the slender style passing through staminal column; D. Reniform anther; E. Ovary with long style and stigmatic branches; F. T.s. of ovary; G. Fruit.**

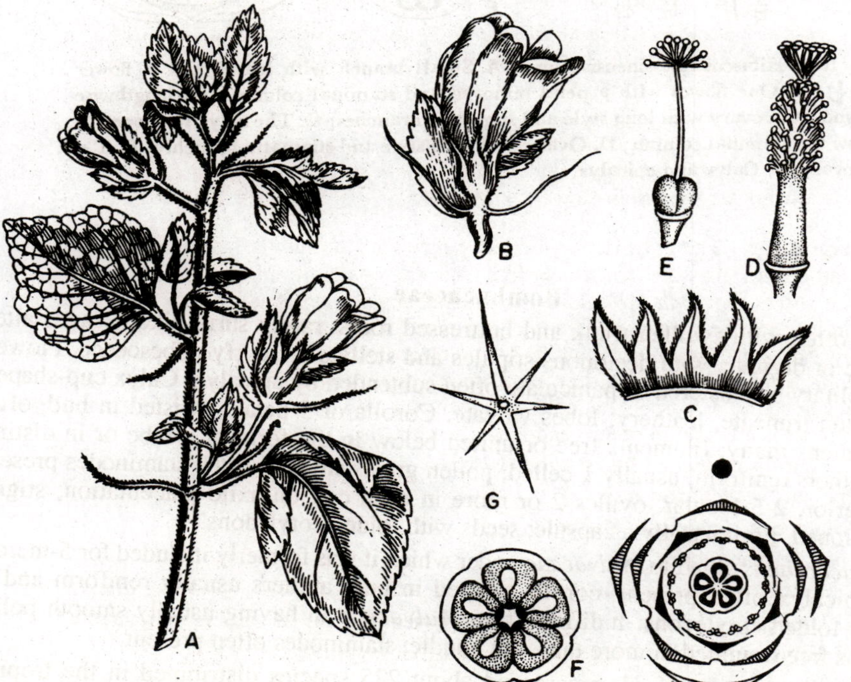

Fig. 108. **Malachra capitata Linn.—A. Leafy branch with flowers (×½); B. One flower (×2); C. Calyx split open; D. Staminal column; E. Gynoecium; G. One stellate hair. F. T.s. of ovary.**

Fig. 109. **Hibiscus rosa-sinensis Linn.—A. Small branch with leaves and a flower ($\times\frac{1}{2}$); B. One flower with a petal removed and staminal column split lengthwise to show the ovary with long style and stigmatic branches; C. The calyx split open to show the staminal column; D. Ovary with long style and stigmatic branches; E. T.s. of ovary; F. Calyx and epicalyx.**

Bombacaceae

Trees, often with swollen trunk and buttressed roots, rarely shrub-like. Leaves alternate, simple or digitate, with deciduous stipules and stellate or scurfy pubescence. Flowers bisexual, solitary or clustered or paniculate often subtended by epicalyx. Calyx cup-shaped, 5-lobed, often truncate, leathery; lobes valvate. Corolla of 5 petals, twisted in bud, often absent. Stamens many; filaments free or united below in the form of a tube or in distinct bundles; anthers reniform, usually 1-celled; pollen grains smooth; often staminodes present. Ovary superior, 2-5 locular, ovules 2 or more in each cell on axile placentation; stigma capitate or lobed. Fruit usually a capsule; seeds with folded cotyledons.

Bombacaceae is allied to *Malvaceae* under which it was formerly included for 5-merous flowers, epicalyx often present, corolla twisted in bud, anthers usually reniform and 1-celled, and folded cotyledons. It differs from *Malvaceae* in having usually smooth pollen and stamens free or united in more than one bundle; staminodes often present.

The family consists of 31 genera and about 225 species distributed in the tropical countries of the world.

	Tiliaceae	Elaeocarpaceae	Sterculiaceae	Malvaceae	Bombacaceae.
1. Plants	Usually trees or shrubs, rarely herbs.	Trees or shrubs.	Trees or shrubs, rarely herbs.	Herbs or shrubs, very rarely tree.	Trees.
2. Leaves	Simple, alternate, stipulate.	Simple alternate or opposite, stipulate.	Simple, stipulate, alternate, rarely digitate.	Simple, stipulate, alternate.	Digitate, alternate.
3. Flowers	Regular, hypogynous, bi- or unisexual.	Regular, bisexual, hypogynous.	Regular or irregular, bi- or unisexual, hypogynous.	Regular, bisexual hypogynous.	Regular, bisexual, hypogynous.
4. Sepals	3-5, free or connate, caducous.	4-5, free or connate.	3-5, free or slightly united at the base.	5, united	5, free or united
5. Epicalyx	Present or not	Absent	Absent	Usually present	Present or absent.
6. Petals	3-5, twisted, often absent.	4-5, valvate, rarely absent.	5, often reduced or absent, twisted.	5, slightly united at base twisted.	5, often absent, twisted.
7. Stamens	∞, free or slightly connate at base, or in 5-10 bundles.	∞, polyadelphous, inserted on a disk.	∞, in 2 whorls, outer sterile or absent, inner fertile, monadelphous.	∞, usually monadelphous.	5-∞, free or polyadelphous, often with staminodes.
8. Anthers	2-celled, pollen smooth.	2-celled, pollen smooth.	2-celled, pollen smooth.	1-celled, reniform, pollen spiny.	1-celled, pollen smooth.
9. Androgynophore	Absent.	Absent.	Present or not	Absent	Absent
10. Carpels	2-∞, syncarpous.	2-∞, syncarpous.	2-5, syncarpous.	2-∞, syncarpous.	2-5, syncarpous
11. Ovary	2-many-celled with 1-many ovules in each cell.	2-many-celled with 1-many ovules in each cell.	4-5-celled with 2-∞ ovules in each cell.	1-many-celled with 1 or few ovules in each cell.	2-5-celled with 2 or few ovules in each cell.
12. Ovules	Horizontal.	Pendulous.	Horizontal or ascending.	Horizontal.	Erect.
13. Fruit	Baccate or capsular.	Capsular or drupaceous.	Capsule or follicle.	Capsule or schizocarp.	Capsule or berry-like.

The family includes the Simul or Red silk-cotton tree *Bombax ceiba* Linn. and the White silk-cotton tree or the Kapok tree *Ceiba pentandra* Gaertn. The floss obtained from the fruit is used for stuffing pilows and cushions and for making life-jackets. *Durio zebethinus* Murr. of Malaya yields the Durion, an edible fruit with custard like flesh. *Adansonia digitata* Linn. the Baobab tree of Africa lives to a great age and the trunk expands steadily to have a circumference of about 50 mtr. *Ochroma lagopus* Sw. is a softwooded tree known as the Balsawood-tree of W. Indies, the wood of which is much used for making canoes.

Segregation of Bombacaceae as a distinct family has been accepted by most botanists. Hutchinson however, places it in **Tiliales,** an order which besides *Tiliaceae* contains the families *Sterculiaceae, Dirachmaceae, Scytopetalaceae* and *Peridiscaceae* while his *Malvales* constists only of a single family *Malvaceae.*

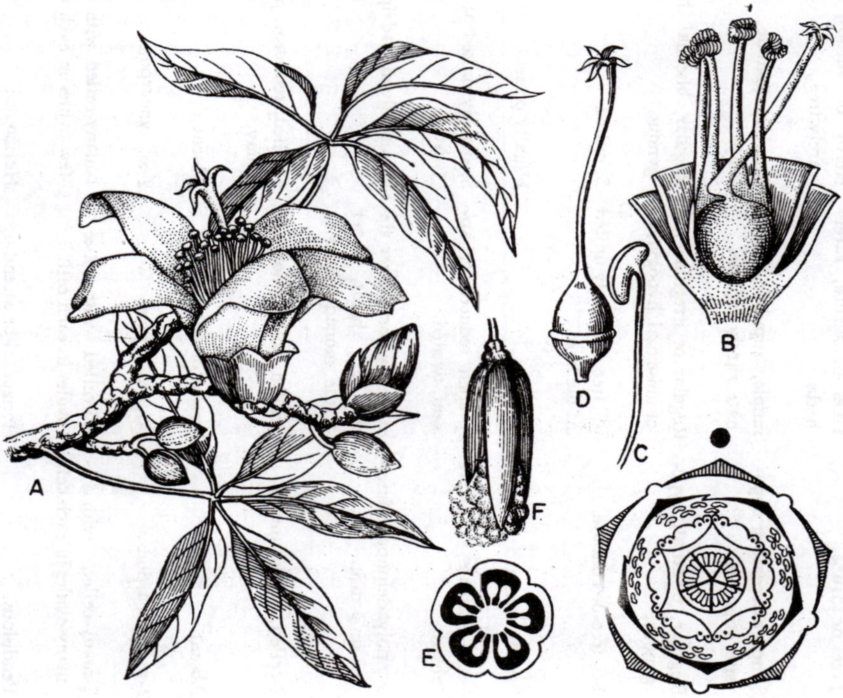

Fig. 110. Bombax ceiba Linn.—A. Small portion of the branch with leaves flowers and buds ($\times\frac{1}{8}$); B. One flower with calyx and corolla removed to show a few united stamens and the gynoecium; C, One stamen; D. Gynoecium; E. T.s. of ovary; F. Fruit ($\times\frac{1}{4}$).

PARIETALES

The 27th order **Parietales** following **Malvales** is a large one comprising 29 families distributed under 11 suborders as noted below:—

Theineae: Dilleniaceae, Eucryphiaceae, Ochnaceae, Caryocaraceae, Marcgraviaceae, Quiinaceae, Theaceae, Guttiferae, Dipterocarpaceae.

Tamaricineae: Elatinaceae, Frankeniaceae, Tamaricaceae.

Fouquierineae: Fouquieriaceae.

Cistineae: Cistaceae, Bixaceae.

Cochlospermineae: Cochlospermaceae.
Flacourtiineae: Winteraceae, Violaceae, Flacourtiaceae, Stachyuraceae, Turneraceae, Malesherbiaceae, Passifloraceae, Achariaceae.
Papaynieae: Caricaceae.
Loasineae: Loasaceae.
Datiscineae: Datiscaceae.
Begoniineae: Begoniaceae.
Ancistrocladineae: Ancistrocladaceae.

The common characters of these famalies are: Flowers hermaphrodite, pentamerous or tetramerous, perianth distinguished into calyx and corolla; sepals imbricate; stamens as many as petals; carperls 3, united to form a unilocular ovary; placentation parietal; seeds many, albuminous. Flowers usually regular and a disc is often present.

The main characters based on which these families have been placed in one order are the nature of placentation and seeds. Such treatment however has not met with the approval of subsequent workers who consider that some of the families included are not phylogenetically close. For instance the family *Winteraceae* has affinity with *Magnoliaceae* and is placed in **Magnoliales** by most taxonomists. *Dilleniaceae* which is included in this order by Engler and placed in **Theineae** is not very close to *Theaceae* or other families of this suborder and has therfore been removed to **Dilleniales.** Cronquist groups the other families under 2 orders, viz., **Theales** and **Violales** while Takhtajan distributes them into 5 orders, viz., **Theales, Violales, Passiflorales, Begoniales** and **Tamaricales** and these orders are arranged close to each other and also to **Dilleniales** in his system. Following Hutchinson he splitted *Theaceae* into *Theaceae*, *Sourauiaceae* and *Actinidiaceae* but removed *Saurauiaceae* and *Actinidiaceae* to **Ericales.** Hutchinson distributed the 29 families of this order **Parietales** of Engler under 13 orders placing *Elatinaceae* under **Caryophyllales** of the division **Herbaceae.** It follows therefore that **Parietales** is not a natural taxon and inclusion of *Winteraceae* is out of place in this group while difference of opinion exists in the cases of other families. According to Cronquist **Theales** has been derived from **Dillaniales** and **Violales** has been derived from **Theales.** These 3 orders are placed by him in **Dilleniidae.** Cronquist takes out the family *Eucryphiaceae* from this group and places it in **Rosales** in the subclass **Rosidae** and as mentioned before *Winteraceae* is placed in **Magnoliales** of **Magnoliidae.**

Dilleniaceae

Trees, shrubs, woody climbers or rarely undershrubs; some are deciduous. Leaves alternate, rarely opposite, simple, usually with a large blade with prominent and parallel lateral nerves; stipules present or absent. Inflorescence is a cyme or a cymose panicle, or solitary and axillary. Flowers regular, usually, pentamerous, bisexual or polygamous or unisexual and dioecious, hypogynous, often large and showy, usually yellow or white, rarely pink. Sepals 5 or fewer or more, free, imbricate and macrescent spirally arranged. Petals 5 or 2-7, free, imbricate, caducous. Stamens ∞, in one or more whorl, rarely less than 10, free or united at base; filaments often broader above; anthers opening by lateral slits or by apical pores. Ovary superior of many carpels, fused partially or completely, conduplicately folded; sometimes carpels free or rarely solitary; ovules anatropous, erect, one to many, with ventral raphe on axile placentation or in monocarpellary ovary on marginal placentation; styles curved, as many as carpels;

stigma capitate or peltate. Fruit baccate or follicular. Seeds arillate or not, with crustaceous testa, copious fleshy endosperm and minute embryo.

Acrotrema is a genus of rhizomatous herbs often with pinnately compound leaves. In *Pachynema* the stem and branches are metamorphosed into phylloclades while the leaves are reduced to scales. In *Acrotrema* leaves are usually radical. *Tetracera* has lianas as well as shrubs. In *Pachynema* the sepals are unequal in size so that the flower is slightly zygomorphic. In *Tetracera empedoclea* Gilg there are as many as 15 sepals spirally arranged on an elongated thalamus. In *Davilla* the 2 inner sepals are larger and in some species become woody in fruit. In *Hibbertia* there are many staminodes surrounding the gynoecium while the few fertile stamens are situated on one side. *Davilla* has free stamens; in *Acrotrema*, *Hibbertia* stamens are polyadelphous; monadelphous stamens are met with in other genera; anther loculi divergent at base in *Tetracera* but parallel in other genera, opening by apical pores, e.g., *Dillenia bracteata* Wight and by slits in other cases. *Acrotrema*, *Tetracera* have follicular fruits; in *Dillenia* the fruit is a baccate pseudocarp.

Floral formula: ⊕ ☿ K_{4-5} C_{3-5}, A ∞ or (∞) $\underline{G_{1-\infty}}$

Anatomical characters have much in common with families under Ranales. Vessels are solitary with scalariform perforation plates and are scattered in the xylem; the wood parenchyma is apotracheal with thick-walled cells. Fibres have bordered pits on transverse walls. Anomalous secondary thickening is met with in climbing plants. The stomata are of ranunculaceous type. The floral anatomy is more or less similar to *Magnoliaceae* and *Annonaceae*.

The family consists of over 500 species under 18 genera mainly distributed in the tropical countries of the world, a large number being Indo-Malayan. *Hibbertia* and *Pachynema* are xerophytes occurring in Australia and a few are found in S. America. In India 10 species are found in the plains and at low elevations in the hills. *Dillenia indica* Linn. a medium sized evergreen tree with solitary pendulous flowers about 20 cm. across and fruits of same diametre is common in the southern and eastern parts of India. This is the Chalta-tree fruits of which are acid and are used to make chutney and jam and jelly. This and several other species of *Dillenia* yield good timber.

The spirocyclic arrangement of the floral parts, free carpels and many stamens point to the primitiveness of the family. The floral anatomy and the anatomy of the stem also speak for its primitiveness. It is similar to *Magnoliaceae* in some respects and to *Theaceae* in floral construction. It is considered that *Dilleniaceae* has been derived from **Magnoliales** and has given rise to **Theales.** Bessey included *Dilleniaceae* in **Ranales** but Hutchinson, Takhtajan and Cronquist place it in an order **Dilleniales** which order is according to them very close to **Magnoliales.**

Ochnaceae

Trees shrubs or undershrubs , rarely herbs. Leaves simple, alternate, stipulate, stiff and leathery; stipules caducous. Inflorescence is a terminal panicle or umbel or axillary umbel or fascicle; rarely flower solitary and axillary. Flowers hermaphrodite, regular, hypogynous, usually bracteate. Receptacle often elongated or expanded in the form of a disc, often enlarged after flowering. Sepals 5 or 4, rarely 10, free, imbricate, leathery and persistent. Petals 4-10, free, imbricate or contorted, deciduous. Stamens 4-5 or 8-10 or numerous in one or more whorls, inserted on the disc when present, often pushed out on one side; staminodes often present; anthers bilocular, dehiscing by lateral slits longitudinally or by apical pores; filaments often persistent and anthers deciduous. Ovary superior, of 5-15 free carpels or carpels more or less fused, or united to form a unilocular ovary; ovules many in each locule, erect or pendulous, with ventral raphe; rarely ovules one in each chamber, styles gynobasic; placentation parietal or axile; stigma lobed or capitate. Fruit a capsule or drupe or a cluster of druplets. Seeds few, rarely numerous or solitary in each druplet; endosperm present or absent, embryo straight or curved.

Some species of *Sauvagesia* are herbs otherwise plants are shrubs or trees. *Godoya splendida* Planch. has large pinnate leaves. Sepals are coloured in *Ochna*. The carpels in *Ochna* and *Ouratea* are partly fused but become completely free when mature, have a single ovule in each carpel-chamber and form an aggregate type of fruit. In the African genus *Lophira* 2 of the persistent sepals enlarge to form the wings of the fruit.

The family consists of about 600 species under 40 genera found in the tropical countries of the world but more in America. *Ochna squarrosa* Linn. and a few other species of the genus are found in India wild and also in cultivated condition for the beautiful flowers.

The family is allied to *Theaceae* and *Dipterocarpaceae* and resembles *Guttiferae* (*Clusiaceae*) to some extent. These 3 families are included in the order **Theales** by Cronquist and Takhtajan while Hutchinson placed *Ochnaceae* and *Dipterocarpaceae* in **Ochnales** and *Theaceae* in **Theales** just before **Ochnales** but included *Guttiferae* (Clusiaceae) in **Guttiferales** of another group.

The family is not of much economic importance. Two species of *Lophira* yield good timber and are known as the African oaks and the seeds of *L. alata* gives an oil which is the *Meni* oil of commerce.

Theaceae

Evergreen shrubs or small trees, bark warty or wrinkled, often shedding in flakes. Leaves coriaceous, simple, alternate or spirally arranged, exstipulate, secondary veins usually conspicuous underneath. Inflorescence an axillary cyme rarely terminal panicle, often axillary and solitary; bracts and bracteoles often gradually pass into sepals and sepals into petals in a spirocyclic order; bracteoles persistent or caducuous. Flowers actinomorphic, bisexual or polygamous or unisexual and dioecious, hypogynous. Sepals 4-7, usually 5, free or slightly connate at base, imbricate or quincuncial, persisent or caducuous. Petals 4-9, usually 5, free or slightly connate at base, imbricate; the outermost usually smaller. Stamens usually many rarely few, in one or more whorls, free or connate at base, sometimes in several bundles, often adnate to petals, anthers globose or oblong, versatile or basifixed, dehiscing longitudinally. Carpels usually 3-5, rarely 2 or 1 or more than 5 and upto 10, fused to form a superior ovary, rarely perigynous; rarely carpels almost free; cells as many as carpels with 2-8 ovules in each cell, or ovules 1 in each cell, rarely many, pendulous, anatropous, with ventral raphe; placentation axile; styles free or partly connate, often persistent; stigma entire and pointed or lobed. Fruit baccate or capsular. Seeds rarely arillate; endosperm absent or scanty, granular or oily; embryo straight or curved.

Plants of the genus *Asteropeia* are climbers, of all other genera are trees or shrubs. In *Ternstroemia* the veins of the leaves are indistinct. In *Sladenia* the inflorescence is a dichasial cyme; it is an umbellate corymb in *Anneslea;* while in *Eurya and Cleyera* flowers are fasciculate. Flowers are unisexual in many species of *Laplacea* and dioecious in *Eurya*; polygamous in *Ternstroemia*. Calyx and corolla are not differentiated in *Gor-*

donia and *Camellia*, gradually passing from bracts to petals in *Camellia*. In *Anneslea* calyx is gamosepalous and tubular. In *Stewartia* there are 6 sepals and 6 petals. The number of stamens vary greatly in different genera. In *Eurya* some times there are only 5 stamens. In *Adinandra* 20-100 stamens are found and in *Ternstroemia* as many as 300 in certain species. Filaments are free or connate at base, monadelphous or polyadelphous; in *Gordonia* the connate filaments form a cup; in *Sladenia* dialated below and constricted near apex. In *Anneslea* ovary is epigynous or perigynous. In some *Ternstroemia* ovary is monocarpellary while in *Laplacea* there may be as many as 10; ovules usually 1-8 in each cell of ovary but in *Adinandra* often 100 ovules have been found in each cell. The seeds of *Sladenia* are winged, and the seeds of *Schima* have foliacious cotyledons.

Sclerides are present in the mesophyll of the leaves as well as in the cortex and pith of young stem. Pallisade layer is one cell thick. Raphides often occur in the ground tissue. The vessels are solitary with scalariform perforation plates. Fibres are bordered pitted. Isolated fibres in the pericycle ultimately unite in a composite mechanical ring. Wood parenchyma is diffuse and usually apotracheal.

The family consists of 23 genera and about 500 species occurring mainly in tropical and subtropical regions of Asia and America. In India it is represented by[33] species in the plains and the hills at lower elevations including the famous tea-plants *Camellia sinensis* (L.) O. Kuntze and *C. assamica* Wt. India, Srilanka and E. Africa are the most important countries for tea-production. Besides the above 2 species of *Camellia*, *C. oleifera* Abel and *C. sasansqua* Thunb. yield the tea-oil from the seeds. *C. japonica* Linn. is a favourite garden-plant having large showy flowers and dark green glossy leaves. Seeds of *Pyrenaria diospyricarpa* Kurz. forms a lather in water and is used as a substitute for soap. *Schima wallichii* Bloemb. and other species of *Schima* are good timber trees. The leaves of *Haploclathra paniculata* Benth. are used as tea of inferior quality.

Theaceae resembles *Dilleniaceae* in floral morphology to some extent as well as in anatomy of the stem. It has also much in common with *Guttiferae* (*Clusiaceae*) and *Marcgraviaceae* and to some extent with *Dipterocarpaceae*, *Ochnaceae*, *Actinidiaceae* and *Caryocaraceae*. It is presumed that *Theaceae* has been derived from *Dilleniaceae* directly or through some allied families.

Guttiferae
(Clusiaceae)

Trees, shrubs or herbs, rarely climbers. Leaves coriaceous, simple, entire, exstipulate, opposite or whorled, rarely alternate. Inflorescence cymose or flowers solitary or clustered. Flowers hermaphrodite or polygamous, or unisexual, actinomorphic, hypogynous, with cyclic or spirocyclic arrangement of parts; bracts and bracteoles often present; thalamus usually large. Sepals 2-6, free, imbricate. Petals as many as or double the number of sepals, imbricate. Stamens usually numerous, monadelphous or polyadelphous, in one or more whorls, rarely free; staminodes sometimes present. Carpels usually 3-5 united to form a superior 3-5 celled ovary, rarely carpels more or fewer; ovules 1-many in each cell on parietal, basal or axile placenta; style very short, with broad stigma depressed above. Fruit capsular or fleshy and indehiscent. Seeds without endosperm and often arillate; embryo straight.

The trees usually have resinous bark. The shrubs of *Hypericum** are rhizomatous. *Clusia* is a genus of epiphytic climbers. Leaves of *Hypericum* are soft and thin; in other

* Placed by most workers in a distinct family Hypericaceae.

genera they are coriaceous and often more or less thick; alternate leaves are found in *Caraipa*, *Kielmeyera*, etc. while in other genera they are usually opposite. In many genera bracteoles gradually pass into sepals and in *Tovomita* sepals and petals cannot be differentiated. The thalamus is usually broad, convex or concave while in *Garcinia* it is elongated with the floral parts spirally arranged. Similar spiral arrangement is also found in *Clusia criuva* Camb. Calyx is persistent in *Mesua*. In *Hypericum* the stamens are many in several fascicles with hypogynous glands in between. The bundles of stamens in *Endodesmia* are free at base but united to form monadelphous stamens near apex. Stamens may be free in some *Calophyllum* or *Garcinia* species. Ovary one celled in

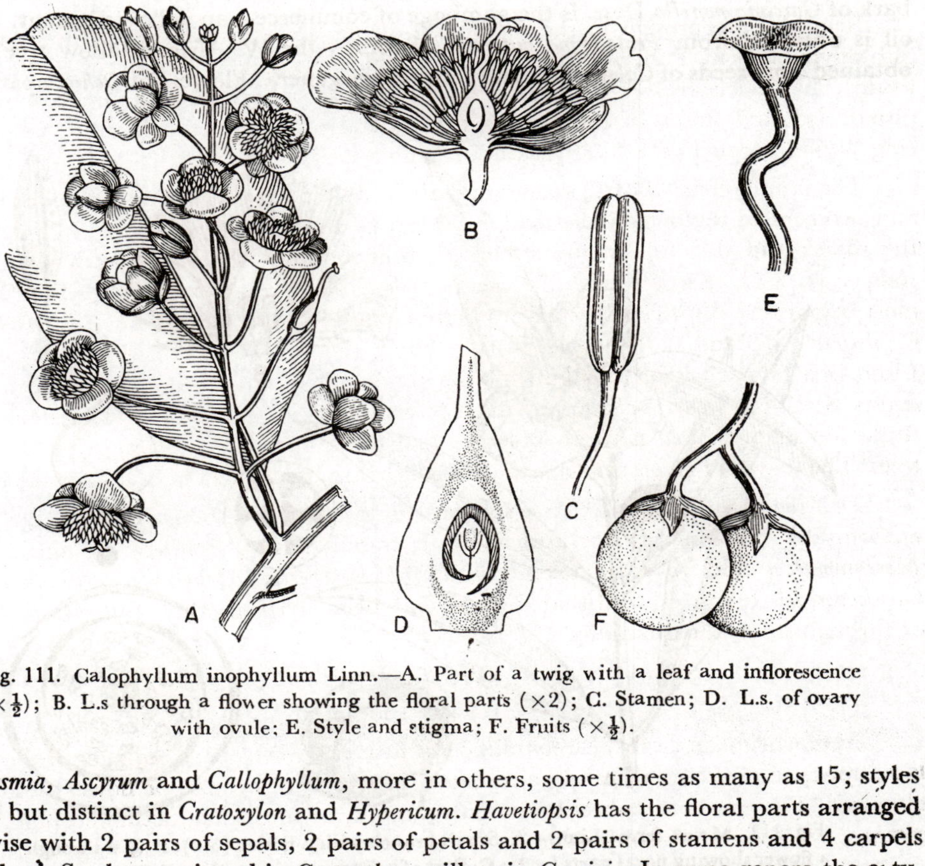

Fig. 111. Calophyllum inophyllum Linn.—A. Part of a twig with a leaf and inflorescence ($\times\frac{1}{2}$); B. L.s through a flower showing the floral parts ($\times 2$); C. Stamen; D. L.s. of ovary with ovule; E. Style and stigma; F. Fruits ($\times\frac{1}{2}$).

Endodesmia, *Ascyrum* and *Callophyllum*, more in others, some times as many as 15; styles united but distinct in *Cratoxylon* and *Hypericum*. *Havetiopsis* has the floral parts arranged crosswise with 2 pairs of sepals, 2 pairs of petals and 2 pairs of stamens and 4 carpels in a whorl. Seeds are winged in *Cratoxylon*, arillate in *Garcinia*. In some genera the cotyledons are very small and often obsolete and the radicle is large, e.g. *Clusia*, *Garcinia*, *Ochrocarpus*, etc.

Schizogenous cavities and ducts are found in leaves and stem with resin or oil. The vessels are solitary or in small multiples; perforation plates simple or mixed with scalariform pits. In *Clusioideae* wood parenchyma is paratracheal, fibres are septate and long, vascicentric tracheids are absent; in *Callophylloideae* wood parenchyma is apotracheal, fibres are of medium length and vascicentric tracheids are present.

The family comprises 45 genera and about 1000 species. *Hypericum* the largest genus with over 300 species stretches up to the temperate parts of the world, other genera being restricted to the tropical region. It is represented in India by several species of *Calophyllum*, *Ochrocarpus longifolius* Benth. & Hk.f. *Mesua ferrea* Linn. (both being called Nag Kesar or Nageswar in Bengali), *Garcinia cowa* Roxb., *G. xanthochymus* Hk. f. and several other species of *Garcinia*. *Hypericum* is found in the hill, while *H. japonicum* Thumb. occurs also in the plains.

The family includes several timber trees, e.g. species of *Calophyllum*, *Mesua*, *Cratoxylon*, *Montrouziera*, *Harungana*, *Platonia* etc. *Garcinia mangostana* Linn. produces the most delicious fruit mangostene the aril being the edible part. The drupes of *Mammea americana* Linn. and *Platonia insignis* Mart. are also edible. The resinous gum obtained from the bark of *Garcinia morella* Desr. is the gamboge of commerce—an yellow pigment. A fatty oil is obtained from *Pentadesma butyracea* Sabine—the W. African tallow tree. Oil is obtained from seeds of *Calophyllum* and some other genera. Flowers of *Ochrocarpus*, *Mesua*

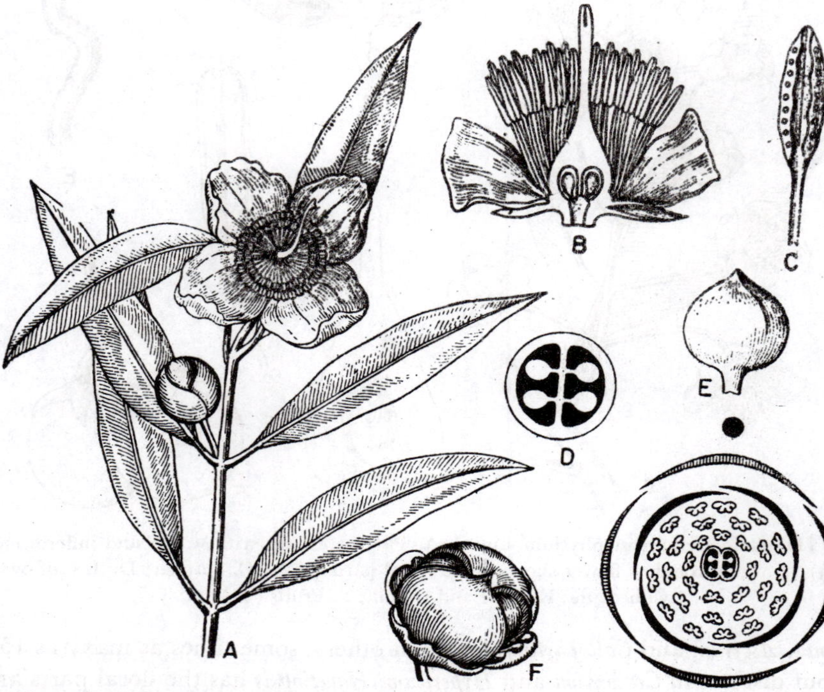

Fig. 112. Mesua ferrea Linn.—A. Small branch with a flower (×1); B. L.s. through a flower showing floral parts (×2); C. Part of a filament with anther; D. T.s. through ovary; E. A small fruit; F. Bursting fruit (×½).

and leaves of *Harungana madagascariensis* have medicinal properties. *Calophyllum inophyllum* Linn.—the Punnag or Sultan Champa, is planted in parks and gardens and as avenue trees for the beauty of the glossy leaves and flowers.

Guttiferae shows close affinity with *Theaceae* and *Dipterocarpaceae*. It resembles *Dilleniaceae* in floral construction as well as floral anatomy. Engler placed the 3 families in **Parietales** in the same suborder **Theineae** while Takhtajan and Cronquist include them in **Theales.** Hutchinson put them in 3 distinct orders, viz. *Theaceae* in **Theales,** *Clusiaceae* (*Guttiferae*) in **Guttiferales** and *Dipterocarpaceae* in **Ochanales.**

The family is subdivided into 5 subfamilies by Engler as given below:

I. Kielmeyeroideae: Flowers usually bisexual; stamens many; ovary 3-5-carpelled, 3-5-celled, style one.—*Caraipa*, *Kielmeyera*, etc.

II. Hypericoideae: Flowers bisexual; stamens many, polyadelphous, ovary of 3-5-carpels, 3-5-celled or one-celled, styles free.—*Hypericum*, *Vismia*, etc.

III. Endodesmioideae: Flowers usually bisexual; stamens many, monadelphous above but polyadelphous at base; ovary monocarpellary. —*Endodesmia*.

IV. Calophylloideae: Flowers bisexual or unisexual; stamens many free or connate at base; ovary of 1-4 carpels, 1-2-celled, style one.—*Mesua*, *Calophyllum*, etc.

V. Clusioideae: Flowers bisexual or polygamous; stamens many, free or connate; carpels and cells of ovary 2 or more, often 12-15, style one very short; cotyledons very small or scaly.—*Clusia*, *Garcinia*, etc.

In the classification of Bentham and Hooker *Hypericineae* was a distinct N.O. other than *Guttiferae*. Engler merged *Hypericineae* into *Guttiferae* as one of the subfamilies of the same, e.g. *Hypericoideae*. Hutchinson and most other workers prefer to treat **Hypericaceae** as a distinct family the characters of which are given below:

Trees, shrubs or herbs, rarely lianes with resinous sap. Leaves simple opposite or whorled, exstipulate, often pellucid-punctate. Inflorescence a terminal, rarely axillary cyme, or flowers solitary. Flowers regular, hermaphrodite. Sepals 4-5, imbricate, often connate at base, unequal. Petals as many as sepals sometimes clawed, claw with nectar-pit or groove, free, imbricate or contorted. Stamens many, hypogynous, usually polyadelphous; filaments in each bundle connate, rarely monadelphous; anthers 2-celled. Ovary superior, 3-5-carpelled, syncarpous, 3-5-celled or only 1-celled, ovules many in each cell, anatropous, on axile, rarely parietal placentation, styles free or basally connate. Fruit a capsule or berry. Seed without endosperm and with straight or curved embryo.

Dipterocarpaceae

Trees, usually very tall, rarely shrubs; branching at first monopodial, later sympodial; younger parts hairy. Leaves simple, coriaceous, alternate, stipulate, usually prominently penni-nerved, frequently with domatia in axils of nerves. Inflorescence is a racemose panicle, rarely cymose, terminal or axillary, with caducous bracts. Flowers hermaphrodite, regular, with a broad receptacle, 5-merous. Sepals 5, unequal, imbricate or valvate, slightly connate at base and adnate to the ovary, persistent and more or less enlarging in fruit in the forms of wings. Petals 5, imbricate or contorted, free or connate at base. Stamens 5, 10, or 15, sometimes more, in one or more whorls, developement centrifugal, usually connate at base, frequently adnate to the base of petals; androgynophore often present; anther lobes unequal, connective usually produced at the apex. Carpels 3, forming a syncarpous 3-celled ovary, rarely 1-celled; ovary superior rarely semi-inferior; ovules 2 or more in each cell on axile placentation; style often trifid at apex, sometimes on a stylopodium; stigma usually obscure, 3 or 6-lobed. Fruit nut-like, with all or some of the persistent sepals enlarged to form wings. Seeds without endosperm; embryo fills the seed, cotyledons often twisted, lobed or laciniate, unequal, enclosing the radicle.

The trees are usually evergreen but *Shorea* is deciduous. Stipules usually caducous but in some species of *Shorea* they are persistent; in *Dipterocarpus* the stipules are large and enclose the young bud. Five stamens are met with only in *Monoporandra;* in most genera there are 15 stamens in 3 whorls, often stamens are 20 in 4 whorls, rarely more stamens are found. *Hopea recopei* Roxb. has monadelphous stamens. In *Marquesia* ovary is one-celled and the placentation is parietal. In *Vatica* ovary is sunk in the receptacle.

Floral formula: $\oplus$ ⚥ $K_5\ C_5\ A_\alpha\ G_{(\underline{3})}$

The resin ducts are lined with epithelium layer. The vessels are mostly solitary, sometimes in small groups and rarely in radial rows; these have simple perforations and alternate intervascular pitting. Vascicentric tracheids are often present. Sometimes vascular bundles are present in cortex.

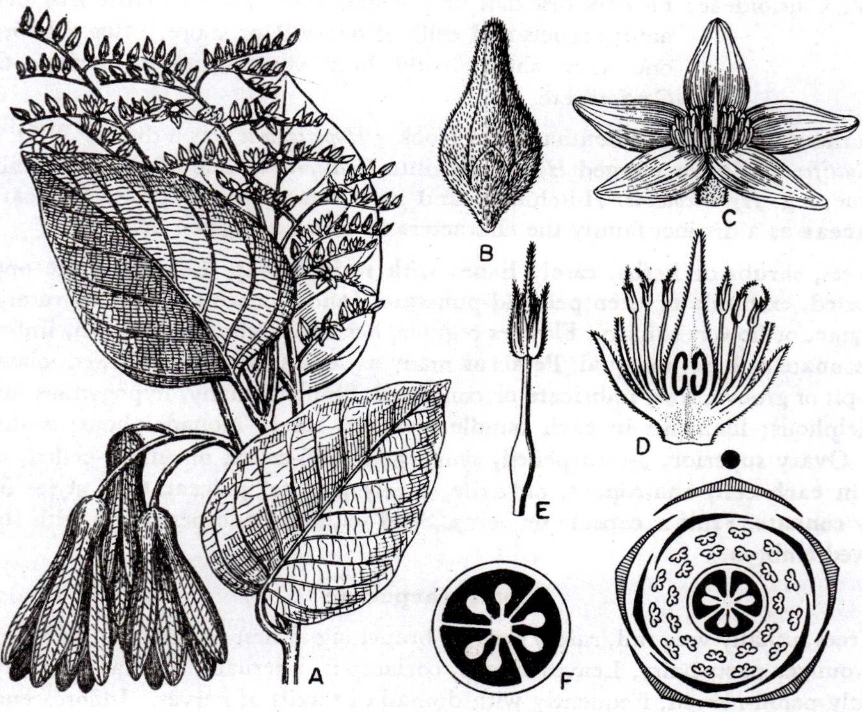

Fig. 113. Shorea robusta Gaertn.—A. Leafy branch with inflorescence and fruits. B. Flower bud (×4); C. Open flower (×4); D. L.s through the flower showing stamens & ovary with ovules; E. Stamen; F. T.s. of ovary.

The family consists of 16 genera and over 500 species found in Tropical Africa and S. E. Asia. Over 50 species occur in eastern and southern parts of India the most important being *Shorea robusta* Gaertn. f.—the Sal tree which grows wild and is cultivated for the valuable timber. *Dipterocarpus* is Indo-Malayan, the species of which are very tall branching only near the top. About 10 species occur in eastern parts of India and are locally called Garjan tree. *Hopea*, *Vatica*, *Vateria*, etc. are other genera having Indian species.

Most species yield hard and durable timber, *Shorea robusta* being most important. Turpentine and dumar resin are obtained from *Shorea robusta* and *S. koordarsii*. Gum-resin obtained from *Vateria indica* Linn. is used to make copal varnish. Fatty oil is obtained from the seeds of *Shorea aptera* and *Vateria indica* Linn. Starchy seeds of *Vateria, Vatica* and *Doona* are edible. A strong smelling dense balsam known as "Chooa" is obtained from *Isauxis lancaefolia* King. "Borneo camphor" or "Sumatra camphor"—the yellow camphor is the product of crystals deposited in the wood of *Dryobalonops aromatica* Gaertn.

Dipterocarpaceae is closely related to *Guttiferae* and *Theaceae*. From the former it differs in alternate leaves and presence of stipules. From *Theaceae* it differs in having resin ducts in the wood and pith, and fruit usually winged. The prominent nerves of the leaves resemble those of *Dilleniaceae* to some extent. It is also close to *Ochnaceae* having somewhat similar arrangement of floral parts. It has some affinity with *Ancistrocladaceae* also which family was included under *Dipterocarpaceae* in the old classification of Bentham and Hooker. According to Hutchinson *Dipterocarpaceae* is much closer to *Ochnaceae* and *Ancistrocladaceae* which 3 are put by him in **Ochnales,** than to *Theaceae* and *Clusiaceae* (Guttiferae) which are placed by him in **Theales** and **Guttiferales** respectively. Further he places **Theales** and **Ochnales** side by side while **Guttiferales** is placed in another group.

Engler divided *Dipterocarpaceae* into 2 tribes as noted below:

I. **Monotoideae:** Anthers dorsifixed; gynophore present; wood without resin ducts; rays uniseriate.—*Monotes, Marquesia*. (Tropical Africa).

II. **Dipterocarpoideae:** Anthers basifixed; gynophore absent; wood with intercellular resin ducts; rays multiseriate.—*Shorea, Hopea. Dipeterocarpus*, etc. (S. E. Asia).

Tamaricaceae

Shrubs or perennial herbs, rarely short trees. Leaves alternate, exstipulate, very small and scale-like or linear, sessile, entire, adpressed and usually glaucous. Inflorescence spikate or racemose, terminal or axillary near the apex of branches, ebracteate. Flowers small and inconspicuous, regular, bisexual, rarely unisexual, hypogynous, pentamerous or tetramerous. Sepals 4-5 free, imbricate; petals as many as sepals, free, imbricate. Stamens 4 or 5, or double this number, or numerous, inserted on a disc, free or connate, anther bilocular, dehiscing longitudinally and laterally. Carpels 4-5 or only 2, united to form a superior unilocular ovary; ovules few or many, anatropous, ascending on basal or parietal placentas; raphe ventral; styles free or united below and branched above. Fruit a capsule dehiscing along the dorsal surface. Seeds hairy with a straight embryo and with or without endosperm, rarely winged.

This is a small family of about 120 species under 4 genera, halophytic or xerophytic, inhabiting the steppes of C. Asia, and on sandy soils on sea-shores on Med. region and banks of large rivers in Asia. In India it is represented by *Tamarix Troupii* Hole, *T. articulata* Vahl., *Myricaria germanica* Linn. etc.

Economically the family is not very important. Those attaining tree-size yield valuable timber, e.g. *Tamarix articulata*. The bark and galls of this tree as well as of *T. gallica* Linn. are much used for tanning and dyeing. *T. gallica* var. *mannifera* Ehren of W. Asiatic countries produce a manna much eaten by the local people and has medicinal properties. The plants being fast growing are a source of fuel and serve as sand-binders.

The affinity of the family with *Frankeniaceae* has been recognised by almost all workers. Hutchinson and Takhtajan place these 2 families along with *Fouquieriaceae* in a distinct order **Tamaricales** which is considered to have been derived from *Bixaceae* and allied families.

Bixaceae

A small family of trees and shrubs with reddish sap. Leaves simple, alternate, stipulate, palmately nerved; petioles usually long and covered with tufted hairs. Inflorescence is a terminal panicle. Flowers large and showy, actinomorphic, bisexual and hypogynous. Sepals 5, free imbricate, deciduous, biglandular at base. Petals 5, free, imbricate or twisted. Stamens many, free; anthers bilocular, theca narrowly horse-shoe shaped, opening by short slits at the apical bend. Carpels 2-4, united to form a superior unilocular ovary; ovules many anatropous, on parietal placentas; style slender and curved, stigma thick, bilobed. Fruit a loculicidal capsule, setose. Seeds with a fleshy red testa; funicle thick; endosperm scanty, starchy; cotyledons large, curved at apex.

This is a unigeneric family with only 4 species indigenous to tropical America. *Bixa orellana* Linn. —the Annatto (Beng. Latkan) is cultivated in almost all tropical countries as an ornamental plant and for the dye obtained from the seed-coat. The dye is used in colouring clothes, cheese, butter and sweet meats.

The family is allied to *Cochlospermaceae*, *Cistaceae*, *Flacourtiaceae* and also to *Violaceae* to some extent. Both Takhtajan and Cronquist include the family in **Violales** while Hutchinson placed it in **Bixales** stating that this order originated directly from **Dilleniales.**

Violaceae

Annual or perennial herbs, rarely erect shrubs or climbers, very rarely trees. Leaves simple alternate or opposite, stipulate, often basal and variously lobed and laciniate; stipules often large and foliaceous. Inflorescence an axillary spike or raceme or panicle, or flowers solitary; bracts and bracteoles present. Flowers pentamerous, actinomorphic or zygomorphic. Sepals 5, free of slightly connate, imbricate, persistent; the posterior often caducous. Petals 5, free or slightly connate below, equal or unequal, in the latter case the anteior petal is much larger and spurred or gibbous. Stamens 5, connivent in a ring round the ovary; filaments often broad and thin, sometimes connate in a tube, very rarely diadelphous; the connectives of the outer pair of stamens often spurred or appendaged. Ovary superior, of 2-5, usually 3 carpels, syncarpous, unilocular; ovules 3-∞ on parietal placentas, anatropous with 2 integuments and ventral raphe; style terminal , simple or in zygomorphic flowers sygmoid or thickened upwards; stigma variable. Fruit a capsule splitting into 3 boat-shaped valves, rarely berry. Seeds with hard and shining testa, often with an elaiosome in the form of an appendage of the raphe; endosperm copious, fleshy; embryo straight.

Anchietia and *Agatea* are climbers, *Rinorea* and *Paypayrola* are trees and *Hymenanthera* are erect shrubs. Some species of *Viola* are rhizomatus and a few are stoloniferous. *Alsodeia*, *Rinorea*,etc. have actinomorphic flowers. In *Paypayrola* corolla is gamopetalous. Androecium in *Agatea* and *Leonia* is monadelphous and in *Anchietia* it is diadelphous. Fruit is a berry in *Hymenanthera*, *Leonia*, etc.

In the case of irregular flower nectar is stored in the hollow spur of anterior petal and this is secreted by the spurs of the anterior anthers. The showy flowers and the nectar attract the insects which pollinate the flowers. In some species self-pollination is effected by means of cleistogamous flowers which appear later in the season after the normal flowering is over. These are small and apetalous with 2 perfect stamens and 3 staminodes.

Floral formula: $\oplus$ ⚥ K_5 C_5 A_5 $G_{(\underline{3})}$
or † ⚥ K_5 C_5 A_5 $G_{(\underline{3})}$

Calcium oxalate crystals are often present in leaf-mesophyll. Stone cells are present in the mechanical tissue in most genera and groups of schlerenchyma fibres form a closed pericyclic ring together with stone cells. The vessels are irregularly distributed. Those in the triba **Violeae** have simple and repand scalariform perforations on transverse walls while in the triba **Rinoreae** there are many scalariform perforations. The fibres are septate with simple and bordered pits.

The family consists of about 1000 species under 18 genera distributed in the tropical and temperate parts of the world, a few occurring in the artic region. The largest genus *Viola* with 500 species is widely distributed, only 15 of which occur in India in the hills. *Hybanthus enneaspermus* Fragm. a small perennial herb is common in the plains.

Many species of *Viola* are cultivated for the showy flowers. *V. tricolor* Linn. is the Pansy, many hybrids of the same are met with. *V. odorata* Linn. is sweet scented and yields an essential oil. A few species of S. American *Hybanthus* are good substitutes of Ipecacuanha plant. Roots of *Anchietia salutaris* are emetic and are used to treat sore throat and lymphatic tuberculosis.

The family appears to be closely related to *Flacourtiaceae*. Hutchinson places the family in an order of its own, viz., **Violales** which is next to his **Tamaricales.** The **Violales** of Takhtajan includes *Flacourtiaceae* and *Bixaceae* as well as *Stachyuraceae*, *Cochlospermaceae* and *Cistaceae* tracing their affinity with *Violaceae*. Affinity of **Violaceae** with *Flacourtiaceae* is also recognised by Cronquist who includes so many other families in his **Violales** besides *Violaceae* and *Flacourtiaceae*. *Violaceae* appears to be related also to *Resedaceae*.

The family is divided into 2 subfamilies as given below:

Subf. I **Violoideae:** Stamens free or slightly united, anthers introrse.

Tribe 1. Rinoreae Flowers regular, sepals free, fruit usually a capsule—*Rinorea*, *Gloeospermums*, *etc*.

Tribe 2. **Hymenantheriae:** Sepals united at base, fruit a berry—*Hymenanthera*, etc.

Tribe 3. **Violeae:** Flowers zygomorphic, posterior petal largest and spurred, posterior pair of stamens larger and appendaged—*Viola*, *Hybanthus*, etc.

Subf. II **Leonioideae:** Stamens monadelphous, anthers sunk in the staminal tube—*Leonia*.

Flacourtiaceae

Trees and shrubs often with spiny branches; rarely climbing. Leaves simple, leathery, alternate, usually distichous, rarely opposite or whorled, stipulate or not. Inflorescence axillary or terminal, racemose or cymose, or of a mixed type, rarely corymbose; rarely flowers solitary. Flowers bisexual, sometimes polygamous or unisexual and monoecious or dioecious, regular, 4-5-merous or with several members in each whorl, cyclic or sometimes partly spiral; peduncle often jointed near base; axis convex with a disc or a ring of glands or scales between corolla and androecium. Sepals 4-15, persistent, free or united, imbricate or valvate. Petals as many as or twice as many as sepals or more, free, imbricate, or petals absent. Stamens many, in one or more whorls, free or polyadelphous, the bundles being antipetalous; filaments long, very rarely petaloid; connective of anthers sometimes appendaged, usually opening by lateral slits; very rarely stamens as many as and alternate to sepals. Ovary of 2-10 carpels, unilocular or rarely multilocular, superior or semi-inferior or rarely inferior; ovules anatropous, many or few on parietal placentas which often project inside and sometimes meeting in centre to form multilocular ovary; styles as many as carpels, free or united, or stigma sessile. Fruit a berry or capsule. Seeds often arillate, with copious endosperm and straight embryo.

The 2 genera *Streptothamnus* and *Dioncophyllum* are climbers while all others are shrubs or trees. The stipules when present are caducous except in *Phyllobotrium* where they are large and persistent. *Bembicia* has a dense corymbose inflorescence with an involucre of scaly bracts. The inflorescence is epiphyllous in *Phyllobotrium.* Monoecious and dioecious plants occur in many genera, e.g., *Flacourtia*, *Xylosma*, *Trichostephanus*, *Pangium*, *Hydnocarpus*, etc., while many genera have hermaphrodite flowers. In *Abatia*, *Flacourtia*, *Trichostephanus*, *Casearia*, *Samyda*, etc., the flowers are apetalous and in the last genus the sepals are petaloid. In *Paropsia* the disc is more or less tubular and like a gynophore, and often a corona is present. In *Paropsiopsis* and *Soyauxia* androphore is also present. *Bembicia* has true epigynous flowers and calyx tubular with stamens on the mouth of calyx-tube.

Calcium oxalate crystals are found in the epidermal cells of many genera. Resin containing cells are found only in *Casearia resinifera.* The pericycle is usually composed of strands of fibres while isolated fibres are present in many genera. Fibres are septate with simple pits. The vessels are solitary or in rows of 2-3 cells radially arranged; perforations simple, rarely scalariform; intervascular pitting also scalariform.

Floral formula $\oplus$ ⚥ K_{4-15} $C_{4-15 \text{ or } 0}$ A_{∞} $G_{(\underline{2-10})}$ for a typical bisexual flower.

Flacourtiaceae contains over 1200 species under 95 genera, distributed in the tropical and subtropical parts of the globe. In India it is represented by several species in the plains, e.g., *Gynocardia odorata* R.Br., *Xylosma longifolium* Clos., *Casearia tomentosa* Roxb., several species of *Flacourtia* and several species of *Hydnocarpus*.

The family is important economically for a few useful plants. Oil obtained from the seeds of different species of *Hydnocarpus* and *Gynocardia* are efficacious in treating skin diseases. The chalmoogra oil obtained from *Gynocordia* is useful in leprosy. *Dovyalis caffra* Warb. produces edible frūits called Key-apples. Berries of different species of *Flacourtia* are also edible. Species of *Pangium* which have fragrant flowers are poisonous. Fruits of *Casearia tomentosa* Roxb. are also poisonous and are used to stupefy fish before catching. *C. praecox* Griseb is the Box-wood that yields valuable timber. The juice of the fruit of *Hydnocarpus venenatus* is strongly intoxicating. *Oncoba* has large flowers and edible berries.

Flacourtiacea is closely related to *Bixaceae.* Many genera of *Flacourtiacea* were formerly iucluded in *Bixaceae.* These genera together with those under *Samydaceae* were brought under a new family *Flacourtiaceae* established by Gilg who placed it among other families of **Parietales.** Hutchinson and Takhtajan place *Flacourtiaceae* in **Bixales** while Cronquist included it in his **Violales** where he puts *Bixaceae* also and many other families. *Flacourtiaceae* appears to be close also to *Tiliaceae* and *Elaeocarpaceae* and to *Euphorbiaceae* to some extent.

Gilg classified the family Flacourtiaceae into 12 tribes as noted below:—

1. Erythrospermae: Fls. ⚥; perianth segments usually numerous; stamens 5-8, anthers linear; fruit a capsule.

2. Oncobeae: Fls. ⚥; K_{3-5}, C_{4-12}, imbricate; stamens, numerous, anthers linear; fruit indehiscent or tardily dehiscent.

3. Pangieae: Dioecious; sepals 2-5; petals 5-8, with scales at base; stamens 5-∞; berry or berry like capsule.

4. Paropsieae: Fls. ⚥; disc tubular, gynophore-like; K_5, C_5, often with corona; stamens many or few, sometimes united, perigynous or at base of gynophore.

5. Abatieae: Fls. ⚥; K_4, valvate, C_0, stamens 8 or many; perigynous; leaves opposite.

6. Trichostephaneae: Monoecious or dioecious; K_{2+2}, C_0, stamens 15-20, united, with adnate corona of 15-20 pubescent staminodes; styles 4.

7. Scolopieae: Fls ⚥; sepals 4-6, valvate; petals small or absent; stamens many, perigynous, anthers short; ovary uni- or multilocular.

8. Homalieae: Fls. ⚥, peri- or epigynous; sepals 4-5; petals 4-5; stamens 4-15 or ∝ in antipetalous bundles; peri- or epigynous; leaves spiral rarely in pairs.

9. Phyllobotryeae: Fls. ⚥ or polygamous; sepals 3-5; petals 3-5; stamens 5-∝, hypogynous; leaves alternate with epiphyllous inflorescence.

10. Flacourtieae: Dioecious; sepals 4-6, imbricate; petals usually absent; stamens ∞, with short anthers; berry or capsule.

11. Casearieae: Fls. ⚥; sepals 4-5, imbricate; petals absent; stamens ∝ or few, staminodes often present; perigynous.

12. Bembicieae: Fls. ⚥; condensed bracteate inflorescence; sepals 7-8, tubular; petals absent; disc annular; stamens ∝ on mouth of calyx tube, filaments filiform; ovary trigonal.

Passifloraceae

Climbing plants, herbaceous or shrubby, often lianous, climbing by axillary tendrils. Leaves alternate, simple or compound, palminerved or pinninerved, palmilobed or entire, stipulate; petiole often glandular. Flowers axillary, solitary or in pairs, with persistent bracts, regular and bisexual or rarely unisexual; receptacle very prominent cupular or tubular or saucer-shaped. Sepals usually 5, free or connate at base, often petaloid or fleshy, imbricate, membranous at the margin. Petals as many as sepals, free or slightly connate at base, imbricate, often smaller than sepals, rarely absent. A fleshy concave or cup-shaped corona is usually present between the perianth and androecium. Stamens as many as petals and opposite to them, or more, arising from the base of the corona or rim of the receptacle or from the apex of the gynophore (thus forming an androgynophore), free or basally connate; anthers 2-celled dehiscing longitudianlly; staminodes rarely present. Carpels 3-5, syncarpous; ovary superior, raised on a gynophore or androgynophore, unilocular; ovules anatropous, numerous on parietal placentas which are usually intruding; styles as many as carpels with capitate or discoid stigmas, or styles united or rarely absent. Fruit a berry or loculicidal capsule. Seeds with fleshy endosperm and straight embryo, rarely with mucilagenous and pulpy aril.

The tendril is a metamorphosed branch or it is part of the axis of inflorescence; it corresponds to the terminal flower of a dichasium or the first flower of a monochasium. Tendrils are absent in few genera, e.g. *Tryphostemma*, *Machadoa*, *Adenia*, etc. *Adenia keramanthus* is erect while in a few other species of the same genus tendrils are replaced by thorns. *Adenia globosa* is another tendril-less species which is xerophitic and has a globular erect fleshy stem and small leaves.

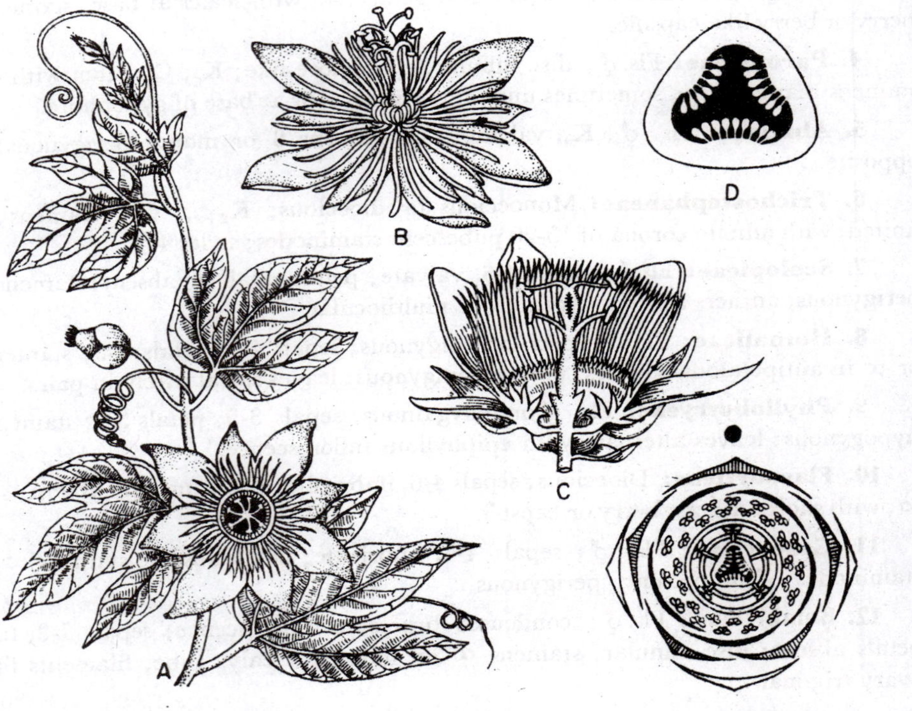

Fig. 114. Passiflora caerulea Linn.—A. Flowering and leafy branch (×½); B. Side view of a flower showing corona and andro-gynophore; C. Flower in vertical section; D. T.s. of ovary.

The corona is interpreted to comprise the hypanthium and all accessory structures situated between the perianth and stamens. The hypanthium is of appendicular origin and not expansion or concavity of the receptacle or torus. The whorls of sterile structures within the petals are called the *radii*, the shorter whorls within the radii are the *pali*, inside the pali there is usually a delicate membrane which is the *operculum*. The operculum usually closes the nectary-chamber from outside. The 3 parts of the corona, radii, pali and operculum represent extra developments of the perianth parts and no part of the androecium. The annulus within the operculum is the nectariferous region. At the base of the androgynophore or inside the hypanthium there is a narrow rim or cup which is often lobed. This is called *limen* and is probably staminodial in nature.

In some genera there is a prominent swelling of the node above the limen. This is called *trochlea*.

The family consists of about 600 species under 11 genera mostly confined to tropical America while a few are found in Africa, Asia and Newzealand. In India several species of *Passiflora* originally of Tropical America have established themselves and are growing wild, e.g. *P. suberosa* Linn., *P. foetida* Linn. etc. *Modeca triloba* Roxb. is indigenous to eastern India. *Passiflora caerulea* Linn. is cultivated in the gardens for the beautiful flowers while *P. edulis* Sims. is cultivated in the hills at lower elevations for the edible fruits.

P. ligularis is another species of which the fruits are edible. A few have showy flowers, viz. *P. racemosa* Brot., *P. incarnata* Linn., *P. holosericea* Linn., *P. caerulea* Linn., etc. and are cultivated in the gardens. Otherwise the family is not of much economic importance.

Passifloraceae is closely related to *Caricaceae* and *Turneraceae*. According to Hutchinson the family *Passifloraceae* is closer to *Malesherbiaceae* and *Achariaceae* than to any other families of **Parietales** of Engler and he places these 3 families in a distinct order **Passiflorales.** Takhtajan also recognises the close relationship of *Malesherbiaceae* and *Achariaceae* with *Passifloraceae* as also of *Caricaceae* and *Turneraceae* and includes these five families in his **Passiflorales.** Cronquist places *Passifloraceae* in **Violales** where several other families, *Caricaceae*. *Turneraceae*, *Malesherbiaceae* and *Achariaceae* are also included.

Caricaceae

Soft wooded trees with milky sap; trunk rarely branched with foliage in a terminal crown, having the appearance of a palm tree. Leaves large, alternate and crowded near the apex of the stem, long petioled and palmately lobed, exstipulate; petiole usually fistular. Panicles or corymbs axillary, or flowers clustered. Flowers hermaphrodite or unisexual, polymorphous. Calyx gamosepalous, very small, 5-lobed. Corolla gamopetalous and tubular in the male flowers and free or connate near base in female flowers, segments or lobes 5, twisted or valvate. Stamens usually 10 in 2 whorls, the inner often absent; the anthers usually sessile, 2-celled, dehiscing longitudinally, inserted on the throat of the corolla tube or the filaments attached near the base of the ovary; connectives often produced upwards. Carpels 5, syncarpous in a superior unilocular ovary; ovules ∞, anatropous, on parietal placentas which some times intrude inside; styles 5, short, with broadly cuneate or fan-shaped simple or five-partite or fimbriate stigmas. Fruit a large globose or pyriform or cylindric berry with a large cavity inside and many small seeds. The seed has 2 coats, an outer fleshy one known as *sarcotesta* or false aril and the inner hard one the *sclerotesta* which is tubercled or echinate with straight or hooked spines; embryo straight and endosperm fleshy.

The trees are short, rarely reaching a height of 10 mtr.; the trunk is rough with leaf scars. *Mocinna heterophylla* Cervo is a climbing shrub. *Carica lanceolata* Hiern. has simple entire leaf. In *Cylicomorpha* and *Jacaratia* the stem is spiny. The flowers are polymorphous and 4 different types of flowers are found: (1) male plants having only staminate flowers in clusters on pendant racemes, stamens 10 in 2 series with sessile anthers, rudimentary ovary usually present; (2) female plants with subsessile pistillate flowers which are solitary or in few-flowered corymbs in axils of leaves, ovary large, globose with 5 sessile fimbriate stigmas, fruits globose or pyriform or ovoid; (3) similar to (2) but with a long many flowered panicle with several 5-6-flowered corymbs, flowers usually bisexual, stamens 10 with sessile anthers, situated at base of petals, fruit long, cylindric; (4) flowers are polygamous, some male flowers have 10 stamens with sessile anthers at the throat of an elongated corolla tube, others with only 5 long-filamented stamens attached near the base of the ovary. Such flowers with variable morphology are mét with in same species, e.g. *Carica papaya* Linn. In *Carica quercifolia* Solms. the ovary is 5-celled. The female flower of ***C. pentagyna*** Heilb. has a much longer corolla-tube than the male.

Branched and articulated latex tubes occur in the tissues in most part of the plant. The cortex is composed of collenchymatous cells with isolated strands of fibres. Xylem vessels are large and have simple perforations. Pith rays are parenchymatous and separate the vascular bundles.

Caricaceae is a small family of 4 genera and 55 species occurring in tropical America and Africa. It is represented in India only by the cultivated species *Carica papaya* Linn.

The family was formerly included in *Passifloraceae* but later treated as a distinct family allied to *Passifloraceae*. Hutchinson places *Caricaceae* in **Cucurbitales** which order however is close to **Passiflorales** according to him. Cronquist includes it in his **Violales** where in with several other families *Passifloraceae* and *Cucurbitaceae* are also iucluded.

The well known fruit tree *Carica papaya* Linn. belongs to this family. It is much cultivated in India and other tropical countries for the delicious fruit as well as for the alkaloid papain obtained from the latex. *C. cundinamarensis* Hook. f. is another species producing edible fruits. No other species is of any economic importance.

Begoniaceae

Succulent herbs or low shrubs, erect or creeping, sometimes accaulescent and often rhizomatous or tuberous; stem more or less jointed. Leaves alternate, usually 2-ranked, simple, palminerved and often palmilobed, stipulate, asymmetrical, petiolate; stipules caducous or early deciduous. Cymes axillary, dichotomous. Flowers unisexual, zygomorphic or actinomorphic, epigynous. Male flower with 2 petaloid valvate sepals and 2 valvate petals smaller than sepals, rarely sepals and petals more than 2, usually free or rarely connate; stamens ∞, in more than one whorl, free or the filaments connate at base; anthers bilocular, variously shaped, basifixed, dehiscing logitudinally or by pores, connective often produced. Female flower with 2-8 perianth segments in one series, all petaloid, imbricate or rarely valvate, free; ovary inferior, of 3-5-carpels, syncarpous, 3-locular, with 3 wings, ovules ∞, on simple or lobed usually axillary placentas, anatropous; styles distinct or basically connate, the stigmas strongly papillose and often twisted. Fruit a loculicidal winged capsule, rarely a berry. Seeds with straight oily embryo and without endosperm.

Calcium oxalate and calcium carbonate crystals are common in the tissues of the leaves. *Begonia socotrana* Hook. has orbicular peltate leaves. Sepals and petals are united in *Begoniella* and also in the female flower of *Symbegonia*. The female flowers of *Begonia* have bracts and bracteoles. In *Hillebrandia* sepals and petals are 5 each, the ovary perigynous and unilocular with 5 parietal placentas.

Extra cauline vascular bundles occur outside the normal ring of bundles. These unite with the vascular ring at the nodes. Vessels are of medium sized and perforations are simple or scalariform at the end walls.

The family consists of 5 genera and 920 species about 900 of which belong to the genus *Begonia* which is distributed in the temperate and tropical regions of the world. *Hillebrandia* is a monotypic genus of Hawaii while *Symbegonia* is another monotypic genus occurring in New Guinea. In India the family is represented by over 50 species of *Begonia*. The plants of this family prefer a damp warm situation.

The family is not economically important except that a few species of *Begonia* are cultivated in the gardens for the beautiful flowers, e.g. *B. rex* Putz., *B. tuberhybrida* Voss, *B. semperflorens* Link & Otto, etc. They are of further horticultural interest for the fact that new plants can be raised easily by leaf cuttings.

The family is allied to *Datiscaceae*. It is also related to *Cucurbitaceae* according to Rendle, Hutchinson, Cronquist and others although according to Engler *Cucurbitaceae* is far removed from the families included in his **Parietales.**

OPUNTIALES

This is a monotypic order placed between **Parietales** and **Myrtiflorae** by Engler The only family included in this order is *Cactaceae*. **Opuntiales** (or **Cactales**) as a distinct monotypic order is maintained by Rendle, Hutchinson, Gunderson and others while Takhtajan and Cronquist place *Cactaceae* in **Caryophyllales** and Wettstein includes it in **Centrospermae** (i.e. **Caryophyllales**). Such treatment is supported by Maheshwari and Erdtman.

Cactaceae

Strongly xerophytic herbs or shrubs, rarely trees; roots elongated, slender, fleshy, occasionally tuberosus, often a well-developed tap-root occurs; stem fleshy, usually modified into phylloclades of various shapes, flat or cylindric, angular, ribbed, often globose, provided with spines or thorns, rarely bearing normal leaves. Flowers solitary or in clusters, rarely paniculate or spikate, usually sessile, hermaphrodite, actinomorphic or zygomorphic, epigynous, on or near the areoles or on the axils of tubercles, often clothed with stiff hairs or spinous structures. The receptacle is a cup-shaped structure on which numerous perianth segments are spirally arranged; the receptacle with bases of perianth segments forms the hypanthium; the perianth segments gradually change from sepals to petals, often spinous at the tips. Stamens numerous, spirally arranged on the inner face of the hypanthium; filaments free, slender, sometimes much exserted, often united to form a column or flat; anthers 2-celled, basi- or dorsifixed, dehiscing longitudinally; pollens minute, globular with finely warted exine. Carpels 2-∞, syncarpous, forming a unilocular inferior ovary; ovules numerous, campylotropous or anatropous, with long funicles, on parietal placentas; style simple, rarely branched, stigma capitate, rarely lobed. Fruit a berry, spiny or bristly or glochidiate, often dry. Seeds numerous, often finely pitted or with smooth testa, rarely winged and with corky aril; endosperm scanty or absent.

The spines are regarded as modified leaves of an axillary branch which is represented by a small tuburcle. The tubercle with the group of spines is termed as the areole. The areoles are often furnished with glochidia or barbed bristles. The areoles are arranged in a definite phyllotaxy. In globose or cylindric species the areoles at regular intervals form the ribs by the confluence of the leaf bases in a vertical row. Broad flat succulent leaves occur in *Pereskia* and *Pereskiopsis*. Fleshy leaves appear also in *Opuntia* which soon fall off. *Carnegiea gigantea* is the tree cactus of Mexico attaining a height of 17-18 mtr. *Pereskia*, *Pereskiopsis* and *Quiabentia* are shrubs or small trees. *Epiphyllum* has unarmed flat leaf-like phylloclades that form a jointed ribon-like stem. *Cereus* is epiphytic and *C. giganteus* attains a great length.

The cell-sap is usually mucilaginous. The internal tissues are mostly parenchymatous where water is stored. Epidermis is thick and heavily cuticularised. Mechanical tissue is present on the ridges and the stomatas are situated on the furrows. Vessles are small, solitary or in multiples, with simple perforations; intravascular pitting alternate or opposite. Fibres are septate with simple pits. Wood parenchyma is paratracheal. Vessels are lacking in some genera due to secondary reduction; here the vessels are replaced by vascular tracheids.

Engler placed *Cactaceae* in the monotypic order **Opuntiales** and considered this order to have been derived from **Parietales.** From serological evidence as well as from floral morphology Mez considered that *Cactaceae* was allied to *Loasaceae* and expressed his opinion that *Cactaceae* should be included in Parietales. Bessey and Hutchinson considered that *Cactaceae* was allied to *Cucurbitaceae* while Wettstein, Hallier, Buxbaum, Maheshwari and Martin suggested on the evidence of embryology, floral morphology and anatomy that *Cactaceae* was allied to the families included in **Centrospermae** (or **Caryophyllales**). Takhtajan and Cronquist also hold the same view. Buxbaum also states that *Cactaceae* has been derived from *Phytolaccaceae* parallelly evolving with *Aizoaceae*.

Britton and Rose divided the family into 3 tribes as:

1. **Pereskieae:** Leaves broad, flat; trees or shrubs with terete stem; glochidia absent; flowers pedicelled, usually clustered.

2. **Opuntieae:** Succulent herbs with jointed flat or columnar stem; leaves small falling off very soon or modified into spines; glochidia present; flowers sessile, rotate.

3. **Cacteae** (or **Cerecae**): Succulents, often epiphytic climbers; leaves rudimentary; glochidia absent; flowers sessile, funnel-shaped or salver-shaped.

The family comprises about 2000 species under 50 genera (or much more genera according to some) occurring in the tropical countries of N. and S. America. *Rhipsalis* grows wild in Africa and Ceylon but is considered to have migrated from Trop. America in the remote past. In India a few species of *Opuntia* have been naturalised and grow wild in the plains, e.g. *O. dillenii* Haw (=*O. elatior* Mill) and *O. vulgaris* Mill. *Cereus hexagonus* (Linn.) Mill is also met with in gardens and also as an escape in villages.

The plants of this family are cultivated for the large showy flowers and for the peculiar shape of the plants. Fruits of different species of *Opuntia*, especially of *O. ficus-indica* Mill. are sweet and edible. This species is cultivated in southern part of Europe as a fruit tree. In drier areas *Opuntia*-plants are used as cattle-fodder. The cochineal insects that yield a red dye are reared on different cactii-plants, viz. *Nopalea coccinellifera* Solm-Dyke, and *Opuntia tuna* Mill. *Anhalonium* species are highly poisonous containing saponine and other alkaloids. *Cereus grandiflorus* Mill. and some species of *Opuntia* have medicinal properties. Species of *Lophophora* are used for prepaıing an intoxicating drink by the American Inidians on religious festivals.

MYRTIFLORAE

The 32nd order **Myrtiflorae** consists of 23 families distributed **under 4 sub-orders** as given below:

Thymelaeineae—Geissolomataceae, Penaceaceae, Oliniaceae, **Thymelaeaceae**, Elaeagnaceae.

Myrtineae—Lythraceae, Heteropyxidaceae, Sonneratiaceae, **Crypteroniaceae**, Punicaceae, Lecythidaceae, Rhizophoraceae, Nyssaceae, **Alangiaceae**, Combretaceae, Myrtaceae, Melastomaceae, **Hydrocaryaceae**, Onagraceae, Haloragidaceae.

Hippuridineae—Hippuridaceae, Thelygonaceae.

Cynomorineae—Cynomoreaceae.

Characters common to these families are: leaves opposite, simple, **exstipulate**; flowers actinomorphic, hermaphrodite, tetra- or pentamerous; androecium diplostemonous or obdiplostemonous; ovary syncarpous, peri- or epigynous, uni- or multilocular; ovules numerous on axile placentas; seeds without endosperm.

In the treatment of the above families later workers did not follow **Engler**. *Cynomoreaceae* is placed in **Santalales** by almost all subsequent workers. Closer affinity of *Nyssaceae* and *Alangiaceae* with *Cornaceae* is recognised and these families are removed from **Myrtiflorae** and placed in another order with *Umbelliferae* (*Apiaceae*). Hutchinson in his revised system placed *Umbelliferae* in a monotypic order **Umbellales** while *Cornaceae*, *Nyssaceae* and *Alangiaceae* together with *Garryaceae*, *Araliaceae* and *Caprifoliaceae* formed his **Araliales**. *Heteropyxidaceae* is merged with *Myrtaceae* by most authors while Hutchinson keeps this as a distinct family under **Rhamnales** together with *Elaeagnaceae* which again is placed under **Proteales** by Cronquist and **Elaeagnales** by Takhtajan. In the system of Takhtajan **Elaeagnales** and **Proteales**, both monotypic orders, are placed one after another thus recognising the affinity between the 2 families. *Lecythidaceae* is removed from **Myrtales** by Cronquist and placed in an order of its own, e.g. **Lecythidales** but others support Engler by keeping this family in **Myrtales**. *Thymelaeaceae* is left in **Myrtales** by Cronquist but is removed to **Thymeleales** by Hutchinson and Takhtajan. **Thymeleales** of Takhtajan is a monotypic order while Hutchinson has six families in that order viz. *Gonystylaceae*, *Aquilariaceae*, *Geissolomataceae*, *Penaeaceae*, *Thymelaeaceae* and *Nyctaginaceae*. *Rhizophoraceae* is placed in **Cornales** by Cronquist but others keep it in **Myrtales** as was done by Engler. *Lythraceae* is removed to **Lythrales** by Hutchinson who places *Onagraceae*, *Trapaceae*, *Haloragidaceae* and *Callitrichaceae* also in that order. As to the inclusion of the following five families, viz. *Myrtaceae*, *Sonneretiaceae*, *Punicaceae*, *Combretaceae* and *Melastomaceae* in **Myrtales** there is no difference of opinion among most authors.

Lythraceae

Herbs, shrubs or trees, often with square stem. Leaves simple, opposite or whorled, entire, exstipulate or with minute stipules. Inflorescence paniculate, racemose or cymose, or flowers solitary, axillary or terminal. Flowers bisexual, actinomorphic or rarely zygomorphic, perigynous, subtended by a pair of bracteoles, large and showy or minute; receptacle cup-shaped. Sepals 4, 6 or 8, rarely more, on the margin of the receptacle, free or united, valvate. Petals as many as sepals, free, usually crumpled, inserted on the margin of the receptacular cup and alternating with the sepals, usually clawed.

Stamens twice as many as petals in 2 whorls, inserted on the receptacular cup lower down, sometimes inner whorl absent, or stamens many with centripetal development, rarely stamen solitary; filaments unequal, bent in bud; anthers bilocular, introrse, dehiscing longitudinally. Carpels 2-6; united to form a semi-inferior or superior, 2-6-chambered ovary; ovules usually many in each chamber, anatropous, ascending on axile placentas; style simple with capitate stigma; rarely ovary unilocular and the placentation is parietal. Fruit a capsule. Seed with a straight embryo and without endosperm.

Plants vary in habit from tiny little herbs like *Ammania*, *Rotala*, etc. to tall timber trees, e.g. *Lagerstroemia speciosa* (L.) Pers., *L. parviflora* Roxb., *L. macrocarpa* Wall., etc. *Hydrolythrum* is a submerged herb while a few *Ammania* and *Rotala* species are also aquatic. *Woodfordia* and *Cuphea* have tubular calyx, in the former the limb of calyx is oblique while in the latter the flower is zygomorphic. *Lythrum salicaria* Linn. has trimorphic flowers where stamens and styles are of different lengths in different flowers. *Lafoensia* has 8-16 segments or lobes in each perianth whorl , while in *Peplis* and some species of *Ammania* flowers are apetalous. Stamen is one in some species of *Rotala*. In *Lagerstroemia* the seeds are winged.

Formula for a typical flower of the family is:

$$\oplus \ ⚥ \ K_{4-8} \ C_{4-8} \ A_{8-16} \ G_{(2-6)}.$$

Vessels are solitary or in multiples of 2-3 cells. Intervascular pitting is alternate. Fibres are with simple pits. Intraxylary phloem is almost always present.

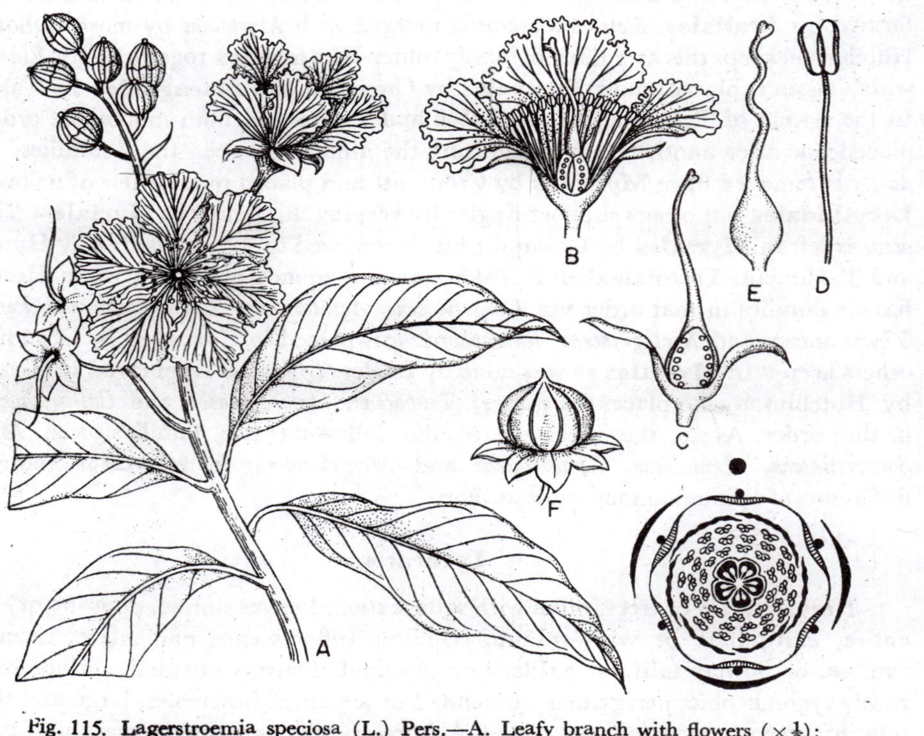

Fig. 115. Lagerstroemia speciosa (L.) Pers.—A. Leafy branch with flowers ($\times\frac{1}{2}$); B. Flower in vertical section; C. L.s. of perigynous ovary on the cup-shaped receptacle; D. Stamen; E. Ovary; F. Fruit ($\times\frac{1}{2}$).

The family comprises about 475 species in 23 genera found in the tropical and subtropical regions with a great majority occurring in tropical America. About 50 species are found in India in the plains while a few ascending to 1500 mtrs. in the hills.

Lagerstroemia speciosa (L.) Pers. yields hard and durable timber suitable for making boats. A few other species of this genus are also good timber trees and most have showy flowers and are planted as avenue trees. *L. indica* Linn. is an arboreous shrub much cultivated in gardens. *Lawsonia inermis* Linn. also a large shrub is cultivated as a hedge plant of which the leaves yield a reddish orange dye known as Mehendi used to stain palms and finger nails by Indian ladies and for dyeing hair or beard by old men. Leaves and barks have medicinal properties also. *Ammania vesicatoria* have leaves which are very acid and are used for raising blisters for relieving pain in rheumatism. The blisters are however too irritating and very painful. The leaves of *Ammania baccifera* Linn. are also used in a similar manner. The leaves and flowers of *Woodfordia fruticosa* (L.) Kurz. are extensively used in tanning and in dyeing silk. *Cuphia platycentra* and *Lythrum salicaria* Linn. are cultivated for their beautiful flowers.

Lythraceae is closely allied to *Onagraceae*, *Melastomaceae* and *Myrtaceae*, and also to *Punicaceae* and *Sonneratiaceae* which families were included in *Lythraceae* in the old system of classification by Bentham and Hooker.

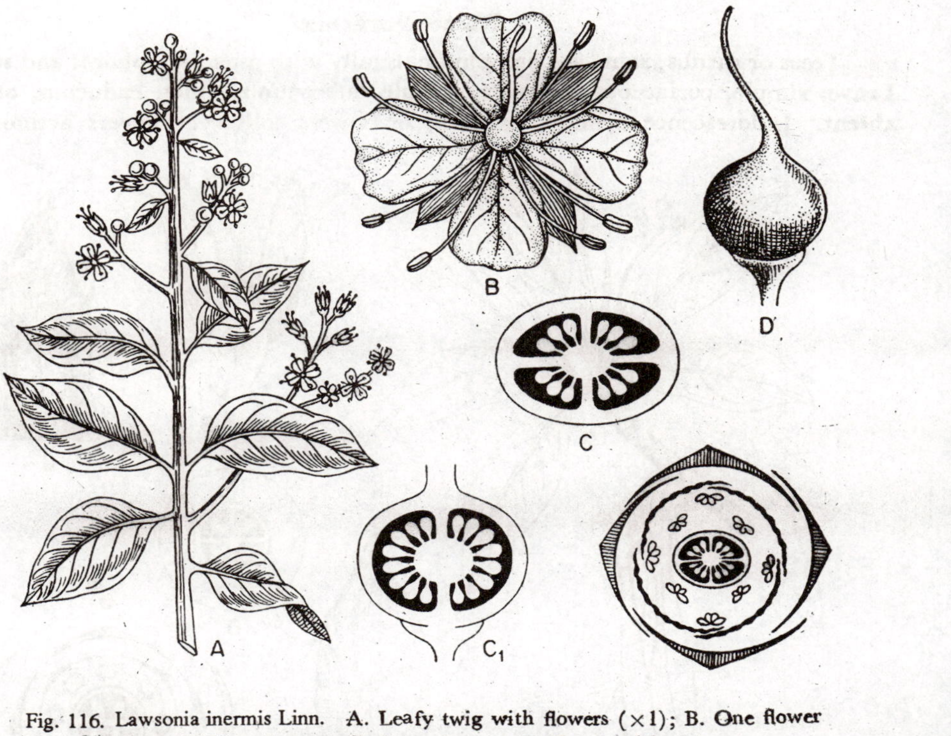

Fig. 116. Lawsonia inermis Linn. A. Leafy twig with flowers (×1); B. One flower (×5); C. T.s. of ovary: C_1 L.s. of ovary; D. Ovary with style.

Punicaceae

Shrubs or small trees, sometimes armed with spines; young branches 4-winged. Leaves simple, opposite or fasciculate, exstipulate. Inflorescence is a terminal few-flowered cyme, or flowers solitary. Flowers regular, hermaphrodite, peri- or epigynous, with a tubular or urceolate hypanthium. Calyx lobes 5-8, fleshy, valvate, persistent. Petals 5-8, imbricate, inserted on the rim of the hypanthium, crumpled in bud. Stamens many in several whorls, inserted on the upper half of the hypanthium, free; anthers 2-celled, dorsifixed, dehiscing longitudinally. Carpels 8-12; ovary syncarpous, inferior or semi-inferior with 8-12 locules in 2 concentric rings at the early stage with axile placentation, gradually in course of development the outer series of 5-9 locules is carried upwards and ultimately superposed over the originally inner series of 3 locules, and the placentas of the upper locules changed to parietal position; the ovules numerous, anatropous; style simple; stigma capitate. Fruit a berry, crowned with persistent calyx lobes. Seeds with a fleshy testa, a straight embryo and without endosperm.

This is a unigeneric family of western Asia with only 2 species of the genus *Punica*, viz. *P. granatum* Linn. and *P. protopunica* Balf. f. The former, the pomegranate plant is much cultivated for the edible fruit in almost all tropical and subtropical countries and has been introduced to tropical America. The edible part of the fruit is the sweet fleshy testa of the seeds.

This is closely related to *Lythraceae* in which it was formerly included. Hutchinson considers it closer to *Myrtaceae* than to *Lythraceae* and keeps *Punicaceae* in **Myrtales** while *Lythraceae* is in his **Lythrales** far removed from **Myrtales**.

Rhizophoraceae

Trees or shrubs; some are halophytic usually with pneumatophores and stilt roots. Leaves simple, coriaceous, opposite; stipule interpetiolar often caducous, or stipules absent. Inflorescence cymose, axillary, or flowers solitary. Flowers actinomorphic,

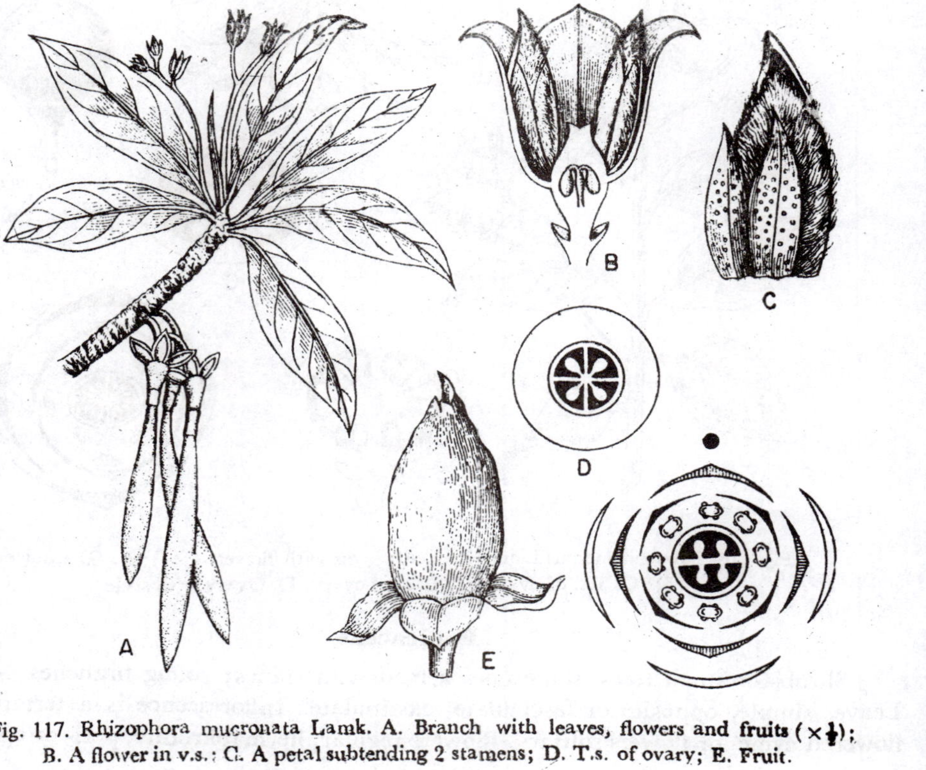

Fig. 117. Rhizophora mucronata Lamk. A. Branch with leaves, flowers and fruits (×½); B. A flower in v.s.; C. A petal subtending 2 stamens; D. T.s. of ovary; E. Fruit.

bisexual or rarely unisexual, perigynous or epigynous; receptacle cup-shaped or pitcher-shaped. Sepals usually 4-8 or sometimes 3-16, valvate, more or less connate at base and adnate to the ovary, leathery and persistent. Petals as many as and smaller than the sepals, free, convolute or inflexed, entire or fringed or flappy. Stamens usually twice as many as petals, each petal embracing a pair of stamens, rarely stamens numerous, situated on the margin of a lobed disc, all in one whorl; filaments short or long; anthers 4-celled, dehiscing longitudinally, introrse, carpels 2-6, syncarpous; ovary 2-6-locular, inferior or semi-inferior, usually with 2 pendulous, anatropous ovules in each cell on axile placentas, rarely ovary unilocular with parietal placentas; micropyle directed outside and upwards; style short, one or more; stigma simple or lobed, usually persistent. Fruit a berry or a capsule, rarely a drupe. Seeds with or without endosperm, rarely arillate; cotyledons 2 or more; embryo straight, small; if endosperm is present—elongated, if endosperm absent cotyledons often contain chlorophyll; usually the germination is viviparous.

Mostly the plants stand on stilt roots, the base of the stem having perished early; the stilt roots are provided with lenticels permitting communication of air through intercellular spaces. In some genera such communication is effected by the pneumatophores. Viviparous germination of the seeds is another characteristic feature of this halophytic family. The hypocotyl grows very long pushing its way through the open wide micropyle and piercing the fruit wall. It reaches a length of 20-30 cm. or more and hangs freely with the fruit which ultimately drops to the soil and the hypocotyl is embedded in the mud and a number of rootlets grows very quickly fixing the seedling rigidly to the soil. *Carallia* and a few other genera growing inland have seeds which are not viviparous.

Floral formula for the family is expressed as: $⚥ K_{(3-16)} C_{3-16} A_{6-\infty} G_{(\overline{2-6})}$.

The flowers of *Anisophyllea* and *Gynotroches* are unisexual. The ovary is superior in *Gynotroches* and *Cassipourea*. *Anisophyllea* has the styles free.

The epidermis of the leaves is thickly cuticularised having one- or more-celled hypodermal layer underneath. Stomata are deep-seated with well developed front cavity. Vessels have simple and scalariform perforations and wood parenchyma is paratracheal. The cortex of the stilt root is spongy due to the presence of a complex type of intercellular spaces. Tannin containing cells are present in almost all parts of plants and often H-shaped and branched idioblasts occur in leaves, roots and younger parts. These also contain tannin and mucilage.

The family contains 17 genera and about 120 species, a few genera growing on the sea-shores and near estuaries forming the mangrove vegetation. In India 9 species are found, 8 in the tidal forests on the coast and one viz. *Carallia brachiata* Merr. in the terai region of N. Bengal, Assam, Bangladesh and west coast of India.

The family is allied to *Myrtaceae* and other families of the order, having inferior ovary and in the structure of ovule. The genus *Cassipourea* is placed by some workers in a different family *Cassipoureaceae*. Similarly *Anisophyllea* is placed by some in *Anisophylleaceae*.

The family contains but a few useful plants. Timber obtained from *Bruguiera gymnorhiza* (Linn.) Lamk. and from *B. sexangula* Poir. is used in house-construction and also as fire-wood. Timber of *Carallia brachiata* Merr. is used in various ways and an edible oil is obtained from the seeds.

Combretaceae

The plants are trees or shrubs, often lianous; armed or not. Leaves simple, alternate or opposite, entire, exstipulate. Inflorescence spicate or racemose or paniculate. Flowers bisexual, rarely unisexual, actinomorphic or zygomorphic, bracteate; the tubular receptacle together with the adnate tubular base of the calyx forming a hypanthium. Calyx with 4-5 or more persistent lobes; lobes valvate. Corolla lobes as many as calyx lobes, small, imbricate or valvate, free, often absent. Stamens 4-5 in one

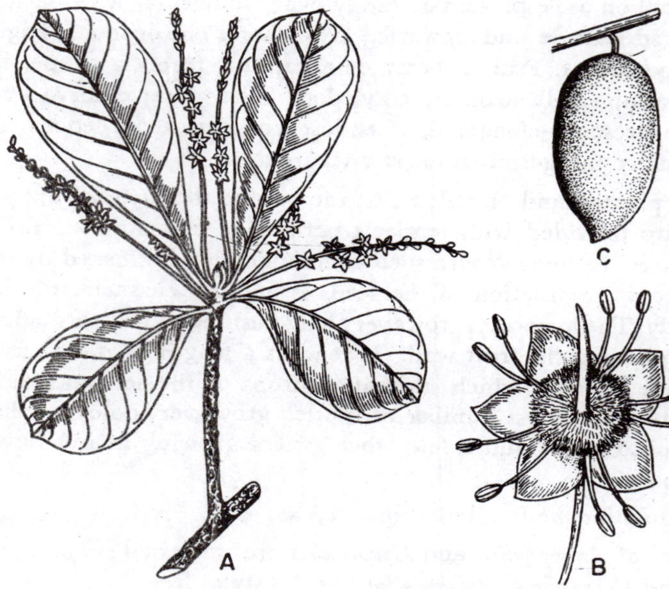

Fig. 118. Terminalia catappa Linn. A. Leafy twig with flowering spikes ($\times\frac{1}{4}$); B. Flower ($\times 10$); C. Fruit ($\times\frac{1}{2}$).

whorl, or double the number and in 2 whorls, inserted on the calyx tube; filaments inflexed in bud; anthers bithecal, versatile. Carpels 4 or 5, or often less, syncarpous; ovary inferior, unilocular, angular or ribbed, the ribs equal in number to calyx lobes; ovules 2-6, anatropous, pendulous from the apex of the ovary chamber by long funicles; micropyle directed upwards and outwards; style slender with a capitate or pointed stigma. Fruit a drupe, 1-seeded, with angled or winged pericarp. Seed without endosperm; embryo with convolute cotyledons or cotyledons often folded, rarely flat.

Floral formula is expressed as: $\oplus$ ⚥ $K_{(4-5)}\ C_{4-5}\ A_{4-5 \text{ or } 8 \text{ or } 10}\ G_{\overline{(4-5)}}$.

The family contains 600 species under 20 genera occurring in the tropical and subtropical countries of the world and a few genera are restricted to the mangrove forests in the sea-shores, e.g. *Lumnitzera*, *Laguncalaria*, *Conocarpus*, etc. which have the characteristic features of the holophyte plants. *Lumnitzera littoria* (Jacq.) Voigt. is found in the Sunderban and other tidal forests of India.

In the vascular bundles of the stem both intraxylary and interxylary phloems are present. Vessels have simple perforations; intervascular pitting is alternate and wood parenchyma is paratracheal. The long fibres have simple pits. Tannin containing cells are found in every parts but more in the pericarp of the fruit.

The family is closely related to *Myrtaceae* and *Rhizophoraceae*, and to the other families of the order to some extent.

Several species of Combretaceae are useful as timber, medicinal plants, source of tannin and as ornamental plants. *Anogeissus latifolia* (Roxb.) Wall., *A. acuminata* (Roxb.) Wall., *Terminalia tomentosa* W. & A. are important timber trees of India. *Terminalia ivorensis* A. Chev. is the Idigbo timber, *T. superba* is the Afara timber and *T. sericea* Burch. is the Asegai of commerce. The bark of *T. Arjuna* W. & A. is highly valued as a cardiac tonic. *T. chebula* Retz. is the chebulic myrobalan and *T. bellirica* Roxb. is the beleric myrobalan. *T. catappa* Linn. a tall tree growing in coastal parts of India and Malaya is often planted as an avenue tree in tropical countries. *Quisqualis indica* Linn.—the Rangoon creeper is a favourite of the Indian gardens. A few species of *Combretum* are also cultivated in the gardens as ornamental plants.

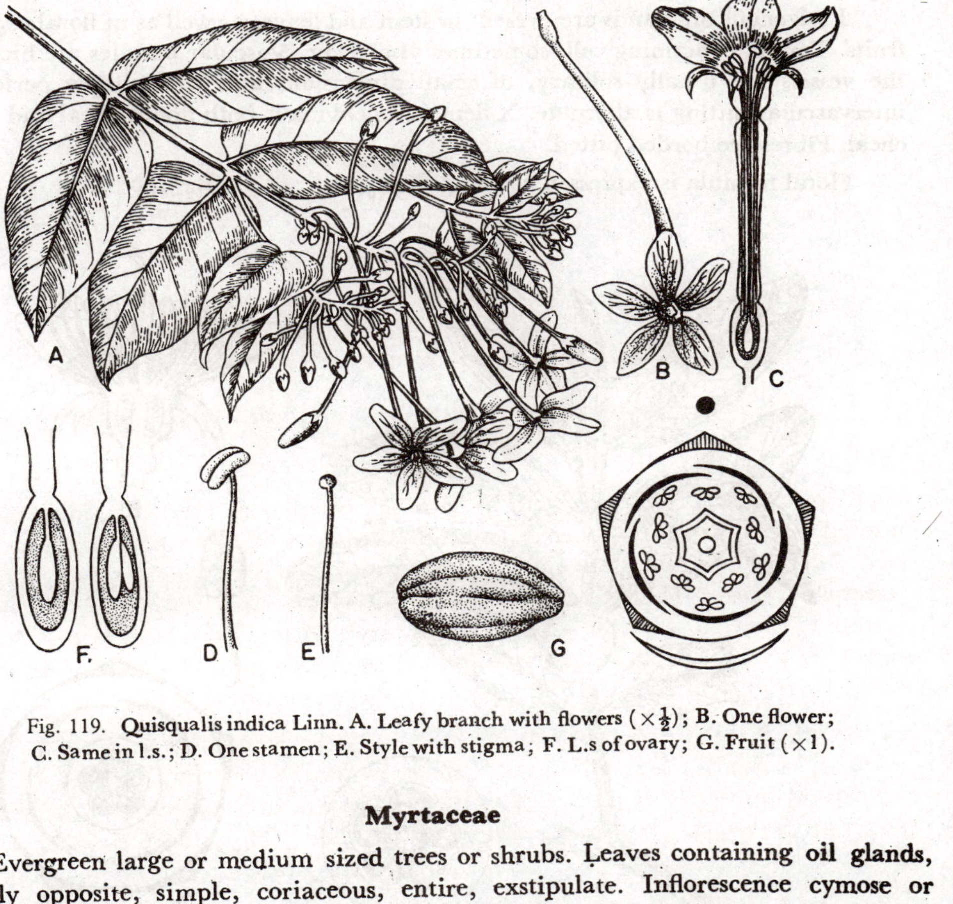

Fig. 119. Quisqualis indica Linn. A. Leafy branch with flowers ($\times\frac{1}{2}$); B. One flower; C. Same in l.s.; D. One stamen; E. Style with stigma; F. L.s of ovary; G. Fruit ($\times 1$).

Myrtaceae

Evergreen large or medium sized trees or shrubs. Leaves containing oil glands, usually opposite, simple, coriaceous, entire, exstipulate. Inflorescence cymose or racemose or paniculate, rarely flowers solitary. Flowers hermaphrodite, regular, usually epigynous, with a pair of bracteoles at base. Sepals 4-5, connate at base and united with the receptacular cup to form a hypanthium, lobes free, quincuncially arranged. Petals

4-5 usually free, imbricate or connate to form an operculum. Stamens numerous, rarely few, free or slightly connate at base, in several whorls on the edge of the hypanthium developed centripetally, sometimes in fascicles opposite to the petals; filament, often coloured; anthers 2-celled, versatile or dorsifixed, introrse, dehiscing longitudinally or sometimes apically, connective often conspicuous and gland-tipped. Carpels 2-5, united to form an inferior or semi-inferior 2-5-locular ovary, often unilocular, rarely many-locular ovary; ovules 2-many in each chamber on axile or rarely parietal placentas, campylotropous or anatropous, obliquely pendulous; the style simple, stigma capitate. Fruit a berry or loculicidal capsule, rarely drupaceous or nut like. Seeds usually few; testa modified into wings or may be horny, leathery or membranous; embryo straight or curved, endosperm absent or scanty.

Myrtus and *Psidium* have solitary flowers. Sepals inconspicuous or absent in *Eucalyptus*. Petals connate in *Eucalyptus* forming an operculum that falls off early and releases the stamens. The anthers are basifixed in *Calothamnus*. Stamens in *Melaleuca* are polyadelphous and in one whorl; the bundles are equal to the number of petals and opposite to them. Nut-like fruit is found in the Australian tribe *Chamaelaucieae*.

Lysigenous oil glands are present in stem and leaves as well as in floral organs and fruits. Tannin containing cells sometimes also occur. Vascular bundles are bicolateral; the vessels are usually solitary, of small dimensions and with simple perforations; intervascular pitting is alternate. Xylem parenchyma is both apotracheal and paratracheal. Fibres are borded pitted.

Floral formula is expressed as: $\oplus$ ⚥ K_{4-5} C_{4-5} A_{∞} $G_{\overline{(2-5)}}$.

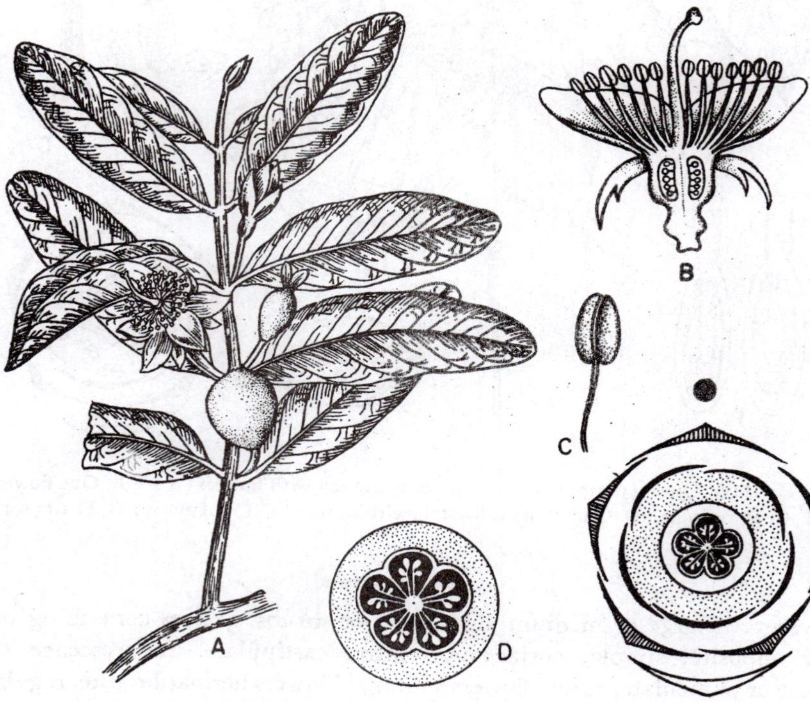

Fig. 120. **Psidium guajava Linn. A. Leafy branch with flower and young fruits (×½); B. A flower in l.s.; C. One stamen; D. T.s. of ovary.**

The family consists of about 3000 species under about 100 genera, with main centres of distribution in Australia and tropical America. The genus *Eucalyptus* with over 300 species is restricted to Australia and adjacent islands in the Pacific and Indian Oceans. The species of this genus are lofty trees some attaining 150 m. in height. The family is represented in India by about 50 species of *Syzygium* which are indigenous and a few species of other genera cultivated as ornamental trees or for their economic importance.

Myrtaceae is allied to *Rhizophoraceae*, *Lythraceae*, *Combretaceae* and *Onagraceae* and to *Sonneratiaceae* and *Melastomaceae* to some extent. The family is divided into 2 subfamilies as given below:

I. **Myrtoideae:** Lvs. usually opposite; flowers epigynous; fruit fleshy, berry or drupe. Trop. America (mainly).

II. **Leptospermoideae:** Lvs. opposite or alternate; flowers epigynous or perigynous; fruit dry, capsule or nut-like. Australia (mainly).

The family includes many useful plants. Many species of *Eucalyptus* yield valuable timber, e.g. *E. crebra* F. Muell., *E. paniculata* Sm., *E. punctata* DC., *E. leucoxylon* F. Muell. etc. Oil of Eucalyptus is distilled from the leaves and younger parts of *E. sideroxylon* A. Cunn., *E. leucoxylon* F. Muell., *E. elaeophora* F. Muell., *E. globulus* Labill., *E. dealbata* A. Cunn. etc. An astringent taniniferous substance called **Kino** is obtained from many species and many are planted in gardens for their grace and beauty. Many species have been introduced into India among which *E. citriodora* Hook is quite common.

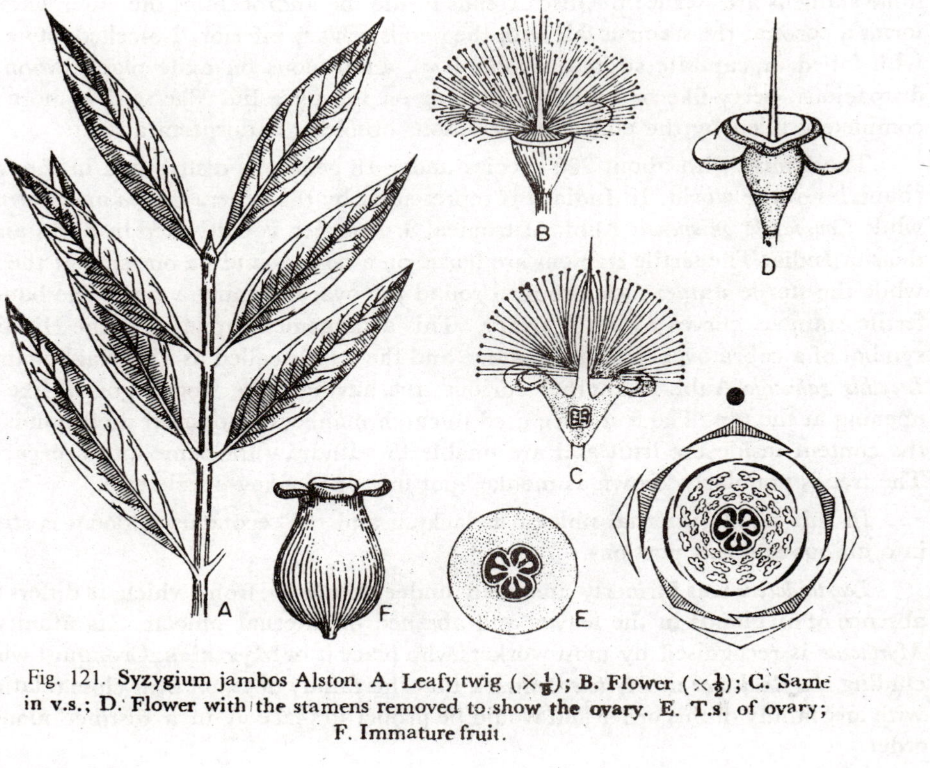

Fig. 121. Syzygium jambos Alston. A. Leafy twig ($\times\frac{1}{8}$); B. Flower ($\times\frac{1}{2}$); C. Same in v.s.; D. Flower with the stamens removed to show the ovary. E. T.s. of ovary; F. Immature fruit.

Many species produce edible fruit, viz. *Psidium guajava* Linn.—the guava, original of Brazil is now cultivated in many tropical countries. *P. cattleianum* Sabine is the Strawberry guava. *Myriciaria cauliflora* Berg. is the Jaboticabo fruit. *Eugenia uniflora* Berg. is the Surinam-cherry. *Feijoa sellowiana* Sabine is the Fekhow fruit. *Syzygium cumini* (L.) Skeels is the Jamoon of India, *S. jambos* (L.) Alston—the Rose apple growing in different parts of India, *S. samarangense* (Bl.) Merr. & Perry, is the Jamrool, indigenous to Malaya and *S. malaccense* (L.) Merr. & Perry, the Malacca Jamrool. *S. aromaticum* (L.) Merr. & Perry is the clove-plant of Zanzibar. *Pimenta dioica* (L.) Merr. is the Allspice and *P. racemosa* (Mill.) Moor is the Bay oil tree, by distilling the leaves of which the oil is obtained. *Melaleuca leucadendron* Linn. yields the Cajuput oil. *Leptospermum scoparium* Forst. is the Tea tree or Manuka. *Callistemon lanceolatus* DC—the Bottle-brush tree of Australia with aromatic leaves is cultivated in many countries as an ornamental plant.

Lecythidaceae

Trees, usually evergreen. Leaves simple, whorled near the tip of the branches, exstipulate. Inflorescence a raceme, spike or small cymose clusters near the end of the branches. Flowers hermaphrodite, regular or zygomorphic due to unequal development of stamens; the axis forms a flat disc to which the petals and stamens are attached. Calyx persistent, of 4-6 or more sepals, united near base, often tubular, rarely the calyx splits irregularly into 2-3 segments, valvate. Petals 4-6 or more, free, imbricate, distinct or adnate at base to the staminal tube. Stamens numerous united in several whorls, often unequally developed resulting in the zygomorphy of the flowers, often some stamens are sterile; the disc extends inside the androecium; the outer whorl often forms a corona; the stamens fall with the petals. Ovary inferior, 2-6-celled; style simple with lobed or capitate stigma; ovules 1-∞, anatropous on axile placentation. Fruit drupacious, berry-like or capsular, opening on top by a lid. The seed is more or less completely filled by the embryo; cotyledons obsolete; endosperm absent.

The family with about 220 species under 18 genera is distributed in the tropical countries of the world. In India it is represented by the genera *Careya* and *Barringtonia* while *Couroupita guianensis* Aubl. of tropical S. America is cultivated in parks and gardens in India. The fertile stamens are borne on a fleshy band on one side of the flower while the sterile stamens are grouped round the ovary forming a ring. The band with fertile stamens curves over the ovary. This arrangement appears to the Hindus as a symbol of a cobra over the lingam-stone and the tree is called as the Naglingam tree. *Lecythis zabucajo* Aubl. is another curious tree having large woody gourd like fruits opening at the top. The fruits are used to catch monkeys who insert their hands to get the content inside the fruit and are unable to withdraw the same and are captured. The tree is popularly known as monkey-pot tree or monkey-puzzle tree.

In this family internal phloem is lacking and the secondary phloem is stratified into fibrous and soft portions.

Lecythidaceae was formerly included under *Myrtaceae* from which it differs in the absence of oil glands in the leaves and absence of internal phloem. Its affinity with *Myrtaceae* is recognised by most workers who place it in **Myrtales.** Cronquist while including *Lecythidaceae* in *Myrtales* remark that this family does not bear close relationship with any family of this order and would be proper to place it in a distinct monotypic order.

Economically the family is not very important. *Barringtonia acutangula* Gaertn.—the Hijal is common in lower Bengal and other parts of India. It yields valuable timber and the bark is used in tanning. The root is supposed to have properties similar to quinine. The fruit is also medicinal. The bark is thrown in water to stupify fish before catching. The timber of *Careya arboria* Roxb. is also used in different ways and the leaves are a food of Tassar-silk-moths. Timber obtained from other trees are also useful. *Gustavia augusta* Linn. and *Couroupita guianensis* Aubl. are often planted as ornamental trees.

Melastomaceae

Herbs shrubs or trees, rarely epiphytes; a few are aquatic and some are root-climbers; the aerial root often swell to form tubers where ants take shelter, an example of myrmecophily. Leaves simple, opposite and decussate or whorled, exstipulate, with multicostate reticulate, convergent venation; the 2 leaves of a pair often unequal, the larger leaf frequently has a sac-like outgrowth having entrance on lower surface; such outgrowths or domatia are found sometimes on the petiole also; the domatia give shelter to ants. Inflorescence cymose or corymbose or paniculate, or the flower solitary or in small clusters. Flowers hermaphrodite, actinomorphic or slightly zygomorphic, peri- or epigynous, 4-5 merous on a bell-shaped receptacle with coloured bracteoles. Sepals 4-5, united to form a tube, adnate to the receptacle, often forming a cap, or free from the receptacle and persistent; often reduced to a mere rim round the floral axis. Petals 4-5, free, generally brightly coloured, twisted or imbricate. Stamens double the number of petals and in 2 whorls, sometimes one whorl reduced to staminodes or suppressed; filaments all equal or alternately long and short, usually geniculate; anthers 2- or 4-celled, rarely unithecal, dehiscing longitudinally or by 1 or 2 apical pores; connectives variously appendaged. Ovary inferior or semi-inferior, carpels and cells usually 4-5, sometimes more or fewer, rarely up to 14 and very rarely only 1; ovules anatropous, usually many on axile or parietal placentas, rarely placentation is free-central; style and stigma simple. Fruit a capsule or a berry; seeds small, straight or curved; embryo small; cotyledons fleshy; endosperm absent.

Pachycentria is epiphytic, the aerial roots of which bear *domatia*. *Memecylon* is a genus of trees where the leaves are unicostate. The leaves of *Mouriria* are also unicostate. *Sonerila*, *Gravesia* and *Bertolona* have variegated or spotted leaves. *Sonerila* has trimerous flowers. *Memecylon* has unilocular ovary and the placentation is free central. In *Osbeckia* the capsule opens apically by pores and the capsule of *Sonerila* opens by apical valves. The seeds of *Osbeckia* and *Melastoma* are curved. The cotyledons in *Memecylon* are convolute.

Floral formula: $\oplus ⚥\ K_{4-5}\ C_{4-5}\ A_{8 \text{ or } 10}\ G_{\overline{(4-5)}}$.

Aerenchyma is formed in the submerged stem and root of aquatic species. Vascular bundles have internal phloem. Concentric cortical and pith bundles also occur. Vessels have simple perforations and alternate intervascular pitting. Wood parenchyma is usually paratracheal or sometimes mixed with apotracheal. Pericycle is not continuous but made up of isolated fibres and sclerotic thickened cells.

Melastomaceae is a large family with about 4000 species under 240 genera. They are distributed in the tropical as well as temperate regions of the globe with a chief centre of distribution in S. America. The family is well represented in India with several species of *Melastoma*, *Osbeckia*, *Oxyspora*, *Memecylon*, *Sonerila*, etc. *Melastoma malabathricum* Linn. has large mauve flowers and occurs in the plains as well as in the hills at low elevations. *Memecylon* has very small flowers in axillary or extra-axillary clusters. Species of *Memecylon* grow in tropical region. *M. edule* Roxb. and *M. capitellatum* Linn. are very common in the plains., *Osbeckia nepalensis* Hook. f., *O. crinita* Benth, *Oxyspora paniculata* Hook. f. are common in the Himalayas and Naga hills at about 2000 m. *Tibouchina semidecandra* Linn. is cultivated in Darjeeling and other hill stations for its large purplish violet flowers.

Melastomaceae is allied to *Myrtaceae* and also to *Lythraceae* to some extent. According to Hutchinson relationship of *Melastomaceae* with *Myrtaceae* is not very clear although he includes *Melastomaceae* in his **Myrtales** and remarks that *Lythraceae* is not at all close to *Melastomaceae*.

Melastomaceae is divided into 3 subfamilies by Krasser, viz.—

I. **Melastomatoideae:** Fruit many seeded capsule, embryo minute, ovules on projecting axile placenta. *Melastoma*, *Osbeckia*, etc.

II. **Astronioideae:** Fruit many seeded capsule, embryo minute, ovules on basal or parietal placenta. *Astronia*, *Kibessia*, etc.

III. **Memecyloideae:** Fruit 1-5 seeded berry, embryo large, placentation axile or free-central. *Memecylon*.

The genus *Memecylon* is placed by some in a family of its own, e.g. **Memecylaceae.**

Hydrocaryaceae
(Trapaceae)

Annual herbs floating in fresh water pools. Leaves dimorphic; the submerged pinnatipartite with filiform segments, opposite; the floating leaves rosulate, simple and rhomboid with rather long spongy petiole dialated near its apex. Flowers solitary, axillary, regular and hermaphrodite, tetramerous, perigynous. Sepals 4, connate in a short tube, adnate to the base of the ovary; lobes persistent, 2 or all becoming spinescent in fruit. Petals 4, small, white, inserted on the margin of the epigynous disc. Stamens 4 in one whorl. Ovary semi-inferior, of 2 united carpels, bilocular; ovule 1 in each cell, often abortive in one cell; pendulous from the top of the inner angle; style subulate; stigma capitate. Fruit an 1-seeded drupe, obpyramidal in shape with an early deciduous fleshy pericarp and a 2-4 horned stony endocarp (i.e. a pyrene); the horns represent the persistent sepals which are often barbed at the apex; persistent base of the style remains as a central apical beak. Seed solitary, inverted, with 2 very unequal cotyledons, one almost filling the seed and the other scale like; embryo small; endosperm absent; during germination the larger cotyledon remains in the seed while the smaller is carried up on the slender hypocotyl.

This is a unigeneric family of 30* species found in the Old World, while *Trapa natans* Linn. has been introduced in tropical America. Fossil fruits of Tertiary period indicate that the family was more widely distributed in that period.

Trapaceae was included in *Onagraceae* from which it was separated by Engler for its perigynous, bilocular ovary and spiny fruit. This treatment has been supported by most subsequent workers. Embryological and cytological data also speak in favour of segregation of *Trapaceae* as a distinct family.

---

* According to some authors *Trapa* consists of only one polymorphic species, *viz.*, *T. natans* Linn. having several varieties.

The family is economically important for the edible fruit of different species of *Trapa* and for this reason different species are cultivated. *T. bispinosa* Roxb. is much cultivated in India and forms an important article of food in most parts.

Onagraceae

Annual or biennial herbs, or shrubs, rarely arborescent, often aquatic. Leaves simple, alternate or opposite, rarely whorled, exstipulate. Inflorescence racemose or spicate, or flowers solitary and axillary, often pendulous. Flowers hermaphrodite, actinomorphic, tetramerous and epigynous; the receptacle adhering completely to the ovary and produced above it forming the hypanthium or the so called calyx-tube. Sepals, petals and stamens arise from upper edge of the hypanthium. Sepals 4, united near base and adnate to the hypanthium, valvate, usually persistent. Petals 4, free, imbricate, clawed. Stamens twice as many as petals and in 2 whorls, free, the inner stamens shorter often sterile or absent; anthers bithecal, dehiscing longitudinally, often transversely divided in 2 or more stories by false partitions; pollens large, spherical, having 3 pores with protruding stoppers and are connected by viscid threads. Carpels 4, united into a 4-celled inferior ovary with numerous ovules; style simple, long and filiform; stigma capitate, 4-rayed or notched; ovules anatropous, ascending, horizontal or descending on axile placenta. A disc-like swollen structure is often present at the base of the style that secrete nectar or nectary is situated at the base of the calyx. Fruit a loculicidal capsule with a central column bearing the seeds, or a berry or 1-2 seeded and nut-like. Seeds with a small straight embryo and without endosperm.

Fig. 122. Ludwigia adscendens Hara. A. Part of a branch with leaves, pneumatophores, adventitious roots, flowers and fruit (×½); B. Flower (×1); C. Fruit (×1).

Species of *Hauya* are trees and some *Fuchsia* species are climbing. *Ludwigia* is aquatic. *Fuchsia* and *Circaea* have small caducous stipules. Calyx in *Fuchsia* is petaloid, the petals small and in some scale-like. *F. apetala* has no petal as is the case in *Ludwigia palustris*. The central American genus *Lopezia* has strongly zygomorphic flower. Here the petals are linear, the 2 anterior are turned obliquely backwards and bent like a knee with a nectary at the bend. Stamens only 2, the posterior is fertile and the anterior one reduced to a spathulate petaloid staminode. Flowers of *Circaea* are dimerous with 2 stamens in one whorl. In *Clarkia* the antipetalous stamens are reduced to staminodes and in *Eucaridium* and *Ludwigia* these are absent. Pollens are in tetrads in *Epilobium*. *Circaea* has 1-celled ovary with 1 ovule in each cell. Seeds of *Epilobium* are hairy on the chalazal end.

Internal phloem is present in the stem. Vessels have simple perforations. Large aerenchyma occurs in the roots and submerged stems of *Ludwigia*. Raphides are also present.

The floral formula is represented as: ⊕ ⚥ K_4 C_4 A_{4+4} $G_{(\overline{4})}$.

The family consists of about 800 species under 38 genera. They are distributed chiefly in the temperate and tropical regions of the northern hemisphere and more so in the New World. *Epilobium* with over 200 species are found in the temperate regions all over the world. Several species of *Epilobium* occur in the Himalayas and hills of Assam. *Ludwigia perennis* Linn. (Syn. *L. parviflora* Roxb.), *L. adscendens* (L.) Hara (Syn. *Jussiaea repens* Linn.) and *L. octovalvis* (Jack) Raven (Syn. *J. suffruticosa* Hook. f) are found in the plains of E. India in marshy areas.

The family is allied to *Melastomaceae*, *Myrtaceae* and *Lythraceae*. Close affinity between these 4 families is recognised by Takhtajan and also by Cronquist while according to Hutchinson *Onagraceae* is closer to *Lythraceae* than to *Melastomaceae* and *Myrtaceae*. Hutchinson includes this family in his **Lythrales** with *Lythraceae*, *Haloragidaceae*, etc. while *Myrtaceae* and *Melastomaceae* are in his **Myrtales**.

The family is of little economic importance, except that the berries of some species of *Fuchsia* are edible and some plants with showy flowers are cultivated in gardens as ornamental plants. The family has become famous for *Oenothera* ***lamarckiana*** which was used by de Vries for his experiments on mutation.

UMBELLIFLORAE

The 33rd order Umbelliflorae of Engler consists of only 3 families, viz. *Araliaceae*, *Umbelliferae* and *Cornaceae*. *Cornaceae* of earlier workers included the genus *Alangium* which was placed in an unigeneric family *Alangiaceae* by Engler who included this new family in **Myrtales** while *Cornaceae* was included in **Umbelliflorae** by him. All subsequent workers agreed in segregating *Alangiaceae* as a distinct family but placed *Alangiaceae* and *Cornaceae* close to each other and in one and same order.

Takhtajan includes all these 4 families in his **Cornales** where he also includes *Nyssaceae*, *Garryaceae*, etc. But all workers do not consider that the affinity between these families is close enough to include them in a single order. Hutchinson places *Umbelliferae* in an order of its own, viz. **Umbellales** while *Araliaceae*, *Cornaceae* and *Alangiaceae* are in his **Araliales** with *Nyssaceae*, *Garryaceae* and *Caprifoliaceae*. He keeps **Araliales** in **Lignosae** while **Umbellales** is in his division **Herbaceae.**

Cronquist keeps **Umbellales** and **Cornales** as 2 distinct orders but unlike Hutchinson he places *Umbelliferae* and *Araliaceae* in **Umbellales** while *Cornaceae* and *Alangiaceae* are placed in **Cornales** along with *Nyssaceae*, *Garryaceae*, *Davidiaceae* and *Rhizophoraceae*. Cronquist considers that **Umbellales** is related to **Sapindales** while **Cornales** is related to **Rosales.** This is the opinion of Hegnauer who on chemical grounds favours the separation of **Umbellales** from **Cornales.**

The common characters of the order **Umbelliflorae** are: leaves alternate, exstipulate, usually sheathing at the base; inflorescence generally umbellate; flowers regular, bisexual, epigynous; stamens episepalous; carpels usually 2, ovule solitary in each cell, anatropous, pendulous, with one integument only; seeds with copious endosperm.

Araliaceae

Perennial herbs or shrubs or trees, rarely lianas, very rarely scandent epiphytes; stem and branches often armed with prickles; profusely lenticelled. Leaves cauline or radical, simple or digitate or pinnate, often peltate, alternate or whorled near the end of branches; stipulate or exstipulate; stipules interpetiolar or intrapetiolar; petiole long, often prickly. Inflorescence terminal or axillary racemes or umbels, or panicles of umbels, sometimes subcorymbose, often a head or capitulum if the flowers are sessile; bracts and bracteoles persistent or deciduous; pedicels articulated or not. Flowers small, regular, bisexual or polygamous, rarely unisexual epigynous. Receptacular tube or hypanthium cupuliform or obconic or cylindrical. Calyx persistent, lobes or teeth short, 5-8, often represented by an undulate rim. Petals 3-10, valvate or imbricate, inserted on the margin of a fleshy disc, free or shortly connate and forming a calyptra. Stamens usually as many as the petals and alternating with them; anthers dorsifixed, often versatile, dehiscing longitudinally. Disc annular, epigynous, fleshy. Carpels 1-5 rarely more, syncarpous; ovary inferior, 1-5-celled or rarely more celled, apex fused to the disc; style single, often 2-4-fid, rarely as many as carpels or wanting; stigmatic surface terminal or along the adaxial surface of the style; ovule 1 in each cell of ovary anatropous, pendulous from the axile placenta, with ventral raphe. Drupes often sulcate, with thin exocarp and fleshy mesocarp, both on drying form a membranous covering over the pyrenes. Seeds with a thin seed coat, usually laterally compressed, with minute straight embryo and copious fleshy endosperm; endosperm often ruminate.

Schizogenous resin passages occur in all vegetative parts. Vessels are disposed in groups, these are often ring porous, sometimes with spiral thickenings; intervascular pitting is usually scalariform. Medullary and cortical bundles are also reported in many genera. Fibres are simple pitted and septate; there is not much fibre in the pericycle.

Floral formula: ⊕ ⚥ K_5 C_5 A_5 $G_{(\bar{5})}$ in case of a typical flower.

The family contains 63 genera and about 750 species in the tropical and temperate regions of the globe, with 2 main centres of distribution, one in tropical America and the other in the Indo-Malesian region. India has 64 species which are found to be growing more in the hills with a few occurring also in the plains. *Hedera nepalensis* Koch is the Himalayan Ivy, while *H. helix* Linn. is the true Ivy of Europe. The fossil records reveal that the family had a wider distribution in the Tertiary period particularly in the northern temperate regions.

Harms divided the family into 3 tribes as noted below:

I. **Schefflereae.** Petals valvate, not clawed, wide at bas.

II. **Aralieae.** Petals imbricate, wide at base.

III. **Mackinlayeae.** Petals valvate, shortly clawed, inflexed above.

A close relationship between *Araliaceae* and *Umbelliferae* has been recognised by most authors. Many workers trace the affinity of *Araliaceae* also with *Cornaceae*. Hutchinson however considers *Araliaceae* to be related to *Cornaceae* and *Alangiaceae* as well as to *Nyssaceae*, *Garryaceae* and *Caprifoliaceae*, and these six families are included in his **Araliales** of **Lignosae** while *Umbelliferae* is in a monotypic order **Umbellales** of **Herbaceae.**

The roots of *Panax ginseng* Linn. are the Ginseng of the Chinese used as medicine for various ailments. *Aralia nudicaulis* Linn. is a substitute for Sarsaparila. A few other species also possess medicinal properties. *Hedera helix* Linn.—the Ivy plant, and species of *Acanthopanax*, *Panax*, *Polyscias*, etc. are cultivated as garden-ornamentals. Leaves of a few species are good fodder for cattle. Timber obtained from the short tree *Schefflera elata* Harms. is used to make soft planks for packing cases. *Polyscias fruticosus* Harms. is said to be an antidote of snakebite.

Umbelliferae

(Apiaceae)

Annual or biennial herbs or shrubs, usually aromatic, often rhizomatous or with tuberous roots; stem ultimately hollow at the internodes. Leaves alternate, rarely opposite, pinnately or palmately compound or decompound, rarely simple, stipulate or not; petiole sheathing at the base; leaves are often basal and sometimes heteromorphic. Inflorescence is a simple or compound umbel surrounded by an involucre of bracts, terminating the main stem and branches, often in compact head, very rarely solitary; umbels often heteromorphic. Flowers bisexual, rarely unisexual, monoecious or dioecious, or polygamous, actinomorphic, epigynous and pentamerous, small, white or yellow, rarely pink or violet. Calyx gamosepalous, 5-toothed or entire, often persistent. Petals 5, free, valvate or imbricate, often unequal in size. Stamens 5, free, usually bent inwards in bud, arising from the epigynous disc and alternating with the petals; anthers basi- or dorsifixed. Carpels 2, syncarpous, forming a bilocular inferior ovary with one pendulous ovule in each cell; styles 2, surrounded at base by a 2 lobed nectar-disc or stylopodium; stigmas capitate. Fruit is a schizocarpic cremocrp splitting into 2 mericarps which remain attached to a slender, often forked carpophore; each mericarp contains a seed, with five ridges or *costae* outside and the furrows or *valecullae*; the ridges contain vascular bundles and under the furrows there are schizogenous oil ducts or *vittae.* Seed with copious endosperm and a small embryo.

A predominantly herbacious group of plants but a few genera are shrubs while *Eryngium bupleuroides*, *E. sarcophyllum* and *E. inaccessum* are small trees with woody trunk. *Hydrocotyle* is a creeper and so is *Lilaeopsis* a rhizomatous herb of the muddy coasts. *Azorella* is a cushion-plant and *Gingidia* forms rosettes. *Schizeilema* is stoloniferous. *Daucus* has a thick taproot. Leaves are simple in *Hydrocotyle*, *Bupleurum*, etc. Venation of leaves often parallel in *Bupleurum* resembling those of the Monocots. *Eryngium* has the leaf-margin spiny and looks like a spiny thistle with compact floral heads.

Aciphylla has also spine-tipped leaves and bract-segments. Umbels are usually compound but simple umbels are found in *Centella*, *Astrania* as well as in most *Hydrocotyle*, rarely solitary flowers occur in *Azorella* and some *Hydrocotyle*. Flowers in *Eryngium* are sessile and crowded in dense heads surrounded by spiny bracts. In *Petagnia* the inflorescence is of a dichasial type. In *Eryngium* and *Bupleurum* bracts are often large and coloured. In *Mathiasella bupleurioides* the involucre is composed of showy petaloid bracts. The flowers are usually regular but the marginal flowers in the umbels of *Daucus carrota* Linn., *Turgenia latifolia* and *Artedia squamata* and species of *Heracleum* are zygomorphic having the anterior petal largest and the posterior pair the smallest. Unisexual flowers occur in *Echinophora*, *Arctopus*, *Mathiasella*, etc. In *Astrania* the flowers are polygamomonoecious. In *Mathiasella bupleurioides* the pistillate flowers are apetalous. In the subfamily *Hydrocotyloideae* the vittae on the mericarps are absent or they are on the ridges.

The development of a flower in this family is peculiar. The stamens are formed first, next are the petals and then the sepals. The carpels are formed last and are distinct at the beginning but ultimately fuse by their margins. The roof of the rudiments of the carpels form the glandular disc or the stylopodium through which the styles come out. Flowers are protrandous but in case of *Hydrocotyle* and *Sanicula* they are protogynous. The floral formula for a typical flower of this family is represented as:

$$\oplus ⚥ K_{(5)}\ C_5\ A_5\ G_{\overline{(2)}}.$$

Oil or resin canals are present in the inner cortex, pericycle and sometimes in secondary phloem. Pericycle is composed of strands of fibres; it is often a continuous ring of fibres. The fibres are simple pitted, vessels are often in clusters and have simple perforations or rarely scalariform. Wood parenchyma is paratracheal. Crystals of calcium oxalate are often present in the pericarp.

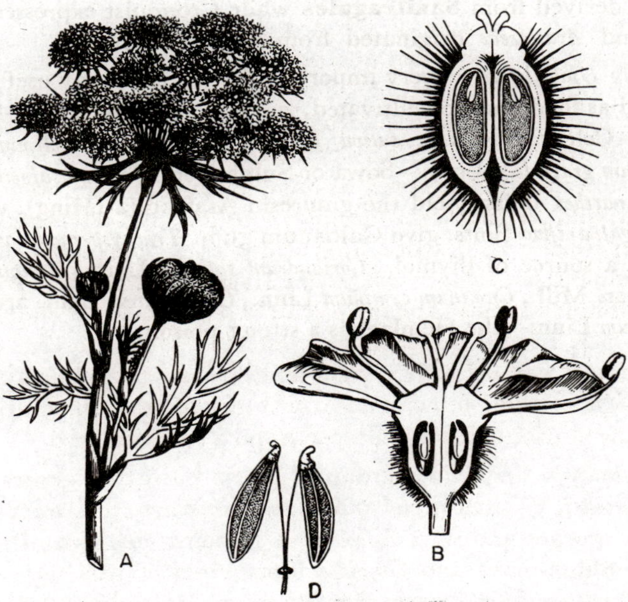

Fig. 123. Daucus carrota L. A. Part of the plant with leaves and inforescence (× 1) B. L. S. of a flower (× 4); C. L.S. of a fruit (× 4); D. Mericarps on Carpophore.

Umbelliferae is a large family of about 3000 species under 275 genera. It is distributed over almost all parts of the globe but more in the north temperate regions. In India 180 species are found mostly in the hills. *Centella asiatica* Urb. is quite common in the plains as well as on the hills up to a height of 1500 m. *Seseli indicum* Wt. & Arn., *Oenanthe benghalensis* Benth., *Pimpinella Heyneana* Wall. etc. are other species that grow wild in the plains.

The family is divided by Drude into 3 subfamilies as noted below:

I. **Hydrocotyloideae:** Stipules present; fruits with no free carpophore, and with hard endocarp; vittae absent or in the ridges only.

II. **Saniculoideae:** Stipules absent; endocarp soft, exocarp rarely smooth, style long, with capitate stigma, surrounded by ring-like disc; vittae various.

III. **Apioideae:** Stipules absent; endocarp soft or hardened by subepidermal fibre layers; style on apex of disc; vittae various.

Umbelliferae is closely allied to *Araliaceae*. That the affinity between the 2 families is close is also supported by pollen characters as well by chemical tests. The 2 families are included in the same order by most workers except Hutchinson who places *Araliaceae* in **Araliales** under **Lignosae** and *Umbelliferae* under **Herbaceae.** According to him *Araliaceae* is a primitive family while *Umbelliferae* is much advanced. *Umbelliferae* resembles *Compositae* (*Asteraceae*) to some extent in the reduction of calyx, bicarpellate syncarpous ovary with 2 distinct styles. It is therefore presumed that *Compositae* originated from *Umbelliferae* through *Rubiaceae*. *Cornaceae* **and** *Alangiaceae* **although put** in a distinct order other than **Umbellifloreae** (**Umbellales**) by Cronquist are considered to be phylogenetically related to *Umbelliferae* by most workers; and these have been derived from **Myrtales** or from **Rosales.** Hutchinson considers that *Umbelliferae* is derived from **Saxifragales** while Cronquist expresses his opinion that *Umbelliferae* and *Araliaceae* originated from **Sapindales.**

The family *Umbelliferae* is very important for having many useful plants under it. A few are used as food and are cultivated, viz. *Daucus carrota* Linn.—Carrot, *Apium graveolens* Linn.—Celery, *Pastinaca sativa* Linn.—Parsnip, *Petroselinum crispum* Nym.—Parsley, *Anethum graveolens* Linn.—Sowa or Sulpha, etc. *Ferula asafoetida* Linn. *F. foetida* Regel and *F. narthex* Boiss. yield the gumresin Asafoetida (Hing), while *F. rubricaulis* Boiss and *F. galbaniflua* Boiss. give Galbanum gum. *Trachyspermum ammi* (L.) Sprague is the Ajwan, a source of thymol. *Coriandrum sativum* Linn., *Pimpinella anisum* Linn. *Foeniculum vulgare* Mill., *Cuminum cyminum* Linn., *Carum carui* Linn. are the spice-plants. *Conium maculatum* Linn.—the Hemlock is a strong poison.

CHAPTER VIII

DICOTYLEDONAE—METACHLAMYDEAE (SYMPETALAE)

In this group flowers have gamopetalous corolla. By this adaptation better protection is provided to the essential organs, i.e. the androecium and gynoecium and the flowers are made more attractive to the insect visitors that pollinate the flower. The families included in this group show much elaboration in the flowers and much reduction of parts without losing attraction. Here is noticed the principle of gain through economy practised in nature. This group therefore is considered advanced over former group, i.e. subclass **Archichlamydeae.**

DIAPENSIALES

This order with a single family **Diapensiaceae** was treated as a distinct and the first order of **Metachlamydeae.** In the revised system this order was merged with the next order **Ericales** where **Diapensiaceae** was included under one of the 2 suborders, viz.: **Ericinae** and **Epacridineae.** Recent workers however prefer to treat **Diapensiales** as a distinct monotypic order close to Ericales.

ERICALES

In this order 5 families were included at first under 2 suborders as given below:

Ericineae: Clethraceae, Pyrolaceae, Lennoaceae, Ericaceae.

Epacridineae: Epacridaceae.

Later on the monotypic order **Diapensiales** was merged with this order and the family Diapensiaceae was transferred to this order and was placed in the suborder **Epacridineae.**

The families included in **Ericales** usually have actinomorphic, bisexual flowers, pentamerous and hypogynous; corolla gamopetalous; stamens obdiplostemonous and inserted on a nectar secreting disc, free and usually not epipetalous; pollens in tetrads; ovules many, unitegmic, on axile placenta; seed with endosperm. Frequently roots are associated with endotrophic mycorrhiza.

The order appears to be a natural taxon with the families well knitted together. Hutchinson has the same families in his order **Ericales** although he treats *Monotropaceae* as distinct from *Pyrolaceae*, and *Vacciniaceae* distinct from *Ericaceae*. *Monotropaceae* as a distinct family has also been recognised by Takhtajan and Cronquist both of whom transfer *Lennoaceae* to **Polemoniales** as this family lacks the embryological peculiarities of **Ericales.**

Ericales appears to be related to and derived from Theaceae having more or less similar floral structure except that the ovules are unitegmic and tenuinucellate. **Ericales** is the most primitive group in the **Metachlamydeae** as corolla is often polypetalous, stamens often double the number of petals and free from each other and from the corolla, and ovary usually superior.

Ericaceae

Mostly shrubs, rarely trees or undershrubs or trailing or scrambling vines. Leaves simple, alternate or opposite or whorled, leathery, exstipulate. Inflorescence axillary

or terminal clusters or raceme or panicle or flowers solitary and axillary. Flowers hermaphrodite, usually actinomorphic, hypogynous or rarely epigynous. Calyx 4-7-lobed, persistent; lobes imbricate; sometimes sepals free. Corolla 4-7-lobed, funnel shaped, campanulate or urceolate, imbricate or convolute, inserted on the margin of the nectariferous disc; rarely petals free. Stamens as many as or twice as many as the petals, inserted on the disc opposite the petals; filaments often flattened or dialated and basally coherent or connate in a tube, straight or curved; anthers 2-celled, the thecae often saccate or bulbous at base, sometimes appendaged, cells dehiscing apically by pores or slits or longitudinally; pollens are in tetrads; anthers inverted during development so as to appear introrse when mature. Carpels usually 5, syncarpous, forming a superior or inferior 5-celled ovary, or carpels 4-10 with as many cells in the ovary; ovules many in each cell, anatropous or obliquely amphitropous; placentation axile; style 1, conical or filiform, rarely with as many branches as carpels; stigma capitate or lobed. Fruit a capsule or berry or baccate; seeds small, with a small straight embryo and fleshy endosperm.

Some *Rhododendron*, *Pieris*, etc. are short trees, a few are trailing, e.g. *Cassiope*, while *Erica* form the characteristic heath. Some *Vaccinium* are epiphytes. In *Rhododendron* and *Vaccinium* the vegetative buds are covered by caducous scales. Endotrophic mycorrhiza occur in the roots of all plants in this family. Leaves are very small in *Cassiope*, *Erica*, *Bryanthus* and *Ledothamnus*; these are scale-like in *Cassiope*, imbricating and covering the stem; in *Erica*, *Bryanthus* and *Ledothamnus* they are needle-like. *Epigaea* has dioecious flowers. In *Erica* and allied genera corolla is persistent. In *Rhododendron* the pollen tetrads are joined by fine viscous threads. *Epigaea* has an expanded 5-lobed stigma. Seeds are winged in *Kalmia* and a few other genera. In *Vaccinium* and allied genera the ovary is partially or completely inferior.

Floral formula may be expressed as: $⚥ K_5 C_{(5)} A_{10} G_{(5)}$ or $⚥ K_5 C_{(5)} A_{10} G_{\overline{(5)}}$.

Stem-anatomy shows small solitary vessels which are semiringporous. Perforations are simple or scalariform; intervascular pitting is opposite. Wood parenchyma is absent or sparse. Fibres are bordered pitted.

Ericaceae consists of about 2000 species under 70 genera. It is widely distributed in the temperate regions of the northern and southern hemispheres and the mountains in the tropics. It is almost absent in Australia. *Rhododendron* has the largest number of species, about 1200 and *Erica* has about 650. The plants prefer acidic soil and are absent from desert areas. The majority of the *Rhododendron* species are concentrated in an area that includes Yunnan province of China, N. Burma and mountainous region of E. India, 72 species growing in the Himalayas and Naga Hills. Common *Rhododendron* spp. of the Himalayas are *R. arboreum* Wall. *R. campanulatum* D. Don., *R. falconeri* Hook. f., *R. Dalhousie* Hook f., *R. cinnabarinum* Hook. f. etc. *Andromeda ovalifolia*, *Cassiope fastigiata* Wall, *Gaultheria fragrantissima* Hook. f., etc. are Himalayan species of this family. *R. Leschenaultianum* Wight. occurs in the Nilgiri Hills of S. India.

The family is divided into 4 sub-families by Drude as noted below:

I. **Rhododendroideae:** Anthers without appendages; fruit septicidal capsule; seeds with loose ribbed testa, often winged.

II. **Arbutoideae:** Anthers appendaged; fruit berry or loculicidal capsule; seeds triangular ovate, not winged.

III. **Vaccinioideae:** Anthers usually appendaged; ovary inferior or semi-inferior; fruit berry.

IV. **Ericoideae:** Anthers appendaged; fruit loculicidal capsule; seeds round, not winged.

Recently Stevens made a critical study of the family and divided the same in a slightly different manner as noted below:

I. **Rhododendroideae:** Winter buds with scales; corolla caducous; stamens usually without appendage, often having fine threads among the pollen tetrads; fruit a septicidal capsule; seeds often winged.

II. **Ericoideae:** No winter buds or scales, habit ericoid; corolla usually persistent; stamens usually appendaged, no threads among pollen tetrads; fruit usually a loculicidal capsule or nut; seeds not winged.

III. **Vaccinioideae:** Winter buds with scales; inflorescence usually a leafless raceme or panicle; corolla caducous, urceolate; stamens usually appendaged; ovary often inferior; fruit a loculicidal capsule or drupe or berry; seeds not winged.

IV. **Epigaeoideae:** Lvs. cordate; dioecious plants; stamens without appendages, anthers with longitudinal slits; stigma much expanded, 5-lobed, ovary densely pubescent; placentae double.

Ericaceae is closely related to the families *Clethraceae*, *Epacridaceae*, *Empetraceae* and *Diapensiaceae* and also to *Theaceae* from which family or from the order **Theales** the order *Ericales* is supposed to have been derived.

The family is not economically important except the oil of winter green is obtained from species of *Gaultheria*, and some *Vacciniums* have edible berries.

PRIMULALES

This order consists of 3 families, viz: *Theophrastaceae*, *Myrsinaceae* and *Primulaceae*. The main characters of the order are: flowers bisexual or unisexual by reduction, regular, sympetalous; inner whorl of stamens fertile, outer whorl absent or represented by staminodes, ovary superior, 1-celled with 2-∞ bitegmic ovules usually on free central placenta. Endosperm present in seeds.

Primulales appears to be a natural taxon and the conscription of the order as given by Engler was accepted by most subsequent workers including Takhtajan and Cronquist. Hutchinson splits this order into **Primulales** and **Myrsinales** keeping *Primualaceae* in the first and the other families in the newly created second order **Myrsinales.** He includes *Plumbaginaceae* in **Primulales** and *Aegicerataceae* in **Myrsinales** which order is put in the **Lignosae** while **Primulales** remains in **Herbaceae.** According to him **Primulales** comes closer to **Plantaginales** and was derived from **Caryophyllales.** Bessey included *Plantaginaceae* and *Plumbaginaceae* in **Primulales** along with *Myrsinaceae*, *Theophrastaceae* and *Primulaceae*, and like Hutchinson considered that the order was derived from **Caryophyllales.** The *Caryophyllaceous* ancestry of this group is the accepted opinion of Wettstein and Hallier also but none supported the splitting of the order into **Primulales** and **Myrsinales** as was done by Hutchinson. Cronquist considers that the order originated from **Theales** although *Caryophyllaceous* ancestry might also be possible. Its relation to **Ebenales** is also suggested both by Takhtajan and Cronquist.

Myrsinaceae

Evergreen trees or shrubs. Leaves simple, alternate, entire, exstipulate; usually leathery. Inflorescence usually axillary, racemose or cymose or corymbose, rarely paniculate. Flowers regular, bisexual, rarely unisexual hypogynous, bracteate. Sepals usually 5, free or connate at base, imbricate, persistent. Petals as many as sepals, mostly united to form a rotate or salver-shaped corolla, rarely free, contorted, imbricate or valvate. Stamens as many as and inserted on the petals; filaments very short; anthers bilocular, introrse; connective slightly prolonged. Carpels 3-6; ovary syncarpous, unilocular, superior, rarely semi-inferior; ovules 1 or few, sunk in the tissue of the free central placenta; style with a slightly lobed stigma. Fruit a berry or drupe. Seeds with copious fleshy endosperm and straight embryo, eodosperm often semi-ruminate.

The ordinary floral formula would be : $\oplus$ ⚥ $K_5\ C_{(5)}\ A_5\ G_{(\underline{5})}$.

Corolla is gamopetalous in most cases but free petals are found in *Embelia*. Stamens are usually free but monadelphous androecium occurs in *Ardisia* and in this genus stamens develop before the corolla as in the family *Primulaceae*. Stamens are syngenesious in *Amblyanthus*. In *Aegiceras* the anther lobes are transversely septate.

The family consists of about 800 species under 32 genera occurring in the tropical and subtropical parts of the old world and also found in Mexico. In India a few species of *Maesa* are found in the lower elevations of the Himalayas, several species of *Ardisia* in the plains and *Aegiceras corniculatum* (L.) Blanco occurring in the tidal forests of Sunderbans.

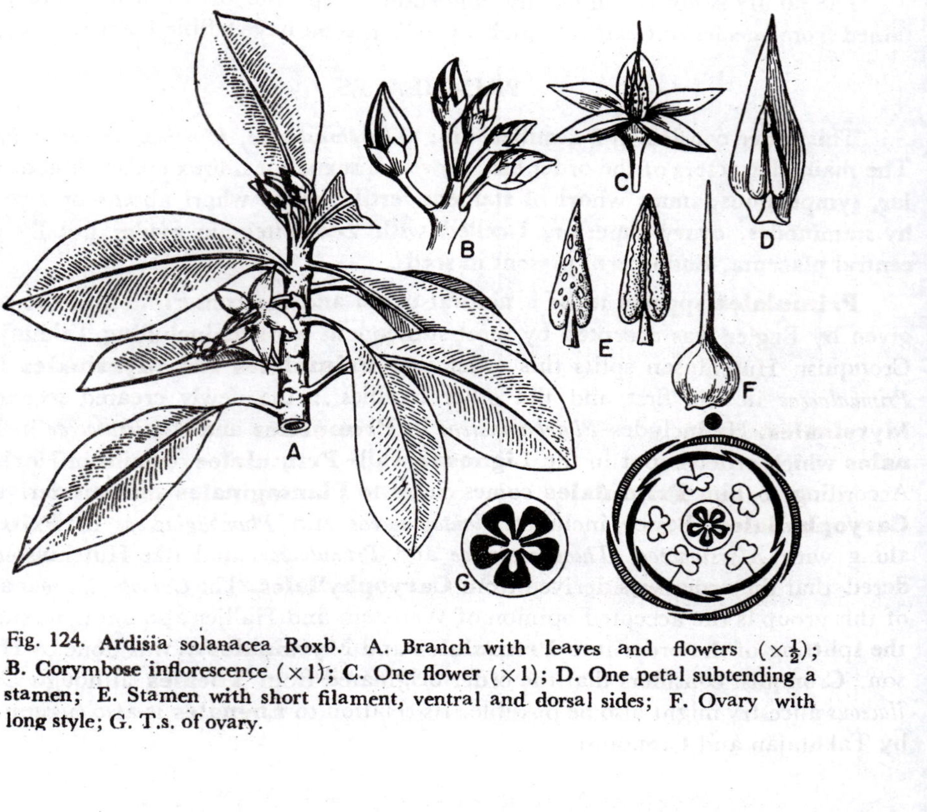

Fig. 124. Ardisia solanacea Roxb. A. Branch with leaves and flowers ($\times\frac{1}{2}$); B. Corymbose inflorescence ($\times 1$); C. One flower ($\times 1$); D. One petal subtending a stamen; E. Stamen with short filament, ventral and dorsal sides; F. Ovary with long style; G. T.s. of ovary.

Myrsinaceae is closely allied to *Primulaceae* and *Theophrastaceae*, the three families being included in one order by most workers.

The family is practically of no economic importance except that a few are cultivated as ornamental trees or shrubs, e.g. *Jacquinia ruscifolia* Linn., *Ardisia solanacea* Roxb. etc. *Embelia ribes* Burm. f. is considered to have medicinal properties.

Primulaceae

Perennial or annual herbs, rarely suffruticose, often with corms, tubers or rhizomes. Leaves simple, alternate, opposite or whorled, exstipulate, sometimes radical, farinose or gland-dotted. Inflorescence umbellate, racemose or spicate, or flowers solitary. Flowers pentamerous, actinomorphic, very rarely zygomorphic, hermaphrodite, usually hypogynous. Calyx 5-partite, imbricate, persistent. Corolla rotate, funnel-shaped or campanulate, lobes usually 5, imbricate or contorted. Stamens as many as corolla-lobes, inserted on the corolla-tube opposite the corolla-lobes; filaments short, free; anthers introrse, dehiscing longitudinally; an outer whorl of staminodes is rarely present. Carpels usually 5, syncarpous; ovary 1-chambered, superior or rarely half-inferior; ovules many on free central placentas, amphitropous or semi-anatropous, with 2 integuments; style long or short with capitate stigma. Capsule dehiscing by valves or transversely; seed with a small embryo and fleshy or horny endosperm.

Corm is found in species of *Cyclamen*. Some species of *Lysimachia* are undershrubs. In the floating aquatic genus *Hottonia* the leaves are heterophyllous, the submerged ones are pinnate. *Coris* has zygomorphic flowers. Flowers in *Primula* are dimorphic, having stamens and styles of different length in flowers of same plant. In *Centunculus* flowers are 4-merous, in *Lysimachia* 6-merous and in *Trientalis* they are 9-merous. The flowers of *Glaux* are apetalous. In *Pelletiera* corolla is polypetalous. An outer whorl of staminodes is present in *Soldanella* and *Samolus*. Corolla is reflexed in *Cyclamen* and *Dodecatheon*. The overy is semi-inferior in *Samolus*. Fruits of *Anagallis*, *Centunculus* and *Soldanella* are pyxis where the top falls off as a lid.

Floral formula: $\oplus$ ⚥ $K_5\ C_5\ A_{5+0}\ G_{\underline{(5)}}$.

The family comprises 28 genera with about 1000 species occurring mostly in temperate countries of the northern hemisphere, having many artic and alpine species. In India several species of *Primula*, *Lysimachia* and *Androsace* are found in the Himalayas and the hills of Assam while *Anagallis arvensis* Linn., *Centunculus tenellus* Duby and *Androsace saxifragaefolia* Bunge occur in the plains.

The family is divided into 5 tribes :

I. **Primuleae** (Androsaceae): Ovary superior; corolla imbricate; capsule usually valvular.

II. **Cyclamineae:** Ovary superior, corolla convolute, petals reflexed; capsule valvular; plants with corm.

III. **Lysimachieae:** Ovary superior; corolla convolute; capsule, valvular or with circumcissile dehiscence; corms absent; petals not reflexed.

IV. **Samoleae:** Ovary semi-inferior; corolla imbricate.

V. **Corideae:** Flower zygomorphic; calyx spiny.

The tribe Corideae with a single genus *Coris* is placed by some in a monotypic family **Coridaceae.**

The family is allied to *Myrsinanaceae* and *Theophrastaceae* and the three families are included in one order **Primulales** by most authors It is also allied to *Plumbaginaceae* which family is placed in **Primulales** by Hutchinson who removes *Myrsinaceae* and *Theophrastaceae* to a distinct order **Myrsinales.** *Primulaceae* is related to *Caryophyllaceae* and also to *Theaceae* to some extent. Bessey, Wettstein, Hallier and Hutchinson are of the opinion that *Primulaceae* and the order **Primulales** originated from **Caryophyllales.** Cronquist considers that *Primulaceae* and the order **Primulales** originated from **Theales** while he does not rule out the possibility of Caryophyllous origin of the group.

The family is not of much economic importance. Species of *Primula* are the Primroses of our garden, the most popular of which are *P. vulgaris* Huds. and *P. sinensis* Sabine. Species of *Cyclamen* are also cultivated for the beautiful flowers. *Lysimachia vulgaris* yields a yellow die and is also a febrifuge. *Cyclamen purpurascence* and *Anagallis arvensis* Linn. are poisonous; the former contains the glucoside cyclamin and the latter a glucoside similar to saponin.

PLUMBAGINALES

The 3rd order **Plumbaginales** of the **Metachlamydeae** consists of only one family **Plumbaginaceae.** This is characterised by trinucleate pollens, polycarpellary syncarpous and superior ovary and single basal crassinucellate, bitegmic, anatropous ovule. The family contains anthocyanin pigments.

Hutchinson does not recognise **Plumbaginales** as a distinct order but includes it in his **Primulales** containing only 2 families *Primulaceae* and *Plumbaginaceae*. Cronquist also does not recognise **Plumbaginales** and places the family *Plumbaginaceae* in **Caryophyllales.** The Caryophyllaceous ancestry of Plumbaginaceae or the order Plumbaginales is quite possible as is considered by most workers but the straight embryo and the peculiar mode of development of the same are characters distinct enough to keep it out of **Caryophyllales** (or **Centrospermae**). This order is closer also to **Polygonales** and Takhtajan keeps **Polygonales** and **Plumbaginales** close to each other and to **Caryophyllales.**

Plumbaginaceae

Perennial herbs or shrubs. Leaves simple, alternate, stipulate or exstipulate. Inflorescence various, racemes, spikes, panicles, cymose heads or dichasial cymes, etc. Flowers bisexual, actinomorphic or slightly zygomorphic, hypogynous and pentamerous. Calyx tubular, 5-lobed, membranous, persistent, lobes valvate. Corolla tubular; lobes 5, often free very near to the base, contorted. Stamens 5, opposite to petals and often epipetalous; anthers bilocular, introrse, dehiscing longitudinally. Ovary of 5 carpels, syncarpous, superior, unilocular with a single basal ovule; funiculus long; styles 5, free or connate at the base; stigmas simple. Fruit a utricle or a capsule dehiscing transeversly, enclosed by persisting membranous calyx; pericarp thin. Seed cylindric with a straight embryo usually surrounded by mealy or fleshy endosperm; rarely endosperm absent.

A few species of *Plumbago* are scandent or climbing, e.g. *P. scandens* Linn. *P. auriculata* Bl., *P. rosea* Linn. and *P. caponsis* Thunb. *Acantholimon* species are dwarf with short tufted stem and branches forming a cushion. In this genus as well as in *Armeria* the leaves are very narrow and linear and often needle-like. In *Armeria* the cymes are clustered in dense heads, the bracts surrounding the peduncle unite at base forming a tubular sheath, the calyx is often spurred rendering the flower zygomorphic. The upper portion of the corolla is deciduous while the tubular lower portion is usually persistent. Pollens are trinucleate.

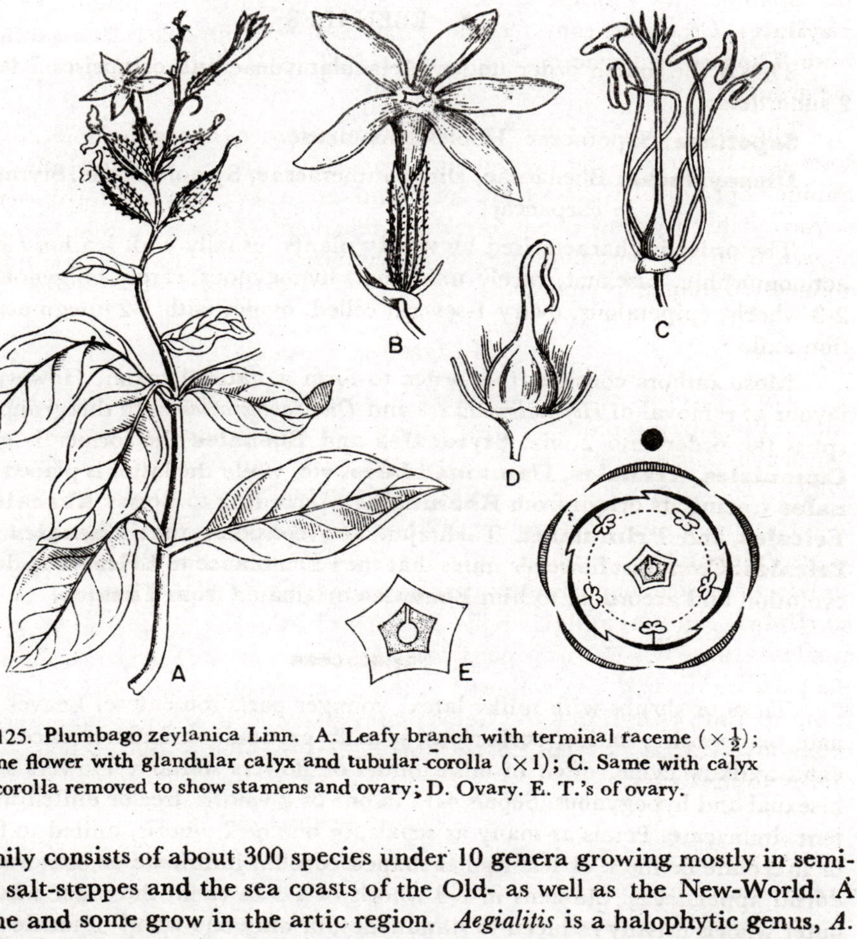

Fig. 125. Plumbago zeylanica Linn. A. Leafy branch with terminal raceme ($\times\frac{1}{2}$); B. One flower with glandular calyx and tubular corolla ($\times 1$); C. Same with calyx and corolla removed to show stamens and ovary; D. Ovary. E. T.'s of ovary.

The family consists of about 300 species under 10 genera growing mostly in semi-arid regions, salt-steppes and the sea coasts of the Old- as well as the New-World. A few are alpine and some grow in the artic region. *Aegialitis* is a halophytic genus, *A. rotundifolia* Roxb. being found in the Sunderban forests of W. Bengal and Bangladesh and the coastal forest of Andaman. *Plumbago zeylanica* Linn. is quite common in some parts of India in the plains.

Plumbaginaceae comes close to *Primulaceae* and also to the families included in **Centrospermae** (or **Caryophyllales**). It is also considered to be related to *Polygonaceae* to some extent.

The family is divided into 2 tribes as given below:

I. **Plumbagineae:** Inflorescence simple; styles connate to a greater extent.

II. **Staticeae:** Inflorescence compound; styles free upto the base.

The family is splitted up by some workers into 3 smaller families, viz. *Limoniaceae*, *Aegialitidaceae* and *Plumbaginaceae*.

Plumbaginaceae is not much important economically. A few species of *Pumbago* is poisonous and have medicinal properties also. *P. indica* Linn. (Syn. *P. rosea* Linn.) has antiseptic properties and is useful in early cases of leucoderma and baldness. *P. zeylanica* Linn. has the same properties and is also used to raise blisters.

EBENALES

This is the fourth order under Metachlamydeae and comprises 7 families under 2 suborders:

Sapotinae: Sapotaceae, Hoplestigmataceae.

Diospyrineae: Ebenaceae, Diclidantheraceae, Symplocaceae, Styracaceae, Lissocarpaceae.

The order is characterised by woody plants, usually with leathery leaves, flowers actinomorphic, bisexual, rarely unisexual, hypogynous, rarely epigynous, stamens in 2-3 whorls, epipetalous, ovary 1-several celled, ovules with 1-2 integuments, placentation axile.

Most authors consider this order to form a natural taxon. However they are in favour of removal of *Hoplestigmataceae* and *Diclidantheraceae* from this group. Hutchinson splits the order into 2, viz. **Styracales** and **Ebenales** the former is grouped with **Cunoniales, Araliales, Hamamelidales,** etc. while the latter is placed after **Myrsinales** tracing its origin from **Rhamnales.** According to Bessey **Ebenales** is allied to **Ericales** and **Primulales.** Takhtajan also considers that **Ebenales** is related to **Ericales.** Cronquist however states that the resemblance to **Ericales** is due to parallel evolution and according to him **Ebenales** originated from **Theales.**

Sapotaceae

Trees or shrubs with milky latex; younger parts tomentose. Leaves simple, alternate or opposite, entire, coriaceous, usually exstipulate. Inflorescence an axillary or extra-axillary cyme, often in false umbel or flowers solitary. Flowers small, regular, bisexual and hypogynous. Sepals 4-12 in one or 2 whorls, free or united at base, persistent, imbricate. Petals as many as sepals, in one or 2 whorls, united to form a rotate or urceolate or more or less funnel-shaped corolla, imbricate or contorted, often with dorsal appendages. Stamens in 2-3 whorls of 4-5 in each, the inner whorl fertile, the outer whorls usually reduced to staminodes, or only one whorl of fertile stamens without the whorls of staminodes, epipetalous; anthers 2-locular, introrse, dehiscing longitudinally. Carpels 4-5, syncarpous forming a superior 4-5-celled ovary; style one, with a small capitate stigma; ovule one in each cell of ovary, anatropous, ascending with a downward micropyle, and with one integument. Fruit a berry or rarely 1-seeded and drupe-like; seed with a hard shining testa and broad hilum; endosperm oily or absent.

Floral formula is represented as: ⊕ ⚥ $K_{(4-12)}$ $C_{(4-12)}$ $A_{4-\infty}$ $G_{\underline{(4-5)}}$.

In this family there is much difference in the number of perianth segments. In *Madhuca* sepals are 4 in 2 whorls, in *Sarcosperma* and *Pouteria* there are 5 sepals in one whorl. *Sideroxylon* flower is also pentamerous where as in *Palaquium* and *Manilkara* it is 3-merous. Corolla is caducous in many genera, e.g. *Madhuca*, *Mimusops*, etc. The petals in *Mimusops* have a pair of appendages and the corolla appears to be 2-seriate with altogether 18-24 lobes.

The family contains about 600 species under 40 genera found in the tropical countries of the world. The family is represented in India by several species in the plains, the common species are *Mimusops elengi* Linn. *Sideroxylon tomentosum* Roxb. *Madhuca indica* Gemel. etc. *Manilkara achras* (Mill) Fosb. is much cultivated for the edible fruits.

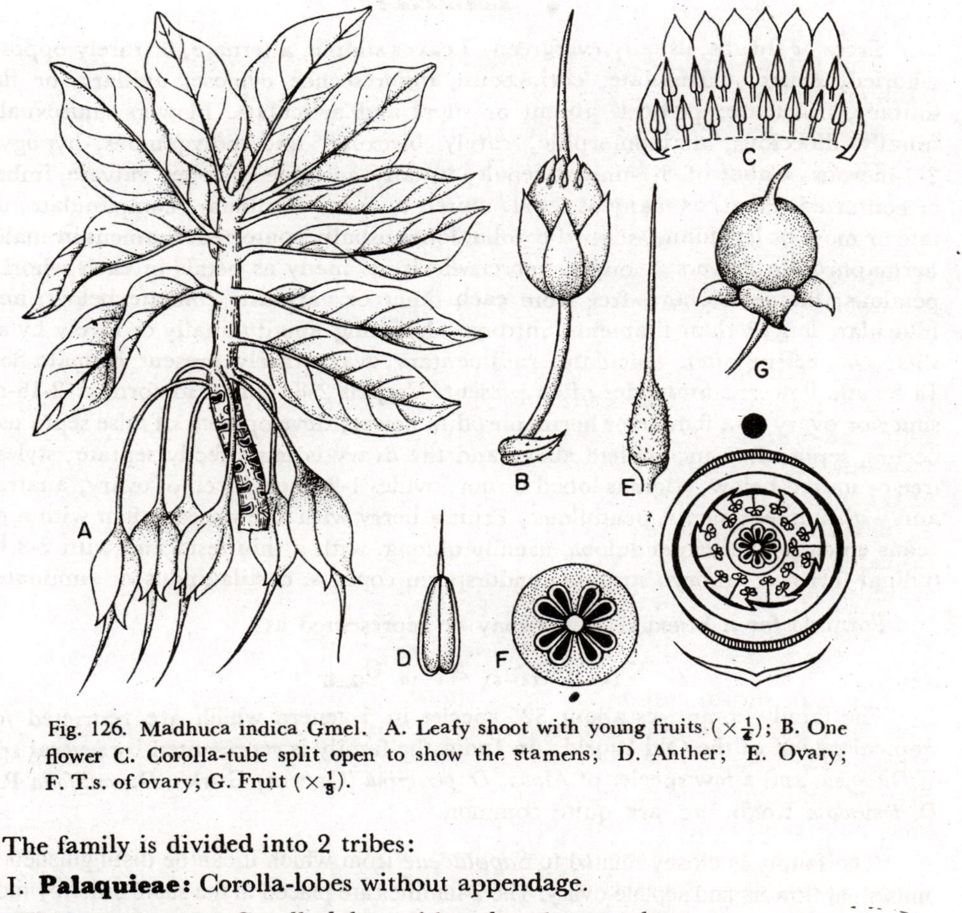

Fig. 126. Madhuca indica Gmel. A. Leafy shoot with young fruits $(\times\frac{1}{4})$; B. One flower C. Corolla-tube split open to show the stamens; D. Anther; E. Ovary; F. T.s. of ovary; G. Fruit $(\times\frac{1}{3})$.

The family is divided into 2 tribes:

I. **Palaquieae:** Corolla-lobes without appendage.

II. **Mimusopeae:** Corolla-lobes with a dorsal appendage.

Sapotaceae is closely allied to *Ebenaceae* and these 2 families are included in the same order by almost all workers. It is also related to *Styracaceae*, *Symplocaceae* and *Lissocarpaceae* although according Hutchinson these 3 families are not at all close to *Sapotaceae* and *Ebenaceae*. Hallier placed the family *Sapotaceae* in a monotypic order **Sapotales** while *Ebenaceae* was included by him in **Santalales.** However he considered **Sapotales** and **Santalales** originated from the same ancestral stock, i.e. *Linaceae* and therefore the families included in these 2 orders were related to each other to some extent.

Many plants of this family are important being useful in different ways. *Manilkara achras* (Mill.) Fosb. is famous for the Sapodilla-fruits, original of Mexico is now cultivated in almost all tropical countries. This tree is also the source of chewing gum obtained from the milky juice. *Vittelaria mammosa* Radlk. f. and *Chrysophyllum cainito* Linn. also produce edible fruits. *Madhuca butyracea* (Roxb.) Macbride yields vegetable butter from the kernel of the seeds. *Madhuca indica* Gmel is the Mohua tree the seeds of which also yield edible oil. Gutta-percha of commerce is obtained from the Malayan tree *Palaquium gutta* (Hk. f.) Baill. *Mimusops elengi* Linn. is the Bakul tree an avenue tree with fragrant flowers.

Ebenaceae

Trees or shrubs, usually evergreen. Leaves simple, alternate, or rarely opposite or whorled, entire, exstipulate, coriaceous. Inflorescence cymose, axillary, or flowers solitary, bracteate; pedicels absent or short and articulate. Flowers unisexual and usually dioecious, actinomorphic, rarely bisexual and polygamous, hypogynous, 3-7-merous. Calyx of 3-7-united sepals, usually accrescent; lobes valvate, imbricate or contorted. Petals as many as sepals united to form a tubular, campanulate, urceolate or more or less funnel-shaped corolla, lobes usually contorted. Stamens in male and hermaphrodite flowers in one or more whorls, as many as petals in each whorl, epipetalous; filaments short, free from each other or variously connate below; anthers bilocular, longer than filaments, introrse, dehiscing longitudinally or rarely by apical slits; connective often apiculate, rudimentary ovary rarely present in male flowers. In female flowers staminodes often present. Carpels 2-8, united to form a 2-16-celled superior ovary in a female or hermaphrodite flower; development of false septa usually occurs, septa often incomplete above and the ovary is imperfectly septate; styles 2-8, free or united below; stigmas lobed or not; ovules 1-2 in each cell of ovary, anatropous and with 2 integuments, pendulous. Fruit a berry with a few seeds often with a coriaceous epicarp. Seeds pendulous, usually oblong, with a thin testa and with 2-3 longitudinal furrows; embryo straight; endorsperm copious, cartilaginous or ruminate.

Formula for a bisexual flower may be represented as:

$$K_{(4-5)}\ C_{(4-5)}\ A_{8-10}\ G_{\underline{(2-8)}}.$$

The family comprises about 325 species in 5 genera which are restricted to the tropical region of the Old World. In India the family is represented by several species of *Diospyros* and a few species of *Maba*. *D. peregrina* (Gaertn) Gurke, *D. cordifolia* Roxb., *D. tomentosa* Roxb. etc. are quite common.

The family is closey related to *Sapotaceae* from which it can be distinguished by the unisexual flowers and septate ovary. The 2 families are placed in the same order by most taxonomists. Hutchinson includes *Sarcospermaceae*, *Ebenaceae* and *Sapotaceae* in **Ebenales** while others favour the inclusion of *Symplocaceae* and *Styracaceae* also in **Ebenales.** *Ebenaceae* is allied to these 2 families in some respects.

The family includes several good timber trees, the most important of which is the Ebony—*Diospyros ebenum* Koen. the natural colour of the wood of which is black and takes high polish. *D. tamentosa* Roxb. and *D. melanoxylon* Roxb. also yield good timber similar to ebony. The tender leaves of *D. melanoxylon* are used as wrapping paper for country-made cigarettes (*bidi*) in India. *D. kaki* Linn. f. is the persimon and is available in eastern India, China and Japan. *D. virginiana* Linn. also yields good fruit which is known as American persimon. *D. discolor* Willd. of the Philppines also produce sweet delicious fruits. *D. peregrina* (Gaertn.) Gurke common in the plains of India yields a hard durable timber and mucilaginous fruits which are used for caulking boats and waterproofing the threads for preparing fishermen's net.

CONTORTAE

This small order of 6 families is the 5th order of Engler's **Metachlamydeae** of the Dicotyledons. The 6 families are grouped under 2 suborders as noted below:

I. **Oleineae:** Oleaceae.

II. **Gentianineae:** Desfontainiaceae, Loganiaceae, Gentianaceae, Apocynaceae, Asclepediaceae.

Desfontainiaceae was later merged with *Loganiaceae*. *Salvadoraceae* was at first included in this order but later transferred to Sapindales.

The order is characterised as:—Herbs, shrubs or trees; leaves generally opposite, simple or pinnately compound, exstipulate; flowers usually actinomorphic, bisexual, hypogynous; corolla gamopetalous, lobes convolute; stamens adnate to corolla near base; nectar secreting disc present; carpels 2, connate or united only by the styles; ovules few to many.

About the relationship between these families different workers hold different opinions. Most of them agree that these families are not close enough to be included in a single order. Rendle and Wettstein splitted the order into 2, viz. **Oleales** (**Ligustrales** of Wettstein) and **Contortae.** In the former are included *Oleaceae* and *Salvadoraceae* while the other families remained in **Contortae.** The orders are put side by side in their systems of classification. Hutchinson breaks the order into 3, viz., **Loganiales, Apocynales** and **Gentianales,** the first and second are placed side by side after **Sapindales** while **Gentianales** is placed in his **Herbaceae** with **Lythrales, Primulales** and **Plumbaginales.** He further splits *Loganiaceae* of Engler into *Loganiaceae, Buddlejaceae* and four other families. *Oleaceae* is placed by him in **Loganiales.** Splitting of the older *Loganiaceae* is supported by Takhtajan who however includes *Loganiaceae* (sensu stricto) and other smaller families in **Gentianales** with *Apocynaceae* and *Asclepiadaceae* while *Buddlejaceae* is placed by him in *Scrophulariales*. *Oleaceae* is placed by him in a monotypic order **Oleales** after **Rhamnales.** Cronquist does not support splitting of *Loganiacea*• into so many small families but recognises *Buddlejaceae* as distinct family which is placed is **Scrophulariales** wherein he includes *Oleaceae* also. In **Gentianales** he includes *Loganiaceae, Gentianaceae, Apocynaceae* and *Asclepiadaceae*. It should be noted that the close affinity of *Apocynaceae* and *Asclepiadaceae* is recognised by all taxonomists. As to the status and relationship of the other families opinions differ. *Buddlejaceae* as a distinct family is also accepted by almost all. *Menyanthoideae* a subfamily of *Gentianaceae* is raised to a distinct family *Menyanthaceae* by Hutchinson and the order **Gentianales** of Hutchinson was constituted only with *Gentianaceae* and *Menyanthaceae*.

Genitianales of Takhtajan is a large order including *Gentianaceae*, *Menyanthaceae* and a few other families. Cronquist however has removed *Menyanthaceae* from **Gentianales** and has placed the family in **Scorphulariales**.

Oleaceae

Trees, shrubs or undershrubs, often scandent or twinning. Leaves opposite, simple or pinnately compound, exstipulate, often pubescent with peltate hairs. Inflorescence is usually cymose, often paniculate, rarely recemose; the cymes often form a dichasium. Flowers actinomorphic, bisexual, rarely unisexual, hypogynous, fragrant or not. Calyx gamosepalous, 4-6 lobed, or entire at apex; lobes valvate; rarely calyx absent. Petals 4-5, connate below to form a salver-shaped or rotate corolla, or petals free, imbricate or valvate; rarely petals absent. Stamens 2 or rarely 4, epipetalous on corolla tube, or hypogynous when petals free or absent; anthers bithecal oblong, dehiscing laterally or subextrorsely, filaments short. Ovary bicarpellary, syncarpous, 2-chambered, superior; ovules usually 2 in each chamber, anatropous, pendulous or ascending; style short, stigma 2-lobed. Fruit a berry, or drupe, or capsular, rarely a schizocarp or samara. Seed with copious fleshy endosperm and straight embryo, or endosperm absent; testa thin or bone-like.

Olea, *Ligustrum*, *Fraxinus*, etc. are trees, *Jasminum* is a genus of shrubs, often scandent or twining. Simple leaves are found in *Olea*, *Linociera*, *Ligustrum*, etc. but *Fraxinus*, *Schrebera*, etc. have pinnate leaves. Inflorescence in *Jasminum* is a true cyme, often a dichasial cyme; in *J. nudiflorum* flowers remain united in threes at the end of scaly shoots. Compound racemes are found in *Ligustrum* and *Fraxinus*. Flowers are unisexual in *Fraxinus* and also in some *Olea*. In *Fraxinus* either calyx or corolla or both may be absent. Perianth segment usually 4 in each whorl but petals may be 5 or sepals and petals may be upto 7 or 9 even 10, as in some *Jasminum*, *Nyctanthes* and *Schrebera*. Ovary has 2 ovules in each chamber but in *Forsythia* ovules may be 4-10 in each cell of ovary. In *Hesperella* and *Tessarandra* stamens are 4.

Extra floral nectaries in the form of peltate hairs are found at the base of the flowers in some genera. In the axils of leaves several buds are sometimes arranged one above the other; these are accessory buds. In *Syringa* the winter bud has a scale which is considered as the sheath of the undeveloped leaf. The vessels in the wood are small, solitary or in multiples of 4 or more cells, usually ring porous. Fibres are simple and bordered pitted. Pericycle is a continuous ring of fibres or of isolated strands of fibres. Wood parenchyma apotracheal or paratracheal. Vascicentric tracheids are present in a few genera.

The typical floral formula is: $\oplus$ ⚥ $K_{(4)}$ $C_{(4-5)}$ A_2 $G_{(\underline{2})}$.

The family with about 500 species under 21 genera are found in the temperate and tropical regions, a few genera confined to the Indo-Malayan region. Many species of *Jasminum* occur wild in India and a few are cultivated, e.g. *J. sambac* Ait.-Beli, *J. auriculatum* Vahl-Juthi, *J. grandifloram* Linn.—Chameli, etc. *Nyctanthes arbor-tristis* Linn. —Shefali grows wild in forest and is also cultivated. *Fraxinus floribunda* Wall. is a timber yielding tree of the Himalayas, *Schrebera sweitenioides* Roxb. with large woody capsules grows in Orissa.

Oleaceae is related to *Loganiaceae* to some extent. It is allied also to *Apocynaceae* in some respects. Hutchinson traces its affinity to *Rubiaceae* and *Melastomaceae*. Cronquist considers it to be allied to *Buddlejaceae* and includes *Oleaceae* in **Scrophulariales.**

Oleaceae is divided into 2 subfamilies as noted below:—

Subf. I. **Oleoideae:** Seeds pendulous; fruit not vertically constricted.

Subf. II. **Jasminoideae:** Seeds erect; fruit divided into 2 parts by a vertical constriction.

The genus *Nyctanthes* of the S.f. *Jasminoideae* was transferred to a monotypic family **Nyctanthaceae** by Agardh while Airy-Shaw transferred the genus to *Verbenaceae*.

The family includes a few plants of economic importance. *Olea europaea* Linn. of the Mediterranean region is the Olive tree from the seeds of which the olive oil is obtained. *Fraxinus excelsior* Linn. yields the Ash wood of commerce. Other species of *Fraxinus* are equally good timber trees. A dye is obtained from the orange tubular part of the corolla of *Nyctanthes arbortristis* Linn. Many species of *Jasminum* are cultivated for fragrant flowers and a few yield essential oil.

Loganiaceae

Loganiaceae of Engler and the older workers was splitted to 6 families by Hutchinson, viz. *Potaliaceae*, *Loganiaceae*, *Buddlejaceae*, *Autoniaceae*, *Spigeliaceae* and *Strychnaceae*. Cronquist recognises *Buddlejaceae* as a distinct family but does not treat *Potaliaceae*, *Autoniaceae*, *Spigeliaceae* and *Strychnaceae* as separate families. *Loganiaceae* of Cronquist is a larger family that includes the above 4 families of Hutchinson.

The conscription of *Loganiaceae* as understood by Cronquist is given here.

Trees, shrubs or herbs, often climbing. Leaves simple, opposite or whorled, stipulate; stipules intrapetiolar, or interpetiolar, often very minute or very rarely absent. Inflorescence cymose, often paniculate. Flowers hermaphrodite, actinomorphic, hypogynous, 4-5-merous; bracts and bracteoles present. Calyx 4-5-lobed or toothed, imbricate. Petals 4-5, united to form a tubular, semi-rotate or campanulate corolla, imbricate or valvate or contorted, often hairy at the throat or at the mouth inside. Stamens 4-5, epipetalous, inserted on the corolla tube or on the mouth of corolla, alternating with the petals; anthers bilocular, introrse, dehiscing longitudinally; very rarely stamen one only. Carpels 2, united to form a syncarpous bilocular ovary; ovary superior with numerous ovules in each chamber on axile placenta; style simple, stigma capitate or bilobed; rarely ovary unilocular with parietal placenta. Fruit a berry or drupe, or a capsule. Seed without endosperm and with a straight embryo.

Strychnos is a genus of trees but a few species are tendril climbers. Species of *Fagraea* are also climbers and some are epiphytes. *Gelsemium* is a stem-twiner. *Mitreola* and *Mitrasacme* are small herbs. Leaves of *Strychnos* are 3-5-nerved. Cymes in *Mitreola* are 2-3-chotomous, in *Mitrasacme* often in umbels and in *Fagraea* sometimes grouped in corymbs. The size of flowers varies great. *Mitreola* has flowers which are about 2 mm. long, while *Fagraea auriculata* Jack has flowers about 20 cm. long and 30 cm. across. Numerous bracteoles are present below the flowers in *Gelsemium*. In *Usteria* the flower has a single stamen. Ovary in *Mitreola* is semi-inferior. In *Strychnos* the ovary is unilocular and the placentation is parietal.

Floral formula of the family may be expressed as: $\oplus$ ⚥ $K_{(4-5)}\ C_{(4-5)}\ A_{4-5}\ G_{\underline{(2)}}$.

Occurrence of internal phloem is a characteristic feature of the family. Vessels are in multiples of 4 or more cells; perforations are simple and the rays are uniseriate. Branched sclerenchymatous idioblasts frequently occur beneath the epidermis.

The family consists of about 600 species under 26 genera which occur in the tropical and subtropical regions. In India several species of *Strychnos*, *Mitreola*, *Mitrasacme* etc. are found in the plains as well as at lower elevations on the hills.

Loganiaceae is allied to *Gentianaceae*. Engler placed *Loganiaceae* in the suborder **Gentianineae** of his order **Contortae** with *Gentianaceae*, *Apocynaceae* and *Asclepiadaceae*. Rendle and Wettstein also included these 4 families in their **Contortae**, recognising the close relation between *Loganiaceae* and *Gentianaceae*. Cronquist also considers these 2 families very close and includes these in his **Gentianales** where he includes *Apocy-*

naceae and *Asclepiadaceae* also. Hutchinson, however, considered *Loganiaceae* to be more allied to *Oleaceae* and placed *Oleaceae* in his **Loganiales** of the **Lignosae** while *Gentianaceae* was placed in **Gentianales** of the **Herbaceae** far removed from *Loganiaceae*.

Several plants of the family are important economically being the source of various alkaloids and are used medicinally. Strychnine and brucine ane obtained from *Strychnos nux-vomica* Linn. *Strychnos potatoram* L. f. is the clearing nut tree the seeds of which purifies muddy water. *Str. toxifera* Schomb. gives the arrow-poison in S. America. *Gelsemium sempervirens* Linn. is also a medicinal plant. *Fagraea fragrans* Roxb., *F. elliptica* Roxb. and *F. crenulata* Maing. are good timber trees.

Buddlejaceae

Shrubs or trees, rarely undershrubs, very rarely herbs; glandular or stellate hairs often present or with lepidote scales. Leaves simple, opposite or verticillate, entire or coarsely dentate, connected by an intrapetiolar stipulary line. Inflorescence cymose, racemose or paniculate or capitate, or flowers solitary. Calyx gamosepalous, 4-lobed; valvate. Corolla tubular with 4 lobes, imbricate. Stamens 4, epipetalous; filaments short or anthers sessile; anthers 2-locular, dehiscing longitudinally. Carpels 2, united to form a superior 2-celled or very rarely 4-celled ovary; ovules many, on axile placentas; stigma capitate or 2-lobed. Fruit a capsule, drupe or berry; seeds often winged or produced at each end; endosperm scanty; embryo straight.

Floral formula: $K_{(4)}\ C_{(4)}\ A_{(4)}\ G_{(\underline{2})}$.

Stem anatomy shows the absence of intraxylary phloem. An integumentary tapetal layer is found and the endosperm is cellular. These characters separate *Buddlejaceae* from *Loganiaceae*.

The family *Buddlejaceae* contains about 150 species under 6 genera, distributed in the tropical and temperate regions. *Buddleja*, the largest genus has over 100 species some of which are cultivated for beautiful fragrant flowers. There are several species of the genus in the lower ridges of the Himalayas and *B. asiatica* Lour. is found in the plains of India.

Buddlejaceae was included in *Loganiaceae* from which it was segregated as distinct family by Hutchinson who considered the 2 families to be close to each other. Hallier included *Loganiaceae* with *Buddlejoideae* as a subfamily in the **Tubiflorae** while both Takhtajan and Cronquist place *Buddlejaceae* in **Scrophulariales.** According to them the affinity of *Buddlejaceae* is closer to *Scrophulariaceae* than to *Loganiaceae*.

Gentianaceae

Annual or perennial herbs, often rhizomatos; branching often dichotomous; rarely floating aquatics. Leaves simple, opposite and decussate, rarely alternate, exstipulate, 3-5-nerved. Inflorescence cymose, often dichasial. Flowers regular, bisexual, hypogynous, 4-5-merous, bracteate. Sepals 4-5, connate at base, imbricate, persistent. Corolla tubular, rotate or salver-shaped or funnel-shaped, 4-5-lobed, contorted or in duplicate valvate. Stamens as many as and alternate to corolla-lobes; anthers 2-celled, introrse, basi- or dorsifixed or sometimes versatile. Ovary superior, bicarpellary, syncarpous, usually unilocular, with many ovules on 2 parietal placentas; ovules anatropous; style simple, stigma capitate or bilobed; glandular hypogynous disc is often present. Fruit a capsule with leathery valves. Seeds with fleshy perisperm and minute embryo.

In most herbs the branching is forked cymose. Some species of *Gentiana* (sec. *Crawfurdia*) are twiners and *Nymphoides* species are floating aquatic herbs. A few genera are saprophitic, e.g. *Voyria, Leiphaimos*, etc. Flowers of *Hoppea* are more or less zygomorphic but regular in other genera. *Cotylanthera* species are parasitic and *Gentiana crassa* Kurz is shrubby. Pitted glands secreting nectar are found at the base of petals in *Swertia*. Stamens have syngenesious anthers in *Voyria* and *Leiphaimos*. Multisporangiate stamens are often found due to the presence of sterile plates between anther lobes. In *Exacum* the dehiscence of anthers is by apical pores. In the same genus the ovary is falsely 2-locular due to the intrusion of the placentas and meeting at the centre. Rarely the ovary is 4-5-locular due to the growth of more false septas. Enantiostyly, i.e. the style bent to one side, is found in *Exacum*. In *Canscora* 1 or 2 stamens with longer filaments have fertile anthers while the rest have shorter filaments and sterile anthers and inserted at lower level, often almost obsolete. The fruit of *Chironia* is a berry.

Floral formula is represented as: $\oplus$ ⚥ $K_{(4-5)}$ $C_{(4-5)}$ $A_{\underline{(4-5)}}$ $G_{\underline{(2)}}$.

Vascular bundles are bicollateral in the subfamily *Gentianoideae* but collateral in the *Menyanthoideae*. The cells contain bitter principles, and stellate hairs are present in intercellular spaces. Cells of the pericycle are thin walled; vessels have simple perforations and fibres are scanty.

Fig. 127. Nymphoides cristata (Roxb.) O. Kuntze. A. One plant ($\times \frac{1}{4}$); B. Flower seen from above ($\times 1$); C. Same with Corolla split open to show glands on the lobes, stamens and ovary; D. T.s. of ovary; E. Fruit ($\times 1$).

The family comprises 80 genera and about 900 species, the largest genus *Gentiana* having about 400. The family is distributed more in the temperate region while quite a large number occur also in the tropics in various ecological situations. A few species of *Gentiana* occur in the artic zone and also in alpine tracts. In India many species of *Gentiana* and *Swertia* are found in the Himalayas and hills of eastern India while *Canscora diffusa* R. Br., *C. decussata* R. & S., *Exacum tetragonum* Roxb., *Erythraea Roxburghii* G. Don, *Nymphoides cristata* (Roxb.) O. Ktze., etc. are common in the plains all over the country.

The family is divided into 2 subfamilies:

I. **Gentianoideae**—Leaves opposite; corolla lobes twisted in bud; vascular bundles bicollateral having intraxylary phloem.

II. **Menyanthoideae,**—Leaves alternate; corolla induplicate-valvate vascular bundles collateral, lacking in internal phloem.

The family is allied to *Loganiaceae* and to *Melastomaceae* in some respects. Hutchinson considers that *Gentianaceae* and *Caryophyllaceae* having same type of inflorescence have close affinity with each other and that **Gentianales** originated from **Caryophyllales.** Hutchinson further raises the subfamily *Menyanthoideae* to the rank of a family, viz. *Menyanthaceae* and most subsequent authors support him in such treatment.

Gentianaceae includes a few economically important plants. *Swertia chirayita* a Himalayan herb is a reputed medicinal plant. *Gentiana lutea, G. campestris, G. punctata, G. Kurroo* (Himalaya) are all medicinal plants. *Canscora decussata* R. & S. is used by the Indian vaids. Many species of *Gentiana*, particularly *G. acaulis* are cultivated in gardens for their beautiful blue flowers.

Menyanthaceae

Treated as a distinct family it is characterised as:

Aquatic or marsh herbs. Leaves simple or 3-foliolate, exstipulate, with a sheathing petiole. Inflorescence cymose or racemose or flowers clustered. Flowers bisexual, actinomorphic, hypogynous. Sepals 5, free or united. Petals 5, united, lobes valvate or induplicate-valvate. Stamens 5, epipetalous, alternating with corolla lobes; anthers versatile, sagittate; hypogynous nectary usually present. Ovary superior, bicarpellary, syncarpous, unilocular; ovules many on 2 parietal placentas; style simple with a bifid stigma. Fruit a capsule, with 2-4 valves or fleshy and indehiscent. Seeds few or many, often winged; endosperm copious; embryo minute.

The family contains about 33 species under 5 genera distributed in the tropical countries. *Nymphoides cristata* (Roxb.) O. Kuntze is very common in fresh water pools all over India in the plains.

The vascular bundles do not have internal phloem as is found in *Gentianaceae.* A tapetal layer is found in the integuments and the endosperm is cellular.

Hutchinson who splitted *Gentianaceae* to *Gentianaceae* and *Menyanthaceae* included these 2 families in his **Gentianales** where no other family is included. **Takhtajan** places these 2 families in **Gentianales** where 9 other families are included by him. Cronquist, however, removes *Menyanthaceae* from **Gentianales** and places it in **Scrophulariales.**

Apocynaceae

Trees or shrubs often twining, rarely undershrubs, usually with milky latex. Leaves simple, opposite or whorled, rarely alternate, exstipulate, entire. Inflorescence cymose, or flowers solitary. Flowers bisexual, actinomorphic, hypogynous, bracteate or not. Sepals 5, united at base, quincuncial, rarely sepals 4 and imbricate; often with basal glands. Petals 5, united in a salver-shaped or funnel-shaped corolla; lobes contorted in bud; a hairy or scaly corona or various outgrowth present at the throat of corolla. Stamens as many as petals and alternate with them, epipetalous; filaments short or almost absent; anthers introrse, often sagittate, free or connivent in a cone over the stigma and often adnate to it, base of anther often produced downward in the form of spines; pollens sometimes in tetrads; an entire, lobed or scaly disc is often present. Carpels 2 forming a syncarpous ovary, or the ovaries united by styles and stigmas; ovaries superior or semi-inferior; 2-celled in the case of syncarpous ovary; or pair of unicellular ovaries; ovules many, anatropous, pendulous from a parietal placenta; style slender; stigma capitate or dumb-bell shaped. Fruit a pair of follicles or berries or capsules or a single fruit in the case of syncarpous ovary. Seeds flat, winged or comose; endosperm copious or rarely absent; cotyledons large and thin.

Branched and unbranched latex tubes are present throughout the plant body. The vascular bundles are bicollateral having intraxylary phloem. Spicular cells are found in the leaf-mesophyll. Nonlignified fibre-like cells occurring in groups or in a ring form the pericycle. Wood parenchyma is apotracheal or sometimes paratracheal. Fibres are septate, with simple or bordered pits. In many twining species anomalous secondary thickening is observed.

The family contains about 300 genera and about 1400 species, occurring in the tropical regions with a few in temperate areas. It is well represented in India by about 85 species. Most common are *Alstonia scholaris* R. Br., *Holarrhena antidysenterica* Wall.,

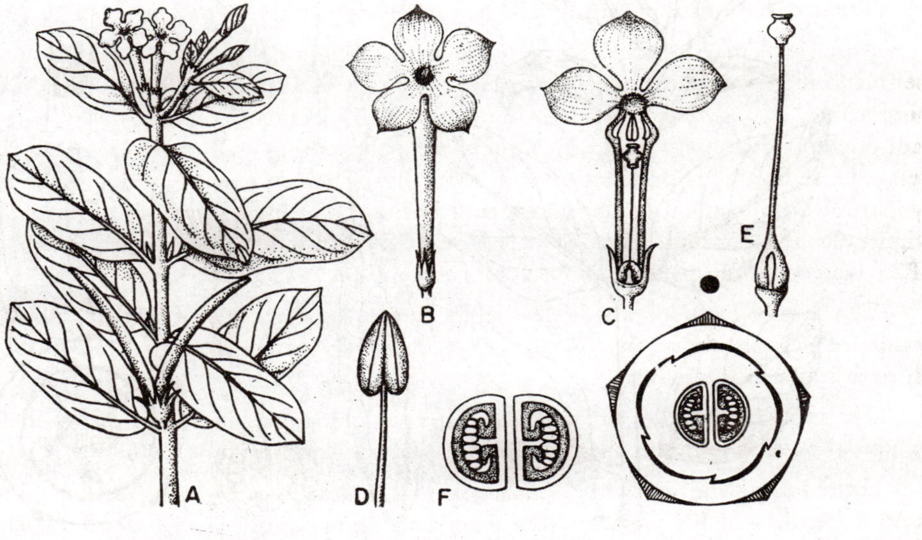

Fig. 128. **Catharanthus roseus (L.) G. Don. A. Leafy branch with flowers and fruits; B. One flower (×1); C. Corolla split open to show androecium and gynoecium; D. Stamen; E. Ovary with style and stigma; F. T.s. of ovary.**

Carissa carandas Linn. *Aganosma dichotoma* K. Schum., *Ervatania divaricata* Burkill, *Ichnocarpus frutescens* R. Br., *Wrightia coccinea* Sims, *Nerium indicum* Mill., *Rauvolfia serpentina* (L.) Benth & Kurz. etc.

Alstonia attains large size; other trees are usually short. *Ervatamia, Carissa, Kopsia,* etc. are shrubs, *Carissa* being spiny. *Aganosma, Vallaris, Beaumontia, Landolphia* are extensive climbers. *Landolphia* climbs by tendrils which are metamorphosed peduncles. *Catharanthus, Vinca,* etc. are undershrubs or herbs. *Adenium* is a succulent xerophyte. *Cerbera odollam* Gaertn. a small tree with drupaceous fruits grows in the magrove forests south of Bangladesh.

Leaves are opposite in most genera; 3 in a whorl in *Nerium, Rauvolfia* etc, 3-7 in *Alstonia,* while in *Cerbera* leaves are alternate, and spiral and crowded in *Thevetia.* Flowers bell-shaped in *Allamanda,* otherwise salver-shaped or funnel-shaped. Anthers are tailed in the subfamily *Echitoideae* but not so in *Plumerioideae.* There is no corona or any such outgrowth within the corolla of *Plumeria* which has a semi-inferior ovary. Fruits of *Melodinus* and *Carissa* are berries, those of *Thevetia, Cerbera, Rauvolfia,* are drupes and in most genera they are follicles. Seeds are peltately attached in *Carissa, Cerbera* etc. Ruminate endosperm is often found in *Ervatamia.*

The floral formula is expressed as: $\oplus$ ⚥ $K_{(5)}$ $\overline{C_{(5)}\ A_5}$ $G_{(\underline{2})}$.

The family is subdivided into 2 subfamilies as noted below:

Sub f. I. **Echitoideae**—Corolla lobes twisted to the right; stamens closely adherent to the stigma; anthers with distinct tails. *Nerium, Vallaris,* etc.

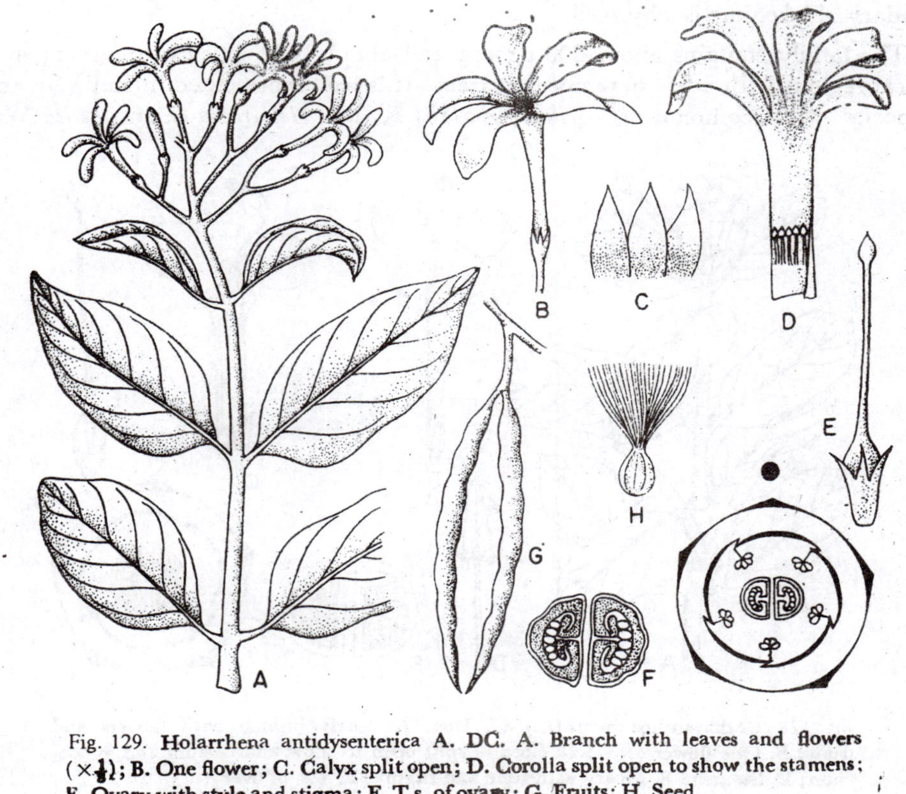

Fig. 129. **Holarrhena antidysenterica A. DC. A. Branch with leaves and flowers ($\times\frac{1}{3}$); B. One flower; C. Calyx split open; D. Corolla split open to show the stamens; E. Ovary with style and stigma; F. T.s. of ovary; G. Fruits; H. Seed.**

Sub f. II. **Plumieroideae**—Corolla lobes twisted to the left; stamens more or less free from stigma; anthers not tailed. *Plumeria*, *Catharanthus*, etc.

The family is closely allied to *Asclepiadaceae* and the two families are always included in the same order. It is related to *Oleaceae* and to *Gentianaceae* in some respects.

The family includes a few important medicinal plants, e.g, *Rauwolfia serpentina* (L.) Benth. ex. Kurz., *R. tetraphytta* Linn., *Holarrhena antidysenterica* Wall. etc. *Wrightia tinctoria* R. Br. yields a blue dye from the leaves. The latex of *Acokanthera* is deadly poisonous and is used in Africa as arrowpoison. Many other species have poisonous properties, and the latex of *Carpodinus lanceolatus* Schum., *Landolphia Kirki* Dyer contains caoutchoc. *Alstonia scholaris* R. Br. is a good timber plant the bark of which is used medicinally. A few are grown in gardens for the showy flowers, viz, *Nerium indicum* Mill. *Thevetia peruviana* Scham., *Plumeria rubra* Linn., *Catharanthus roseus* G. Don., etc.

Asclepiadaceae

Erect or climbing shrubs or herbs, rarely short trees, with milky latex. Leaves simple, entire, exstipulate, usually opposite or decussate Inflorescence cymose, often umbellate. Flowers bisexual, actinomorphic, hypogynous. Sepals 5, slightly united at the base, 5-partite. quincuncial. Corolla rotate or campanulate, 5-lobed, contorted or valvate in bud; often provided with appendages forming a corona. Stamens 5; filaments connate in a hollow column enclosing the style; the anthers adnate to the stigma in a 5-angled disc-shaped gynostegium; the pollens united in 1 or 2 pollinia in each anther lobe (Subfam. *Cynanchoideae*) or remain in tetrads (Subfam. *Periplocoideae*) or granular; the pollinia usually united in pairs to a gland on the pentangular stigmatic disc and are covered by a membrane. Carpels 2, free below and united by the styles and stigmas. Ovaries superior, with numerous anatropous ovules, pendulous from the ventral suture. Fruit a pair of follicles, seeds comose, with scanty cartilaginous endosperm and a large embryo.

The corona in *Asclepiadaceae* may be a true-corona of elaboration of fleshy filaments of stamens, or it may be a faucal annulus of the corolla tube, or appendages of the anthers. A pair of pollinia consists of the contents of adjacent anther cavities of contiguous anthers. Each pollinium has a translator arm, the translators with gland are formed between neighbouring anthers. The translator arm is often called retinaculum or connective and the gland the corpusculum.

In this family erect or climbing shrubs predominate. *Calotropis* often attains the size of a small tree. A few are xerophytes and are succulents, e.g. *Stapelia* where the leaves are modified to spines or reduced to scales. *Dischidia* and some species of *Hoya* are epiphytes. In *Dischidia* one of a pair of leaves is often transformed into a pitcher where rain water and dust particles collect and are absorbed by the plant by means of a few adventitious roots that grow inside the pitcher.

There is not much variation in the structure of flowers in this family, which has 2 distinct types of pollens, i.e. granular tetrads and pollinia. The flowers of *Ceropegia* is jug-shaped and slightly zygomorphic. *Secamone* has 4-celled anthers.

Floral formula is represented as: $\oplus$ ⚥ $K_{(5)}\ C_{(5)}\ A_{(5)}\ G_{(\underline{2})}$.

The family contains about 1800 species under about 250 genera in the tropical countries. In India *Asclepiadaceae* is well represented by about 330 species. *Calotropis gigantea* R. Br. and *C. procera* R. Br. are the Arka-puspa or Akanda common almost every where in the plains. *Hemidesmus indicus* R. Br., the Anantamool, is called the Indian Sarsaparila. *Finlaysonia maritima* Backer is a halophytic plant found to grow in Sundriban forests. *Dischidia* occurs in Assam and Chittagong. *Hoya* has several species in different forests in India. *Pergularia daemia* Chiov. is common in the plains.

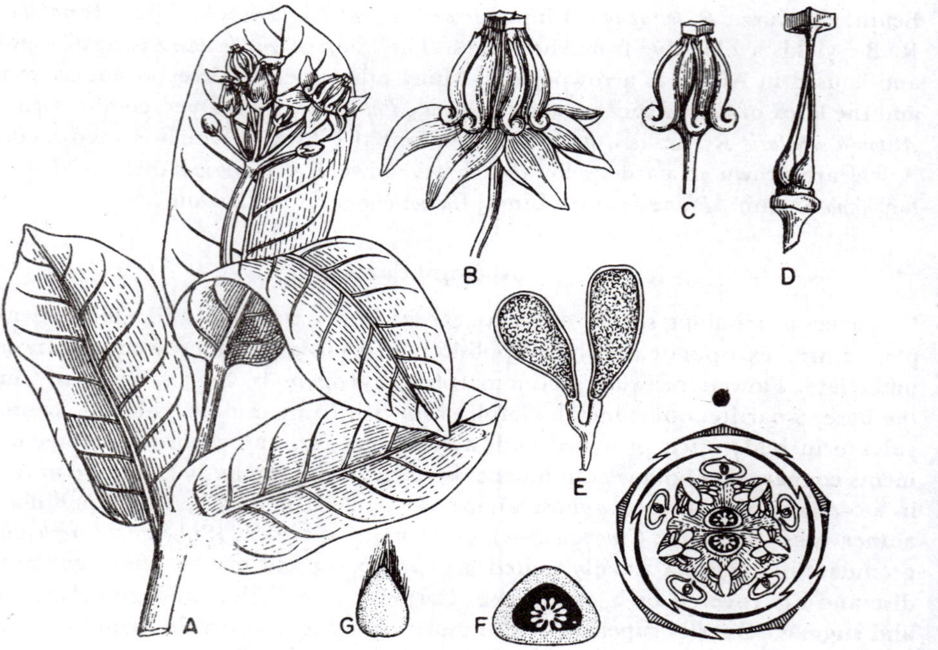

Fig. 130. Calotropis gigantea R. Br. A. Branch with leaves and flowers ($\times\frac{1}{3}$); B. Flower ($\times$1); C. Staminal corona; D. Ovary-free at base united by styles above with a pentagonal stigmatic disc; E. Pollinia; F. T.s of ovary; G. Seed.

The vascular anatomy shows the presence of intraxylary phloem. Latex tubes are present in almost all parts. In the erect plants vessels are usually small in dimensions but these are large in the climbers. Perforations are simple, sometimes ring porous and the intervascular pitting is alternate. Fibres are bordered or simple-pitted. Sunken stomata are found in most of the xerophytic plants.

The family is divided into 2 subfamilies based on pollen characters:—

I. Subf. **Periplocoideae:** Pollen granular, in tetrads; filaments free.

II. Subf. **Cynanchoideae:** Pollen grains united in pollinia; filaments united in a tube, surrounding the gynoecium.

The subfamily Periplocoideae is raised by some workers to the rank of a distinct family, viz. **Periplocaceae.**

Asclepiadaceae is closely allied to *Apocynaceae* and the 2 families are placed side by side in the different systems of classifications of the Angiosparms.

Economically the family is not very important. *Cryptostegia grandiflora* R. Br. yields a caoutchouc and is grown in some countries commercially. *Gymnema lactiferum* Linn. of

Ceylon yields edible milky latex. *Hemidesmus indicus* R. Br. is the Inidian Sarsaparila and is also used in snake-bite and scorpion-bite. Many species are poisonous and the latex of *Matelea* species is used as arrow-poison. *Gonolobus condurango* Linn. yields the medicinal condurango bark.

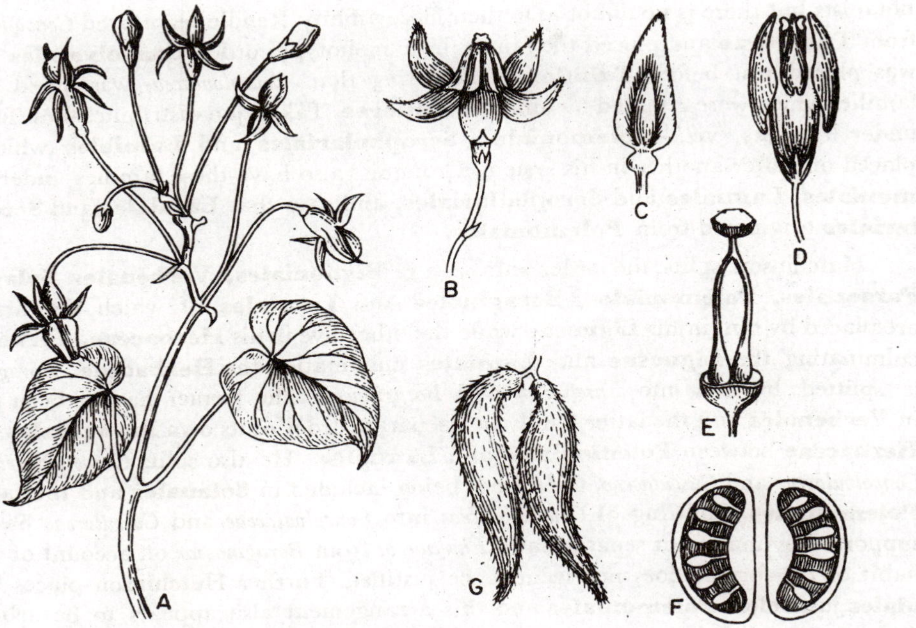

Fig. 131. Pergularia daemia A. Branch with leaves and flowers ($\times\frac{1}{8}$); B. One flower ($\times 1$); C. One petal; D. A flower with petals removed showing the staminal column; E. Gynoecium with 2 carpels—free at base united above with a peltate disc-like stigma; F. T.s. of ovary; G. A pair of follicles.

TUBIFLORAE

This is the 7th order under Metachlamydeae (or Sympetalae) and consists of 22 families under 8 suborders, viz.—

Convolvulineae: Convolvulaceae, Polemonaiceae, Fouquieraceae.

Lennoineae: Lennoaceae.

Boraginineae: Hydrophyllaceae, Boraginaceae.

Verbenineae: Verbenaceae, Labiatae.

Solanineae: Nolanaceae, Solanaceae, Scrophulariaceae, Bignoniaceae, Pedaliaceae, Martyniaceae, Orobanchaceae, Gesneriaceae, Columelliaceae. Lentibulariaceae, Globulariaceae.

Acanthineae: Acanthaceae.

Myoporineae: Myoporaceae.

Phyrmineae: Phyrmaceae.

The characters of the order are given as: Plants usually herbaceous, rarely woody. Leaves mostly simple, opposite or alternate. Flowers bisexual, actinomorphic or zygomorphic, hypogynous, rarely epigynous, tetracyclic. Petals united, induplicate-valvate in bud. Stamens 4, epipetalous, Ovary bicarpellary and 2 to 1-celled or rarely 3-5-carpellary with as many cells; ovules many or few in each cell with one integument only; placentation marginal.

These families have been distributed under more than one order by subsequent botanists but there is no doubt as to their close affinity. Rendle segregated *Convolvulaceae* from **Tubiflorae** and placed the family in a monotypic order **Convolvulales** which was placed just before **Tubiflorae** indicating that *Convolvulaceae* was allied to the families which were retained by him in **Tubiflorae.** Takhtajan distributes these families under 3 orders, viz.—**Polemoniales, Scrophulariales** and **Lamiales** which are placed one after another in his system. Cronquist also have these families under **Polemoniales, Lamiales** and **Scrophulariales,** and says that **Lamiales** and **Scrophulariales** originated from **Polemoniales.**

Hutchinson splits the order into 7, e.g. **Bignoniales, Verbenales Solanales, Personales, Polemoniales, Boraginales** and **Lamiales** of which the first two are placed by him in his **Lignosae** while the other five in his **Herbaceae. Verbenales** culminating the **Lignosae** and **Lamiales** culminating the **Herbaceae.** *Boraginaceae* is splitted by him into *Ehretiaceae* and *Boraginaceae*, the former having been placed in **Verbenales** and the latter family in a separate order of its own **Boraginales** in the **Herbaceae** between **Polemoniales** and **Lamiales.** He also splits *Convolvulaceae* into *Convolvulaceae* and *Cuscutaceae*, the former being included in **Solanales** and the latter in **Polemoniales.** Splitting of *Convolvulaceae* into *Convolvulaceae* and *Cuscutaceae* has been supported by many but separation of *Ehretiaceae* from *Boraginaceae* on account of woody habit of the former does not seem to be justified. Further Hutchinson places **Geraniales** just before **Polemoniales** and this arrangement also appears to be arbitrary. *Verbenaceae* and *Labiatae* (*Lamiaceae*) are considered by almost all workers in taxonomy to be very closely related to each other but Hutchinson not only puts them under two separate orders, viz. **Verbenales** and **Lamiales** but these two orders are placed far apart in his system of classification, **Verbenales** in **Lignosae** and **Lamiales** in **Herbaceae.**

Convolvulaceae

Annual or perennial herbs or shrubs, usually twining or trailing, rarely erect and rarely leafless parasite (e.g., *Cuscuta*, now transferred to *Cuscutaceae*). Leaves alternate, simple, entire or pinnately or palmately lobed, exstipulate. Inflorescence is a biparous cyme or cymose or racemose panicle, or flowers solitary, bracteate. Flowers actinomorphic, bisexual, hypogynous, usually showy. Sepals 5, usually free to the base, quincuncial, often persistent; the outermost sepal sometimes larger. Petals 5, united to form a funnel-shaped or salver-shaped corolla, induplicate-valvate or twisted in bud; lobes often with median folds. Stamens 5, epipetalous, inserted at the base of the corolla tube and alternating with the lobes of the corolla; anthers 2-celled, usually introrse; pollens ellipsoid or globose, smooth or spinulose; annulār or cupular intrastaminal disc usually present. Carpels 2, rarely 3-5, united to form a superior ovary; ovary 2-celled with 2 ovules in each cell, or 4-celled due to presence of false septa with one ovule in each cell, or when more than 2 carpels are present cells of ovary as many as carpels; ovules erect, anatropous; style 1, filiform, bipartite or not, rarely styles 2; stigma capitate or bilobed. Fruit a capsule, rarely berry; seeds smooth or hairy, with cartilagenous endosperm; embryo curved with folded cotyledons.

A family of predominantly twining or trailing plants includes a few erect shrubs, rarely attaining tree size. *Ipomoea wolcottiana* Rose. is a tree often as tall as 10 m. *I. arborescens* Don. is a large shrub or a short tree. *Erycibe paniculata* Roxb. is a diffuse shrub or a short tree. Leaves are simple, lobed or entire, but palmate leaves are found in *Ipomoea pulchella* Roth.,—the Railway creeper. Flowers are actinomorphic and bisexual, but *Mina lobata* Ll. & L. has slightly zygomorphic flowers and in *Hildebrandtia* the flowers are unisexual.

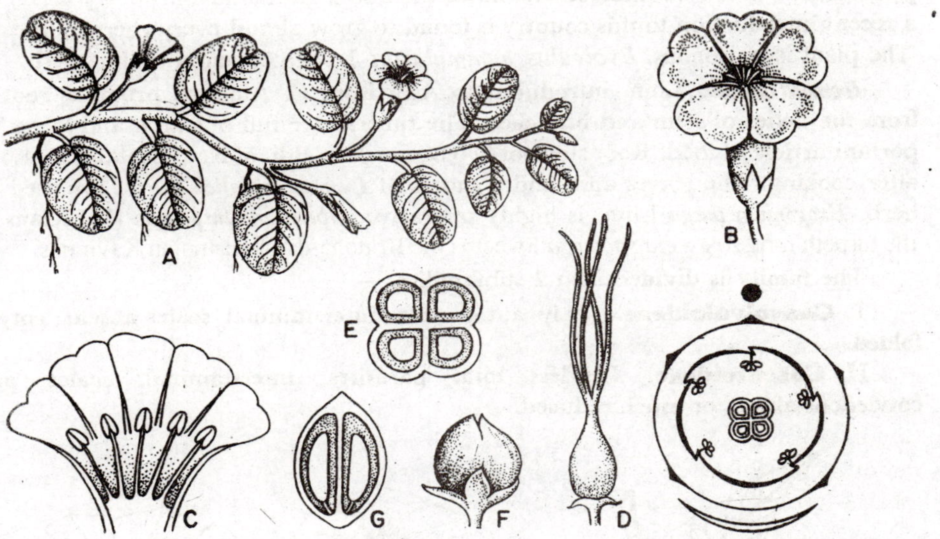

Fig. 132. Evolvulus nummularius Linn. A. Leafy branch with flowers (×1); B. One flower (×2); C. Corolla split open to show insertion of stamens; D. Ovary with 2 bicleft styles; E. T.s. of ovary; F. Fruit G. L.s. of ovary.

Cuscuta is a total parasite. It is leafless and rootless. A corona is present at the base of the corolla formed of staminodes alternating with stamens. This genus is now placed in a distinct unigeneric family *Cuscutaceae*.

Adventitious roots from the nodes of stems come out in many species and in *I. batatas* Linn. they form tubers which are edible. Extra floral nectaries on the leaves of many species are found.

Presence of intraxylary phloem in the stem is a constant character. Anomalous secondary growth occurs in many climbing species due to formation of successive rings of intraxylary phloem and secondary accessary vascular bundles. Fibres in the pericycle is usually scanty, rarely in a continuous ring. Vessels solitary or in multiples; intervascular pitting is alternate. Wood parenchyma scanty, paratracheal or apotracheal; fibres are bordered pitted.

The family consists of about 1200 species in about 50 genera and is cosmopolitan in the tropical and temperate regions. About 177 species are found in India of which a few are cultivated for large showy flowers.

The floral formula of the family is represented as: $\oplus$ ⚥ $K_5\ C_{(5)}\ A_5\ G_{(\underline{2})}$.

Convolvulaceae is closely related to *Solanaceae* as well as to *Nolanaceae* and also to

Polemoniaceae, *Boraginaceae* and *Hydrophyllaceae* to some extent. According to Takhtajan *Convolvulaceae* is more allied to *Polemoniaceae*, *Boraginaceae* and *Hydrophyllaceae* than to *Solanaceae* and *Nolanaceae*. *Convolvulaceae* is placed by him in **Polemoniales** while *Solanaceae* and *Nolanaceae* are included by him in **Scrophulariales.**

The family is well-known for the ornamental plants with large showy flowers. *Ipomoea purpurea* Lamk. is the Morning glory. *I. pulchella* Roth. is the Railway creeper. Many other species of the genus are cultivated in gardens. *I. quamoclit* Linn. with linear-pinnatisect leaves and small scarlet flowers is also a garden favourite. *I. fistulosa* Choisy a recent introduction to this country is found to grow almost everywhere in the plains. The plant is poisonous. *Evolvulus nummularius* L. is a common trailing herb.

Ipomoea batatas Linn. introduced to Asia from C. America produces root-tubers from the nodes of stem and branches. The tubers are full of starch and forms an important article of food. Root stock of *Colystegia sepium* Bth. of New Zealand is also edible after cooking. The leaves and tender shoots of *Ipomoea aquatica* Forsk. are used as pot-herb. *Exogonium purga* Linn. is highly purgative. *Operculina turpethum* (L.) Mans. yields the turpeth root. *Argyreia speciosa* Sweet is the Briddha-darak of Indian Kavirajas.

The family is divided into 2 subfamilies:—

I. **Convolvuloideae.** Leafy autophytes; interstaminal scales absent; cotyledons folded.

II. **Cuscutoideae.** Leafless total parasites; interstaminal scales present; cotyledons absent or much reduced.

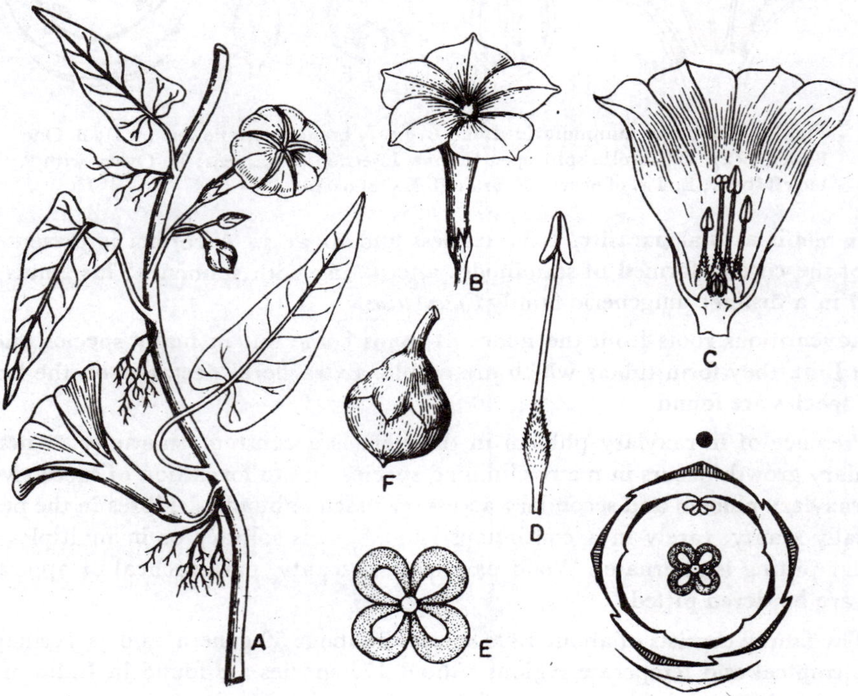

Fig. 133. Ipomoea aquatica Forsk. A. Part of a branch with leaves and flowers, rooting at the noxes ($\times\frac{1}{2}$); B. One flower; C. Vertical section of the same to show stamens and ovary: D. One stamen; E. T.s. of ovary; F. Fruit.

The subfamily *Cuscutoideae* is treated as a distinct family *Cuscutaceae* by Hutchinson. The conscription of the new-family is given below :

Rootless, leafless parasitic climber with thread-like herbaceous stem. Flowers actinomorphic, bisexual, small, in stalked or sessile clusters. Sepals minute, 4-5, free or united. Petals 4-5, united, bell-shaped; lobes imbricate. Stamens 4-5, inserted on the throat of the corolla and alternating with corolla lobes; staminodial scales are present at the base of corolla alternating with the stamens, scales fimbriate or lobed. Ovary superior, 2-locular, with axile ovules in each chamber; styles 2, distinct or more or less connate. Fruit a dry or fleshy capsule, dehiscing irregularly or transversely. Seeds tubercled; embryo linear, curved or spirally twisted; cotyledons much reduced or absent.

The family with the single genus *Cuscuta* contains about 170 species spread over the tropical and temperate regions of the world. A few species of the genus are Indian and *C. reflexa* Roxb. is common as pest all over the country in the plains.

Boraginaceae

Annual or perennial herbs or shrubs or trees, usually pubescent. Leaves simple, entire, exstipulate, usually alternate. Inflorescence a simple or double scorpioid cyme, coiled in young stage. Flowers bisexual, actinomorphic or slightly zygomorphic, hypogynous. Sepals 5, free or united in a bell-shaped or tubular calyx, imbricate or rarely valvate, usually persistent. Petals 5, blue or white, united in a funnel-shaped or rotate corolla with spreading lobes, imbricate or rarely contorted; throat with scale-like outgrowths. Stamens 5, epipetalous, alternating with corolla lobes, filaments equal or rarely unequal; anthers 2-celled, introrse; an annular nectar secreting disc is usually present. Carpels 2, syncarpous, forming a superior 2-celled ovary with 2 basal ovules in each cell; often each cell at maturity is divided into 2 parts, so that the ovary becomes 4-celled with 1 ovule in each cell; style usually gynobasic, rarely terminal, when terminal styles often 2; stigma capitate or lobed. Fruit a cluster of 4 nutlets or a drupe. Seeds with or without endosperm; embryo straight or curved with radicle turning upwards.

The family includes herbs as well as trees or shrubs, e.g. *Cordia*, *Ehretia*, etc. The herbaceous plants are usually pubescent with thick-walled stiff hairs with cystolith like bodies in the basal region. Heterophylly is found in a few genera, viz. *Pulmonaria*, *Cynoglossum*, etc. where the cauline leaves are different from the radical leaves. Flowers are more or less zygomorphic in *Echium* and *Lycopsis*. The style is terminal in the subfamilies *Cordioideae*, *Ehretioideae* and *Heliotropioideae* but gynobasic in others. In *Echium* the style is bipartite.

Floral formula: ⊕ ⚥ $K_5\ C_{(5)}\ A_5\ G_{\underline{(2)}}$.

Vessels are often in clusters with simple perforations and the intervascular pitting is alternate. Wood parenchyma is apotracheal. Fibres have small bordered pits. Pericycle is usually without fibres.

The family consists of about 100 genera and about 2000 species and is distributed mostly in the temperate regions while a good number of species are found also in the tropics. In India 145 species are found. Species of *Myosotis* (*M. palustris* Bth.) are the Forget me-not flowers of European medows, also available in the Himalayas. *Cynoglossum* is another Himalayan genus of herbs with small blue flowers. *Heliotropium indicum* Linn.-Beng. Hatishura is a common weed of the road side in the plains. *Cordia dichotoma* Forst.

the Lasora, a short sized tree is found all over India in the plains. *Ehretia serrata* Roxb. is another Indian tree found near the foot hills of the Himalaya. *Coldenia procumbens* Linn. is a prostrate herb common in the dry fields.

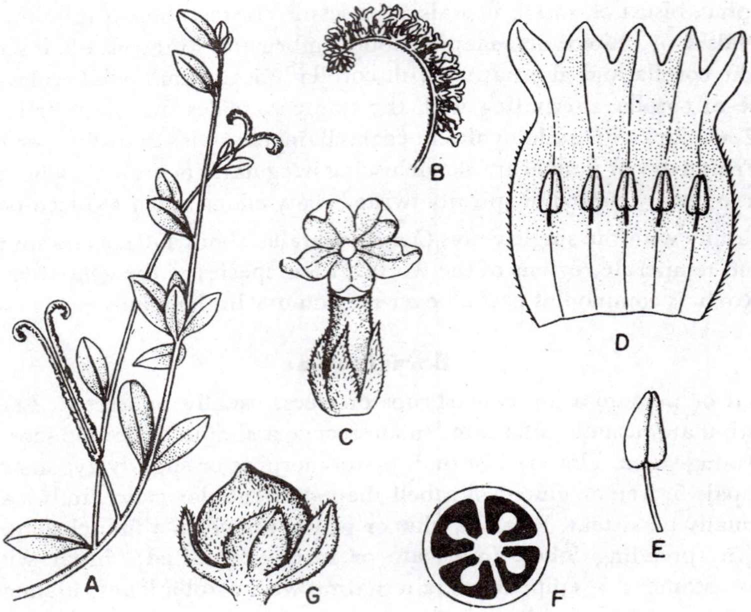

Fig. 134. Heliotropium ovalifolium Forsk. A. Leafy shoot with scorpioid cymes ($\times\frac{1}{3}$); B. Part of the inflorescence ($\times 1$); C. One flower (much enlarged); D. Corolla split open to show the stamen; E. Stamen; F. T.s. of ovary; G. Fruit.

The family is not important from the economic point of view. A dye is obtained from *Alkanna tinctoria* Linn. and also from different species of *Arnebia*. The wood of *Ehretia serrata* Roxb. is very hard and is used as tool-handles. *Cordia sebestena* Linn. is cultivated in gardens for the large orange-red flowers. Many species of *Myosotis* and *Cynoglossum* are also cultivated in gardens in the cold countries.

The family is divided into 5 subfamilies as noted below:

I. Style terminal; fruit a drupe.

Subfam. 1. **Cordioideae:** Style 4-fid; drupe 4-celled.

Subfam. 2. **Ehretioideae:** Style bifid or styles 2; drupe 2-seeded or of four 1-seeded pyrenes.

Subfam. 3. **Heliotropioideae:** Style simple or bifid; a ring of hairs present below stigma, fruit drupe or nutlets.

II. Style gynobasic; fruit of 4 nutlets.

Subfam. 4. **Boraginoideae:** Corolla with scales inside or not, often bent or zygomorphic; nutlets 4 or less.

Subfam. 5. **Wellstedioideae:** Flowers 4-merous; ovary 2-celled with 1 ovule in each cell.

The family is closely allied to *Polemoniaceae* and *Hydrophyllaceae*. It is also related to *Solanaceae* and *Nolanaceae* on one side and to *Convolvulaceae* on the other. Hutchinson splitted *Boraginaceae* into *Boraginacea* and *Ehretiaceae* and these 2 families are placed wide apart. *Boraginaceae* is placed by him in a monotypic order **Boraginales** which is placed between **Polemoniales** and **Lamiales.** *Ehretiaceae* is included by him in his **Verbenales.** This treatment of the family by Hutchinson has not been supported by subsequent botanists.

Verbenaceae

Herbs, shrubs or trees, usually with square stem. Leaves opposite or whorled, simple or pinnately or palmately compound, exstipulate. Inflorescence cymose or racemose, often paniculate, or a dense spicate head, usually bracteate. Flowers usually zygomorphic, bisexual, rarely polygamous. Calyx of 5 united sepals, tubular or bell-shaped, persistent; teeth or lobes valvate, often more than 5. Corolla of 5 united petals,

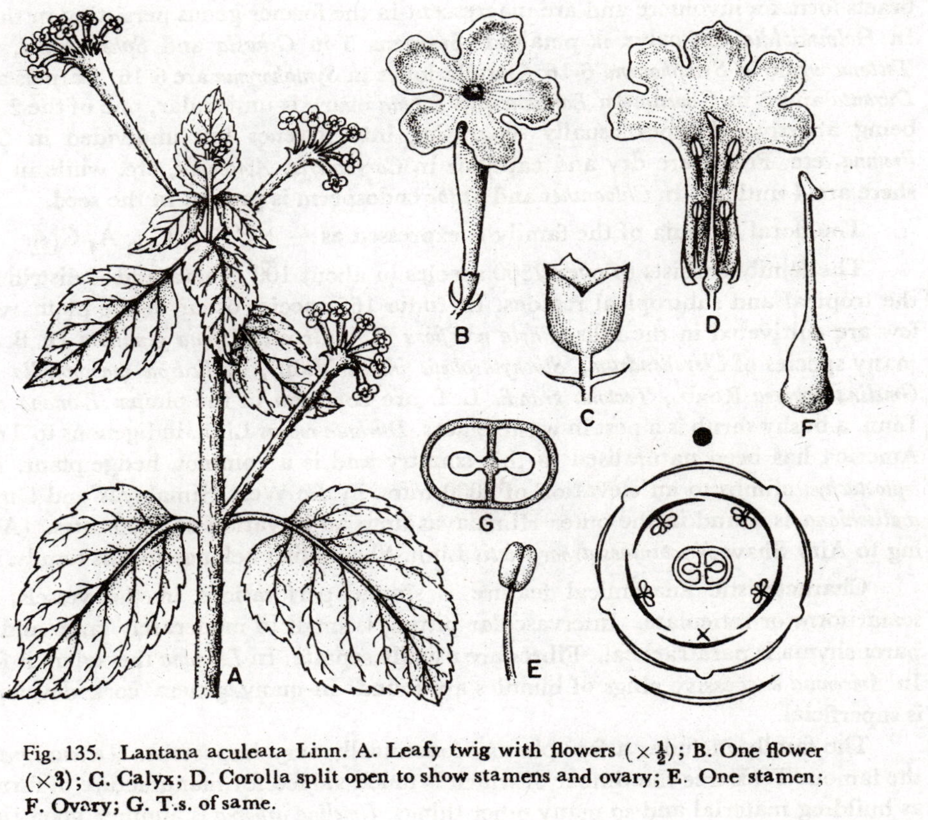

Fig. 135. Lantana aculeata Linn. A. Leafy twig with flowers ($\times \frac{1}{2}$); B. One flower ($\times 3$); C. Calyx; D. Corolla split open to show stamens and ovary; E. One stamen; F. Ovary; G. T.s. of same.

bilabiate or bell-shaped and oblique with spreading limb; lobes imbricate. Stamens 4, epipetalous, didynamous, often only 2, rarely 5; staminodes often present in diandrous flowers; filaments free, usually pairs unequal in length; anthers 2-celled, opening lengthwise; often an inconspicuous disc is present. Carpels 2, syncarpous in a superior 2-celled or 4-celled or rarely 1-celled ovary; ovules 1 or 2 in each cell with downwardly directed micropyle; style terminal; stigma 2-lobed or entire. Fruit usually drupaceous,

1-4-seeded, often enclosed in the persistent calyx. Seed usually without endosperm; embryo straight.

The plants vary in habit from small trailing herb like *Phyla nodiflora* (L.) Green to lofty trees like *Tectona grandis* L. f. and *Gmelina arborea* Roxb. *Petrea volubilis* Linn. is a climber or a scandent shrub. *Avicennia* a genus of trees in mangrove forests develop pneumatophores and have fruits that germinate viviparously. Several species of *Clerodendrum* are myrmecophilous, e.g. *C. fistulosum* Becc. that shelter ants in the hollow internodes. Leaves are usually simple but compound leaves are found in *Vitex*. The leaves of *Verbena* is often very finely sected. Inflorescence is racemose or cymose. In *Lippia*, *Stachytarpheta* it is a spike, dense cylindrical head in the former and long and slender in the latter. Pendulous spike occurs in *Citharexylum*, *Petrea*, etc. and in some *Verbena*. Dichasial cyme is found in most *Clerodendrum* while in *C. fragrans* Vent it is compact and corymbose. Unisexual flowers are found in *Aegiphila*, actinomorphic in *Callicarpa* and tetramerous in *Physopsis*, *Callicarpa*, etc. In *Symphorema* and *Sphenodesma* the bracts form an involucre and are macrescent in the former genus persisting in the fruit. In *Holmskioldia* the calyx is petaloid. Stamens 5 in *Genusia* and *Sphenodesma*, 5-6 in *Tectona* while in *Symphorema* 6-16. Corolla lobes in *Symphorema* are 6-16. Carpels are 4 in *Duranta* and 5 in *Genusia*. In *Lantana* and *Lippia* ovary is unilocular, one of the 2 carpels being abortive. Drupes usually separating into pyrenes but undivided in *Gmelina*, *Premna*, etc. Fruits are dry and capsular in *Caryopteris*, *Avicennia*, etc. while in *Verbena* there are 4 nutlets. In *Chloanthes* and *Stilbe* endosperm is present in the seed.

The floral formula of the family is expressed as:— † ⚥ $K_{(5)}$ $C_{(5)}$ A_4 $G_{\underline{(2)}}$.

The family consists of over 2500 species in about 100 genera and is distributed in the tropical and subtropical regions. In India 165 species occur in the plains while a few are cultivated in the hills. *Phyla nodiflora* (L.) Green, *Lippia geminata* H. B. & K., many species of *Clerodendrum*, *Stachytarpheta indica* Vahl., *Callicarpa macrophylla* Vahl., *Gmelina arborea* Roxb., *Tectona grandis* L. f. are common in the plains. *Lantana aculeata* Linn. a bushy shrub is a pest in waste places. *Duranta repens* Linn. indigenous to Tropical America has been naturalised in this country and is a common hedge plant. *Phryma leptostachya* climbs to an elevation of 2000 mtrs. in the West Himalayas and *Caryopteris wallichiana* is found in the outer Himalayas upto an elevation of 1500 mtrs. (According to Airy Shaw *Nyctanthes arbor-tristis* Linn.-Shephalika belongs to this family.)

Characteristic anatomical feature is simple perforations in the vessels, rarely scalariform or reticulate. Intervascular pitting is small to moderately large and wood parenchyma is paratracheal. Fibres are usually septate. In *Lantana* the xylem is forked. In *Avicennia* successive rings of bundles are found. In many genera cork development is superficial.

The family includes a few plants economically very important. *Tectona grandis* is the famous Teak tree the timber of which is much valued for manufacture of furniture, as building material and so many other things. *Gmelina arborea* is another good timber tree. *Vitex negeundo* Linn. is a febrifuge and *V. peduncularis* is effective in Kalazar or Black fever *Clerodendrum indicum* (L.) O. Ktz. (Syn. *C. siphonanthus* R. Br.) is also said to have medicinal value *Clerodendrum fragrans* is often cultivated for beautiful flowers in a compact inflorescence. Sp. of *Verbena* is cultivated in the plains as well as in the hills. Bark of *Avicennia* is used in tanning. *Premna barbata* and *P. latifolia* of the outer Himalayas have the wood very hard and are useful in different ways. They yield good fuel and can be ignited by friction.

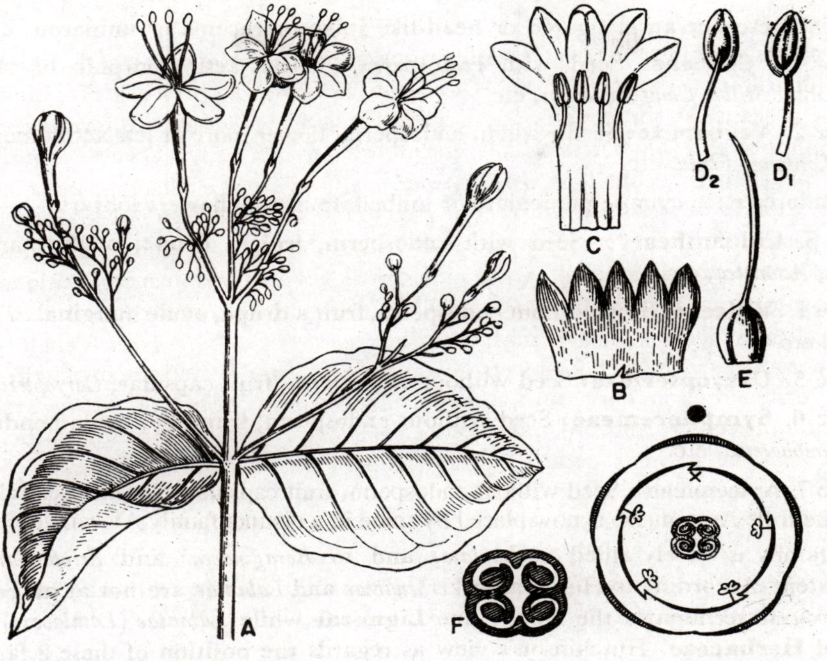

Fig. 136. Clerodendrum viscosum Vent. A. Terminal panicle with a pair of leaves below (slightly reduced); B. Calyx tube split open; C. Corolla split open to show the stamens; D_1 & D_2. Stamens showing front and back of anther; E. Ovary; F. T.s. of ovary.

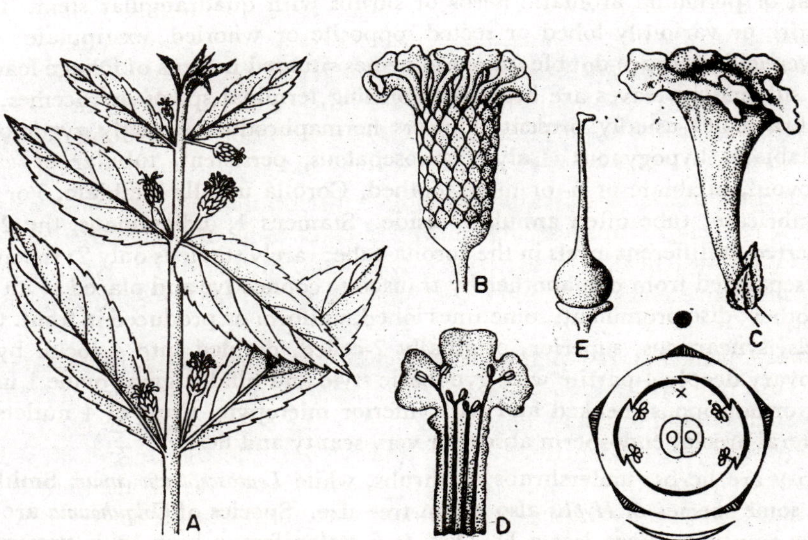

Fig. 137. Lippia geminata H. B, & K. A. Leafy branch with axillary spikes ($\times\frac{1}{3}$); B. A. spike with imbricating bracts and flowers ($\times 1$); C. One flower with bracteoles ($\times 3$); D. Corolla split open to show the stamens; E. Ovary.

The family is divided by Briquet into 7 tribes as noted below:—

A. Inflorescence an elongated or head-like spike or raceme or uniparous cyme.

Tribe 1. **Stilbeae:** Seed with endosperm, flower actinomorphic or slightly zygomorphic. *Stilbe*, *Campylostachys*, etc.

Tribe 2. **Verbeneae:** Seed without endosperm, flower more or less actinomorphic. *Verbena*, *Lantana*, *Phyla*, etc.

B. Inflorescence cymose paniculate or umbellate, rarely flowers solitary.

Tribe 3. **Chloantheae** : Seed with endosperm, fruit a drupe, ovule marginal. *Chloanthus*, *Acharitea*, etc.

Tribe 4. **Viliceae:** Seed without endosperm, fruit a drupe, ovule marginal. *Tectona*, *Callicarpa*, etc.

Tribe 5. **Caryopterieae:** Seed without endosperm, fruit capsular. *Caryopteris*, etc.

Tribe 6. **Symphoremeae:** Seed without endosperm, fruit dry, ovule pendulous. *Congea*, *Symphorema*, etc.

Tribe 7. Avicenneae : Seed without endosperm, fruit capsular, placenta central. *Avicennia*. The tribe Avicenneae is now placed by some in a distinct family Avicenniaceae.

The family is closely allied to *Labiatae* and to *Boraginaceae* and *Scrophulariaceae* to some extent. According to Hutchinson *Verbenaceae* and *Labiatae* are not at all related and *Verbenaceae* terminates the woody line **Lignosae** while *Labiatae* (*Lamiaceae*) is at the end of **Herbaceae**. Hutchinson's view as regards the position of these 2 families in the system of classification has not been accepted by subsequent workers.

Labiatae
(Lamiaceae)

Annual or perennial aromatic herbs or shrubs with quadrangular stem. Leaves simple, entire or variously lobed or sected, opposite or whorled, exstipulate. Floral whorls or verticillasters are double unipared cymes situated in axils of foliage leaves, or where the subtending leaves are bract-like forming terminal spikes or racemes, often panicled; bracteoles usually present. Flowers hermaphrodite, strongly zygomorphic, usually bilabiate, hypogynous. Calyx gamosepalous, persistent, tubular or campanulate or ovoid, bilabiate or 5- or more-toothed. Corolla usually bilabiate, 5 or rarely 4 lobed, imbricate; tube often annulate inside. Stamens 4, didynamous, the 2 pairs usually inserted at different levels in the corolla-tube; rarely stamens only 2; the anther-cells often separated from one another by transverse connective and placed at an angle with each other; disc prominent, sometimes lobed, uniform or produced in front. Ovary of 2 carpels, syncarpous, superior, originally 2-celled, divided into 4 loculi by false partition, ovary deeply 4-partite with gynobasic style and bifid stigma; ovule 1 in each cell, erect, orthotropous, beaked and with inferior micropyle. Fruit of 4 nutlets with basal or lateral areola, endosperm absent or very scanty and fleshy.

Majority are herbs, undershrubs or shrubs, while *Leucosceptrum canum* Smith is a short tree; some species of *Hyptis* also attain tree size. Species of *Colquhounia* are often scandent or rambler. *Ajuga lobata* D. Don. is a stoloniferous herb with prostrate or creeping stem. *Leucas biflora* R. Br. has long procumbent branches. Leaves are whorled in *Plectranthees ternifolius* D. Don (*Rabdosia ternifolia*), *Leucas ternifolia* Desf. etc. and fascicled in *Leucas rosamarinifolia* Bth.. Pinnately compound leaves are found in *Salvia hydrangea* DC. and *S. plectranthoicles* Griffith, trifoliate in *Rubiteucris palmata* Kudo, finely seeted in *Dracocephalum tanguticum* Maxim. and more or less lyrate in *Eremostachys*. The terminal spikes are often very dense and head-like. In *Notochaete hamosa* Benth. the axillary inflorescence is a globose head. Globose head-like inflorescence also occur in some *Hyptis*. Calyx 2-lipped in many genera with unequal teeth or tubular with the teeth equal in others. In *Scutellaria* the upper lip with a pouch or shield-like protuberance. In *Otostegia* the calyx limb is very much expanded at the mouth. Corolla almost always bilabiate but in *Teucrium* there is no upper lip, the limb is slit behind to form a 5-lobed lower lip. In *Coleus* the stamens are monadelphous, the filaments connate below in a sheath separate from the corolla. Perfect stamens only 2 in *Salvia*; the connective linear, transverse with an upper arm having one fertile anthercell and a lower arm with or without any anthercell. In *Leucosceptrum* the anther is unilocular and reniform. In *Lycopus*, *Perowskia*, *Ziziphora* etc. there are only 2 perfect stamens. Nutlets with a thick and more or less fleshy pericarp in *Gomphostemma*. In *Ajuga*, *Cymaria*, *Leucosceptrum* and a few other genera the areola of the nutlets are lateral.

The family Labiatae is mainly distributed in the temperate regions and consists of about 200 genera and 3000 species. About 350 species are found in India in the Himalayas and in the hills of Assam and Peninsular India. Quite a good number are also common in the plains, e.g. *Ocimum sanctum* Linn., *Salvia plebeja* R. Br.; *Leonurus sibiricus*

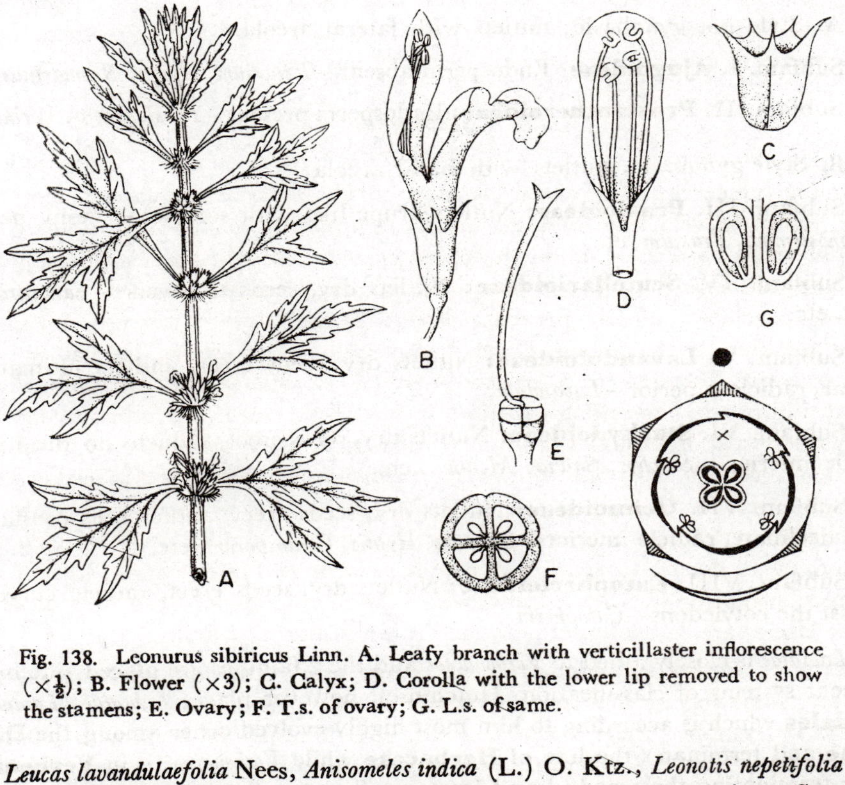

Fig. 138. Leonurus sibiricus Linn. A. Leafy branch with verticillaster inflorescence (×½); B. Flower (×3); C. Calyx; D. Corolla with the lower lip removed to show the stamens; E. Ovary; F. T.s. of ovary; G. L.s. of same.

Linn., *Leucas lavandulaefolia* Nees, *Anisomeles indica* (L.) O. Ktz., *Leonotis nepetifolia* R. Br. *Pogostemon plectranthoides* Dcsf., *Leucas cephalotes* Spr. etc. *Leucosceptrum canum* Sm., many species of *Nepeta*, *Salvia*, *Thymus serpyllum* Linn., *Mentha arvensis* Linn., *M. sylvestris* Linn.,

Royllea calycina Briq., a few species of *Phlomis*, *Dracocephalum*, *Stachys*, *Scutellaria*, etc. are Himalayan.

Vessels occur in multiples in many vascular bundles., very small in dimension, usually with spiral thickenings and are semi-ringporous; perforations are simple and intervascular pitting is alternate. Wood parenchyma is poorly developed and paratracheal. Fibres are simple-pitted and sometimes septate. In pericycle schlerenchyma fibres are few in isolated strands. Endodermis is often indistinct.

Many species contain volatile oil. *Lavandula vera* DC. is the source of lavender oil. Oil of rosemary is obtained from *Rosmarinus officinalis* Linn. *Thymus vulgaris* Linn. yields thymol, while menthol is obtained from *Mentha piperata* Linn. *Mentha viridis* Linn. is Pudina, much used to flavour curries and chutney. *Mentha cablin* Bth. gives patchouli oil and *Pogostemon Heyneanus* Benth. the Indian Patchouli is a substitute. The root-tubers of *Stachys palustris*, some species of *Coleus* and *Ocimum* are edible. *Ocimum Kilimandscharicum* Gurke is the camphor basil, from the oil of which camphor is manufactured. Seeds of *Ocimum americanum* Linn. *O. basilicum* Linn. and *Lallemantia Royleana* Benth. become mucilagenous when wetted and a poultice of the same is applied to abscesses and boils. The juice of the leaves of *Ocimum sanctum* Linn. is used in catarrhal affections of children. *Leucas cephalotes* Spr. is also reputed to have medicinal properties.

The family has been divided into 8 subfamilies by Briquet as noted below:

A. Style not gynobasic; nutlets with lateral areola.

Subfam. I. **Ajugoideae:** Endosperm absent—*Teucrium*, *Ajuga*, *Rosmarinus*, etc.

Subfam. II. **Prostantheroideae:** Endosperm present—*Prostanthera*, *Wrixonia*, etc.

B. Style gynobasic, nutlets with basal areola.

Subfam. III. **Prasioideae:** Nutlets drupe like with somewhat fleshy pericarp—*Gomphostemma*, *Prasium*, etc.

Subfam. IV. **Scutellarioideae:** Nutlets dry, seeds transverse—*Salazaria*, *Scutellaria*, etc.

Subfam. V. **Lavanduloideae:** Nutlets dry, seeds erect, anthers ultimately unilocular, radicle superior—*Lavandula*.

Subfam. VI. **Stachydoideae:** Nutlets dry, seeds erect, stamens on the upper lip, radicle inferior.—*Stachys*, *Salvia*, *Mentha*, etc.

Subfam. VII. **Ocimoideae:** Nutlets dry, seeds erect, anther cells confluent, stamens declinate, radicle inferior—*Ocimum*, *Hyptis*, *Geniosporum*, etc.

Subfam. VIII. **Catopherioideae:** Nutlets dry, seeds erect, radicle curved lying against the cotyledons—*Catopheria*.

Labiatae is closely allied to *Verbenaceae* and the 2 families are placed side by side in different systems of classification. Hutchinson however places *Labiatae* (*Lamiaceae*) in **Lamiales** which is according to him most highly evolved order among the **Dicotyledonae** and terminates the line of **Herbaceae** while *Verbenaceae* is in **Verbenales** an order terminating the woody line **Lignosae.** So according to Hutchinson *Verbenaceae* and *Labiatae* are not allied to each other.

Solanaceae

Herbs or shrubs, rarely small trees or climbers; the juice is often poisonous. **Leaves** simple, alternate, exstipulate, often lobed. **Inflorescence** a cyme or cymose panicle, often helicoid cyme, terminal or axillary or lateral or extra-axillary, often solitary or in clusters; bracts and bracteoles absent. **Flowers** actinomorphic or zygomorphic, bisexual, hypogynous, with a flat thalamus. **Calyx** gamosepalous, usually 5-lobed, persistent and enlarging in fruit. **Corolla** gamopetalous, rotate or funnel- or bell-shaped, rarely bilabiate, plicate-imbricate or plicate-convolute. **Stamens** 5, epipetalous, alternating with corolla-lobes, sometimes 4 and often didynamous; anthers 2-celled or 1-celled, often connivent, dehiscing longitudinally or by apical pores; connective often prolonged; a hypogynous disc usually present. **Carpels** 2, syncarpous in an obliquely placed superior ovary, 2-celled or 3-5-celled due to false partitions; ovules anatropous, numerous on thick axile placentas; style terminal, simple; stigma capitate or bilobed. **Fruit** a capsule or a berry, often enclosed within the enlarged calyx. **Seeds** compressed, discoid or reniform, with fleshy and translucent endosperm and straight or curved embryo.

The leaf arrangement is peculiar in some species. The leaves are in pairs of which one is larger than the others. Often both the leaves of a pair are raised to a higher position or only one is raised and the other remains in original place. In the former case they appear to be the leaves of the axillary branches which terminate in a flower. In the other case the larger leaf of the pair has a branch in the axil and is raised to a higher position in the axillary shoot, while the smaller leaf without any axillary

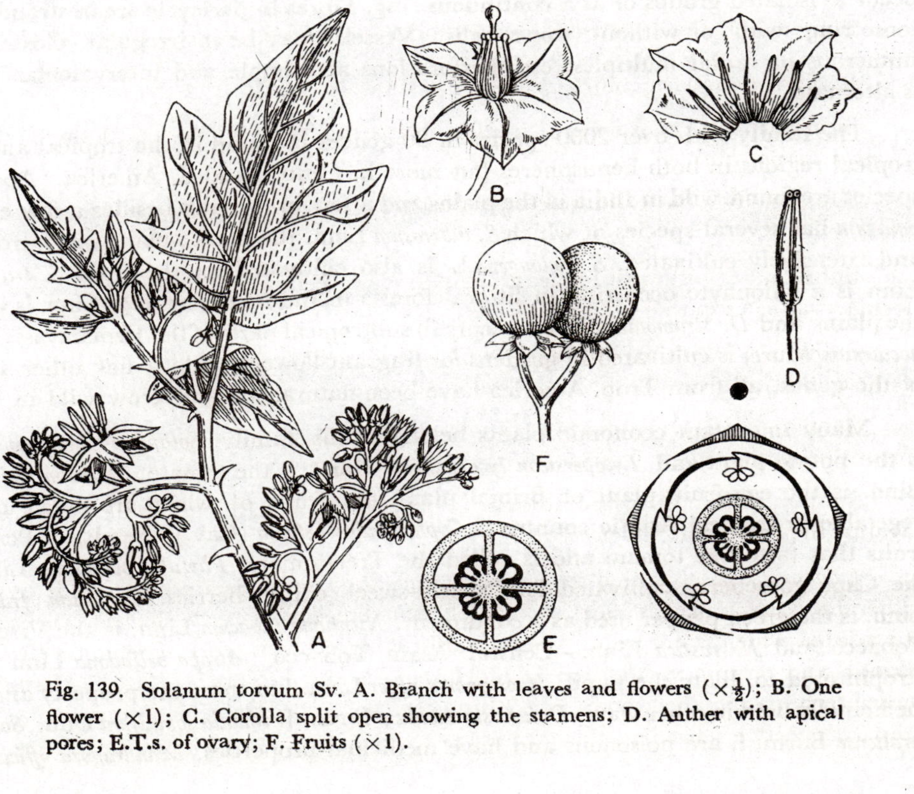

Fig. 139. Solanum torvum Sv. A. Branch with leaves and flowers (×½); B. One flower (×1); C. Corolla split open showing the stamens; D. Anther with apical pores; E.T.s. of ovary; F. Fruits (×1).

vegetative bud remains in its place. So that a pair of leaves at each node contains leaves belonging to two successive shoots of a sympodial stem.

The family predominantly of herbaceous or shrubby plants includes a few trees and some lianas. *Solanum jasminoides* Paxt and *S. Wendlandii* Hook.f. are climbers while species of *Dunalia* and *Cyphonandra* are short trees. *Solanum tuberosum* Linn. and a few other species have stem-tubers. *S. tuberosum* and *S. jasmininoides* have pinnate leaves. Flowers are actinomorphic but may be termed zygomorphic due to the obliquely placed ovary. Corolla is regular but in *Hyoscyamus* and *Schizanthus* it is bilabiate. *Salpiglosis* also has strong zygomorphic flowers. Calyx is persistent and accrescent. In *Physalis* it becomes dry and papery and encloses the berry completely. It is scarlet in *P. alkekengi* Linn. the "Chinese lantern." In *Datura* the long limb of the tubular calyx falls off leaving a disc-like basal portion that enlarges in fruit. The corolla in *Brunfelsia* changes colour and in *B. latifolia* Benth. the corolla is violet in the beginning then turns white and from white changes to yellow. For this reason the plant is called popularly as the "Yesterday—Today and Tomorrow" —plant. Fertile stamens only 2 in *Schizanthus*. The anthers in *Solanum* fuse together in a cone over the style and the dehiscence is by apical pore, in other genera they are distinct and dehisce by longitudinal slits. In *Browalia* the anther is 1-celled. *Cyphonandra* has an enlarged connective. Ovary unilocular in *Henoonia*, while in *Capsicum* it is 2-locular below but 1-locular in upper part.

The floral formula is expressed as : $\oplus$ ⚥ $K_{(5)}\ C_{(5)}\ A_{(5)}\ G_{\underline{(2)}}$

Stem anatomy shows that intraxylary phloem is invariably present. The fibres occur as isolated groups or as a continuous ring. Fibres in pericycle are in strands or in loose ring with or without stone cells. Vessels may be in irregular clusters, in numerous or radial multiples, etc. Perforations are simple and intervascular pitting is alternate.

The family with over 2000 species in 90 genera is found in the tropical and subtropical regions in both hemispheres but more in Central and S. America. About 60 species are found wild in India in the plains and a few in the hills besides a few exotics. *Solanum* has several species of which *S. tuberosum* Linn. the potato-plant was introduced and extensively cultivated. *S. melongena* L. is also cultivated for the fruit. *S. trilobatum* Linn. is a halophyte occurring in littoral forests in India. *Datura metel* Linn. is wild in the plains and *D. stramonium* Linn. occurs in subtropical parts of the Himalayas. *Cestrum nocturnum* Murr. is cultivated in gardens for fragrant flowers while a few other species of the genus, all from Trop. America have been naturalised and grow wild in India.

Many important economic plants belong to this family. *Solanum tuberosum* Linn. is the potato-plant and *Lycopersicon lycopersicum* Karst. is the tomato. *Solanum melongena* Linn. is the egg-fruit plant or Brinjal plant the fruits of which are much used as vegetable in tropical Asiatic countries. *Cyphonandra betacea* (Cav.). Sendt. of Peru has fruits that taste like tomato and is called the Tree-tomato. *Physalis peruviana* Linn. is the Cape gooseberry cultivated for its acid-sweet edible berries. *Capsicum frutescens* Linn. is the green pepper used as a condiment. *Nicotiana tabacum* Linn. is the Virginian Tobacco and *N. rustica* Linn.—Central Asain Tobacco. *Atropa belladona* Linn. gives atropin used to dilate the pupil. *Hyoscyamus niger* Linn. has the same property and also medicinally used in other ways. *Datura stramonium* Linn., *Withania somnifera* Dun., *Solanum surattense* Burm. f. are poisonous and have medicinal properties. *Mandragora officinarum*

Linn. the Mandrake, is a medicinal plant and is notorious for its so called magic properties. *Petunia* is a genus of herbs several species of which are cultivated in gardens for the large showy flowers. Species of *Browalia*, *Cestrum*, *Datura*, *Solanum*, *Brunfelsia* etc., are also cultivated either for the beauty or the fragrance of the flowers.

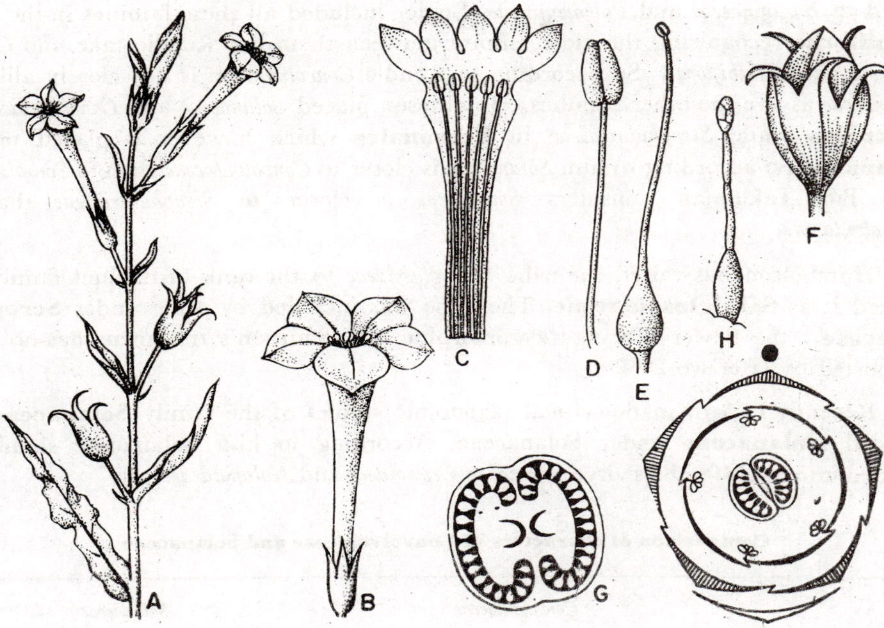

Fig. 140. Nicotiana plumbaginifolia Viv. A. Branch with leaves and flowers ($\times \frac{1}{2}$); B. One flower (slightly reduced); C. Corolla split open to show the stamens; D. One stamen; E. Ovary; F. Fruit; G. T. s. of ovary; H. A glandular hair.

Wettstein divided the family into 5 tribes:

Group A. Embryo strongly curved forming a semicircle; fertile stamens 5, filaments equal.

Tribe I. **Nicandreae:** Ovary 3-4-chambered; the wall of the ovary dividing the placentas irregularly.

Tribe II. **Solaneae:** Ovary 2-chambered.

Tribe III. **Datureae:** Ovary 4-chambered; the wall of the ovary equally dividing the placentas.

Group B. Embryo slightly curved or not.

Tribe IV. **Cestreae:** Fertile stemens 5; seeds small, not compressed.

Tribe V. **Salpiglossideae:** Fertile stamens 2-4; flowers zygomorphic.

According to some workers *Solanaceae* is closely allied to *Convolvalaceae* both having 5-merous flowers, actinomorphic corolla, persistent calyx, usually bicarpellary 2-celled ovary, etc. *Convolvulaceae* is a family of predominantly climbers or twiners while plants of *Solanaceae* are predominantly erect. The obliquely placed ovary in *Solanaceae* is a very distinct character that separates it from *Convolvulaceae* and other allied families.

Solanaceae is also very close to *Scrophulariareae* so much so that a plant of *Solanaceae* with irregular flower can be distinguished from *Scrophulariaceae* only by the position of the ovary. Flowers of *Solanaceae* are usually regular while in *Scrophulariacea* they are usually irregular. In *Solanaceae* stamens are usually 5 in number while in *Scrophulariaceae* they are usually 4 and didynamous. *Solanaceae* is also considered to be allied to *Boraginaceae* and *Polemoniaceae*. Engler included all these families in the order **Tubiflorae** recognising the close affinity between them but Rendle takes out *Convolvulaceae* from *Tubiflorae*. So according to Rendle *Convolvulaceae* is not closely allied to *Solanaceae* as are the other families. Hutchinson placed *Solanaceae* and *Convolvulaceae* in **Solanales** while *Scrophulariaceae* in **Personales** which however is placed next to **Solanales.** So according to him *Solanaceae* is closer to *Convolvulaceae* than to *Scrophulariaceae*. But Takhtajan considers *Solanaceae* is closer to *Scrophulariaceae* than to *Convolvulaceae*.

Hutchinson has raised the tribe *Salpiglossideae* to the rank of distinct family and named it as **Salpiglossidaceae.** The tribe was included by some under **Scrophulariaceae,** the flowers being zygomorphic. Hutchinson's treatment has not been supported by later workers.

Recently D'Arcy made critical taxonomic studies of the family **Solanaceae** and merged **Nolanaceae** under Solanaceae. According to him Solanaceae should be divided into 3 sub-families viz. *Solanoideae*, *Cestroideae* and *Nolanoideae*.

Comparison of characters of Convolvulaceae and Solanaceae

	Convolvulaceae	*Solanaceae*
Habit	Herbs, shrubs or twiners, often with milky juice.	Herbs, often shrubs.
Wood anatomy	Absence of bicollateral bundles.	Presence of bicollateral bundles.
Leaves	Simple or compound, alternate, exstipulate.	Simple, rarely compound, alternate, exstipulate.
Inflorescence	Solitary or cymose.	Usually cymose
Flowers	Penta — or tetramerous, actinomorphic rarely zygomorphic (*Mina*). Bisexual, hypogynous.	Pentamerous, actinomorphic rarely zygomorphic (*Schizanthus*). Bisexual, hypogynous.
Calyx	Sepals 5, free, imbricate or quincuncial, persistent.	Sepals 5, united, imbricate, persistent.
Corolla	Petals 5, united, regular, funnel-shaped, rarely with oblique mouth (*Mina*), induplicate valvate, or twisted.	Petals 5, united, usually regular, rotate, campanulate or funnel-shaped, rarely bilabiate, imbricate, plicate or convolute, rarely valvate.
Androecium	Stamens 5, epipetalous, free	Stamens 5, epipetalous, free.
Gynoecium	Carpels 2, syncarpous, 2-4-celled, superior, not oblique; ovules 1-2 in each cell; placentation axile.	Carpels 2, syncarpous, 2-celled, superior, oblique, ovules many in each cell, placentation axile.
Fruit	Capsule, rarely berry.	Capsule or berry.
Seed	Not compressed.	Compressed.

Scrophulariaceae

Herbs or undershrubs, sometimes twining or trailing, rarely parasitic. Leaves usually simple, alternate or opposite or whorled, exstipulate. Inflorescence is a raceme or spike or cymose, rarely flowers solitary. Flowers bisexual, zygomorphic, hypogynous, bracteate, Calyx gamosepalous, 4-5-partite, with imbricate or valvate lobes. Corolla gamopetalous, with 5 lobes, personate or rotate or bilabiate, often spurred or saccate; lobes imbricate; rarely corolla regular. Stamens usually 4, didynamous, sometimes 5, rarely only 2, epipetalous; anthers 2-celled, one cell larger than the other, often 2-celled at the initial stage and later 1-celled. A hypogynous annular or unilateral or lobed disc is present. Carpels 2 in a syncarpous, superior, 2-celled rarely 4-celled medianly placed ovary; ovules numerous on thick axile placenta, anatropus or amphitropous; style simple terminal; stigma entire or bilobed. Fruit a capsule or a berry; seed with endosperm and a straight or slightly curved embryo.

Herbaceous plants predominate in this family with few shrubs, e.g., *Scrophularia*, ***Verbascum***, etc., species of *Rhodochiton* and *Maurandia* are climbers, climbing by means of sensitive petioles. *Paulownia** is a tree while *Harveya* and *Hyobanche* are total parasites. Some species of *Pedicularis*, *Striga*, *Sopubia* are root-parasites. *Melamporum* and *Castilleja* are saprophytes. Some species of *Limnophila* and *Aubulia* are heterophyllous. The leaves of *Verbascum* are decurrent and give the stem a winged appearance.

The family shows a wide range of variation as regards flower-structure. Flowers

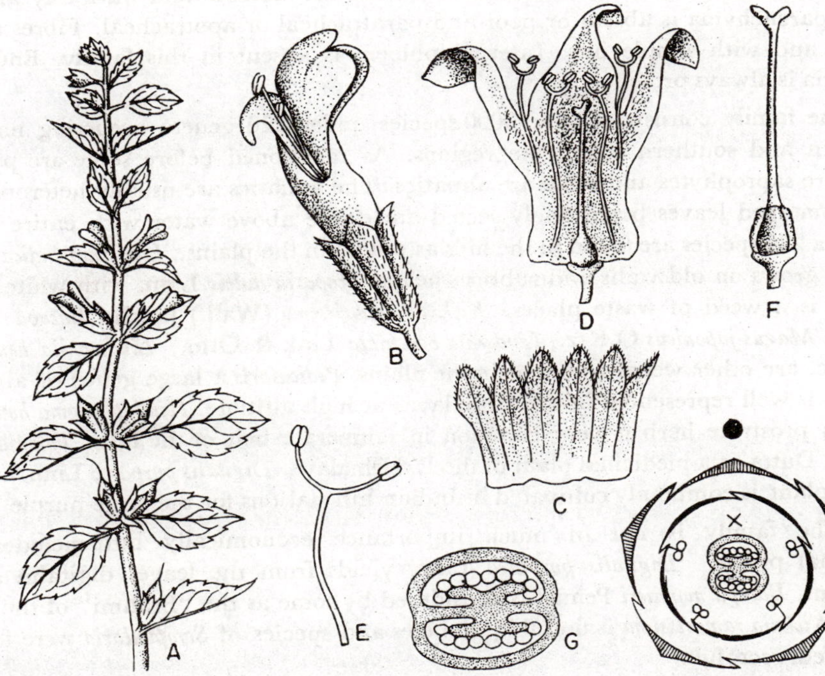

Fig. 141. Lindenbergia indica (L.) O.Ktz. A. Leafy branch with flowers ($\times\frac{1}{2}$); B. Flower ($\times 3$); C. Calyx opened out; D. Corolla split open to show stamens and ovary; E. Stamen with divaricate anther; F. Ovary with style and stigma; G. T.s. of ovary.

* Some authors include this genus in Bignoniaceae.

are solitary in *Bacopa*, *Kickxia*, etc., but usually in racemose or cymose inflorescence in other genera. In *Verbascum* repeated dischasia are formed. In *Antirrhinum* the terminal flower is different from the rest. *Castilleja* has brightly coloured bracts. Flowers are usually zygomorphic but *Scoparia*, *Bacopa* and *Verbascum* have flowers which are regular or almost so. Calyx is 5-lobed but 4 in *Euphrasia* where the posterior sepal is supressed, and in *Calceolaria* where the 2 posterior sepals are united. Limbs of corolla are spreading as in *Veronica* while the 2 lips of corolla in *Linaria* and *Antirrhinum* touch each other so that the mouth of the corolla is closed. In *Linaria* and *Diascia* the corolla is spurred. In *Digitalis* corolla is bell-shaped. In *Scoparia*, *Verbascum*, *Bacopa*, etc., the lobes of corrolla are similar and equal or subequal so that corolla in these genera are regular. In *Verbascum* and *Capraria* there are 5 fertile stamens. *Scrophularia* and *Pentstemon* have 4 fertile stamens and 1 staminode. *Castilleja*, *Linaria* and most other genera have 4 fertile stamens, *Stemotria* has 3 and *Calceolaria*, *Hebe* and *Veronica* have 2 only. In the genus *Lindernia* some species have 4 fertile stamens while others have 2 and 2 staminodes. In *Euphrasia* the anther is appendaged and the pollens are loose and powdery. Carpels are mostly 2 and equal but in *Antirrhinum* the anterior carpel is larger. Capsules are septicidal or loculicidal while in a few genera the dehiscence is by apical pores. Fruits of *Halleria* and *Leucocarpus* are berries.

The floral formula for the family is: † ⚥ $K_{(5)} C_{(5)} A_{(4) \text{ or } (5)} G_{(\underline{2})}$.

The pericycle is present as a continuous ring of fibres which often occur as isolated strands, or these may be absent. Vessels are narrow and variously arranged. Wood parenchyma is absent or poor and paratracheal or apotracheal. Fibres are thin walled and with simple pits. Internal phloem is absent in this family. Endosperm haustoria is always present.

The family consists of over 3000 species under 220 genera occurring mainly in northern and southern temperate regions. As mentioned before some are parasites, a few are saprophytes and some are aquatics. The aquatics are usually heterophyllous, the submerged leaves being finely sected and those above water with entire lamina. In India 275 species are found in the hills as well as in the plains. *Lindernia indica* O.Ktz. usually grows on old walls and rubbish heaps. *Scoparia dulcis* Linn. with white regular flowers is a weed of waste places. *Kickxia ramosissima* (Wall.) Janch., *Bacopa monniere* Pennel, *Mazus japonicus* O.Ktz., *Lindernia brachiata* Link & Otto., *Limnophila heterophylla* Bth. etc. are other weeds common in the plains. *Pedicularis* a large genus of about 500 species, is well represented in the Himalayas at high altitude. *Hemiophragma heterophylla* Linn. a prostrate herb is very common in temperate belt of the hills. *Torenia cordata* (Griff.) Dutta is a medicinal plant of the E. Himalaya. *Digitalis purpurea* Linn. an introduced plant is commonly cultivated in Indian hill stations for the large purple flowers.

The family is not of much importance economically but includes a few medicinal plants. *Digitalis purpurea* Linn. yields from the leaves digitalin a heart stimulant. *Bacopa monnieri* Pennel is considered by some as the "Brahmi" of the Indian Vaids. *Kickxia ramosissima* is useful in diabetes and species of *Scrophularia* were formerly used to cure scrofula.

Wettstein divides the family into 3 subfamilies as mentioned below:

Group A. Two lateral lobes of corolla covered by two posterior lobes.

Subfam. 1. *Pseudosolanioideae:* Leaves alternate, stamens 5.

Subfam. 2. *Antirrhinioideae:* Leaves opposite (at least the lower), stamens 4.

Group B. Two lateral lobes of corolla not covered by posterior lobes.

Subfam. 3. ***Rhinanthoideae:*** Stamens 4 or 2.

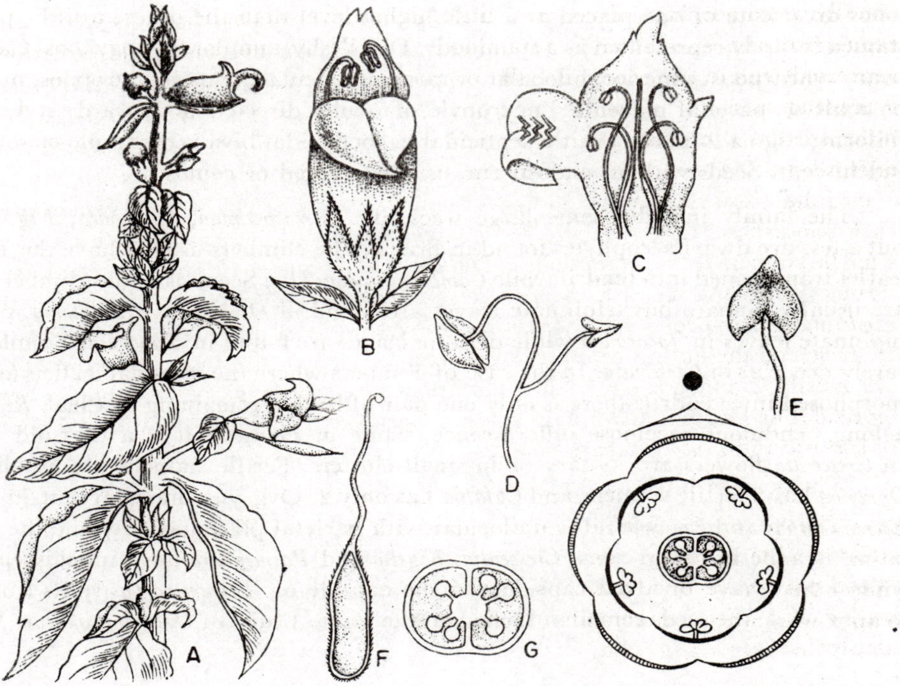

Fig. 142. Antirrhinum majus Linn. A. Leafy shoot with flowers ($\times \frac{1}{2}$); B. One flower ($\times 1$); C. Corolla split open to show stamens; D. & E. Stamens; F. Ovary; G. T.s. of same.

Scrophulariaceae is closely allied to *Labiatae* and *Acanthaceae*, being predominantly herbaceous, flowers usually zygomorphic, stamens usually 4 and didynamous, and fruit usually dry. It is also very close to *Solanaceae* and *Convolvulaceae*, having exstipulate leaves, persistent gamosepalous calyx, bicarpellary superior ovary, etc. A plant of *Solanaceae* with irregular flower resembles much like a *Scrophulariaceae* while some *Scrophulariaceae* with regular flowers resemble plant of *Solanaceae* or *Convolvulaceae.* Intraxylary phloem present in *Solanaceae* and *Convolvulaceae* is however absent in *Scrophulariaceae*. *Scrophulariaceae* is also related to *Bignoniaceae* having zygomorphic flowers, exstipulate leaves, usually 4 didynamous stamens, presence of hypogynous disc and superior bicarpellary ovary. The genus *Paulownia* seems to be the connecting link between the two families. *Bignoniaceae* however is a predominantly woody family with compound leaves, and seeds without endosperm.

Bignoniaceae

Woody plants, trees, shrubs or climbers. Leaves opposite, pinnately compound, exstipulate; trees often have very large leaves. Inflorescence a dichasial cyme or helicoid or paniculate, often racemose, or rarely clustered on the old branches or stem. Flowers zygomorphic bisexual, hypogynous, usually large and showy. Calyx gamosepalous,

5-lobed or toothed or 2-lipped; lobes imbricate or valvate. Corolla gamopetalous, funnel-shaped or campanulate and oblique or sometimes bilabiate; lobes imbricate. Stamens 4, didynamous, inserted on the basal part of the corolla tube; anthers bilobed, lobes divaricate or one placed at a little higher level than the other; a fifth posterior stamen is rarely represented as a staminode. Disc fleshy, annular, hypogynous. Carpels 2; ovary syncarpous, superior, bilocular or rarely unilocular; ovules anatropous, numerous on axile or parietal placenta; micropyle of ovules directed downward; style simple, filiform; stigma 2-lobed. Fruit a septicidal or loculicidal bivalved capsule or sometimes indehiscent. Seeds without endosperm, usually winged or comose.

The family includes some large trees like *Stereospermum*, *Spathodea*, *Kigelia*, etc., but a few are dwarf xerophytes found in Brazil. The climbers usually have the terminal leaflet transformed into tendril while *Campsis radicans* (L.) Seem. is a root climber. Leaves are usually pinnate but tripinnate leaves are found in *Oroxylon*, *Millingtonia*, etc., and bipinnate leaves in *Jacaranda* while digitate leaves are found in *Tabebuia*. Simple leaves rarely occur as in *Crescentia*. In the case of climbers where the terminal leaflets are metamorphosed into tendrils there is only one pair of leaflets remaining in a leaf. *Kigelia* has a long pendulous racemose inflorescence, while in *Pajanelia* it is a thyrsoid panicle. In *Crescentia* flowers are solitary or in small clusters. Fertile stamens are usually 4 but *Oroxylon* has 5 fertile stamens and *Catalpa* has only 2. Ovary is bilocular but in *Kigelia*, *Eccremocarpus* and *Crescentia* it is unilocular with parietal placentation while the placentation is axile in other cases. *Crescentia*, *Kigelia* and *Parmentiera* have indehiscent fruits while others have bivalved capsule and the capsule of *Eccremocarpus* splits from base to apex while the seeds remain attached to the septa. Fruits of *Oxoxylon indicum* Vent. is

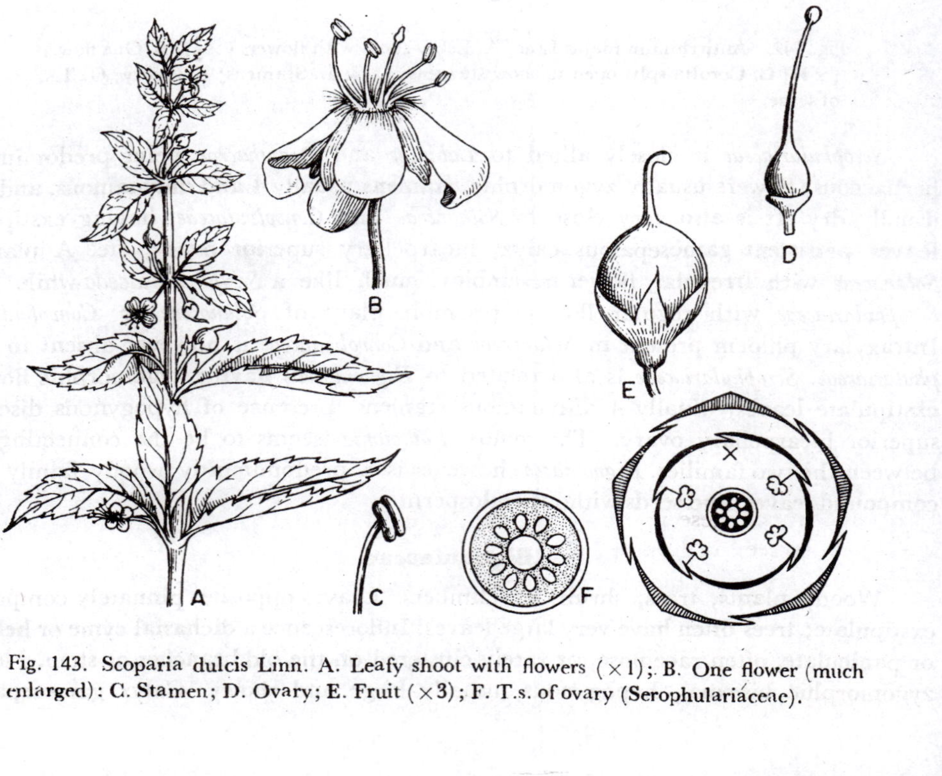

Fig. 143. Scoparia dulcis Linn. A. Leafy shoot with flowers (×1); B. One flower (much enlarged): C. Stamen; D. Ovary; E. Fruit (×3); F. T.s. of ovary (Serophulariaceae).

about a metre. or more long, flat and 5-7 cm. broad. Those of *Crescentia cujete* is round and as big as a human head. Seeds are winged but those of *Crescentia*, *Kigelia*, etc., are wingless. The seeds of *Bignonia* have very fine markings on the wing.

Floral formula for the family is represented as: ⚥ $K_{(5)}\ \overline{C_{(5)}A_{(4)}}\ G_{(\underline{2})}$.

Anomalous secondary thickening in the stems of climbing species is a characteristic feature; the thickening is not uniform and formation of secondary xylem and phloem varies greatly at different parts in the stem so that steler cylinder develops ridges and furrows. Vessels are irregularly disposed with simple perforations and alternate intra-vascular pitting. There is paratracheal wood parenchyma and the pericycle is usually composed of fibrous strands. Fibres are septate in twining plants.

Bignoniaceae with about 650 species under 120 genera is found in the tropical countries of the world but chiefly in S. America. It is represented. in India by several tree-genera e.g., *Stereospermum*, *Oroxylon*, *Heterophragma*, *Dolichondrone*, etc., which are indigenous, but the family is better known in this country for the introduced trees, climbers and shrubs having large showy flowers.

Bignoniaceae is closely allied to *Scrophulariaceae* which however is a predominantly herbaceous family. Didynamous stamens, bi-carpellary superior ovary, presence of hypogynous disc, zygomorphic flowers and usualy capsular fruits are characters common to both. It is also allied to *Acanthaceae* and *Pedaliaceae*. Hutchinson however placing more importance on the woody habit places **Bignoniales** with *Cobaeaceae*, *Bignoniaceae*, *Pedaliaceae* and *Martyniaceae* near the end of his **Lignosae** far removed from his **Personales** of **Herbaceae** where *Serophulariaceae*, *Acanthaceae*, etc., are included Hutchinson's arrangement of these families has not been followed by subsequent workers.

The family has been divided into 4 tribes, e.g.

I. **Bignonieae:** Ovary bilocular cylindric or compressed, parallel to the septum; capsule septicidal; seeds winged. —*Bignonia*, *Pyrostegia*, *Oroxylon*, *Millingtonia*, etc.

II. **Tecomeae:** Ovary bilocular, cylindric or compressed, at right angles to the septum; capsule loculicidal ; seeds winged.—*Tecoma*, *Pajanelia*, *Spathodea*, *Catalpa*, *Heterophragma*, etc.

III. **Eccremocarpeae:** Ovary unilocular; capsule dehiscing from base to apex; seeds winged.—*Eccremocarpus*.

IV. **Crescentieae:** Ovary uni- or bilocular; berry or dry and indehiscent fruit; seeds not winged. —*Kigelia*, *Crescentia*. etc.

Bignoniaceae gains importance for many species having showy flowers. Among these *Stereospermum suaveolens DC*. and *St. personatum* (Hassk.) Chatterjee are the Parul trees or Patala of Sanskrit literature. *Millingtonia hortensis* Linn. f. with long, white, fragrant flowers is the Akas-nim, met with in parks and gardens and on roadsides as an avenue trees. These are indigenous to India. But quite a number of foreign species are very often seen in Indian gardens and a list of the most common ones is given here. These are all tropical plants and are cultivated in the plains.

Spathodea campanulata Beauv.—Central Africa, tall tree with large crimson flower.

Jacaranda ovalifolia R. Br.— Brazil; small tree with purplish blue flowers.

J. filicifolia D. Don.— same, leaflets smaller.

Tabebuia rosea DC.—Trop. America, small tree with pink flower.
T. chrysantha Nichols—same with yellow flowers.
T. donnell-smithii Rose—same.
Catalpa ovata Don.—W. China, small tree with yellow flowers.
Pyrostegia venusta (K.G.) Miers.—Brazil, twining shrub with orange flowers.
Bignonia capreolata Linn.—Argentina, twining shrub with reddish yellow flowers.
Clyptostoma callistegioides (Cham.) Bur.—Syn. *B. speciosa* R. Grah. Trop. Am. twiner, flowers with yellow tube and pink limb.
Saritaea magnifica (Sprague) Dug. (known to the gardeners as *Bignonia magnifica*)—Colombia; twiner with mauve flowers.
Campsis radicans (L.) Seems—N. Am. root climber; fls. orange-red
Tecomaria capensis (Th.) Spach.—S. Africa; rambling shrub, fls. flame-coloured.
Tecoma stans (L.) H.B.K.—Trop. Am. tall shrub, fls. golden yellow.

Orobanchaceae

Annual or perennial herbs , root parasites with very little or no chlorophyll; stem short, usually simple with scale-like alternate leaves. Inflorescence a simple spike or panicle, or flowers solitary at the axil of bracts. Flowers hermaphrodite, medianly zygomorphic and hypogynous. Bracts and bracteoles scale-like; bracteoles 2 or 1, often absent . Calyx gamosepalous, 2-5 lobed, tubular or spathe-like, persistent; lobes valvate or open in bud. Corolla gamopetalous, bilabiate or 5 lobed; tube curved, usually villous at the throat; lobes imbricate. Stamens 4, didynamous, epipetalous, inserted below the middle of the corolla tube; anthers 1- or 2-celled, one cell often abortive, cells frequently spurred at the base; dehiscence by slits or by apical pores. A glandular or unilateral disc usually present. Carpels 2, rarely 3; ovary syncarpous, superior, 1 or 2 celled, with numerous anatropous ovules on parietal placentas which are often confluent; style short; stigma peltate. Fruit a capsule, 1-celled or perfectly or imperfectly 2-celled. Seeds minute, with a pitted, tubercled or reticulated testa; endosperm oily or fleshy; embryo undifferentiated.

The plants derive their nourishment from the host plant by means of exogenous haustoria that enters into the root of the host by enzyme action. Where haustoria is absent a contact between the vascular bundles of the host and the parasite is established and the nutrient material passes from the host to the parasite.

Floral formula: $K_{(2-5)}\overline{C_{(5)}A_{(4)}}G_{\underline{(2)}}$

This is a comparatively small family with about 140 species under 12 genera found mainly in the temperate and subtropical parts of the Old World, the largest genus *Orobanche* with about 100 species extends also to the tropical region. In India the family is represented by a few species of *Orobanche*, *Aeginetia*, *Christisonia*, etc.

Orobanchaceae is closely allied to *Scrophulariaceae* in which family a few genera are also root parasites. The floral construction in both the families are more or less similar and in this respect it is also allied to *Gesneriaceae*. The 3 families are considered to be closely associated to each other by almost all workers on taxonomy.

Pedaliaceae

Annual or perennial herbs, rarely shrubs, usually viscid. Leaves simple opposite, or the upper alternate, exstipulate; the lower leaves very rarely trifoliate; hydathodes usually present. Inflorescence a dichasial cyme, axillary, rarely flowers solitary. Flowers bisexual, zygomorphic, hypogynous. Calyx gamosepalous, tubular, or campanulate, or spathe like, persistent, hairy; lobes 5, imbricate. Corolla gamopetalous, indistinctly bilabiate and ventricose; lobes 5, imbricate. Stamens 4, epipetalous, didynamous; a short staminode is often present; anthers bilocular, introrose, dehiscing longitudinally. Carpels 2, syncarpous, forming a superior uni- or bilocular or quadrilocular ovary due to development of false septa; ovules $1-\infty$ in each locule on axile or parietal placenta, anatropous; style long and filiform, persistent; stigmas 2, leafy, elliptic. Fruit a capsule or a nut with smooth or hairy pericarp, often with hooked or spiny outgrowths. Seed with a straight embryo and scanty endosperm.

The usual floral formula is: $K_{(5)}C_{(5)}A_{(4)}G_{(2)}$.

Species of the genus *Trapella* are aquatic herbs having dimorphic leaves, and flowers with 2 stamens and inferior ovary. *Martynia* has 2 fertile stamens and 3 staminodes.

Pedaliaceae is a small family comprising about 60 species only under 17 genera, occurring in S. Africa, Indo-Malayan region and Australia. They are found more in the arid region and on sea shores. *Martynia annua* Linn, native of Mexico grows wild in the plains of India and *Sesamum indicum* Linn. is widely cultivated.

The family is closely allied to the other families of **Tubiflorae** and particularly to Acanthaceae. Many authors prefer to segregate 3 genera, viz., *Probscidia, Craniotia* and *Martynia* under a distinct family **Martyniaceae** mainly on parietal placentation.

The family includes *Sesamum indicum* Linn. a very important oil yielding plant. Oil is also extracted from *S. angustifolium* Engl. and *Pedalium murex* Linn.

Lentibulariaceae

Insectivorous herbs, often aquatic or marsh-plants, and often rootless. Leaves in submerged plants multifid with capillary segments bearing bladders; small and rosulate in terrestrials and obsolete in the epiphytes. Flowers hermaphrodite and strongly zygomorphic, borne on racemes or spikes; bract and bracteoles small or absent; in case of submerged plants the raceme projects above water surface and are often provided with inflated modified leaves serving as floats. Calyx persistent, 2-lipped or 2-5-lobed or partite. Corolla bilabiate, the upper lip smaller, entire or emarginate, the lower much larger, 3-5 lobed and saccate or spurred. Stamens 2, attached to the base of the corolla, filaments broad and curved, anthers 2-celled, cells transversely confluent and in some cases ultimately becoming 1-celled; anthers dorsifixed and dehiscing longitudinally.

Ovary superior, bicarpellary syncarpous, unilocular with many anatropous ovules, more or less sunk in the tissue of a free central placenta, rarely ovules only 2; style short or absent, stigma unequally 2-lobed. Fruit a many seeded capsule dehiscing by 2-4 valves or irregularly, or opening circumscissously, rarely fruit indehiscent and 1-seeded. Seeds minute, without endosperm.

The bladder of *Uticularia* is an egg-shaped structure with a horseshoe-shaped mouth on one side. The mouth is surrounded by a thick ridge or 'collar' which is produced at the two ends of the base of the horse-shoe. The two projections bear branched hairs called 'antenna". The mouth is closed by a valve which is attached along the base of the horse-shoe and opens towards inside. Irritable hairs are situated at outer side of the dome which on coming into contact with an insect pass on stimuli that cause the valve to open and the insect is sucked in. The valve quickly comes back to its original position and the insect is entrapped. The inner wall of the bladder is provided with scattered quadrifid or quadripartite glandular hairs that absorb the decaying material of the insect trapped inside the bladder.

In *Pingiucula* the simple entire leaves bear glandular hairs which capture tiny insects by a sticky secretion while the margin of the leaf also bends over the insect The decaying material is made soluble by the secretion and then absorbed.

Bladder or pitcher formation is also noticed in other genera of the family.

The floral formula is represented as: † ⚥ $K_5\ \overline{C_5\ A_2}\ G_{(\underline{2})}$.

The family is distributed in the tropical and temperate parts of the world and has about 250 species of which *Utricularia* alone contains about 200. This is represented in India by several species of *Utricularia* in the plains and the hills and a few species of *Pinguicula* in the temperate region of the Himalayas.

Acanthaceae

Annual or perennial herbs or shrubs, sometimes climbers or twiners, rarely small trees. Leaves opposite, simple, exstipulate; cystoliths usually present in the leaves. Inflorescence racemose or cymose usually with prominent bracts and bracteoles. Flowers small or large, bisexual, hypogynous, strongly zygomorphic. Calyx gamosepalous, 5-partite or 4-partite; lobes unequal, imbricate. Corolla usually bilabiate, sometimes oblique, imbricate or twisted. Stamens 4, didynamous, epipetalous.; anther 2-celled or rarely 1-celled, often spurred and hairy; anther-cells sometimes divergent or one placed slightly above the other; dehiscence of anthers longitudinal or by apical pores; stamens sometimes only 2 with or without staminodes; pollens usually variously sculptured. Carpels 2; ovary syncarpous, superior, 2-celled with 2 or more anatropous ovules in each cell on axile placenta; style slender, terminal; stigma bilobed, lobes often unequal, sometimes spathulate. Fruit a loculicidal capsule, hard or leathery. Seeds usually supported on hook-like outgrowths of the funicle, the so called retinacula or jaculators; endosperm absent; embryo curved.

Acanthaceae has the floral formula as: † ⚥ $K_{(5)}$ $\overline{C_{(5)}\ A_{(4)\ \text{or}\ (2)}}$ $\underline{G_{(2)}}$.

There is comparatively less variation in general habit as well as in floral structure although it is a fairly large family. A few species of *Thunbergia* and *Mendoncia* are climbers. Among the shrubby genera a few are arboreal, e.g. *Adhatoda, Phlogacanthus, Strobilanthus* etc. Some have axillary spines, as in *Barleria*, *Hygrophila*, etc. The calyx in *Thunbergia* is reduced to a narrow ring. Sepals usually connate and 5-lobed, but in *Elytraria*, *Nelsonia*, *Blepharis*, *Acanthus*, *Barleria*, etc. calyx is 4-lobed or there are 4 free sepals in opposite pairs. The corolla is 2-lipped in most cases but in *Acanthus*, *Blepharis*, etc. the upper lip is absent. In *Symplectochilus* the lower lip is roled. In *Thunbergia*, *Ruellia*,

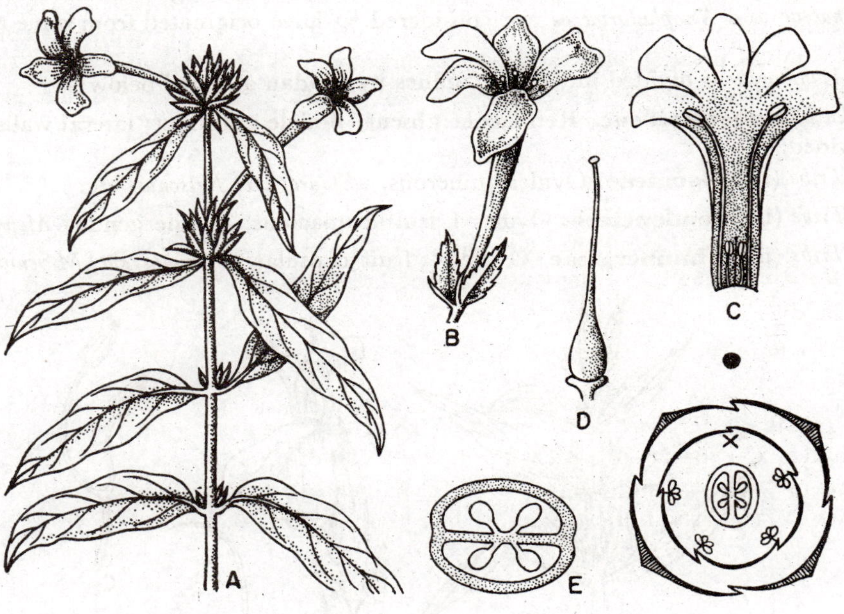

Fig. 144. Barleria cristata Linn. A. Leafy shoot with flower clusters (×½); B. One flower with bracts (×1); C. Corolla split open to show the stamens; D. Ovary; E. T.s. of ovary.

Hemigraphis, etc. the corolla is 5-lobed. In *Pentstemonacanthus* five fertile stamens are present. In other cases they are either 2 or 4. Anther cells are distinct and wide apart in some species of *Justicia*, *Beloperone*, *Salviacanthus*, etc., sometimes one placed higher than the other, e.g. *Justicia*, *Adhatoda*, *Rhinacanthus*, *Peristrophe*, etc., and rarely spurred, e.g., *Dyschoriste*, *Justicia*, *Monechma*, etc. Pollens are of different shape and size and vary much as regards the sculpturing of the exine. A hard retinaculum is present in the fruit of many genera and is absent in the others and the family is divided into 2 subfamilies mainly on this character.

The family comprises about 2500 species under 250 genera and is cosmopolitan in its distribution but the majority are in the tropics. Over 500 species occur in India and a few are often gregarious in the hills of S. India, e.g. *Carvia callosa* Bremek. which is endemic in Malabar hills. Other species common in India are *Ecbolium viride* (Forsk) Alston, *Lepidagathis incurva* Don. *Rungia repens* (L.) Nees., *Justicia procumbens* Linn., etc. *Strobilanthes* usually are found in the hills and many species are in S. India and in the Himalayas upto and elevation of 2000 mtrs. *Thunbergia coccinea* T. Anders a climber with scarlet flowers occurs in the Himalayas in the subtropical region. *Justicia gendarusa* Burm. f. an African species is commonly cultivated as a hedge plant and so is *Adhatoda zeylanica* Med. which is also found wild. *Acanthus ilicifolius* Linn. is a semihalophytic plant growing in Sunderbans and also in marshy places.

Acanthaceae is closely related to *Scrophulariaceae*, *Labiatae*, *Verbenaceae* and *Bignoniaceae*. *Bignoniaceae* is quite distinct being predominantly woody and having compound leaves among other characters. Fruits of *Verbenaceae* are drupaceous and of *Labiatae* are nutlets. *Scrophulariaceae* has many characters similar to *Acanthaceae* but may be easily distinguished by absence of retinacula in fruits and pollen grains not ornamented. *Acanthaceae* and *Scrophulariaceae* are considered to have originated from same ancestral stock.

Acanthaceae is divided into 2 subfamilies by Lindau as noted below:—

I. **Thunbergioideae.** Retinacula absent, funicle indistinct; lateral walls in fruit undivided.

Tribe (i) **Nelsonieae:** Ovules numerous,—*Staurogyne*, *Nelsonia*, etc.

Tribe (ii) **Mendoncieae:** Ovules 4, fruit drupacious,—single genus—*Mendoncia*.

Tribe (iii) **Thunbergieae:** Ovules 4; fruit capsular.—*Thunbergia*, *Meyenia*, etc.

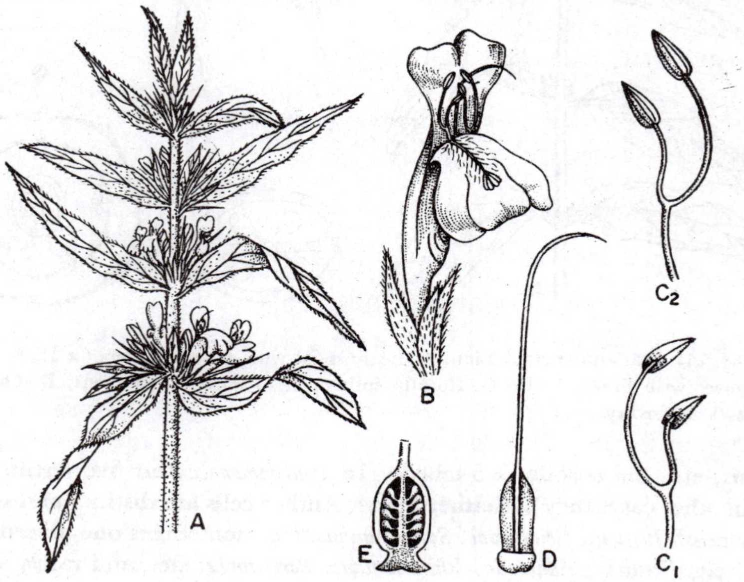

Fig. 145. Hygrophila auriculata Heine. A. Leafy shoot with flowers ($\times\frac{1}{8}$); B. One flower ($\times 2$); C_1 & C_2. Stamens; D. Ovary; E. L.s. of same.

II. **Acanthoideae.** Retinacula and funicle distinct; lateral walls of the fruit bipartite.

Tribe (iv) **Contortae:** Corolla lobes usually contorted, never imbricate.—*Hygrophila*, *Ruellia*, etc.

Tribe (v) **Imbricatae:** Corolla lobes imbricate.—*Andrographis*, *Barleria*, *Justicia*, etc.

Economically the family is not very important. A few are reputed for medicinal properties, viz. *Adhatoda zeylanica* is recommended in cough and cold, *Phlogacanthus thyrsiflorus* is a febrifuge. *Andrographis paniculata* Nees. is efficacious in liver troubles, and kills worms. Roots of *Ecbolium* are used in jaundice and roots of *Rhinacanthus* cure skin disease. The juice of the leaves of *Justicia gendarusa* or a paste of the same is very good for cuts and for ulcers. The juice is taken in cases of internal haemorrhage with good results. A few species are cultivated in gardens for their large and beautiful flowers e.g. *Thunbergia grandiflora Roxb*., *Barleria prionitis* Linn., *Crossandra undulifolia* Salisb., *Justicia betonica* Linn., etc.

RUBIALES

This is the 9th order under **Metachlamydeae** and consists of 5 families viz. *Rubiaceae*, *Caprifoliaceae*, *Adoxaceae*, *Valerianaceae* and *Dipsacaceae*. Characters common to these families are: (1) opposite leaves, (2) cymose inflorescence, (3) tetracyclic, bisexual, epigynous flowers, (4) petals 4-5, (5) stamens as many as petals and (6) ovary inferior, usually 2-3-celled. Plants may be herbs, shrubs or trees, flowers actinomorphic or zygomorphic, inflorescence usually compact and the cells of the ovary may vary from 1-5 or more.

Depending on these characters Engler considered that these 5 families are very close to each other and included them in a single order. Rendle and Bessey supported this treatment. Hutchinson included only *Rubiaceae* and *Dialypetalanthaceae* in his **Rubiales** while *Caprifoliaceae* was transferred to **Araliales,** *Adoxaceae* to **Saxifragales** and *Valerianaceae* and *Dipsacaceae* to **Valerianales.** Removal of these 4 families from Rubiales has been supported by Takhtajan who places these 4 families in a single order **Dipsacales** while he merges Rubiales of Hutchinson with **Gentianales,** where he includes *Gentianaceae*, *Loganiaceae*, *Apocynaceae*, *Asclepiadaceae*, etc. Takhtajan places **Dipsacales** and **Gentianales** side by side while Hutchinson placed **Rubiales** near **Loganiales** and **Apocynales.** These 3 orders are in his **Lignosae** while **Gentianales** with 2 families *Gentianaceae* and *Menyanthaceae* is in **Herbaceae.** Inclusion of *Caprifoliaceae* in **Araliales** by Hutchinson means that he considered this family to be more primitive than the other 4 included in **Rubiales** of Engler.

Like Takhtajan Cronquist keeps the 4 families *Caprifoliaceae*, *Adoxaceae*, *Valerianaceae* and *Dipsacaceae* in **Dipsacales,** but he places *Rubiaceae* in a monotypic order **Rubiales.** *Rubiaceae* has much in common with *Loganiaceae*, such as well developed stipules, alkaloid contents, opposite leaves, bicarpellate ovary, etc. With **Dipsacales** and particularly with *Caprifoliaceae* *Rubiaceae* has a close affinity in having inferior ovary and lacking internal phloem, besides opposite leaves, cymose inflorescence, etc. Hallier therefore stated that *Rubiaceae* and *Caprifoliaceae* originated from *Loganiaceae* while *Dipsacaceae* and *Valerianaceae* originated from *Caprifoliaceae*.

Rubiaceae

Herbs, shrubs or trees, rarely climbing. Leaves simple, opposite or rarely whorled, stipulate; stipules interpetiolar or intrapetiolar. Inflorescence a cyme or cymose panicle or umbel or a compact globose head. Flowers hermaphrodite, actinomorphic, epigynous or semiepigynous, 4-5-merous. Sepals 4-5, valvate, often united, persistent. Petals

4-5, connate in a tube below with funnel-shaped, salver-shaped or rotate limb, valvate, imbricate or contorted. Stamens as many as petals and alternate to them, epipetalous; anthers 2-celled, introrse. Carpels 2, united to form a 2-celled inferior or semi-inferior ovary; ovules 1-many in each cell, anatropous, on axile plancenta; integument one and thick; style filiform with a bifid or multifid stigma; ovary is crowned by a fleshy disc. Fruit a capsule, berry or drupe, sometimes an aggregate. Seeds often winged, with copious fleshy or cartilaginous endosperm and straight or curved embryo: endosperm absent in some genera.

The large family varies much in habit from prostrate or trailing herbs like *Dentella*, *Spermacoce*, *Galium*, etc., to shrubs, e.g. *Ixora*, *Gardenia*, etc. trees, e.g. *Anthocephalus*, *Adina*, etc. and climbers like *Uncaria*, *Paederia*, etc. In *Uncaria* some branches are modified into hooks that help the plants to climb. Some are epiphytes, e.g. *Myrmecodia*, *Hydnophytum*, *Hymenopogon*, etc. *Myrmecodia* and *Hydnophytum* are myrmecophilous,

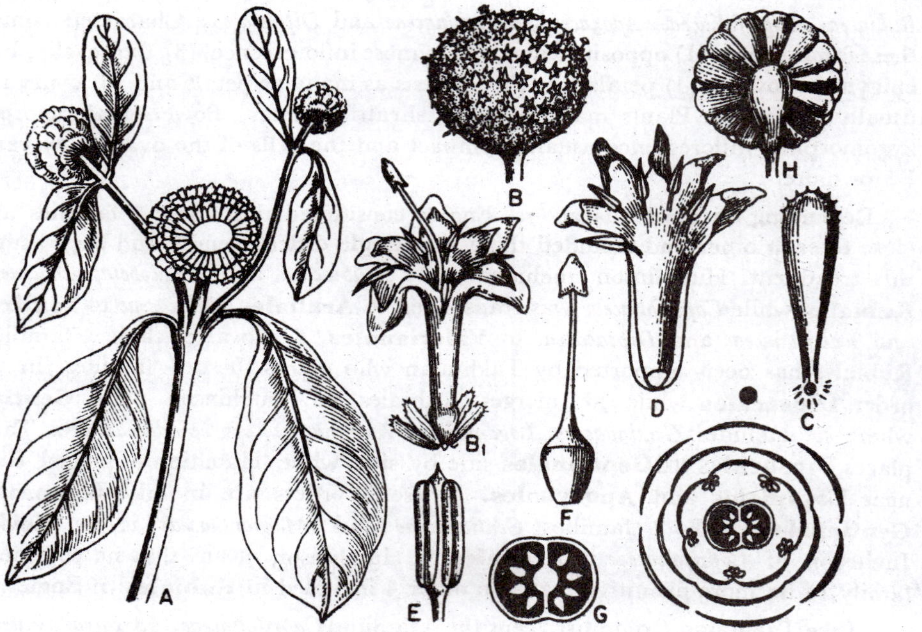

Fig. 146. Anthocephalus chinensis **A. Rich.** **A.** Branch with leaves and floral heads (reduced); **B.** One capitate inflorescence ($\times\frac{1}{8}$); B_1. One flower (much enlarged); **C.** Bract; **D.** Corolla split open to show the stamens; **E.** One stamen with short filament and anther; **F.** Ovary with style and dilated stigma; **G.** T.s. of ovary; **H.** Aggregate fruit.

that shelter ants in hollow tuber-like swellings at the base of the stem. Stipules are interpetiolar in most genera, while intrapetiolar stipules occur in *Gardenia*, *Randia*, *Pavetta*, etc. In *Gardenia* the stipules are connate and cover the growing apical bud of the shoot and are deciduous. In *Adina*, *Nauclea*, etc. the stipules are very large, while in *Galium* and *Rubia* they are like ordinary leaves. Solitary flowers are often found in *Gardenia*; in *Rubia* a perfect dichasial cyme occurs while in *Hamelia* the inflorescence is 2-3-chotomous subscorpioid cyme. The dichasial cymes are condensed into heads in *Anthocephalus*, *Nauclea*, *Adina*, etc. In *Morinda* and *Sarcocephalus* the flowers are also aggregated and basally connate. *Cinchona* has a paniculate inflorescence. Flowers are more or less zygomorphic and bilabiate in *Henriquezia* and *Posoqueria*. In *Coprosma* and *Anthospermum* the flowers are unisexual. One of the calyx segment is much larger than the others and petaloid in *Mussaenda* rendering the flower very attractive. In *Nematostylis* the calyx lobes enlarge in fruit. Ovary is half inferior in *Synaptantha* and superior in *Pagamea* and *Gaertnera*. In *Gardenia* ovary is unilocular and the placentation is parietal. *Hamelia* and *Hamiltonia* have typical 5-merous flowers with 5-celled ovary. In *Vangueria* the ovary is 3-6-celled and in *Lasianthus* 4-9-celled. In *Morinda*, *Sarcocephalus*, etc. the basal parts of the densely aggregated flowers fuse to form a syncarp. The seed is winged in *Cinchona*.

The floral formula of *Rubiacea* is represented as: $\oplus$ ⚥ $K_{(4-5)}, C_{(4-5)}, A_{(4-5)}, G_{(\overline{2})}$.

The family consists of about 7000 species under 500 genera, occurring in the tropics and subtropics and extending to the temperate and even to the frigid zone. About 550 species are found in India mostly in the plains and at lower elevations in the hills. ***Rubia cordifolia*** Linn. grows in the Himalayas upto an elevation of 2500 mtr. Species of ***Galium*** are often found at an altitude of 4000 m. *Luculia*, another Himalayan genus, has beautiful mauve flowers in terminal corymbs. In the plains trees are *Anthocephalus chinensis* A Rich. *Adina cordifolia* Hook. f., *Mitragyna parvifolia* (Roxb.) Korth, etc. *Gardenia, Ixora, Pavetta, Coffea,* etc. are shrubs, while a large number of herbs like *Oldenlandia, Hedyotis, Borreria, Anotis,* etc. are quite, common. *Uncaria* and *Paederia* are climbers or twiners occurring in foot hills of the outer Himalayas and Assam.

In this family presence of raphides in the cells is a characteristic feature. Crystal sands are also present in the cells of many genera. Vessels are solitary or in multiples of 4 or more. Perforations are simple, rarely scalariform, and the intervascular pitting alternate. Wood parenchyma is apotracheal. Fibres are usually simple pitted. In some genera fibres are present in the pericycle. Anomalous secondary thickening is met with in *Basanacantha* and *Rhabdodendron*.

The family is divided into 3 sub families as noted below:

Subf. I **Rubioideae:** Calcium oxalate crystals present in leaves, hairs on stem and leaves often with transverse walls, heterostyly is common; stipules often with several long slender teeth, seeds without endosperm, (usually herbaceous).—11 tribes.

Subf. II **Cinchonoideae:** Calicium oxalate crystals absent, hairs without transverse walls, heterostyly usually absent, stipules usually entire, seeds with plenty of endosperm (Woody plants).—17 tribes.

Subf. III **Guettardoideae:** Calcium oxalate crystals absent; hairs without transverse walls, heterostyly absent, seeds without endosperm (Woody).—1 tribe.

Affinity of *Rubiaceae* is rather controversial. It has much in common with *Loganiaceae*, such as opposite leaves, well developed stipules, bicarpellate ovary, etc; both families contain similar type of alkaloids. But in *Loganiaceae* the ovary is superior and there is internal phloem in the vascular bundles. *Rubiaceae* comes closer to *Caprifoliaceae* both having opposite leaves, cymose inflorescence, stamens as many as petals, bisexual and tetracyclic flowers, inferior ovary, etc. In *Caprifoliaceae* stipules are absent and no alkaloid is present in any part of the plants. With *Cornaceae* and *Umbelliferae* it seems to be related also having epigynous flowers and an epigynous disc and the dense cymose inflorescence, bicarpellate ovary and integument one only.

The family Rubiaceae includes several species economically important. *Anthocephalus chinensis* A. Rich.—the Kadamba tree, *Adina cordifolia* Hook. f.—the Haldu, and a few other trees yield timber which is light and strong and suitable for making tool-handles, toys, picture-frames, etc. Species of *Cinchona* is the source of the alkaloid quinine. This genus is indigenous to Brazil and Mexico and a few species are cultivated

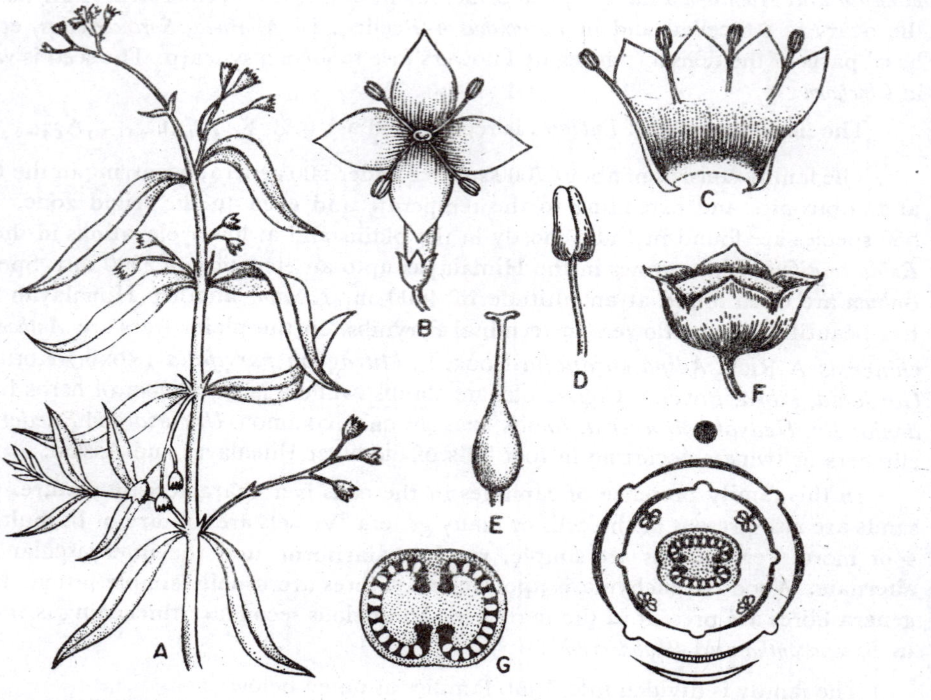

Fig. 147. Oldenlandia corymbosa Linn. A. Part of a branch with leaves and flowers (×1); B. One flower (much enlarged); C. Corolla split open to show the stamens; D. One stamen; E. Ovary; F. Fruit; G. T.s. of ovary.

in different tropical countries. In the E. Himalaya there are a few plantations where *C. officinalis* Linn. *C. succirubra* Pav., *C. calysaya* Wedd. and *C. Ledgeriana* Moens. are cultivated. A factory for the manufacture of quinine has been established at Mungpoo. Another important medicinal plant is *Cephaelis ipecacuanha* (Brot.) A. Rich.—Ipicac plant, a native of Brazil is the source of the alkaloid emetine obtained from its gnarled roots. *Paederia foetida* Linn.—Bhadali, growing in the Terai region is recommended in indigestion and stomach troubles. *Oldenlandia corymbosa* Linn.—Khetra parpati, is much used by the Indian Vaids.

Coffea arabica Linn. is an important beverage plant of N. Africa and W. Asia. It is much cultivated in S. India, Java, Ceylon, Brazil and W. Indies. Coffee-powder is obtained by grinding the roasted seeds of this plant and of *C. liberica* Linn. *Rubia cordifolia* Linn.—Manjistha, growing in temperate Himalayas, and *R. tinctoria* Linn, of Europe yield a red dye. *Uncaria gambier* Roxb.—an Indo-Malayan plant yields gamber-catechue which is used medicinally and also as a dye. A yellow dye is obtained from *Morinda tinctoria* Roxb. A few shrubby plants are cultivated for the showy flowers, e.g.

Gardenia jasminoides Ellis, *Luculia gratissima* Hook. f., *Hamelia patens* Jack, *Ixora arborea* Roxb. ex Smith. *I. coccinea* Linn., *Mussaenda glabra* Vahl., etc. *Anthocephalus chinensis* a timber tree is also cultivated in parks and gardens. *Vangueria edulis* Vahl. has edible fruits.

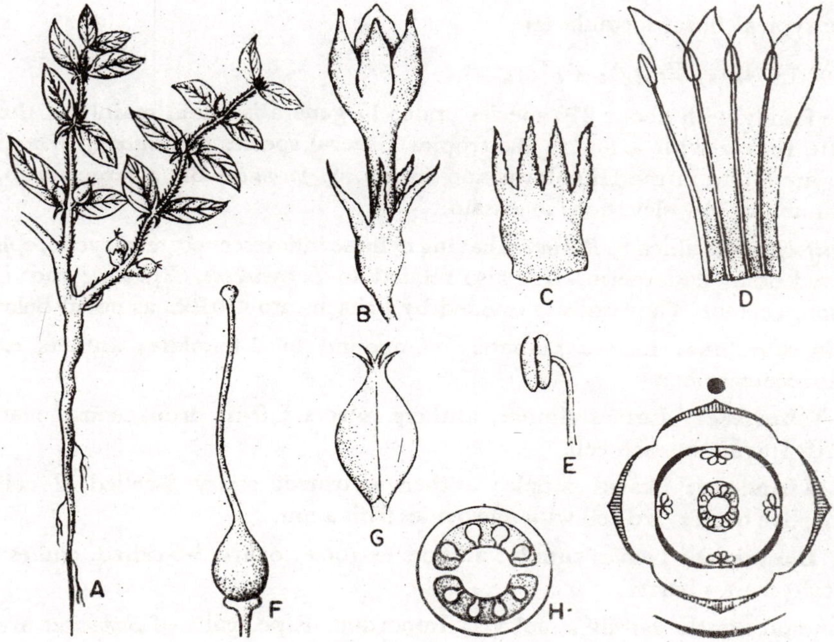

Fig. 148. Borreria articularis (L.f.) K. Schum. A. Part of the plant (×½); B. One flower ((much enlarged); C. Calyx; D. Corolla split open to show the stamens; E. One stamen; F. Ovary; G. Fruit.

Caprifoliaceae

Erect shrubs, often attaining tree-size, rarely twiners. Leaves simple, rarely compound, usually opposite, exstipulate or with reduced stipules. Inflorescence cymose in 3- or 2-flowered dichasia; cymes are often grouped in an umbel-like arrangement. Flowers fragrant, bisexual, regular or irregular, epigynous, usually pentamerous. Calyx 5-lobed, valvate. Corolla 5-lobed, rotate or salver-shaped, or bilabiate; lobes valvate or imbricate. Stamens inserted on corolla tube and alternating with corolla lobes; anthers 2-lobed, introrse. Carpels 2-8, syncarpous; ovary inferior, 1-8-celled; style one or as many as carpels; ovules 1 or more in each cell of ovary on axile placenta. Fruit a berry or drupe. Seeds with fleshy endosperm and straight embryo.

The opposite leaves in some *Lonicera* unite and form a broad collar encircling the stem. Stipules are present in *Sambucus*. In *Viburnum* and *Lycesteria* the stipules are modified to extra floral nectaries. In *Symphoricarpus* and *Diervilla* the inflorescence becomes racemose. In *Sambucus* and some *Viburnum* the small flowers are massed together in an umbellate inflorescence. In *V. opulus* Linn. the marginal ray florets are much larger than the others making the inflorescence conspicuous and attractive. These ray florets are barren. In *Dipelta* and *Linnaea* stamens are 4 in number and didynamous. In *Leyces-*

teria and some *Sambucus* carpals are 5 and in *Diervilla* carpels are only 2. In *Symphoricarpus* carpels are 4 and the ovary is 4-celled; the median cells have many ovules in each in 2 rows, all of which are abortive while the lateral cells have solitary ovules which develop into seeds. In *Linnaea* ovary is 3-celled with several abortive ovules in 2 of the cells while the third cell has a single ovule which develops into a seed. The fruit in *Linnaea* is a nut which remains enveloped by pair of large persistent bracteoles.

The typical floral formula is:—

$\oplus$ or † ⚥ $K_{(5)}\ C_{(5)}\ A_{5\text{ or }4}\ G_{\overline{(2-8)}}$

The family with about 270 species under 17 genera is found mainly in the north temperate region with a few in the tropics. Several species of *Lonicera*, *Viburnum* and *Sambucus* are found in the Himalayas and Assam. *S. javanicus* Bl., a large shrub, grows in Bengal and at low elevations in Assam.

Caprifoliaceae is allied to *Rubiaceae* having cymose inflorescence, tetracyclic, epigynous flowers and fleshy endosperm. It is also related to *Loganiaceae*, *Cornaceae* and *Umbelliferae* to some extent. The family is divided by Fritsch into 4 tribes as noted below:—

I. **Sambucieae:** Leaves pinnately compound or 3-foliolate; anthers extrorse; fruit drupaceous or berry.

II. **Viburneae:** Leaves simple; anthers introrse; fruit drupaceous; ovary 1-5-celled with 1 ovule in each cell.

III. **Linnaeae:** Leaves simple; anthers extrorse; ovary 3-celled, 2 cells with many abortive ovules, 3rd cell with one ovule; fruit a nut.

IV. **Lonicerae:** Leaves simple; anthers extrorse; ovary 2-8-celled, ovules several in each cell; fruit a berry.

Economically the family is not very important. Ripe fruits of *Sambucus* are made into wine and those of *Viburnum* are edible. The leaves of some species of *Sambucus*, *Viburnum*, *Lonicera* and *Triosteum* are strong purgative and emetic. A few species of *Lonicera*, *Viburnum*, *Sambucus* and *Symphoricarpus* are cultivated for the beautiful fragrant flowers.

Valerianaceae

Annual and perennial herbs with aromatic rhizome, rarely undershrubs. Leaves simple or compound, opposite, exstipulate, often radical. Inflorescence a dense panicle of cymes, or the cymes often condensed into a head; bracts and bracteoles present. Flowers small, more or less zygomorphic, bisexual or unisexual, epigynous. Calyx in flower represented by an epigynous ring, persistent and later developing into pappus or plumose outgrowths or a 4-5-toothed structure. Corolla tubular, slightly irregular above with 5 unequal lobes or bilabiate, saccate or spurred at the base; lobes imbricate. Nectar is secreted in the sac or spur. Stamens 1-4, epipetalous; anthers bilocular, introrse. Ovary 3-carpellary, syncarpous, 3-celled, inferior; style with a bipartite or simple stigma; ovule 1 in one of the cells, pendulous and anatropous, and develops into a seed, while the other 2 cells of the ovary are empty. Fruit an achene; seeds without endosperm.

The family consisting of about 350 species under 10 genera distributed in the north temperate zone of the globe; a few are found in the high mountain of S. America. There are 16 species in India all being in the hills.

Valerianaceae is placed in **Rubiales** by Engler and its affinity with *Rubiaceae* and other families of the order has been recognised by most workers in taxonomy. It resembles *Compositae* by the compact type of inflorescence, formation of pappus in some genera and epigynous ovary. The family appears to be much advanced as is evident from the following characters:—

1. Predominantly herbaceous.
2. Aggregation of small flowers in dense inflorescence.
3. Reduction of calyx which is modified into pappus or scales.
4. Ovary inferior.
5. Special adaptation for cross pollination by insects, e.g., nectar secreted and stored in sac or spur, and protandrons androecium.
6. Distribution of fruit over wide area with help of pappus.

The family includes a few plants reputed for medicinal value. *Valeriana officinalis* Linn. yields the Valerian root. *Nardostachis jatamansi* DC. is an Ayurvedic drug available in the Himalayas. Leaves of *Valeriana olitoria* Linn. are used as salad. A few are cultivated as ornamental plants among which *Centranthus ruber* DC is very popular.

CUCURBITALES

In this order Engler included only one family *Cucurbitaceae* with tetracyclic, actinomorphic, unisexual, pentamerous flowers with tricarpellary inferior ovary. Here the ovules are bitegmic and seeds are exalbuminous.

Cucurbitaceae

Climbing or procumbent herbs, annual or perennial, with extra-axillary simple or branched tendrils; monoecious or dioecious; stem usually 5-angled. Leaves simple, alternate, palmiveined and palmilobed or rarely pinnately veined and lobed; exstipulate. Inflorescence racemose or cymose or flowers solitary. Flowers unisexual, regular, pentamerous, epigynous, usually large, yellow or white. Calyx more or less tubular, lobes 5, imbricate or open in bud. Corolla inserted on the calyx tube, gamopetalous, campanulate or rotate; lobes 5, imbricate or induplicate-valvate; rarely corolla lobes free almost to the base or very rarely completely free. Stamens 5 in male flowers but usually appearing 3 as filaments of 4 stamens unite in pairs; filaments usually coherent and often fused and monadelphous; anthers all unithecal and synandrous; anther lobes sigmoid or convolute or conduplicate, extrorse. In female flowers ovary tricarpellary, syncarpous, inferior, 3-celled with ∞ ovules on axile placentation; ovules anatropous with 2 integuments; style short and thick usually divided in 3 stigmatic branches: stigmas thick, often horse-shoe shaped. Fruit usually a pepo with tough or hard pericarp, dehiscent or indehiscent, often opening by a hole at the apex; sometimes of great size. Seeds without endosperm and with a large embryo; cotyledons oily.

Dendrosicyos is a soft wooded tree of Socotra Island. *Acanthosicyos* is a thorny leafless shrub of S. Africa with a branched greatly swollen tap root running to a length of about 15 m. *Ecballium* a trailing or prostrate herb of the Mediterranean region is without tendril.

Bisexual flowers occur in *Schizopepon*. The petals are free in *Fevillia*, *Luffa*, *Lagenaria*, etc. In *Fevillia* there are 5 free stamens. Four other types of androecium are met with viz. (1) filaments of 4 stamens coherent below in 2 pairs, the 5th remaining free; (2) the coherent filaments unite completely so that the andoecium seems to be made up of 3 stamens.

2 with 2-celled anthers and one with 1-celled anther, (3) filaments free below and united above or completely united and the anthers all united and spirally twisted, (4) stamens completely united with the lobes of the anthers forming 2 horizontal rings surrounding a peltate mass of connectives. The first type is exemplified in *Thladiantha*, the second type is met with in *Bryonia*, *Citrullus*, *Momordica*, etc., the third type in *Cucurbita*, and in *Cyclanthera* the fourth type is found.

Difference of opinion exists regarding the true nature of the placentation and the ovary being unilocular or trilocular. Engler, Eichler, Wettstein and Willis considered that the ovary was trilocular, the carpels intruding and meeting at the centre and the placentation was axile. Rendle and others are of the opinion that the ovary is unilocular and the placentation is parietal, the placentas growing inside and meeting at the centre often filling the cavity of the ovary cell.

Sicyos and *Sechium* have a sloitary ovule and the seed of *Sechium* germinates viviparously. The fleshy fruit of *Momordica* splits into 3 parts and the seeds are ejected. *Luffa* has a dry fruit with a fibrous network of vascular bundles. The fruit opens by an aperture at the apex through which the seeds come out. The fruit of *Ecballium* gets detached when fully ripe and the seeds together with the watery fluid that it contains are ejected violently through the aperture at the base of the fruit. The fruit of *Lagenaria* has a hard pericarp which when breaks due to some external pressure the seeds come out. In other cases the seeds are released when the fruit rots.

The seeds are smooth but in some genera corrugated or sculptured. In *Zanonia* the seeds are winged.

Regarding the morphological nature of the tendril different hypothesis have been put forward. Engler's view is that the tendril is a modification of the stipule. Of a pair of lateral stipules one is suppressed while the other is transformed into a tendril. *Kedrostis spinosa* Med. seems to be a good example of this. Naudin considered the tendril to be an axillary branch the axis of which was united with the main stem and the tendrilar portion represented the midrib of a reduced leaf. Payer expressed the view that the tendril resulted due to the splitting of the petiole. According to Braun and Wydler the tendril is a modified bracteole which is displaced from its original position. This view is supported by Eichler. The widely accepted view however is that of Muller who stated that the tendril was a metamorphosed branch, the lower thick portion representing the axis and the upper coiled portion representing the leaf. This view is based on different transitional forms of the tendril of *Cucurbita pepo* DC. where the upper portion often becomes flattened and winged like a leaf blade. Hagerup supported Muller's hypothesis.

Floral formula for male and female are expressed as:

$$♂ \oplus K_{(5)}\ C_{(5)}\ A_{5 \text{ or } 2+2+1}\ G_0$$

$$♀ \oplus K_{(5)}\ C_{(5)}\ A_0\ G_{\underline{(3)}}$$

Cystoliths are present in the epidermal cells of the leaves. The vascular bundles are arranged in 2 rows. These are bicollateral with 2 strands of fascicular cambium and 2 patches of phloem. The vessels and sieve tubes are very large. Perforations are simple. The stomata are Ranunculaceous.

The family consists of about 100 genera and 850 species, distributed in the tropical and subtropical countries and a few species occurring also in the temperate regions.

Some are found in very humid areas while quite a fair number inhabit the arid zones. In India about 90 species are found many of which are cultivated. Of the wild plants *Trichosanthes bracteata* (Lamk.) Voigt.—Makal, *T. cucumerina* Linn.—Banchichinga, *Coccinia grandis* (L.) Voigt.—Telakucha, *Momordica cochinchinensis* (Lour.) Spreng-Kakrol, *Zehneria umbellata* Thw.—Kudari, etc. are very common in the plains.

Many are cultivated for the luscious fruits, viz. *Citrullus lanatus* (Thunb.) Mak. Tarbuz (Water melon), *Cucumis melo* Linn.—Kharbuz, Phunti, Sarda, etc. (Melon), *C. sativus* Linn.—Sosha, Khira (Cucumber), etc. As vegetables most important are,—*Trichosanthes dioica* Roxb.—Palwal, *T. anguina* Linn.—Chichinga (Snake gourd), *Benincasa hispida* Cogn.—Chal Kumra, Petha (Wax gourd), *Lagenaria leucantha* (Duch.) Rusby, Louki (Bottle gourd), *Momordica charantia* Linn.—Karela (Bitter gourd), *Luffa cylindrica* (L.) Roem.—Dhundul, Ghia Toroi (Bath sponge), *L. acatanguta* (L.) Roxb.—Jhinga, Kali Toroi, etc. *Cucurbita maxima* Duchesne—Mitha Kadu, Mitha Kumra (Gourd, Spanish gourd) originally of Africa, *C. pepo* DC.—Kumra, Safed Kadu (Pumpkin) originally of S. America and *C. moschata* Duchesne—Safra Kumra (Musk melon) originally of S. America are widely cultivated. *Sechium edule* Linn.—Chocho or Chyota also of S. America is much cultivated in Darjeeling and Shillong.

Tender shoots of many of the above species are also used as pot herbs. A few have medicinal properties, e.g. the stem and leaves of *Trichosanthes dioica* are much used by Indian Kabirajes as febrifuge, stomachic and for killing worms. *Citrullus colocynthis* Schrad. has extremely bitter fruits, the pulp of which is purgative and with sugar given in dropsy and is applied in discoloration of skin. Different species of *Bryonia* also possess medicinal properties.

Pax and Muller divided the family into 5 subfamilies as noted below:—

Group A. Anther lobes not united in a ring.

Subf. I **Fevilleae:** Stamens 5, rarely 4; free or united only at base.

Subf. II **Melothrieae:** Stamens 5 but apparently 3, rarely 2 or 4; anther lobes usually straight.

Subf. III **Cucurbiteae:** Stamens 5 but apparently 3; anther lobes sigmoid.

Subf. IV **Sicyoideae:** Stamens united in a column.

Group B. Antherlobes united in a ring.

Subf. V **Cyclanthereae:** Stamens united in a column; anther lobes fused in 2 rings round the top of the staminal column.

The family has recently been divided in a different manner into 3 tribes:

I. **Cucumerineae:** Female flowers always solitary; ovules transversely placed rarely pendulous.

II. **Orthospermeae:** Ovules not transverse, erect or ascending.

III. **Zanonieae:** Female flowers in racemes or panicle, never solitary: ovules pendulous.

The affinity of the family is not very clear and difference of opinion exists among the taxonomists regarding the systematic position of *Cucurbitaceae*. This is no doubt an advanced family, being predominantly herbaceous, having unisexual epigynous flowers, gamopetalous corolla, synandrium formation of stamens often with curved anther lobes and also having bicollateral vascular bundles. Engler therefore placed his monotypic order **Cucurbitales** between **Rubiales** and **Campanulatae** and considered this family to be closely allied to *Campanulaceae* with gamopetalous corolla, open type of calyx, more or less synandrium formation, epigynous ovary and bicollateral vascular bundles in some genera. Eichler and Wettstein supported Engler. Bentham and Hooker placed *Cucurbitaceae* in the cohort **Passiflorales** with *Passifloraceae*, *Loasaceae*, *Begoniaceae*, *Datiscaceae*, etc. Hallier considered that *Cucurbitaceae* was closely allied to *Begoniacee* and *Datiscaceae* which belonged to the order **Peponiferae** and according to him this order was derived from *Passifloraceae*. Rendle and Hutchinson more or less agreed with Hallier due to the following common characters, viz.—bitegmic ovule, persistent nucellus and extensive tapetal tissue. Free petals in *Fevillea* (Cucurbitaceae) however bring it closer to *Passiflora*. Flower of *Fevillea* resembles those in *Rosaceae* to some extent and therefore Bessey considered that the order **Loasales** consisting of *Loasaceae*, *Cucurbitaceae*, *Begoniaceae*, *Datiscaceae* and *Ancistrocladaceae* originated from **Rosales.** Takhtajan places only *Cucurbitaceae* in his **Cucurbitales** and the order is placed by him between **Passiflorales** and **Begoniales.** So according to Takhtajan *Cucurbitaceae* is allied to *Passifloraceae* on one side and to *Begoniaceae* and *Datiscaceae* on another side.

Cronquist includes *Cucurbitaceae* in **Violales** a large order wherein are included *Passifloraceae*, *Loasaceae*, *Turneraceae*, *Begoniaceae*, *Datiscaceae*, *Ancistrocladaceae*, etc. Cronquist considers **Violales** to be a natural taxon derived from **Theales.** According to him all the families included in **Violales** are related to each other although the order appears to be a heterogenous assemblage. It is therefore clear that most workers consider that *Cucurbitaceae* is related to *Passifloraceae*, *Begoniaceae*, *Loasaceae* and *Datiscaceae*.

CAMPANULATAE

This is the last order of dicotyledons in the system of Engler and Prantl and the 11th order in their **Metachlamydeae.** The order consists of 6 families, viz. *Campanulaceae*, *Goodeniaceae*, *Brunoniaceae*, *Stylidiaceae*, *Calyceraceae* and *Compositae*. These families are according to them and most other authors very highly evolved and rather recent, the family *Compositae* being the highest. Characters common to these families are:—herbs or shrubs, flowers bisexual or unisexual, actinomorphic or zygomorphic, epigynous, pentamerous, anthers more or less united, ovary usually bicarpellary, 1-celled and 1-ovuled.

This order is considered by many as a natural taxon and the families are related to each other. According to Bessey **Campanulatae** (or **Campanulales**) originated from **Rubiales** where also flowers had bicarpellary inferior ovary. Dense compact type of inflorescence is met with in *Anthocephalus*, *Adina*, *etc.* In some genera in *Valerianaceae* the sepals are reduced to pappus.

Both Takhtajan and Cronquist split **Campanulatae** of Engler into 3 orders and place *Compositae* (*Asteraceae*) in a monotypic order **Asterales. Campanulales** according to Takhtajan consists of 7 families, viz. *Campanulaceae*, *Lobeliaceae*, *Sphenocleaceae*, *Donatiaceae*, *Stylidiaceae*, *Goodeniaceae* and *Brunoiaceae* while Cronquist places 6 families in that order, viz. *Campanulaceae*, *Goodeniaceae*, *Stylidiaceae*, *Pentaphragmataceae*, *Sphenocleaceae* and *Brunoniaceae*. Cronquist does not separate *Lobeliaceae* from *Campanulaceae*. *Calyceraceae* is placed in a monotypic order **Calycerales** by Takhtajan while Cronquist includes this family in **Dipsacales.** So from the treatment of the families included in **Campa-**

nulatae of Engler by different authors it appears that these families are close to one another and are more recent in the course of evolution. Further the origin of these families from *Rubiaceae* or **Rubiales** appears to be quite feasible.

Hutchinson also distributes these families under 3 orders, splitting **Campanulatae** into **Campanulales, Goodeniales** and **Asterales.** He places these orders close to one another recognising their affinity but according to him these do not occupy the highest position in the scale of evolution.

Campanulaceae

Annual or perennial herbs, undershrubs or rarely shrubs, very rarely trees; milky latex often present. Leaves simple, exstipulate, alternate or rarely opposite. Inflorescence racemose or cymose, often paniculate or clustered in heads, rarely solitary and axillary. Flowers bisexual, actinomorphic or zygomorphic, pentamerous, epigynous or semi-epigynous and usually with 2 bracteoles. Calyx lobes 5, valvate or open in bud. Corolla funnel-shaped or bell-shaped, regular, 5-lobed, valvate, or irregular and bilabiate, the upper lip being resupinate to 180°. Stamens as many as petals and alternate to them, free or variously united and syngenesious; filaments often wider at base. A nectar-secreting epigynous disc is usually present. Ovary of 2-5 united carpels, inferior or semi-inferior, 2-5-celled, rarely 6-10-celled or one celled; ovules many, anatropous on axile or parietal placentas; style simple or branched. Fruit a capsule or berry. Seed with a small embryo and copious fleshy endosperm.

Clermontia is a small tree while *Codonopis* and *Cyphia* are twiners. *Cyanea* of Hawai has a palm like appearance. In *Phyteuma* the small flowers are aggregated in heads. In *Lobelia*, *Pratia*, *Cyphia*, etc. the corolla is zygomorphic. In the subfamily **Lobelioideae** sepals, petals and stamens are 6-10. In *Michauxia* and *Phyteuma* the petals are almost free to the base. Stamens are more or less completely unified in *Cyphia*. The ovary in *Merciera* is unilocular.

The floral formula is represented as:

$$\oplus \ ⚥ \ K_{(5)} \ C_{(5)} \ A_{(5)} \ G_{(\overline{2})}$$

or $$\dagger \ ⚥ \ K_{(6-10)} \ C_{(6-10)} \ A_{(6-10)} \ G_{(\overline{2})}.$$

Articulated latex tubes are present in the stem in many species. Bicollateral bundles sometimes occur.

The flowers are protandrous. The style pushes up the pollens to be easily collected by the insect visitor. The nectar in the epigynous disc is protected by the broad bases of the filaments forming a dome-like structure over it.

Campanulaceae contains about 1,500 species under 61 genera and is distributed mainly in the temperate and subtropical parts of the world with a few in the tropics. It is well represented in India having several species of *Campanula* in the hills, a few species of *Lobelia* in the plains and at low elevations in the hills and some other genera. *Wahlenbergia marginata* A. DC. (Syn. *W. gracilis* Schrad) and *Sphenoclea zeylanica* Gaertn. are quite common all over India in the plains, the latter in marshy habitats.

Campanulaceae has a close affinity with *Compositae* and the 2 families are placed under the same order by many workers. In both families herbs predominate, corolla more or less similar, syngenesious androecium in some genera of *Campanulaceae*, similar arrangement of exposing the pollens, inferior ovary, more or less similar style and stigma and compact h.. d-like inflorescence in some *Campanulaceae*. It is allied to *Rubiaceae* where too the small flowers are aggregated in compact type of inflorescence, the corolla is tubular and the ovary inferior. Many workers consider that *Campanulaceae* and the families included in the order **Campanulatae** originated from *Rubiaceae* or the order **Rubiales.**

Campanulaceae appears to be a much advanced family in the scale of evolution, being predominantly herbs, having a special arrangement for cross pollination by insects, gamopetalous corolla, anthers usually united, inferior ovary, etc. Inclusion of *Compositae* the most highly evolved family, by Engler in the same order with *Campanulaceae* appears to be justified. Some authors trace the affinity of *Campanulaceae* with *Cucurbitaceae* having similar calyx and often similar corolla, syngenesious *androecium* (with tendency of synandrium in some cases), inferior ovary and bicollateral vascular bundles, in some genera of *Campanulaceae*. However, the flowers in *Cururbitaceae* are unisexual while in *Campanulaceae* they are bisexual.

The family is divided into 3 subfamilies as mentioned below:—

Subf. I. **Campanuloideae:** Flowers actinomorphic; anthers free.

Subf. II. **Cyphioideae:** Flowers zygomorphic; filaments of stamens more or less united.

Subf. III. **Lobelioideae:** Flowers bilabiate, anthers united; carpels 2.

The subfamily Lobelioideae is raised to the rank of a distinct family *Lobeliaceae* by some authors, e.g., Hutchinson and Takhtajan and the genus *Sphenoclea* is placed by some in a distinct monotypic family *Sphenocleaceae*. Characters of these 2 families when treated as distinct, are given below:—

Lobeliaceae

Herbs, undershrubs or shrubs, rarely trees, often with milky juice. Leaves alternate, simple, exstipulate. Flowers hermaphrodite or unisexual, epigynous, bilabiate. Calyx adnate to the ovary, 5-lobed. Corolla gamopetalous, bilabiate; lips resupinate due to twisting of the pedicel; lobes valvate. Stamens 5, epipetalous or not; filaments free, anthers cohering into a tube round the style. Ovary more or less inferior, 2-3-locular (rarely 1-locular); style simple or 2-3-lobed and surrounded by a ring of hairs; ovules ∞ ; placentation axile. Fruit a capsule or fleshy and indehiscent. Seeds small and numerous, with small straight embryo and copious endosperm.

Sphenocleaceae

Herbaceous plant of marshy area, stem hollow. Leaves simple, alternate, exstipulate. Inflorescence a dense cylindric spike. Flowers regular, bracteate, bisexual, pentamerous. Calyx gamosepalous; lobes 5, valvate. Corolla gamopetalous, 5-lobed, campanulate, valvate, stamens 5, epipetalous, anthers free. Ovary semi-inferior, bicarpellary, 2-locular; ovules many in each locule, pendulous from axile placentas. Capsule circumscissile, seeds many, with plenty of endosperm.

Only one species *Sphenoclea zeylanica* Gaertn. found in India and S. E. Asia. This genus appears to be anomalous when placed in *Campanulaceae* and some workers transfer it to *Phytolaccaceae*. Takhtajan segregates **Sphenocleaceae** as a distinct family and Cronquist supports this treatment.

Economically *Campanulaceae* (sensu lato including *Lobeliaceae* and *Sphenocleaceae*) is not very important. Many species of *Campanula* are cultivated as garden annuals and are known as Canterbury-bells, Hair-bells, etc. Some species of *Lobelia* and *Siphocampylos* are also cultivated for their showy flowers. The young roots and shoots of some *Campanula* are edible and the tender leaves and shoots of *Specularia* are used in salad.

Some species are strong poisons, e.g. *Lobelia inflata* Linn. *L. tupa* Linn., *Laurentia longiflora* (Linn.) E. Wimm. etc. In small doses *L. inflata*—the Indian tobacco, cures whooping cough and gives relief in spasmodic asthma. The milky juice of *Isotoma longiflora* Linn., also a strong poison, contains couchouc.

Compositae

(Asteraceae)

Herbs, under shrubs or shrubs; sometimes with milky latex, rarely aromatic, usually unarmed. Leaves radical or cauline, simple or rarely compound, pinnately or palmately lobed, alternate or opposite, rarely whorled, exstipulate. The inflorescence is a capitulum surrounded by an involucre of bracts. Flowers actinomorphic or zygomorphic, bisexual or unisexual, epigynous. Calyx represented by pappus consisting of scales or hairs, persistent. Corolla tubular or bilabiate, ligulate in the marginal ray florets. Stamens 5, filaments attached to the corolla tube, anthers syngenesious, bilobed, connective often prolonged. Carpels 2, syncarpous, forming a unilocular inferior ovary; ovule solitary, basal, with one integument; style short with 2 recurved or spreading stigmas. Fruit a cypsela; seeds without endosperm.

The capitulum inflorescence may be heterogamous or homogamous. In the former the ray florets are either female or sterile and the disc florets are bisexual. Ray florets are zygomorphic, with a ligulate corolla or rarely bilabiate; disc florets are actinomorphic. In homogamous capitulum all flowers are usually bisexual and similar, actinomorphic or zygomorphic, rarely all unisexual. A capitulum may have few flowers or numerous and often not less than a thousand. It may be simple or compound, arranged in heads, corymbs or paniculate. The involucre may be uniseriate, biseriate or multiseriate. In a compound capitulum each smaller capitulum has its own involucre. The axis of the capitulum (usually called receptacle) is usually flat or convex but may be cone-like or elongate (*Rudbeckia, Spilanthes*) or concave and cup-like (*Epaltes*). The pappus is regarded as modified calyx but Small interpreted these as trichomes of the ovary. Ramiah and Sayeduddin supported Small.

The plants are usually herbs or shrubs but rarely also climbers, e.g. *Mikania* and very rarely are trees, e.g. *Wilkesia* (Sandwich Isl.), *Leucomeris* (Nepal), *Vernonia arborea* Buch. Ham. (India), etc. Tuberous roots are found in few genera, e.g. *Dahlia, Helianthus* etc., where the tubers store reserve food in the form of inulin grains. In the armed species the lobes of the leaves and the involucral bracts are spine tipped, e.g. *Cirsium, Cnicus, Carthamus*, etc. One-flowered capitulum occurs in *Lagascea*, some species of *Vernonia*, etc. In *Hoplophyllum*, a xerophytic genus, the leaves are modified into spines. The stem is flat and leaf-like in *Baccharis*. Capitula of *Xanthium* are unisexual, the female consists of 2 florets in an urnshaped 2-beaked involucre clothed with hooked bristles. In *Schoenia* the disc florets are sterile and the ray florets are bisexual. In *Lactuca, Cichorium*, etc. all florets are ligulate while in *Mutisia* all florets are bilabiate. In *Silybium* the stamens unite by anthers as well by filaments.

The bracts in *Elveria* are accrescent and act like wings giving the capitulam a samara-like appearance.

In *Wilkesia* the floral bracts are prominent and the involucre of bracts is wanting. In *Millenia* one bract is larger than the others and covers the capitulum in fruit.

A ring-like tubular nectary is present at the base of the style. In many genera vascular bundles are present in the cortex and in pith. Anomalous secondary thickening occurs in some cases. In the African genus *Metalasia* the vascular bundles are in several successive rings.

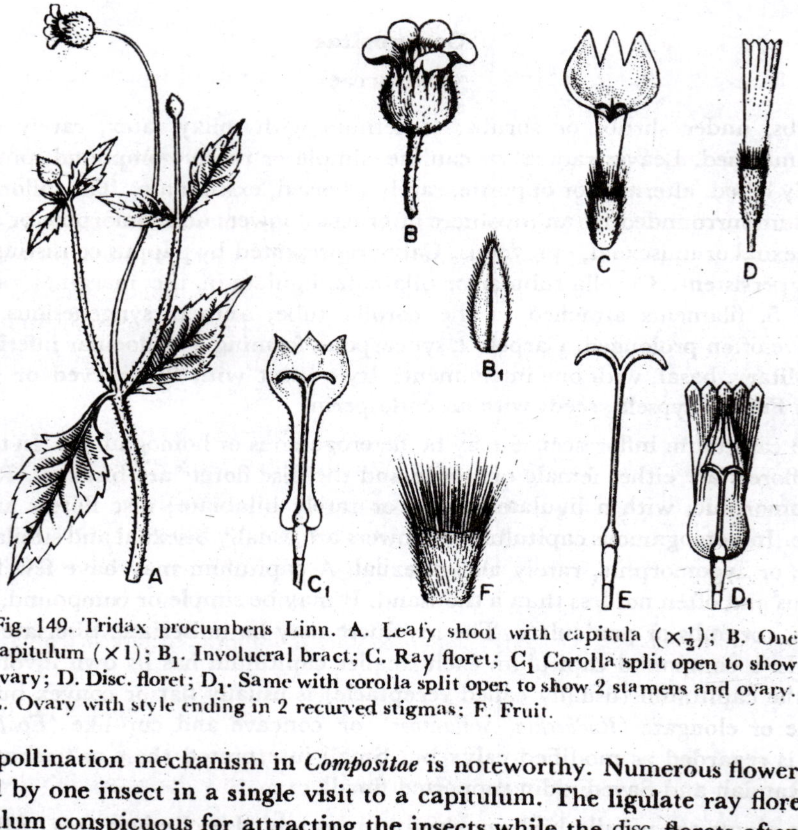

Fig. 149. Tridax procumbens Linn. A. Leafy shoot with capitula ($\times\frac{1}{2}$); B. One capitulum ($\times 1$); B_1. Involucral bract; C. Ray floret; C_1 Corolla split open to show ovary; D. Disc. floret; D_1. Same with corolla split open to show 2 stamens and ovary. E. Ovary with style ending in 2 recurved stigmas; F. Fruit.

The pollination mechanism in *Compositae* is noteworthy. Numerous flowers can be pollinated by one insect in a single visit to a capitulum. The ligulate ray florets make the capitulum conspicuous for attracting the insects while the disc florets often inconspicuous, get the benefit. The nectar is easily accesible to the insects and is protected from rain. The protandrous condition of the androecium is another help for cross pollination. The pollens are carried up and preserved by the stigma of the same flower to be easily carried away by the insect visitor. Arrangement of self-pollination also exists if cross-pollination fails.

The family consists of more than 19,000 species under 950 genera and is the largest among the dicotyledonous families if not among the whole of angiosperms. They are found in almost all parts of the world from sea-level to the alpine region, from the tropics to the arctic zone, from the arid region to very humid tracts. A few are true aquatics and some are halophytes. In India about 700 species are found among which *Senecio*, *Vernonia*, *Blumea*, *Saussurea* etc. are represented with large number of species. *Ageratum conyzoides* Linn., *Blainvillea acmella* (L.) Philip., *Caesulia axillaris* Roxb., *Echinops echinata* Roxb., *Eclipta prostrata* (L.) Linn., *Siegesbeckia orientalis* Linn., *Sphaeranthus indicus* Linn., *Xanthium strumarium* Linn., *Tridax procumbens* Linn., *Lagascea mollis* Cav., *Grangea maderaspatana* (L.) Poir., *Gnaphalium luteoalbum* Linn., *Eupatorium odoratum* Linn., *Emilia sonchifolia* (L.) DC., *Elephantopus scaber* Linn. etc. are very common in the plains. *Anaphalis contorta* Hk. f., *Artemisia nilagirica* (Cl.) Pamp., *Saussurea candicans* Clarke are common in the hills. *Tragopogon gracile* Don. are common in the Himalayas between elevations of 2000 to 3000 mtr.

Floral formula for a bisexual flower:

$$\dagger \text{ or } \oplus ⚥ \text{ K pappus } C_{(5)}, A_{(5)}\ G_{\overline{(2)}}.$$

The family is divided into 2 subfamilies and 13 tribes of which 12 are under one subfamily and the 13th is under the other.

Subf. I. **Tubuliflorae:** Corolla of disc florets not ligulate; laticiferous vessels absent.

Tribe (i) *Vernonieae:* Capitula homogamous; corolla tubular; anthers sagittate: pappus hairy; stigmatic branches long with papillae all over the inner surface.

Tribe (ii) *Eupatorieae:* Capitula homogamous; corolla tubular; pappus bristle or scale-like; anther-base not sagittate; stigmatic branches papillose on margin only.

Tribe (iii) *Astereae:* Capitula heterogamous with female or neuter ray florets: anthers not sagittate; stigmatic arms flat.

Tribe (iv) *Inuleae:* Capitula homo- or heterogamous; all or only central florets tubular; pappus hairy or bristly; anthers tailed; stigmas with marginal papillae.

Tribe (v) *Heliantheae:* Capitula heterogamous with female or neuter ray florets; involucral bracts not membranous at margin; pappus not hairy; anther base not prolonged; ray florets often with 3 petals; disc florets paleaceous, i.e. with bracteoles.

Tribe (vi) *Helenieae:* Like *Heliantheae* but disc florets without palea.

Tribe (vii) *Anthemideae:* Like *Heliantheae* but involucral bracts scarious at margin and pappus small, annular or absent.

Tribe (viii) *Senecioneae:* Capitula homo- or heterogamous; involucral bracts with scarious margin and with extra scales; pappus hairy.

Tribe (ix) *Calenduleae:* Capitula heterogamous with female ray florets and small disc florets; floral bracts absent; pappus absent; anther-base pointed; stigma entire.

Tribe (x) *Arctotideae:* Capitula heterogamous; ray florets female or neuter, ligulate; pappus not hairy or absent; anther-base pointed or not; style thickened at base or with a ring of hairs.

Tribe (xi) *Cynareae:* Capitula homogamous or heterogamous; ray florets not ligulate, female or neuter; involucral bracts spiny; base of anther tailed.

Tribe (xii) *Mutisieae:* Capitula homo- or heterogamous; ray florets with bilabiate corolla; disc florets regular with deeply seated corolla-limb.

Subf. II. **Liguliflorae:** All florets in the capitula with ligulate corolla; laticiferous vessels present.

Tribe (xiii) *Cichorieae:* Capitula homogamous: anthers sagittate.

Compositae is related to *Campanulaceae* and *Goodeniaceae* having 5-merous flowers and inferior ovary. In the 3 families the arrangement for collecting the pollens is elaborate. In *Campanulaceae* the stamens often have syngenesious anthers. In *Goodeniaceae* also anthers are sometimes united and the ovary is bicarpellary. *Compositae* is also allied to *Stylidiaceae*, both having inferior bilocular ovary and on this character it comes near to *Rubiaceae*. The affinity of *Compositae* with *Valerianaceae* and *Dipsacaceae* is also traced from dense inflorescence and inferior ovary. It is presumed that *Compositae* and the other families in the order **Campanalatae** originated from *Rubiaceae*.

The family is generally regarded as occupying the highest position among the angiosperms or at least among the dicots in the course of evolution as is evident by the presence of largest number of species and by the cosmopolitan distribution from the arctic to the tropical zone. The highest position reached by the family is due to the following advanced characters:

(a) The herbaceous habit.

(b) The capitulum inflorescence with numerous inconspicuous florets surrounded by a ring of ligulate marginal florets that make the whole capitulum very prominent and showy for attracting insect visitors for pollination. Aggregation of so many flowers in a small space makes it possible to pollinate a large number of them by an insect in a single visit.

(c) Reduction and modification of calyx.

(d) Cohesion of stamens in the form of syngenesious anthers or completely; protandry of the androecium.

(e) Reduction of carpels to 2 and in the number of ovules to one only; inferior ovary.

(f) Easily accessible nectar which is protected against rain.

(g) Arrangement for cross pollination and prevention of self-pollination till last moment with certainty of the same when cross pollination fails by curling back of stigmas and coming in contact with pollens of the same flower.

(h) Distribution of fruit with help of the pappus that act as parachute mechanism.

The family includes a few plants of economic importance some of which are cultivated as ornamental plants, e.g. *Dahlia pinnata* Cav., *Chrysanthemum coronarium* Linn. and other species of the same genus, *Zinnia pauciflora* Linn., *Z. elegans* Linn., *Tagetes patula* Linn., *T. erecta* Linn. (Marigold), *Helianthus annuus* Linn. (Sun flower), *Aster tripolium* Linn., *Calendula officinalis* Linn., *Gaillardia* species, *Cosmos bipinnatus* Cav., etc. Species of *Helichrysum* and *Heliptarum* produce the so called "Everlasting flowers" where the bracts of the involucre are brightly cloloured and dry and papery. These do not change long after the fruits mature.

Artemisia cina Berg. is the source of santonin. *Centratherum anthelminticum* O. Ktze. is the Someraj of Indian Kavirajes the seeds of which have anthelminitic properties. Leaves of *Eupatorium ayapana* Vent. stop internal haemorrhage. The juice of *Wedelia calendulacea* Less. promotes the growth of hairs. *Eclipta prostrata* Linn. possess the same property and the juice is also used in tattooing. *Saussurea lappa* Clarke, the Kuth or Kustha is used medicinally in various ways and also in the preparation of a hair tonic.

The juice of *Enhydra fluctuans* Lour.—Hingcha, Hilomochika kills worms and induces sleep.

Lactuca sativa Linn. is cultivated for the leaves which are used as salad. *Cichorium endivia* Linn. is the Endive which is also a salad plant. *C. intybus* Linn. is also used similarly and the roots of which are much used as a beverage after roasting. The tuberous

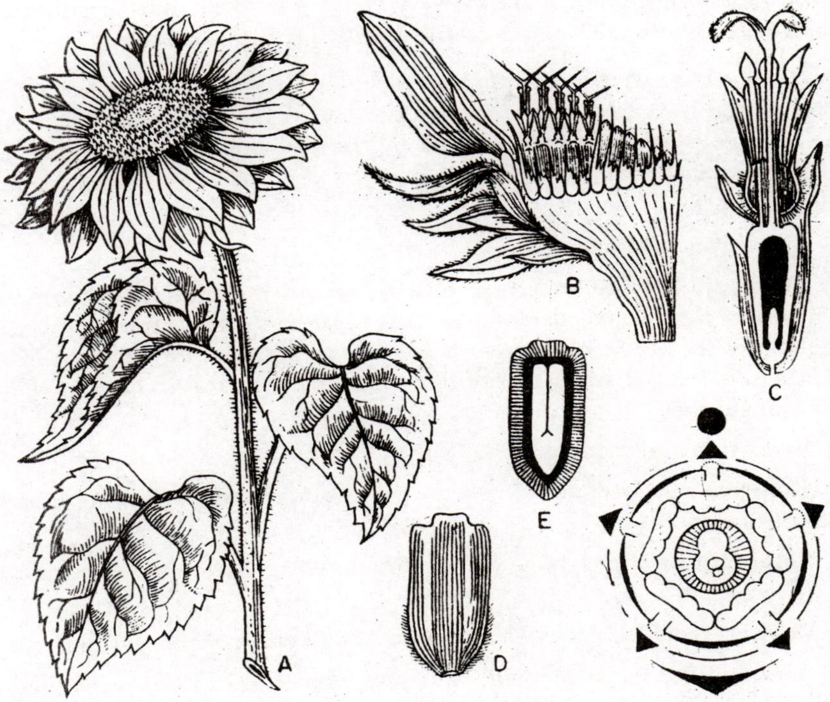

Fig. 150. Helianthus annuus Linn. A. Shoot with leaves and a capitulum. B. A portion of the capitulum showing involucral bracts, ray florets and disc florets; C. One flower in l.s. (much enlarged); D. Fruit; E. L.s. of the fruit.

roots of *Helianthus tuberosus* Linn.—the Jerusalem Artichoke are edible. The young shoots of *Scolynus hispanicus* Linn. and *S. maculatus* Linn. are eaten as asparagus. The roasted seeds of *Helianthus annuus* Linn. are also eaten.

Flowers of *Carthamus tinctorius* Linn. yield a dye and an oil is extracted from the seeds of this and of *Guizotia abyssinica* Cass. Pyrethrum, an insecticide, is obtained from *Tanacetum cinerariefolium* Schr. (Syn. *Chrysanthemum cineraiefolium* Vis.) *Parthenium argentatum* A. Gray yields rubber.

PART III
PHYTOGEOGRAPHY

CHAPTER IX

PHYTOGEOGRAPHY

The cradle of primitive Angiosperms

It was in the Jurassic period when the Angiosperms first appeared on the globe. In the early Cretaceous the Angiosperms were confined to areas lying between latitudes 45°N and 45°S. The angiospermic flora was gradually replacing the non flowering vegetation of the Jurassic and in the northern part of the globe Angiosperms established themselves only in late Cretaceous period. Teslenko proved that no Angioperm existed in Siberia before the late Cretaceous and that Angiosperms migrated to Siberia from the south. Teslenko observed that the Angiosperms did not originate in the northern part of Angaria or the ancient Angara land.

In the present century many workers suggested a tropical origin of the Angiosperms. Hallier assumed that this group of plants originated in a continent in the south of pacific ocean. But no such continent ever existed. However, other workers, e.g. Diels Golenkin, Bailey, Axelrod, A.C. Smith, Thorne, etc. all agreed that the cradle of Angiosperms was situated in the S. Pacific, or western part of S. Pacific. It is an wide area stretching from Assam in the West and Australia and Fiji Isls. in the east including Burma, S. China, Japan, Malaysia, New Zealand, New Caledonia, etc. The fossil evidences do not indicate the exact centre of origin but these established the fact that Angisperms arose in the tropical belt and spread to higher latitude areas.

In this wide area, i.e. S.W. Pacific Basin the primitive Angiosperms are found in abundance. Many primitive families are confined in this area and primitive representatives of many other families are to be found here. Croizat points out that Malaysia is one of the most important phytogeographic zones of the world and all the five continents can easily be reached from its boundaries. It is however, a well known fact that the continental S.E. Asia was connected to the Malayan Archipelago for a long time, the mountains forming prolonged link. The high lands of the Burma-Yunnan area ran as far as Antartica through Malaysia, New Caladonia, N.E. Australia. Tasmania, etc. In the Jurassic and early Createaceous these highlands served as the migratory route from Malaysia to Australia and Antartica.

Van Steenis advanced a hypothesis that a land-bridge connection existed between S.E. Australia, Tasmania, New Zealand, Patagonia and the Antartic continent. But Smith, Zimmerman, Axelrod are of the opinion that no such continuous land connection existed although there was insular chain and served as stepping stones for migration of plants.

The lowlands in the tropical regions were very damp throughout the year and were unsuitable to support Angiospermic vegetation. Axelrod therefore suggested that the Angiosperms originated not in the lowlands but in the mountains, under the most diverse and variable environmental conditions. From the very beginning they had developed a high degree of adaptability to variations in atmospheric and soil moisture. The rapid ecological and morphological differentiations began in the very earliest stages of their evolution and as they migrated along different geographical and ecological pathways they underwent further transformation enroute.

Krassnov considered that temperate flora orginated from tropical plants that migrated northwards and proved hardy to temperate climate. The periodicity of growth in temperate plants is an attribute which had already developed in the tropics. Axelrod as well as Holttum said that the deciduous habit developed in plants in the tropics and permitted such trees to spread from the equatorial belt to regions having marked alternating seasons.

From the above discourses it is inferred that the Angiosperms originated in the mountains of S.W.Pacific basin lying between Assam and Fiji Isls.. and from which area they spread to other tropical countries and in course of evolution gave rise to plants capable to survive in varied types of soil and climate. They spread by land route and crossed the ocean-barrier by insular chains that existed in the Creataceous period and earlier. The earliest primitive Angiosperms gave rise to different types of tropical plants as well as temperate and alpine. Thus we find that the extremely rich tropical flora of America is rather poor in primitive Angiosperms while the flora of tropical Africa has such Angiosperms.

According to a second and older theory the Angiosperms originated in the north polar region. This theory was proposed by Heer in 1868. J.D. Hooker and A. Engler were among others who supported this theory. The theory of northern origin of Angiosperms has now been discarded as a result of investigations by the paleo-botanists.

Migration of Plants

From their original abode the Angiosperms covered the whole of the earth migrating to different countries along different routes. Moving northwards they covered the whole of Asia and following a coastal route reached the Bearing Straight and crossed over to America. Mountains of Malaya and Burma brought them to the Himalayas by which route they had access to Europe. In N. Vietnam, Upper Burma, Assam, Yunnan and E. Himalayas a series of phylogenetic links do exist that connect the temperatre forms of plants to the subtropical and tropical forms. Those plants that reached Antartica travelled westwards and ultimately reached S. America.

Migration of plants depends on dispersal of seeds. Vegetative propagation is also responsible in few cases but this must have played an insignificant role at the early stages of plant migration. Seeds are carried over to wider and wider areas by different agents. The plants that come out of the seeds that fall in new areas need to acclimatise themselves in the new situations for survival. This depends on a few factors, viz :- (a) Character of the seed or fruit that makes it easy or difficult for the dispersal of a particular plant; (b) Natural barrier that stops further dispersal; (c) Ecological conditions that make it easy or difficult for the seed to germinate, for the seedling to survive for the new-comer to compete with the local plants. Dispersal of seeds is a continuous process by which a species survives and spreads. Migration of plants as a result of dispersal of seeds to wider areas is also a constant phenomenon in the plant kingdom.

The range of distribution of a species, genus or family may be *continuous* or *discontinuous.* Discontinuous distribution means the presence of gaps in the range of distribution. Such gaps appear due to ecological conditions, failure of survival in competition with other pre-established plants, changing of climate and composition of the soil in geological periods, etc. Examples of discontinuous distribution are : *Ranalisma, Magnolia,* etc. *Ranalisma rostrata* Stapf occurs in Malaya while *R. humile* (Ktz) Hutch. is found in Africa. No species of the genus is found in between. A few species of *Magnolia* occur in S.E. Asia while some are found in tropical America; and this is the distribution pattern of the family *Magnoliaceae. Calycanthaceae* is restricted in 2 areas widely apart, i.e. in, southern part of tropical N. America and Upper Burma and Yunnan. *Cochlospermaceae* is confined to W. Tropical Africa and India, Malaysia to Australia, *Schizandraceae* has a Malaysian distribution but one species *Schizandra glabra* occurs in N. America. *Illiciaceae* is distributed in Atlantic N. America and in E. Asia including Japan.

Due to same reasons we find many groups of plants are restricted to smaller areas, e.g. *Ruscus*, found only in the Mediterranean region. Taxa with a very restricted distribution are called *endemic* taxa. *Degeneriaceae* a monotypic family is endemic in Fiji Islands. *Amherstia* with a single species is endemic in Burma. *Calacanthus* a monotypic genus is endemic in Western India. Many larger genera have some species distributed over wide areas and some are endemic and restricted to smaller areas. *Primula*, *Impatiens*, *Gentiana*, *Rhododendron*, etc. include many endemic species as well as many distributed over wide areas. *Gomphostemma* an East Asiatic genus has a few species endemic in Assam. *Rhododendron nilagiricum* Zenc. is endemic in the Nilgiri hills of S. India while quite a number of species of the genus occur in the Himalayas and a few of them are endemic.

Two factors are considered to be responsible for endemism. Areas which are widely separated from other areas by natural barriers, viz : islands in the middle of wide oceans, alpine regions of the high mountains or oasis in vast deserts. In these areas when new species are evolved fail to spread over other areas due to the natural bariers. The other factor is the change of eological conditions for a particular species making it too difficult for the species to survive except in some niches and corners. Examples of such endemic genera as mentioned by Ridley are *Metasequoia* and *Ginkgo* endemic in China and Japan. These are considered to have had an wide distribution in the past but due to change of conditions from favourable to unfavourable for their survival they perished in most of the areas. Unsuccessful competition with other species might also have played an important part in their elimination from different areas.

New species originate by natural hybridisation between closely related species growing in a particular area. They spread over wide area in course of time unless the place of origin is not cut off by natural bariers. Therefore percentage of endemic species in wide landmassess is much less than islands, high mountainous regions, etc. For example in the Hawai Islands. the percentage of endemic species is as high as 82%. According to Willis a very widely distributed species originated in the long past while an endemic species or a species with a restricted distribution is a recently evolved species. In other words the span of existence of a species on the face of the earth is proportional to its range of distribution. This theory is known as the age and area theory of Willis. This theory however is not applicable in all cases. As is evident from the examples given by Ridley the genera like *Metasequoia* and *Ginkgo* having restricted distribution are not at all recent plants but are representatives of very primitive group of plants. Therefore we can distinguish two types of endemic taxa viz : those which are newly evolved and those primitive taxa the distribution of which becomes restricted to small areas due to unfavourable ecological conditions or due to competition with other taxa. The former type is called *Neoendemic* while the other type is *paleoendemic*.

Along with endemic species we may also discuss about *rare species* and *vicariads*. A species is a rare species in an area if only few individuals of that species are found in that area. The range of its distribution may be wide but if the percentage of its occurrence in a particular locality is low it is said to be a rare species in that locality. Similarly if a large number of individuals occur in a particular area it is said to be *abundant* species in that area. A rare species may be a newly evolved species or a remnant of a primitive species which is on its way to extinction. When a widely distributed species becomes rare in a particular area it may be due to unfavourable ecological condition or due to its incapability to compete successfully with other local plants.

When 2 or more species of a genus are considered to have originated from a common species i.e, a common ancestor then these species are called *vicariads.* Vicariads are new and distinct taxa produced in course of evolution by a single widely distributed species. *Ranunculus ambigens* and *R. lingua* are cited as examples of vicariads as these are supposed to have originated from a common ancestor. The former is an American species while the latter is Eurasian. Morphological and genetical differences are manifested in the case of vicariads after the individuals of ancestral species established themselves in their new abodes. When such differences make their appearance before the individuals spread in new areas the new taxa are called *pseudovicariads.*

In India the percentage of endemic species is very high, about 50%. These are concentrated in the Himalayan region and in S. India. In the Indo-Gangetic plain on the other hand comparatively few endemic species occur. Preponderance of endemic species in the Himalayas and S. India is due to their separation from other areas by the altitude in the former case and by sea in latter. The dry Tibetan plateau on the north and the hot plain area on the south checked the spreading of the species evolved in the Himalayas. Similar is the case with S. India bounded by sea and the northern alluvial plain. Due to the presence of high percentage of endemic species some authors consider that India has an original flora. Hooker, Champion, etc. are of the opinion that the Indian flora is a derived flora composed of elements that migrated from different adjacent countries. The families having greater number of endemic species in India are, Leguminosae, Rubiaceae, Compositae, Euphorbiaceae, Acanthaceae, Primulaceae, Asclepediaceae, Rosaceae, Gesneriaceae, Balsaminaceae, etc. None of these can however be called a typical Indian family. It further appears that the endemicity in case of Indian genera has not been properly assessed. For example it has been stated that in India the endemic species of *Ranumculus* is 36%; on a critical review however it is found to be not more than 16.5%. *Sapria himalayensis* of Raflesiaceae was considered to be endemic in E. Himalaya but it was recently discovered in Manipur. Hooker's view that India's flora is a derived flora appears to be quite correct and therefore the statement that India has a flora of its own is nothing but a fallacy.

Major phytochoria or phytogeographic divisions of the world's flora. (Map.I)

After their appearance in the South East Asiatic basin the Augiosperms gradually covered the whole of the earth. In early Tertiary (Eocene) the climate all over the world was tropical and subtropical. Then from middle to later Tertiary times there was a general lowering of temperature and this dragged in the glacial Epoch. Such climatic changes occurred more than once and in course of such changes different types of plants evolved that were able to adapt themselves to different types of climate and soil, until we had the present green cover of the earth.

Plant geographers have divided the world into serveral phytogeographic divisions depending on the nature of soil and climate and the types of plants growing in such areas. Schow (1921) divided the world into 25 phyto-kingdoms each having several smaller subdivisions. Good (1964) divided the world into 6 kingdoms and 37 smaller areas under them. Turrill (1959) divided it into 4 major phytogeographic realms with several smaller subdivisions under each. The major realms according to Turrill are given below :

I. Northern Realm.
II. Paleotropical Realm.
III. Neotropical Realm.

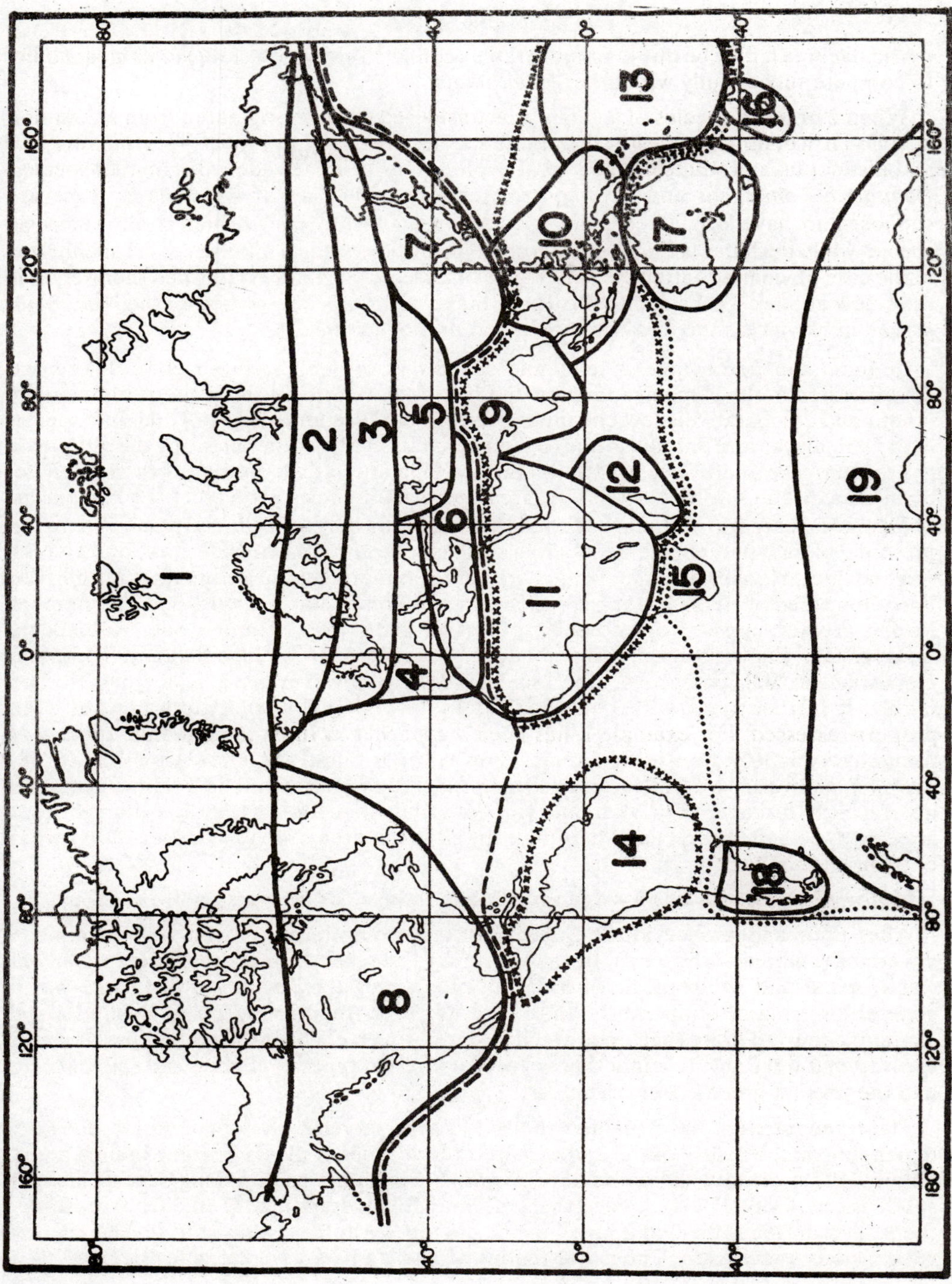
1
2
3
4
5
6
7
8
9
10
11
12
13
14
15
16
17
18
19
80°
40°
0°
40°
160°
120°
80°
40°
0°
40°
80°
120°
160°
180°

IV. Southern Realm.

I. The Northern Realm is subdivided into following 8 regions :

1. Artic and Subartic Region : Includes Alaska, Greenland, Iceland, northern part of Scandinavia, Northernmost part of Russia. Predominating plants are Willows, Birches, Junipers, some plants of Ericaceae, etc.

"The Artic flora is fairly old; it is preglacial and extended much further south in the glacial Epoch".

2. Boreal Region : Northern part of Eurasia with a coniferous belt.

3. Central European Region : Major part of Europe, Siberia and Mongolia with broad-leafed forests, *Quercus robur, Q. petraea, Fagus sylvatica,* species of *Fraxinus, Tilia, Acer, Populus,* etc. predominating.

4. Mediterranean Region : Areas on the north and south of Mediterranean sea and Madeira, the Canaries, the Azorses, and the Cape Verde Islands; the characteristic vegetation represented by *Pinus halepensis, Quercus ilex, Q. coccifera, Arbutus, Myrtus, Olea, Juniperus, Laurus, Spartium, Ruscus, etc.*

Mediterranean flora is a relatively old one with a large number of Tertiary relics. The area was not glaciated during the glacial Epoch.

5. Central Asiatic Region : Asiatic Russia, Mongolia, Turkistan, N. Tibet; mostly arid tracts. The aridity in central Asia is of very ancient in character having originated in the end of Cretaceous. Plants of Mediterranean Realm and of the Near East migrated to this area to some extent.

6. Region of Near East : Includes N. Africa, the Balkan peninsula, Anatolia, Israil, Jordan, Syria, Iraq, Iran, Affghanistan and Pakistan, — home of the Date Palm and Smyrna fig; mainly xerophytic plants and those comming from neighbouring countries.

7. Eastern Asiatic Region : Includes China, East Tibet, Upper Burma and Japan. Vegetation is sparse in N. China with **Metasequoia, Larix** and deciduous Angiosperms. Grassland is characteristic of E. Tibet, **Rhododendron, Mahonia, Camelia,** etc. grow in Yunnan and N. Burma and mixed evergreen vegetation covers the rest of China. Japan has forests of **Larix, Cryptomeria, Thujopsis, Cercidiphyllym, Salix, Prunus, Pyrus,** etc. in the north and **Qucrcus, Myrica, Bauhinia, Ficus, Hibiscus, Cycas,** etc. are found in the South. **Cycas revoluta** is Japanese while **C. circinalis** grows in China.

8. North American Region : Comprising Artic and subartic zones and temparate zone of N.America, Mexican subtropical zone and tropical zone of N.America also included here. **Tsuga, Pseudotsuga, Thuja, Taxodium, Sequoiadendron, Quercus, Lithocarpus, Robinia, Opuntia** and other cacti, **Magnolia, Crossosomataceae, Garryaceae** are predominating; wide belt of Conifers present in the north.

II. Paleotropical Realm is subdivided into 5 regions as noted below

9. Indian Region : Indian subcontinent excluding Pakistan, but including central and lower Burma and Sri Lanka. Conifers in the Himalayas and Assam with **Rhododendron, Rosaceae, Magnoliaceae, Primulaceae; Shorea** at the foot of the hills; **Dipterocarpaceae. Ficus, Palms,** etc. in other parts; **Rhizophoraceae** and other halophytes in the littoral forests; Ferns and Orchids abound in Malabar, Sri Lanka, Central and South Burma.

10. Malayasian Region : Malayan peninsula, Malayan Archipelago, Phillippines, Formosa, New Guinea. One of the richest floras of the world; **Dipterocarpaceae, Rafflesiaceae, Moraceae,** Palms, Bamboos, Orchids, etc.

11. Tropical African Region : Major part of Africa south of Sahara; **Myrsinaceae, Cyanastraceae, Oliniaceae,** Palms, etc.

12. Mascarene Region : Malagasi and other adjacent islands; natural vegetation almost totally destroyed. **Chlaenaceae, Didieriaceae,** etc. are however characteristic.

13. Pacific Region : Comprising Hawai groups of Islands, Fiji, Samoa, New Caledonia, Tahiti, The Marquessas, etc. **Degeneriaceae** among others is the predominant family.

III. Neo tropical Realm consists of only one region :

14. Tropical and subtropical American region : Mexico, Central America, West Indies, Northern S. America. Forests are characterised by the presence of **Cunoniaceae, Lecythidaceae, Malpighiaceae, Cyclanthaceae, Julianiaceae, Alstroemeriaceae, Andropogon, Cymbopogon, Trachypogon,** etc.

IV. Southern Realm is divided into 5 regions :

15. S.African Region : Families, like **Achariaceae, Grabbiaceae, Geissolomataceae, Roridaceae,** etc. and the genera **Crassula, Pelargonium, Rochia, Erica, Protea, Leucadendron, Mesembryanthemum** etc. predominate.

16. Newzealand Region : Agathis australis forms a mixed evergreen forest with **Nothofagus, Hebe, Perenthya, Drimys, Uncinia,** etc.

17. Australian Region : Families like **Pittosporaceae, Epacridaceae, Tremandaceae, Stackhousiaceae,** and genera like **Grevillia, Boronia, Callistemon, Casuarina, Dryandra, Banksia, Eucalyptus, Melaleuca, Acacia, Leptospermum, Prostranthera, Xanthorrhoea,** etc. predominating in the forests.

18. Temperatre S. America : Including Chili, Argentina, Uruguya, Paraguya, etc. having **Bignoniaceae, Bromeliaceae, Aexotoxicaceae, Myzodendraceae,** etc. as components of the vegetation.

19. Antartic Region : Only a few species like **Deschampsia antartica, Colobanthus crassifolius,** etc.

PHYTOGEOGRAPHIC DIVISIONS OF INDIA

J.D.Hooker, the auther of Flora of British India marked 9 distinct areas according to the nature of vegetation. By "British India" he meant the vast tract that included the sub continent of India, Burma, Malaya, Sri Lanka and the Maldiva and Laccadiva Islands. These nine phytogeographic divisions are :

1. East Himalaya : Sikkim, Bhutan and North Assam.

2. North West Himalaya : From Kumaoon to Chitral (now in Pakistan).

3. Indus plain : Undivided Punjab, Sind, Baluchistan, Kutch, North Gujrat, Rajasthan.

4. Gangetic Plain : From the Aravalli Hills in the west to Sylhet and Assam in the East and Orissa as far south as Mahanadi. This is subdivided into **Upper gangetic plain, Lower gangetic plain** and the **Sunderbans.**

5. Malabar : This stretches from the south of Gujrat to Kanyakumari and the Laccadiva Islands.

6. The Deccan : The elevated land east of Malabar and south of the Indo-Gangetic plain, including the Coromandel coast on the east.

7. Ceylon (Sri Lanka) and the Maldiva Islands.

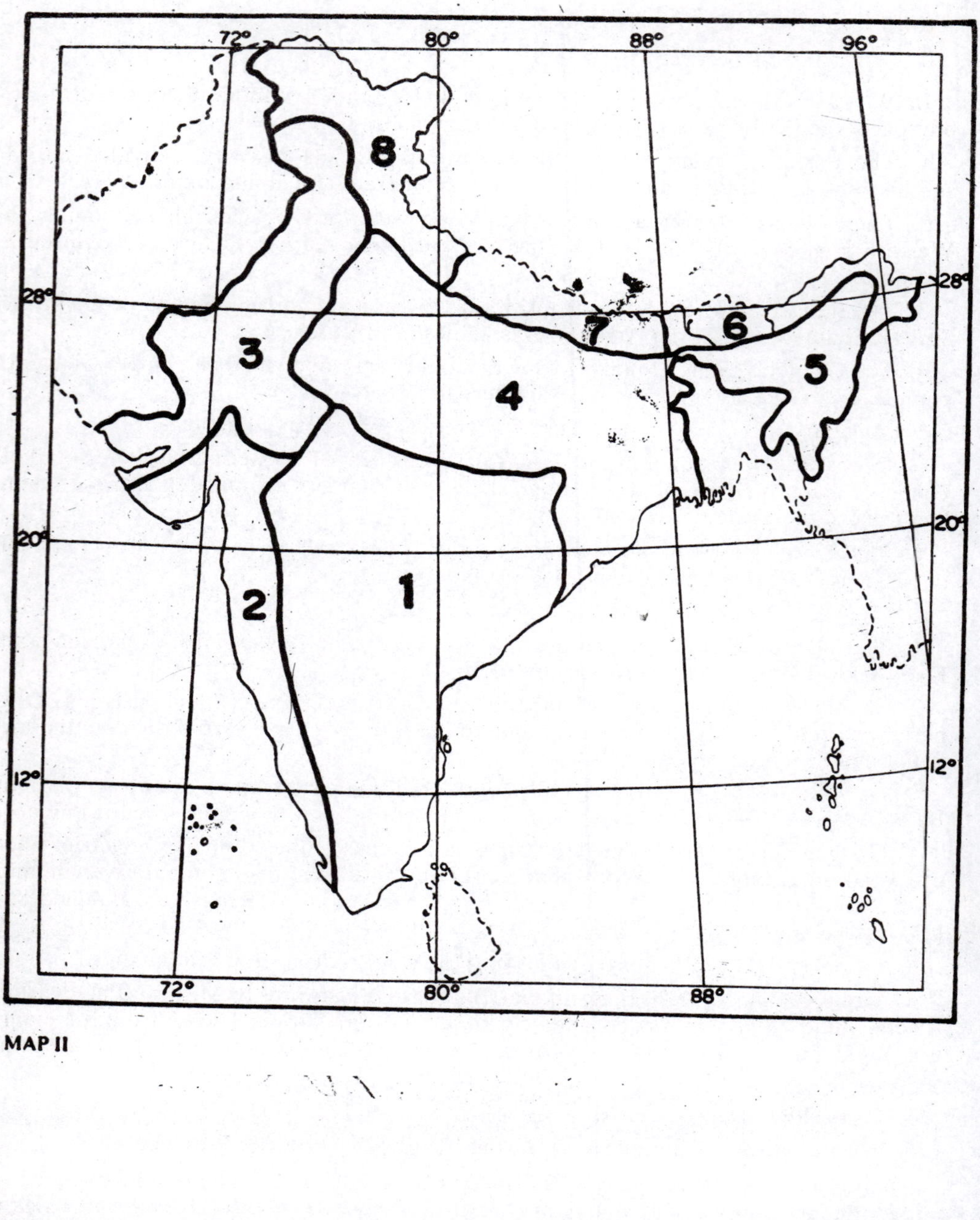

MAP II

8. Burma.

9. Malaya.

In 1937 C.C. Calder published an account of the vegetation of India and distinguished 6 phytogeographic divisions (which he called regions) as noted below :

1. The Eastern Himalaya : Sikkim and the hilly tracts eastwards; divided into 3 subdivisions according to altitude as tropical, temperate and alpine zones.

2. The Western Himalaya : From Kumaoon westwards to Chitral, i.e. similar to Western Himalaya of Hooker. Like the Eastern Himalaya here also he recognised 3 distinct zones according to altitudes.

3. The Indus Plain : Similar to Hooker's 3rd division, comprising Punjab (undivided), Sind, Rajputana west of the Aravalli Hills, Gujrat and Kutch.

4. The Gangetic plain : Similar to that of Hooker and subdivided into Upper Gangetic plain, Lower Gangetic plain and the Sunderbans.

5. Malabar : The hilly strip of land known as the Western Ghats.

6. Deccan : The plateau of the Peninsular India east of Western Ghats and south of Gangetic plain. A subdivision is distinguished in the east as Coromandel, a strip of plain land east of the Eastern Ghat hill-range.

D. Chatterjee while making a study of the endemic flora of India divided the subcontinent into 8 divisions excluding Burma. These subdivisions are :

Map.II –

1. The Deccan : Mysore, Madras and major part of Hyderabad, i.e. the states of Karnataka, Tamil Nadu and Andhra Pradesh.

2. Malabar : Comparable to Malabar division of Hooker and Calder consisting of the narrow strip of land south of Sind running to the southern most part of the country and including the Western Ghat hills.

3. Indus plain : Areas on either sides of the Indus, divisible into a drier tract of Sind, Baluchistan and Rajputana (or Rajasthan) and a comparatively humid tract of Punjab.

4. Gangetic plain : Divisible into 3 smaller areas as (a) the comparatively drier tract of Punjab including Delhi upto Alahabad of Uttar Pradesh, (b) a comparatively humid tract including the rest of Uttar Pradesh, Bihar, Bengal (i.e. W.Bengal and Bangladesh) and (c) the Sunderbans.

5. Assam : The Brahmaputra valley and the Naga, Khasia and Jaintea hills.

6. East Himalaya : Darjeeling, Sikkim, Bhutan and eastwards to Mishmi. This division is subdivided into 3 zones according to altitude, viz. (a) Tropical zone, from the plains upto 1800 mtr., (b) Temperate zone stretching from 1800-3500 mtr. and (c) Alpine zone above 3500 mtr.

7. Central Himalaya : Nepal

8. West Himalaya : Kumaoon to Kashmir and N.W. Frontier Province.

Chatterjee's classification deviates from that of Hooder and Calder that he divided the subcontinent into 8 divisions in place of 6. He distinguished a Central Himalayan division and an Assam division. Hooker and Calder are both silent about Nepal Himalaya which is the Central Himalayan division of Chatterjee. Here we do not find a type of vegetation characteristic of a distinct phytogeographic division like other divisions but it is an area of transition of Western and Eastern Himalayan flora. His Assam division however is very distinct. It is similar to the East Himalayan division in certain respects but there is no alpine zone. The temperate zone has many species of plants allied to those growing in

East Himalaya while there are many species which are allied to the hills of Burma and Malaya. Hooker and Calder included this hilly area in the gangetic plain division where it hardly fits in. Further Chatterjee arranges his phytogeographic divisions starting from S. India where according to him is found the relic vegetation of India.

Map.III

Making an adjustment of the views of different authors and depending on the reports of the explorers visiting different parts of the country in recent times we may recognise 7 phytogeographic divisions of the subcontinent of India which are named below :

(i) West Himalaya
(ii) East Himalaya
(iii) Arid zone
(iv) Gangetic Plain
(v) Assam
(vi) Malabar
(vii) Deccan

The 2 Himalayan divisions are divided into 3 distinct zones according to altitude, viz. (a) Tropical zone, (b) Temperate zone and (c) Alpine zone. The Tropical zone stretches upto 1800 m. from the foot of the hills. The Temperate zone occupies a belt from 1800 m. to 3500 m. and above this is the Alpine zone. In the Western Himalaya Temperate zone starts from 1000 m.

West Himalaya stretches from western part of Nepal westwards to Chitral and East Himalaya includes the rest of Nepal, Darjeeling district, Sikkim, Bhutan, northern part of Assam and Arunachal Pradesh.

The arid zone is the division designated as the Indus Plain by the previous authors.

The gangetic plain is the area as described by D. Chatterjee and is divisible into (i) a drier tract including a portion of drier Punjab, Delhi and Uttar Pradesh upto Allahabad, (ii) a comparatively humid tract including the rest of Uttar Pradesh, Bihar, West Bengal and Bangladesh, and (iii) the littoral forests of the Sunderbans.

Assam division is also the same as that of Chatterjee including the Brahmaputra valley the Naga, Khasia and Jaintea hills.

Malabar division is the same as that of Hooker, Calder and Chatterjee a narrow stretch of land south of Gujrat running to the southern most point of the country and including the Western Ghat hills.

The seventh division Deccan includes a vast area east of the Western Ghats and south of the Gangetic plain. This is the same as Hooker, Calder and Chatterjee, and as has been shown by Calder is divisible into 2 subdivisions, viz. (i) the plateau of the Peninsular India and (ii) Coromandel, a strip of plain land east to Eastern Ghats.

VEGETATION OF INDIA

Influenced by the climate and topography the vegetation of India varies considerably in different areas of the country. As described in the previous chapter the country has been divided into seven phytogeographic regions, viz., 1. Western Himalaya, 2. Eastern Himalaya, 3. Arid zone, 4. Gangetic plain, 5. Assam, 6. Malabar and 7. Deccan. The types of vegetation met with in these regions are briefly described below.

1. Western Himalaya : In the tropical belt extending upto an altitude of 1000 mtr. we find a Sal forest (**Shorea robusta Gaertn**) of stunted trees in Kangra and Hoshiarpur

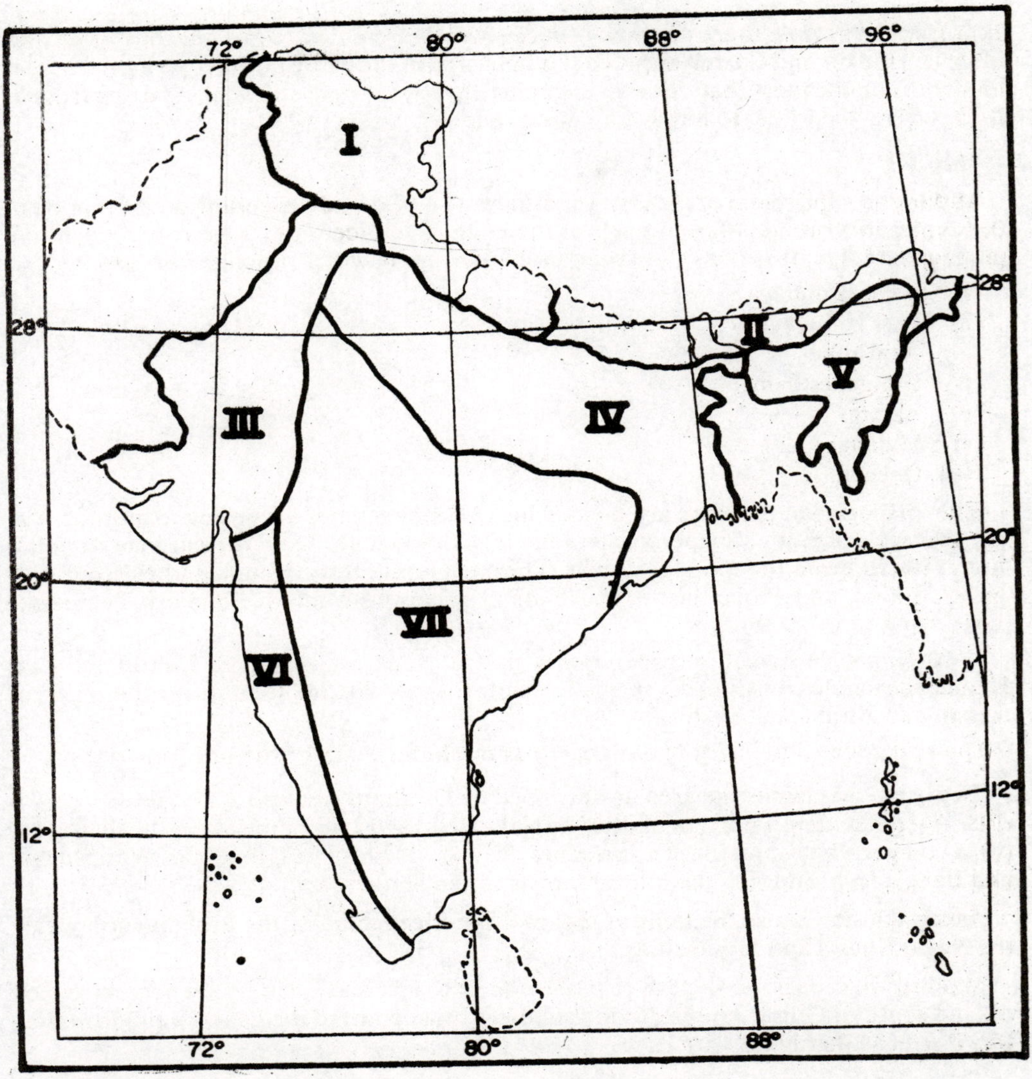

MAP III

but lofty trees in the Siwaliks and West Nepal. Associated with Sal are found **Terminalia tomentosa, Buchanania lanzan, Anogeissus latifolia, Ougenia oojeinensis** etc. Bamboo groves of **Dendrocalamus strictus** are also met with. The most important climbers are **Bauhinia Vahlii, Spatholobus Roxburghii** and **Milletia auriculata.** "Bhabar" tracts are met with where the forest is of open character with trees like **Holoptelea integrifolia, Bombax ceiba, Garuga pinnata** and **Acacia catechu.** In moist situation **Trewia nudiflora** and **Syzygium cumini** occur. Near rivers Sal does not occur but **Acacia catechu, Dalbergia sissoo** and Bombax ceiba form alluvial forests with other deciduous trees. There are grassy tracts — the "savannah" — where the dominant grass is **Saccharum narenga. Anthistiria gigantea** and **Imperata cylindrica** are other grasses found on savannahs and other open Sal forests.

Above 1000 meters we come across a broad belt of coniferous forest with **Pinus Roxburghii** lining the base, and Deodar (**Cedrus deodara**), Blue Pine (**Pinus wallichiana**), **Pinus Gerardiana, Picea morinda, Cupressus torulosa, Abies pindrow — A. spectabiles** and Junipers forming the upper limit.

Along with the Conifers, species of Oaks (**Quercus ilex, Q.incana, Q.dilatata**, etc.). **Cornus capitata, Populus cilia, Betula utilis, Ulmus Wallichiana, Rhododendron arboreum, Aesculus indica**, and species of **Acer, Alnus**, etc. are found. Shrubby **species** of **Rosa, Pyrus, Crataegus** etc. are found in the open. The orchids are mostly terestrial and **Eriophorum comosum** is quite common. Species of **Aquilegia, Paeonia, Adoxa** and several herbs of **Ranunculaceae, Labiatae**, etc. and many grasses cover the forest floor.

Above the Coniferous temperate zone there is the alpine zone extending upwards from about 3000 mtr. Here wide fields of grassland are found with herbs like — **Corydalis, Primula, Delphinium, Anemone, Astragalus, Arenaria, Saxifraga, Epilobium**, etc. Shrubby **Rhododendron, Salix, Betula** are also met with. **Juniperus religiosa, Abies spectabiles, Picea Smitheana** and **Ephedra Gerardiana** represent the Gymnosperms.

2. Eastern Himalaya : The tropical zone is covered with a luxuriant flora. Here also we find a mixed Sal forest composed of tall trees with many climbers and sheltering many epiphytic orchids and ferns. The Sal forests stretch upto an elevation of about 1000 mtr. and are reserved forests. According to Cowan 2 distinct types of Hyliums or associations are here met with viz. (1) **Shorea — Terminalia — Garuga** Hylium and (2) **Shorea-Stereospermum** Hylium. In the former type along with Sal **Terminalia bellirica, T.crenulata, Garuga pinnata** and **G.Gamblei** predominate, while in the latter type **Stereospermum** is the predominant species along with Sal, and **Terminalia crenulata** is also common. **Schima Wallichii, Bauhinia purpurea, Sterculia villosa, Gmelina arborea, Dillenia pentagyna, Duabanga grandiflora, Lagerstroemia parviflora, Ficus cunia**, etc. occur in both types of association, and in addition to these **Toona ciliata, Tetrameles nudiflora, Stereospermum tetragonum, Premna mucronata, Dysoxylum binectariferum, Bombax ceiba, Callicarpa arborea, Litsaea polyantha, Albizzia odoratissima, Appanamyxis polystachya, Bischofia javanica** are found in the former hylium and **Grewia vestita, Elaeocarpus aristatus, Syzygium formosum, Meliosma simplicifolia, Terminalia chebula, Alstonia scholaris,Trewia nudiflora, Beilschmiedia Roxburghiana, B. sikkimensis, Abbizzia procera, Micromelum pubescens**, etc. are found in the other, i.e. Shorea — Stereospermum hylium. **Dendrocalamus Hamiltoni** a giant bamboo is frequent in both the hylii.

In places where rainfall is very high an evergreen type of forest is met with where Sal is totally absent or almost so. Here also we find 2 distinct hylii, e.g. **Schima — Bauhinia** Hylium and **Syzygium — Phoebe** Hylium.

Common shrubs found in the forests of this zone are **Bridelia stipularis, Capparis olacifolia, Leea robusta, L. crispa, Moghania macrophylla, Phlogacanthus thyrsiflorus, Coffea bengalensis, Morinda angustifolia, Ixora undulata, Ervatamia coronaria, Melastoma malabathricum, Clerodendrum viscosun C. nutans, C. serratus, Grewia sapida, G. serrulata, Pandanus furcatus,** etc. Three species of **Calamas,** viz. **C. flagellum, C. guruba** and **C. leptospadix** are found here. Among the common climbers are **Bauhinia Vahlii, Entada pursaetha,** species of **Mucuna, Ipomoea, Hoya,** etc. Epiphytic orchids are many and there are many terestrial and epiphytic ferns. **Angiopteris evecta** with very large fronds is frequently found.

Near rivers **Acacia catechu, Dalbergia sissoo, Bombax ceiba** and a few deciduous trees form a low alluvial forest. Grasslands are formed on dry beds of rivers that have changed their course. Here **Saccharum spontaneum** is gregarious. Other tall grasses are **Imperata cylindrica, Themeda arundinacea, Arundinella nepalensis,** etc. **Capillipedium assimile** is gregarious on lower hills.

In East Himalaya Coniferous forests are not met with immediately above 1000 mtr. Instead there are forests of broadleaved species. Thus we have **Castanopsis tribuloides, C.indica, Schima Wallichii, Phoebe Hainsiana, P.attenuata,** as the predominating trees in the forests. **Bauhinia purpurea, Stereospermum tetragonum, Callicarpa arborea, Erythrina stricta** are other common trees in these forests.

At an altitude of about 2000 mtr. the forests are composed chiefly of **Mchilus edulis, Michelia Cathcartii, Engelhardtia spicata, Castanopsis tribuloides, Cinnamomum obtusilobium, Prunus nepalensis, Nyssa javanica, Casearia glomerata, Ehretia Wallichiana, Actinodaphne sikkimensis,** etc. **Ardisia macrocarpa, Boehmaria polystachya, Osbeckia crinita, O.nepalensis, Maesa chisia, Polygonum molle** are common shrubs and are gregarious at certain places. On marshy areas **Acorus calamus** grows often in pure formations.

This zone lying between 1000 and 2000 mtr. is called subtropical zone where the climate is humid and warm. The trees are usually covered with Mosses and Lichens and support many epiphytic Orchids and other Angiosperms and many ferns.

At the foot of the hills and upto 2000 mtr. in Darjeeling district many tea gardens form a characteristic feature of the vegetation.

Above 2000 mtr. plants of temperate region appear, e.g. **Quercus lamellosa, Q.pachyphylla, Acer Campbelli, Michelia excelsa, Echinocarpus dasycarpus Meliosma Thomsoni, Turpinia nepalensis,** species of **Machilus, Litsaea,** etc. **Taxus baccata, Cupressus torulosa, Juniperus recurva** and **Tsuga damosa** are found with Oaks, **Ilex, Mahonia** and **Rhododendron.** Higher up the conifers predominate in the forests and the common species are **Abies spectabillis, A.densa, Picea spinulosa, Larix Griffithiana, Juniperus squamata** and **J. Wallichiana. Rhododendron campanulatum** a shrubby species grows gregariously. Many other species of **Rhododendron** are found at an altitude of about 3000 mtr. of which **R.lepidotum, R.setosum** and **R.anthogonium** are dwarf species and are found also in alpine region. **Prunus undulatus, Acer caudatum, A. pectinatum, A.sterculiaceum-Brassaiopsis alpina, Schefflera, Sorbus,** etc. are other broad-leaved species growing at that height.

In the alpine zone along with a few dwarf **Rhododendron** and **Juniperus squamata Salix** and **Ephedra** are also found. The herbaceous flora consists of species of **Pedicularis, Primula, Cassiope, Arenaria, Iris, Meconopsis,** etc. The grasses are species of **Stipa, Phleum, Avena, Festuca** and **Agropyron.**

3. Arid Zone : The arid zone of India has an open forest mainly of **Prosopis spicigera, Salvadora oleioides, Acacia nilotica** and **Capparis decidua.** On irrigated lands **Albizzia lebbek, Dalbergia sissoo, Azadirachta indica, Cordia dichotoma** and **Ficus glomerata** are found. On Aravalli hills and its outliers forest patches purely of **Anogeissus pendula** are frequently found. Other trees found there are **Boswellia serrata, Grewia salvifolia, G.pilosa, Balanites aegyptiaca, Acacia senegal, A.leucophloea, Commiphora mukul, Zizyphus numularia** and **Euphorbia nivulia.**

In the western part of this region there are extensive tracts covered by **Euphorbia neriifolia** composing the 'Thor' vegetation. Scrub jungles cover the rest of the area and are composed of **Capparis decidua, Zizyphus glabrata, Commiphora mukul** and shrubs and herbs like **Solanum indicum, S.suratense, Scaevola frutescence, Atriplex Stocksii, Salicornia brachiata, Suaeda maritima, Fagonia cretica** and **Ephedra foliata.**

4. The Gangetic Plain : The vast tract is divided into 3 subdivisions, viz. (i) Upper Gangetic Plain (ii) Lower Gangetic Plain and (iii) the Sunderbans. The whole area excepting the Sunderbans forming the littoral forests at the extreme southeastern part, is thickly populated and open lands are none but cultivated fields. The natural vegetation is represented by a weed flora and trees planted in orchards and on road sides or growing self-sown in villages.

In the Upper Gangetic Plain trees common on roadside and villages are **Azadirachta indica, Ficus religiosa, F. glomerata, F. benghalensis, F. Rumphii, Cordia dichotoma, C.Rothii, Acacia nilotica, Tamarindus indica, Albizzia lebbek, Pithecellobium dulce, Syzigium cumini, Manilkara hexandra** and a few others. **Euphorbia neriifolia** is planted in hedges and is often found gregarious. **Agave cantalla** an American fibre-plant is grown as a hedge-plant or in plantations. **Lantana aculeata** an exotic shrub is common all over the area. **Dodonaea viscosa, Acacia farnesiana, Carissa carandas, Calotropis procera, C.gigantea,** etc. are other shrubs common in the sub-region.

Open forests of **Acacia catechu, Dalbergia sissoo, Tamarix Troupii, T.dioica** and a few other trees are met with on sandy river banks with **Asparagus racemosus, Solanum suratense, Alhagi pseudalhagi,** etc. and tall grasses like **Erianthus munja, Saccharum spontaneum, Vetiveria zizanioides** and **Themeda arundinacea. Borassus flabellifer** and **Phoenix sylvestris** occur wild and the former is occasionally planted. The weed flora is composed of **Xanthium strumarium, Blumea lacera, Cassia tora, Crotalaria medicaginea, Amaranthus spinosus, Argemone mexicana,** etc. while the aquatic flora is represented by **Nymphaea nouchali, Nelumbo nucifera, Ottelia alismoides, Ipomoea reptans, Trapa bispinosa, Nymphoides cristatum, Potamogeton crispus, Utricularia stellaris,** etc. **Eichornia crassipes** is found in stagnant pools and in canals where the current is not strong.

In the Lower Gangetic Plain the rainfall is higher and consequently the vegetation denser. The trees noticed in the Upper Gangetic Plain are met with in this subregion also where **Trewia nudiflora, Diospyros peregrina, Polyalthea longifolia, Trema orientalis, Terminalia catappa, Alstonia scholaris, Gelonium multiflorum, Ficus hispida, Alangium salvifolium, Streblus asper** are other common trees.

In addition to the shrubs found in the Upper Gangetic Plain **Cassia sophera, Ecbolium viride, Blumea lacera, Abutilon indicum, Capparis zeylanica, Sida rhombifolia,** Urena lobata, Sesbania sesban, Hyptis suaveolens, are very common. Calotropis **procera** is absent in this tract. There are many climbers forming impenetrable thickets in places with the shrubby and herbaceous vegetation. Common among them are **Coccinea cordifolia, Luffa cylindrica, Daemia extensa, Tylophora asthmatica, Cissus lanceolaria, Dioscorea pentaphylla, Smilax macrophylla, Tiliacora racemosa,** and the exotic **Mikania micrantha.** The **aquatic** flora is similar to that met with in the Upper Gangetic Plain. Here are found some tall herbaceous plants which are often gregarious, e.g. **Polygonum orientale, Aeschenomene aspera, Typha elephantina, Cyperus exultatus, C. corymbosus, Phragmites karka, Panicum tripheron,** etc. **Azolla** and **Salvinia** often cover the surface of water in the jheels and **Marsilea** is found on wet ground.

The Sunderbans occupy the southernmost area of the Lower Gangetic Plain, a comparatively small portion of which is within Indian Union. Here **Phoenix paludosa,** a dwarf palm is gregarious near inlands. This is replaced by species of **Avicennia** further down. **Bruguiera gymrorhiza, Ceriops candolleana, Kandelia Rheedii, Aegiceras majus, A.rotundifolia, Xylocarpus granatum, Lumnitzera racemosa** are other species common in that area. **Nypa fruticans** a stemless palm with very large leaves and a few species of **Heritiera** grow where sweet and saline waters meet.

5. Assam : Vegetation of Assam is similar to that of E.Himalaya except that there is no alpine flora. Here also we find sal forests at the foot of the hills and at lower elevations on the hills. **Amoora Wallichii, Vatica lancaefolia, Artocarpus chaplasha, Michelia champaka, Cinnamomum cecicodaphne, Dillenia indica, Aquilaria agallocha, Morus laevigata,** etc. often form dense evergreen type of forests. Species of **Dipterocarpus** and **Connarus** also occur in Assam.

Hill forests are ever green broad-leafed forests or Pine-forests. The former includes species of **Magnolia, Manglietia, Michelia, Schima, Acer, Pyrus, Prunus, Andromeda, Alnus nepalensis, Litsaea citrata, Betula alnoides** and many species of **Quercus** and a few of **Rhododendron** at higher elevations. **Camelia drupifera** is very common with **Leucosceptrum canum, Eleagnus latifolia** and **Saurauja nepalensis. Berberis** and **Mahonia** occur at higher altitude and **Rubus, Zanthoxylon, Osbeckia** and **Polygala** are common at about 2000 mtr. **Gomphostemma, Hedychium** and many species of **Impatiens** and **Polygonum** are found at lower elevations. Presence of **Nepenthes Khasiana** is noteworthy.

Orchids, epiphytic and terrestrial are abundant and at some places the tree fern **Cyathea** imparts a characteristic form to the forest. There are many other ferns terestrial or epiphytic in the valleys and on the hills.

6. Malabar : In Malabar tropical evergreen forests are found from Kanara southwards and have lofty trees like **Dipterocarpus indicus, Hopea parviflora, Calophyllum tomentosum, Dysoxylon malabaricum, Toona ciliata, Vateria indica, Canarium strictum, Mesua ferrea, Artocarpus lakoocha, Hydnocarpus Wightiana, Garcinia morella, Ochrocarpus longifolius** and many other trees. A reed like bamboo **Ochlandra travancorica** is common along hill streams. **Barringtonia racemosa** occurs in swampy areas.

Mixed deciduous forests occur in the north containing **Tectona grandis, Dalbergia latifolia, Terminalia tomentosa, T. paniculata, T. bellirica, Lagerstroemia lanceolata,**

Pterospermum marsupium, Xylia xylocarpa, Grewia tiliaefolia and a few other species.

On Nilgiri hills at about 2000 mtr. a forest of subtemperate or temperate nature is encountered. Here we find short trees like **Michelia nilagirica, Ternstroemia japonica, Eurya japonica, Rhododendron nilagiricum, Gordonia obtusa, Ilex, Euonymus, Symplocos** and many **Lauraceae.** There are shrubs like **Berberis tinctoria, Mahonia Leschenaultii, Polygala arillata, Xanthoxylum, Strobilanthus,** etc. and herbs like **Anemone rivularis, Thalictrum javanicum, Viola serpens, Geranium nepalense, Parochaetus commanis,** etc.

7. Deccan : In Deccan proper mixed deciduous forests occupy the major part of the plateau with thorn forests in drier parts of central India and Mysore. The thorn forests are open in character and consists of **Acacia nilotica, A.leucophloea, Dichrostachys cinera, Balanites aegyptiaca, Butea monosperma, Emblica officinalis, Zizyphus nummularia, Z.oenoplia, Xylia xylocarpa, Boswellia serrata, Sterculia urens** and **Cochlospermum religiosum** with grasses like **Pennisetum setosum, P.pedicellatum, Heteropogon contortus, Chrysopogon lanceolarius, Ischaemum angustifolium, Cymbopogon martini etc.** The mixed deciduous forests are composed of **Tectona grandis, Terminalia tomentosa, T. bellirica, T. chebula, Anogeisus latifolia, Lagerstroemia parviflora, Pterocarpus marsupium, Dalbergia latifolia, Cassia fistula, Butea monosperma, Lannea coromandelica, Schleichera oleosa, Buchanania lanzan** and a few others. The prevailing bamboo is **Dendrocalamus strictus.** In some parts **Anogeissus pendula** grows gregariously and **Phoenix humilis** a dwarf palm is frequent. **Cymbopogon martini** the Russa grass is very common.

Sandal wood **Santalum album** grows in open forest in the uplands of Mysore, Coorg, Salem and N.Arcot. **Pterocarpus santalinus,** the Red sandal wood occurs in a dry type of mixed forest. In the extreme south a special type of thorn forest exists consisting of **Acacia planiformis, A.latorum, Prosopis spicigera, Cassia auriculata, Capparis divaricata, C. aphylla** and a few fleshy Euphorbiaceae.

Sal forests occur on the hilly tracts of Orissa, Chota Nagpur and Santal Parganas. Chief companions of Sal in these places are **Terminalia tomentosa, Pterocarpus marsupium,** Anogeissus latifolia, Diospyros melanoxylon, Madhuka latifolia, Dalbergia latifolia, **Schleichera oleosa, Holarrhena antidysenterica, Butea monosperma** and **Emblica officinalis.**

The Coromandal subregion supports the same type of vegetation but is rather sparse. The steep slopes of Eastern Ghats are densely wooded. In Carnatic a dry evergreen forest occurs with **Mimusops hexandra, M.elengi, Diospyros peregrina, Strychnos nux – vomica, Pterospermum suberifolium, P.heyneanum, Memecylon edule, Chloroxylon swietinia** and species of **Syzygium** predominating, Mangroves occur in the estuaries of Coromandel. At the southern end **Acacia planiformis** and **Cassia angustifolia** are very common.

Composition of Indian Flora

Of the predominating families of plants in the flora of India **Gramineae** outnumbers all the other families with over 1100 species in India. There are meadowlands in the plains as well as on the hills, the savannahs of the tarai and dooars and the rolling downs of Ootacamund and other hills. Bamboo groves are common in warm and humid parts.

Next to Graminae in magnitude is **Fabaceae (Papilionaceae)** with about 900 species. Plants of this family are found all over the country in different ecological conditions and are often predominant in dry situations with herbaceous or shrubby species while the trees and climbers are met with more in humid forests.

Compositae has about **800** Indian species and are almost all herbaceous or shrubby. These are conspicuous in open situations on the hills and occur as road side weeds in the plains. **Eupatorium odoratum** an exotic herb is gregarious in many parts of eastern India. **Orchidaceae** is another large family with over 700 species. This family is concentrated mostly in E. Himalaya and Assam and in Malabar. These herbs with showy flowers lend a colour to the forests during the summar and monsoon months. **Acanthaceae** with over 500 species in India is more abundant in the Deccan peninsula. This is predominantly a herbaceous family, some species being gregarious in Nilgiri and Malabar hills. Labiatae is another herbaceous family with over 400 species mostly confined to the hills. The family Rubiaceae has about 550 species in India, the majority being in southern India.

Euphorbiaceae also has over 400 species of trees shrubs and herbs, some of which are succulents inhabiting warm and dry localities where some species are gregarious. Scrophulariaceae has about 300 herbs mostly confined to the hills. Rosaceae with about 250 species of trees and shrubs are conspicuous in the temperate parts where Ericaceae, Lauraceae, Betulaceae and Fagaceae predominate. The Pines play an important role in the composition of temperate forests in the Himalayas. In the plains Meliaceae, Anacardiaceae, Sapindaceae, Dipterocarpaceae, Myrtaceae, Combretaceae being predominantly trees, help in climax forest formation.

The family Palmae is represented in India with a comparatively few species. But the tall unbrached palms are a conspicuous feature of the landscape in many parts of the country. The Palmyra palm — Borassus flabelifer is the most widely distributed palm in India. The Coconut — Cocos nucifera and Betlenut — Areca catechu are much cultivated in the states near the sea. In the Sunderbans and other mangrove areas Phoenix paludosa a dwarf palm is very common and often form pure associations. Nypa fruticans is another palm of mangrove forest but is represented by a few individuals in the Sunderbans within Indian Union. Nannorhops ritchieana a desert palm of tufted habit having short or often prostrate stem occurs in Rajasthan. The climbing palms or the Rattans are found mainly in the humid parts of the country and often form impenitrable thickets.

Succulents in India include a few shrubs of **Euphorbiaceae and herbs like Portulaca, Sedum, Kalanchoe, Suaeda,** etc. Cactaceae, **although represented in India by a single** introduced species, viz. **Opuntia monacantha requires a special mention** as this species is widely distributed all over the country **in the plains usually in drier areas.**

The Pteridophytes are also well-represented **in Indian Flora and there are** about 500 species of Ferns and Fern-allies in India. **There are a few species of Cyathea** which attain tree-size and look like palms. These are common **in some parts of E. Himalaya,** Assam and Western Ghats.

A study of the vegetation of different areas of India and of the adjacent countries reveals that it has close affinities with the vegetation of these countries and is composed of elements which are (1) Gondowana-relic (2) Malaysian, (3) African & Oriental, (4) Eurasian and (5) Sino-Himalayan.

The peninsular India is one of the oldest known land masses of the earth. In this area there are many trees and shrubs of the rain forest type which form part of a flora that extends from Malaysia through India to N.E. Africa and in Eastern S. America. This flora originated in the Oligocene period on Gondowanaland and disappeared in the thickly populated and long-cultivated regions of India and Central Africa which gradually turned to deserts or arid lands. Relies of the old flora occasionally persist in distant mountainous localities unaffected by man as examples of discontinuous distribution. A large number of genera common to Malaya, India, Africa and Eastern S. America may be mentioned which formed the components of this flora, e.g. **Tetracera, Eriodendron, Sterculia, Erythroxylon, Bauhinia, Cynometra, Crudia, Parkia, Acacia, Casearia, Homalium, Ixora, Ardisia, Rauvolfia, Buddleia, Strychnos, Piper, Croton, Acalypha, Alchornea** and many others.

Anaxagorea is found in Malaya, Andaman Isls., Ceylon and in West Indies, but not in peninsular India or Africa. **Klugia** occurs in India and S.America. There are more such examples of discontinuous distribution which prove the existence in the past of same type of vegetation in India, Africa, and S.America.

The Malaysian element is represented in the Indian flora by Dipterocarpaceae, Myrtaceae, Guttiferae, Dilleniaceae, Meliaceae, Connaraceae, **Tectona, Schleichera** etc. and by a few mangrove species. Most of these evolved in the coral islands and travelled westwards by sea as well as by land.

After the closing of the east end of the Mediterranean a desert flora came from Africa and Arabia via Buluchistan to Sind and Rajasthan, and penetrated as far south as Travancore. **Azima, Salvadora, Prosopis, Dodonea, Heliotropium, Indigofera,** many species of Zygophyllaceae, Capparidaceae, **Farsetia, Malcolmia, Zoysia, Andropogon** etc. are characteristic of this xerophytic invasion.

A few families developed chiefly in the Mediterranean region and these are Cruciferae, Caryophyllaceae, Labiatae, Polygonaceae, Liliaceae etc. These have entered India from the north-west. Along with these came species of Juniperus, Cedrus, Crataegus, Astragalus, many Compositae and Euphorabiaceae. These constitute the Oriental element in Indian Flora.

During the Pleistocene ice age the circumpolar flora was pushed fanwise southwards. The part of the flora which followed the direct route through Central Asia, which might have been partly desert, had to cross the Tian Shan Mts. and Tibet plateau to reach the Himalayas which were also glaciated. These artic plants therefore did not survive. Those which followed other routes entered the Himalayas from the north-west and the east during interglacial periods and after. The alpine plants of the Himalayas which are common to the Artic regions are considered to have come by the north western route and form the Eurasian element. These include Saxifragaceae, **Thalictrum, Corydalis, Aconitum,** etc.

The Sino-Himalayan element is represented by a great number of genera, viz. **Camellia, Saurauja, Schima, Altingia, Rhododendron, Engelhardtia, Tsuga, Primula, Androsace, Meconopsis, Gentiana, Pedicularis, Stachyurus, Mahonia, Rubus, Cotoneaster, Photinia, Eurya, Gordonia, Podophyllum, Actinidia,** etc. These genera followed the coast line of China while migrating towards south and reached the highlands of S.China. Then as the ice receded they eventually turned north-westwards towards the Himalayas. This happened several times and the resultant Sino-Himalayan flora is a composite flora, a mixture of floras that originated in different parts of northern and eastern Asia in different geological times.

PART IV

1 ECONOMIC BOTANY
2 PHARMACOGNOSY

CHAPTER X

ECONOMIC BOTANY

USEFUL PLANTS

The animals as well as man depend much upon plants for the sustainance of their lives. Many animals, birds and insects are herbivores and the plants provide them shelter. The mankind use plants as food, medicine and fuel, as materials for constructing their houses, for manufacturing their clothings, furniture and articles of luxury and as fodder for their cattle. Plants with beautiful flowers and foliage please them and they use them to decorate their abode. The plants also provide them with weapons, and plants which are poisonous are made use of in killing or repelling insects that are injurious to their health and destory or damage household articles. There are plants which are sand-binders, and prevent land-erosion. Plants in general attract rain-clouds, retain moisture of the soil and atmosphere and prevent lands from turning into deserts, thus serving the mankind indirectly.

Plants which are directly useful to human being fall in the following categories :

(i) Plants supplying food.
(ii) Medicinal plants.
(iii) Fibre-plants.
(iv) Plants for paper-pulp.
(v) Timber plants, bamboos and canes.
(vi) Beverages, masticatory and narcotics.
(vii) Rubber yielding plants and plants yielding gum, dye and resin.
(viii) Insecticides.
(ix) Spices.

Those which are indirectly useful are also of no less importance and these are fodder plants, sand binders, plants for erosion control and ornamental plants.

India is a large country with varied conditions of soil and climate. The vegetation of India therefore is varied and plants of economic importance of almost all categories have their representatives in this country in the plains as well as in the hills, in deserts and in marshy areas and innundated fields.

These useful plants are mostly indigenous to this country, while a good number are exotics. The exotics have all been introduced through human agencies, some quite recently and some in the remote past. Among the introduced plants are *Cinchona,* Ipecac, *Digitalis, Eucalyptus,* Maize, Potato, Tomato, French bean, Soya bean, Cabbage, Cauliflower, Sweet potato, Custard apple, Papaw, Guava, Pine apple, Tobacco, Coffee, Chilies, Sisalhemp, Cashewnut, Casava (or Tapioca), Zapota, etc.

Mahogany tree was introduced to enrich our timber resources but in this country the trees do not produce timber of the same quality as obtained from trees grown in West Indies. Many trees have been introduced as avenue-trees and ornamantal trees in parks and gardens, e.g. *Peltophorum inerme* (Roxb) Llanos, *Acacia moniliformis* Griseb, *Delonix regia* Raf., *Samanea saman* Merrill, *Grevillea robusta* A. Cunn., *Spathodea campanulata* Beauv., different species of *Eucalyptus,* etc. *Bougainvillaea* is very popular all over India, and this has come from Brazil.

PLANTS FOR FOOD

Plants that yield our food fall into the following groups, viz. cereals, pulses, fruits, vegetables and sugar yielding plants. Important cereals of India are rice, wheat, barley, maize, jowar and bajra. Of these plants maize has been introduced in this country and is cultivated in the plains as well as in the hills. Others are indigenous. Among the pulses peas, mung, mashkelai, lentil and Cajanus are important. Fruits are many introduced and indigenous. Important fruits are mango, litchi, orange, banana, melon, watermelon, cucumber, grapes, apple, peach, prunes, walnut, pomegranate, bael, wood-apple, jamoon etc. These are indigenous. Introduced fruit-plants are guava, custard-apple, papaw, pine-apple, zapota, raspberry, cashewnut, etc. Ripe tomato is eaten as fruit and also cooked for preparing chutny. The sweet root-tuber of *Pachyrhizus angulatus* Rich is eaten raw as a fruit and carrot and beet-root are also taken as fruits. All these fruit *plants are* Angiosperms, while among the Gymnosperms we have *Pinus Gerardiana* Wall, the chilguza plant, the seeds of which are taken as nuts.

In the tropical countries many plants are used as vegetables and different parts of the plants are used as such, e.g. fruits and seeds, root-tubers and rhizomes, leaf and stem. Most important of the vegetables in India is at present the potato for which the Old World is indebted to the New World. Tomato, cabbage, cauliflower, knolkhol are other important vegetables which were also introduced into this country. Among the indigenous vegetables the parbal, lady's finger, louki, arum, brinjal, elephant's foot, etc. are important. All these are cultivated but a few pot herbs and other vegetables grow wild and are collected. Tender leaves of *Marsilea* and *Athyrium* which belong to the Filicales are used as pot herbs. Then we have some mushrooms which are also used as vegetables and considered by some as delicacies.

Most important sugar yielding plant is the sugarcane. Species of *Sorghum* are also used for producing sugar and jaggery. Different species of palms, especially *Borassus flabelifer* Linn.and Phoenix sylvestris Roxb. yield copious sugary juice which is used to produce jaggery but not sugar. In many countries sugar-beet, a variety of *Beta vulgaris* Linn.is cultivated for purpose of manufacturing sugar but in India production of this article from the juice of sugarcane is practiced being commercially more profitable. Sweet juice obtained from some other palms, e.g. Corypha, Caryota, etc. are taken as soothing drink or as fermented liquor. *Acer saccharum* Marsh.and *A. nigrum* Michx. produce copious sweet sap but are not found in India.

CEREALS

ORYZA SATIVA LINN : Poaceae

The Rice

An annual grass; culms up to 1.5 mtr. tall, or more in deep water varieties, rooting at the nodes below, smooth and glabrous. Leaves with flat linear acuminate blades, more or less scabrid below and on the margins, 30-60 cm. long, 0.6-0.8 cm. broad, sheathed at the base; sheaths smooth with ciliate auricles; ligules long, lanceolate, scarious, finally splitting. Inflorescence a lax erect panicle, 15-30 cm. long; rachis more or less robust, angled and channelled, scaberulous. Spikelets 3 - flowered, ovate - oblong or ovoid, erect, 0.8 - 1.2 cm. long, awned or not; the terminal floret fertile, the lower 2 sterile; the glumes are represented by obscure scales at the apex of the peduncle; pedicels angular, short, swollen at the top; fertile lemma strongly laterally compressed, as long as the spikelet, coriaceous, finely granulate, folded and keeled, acute with a short awn, strongly 3 - 5 - nerved; the lateral nerves forming a thickened margin, hispid-ciliate; lower empty lemmas oblong-lanceolate, acute or subulate, entire or toothed at the top, about 2 mm. long; palea of the same texture as the lemma and as long, linear, 3-nerved, keeled, with membranous margin; lodecules 2, entire or 2-lobed; stamens 6, with slender filaments; anthers linear; ovary superior, 1-celled with one anatropous.ovule; styles 2; stigmas 2, laterally exserted, plumose. Fruit a caryopsis, oblong, angular, lightly enclosed in the lemma and palea, more or less 1 cm. long.

Rice is the staple food of a large number of people in Asia. It is widely cultivated in India, China, Japan, Pakistan, Sri Lanka and countries of South eastern Asia and adjacent islands of the Pacific. It is also cultivated in East Africa, some parts of S. Europe and S. America. In ancient period rice used to be cultivated in India, Malaya, Java, Sri Lanka and S. Africa. Use of rice in India as food dates back to about 2300 B.C. It is considered that rice originated in the south and south eastern Asia and S. India might have been its original home.

Rice is a crop of wide physiological adaptability and is grown in both tropical and temperate countries from sea level to an altitude of over 2000 m. above sea-level and from semiarid tracts to very wet areas. A large number of varieties are under cultivation in India which differ in their season of growth, maturity, adaptability to different conditions of soil, rainfall, temperature, etc.

The method of cultivation of the crop varies with the adaptability of the varieties. The crop grows best on clayey loams but it can be cultivated on various types of soils, viz — damp alluvial soil, high sandy soil, gravelly or stony soil, boggy soil, or terraces, hill-slopes, high lands or low lands subject to flooding. It can grow even on lands on which 2-6 m. of water is standing for several weeks. High temperature and high humidity are very good for the crop but there are certain varieties which can grow under very low rainfall.

Under tropical and subtropical conditions, as in S. India rice can be grown practically throughout the year. In temperate region and high altitude-areas the crop is grown only in the warm part of the year. The varieties grown in the plains fall into 3 categories, viz :

	Sowing time	Harvesting time
1. Ashu or Aus, (autumn crop)	May — June	Sept. — Oct.
2. Aman (winter crop)	June — July	Nov. — Dec.
3. Boro (summer crop)	Nov. — Dec.	March — April

The crop is grown unden dry or puddle system. Under the former the field is ploughed repeatedly after the harvest of previous crop to bring it to good tilth, while under the other system, the land is ploughed in standing water. Under the dry system of cultivation the seeds are sown in rows or by broadcasting. In the puddle system the seeds may be sown after sprouting or unsprouted. For transplanted crop, seedlings are raised in nurseries or seed beds. Seedlings are transplanted when they are of 4-6 weeks old. Usually transplanting is done in rows to facilitate weed control operation and easy harvesting.

Rice responds well to nitrogen application and the optimum dose being 20 kg. of nitrogen per acre in organic or inorganic form or as a mixture. Farm yard manure, compost, oilcakes, tank-silt, fish manure, leaves of **Gliricidia maculata, Indigofera, Tephrosia,** etc. and green manure in situ with sunn hemp are commonly used in different rice growing areas in our country. When organic manures are not available and green manuring not practicable 10-15 kg. of nitrogen in the form of ammonium sulphate should be applied immediately before sowing or transplanting and an equal quantity as top dressing when plants are about one month old would be necessary. Super phosphate at 10-20 kg of P_2O_5 per acre and oil-cake giving 10 kg.of nitrogen may also be added during puddling.

After transplanting water is allowed to stand in the field to a depth of 2-3 cm. until the seedlings are well established. About 6 cm.of water is always maintained in the field by frequent draining and re-irrigating the field and the water is drained off the field about a week or two before harvesting unless the water dries up in natural course. The right stage of harvesting is when the ears are nearly ripe and the straw is slightly green. In the case of plants about a metre tall or more these are cut with a sickle and left in the field for drying for 3-4 days and afterwards carried and stacked in the threshing yard. Threshing is done by beating the sheaves against a wooden log or with sticks or trampling the crop under the feet of bullocks. A pedal thresher machine is also used for the purpose for quick work.

Varieties of rice plant grown in India easily run to about three thousands, majority of them are suitable for cultivation in the plains. The yield of paddy varies from 400 to 2000 kg per acre depending on the soil, season of cultivation, manuring and the variety grown. The total area under rice in India is about 83 million acres and the annual production is about 33 million tons.

Rice plant is suceptible to Blast disease, Brown-spot or Sesame Leaf-spot, and Bakanae disease caused by fungal infection. Blast disease is caused by *Piricularia oryzae* Cav. This can be controlled by spraying Bordeaux mixture repeatedly. Growing resistant types, avoiding excessive nitrogenous manure, adjusting planting date, spraying the crop 3-4 times with copper fungicides are also recommended. The 2nd disease is caused by *Helminthosporium oryzae* Br.de Haun. To get rid of this disease a seed treatment before sowing gives good result. In this case the germinating seeds are soaked in cold water extract of this fungus and this treatment makes the plants immune to this disease. The 3rd or the Bakanae disease or Foot Rot is caused by *Gibberella fujikuroi* (Saw) Wollenw. This can be controlled by applying Ceresan and Agrosan G.N. A seed treatment with organomercurial drips is also recommended. Insect pests are controlled by dusting BHC or DDT powder or spraying a solution of the same.

TRITICUM AESTIVUM Linn — Poaceae

The Wheat

Annual grass with fibrous roots; culms 80-150 cm. tall, smooth. Leaves flat, linear-lanceolate, acuminate, ligulate; sheaths smooth, ligules short, truncate. Inflorescence an erect terminal spike, irregularly 4-sided, more or less compact; rachis continuous, excavated opposite the spikelets, hairy on the margins; spikelets solitary, distichous, tumid, few-flowered, imbricate, on the opposite sides of the rachis, laterally compressed, ovoid, glabrous or hairy. Flowers bisexual, the uppermost flower sterile, glumes 2 persistent, about 1 cm. long, rigid, subequal, broadly ovate oblong, unequal sided, obtuse or shortly awned. Lemmas oblong or ventricose, rounded or keeled on the back, muticous or 1-3-awned. Paleas as long as lemmas, 2, entire, ciliate. Stamens 3. Ovary superior, 1-celled, with 1 anatropous ovule; styles 2, very short, stigmas pulmose. Caryopsis oblong, ventrally grooved, about 1 cm. long, free within the lemma and palea or adhering to the latter.

Besides T. aestivum a few other species of the genus also give us the wheat, viz :

1. T.monococcum Linn — Diploid.
2. T.dicoccum Schrenk-Tetraploid.
3. T.durum Desf-Tetraploid.
4. T.polonicum Linn-Tetraploid.
5. T.turgidum Linn-Tetraploid.
6. T.spelta Linn-Hexaploid.
7. T.sphaerococcum Perc — Hexaploid.

T.aestivum is also hexaploid and is cultivated in the major part of this country, e.g. in the Punjab, Uttar Pradesh, Bihar and northern Rajasthan. T. durum is next in inportance and is widely grown on the black soils of central and Peninsular India. T. dicoccum is grown in small areas in the Nilgiri Hills, Karnataka, Andhra Pradesh and Maharashtra. T.sphaerococcum is the Shot or Indian Dwarf wheat often cultivated in a smaller scale.

Wheat is the staple food of the people of all European and W. Asiatic countries, and of Africa, America and Australia. It is also consumed in a number of other countries in good quantities although rice forms there the staple food. The use of wheat as staple food by man started in prehistoric times. The Babylonians, early Greeks, the Romans, the Egyptians and the people of Crete left records of their dependance on wheat. Archeological findings from Iraq date the use of wheat in 6700 B.C. The excavations of Mahenjodaro reveal that the grains of T. *sphaerococcum* were in use by the people 5000 years ago. It is also known that in China wheat used to be consumed as early as 2700 B.C.

Wheat grows very well in the Indo-Gangetic plain, where the winter is cool and dry and the crop can grow for a period of 5 to 6 months. The crop can also be cultivated upto an elevation of 2700 m. Prolonged drought in the irrigated tracts reduces production considerably. Rainfall in wheat areas ranges from 12.5 to 100 cm., irrigation being necessary for good yield in areas where rainfall is scanty. About 30 to 50% of the crop in the Indo-Gangetic tract is irrigated while in Peninsular India it is rainfed.

Well drained loams and clay loams are very much suitable for wheat cultivation. It further requires well pulverised but compact seed bed for germination. Sowing usually starts in the second half of October and continued till the middle of next month. In Punjab, Delhi and adjacent parts of U.P. the sowing starts in November and may go up to December. Seed is sown by broadcasting, drilling or dibbling. Generally speaking, deeper sowing is advisable in rough, dry and light soils while comparatively shallow sowing is desirable in moist or heavy soils. Where sowing is delayed on account of water logging, transplating seedlings of about a month old in December can give a normal crop. Usually 90 kg. of seeds per hectare is sown but the rate may vary in different areas. For dibbling 13 to 15 kg. per ha. is adequate and for the transplanted crop 25 kg.of seed in the nursery should provide sufficient seedlings to cover one hectare.

The first irrigation should normally be given one month after sowing, 3-4 irrigations especially at tillering, heading and grainfilling stages, should be enough while in Rajasthan 5-6 irrigations may be necessary. Excessive irrigation is however harmful.

For manuring it is advisable to apply about 180 to 275 q. per ha. of well rotted farmyard manure or compost, or an equivalent quantity of oilcake six weeks before sowing. If sufficient rain is received in August and September application of 15 to 25 kg.of nitrogen and 10 to 15 kg. of phospherous per ha. at sowing time produces good result. For irrigated wheat a split application at sowing time and 35 to 45 kg of nitrogen together with 25 to 35 kg. of phosphoric acid per ha. after 30 - 45 days is recommended. These may be increased to 75 kg. nitrogen, 50 kg. phospherous and 50 kg. potash per ha. under intensive cultivation. Green manuring of irrigated crop with guar, cowpeas or sunnhemp is also practised.

Wheat is susceptible to diseases such as Rust, Smut and Bunt. Rust-disease is caused by *Puccinia graminis Pers.* var *tritici* Eriks & Henn. *P. recondita* Rob.ex Desm. and *P. glumarum* Eriks. & Henn. Smut-disease is caused by *Urocystis triticyi* Koen and *Ustilago tritici* Rotr., while Bunt is caused by infection of *Neovassia indica* (Mitra) Mundkur. These can be controlled to some extent by spraying solutions of Agrosan — G.N., Ceresan, Tritisan, Panogen or Vivatex. Seed dressing with copper sulphate also gives good results. There are a few resistant varieties and selection of such varieties for cultivation gives effective control. Termite of the soil causes much harm and to cope with this Aldrin dust is mixed with the soil during preparation before sowing.

The crop is harvested when the grain is dead ripe and the straw is golden yellow and brittle. Plants are either uprooted or cut with a sickle. Harvesting begins in mid-January in Karnataka, in February in some areas of Maharashtra, in March-April in Bihar, U.P., Delhi and Punjab and in May-June in the hills of the north. The grain is generally threshed out by treading under the feet of cattle. Simple mechanical threshers are also used for the purpose. The yield of grain of rainfed crop varies from 450 kg. to 775 kg per hect. depending on the condition of the soil. In irrigated areas the yield ranges from 1000 kg. to 1400 kg. per ha. Under favourable conditions the crop may produce over 1.2 tonnes of grains per acre. Wheat is grown in India on an area of about 13.3 million ha. producing nearly 11.5 million tonnes of grain.

As mentioned before wheat is obtained from 8 species of Triticum. Numerous cultivated varieties of each species are known. The Russian scientists have developed a new perrenial hybrid variety of wheat that flowers and fruits for several consecutive years. After the first harvest the stumps that remain in the soil start tillering in the next sowing season and flower and fruit in proper time. This saves much of the cost. The yield however is less than the other varieties and gradually decreases every year.

ZEA MAYS Linn — Poaceae

The Maize

This is a tall annual herb with a stout stem which is solid and jointed at the nodes. It has a fibrous root system with 3 types of roots, viz : (1) seminal roots developing from the radicle and forming the primary root system which may later perish or persist; (2) advantitious roots produced from the nodes at the basal portion and penetrating the soil; (3) prop roots, which come out in whorls from one or two nodes above the basal part. The prop roots are much thicker than the other roots and on entering the soil help the plant to stand erect,and also function as ordinary absorbing roots. Leaves alternate and distichous, simple, linear - lanceolate, acuminate, with an entire ciliate margin, multicostate with a firm midrib, with a sheathing leaf-base; sheath split on the side opposite the blade, villous at the margin; leaf blade 30-45 cm long, 3.5-12 cm. broad.

Maize plant is monoecious, but has 2 types of inflorescences; the male is a terminal panicle and the pistillate an axillary spadix. The panicle consists of a central axis with several rows of paired spikelets and a few lateral branches with only 2 rows of paired spikelets. One of each pair of the spikelets is pedicellate while the other sessile. Each spikelet consists of 2 flowers subtended at the base by a pair of glumes. The glumes are atmost equal in size, densely covered with minute stiff hairs and the outer or lower one more or less overlapping the other so that the 2 flowers are completely enclosed when young. Each flower has 2 opposite bracts; the outer one is called the lemma and the inner one the palea. At the base of the lemma are found 2 fleshy scales representing the perianth and are called lodicules. Androecium consists of 3 stamens, 2 opposite the lemma and one opposite the palea; filaments long with 2-lobed versatile anthers. In the centre of each staminate flower lies a rudimentary gynoecium. Of the 2 flowers in a spikelet the upper one matures first.

The spadices are borne in the axils of the lower leaves. A spadix, commonly called a cob, is enclosed by a number of large bracts or spathes. The axis of the cob on which the spikelets are arranged in vertical rows is thick and spongy and represents the fused axis of several spikes. The stalk of the axis is called the *shank* and is in reality a condensed shoot having compressed internodes. The spathes or the husks are the leaves comming out form the nodes of the shank. There are rows of female spikelets all round the axis. Each female spikelet is 2-flowered and has 2 glumes at the base. The lower flower is barren and the upper is fertile. Like the male, the female flower has a lemma and a palea. The sterile one has 2 lodecules, 3 rudimentary stamens and a rudimentary carpel; the fertile flower on the other hand has the carpel very well developed but the lodecules and staminodes are not recognisable. Ovary is 1-celled with 1 campylotropous ovule; style filiform with long hairy stigma. The apparently monocarpellary ovary is in reality tricarpellary of which only one carpel bears the ovule and the other 2 extend and form the style. The palea and lemma of a female floret are persistent and form the chaff of the grain on maturity. Caryopsis subglobose, hard and shining.

The maize is not indigenous to India or to any part of the Old World. It originated in the low lands of Central America and most probably in Southern Mexico. The antiquity of its domestication is shrowded in mystry but it is known that the Mayas and the Incas depended on maize as a cereal. It is now grown in almost all countries of the world even upto an elevation of 3600 mtrs in the hills. In India it is widely cultivated and a total area of about 6 million hectares is under maize cultivation.

Maize is a warm weather crop. It prefers a well-drained loamy soil, moist but not water-logged. In India sowing starts on the onset of monsoon or earlier in irrigated areas. Seeds are dibbled by hand or sown by broadcasting. The field is prepared before sowing by ploughing several times and spraying the soil by 2,4D solution or by triazine weedicide to make it free from insects or spores of fungi. Compost and farmyard manure are usually applied and potassium chloride and superphosphate are also used. To control viral, fungal and bacterial infection a mixture of Aureofungin and coppersulphate or Bordeaux mixture is sprayed over the plants. Caterpillars do a lot of damage to the crop and to kill them dusting with 5% DDT or spraying with 0.25% DDT gives the desired result. The crop is ready for harvesting in 80 - 100 days from the time of sowing. Cobs are collected and the grains are separated by beating with sticks or by other mechanical means.

FRUITS

MANGIFERA INDICA Linn : Anacardiaceae

THE MANGO

A large or medium sized evergreen tree with thick rough or nearly rough bark. Leaves simple, alternate coriaceous, oblong-lanceolate or oblong, entire, acute or acuminate, narrowed at base, often with wavy margin, 12-25 cm. long, 3-5 cm. broad, crowded near the ends of the branches; petioles 2-3.5 cm.long. Inflorescence a much branched terminal panicle; pubescent; bracts deciduous. Flowers very small, polygamous or monoecious, on very short jointed pedicels. Calyx 4-6-partite, segments imbricate, deciduous. Petals 4-5, free, often adnate to a disc, imbricate. Disc 5,lobed. Stamens 1 or 2 perfect,and 2-4 sterile with imperfect anthers or without anthers, inserted on the inner side of the disc. Carpel 1; ovary superior, sessile, oblique, 1-locular with a lateral style and simple stigma; ovule solitary, pendulous from a basal or lateral, rarely horizontal funicle. Fruit a large fleshy drupe with a compressed fibrous stone and glabrous skin; ripe fruits 5-15 cm.long and 2-8 cm.broad near base, generally slightly flattened and elongated with a tendency to be curved at the thinner end opposite the stalk and a pointed swelling indicating the position of the style.

When ripe the basal part or the whole of it turns yellow, some times with flush of red or purple; some varieties remain green even when fully ripe. The flesh is yellow or orange, sweet and delicious with a characteristic flavour of its own. A great number of varieties are found in different parts of India of which the "Alphonso" of Bombay is perhaps the best. The "Langra" of U.P. and Bihar is also very tasteful while S.India can boast of some with fruits of excellent qualities. The "Fazli" of Bengal has the largest fruits each weighing 1 kg. or more. It is also very tasteful. The good fruits come from grafted trees which are usually short sized. Trees raised from seeds attain large size, yield numerous fruits which however have larger stone covered by fibres. Fruits from grafted trees have smaller stones and almost fibreless.

Mango is in great demand in countries outside India and is exported in considerable quantities as fresh fruits or tinned fruits and also as chutneys and preserves. The juice of ripe fruits dried on plates forms thin cakes known as "amsath" which can be preserved for a long time. The unripe fruit is acid, and has a flavour of terpentine. It is cooked and made into pickles.

Besides producing fruits the mango tree is useful in many other ways. It is a good timber tree. The bark and leaves yield a yellow dye and the bark is used for tanning. The unripe fruit is a cure for opthalmia. The smoke of burning leaves stops hiccough and is a remedy for sore throat. A paste of the leaves is applied to remove pain in scorpion sting. The large evergreen tree with dense foliage is very often planted as an avenue tree.

Mango is indigenous to India but is seldom found truely wild although it grows as self sown tree almost everywhere in the plains near human habitations. It is planted in almost all gardens in the villages and is cultivated in the orchards. It is also indigenous to Ceylon and Malaya and has been introduced into other tropical countries including Mexico.

The mango tree comes to flower towards the close of winter season and fruits ripe in 3 months. Ripe fruits are available in market from April to July. The tree has been associated with Hindu-religion. The leaves are used in decorating the place of worship and from an important ingredient in all pujas. The tree is mentioned in old Sanskrit and

Pali literature and travellers from Persia and Arabia spoke highly about the fruits. From the ancient times the kings encouraged planting of mango trees and being patronized by the rulers and rich people the gardeners were able to raise so many different varieties.

In different parts of the country there are many mango orchards where trees are grown on a commercial scale. These are all raised from grafts and trees are about 15 mtr. high. Trees are planted in rows 4-8 mtrs apart and same distance between trees in the same row. The grafts are planted in holes 50-60 cm. in diam. and so deep. The holes are filled with 90% of farmyard manure, 10% of wood ash and a little quantity of bonemeal. Where white ants prevail Neem or Mahua cakes are mixed with the manure to get good result. Mango grows in varied types of soils from rich clayey loam to poor sandy and gravelly soil, but it can not stand water-logging. Those growing on loamy soil containing 5-10% of lime and enough peroxide of iron produce best fruits. Irrigation for first 3-4 years is necessary and in drier areas irrigation is done 4-5 times before monsoon. Manuring is done for young plants in trenches at the beginning of monsoon. To control white ants DDT in water is sprayed to the young plants in October.

Inarchining or simple approach-grafting is commonly practised. Seeds are sown on the onset of monsoon and seedlings of a year old are used as a stock. Potted seedlings are carried to the scion tree and placed on an elevated scaffolding to meet the branches. The graft is ready in about 2 months which is then removed by cutting the scion branch below the grafted portinon and the top of the stock. The graft is nursed for about six months or more before planting.

Varieties of mango run to over a thousand and a few best varieties are named below :

Alphonso	Maharastra, Kerala, Mysore, Tamil Nadu, Andhra Pradesh.
Bangan palli	Tamil Nadu; Andhra Pradesh;
Bombai	U.P; Bihar;
Dusheri	U.P; Hariana;
Fazli	W.B; U.P; Bihar
Gulabkhas	Bihar
Langra	U.P; Bihar
Himsagar	W.B.

MUSA X PARADISIACA LINN : Musaceae

THE BANANA

Tree-like herb with a pseudostem and an underground larger globose perennial rhizome, stoloniferous; the pseudostem composed of leaf-sheaths rolled round one another, 1-3 mtr. high and 15-25 cm. thick at base. Leaves radially arranged with a large oblong blade on a channelled spongy petiole on the top of a cylindrical leaf-sheath split on one side; the blade 1-2 mtr. long, 25-60 cm. broad, bright green above and pale green and glaucous beneath, with a stout channelled spongy midrib and parallel secondary nerves, slightly unequal at base. Inflorescence is a large decurved pendulons spadix, terminating the arial stem that pushes itself through the pseudostem and the crown of leaves, comming from the centre of the rhizome; the spadix bears a number of cymose groups of flowers arranged acropetally on the stout axis each subtended by a spathe, the largest is the first from the base and covering the whole inflorescence above it; the next spathe is slightly smaller and covers the rest of the inflorescence and successive spathes are smaller by degrees and cover the portion of the inflorescence above each; the spathes are caducous and each spathe after opening and exposing the cyme of flowers subtended by it is shed off. The spathes are thick and leathery in texture, ovate and boat shaped and of a dull purple colour; cymes dense flowered. Flowers functionally unisexual, the females on the basal portion of the spadix and males on the upper part, zygomorphic, epigynous. Sepals 3 and petals 3; the 3 sepals and 2 petals unite to form an anterior, 5-toothed perigonium, while the 6th posterior petal is free, hyaline, notched or pointed at apex; the perigonial tube is split on one side. Stamens 5, with a sixth rudimentary one or the sixth stamen altogether absent; anther linear, 2-celled. Carpels 3, united in an inferior 3-locular ovary with many ovules superposed on axile placentation; style filiform from a thickened base; stigma globose or 6-lobed. Fruit an oblong or fusiform trigonous berry, often slightly curved on one side; seeds absent, although in wild species of Musa the fruit is full of globose or angular seeds.

The above description of the edible banana is that of a cultivar, a natural hybrid between *M.acuminata* Colla and *M.balbisiana* Colla. Edible banana of hybrid origin comprises all the deploid, triploid and tetraploid clones. Edible forms of *M.acuminata* Colla are also known and cultivated.

Musa is indigenous to Indo Malayan region and cultivation of edible bananas started in that region in prehistoric times. It is now extensively cultivated in the tropical countries of Asia and Africa, in the Caribbean Islands, Central America, Ecuador, Columbia, Brazil and Canary Islands. In India Kerala, Mysore, Tamil Nadu, Maharastra and West Bengal are the chief banana growing states. In addition to growing the plant in large plantations or orchards, it is extensively grown in village gardens with other fruit trees. The total area under banana cultivation in India is about 3,83,000 acres.

Banana is a rain-fed crop and grows best in areas with a well-distributed rainfall from 175 cm,- 250 cm.in a year. In some drier areas irrigation during December — March is necessary. The crop requires a well-drained soil. The soil is well dug or deeply tilled before planting. Suckers are used for propagation. Pits are dug 45 cm. in length, breadth and also of same depth at distances of 1.5 - 3 mtr-on either sides depending on the size of the plants. Farm-yard manuring of 20 - 30 cart loads is recommended per acre before planting. Green manuring is also done. After planting a top dressing of farm-yard manure or compost, oil cakes and artificial fertilizers is practised. Nitrogen - 150 kg, phosphoric acid 75 kg. and potash - 50 kg. are used per acre. Fish meal is also good for the crop. Only one or two suckers are allowed to remain with the mother plant. In the hills banana is planted in terraces.

The plants start fruiting 8 — 18 months after planting depending on the variety. Some varieties fruit much earlier. The top portion of the spadix with the male flowers is usually cut off and this is beneficial to the maturing fruits. The fruiting spadix is often covered with dry leaves to give the fruits a beautiful pale yellow colour.

The area under banana cultivation in India is 383362 acre and the annual production is 1.7 - 2.0 million tons. These figures are exceeded if we take into account the plants grown in village orchards. A small portion of the total yield is exported outside India while the rest is consumed inside the country.

Banana plant is susceptible to Panama disease caused by *Fusarium* species. To check the spread of the disease in a plantation the infected plant is uprooted and the soil is treated with quicklime. Flooding the soil under 5 cm.of water for 45 days and application of lime is recommended. Banana weevil or borer does a lot of damage to the crop and to kill the beetle paris green mixed with flour is dusted. Dry Dieldrin mixed with gypsum powder around the base of a clump affords effective control.

A few important types of edible banana cultivated in India are noted below :

Group	Types or clones	Indian names	Where cultivated
M.acuminata	Sucrier (Diploid)	Chingam, Matti, Kadali	West Cost, Kanyakumari
M.acuminata	Dwarf Cavendish (Triploid)	Basrai, Kabuli, Loton	Maharastra, Tamil Nandu
M.acuminata	Giant Cavendish (Triploid)	Harichal, Bombay-green	Maharastra, Tamil Nadu, Andhra Pradesh
M.acuminata	Red or Green red (Triploid)	Chen kadali, Anupam, Lal Kela	Kerala, Tamil Nadu
M.X.paradisiaca	Mysore (Triploid)	Poovam Champa	Maharastra, Andhra Pradesh, W.Bengal, Bihar
M.X.paradisiaca	Silk (Triploid)	Martaman, Sabari Kala	W.Bengal, Karnataka, Tamil Nadu
M.X.paradisiaca	French Plantain (Triploid)	Neudrin	Kerala, Maharastra
M.X.paradisiaca	Pome (Triploid)	Dhakai Marta-man, Virupakshi	Tamil Nadu, W.Bengal
M.X.paradisiaca	Ney Poovam (Diploid)	Soveri	Maharastra, Karnataka, Kerala
M.X.paradisiaca	Bluggo (Triploid)	Kachkela, Moutham	Plains of India except dry areas.

ANACARDIUM OCCIDENTALE — Anacardiaceae

THE CASHEW NUT

A short spreading evergreen tree, upto 12 m. high; milky latex present in all parts. Leaves alternate, simple, petiolate, oblong obovate, 10 - 20 cm. long. Inflorescence a branched terminal panicle, 15 - 25 cm. long. Flowers hermaphrodite and unisexual in the same panicle, small, yellow or pinkish, 1.5 cm.across. Sepals 5; deciduous. Petals 5, very narrow. Stamens 8 - 10, a few often reduced to staminodes. Ovary 1-celled; style simple, lateral. The fruit is a kidney shaped nut seated on fleshy, swollen receptacle, much enlarged in fruit; the nut 2.5 cm. long, the receptacle or the cashew-apple is 5 - 8 cm. long, pyramidal in shape yellow or scarlet when ripe.

The tree is indigenous to tropical America and was introduced to India by the Portugese some 450 years ago. Gradually it became popular and cultivation started in commercial scale and is now cultivated in Maharastra, Kerala, Tamil Nadu, Karnataka, Orissa and on a small scale in W.Bengal.

It can be grown in various types of soil but a sandy loam appears to be the best for its cultivation. It is drought resistant and grows well where average annual rainfall does not exceed 1000 mm,and is quite at home in place with a rainfall of 3000 mm. or over. It can not however stand waterlogging and is not frost resistant. Plants are grown from seeds although saplings are raised from grafts and layerings. About 100 trees are recommended for a plot of an acre. No manure is usually applied although organic manure increases the yield.

Flowering starts in February and the fruits mature in 70 - 80 days. The fruits are gathered before they are fully ripe. They are then dried in the sun or sometimes roasted. The nuts are then broken and shelled. Shelling and peeling are done by hand.

About 15 kg of nuts are obtained annually from each tree and the yield per acre is about 1500 kg. The total annual production of nuts in India is about 20,000 tons. The nuts give us the kernels which are used as dessert and also the shell oil is much in demand in insulating and varnishing industries. India meets 95 per cent of the world demand for kernels by exporting 75 per cent of her total production and only 25 per cent is consumed in this country.

SUGAR YIELDING PLANTS

SACCHARUM OFFICINARUM LINN : Poaceae

The Sugar Cane

Tall erect grass, usually unbranched, culms 2.6 mtr. high, glabrous or with appressed hairs below the panicle, waxy below the nodes. Leaves linear lanceolate, acuminate, narrower at base, spreading and drooping at the tip, scabrous above and on margins, scaberulous and more or less glaucous underneath, upto 1.5 mtr.long and 6 cm broad; median nerve thick, white above; sheath pubescent on the throat or at first covered with appressed hairs; ligule very short, membranous, ciliate.

Inflorescence a large panicle, ovate-pyramidal, dense and spreading, about 25 cm. long, silvery silky; principal axis glabrous, channelled, bearded at the nodes; primary branches slender, 5-10 cm. long, more or less verticillate, glabrous, bearded at the nodes; secondary branches simple, distant, internodes fragile, equalling or exceeding the spikelets in length, somewhat thickened at the top, glabrous; pedicels glabrous. Spikelets linear oblong, pale or almost brownish, muticous, 3.5 - 4 mm. long, callus covered with dense white silky hairs 7 - 12 mm.long, one spikelet sessile the other pedicelled on the articulate fragile rachis; the pedicelled one falling from the pedicel, the sessile falling with the contiguous joint of the rachis and pedicel. The florets 2; the lower reduced to an empty lemma, the upper hermaphrodite. Glumes equal, 3.5 - 4 mm. long, lower with inflexed margins in sessile spikelet, papyraceous-membranous, acute, entire, obscurely nerved; upper glume membranous, acute, 1-3 nerved, keels scabrous above. Lemmas hyaline, as long as the spikelet in the lower empty floret, lanceolate, acute, membranous, nerveless; lemma of upper hermaphrodite floret very reduced or absent; palea lanceolate, acute, ciliate at the apex. Lodicules 2, cuneate. Stamens 3. Ovary superior, 1-celled with one anatropous ovule; styles 2, laterally exserted; stigmas plumose. Caryopsis oblong.

The cultivated sugarcanes are hybrids of *S. officinarum* Linn, and *S. sinense* Linn. and also of *S. spontaneum* Linn. As a result of continued research in many countries and in Coimbatore in India many varieties were raised to suit various types of soil and climate and as resistant to diseases. Some are given code number instead of any varietal name, e.g. Co. 997, Co. 658, Co. 775, etc. These three are the best of the different types cultivated in India and mature early.

S. officianrum is supposed to have originated as a desirable mutant from the wild species *S. robustum* Linn, in New Guinea. From New Guinea it came to Indonesian islands and then to India where it was taken into cultivation. The art of making sugar from the juice also developed in India many centuries before the Christian era. The art of making sugar spread to Malay and China and west wards to Persia and Egypt where sugar cane cultivation was also started. There were many natural varieties which were gradually replaced by improved hybrid varieties raised in different Research Stations.

For most varieties a period of about 18 months is required for maturation although some varieties mature in course of one year. It is propageted by planting small pieces having usually 2 nodes with buds. These pieces are called seed-pieces or seed - sets. Planting is done in spring, i.e. from January to March. Seed-pieces are collected from immature canes and 3-budded sets are preferred. Soaking the sets in water for 36 - 48 hours gives better "germination". After planting water is sprinkled for 15 days. Careful weeding in early stages is necessary and several weedicides are used of which 2.4 – D is very suitable in Indian conditions. Gramoxone is also very effective provided it is sprayed only on the weeds avoiding the cane-plants. Hoeing and manual weeding is also done and that is more economical. Earthing up the plants keeps them erect and induces tillering. In coastal areas, particularly in Andhra Pradesh propping is necessary to keep the plants erect. Inter-cropping is done some times to raise a second crop of vegetable or ground nut but that reduces the yield of canes.

Bulk of the sugarcane is grown on alluvial soil, but black soil and red soil are equally good which are not subjected to innundation. Ploughing the field several times to a fine tilth is necessary and ridges and furrows are to be made. Planting is done in the furrows. Basal dressing of compost and green manuring are done before planting. Frequent irrigation in formative phase of the crop is necessary and at post monsoon period irrigation is done at intervals of 25 days.

Manuring is done 3 months after planting and in 1 h.a. area nitrogen 200 kg, phosphorus 75 kg and potash 900 kg are applied by instalments. Oilseed cakes are liberally used. Harvesting is done after 18 months of planting but in good varieties in much less time. The plants are cut down at the base and made into bundles which are taken to the sugar mills or to the crushing machines.

Sugar cane is susceptable to Red-rot, Smut, Wilts, Yellow-spot and Virus diseases. Planting of disease free varieties is the best means to avoid such diseases. Diathene, Fermate, Bordeauxe mixture are useful in controlling the diseases. Treatment of the seed-pieces with different fungicides makes them immune to such diseases.

About 2 million h.a. of land is under sugarcane cultivation in India, the major part lying in U.P. About 6% of the extracted juice is used for preparing molasses and khandseri sugar and the rest is manufactured to refined sugar. India exports a fair quantity of sugar to U.S.A., Canada and United Kingdom.

PULSES

PISUM SATIVUM LINN : Leguminosae

The Pea

A glaucous annual herb. Leaves paripinnate, alternate; the leaf-rachis produced to form a branched tendril; leaflets 4-6, sharply toothed; stipules large, ovate, semicordate, irregularly toothed at base; leaflets 2 × 1 cm; stipules 3 × 1.5 cm. Flowers in short axillary racemes or solitary, bisexual, zygomorphic, white, pink, bluish or purplish in colour, about 2 cm long and as much broad. Calyx tubular-campanulate, gamosepalous, oblique. Corolla papilionaceous, longer than calyx; petals 5, the upper most or the outer most is the standard or vexillum covering the other petals in bud; the 2 lateral petals, linear-oblique, forming the alae or wing-petals; the innermost pair, shorter than wing-petals, linear oblique, loosely uniting along the ventral margins constitute the keel or carina. Stamens 9 + 1, diadelphous, the free stamen is the uppermost. Ovary superior monocarpellary, linear, narrowed near base with 2 rows of ovules on marginal placentas which lie so close to each other that the ovules appear to be in a single row; style hard, inflexed and almost perpendicular to the axis of the ovary, flat and wider above, with margins bent back forming a sort of channel; stigma bearded on the inner face; ovules few to several, campilotropous. Pod linear-oblong, terete or slightly compressed, 4-8 cm. long, obliquely beaked at the apex and with a short claw at base. Seeds globose, pale yellow, about 1 cm across.

Several varieties of *P. sativum* are known, of which *P. sativum* var. *speciosum* (Dirb.) Alef is commonly cultivated in India and other countries. *P. exiphiens* Alef is the Sugar-pea. A large number of cultivated types have evolved as a result of breeding and horticultural manipulations by the agriculturists in Europe and America. In India 3-4 types are usually cultivated. A type of sugar-pea known as Sylviapea is now cultivated in India which has been introduced from Sweden. This has the pods very soft and tender, and is used as a vegetable like the beans. Besides P. sativum *P. arvense* Linn. is also cultivated in India. This has smaller seeds which are angled and mottled with red. This is used as a substitute for pea.

Original home of pea is supposed to be in Europe where cultivation of the crop started during the Bronze-age. Cultivation of pea in W. Asia and in India dates back also to prehistoric ages. At present in India about 1122000 h.a. of land are under pea cultivation and the total yield is about 1100000 tones per year. In the plains pea is cultivated after the rainy season, while in the hills it is cultivated in the summar and in the rains and 2 crops can be raised successively from the same field. It can be grown in different types of soil but it can not stand water logging. In the plains seeds are sown by broadcasting in Oct — Nov. and green pods can be collected in course of 2 months. For ripe seeds a period of few weeks more is necessary and the plants are uprooted about 3 months after sowing. The dried plants are carried to the threshing floor in bundles and the grains are separated by trampling under foot of cattle or by beating with rods. The impurities are got rid off by winnowing.

The land, still moist after the rains is ploughed and seeds sown without application of any manure, or well - rotted farmyard manure at the rate of 20 cart loads per hectare is added when preparing the soil. Like other leguminous crops pea collects its nitrogenous manure and no other chemical manuring is usually applied. In irrigated areas 22.5 kg of nitrogen and 67.5 kg of phosphorus are recommended. Manuring with cattle dung is also practised. Irrigation is necessary in drier areas and for late crops.

Early crops are more susceptable to diseases and Fusarium causes foot rot and wilt. Powdery mildew also causes much damage. These can be checked by dusting with sulphur or spraying with ultra sulphur.

CICER ARIETINUM LINN : Leguminosae

The Gram

Small, much-branched annual herb, viscously hairy all over. Leaves even-pinnate, alternate, stipulate; the rachis ending in a bristle or tendril or rarely with a terminal leaflet; leaflets elliptic-ovate, dentate, 6-8 mm long; stipules strongly veined, foliaceous, deeply toothed. Flowers solitary axillary, small, bluish purple, on slender peduncle. Calyx oblique, gamosepalous, tubular, with 5 lanceolate teeth, longer than the tube. Corolla short, papilionaceous; standard petal largest, covering the wing petals and keel; wing petals obliquely obovate, free; keel incurved. Stameus 9 + 1, diadelphous, the vexillary one free; anthers uniform. Ovary superior-sessile, 2-many ovuled on marginal placentas; style filiform, incurved, persistent, not bearded; stigma capitate. Pod oblong, turgid, sessile, 2-seeded, 2-2.5 cm long. Seeds obovate or subglobose, beaked, reddish brown, pale brown or often dark brown in colour, 0.5-0.8 cm long.

This is called the Desi or brown gram to distinguish it from the Kabuli-or White gram with larger and pale coloured seeds, which according to some is a different species, viz. C.kabulinum. This has the seeds larger but the yield is poor.

Gram is important as a pulse but it is consumed much as *sattu* a powdered form of the parched seeds. Bason is the powder obtained by grinding the seeds and is also much used. Gram soaked in water is given to the cattle and especially to the horses to make them strong. The husks with broken particles of the seeds make the *chuni* that is also given to the cattle.

Gram is cultivated as a cold weather rabi crop. It is grown as a pure crop or as a mixed crop with wheat and other winter crop and as a catch crop in sugarcane fields. Like other leguminous plants nodular swellings are found on the roots of gram-plant harbouring bacteria that fix atmospheric nitrogen. For this reason gram is often cultivated as a rotation crop to increase the fertility of the soil.

Light loany soil is best for cultivation of gram. Black cotton soil and alluvial soil are also quite suitable. Soil should be well drained and there should not be any waterlogging. A cool dry climate is preferred. Seeds are sown by broadcasting or by drills in rows about 2.5 cm. apart. September — October is the sowing season but seeds can be sown till the month of January. Frost, hailstorm and excessive rain are harmful to gram-crop.

The crop is ready for harvest in 4-6 months and when the plants start drying they are uprooted. Bundles of plants with the pods are taken to the threshing floor and the pods are threshed by beating with sticks or trampling under the feet of cattle, preferably of goats. The grains are then separated by winnowing. The yield of grain per acre is 400-600 kg per acre and in some good variety it is as high as 800 kg.

Irrigation is seldom necessary and usually no manure is applied. Sometimes organic manure is mixed with the soil before sowing. Gram blight and Rust disease are caused by *Meyosphaerella rabiel* Kov. and *Uromyces cicerisarietina* J & B. These come from infected seeds and to use disease free seeds is the best means to get a crop unaffected by such diseases. Caterpillar and white ants also cause serious damage. Dusting DDT powder and spraying solution of the same make the plants free from the pests.

In India 18-19 million acres of land are usually cultivated for gram every year and the anual yield is about 4.5 million tons.

VIGNA RADIATA (L) R. WILCZ — Leguminosae

(Syn. Phaseolus radiatus Linn)

The Mung

Scandent or subscandent shrub or under shrub with long trailing branches, more or less densely pubescent with reddish brown hairs. Leaves pinnately 3-foliolate, stipulate and stipelate; leaflets ovate-lanceolate, the terminal rhomboid ovate, 5-8 cm. long, sparsely setosely hairy; stipules 5-7 nerved, usually ciliate, about 1 cm long. Racemes axillary, few-flowered; bracts and bracteoles present; peduncle short at first, elongating in fruit. Flowers pale yellow 6-7 mm. long, bisexual and zygomorphic. Calyx campanulate with linear teeth. Corolla papilionaceous; standard petal orbicular, much the largest and covering the wings and keel; wings obovate-falcate, slightly adnate to the keel; keel incurved, shortly beaked. Stamens 9 + 1, diadelphous, vexillary stamen free, anthers uniform. Ovary superior, monocarpellary, with many ovules on marginal placenta; style filiform, longitudinally bearded on the inner face; stigma oblique with a short beak. Pod linear, nearly erect, 4-7 cm. long, very hairy when young, glabrescent afterwards, septate between the seeds; seeds subquadrate, about 2 mm long, brown or dull greenish grey; cotyledons yellow in some varieties and white in others.

(In using the vernacular name as the specific epithet Linnaeus made a confusion. The name "Mung" was used for the pulse "Mas-kelai" or "Urud" which was named by him as *Phaseolus mungo* Linn.)

About 40 different types of Mung are met with in cultivation which can be botanically grouped under 5 varieties, viz :

1. var. *radiatus* (typical variety) leaves drak green, pods spreading, seeds green.
2. var. *aurea* (Roxb) R.Wilcz (Sonamung) Leaves pale, pods reflexed, seeds dull yellow.
3. var. *grandis* (Prain) R. Wilcz. Leaves large, pods spreading, flowers with prominent bracts, seeds green.
4. var. *brunea* (Bose) R. Wilcz. Leaves bright green, spreading pods, brown seeds.
5. var. *glabra* (Roxb) R. Wilcz. Leaves and other parts more or less glabrous.

Another variety occurs wild in the subtropical region of the Himalaya. viz. var. *sublobatus* (Roxb) R.Wilcz. This is regarded as the progenitor of Mung as well as Urud.

Mung is cultivated all over India in the plains as a Kharif crop, except in Gujarat and Maharastra. It is grown as a pure crop or a mixed crop with jowar, bajra or cotton. Well-drained loamy soil is most suited for mung. Seeds are sown by broadcasting or drilling in

May-June or June-July or in July-August in some places. In Karnataka 3 types are grown, the early type sown in July-August, midseason in Aug-Sept and late in Dec-Jan. Hoeing after 20 days and hand-weeding also are practised. Being a legume it enriches the soil of its nitrogen content and when grown as a pure crop no manure is applied to the soil. Water-logging as well as heavy and continuous rainfall has harmful effects. Pods mature in 70 days and are collected green when these are used as beans. The mature pods ripen in about a months time and the crop is harvested before the pods are fully ripe. Plants are pulled out and bundles are left in heaps for drying. These are then threshed by beating with sticks or trampling under the feet of oxen and cleaned by winnowing. Empty pods and chaffs are used as fodder.

The crop suffers from stem-rot and mildew. The former can be controlled by Agrosan G.N. before sowing while the other by spraying with ultrasulphur and dusting with sulphur and also by spraying with one percent Bordeaux mixture.

FIBRE PLANTS

CORCHORUS CAPSULARIS Linn – Tiliacae
&
C. OLITORIUS Linn

The Jute plants

Undershrubs up to 75 cm. high or taller. Leaves simple, ovate to elliptic, stipulate, serrate, acute or shortly acuminate, rounded at base and often tailed on both sides, pubescent or almost glabrous; lamina upto 7.5 cm. long, 3.5 cm. broad; stipules filiform or subulate. Cymes axillary, 1-few-flowered, bracteate. Flowers bisexual, short pedicilled, yellow; buds obovoid. Sepals 4-5, free, oblong-lanceolate 3-4 mm. long. Petals 4-5, free, spathulate, with a short claw, ciliate, 5 mm.long. Stamens twice as many as petals or numerous; anthers 2-celled, dehiscing laterally and longitudinally. Ovary sessile or on a short gynophore, 2-6 celled with many ovules in each; style thick, stigma cup-shaped, fimbriate. Fruit a loculicidal capsule, many seeded; seeds smooth, brown or black, trigonous or not, about 2 mm.long.

Capsule globose, 1 cm. in diam., not beaked...C. capsularis
Capsule elongated, 3-8 cm. long, beaked...C. olitorius.

Jute is a rainy season crop. It prefers an alluvial soil although it can be grown in other types of soil. The soil is prepared by ploughing 5 or 6 times and all clods of earth should be broken to fine particles. Seeds are then sowed by broad-casting or sometimes by dibbling. Cowdung and wood ash is liberally applied to the soil before sowing. The seeds are sown during March to May and germinate when they receive a premonsoon shower. Weeding and thinning is necessary at seedling stage and the land is harrowed with a rake. Weeding operation is done 2-3 times and after final thinning the spacing between the plants is 10-15 cm. wide. The plants are unaffected by water standing on the field due to excess rainfall but at seedling stage water logging is harmful. Manuring with sulphate of ammonia, potash and lime results in a quick growth. Harvesting is done after 60-90 days when the pods are still green or at flowering stage. The plants are cut down very near to the base tied into bundles and carried to a pool or a canal of slow running water.

The bundles are arranged in 2 or 3 layers. Logs, psudostems of banana and mud are put on the floating layers as weights. Complete submersion is essential. In a period of 10-15 days the soft tissues of the stem disintigrates and the fibre-strands separate from the woody portion. Fibres are then stripped out and washed and are spread in the sun for drying for 2 to 3 days. The bundles of fibres are then made into bales and stored or sent to the market. The average yield per acre is about 600 kg.

The chief jute growing areas in India lie in W.Bengal and Assam. The crop is raised in Bihar, U.P. and Orissa also and in smaller scales in Andhra Pradesh. Outside India major jute producing countries are Bangladesh, Ceylon, Nepal, Siam, China and Taiwan and also some parts of Africa and in Brazil. Land under jute cultivation in India is about 1200000 acres and the jute obtained each year is about 3 million bales of 200 kg. each. About 70% of jute produced in India is exported outside every year.

The jute is used for the manufacture of hesian, ropes, etc. The woody material or the sticks after the removal of the fibres are also made use of in different ways. They are good as fuel and are much in demand in the field of betel vine. The vines are grown in partial shade under a roof covered by the jute-sticks. The sticks are also used as supports of betel vine and also other climbers producing vegetables. The leaves of **C. olitorius** are used as pot herbs and leaves are collected from the seedlings which are uprooted in thinning operation. They are also considered to have some medicinal value.

GOSSYPIUM species — Malvaceae

The Cotton Plants

The cotton fibre is the hairy outgrowth of the seed of different species of Gossypium Linn. Those cultivated in India for the fibre are :-

1. G. arboreum Linn.
2. G. herbaceum Linn.
3. G. barbadens Linn.
4. G. hirsutum Linn.

The first 2 are old world species and are diploid having chromosome number, n = 13. The other 2 are New world species and tetraploid with n = 26. The genus **Gossypium** is described below :

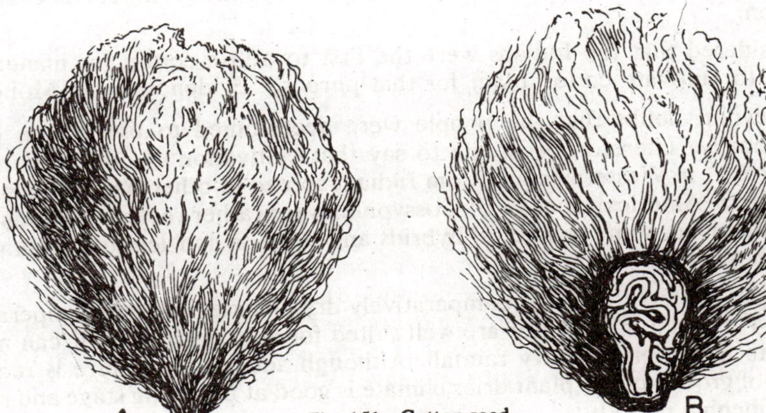

Fig. 151. Cotton seed

Shrubs or short trees. Leaves simple, palmately lobed, alternate, stipulate; stipules 2, lateral. Flowers solitary on jointed peduncles, axillary, regular, hermaphrodite, large, yellow, usually with crimson or purple centre; bracteoles 3, large, leafy, cordate, broadly ovate, deeply toothed or laciniate near apex, persistent. Calyx cupular, truncate or slightly 5 - toothed. Petals 5, slightly conate at base and adnate below to the staminal column. Stamens numerous, connate in a tube which is truncate or 5 - toothed at the top and giving off below the apex many short antheriferous filaments; anthers 1 - celled, reniform, dehiscence longitudinal, extrose. Disc small. Carpels 5, syncarpous, forming a superior 5 - locular ovary; ovules many in each cell on axile placenta; style clavate, 5 - grooved at the apex with 5 stigmas. Fruit a 3-5 valved capsule; seeds densely clothed with wooly hairs.

1. **G.arboreum** : Shruby, younger parts finely pubescent. Leaves deeply cut into 3-7 lobes. Bracteoles triangular, longer than broad, entire or with 3-4 coarse teeth. Capsule tapering, profusely pitted, 3-4 locular, opening widely. Seeds with 2 coats of haris.

Old world species, found wild and cultivated in Africa, Arabia, India, China, Japan and Malaysia.

2. **G.herbaceum** : herbaceous or shruby, 1.7 mtr. to 2.5 mtr. high, sparsely hairy or glabrous. Leaves cleft to the middle, 1-7-lobed. Bracteoles triangular, usually broader than long, with 6-8 teeth, loosely attached to the flower or capsule. Capsules rounded, with few oil glands, opening slightly when ripe. Seeds with 2 coats of hairs.

Old world species, found wild and cultivated in Africa, Middle East and Central Asia and Western India; cultivated in China.

3. **G.hirsutum** : Shrubes or short trees, 1-5 mtr. high. Leaves ovate-cordate, with 3-5 acuminate lobes. Bracteoles ovatecordate, longer than broad, with 7-12 acuminate teeth. Capsules rounded, 3-5 locular, oilglands few and inconspicuous.

New world species, found in India and other Asiatic and African countries only in cultivation. Different races are known in cultivation and some are annual.

4. **G.barbadense** : Shrubs or small trees, upto 5 mtr. high, glabrous to densely hairy. Leaves with 3-5 long tapering lobes. Bracteoles as broad as long, cordate, with 10-15 long acuminate teeth. Capsules 3-4-locular, broad at base, acute, rough and pitted.

New world species cultivated in African and Asiatic countries. Annual races are known in cultivation.

It is considered that the Indians were the first to utilise cotton for manufacturing fabrics and to cultivate cotton plant for that purpose. Evidences from Mohenjodaro establish beyond doubt that the people were accustomed to use cotton garments produced locally. Therefore it is safe to say that cultivation of cotton plant started before 3000 B.C. in Western India. From India it spread to other Asiatic countries and to North Africa. American species of Gossypium were rather recently introduced, and many races evolved, some as natural hybrids and some by horticultural manipulations and researches.

Cotton plant prefers a hot and comparatively dry climate. Summer temperature not exceeding 44°c and a mild winter are well suited for cotton growing. It can not stand frost and can not tolerate heavy rainfall. Although adequate moisture is required in early stages of growth of the plant drier climate is good at flowering stage and rainfall is harmful at ripening period.

The black cotton soil of western and central India and the red soil of S. India are very suitable for cotton cultivation. The former type is deep heavy and black soil rather clayey, cracking when dry, swelling and loosening after rains. This type of soil contains calcium and low in organic matters. This soil is very fertile and retains moisture and cotton is grown here under rainfed condition. Red soil is light, porous and friable, contains much iron and alumina and less of calcium. American races are usually grown on such soil under irrigated condition. Clayey or sandy alluvial soil of Indo-Gangetic plain is also suitable for cotton cultivation.

Land is prepared by ploughing and harrowing 2-3 times with a blade-harrow. Seeds are then sown in lines with wooden seed drillers or by broadcasting. Seeds are pretreated with mud and cowdung. Delinting with chemicals is also recommended. Soaking the seeds in water for 12-24 hours is also practised as it facilitates germination. Seeds are sown in Summer from April to June usually after the first shower. Plants are thinned out when one or one and half month old so that the spacing between the plants is 30-100 cm. American plants are sometimes topped when about 1 mtr. tall to induce branching. Small quantities of farm yard manure or oil cakes are applied. If the soil is not saline and rainfall is adequate nitrogenous fertilisers and organic manures are given. Rotation of crops is usually practised with wheat or jowar after the cotton is harvested.

Flowering starts after about 2 months or more and the boll or the fruit attains full size in a period of about 4 weeks. Three to four pickings are done from a field as the blooming is not simultaneous and all fruits are not fully ripe at one time. In rainfed areas the yield is 15-70 kg. per acre while in irrigated fields it is much more, about 125 kg per acre.

Wilt and root rot are the two serious diseases of cotton plant. As these are seed borne diseases seed treatment is necessary for the control. Seeds are immersed for 1 hr. in 0.25% Uspulum, or are dusted with the same. Delinting with sulphuric acid also gives good result. Spraying of Bordeaux mixture in the field when the plants are at seedling stage is recommended. **G. hirsutum** and **G. barbadense** are immume to such diseases in India and there are some wilt resistant strains of other species. Selection from amongst these for cultivation eleminates the diseases.

Ginning is done in factories by power-driven machines but in villages charkha gins are still in use. After ginning the cotton is compressed into bales each weighing about 175 kg. The total production is about 4298000 bales every year while total area under cotton cultivation is about 18346000 acre.

AGAVE SISALANA PERR : Amaryllidaceae
(Placed by some under Agavaceae)

Sisal Hemp

Shrubby herbs with usually a very short thick woody root stock. Leaves large, thick and fleshy, densely clustered at the top of the root stock, bluish green, spiny at the tip and at the edges; 1.5 - 2 mtr. long and about 15 cm. broad. Inflorescence is a long thyrsoid panicle on a stout pole like peduncle arising from the centre of the plant and rapidly growing to a height of 7-10 mtr. Flowers bisexual, with a tubular perianth. Stamens 6; filaments adnate to the base of and longer than the perianth. Carpels 3; ovary inferior, 3-celled with many ovules in each cell; style filiform; stigma 3-lobed. Fruit an ovoid capsule; seeds many, flattened, cuneate, with a black testa. Fruit sometimes replaced by viriparous bulbils.

Agave flowers only once in their life time and the plant dies after fruiting. On cutting the young peduncle a large quantity of sugary juice is obtained. The fibres are obtained from the leaves and are bast fibres. Besides **A. sisalana,** two other species are cultivated in India, e.g. **A. americana** Linn. (Syn. **A. cantala** Roxb.) and **A. vera-cruz** Mill. The leaves of these 2 species are smaller than those of **A. sisalana.**

Agave plants are indigenous to Tropical America wherefrom these were introduced to India by the Portugese in the 15th century. In this country cultivation of Agave was not taken up at the beginning for fibre production but occasionally it was cultivated as a hedge plant. Cultivation on a commercial scale was taken up only in the middle of this century.

The plants prefer a hot and more or less dry climate and grow on clayey, gravelly or sandy soil. They are propagated by bulbils or by suckers. Not much care is taken to grow the plants which start producing full size leaves in course of 3-4 years. The leaves are then collected from time to time, few at a time from each plant which continues to grow for several years. The leaves are crushed in the crushing mills and the fibrous materials are retted in water, washed and dried. The fibres are made into ropes and woven into a type of hesian cloth for making sacks and bags. Agave fibres or Sisal hemp does not rot in water and for this Sisal-rope is in great demand in the navy.

OIL YIELDING PLANTS

Different kinds of oil are obtained from different plants and are used mainly for cooking, in paints and varnish and for manufacturing soap and essence. Some kinds of oil are also used medicinally. Cooking oil and varnish oil are obtained from seeds while essential oil is obtained usually from fragrant flowers. Cooking oil or edible oil are often used for anointing the body, e.g. mustard oil, coconut oil, sesame or jinjili oil, etc. Such oil is some times used also for burning in lamps. Mustard oil cake is used as a fertiliser and cattle feed. Other cakes are used as food or food-adjuncts.

BRASSICA CAMPESTRIS Linn — Cruciferae or Brassicaceae

Mustard

Tall herbs, a metre high or more, with pungent juice. Leaves large alternate, lyrate, rounded at apex; petiole stemclasping, the upper usually auricled, 10-25 cm. long, 5-10 cm. broad. Inflorescence a raceme or panicle. Flowers actinomorphic, hermaphrodite hypogynous. Sepals 4, imbricate, pouched at the base. Petals 4, set crosswise, distinctly clawed, yellow. Stamens 6, tetradynamous; filaments of inner 4 stamens longer than the outer 2; anthers oblong, basifixed. Carpels 2; ovary superior, 2-celled by a placental replum; style beaked, stigma 2-lobed; ovules many, on opposite sides of the replum on 2 parietal placentas. Fruit an elongated capsule with a seedless indehiscent beak at the apex; valves deciduous, replum and placentas persistent; in cultivated forms valves often more than 2. Seeds globose, with large cotyledons.

Different varieties of the above species are cultivated in India, viz. **B. campestris** (1) var. **sarson** Prain, (2) var. **toria** Duthie & Fuller, (3) var. **dichotoma** Watt., etc. Besides this 2 other species are also cultivated, viz. **B. juncea** Czern & Cess and **B. nigra** Koch. A great diversity of forms is met with in the varieties of **B. campestris.** In var. **sarson** the ripe fruits are erect in some and directed downwards in others. The number of valves in a pod and the colour of seeds also vary. In case of var.**toria** the plants have a more open habit with many dichotomous branches and stem-clasping leaves. The pods are torulose and the seeds are bluish brown and finely rugose. The variety **dichotoma** is more or less like var. **toria** and has the seeds with a mucilaginous coat. **B. juncea** is the Rai-sarisha the seeds of which are yellow. **B. nigra** has almost back seeds which are usually used to flavour curries.

Mustard is grown as a winter crop. It requires a loam soil prepared by 2-3 ploughings. Seeds are scattered or sown by seed driller. It is usually grown in rainfed areas in Himachal Pradesh toBengal with plentyof moisture in the soil while in some parts of Uttar Pradesh it is cultivated in irrigated fields. Seeds are sown in Sept-Oct. and the crop is ready for harvesting in Jan-Feb. No manuring is usually applied; it has however been observed that 15 kg. of amonium sulphate per acre increases the yield. Mustard is grown as a pure crop or mixed with pea, wheat or barley.

While harvesting the whole plants or the top portions only are collected before the pods dehisce. These are carried to the threshing floor and left for 2-3 days. The seeds are then separated by beating by sticks or under the feet of goats, The yield per acre varies from 400-700 kg.

COCOS NUCIFERA Linn — Palmae or Arecaceae

The Coconut

A tall palm with an unbranched trunk, upto 25 m. high, with a crown of long feathery leaves; base usually swollen. Leaves pinnate, 2-4 m. long; leaflets equidistant, upto a mtr. long, linear lanceolate. Inflorescence a branched spadix about a mtr. long. axillary, erect but ultimately drooping, flowers small, unisexual; female flowers scattered near the base of the branches of the panicle, often between 2 males, the upper portion of the branches having male flowers only. Male flowers unsymmetric, with 2 series of perianth. Perianth segments 3 in each series, coriaceous, 2-5 mm. long, valvate. Stamens 6, filaments short, anthers linear. Perianth segments of female flowers about 1.2 cm. long, persistent, inbricate. Carpels 3, connate in 3-celled, superior ovary, ovules solitary, basal; style short; stigmas 3, recurved. Fruit a large drupe, 20-30 cm. long, ovoid, trigonous or almost terete, 1-seeded, with a thick fibrous pericarp and hard endocarp with 3 basal eyes, the remains of 3 ovarian cells. Embryo lying opposite to one basal eye, embeded in the fleshy endosperm lining the endocarp with a fluid filling the central portion.

No other plant appears to be more important economically than the coconut palm. Besides the "copra" or the kernel which is an article of food and is the source of the oil, the fruit is in great demand for the milk of green coconut which furnishes a cool and refreshing drink. The fibre of the husk of the fruit is also an important article of trade for the manufacture of matting, brushes, ropes, etc. The other parts of the tree are also used in various ways often in different ailments.

The coconut palm is cosmopolitan in the tropics but not found inland far from the sea. Probably it originated in the western parts of tropical America or in the ancient land of Papua. The fibrous coat helped the fruit to float and to be carried to distant countries adjoining the sea. It reached Africa very recently and also to West Indies although it was growing all the time on western parts of America.

It came to India in the remote past either by human agency or by ocean currents and established in the costal districts of Peninsular India. It is in Kerala and Tamil Nadu that there are some plantations; in other states Coconut is cultivated in village orchards with other fruits and such states are Maharastra, Karnataka, Andhra Pradesh, Orissa and W.Bengal. Coconut prefers a typical tropical climate, hot and humid. Soil must be well drained. Light alluvial sandy soil near the coast is ideal for coconut growing. Rainfall of 1250-1750 mm. well distributed throughout the year favours healthy growth of the plant. It can stand much higher rain fall if the soil is well drained. Where rainfall is lower than 1000 mm. per year irrigation is necessary. Plenty of sunlight is necessary at all stages.

Seedlings are raised in nurseries where the soil should be sandy or light loamy. Seed beds are long and narrow, raised 20-25 cm. above general ground level. Beds are 25-30 cm. apart and the nuts are placed with same spacing. Shallow drains are made between, the beds. Seedlings are fit for transplanting after 7-8 months. Pits should be dug 1 × 1 × 1 mtr. in rows, 3 mtr. spacing between pits in the rows and 8-10 mtr. between the rows, so that a field of 1 acre can accommodate 40-50 plants, or if the soil is rich the rows can be made closer increasing the number of plants per acre. Some times triangular planting is done to have more plants in the field.

Watering in the dry seasons is necessary for 2-5 years planting. Cereals, pulses or herbs with underground tubers are often grown in the spaces between rows as inter crops. Bananas and pineapple are also cultivated. **Crotalaria and Tephrosia** are often grown as cover crops that are used for green manuring and also for checking other undesirable weeds. Artificial fertilisers are seldom applied but wood ash, cattle manure and oil cake are recommended at the rate of 10 kg. per palm per year.

Plants begin to yield 5-6 years after planting. A mature tree gives 60-100 nuts per year in 6-8 gatherings. Sometimes much damage is done to the trees by beetles. These are to be collected and distroyed and the decaying refuse in the field that serve as the breeding medium should be burned.

The fruits are sundried or kiln dried. Dehusking is done with manual labour. Dehusked nuts are broken into 2 halves and these are again dried in sun or over fire when the meat or the kernel shrinks and is easily detached from the shell. The meat is further dried. Oil is then extracted from the dried meat or copra by pressing in bullock-driven ghanis or in rotary ghanis or expellers and hydraulic presses. The copra contains 57-75% of oil.

The oil serves as an edible oil, hair oil, an ingradient in soap manufacture, a constituent of margarine, a base of pharmaceutical ointment and also as a substitute of ghee. The cake is a cattle-feed and also a fertiliser. The coir is the fibrous element of the husk and is used in making ropes and matting and in stuffing cushions. A sugary juice in copious quantity exudes from the stalk of the young inflorescence when the upper portion is chopped off and this is made into toddy and jaggery.

ARACHIS HYPOGEA Linn — Leguminosae

The ground nut

An annual herb, with erect stem and branches, or branches prostrate. Leaves even pinnate with 2 pairs of leaflets; stipules adnate to the petiole; leaflets rounded or acute at apex, 2-3 cm. long. Spikes axillary, near the base of the stem and branches, or flowers solitary, often from underground stem. Flowers bisexual, zygomorphic, hypogynous 1 cm. long. Calyx of 5 sepals, united in a slender tube with 2 lips; the upper 4-lobed, the lower with 1 lobe membranous. Corolla of 5 yellow petals, papilionaceous; standard petal or bicular; wings oblong, free; keel incurved beaked. Stamens 10; filaments connate in a tube alternately long and short. Ovary superior, monocarpellary; ovules 2-3, marginal; style long, filiform, with a small stigma; the recptacle elongating after fertilisation, becoming reflexed and burying the fruit underground; fruit an oblong lomentum, more or less torulose, continuous within, 1-3-secded, ripening under ground. Seeds ovoid, slightly depressed at one side at base, with a brown testa.

The ground nut originally came from Brazil. It is now cultivated in all tropical and subtropical countries and in a large scale in India, China, U.S.A. and W.Africa. To India it was introduced in the 16th century and at present the total production of nuts in India exceeds 400000 (four lacs) tons being 35% of the world total.

The plant has about 100 cultivated varieties or forms which however are commonly divided into 2 groups or types — (1) the bunch — or erect-type and (2) the runner or spreading type. In the former several branches come up from the base of the main stem and grow erect. These branches bear clusters of fowers at the base. The fruits are smaller, thin shelled and with rounded seeds. Plants of this type come to flower in 3-4 months. The spreading type has long creeping branches flowering along their length. The fruits are longer with thicker shell. These plants come to flower in 4-6 month's time.

The plants are grown in sandy or loamy soil, or in black soil, but grow best in light sandy loam soil. It is grown as a rainfed monsoon crop. In some places it is grown in irrigated fields.

The land is prepared by 2-4 ploughings, and the seeds are sown by dribbling method in the furrows. Spacing is about 30 cm. between rows and 25 cm. between the plants. In rich soil wider spacing is necessary. Two hoeings and weeding are practised, one 3-4 weeks after sowing and a second time after another month. No fertiliser is given but just before sowing time 2-5 tons of cattle manure per acre is often applied. On sandy soil tank-or channel-silt, 15-20 tons per acre is recommended. Ground nut cultivation enriches the soil with respect to nitrogen.

Seeds are sown in February-March after a shower and the crop is harvested in June to August. Bunch type plants are lifted by working a harrow or by using a hand hoe. The fruits are removed by hand or by beating the plants against a bar. In the case of spreading type the field is dug up with spades, ploughed or harrowed and the pods are hand picked. The pods are then dried. The dried pods are shelled by beating with sticks or by machinery.

The seeds are pressed to obtain the oil which edible as such, or by hydrogination is converted to vegetable ghee. The oil is often used as a substitute for diesel. It is used in soap manufacture, in cosmetics, leather dressing and as tallow substitutes. The yield of oil is 36 - 40% of the seed. Peanut butter is also prepared from the seeds which is used as a substitute of butter or is mixed with butter. Pea nut flour is also made which is used as wheat flour.

The oil cake of groundnut is an important cattle feed. It is also a valuable organic manure.

LINUM USITATISSIMUM Linn. — Linaceae

The Linseed

Herbs. 60 - 120 cm. or taller. Leaves simple, narrowly linear, entire 3-5 cm. long; stipules are replaced by glands. Flowers few at the end of the branches near the top of the stem, regular and hermaphrodite. Sepals 5, white — margined. Petals 5, contorted, obovate, 1-1.5 cm. long, blue, pale purple or white. Stamens 5, alternating with small staminodes; filaments connate below; anthers versatile. Ovary superior, 5 locular, each locule again 2-locullate; styles 5, free, with clavate stigma; ovule one in each locule. Fruit a 5-celled capsule, slightly exceeding the sepals, splitting into 5 2-seeded or 10 1-seeded cocci. Seeds narrowly ovate, compresed, more or less shining, about 0.5 cm. long with scanty endosperm and straight embryo.

This species is not found wild in any part of the world although it has been in cultivation in the Mediterranean region since antiquity. It is very close to Linum trienne Mill. growing wild in S.Europe and is considered to have been derived from the latter species. Those growing in S.Europe and N.Africa are tall plants and yield the "flax". The oil content in the seeds of these plants is scanty. The oil yielding variety is cultivated in Turkistan, Afghanistan and India. This variety has shorter stem, much branched and is tillering. Oil content in the seeds is much higher. In India it has been introduced from Central Asia. In S. Russia and Asia Minor transitional forms are grown that give fibre as well as oil seeds.

In India two distinct types are cultivated viz. the Gangetic type of N. India and the Peninsular type of Rajasthan and Central India. The former has a shallow tap root, is slow growing and late maturing but produces much more fruits and seeds. The other has a long tap root, quick growing early maturing with larger seeds rich in oil but production of fruits and seeds is low.

Linseed plant is grown as a pure or a mixed crop. Almost all types of soil having sufficient moisture are suitable for growing **Linum.** Black soil and havey soil of central and Peninsular India are equally good for linseed growing. In northern India it is grown chiefly in the submontane districts and does best on heavy loam soil. Areas with moderate rain-fall of 75 - 175 cm. per annum appears to be best suited for linseed growing. In northern India it is grown in the cold season. Seeds are sown in November and the crop is harvested in March-April. In the hilly districts of Uttar Pradesh seeds are sown in Sept-Oct. In Kashmir seeds are sown in Feb-March. In Peninsular India seeds are sown in Sept-Oct. and the crop is harvested in February.

Seeds are swon in lines and the lines are about 30 cm. apart. In case of growing as a mixed crop where there are standing crops in the field seeds are sown by broadcasting. Nitrogenous fertiliser increases the yield of seeds.

The crop is harvested when the capsule matures but before it dries up and splits. The plants are cut close to the ground or are uprooted. They are left in the field to dry and then threshed. The chaffs are separated from the seeds by winnowing. Threshing is done by beating with sticks or wooden mallets or by hand driven deseeding machines. The stems are collected and treated for the extraction of fibres. India produces about 150,000 tons of linseed oil all of which is used internally.

The demand of linseed oil is mainly for the manufacture of paints and varnishes. It is also used in the manufacture of linoleum and oil cloth, printing and lithographic ink and soft soap. It has a medicinal value and is laxative.

Linseed cake is used as a nutritive food, as a protein supplement to live stocks. For dairy cattle and young stocks it is very valuable. It is also used as an organic manure. The mucilage from the seeds or from the cakes is used in cosmetics and in pharmaceutical industries.

Flax is obtained from stalks of the plants grown especially for this. These plants are harvested when the capsules are still immature. Flax fibre is woven into different types of fine fabrics as well as canvas, buckram etc. Strong ropes and twine threads are also manufactured from flax.

Linseed fibre is obtained also from types that are grown for oil seeds. These fibres are extracted from the straw after the seeds are collected. Linseed fibre is also spun into fine or course yarn. It is inferior to flax but is strong. It may be spun into textile by itself or mixed with cotton or wool. This fibre is very suitable for making paper pulp.

Linseed straw is also useful. It is used in the manufacture of card board and wrapping and insulating material.

BEVERAGES

Tea and coffee are the 2 important beverages very popular in India. Tea is obtained from CAMELIA SINENSIS (L) O.Ktz. and coffee from COFFEA ARABICA Linn. and a few other species and their hybrids.

CAMELIA SINENSIS (LINN.) O.Ktz — Theaceae

The Tea Plant

Evergreen shrubs or short trees, branches glabrous. Leaves simple, alternate, exstipulate; elliptic oblong, serrate, acute at both ends or cuspidate acuminate at apex, silky puberulous beneath when young, 10-20 cm. long 3-7 cm. broad. Flowers solitary, axillary, often in a cluster of 2-4 bisexual, about 3 cm. in diam, bracteate; bracts 2-3, small. Sepals 5-6, unequal, orbicular, glabrous, with membranous ciliate margin. Petals white, 5-6, broadly obovate, slightly coherent at base. Stamens many in several whorls, 5-12 of the inner most whorl free, others unite to form a monadelphous ring, adnate to the base of the petals. Ovary superior, 3-5-celled with 4-5 pendulous ovules in each cell, styles 3-5, united upto 2/3rd of their length. Fruit a loculicidal capsule, trigonous, with leathery pericarp. Seeds 1-2 in each cell of the fruit, 1.5-2 cm. in diam., globose or obtusely angled, pale brown and smooth.

As a beverage tea was known to the people of China from ancient times and by the 5th century A.D. it was very popular. It is not known when cultivation started on a commercial scale but it is now grown in many tropical and subtropical countries of the world. In India tea is cultivated in the districts of Dehra Dun, Kangra and Kumaun of U.P Darjeeling and Jalpaigooree of West Bengal, Brahmaputra — valley and Surma — valley of Assam and in Ranchi area of Chota Nagpur. In southern India it is grown in Malabar, Coimbatore, Nilgiris and hills of Kerala. In Drajeeling district tea is cultivated from the Duars to an elevation of about 2000 mtr.

Tea prefers a wet and warm climate. The optimum condition is considered to be a narrow range of temperate variation, generous rainfall throughout the year, absence of strong dry wind and temperature well above freezing point. Rainfall of 150 cm. to 370 cm. per year is well — suited for tea growing but in S.India annual rainfall as high as 750 cm. appears to have no harmful effect on tea plant provided the soil is well drained. Waterlogging in the soil is detrimental. Acid soil free from Calcium carbonate or reactive Calcium is best suited for tea growing. As a manure Ammonium sulphate is used at the rate of 20 kg. per acre.

Tea plant is shade loving. Partial shade is therefore provided to the bushes in a plantation by planting medium sized trees at intervals, preferably at distances of 16-17 mtr. The trees preferred for this purpose are : *Dalbergia assamica* Roxb; *Derris robusta* Benth; *Leucena glauca* Benth, *Gliricidia maculata* H.B.K., *Grevillia robusta* A. Cunn., and species of *Acacia, Erythrina* and Albizzia.

Regular pruning is done to induce vigorous vegetative growth and to keep the bushes at a suitable height for easy plucking of the leaves. Pruning starts mwhen the plants are two and a half years old. It is done annually or biennially in northern India but at an interval of 2-3 years in S. India. Heavy pruning is necessary when the bush is high.

Tea plants are propagated from seeds and also from root-cuttings. The viability of tea seeds is poor and the seeds should be sown soon after collection. In nurseries seeds are sown in beds 10-20 cm. apart and are properly shaded. When about 30 cm. high the

Fig. 152. **Tea plant**

seedlings are transplanted. On flat land and on gentle slopes seedlings are planted 1.5 mtr. apart and on terraces of the hills at a distance of 1 mtr. from each other. The holes dug for receiving the seedlings are partly filled with well rotted cattle dung and compost, and then seedlings are planted with a large lump of undisturbed soil attached round the roots. In the case of root cuttings, these are allowed to root under bamboo shade or ferns.

Tanin content is highest in the apical bud and the 1st leaf. The bud and 2 leaves just beneath are therefore plucked and the plucking is done at an interval of one week.

Tea is obtained from another species which is much cultivated in E.India and this is Camelia Kissi Wall. This does not have a very good flavour but gives a good liquor.

As a beverage tea is used in 4 forms viz. -- Black tea, Green tea, Oolong tea and Brick tea. Drinking of black tea is popular in almost all countries and green tea is popular in central Asia and to some extent in other countries. Oolong tea is a semifermented product manufactured in Formosa and outside Formosa used in some parts of America. Brick tea is liked by the people of Mongolia and Tibet.

Manufacture of Black tea consits of 4 stages, viz. Withering, Rolling, Fermenting and Drying or Firing. The process of withering is to spread out the collected leaves from the garden on racks and shelves of the withering room. They are left there for partial drying until the leaves are soft and flaccid. This is done by allowing natural breeze to pass through the room or by blowing warm wind with the help of power driven fan. In the rolling process the flaccid leaves are passed on to rollers where the leaves are twisted. The process is repeated for 1st, 2nd and 3rd rolling. For fermentation the rolled or twisted leaves are spread on platforms,3 - 10 cm. thick and left there for 2-6 hrs. in an atmosphere of high humidity and low temperature. Then for firing or drying hot air-current is passed over the leaves for 30 - 40 mts. The dried material contains 3-5% of moisture. The material is then packed in aluminium-lined packing cases. In the preparation of green tea the plucked leaves are first heat-treated. This consists of pan-firing or steaming for a few minutes not to show any sign of scorching or reddenning. The heat-treated leaves are then rolled and dried. In this preparation withering and fermentation is omitted.

Oolong tea is manufactured in Taiwan and is a semifermented product. It has a special flavour peculiar to its own. In preparing brick tea the plucked leaves are steamed over a boiler and when flaccid and soft passed in heavy moulds under hydraulic pressure into bricks.

In India tea gardens cover a total area of about 900,000 acre and the annual production is about 28900000 kg. about half of which is exported outside.

Camelia Kissi Wall is another species grown in Assam on a small scale and is used as a substitute for *C. sinensis*.

COFFEA ARABICA Linn. — Rubiaceae

The Coffee Plant

Shrub or small tree; branches compressed. Leaves simple, opposite, with broad interpetiolar stipules. Flowers in axillary clusters, hermaphrodite, regular, epigynous, white and fragrant; bracteate. Calyx tubular, 4 - toothed, persistent. Corolla tubular below; lobes 4-5, contorted. Stamens 4-5, with narrow sessile anther, inserted on the corolla tube. Ovary inferior, 2-celled; ovule solitary in each cell, pendulous; style stout with large capitate stigma. Fruit a drupe with 2 pyrenes, scarlet when ripe. Seeds (known as coffee-beans) usually 2, enclosed in a common husk like membrane with horny endosperm, short and curved embryo and thin cordate cotyledons.

C. arabica is native of Abyssinia and is grown in many tropical countries. In India it is cultivated in the Western Ghats in Mysore and Kerala and in small scale in Chotanagpur. The total area under coffe plantation in India is about 197800 acre with an annual production of beans of about 15145 tons.

C. arabica may attain a height of about 10 m. if not pruned but is usually pruned down to 1½ m. It prefers a rich well drained friable loamy soil with pH value of 6.0 -

6.5. Areas exposed to strong wind are not suited for good growth. Partial shade is beneficial to coffee plants. To start a plantation a virgin forest is cleared on a hill-slope. Pits are dug 45-60 cm. deep, 30-45 cm. wide and 2-3 mtrs. apart. Seedlings or grafts are planted in the pits during July-September. In India overhead shade trees are provided but in other countries the young plants are left exposed to direct sun.

Seedlings are raised in specially prepared seed beds and transplanted to nurseries when 7-8 cm. tall. In seed-beds seeds are sown in Jan. to March, covered with earth about 1 cm. thick and then covered with moss or grass and watered daily. The seeds germinate in 4-8 week's time and the moss — or grass covering is removed after the germination of seeds. Light overhead shade is provided. In nurseries small seedlings are often transplanted in baskets from the seed beds. After about a year in July-Sept. the seedlings are transplanted to pits in the plantations. If they are in baskets the seedlings are not removed from them and the baskets are placed in the pits with the seedlings.

Besides planting shade trees in the plantations cover crops are grown to cover the ground between the rows and keep down the weeds. Weeding is necessary till the coffee-plants form small bushes. Proper arrangement for good drainage is always made in a plantation. Cattle dung, oil cake and bone-meal are used as manure at early stages, later replaced by chemical manuring. Topping and pruning is regularly done when the plants are more than 1½ mtr. tall and all unnecessary suckers are removed.

Plants start producing the berries when 3 years old and go on bearing for 30-50 years. Berries ripen in Oct-Nov. and are plucked when properly ripe. Unripe berries give defective beans (i.e. seeds) and overripe berries are difficult to pulp. Berries are sun-dried for 2-3 weeks and the covering is removed by hulling. They are then cured in a curing shed. Wet beans are pulped, fermented, washed and dried. The beans are then put in a peeler and the parchment cover and silver skin are removed. They are then roasted, powdered and packed for marketing. For outside trade the beans usually exported as such and the powder only in a small quantity.

The seeds if left in warm damp place for some time develop a change in flavour and taste and coffee with such flavour and taste is liked by some people. To prepare such special type of coffee the beans are spread evenly on the floor or platforms of a room through which monsoon air is permitted to pass. After 2 weeks the seeds are turned and left as such for another week. These are then packed in bags and the bags are also left in the floor or platform in such a manner that the damp air current can freely pass through them. After a few days the bags are packed for export. This process is called monsooning of the beans.

The beans are also used in manufacturing a plastic material, known as caffelite. The leaves of coffee are also used as beverage in Malaya.

Coffee is obtained from the seeds of a few other species of COFFEA viz. *C. liberica* Bull exHiern, *C. robusta* Lind., *C. stenophylla* G. Don, etc. *C. robusta* is a native of Congo in Africa and grows in varying conditions of soil and climate. It is much cultivated in Java and Sri Lanka. This has been introduced into India and has been successfully established in Kerala.

TIMBER TREES

India can boast of many timber trees, hard, strong and durable, and some are light and comparatively soft. Some take high polish and suitable for cabinet work. Most of these trees grow in plains while a few are found in the subtropical and temperate belts of the Himalayas, e.g. *Juglans regia* Linn. *Michelia excelsa* Bl., the Oaks - different species of *Quercus*, etc. The Mahogany tree is indigenous to central America. It is found to be growing in many places planted for shade and as an ornamental tree. It was introduced into India towards the end of the 18th centry. Most famous of the timber trees in India are the Teak — *TECTONA GRANDIS* L.f. and the Sal-*SHOREA ROBUSTA* Gaertn. which are described below.

TECTONA GRANDIS L.F. — Verbenaceae

The Teak

A tall tree, deciduous, with chanelled quadrangular branches. Leaves simple, opposite, elliptic or slightly obovate, acute or acuminate at apex, cuneate at base, scabrous above and stellately tomentose beneath, with entire margin, 25-50 cm. long 20-40 cm. broad; peiole 2.5-4 cm. long. Panicles large, terminal, with small bracts. Flowers small white, hermaphrodite, slightly irregular. Calyx persistent, gamosepalous, 5-6-lobed, much enlarged in fruit. Corolla tubular below, with 5-6 lobes above. Stamens 5-6 epipetalous, longer than the corolla. Ovary superior, 2-4 celled with 1 ovule in each; style long and slender. Fruit a drupe, subglobose, somewhat 4-lobed, about 1.2 cm. in diam., enclosed by the expanded calyx. Seeds usually 1-2.

The timber is of an excellent quality. It is fairly hard and very strong and contains an oil that acts as a preservative of the timber. It is durable and takes a high polish. The timber is golden yellow at first but gradually turns dark brown. It is in great demand for cabinet — making, as building material, railway sleepers, ship-building and for various other purposes.

The teak is indigenous to India, Burma, Sri Lanka and the Malaysia. It grows over a wide area in the Peninsular India and planted in Uttar Pradesh, Bihar, Orissa and W.Bengal Total area under teak forest in India is about 7,285,000 h.a. of which 3,119,000 h.a. being in Madhya Pradesh. It grows as one of the natural components of deciduous forests and there are plantations of teak in different states.

Teak is a fairly quick growing tree. It thrives best in fairly moist and warm climate with a rainfall of not less than 125 cm. a year and a dry season of 3-5 months. It prefers a rich soil, deep and moist and sandy. It is a great light demander and can not stand frost. Laterite soil is unsuitable for growing teak and so is water-logged area.

Deficiency of Nitrogen in the soil results in stunted growth and Potassium and Calcium deficiency are harmful in the seedling stage.

In India teak regenerates naturally. For plantation purpose seedlings are raised in nurseries. Seeds are sown in April-May with spacing of 1.8 m x 1.8 m or more. Regular weeding is necessary to protect the seedlings from being choked up by the aggressive grasses and other pests. Seedlings are transplanted when 30 cm. or more long. To get good quality of timber, trees are felled in plantations after 50 years. The rotation period may however be more and upto 80 years. In plantations teak is grown as in a mixed forest with other trees, or as a pure forest.

Besides yielding excellent timber teak provides us with paper pulp and other materials from wood waste. A dye is obtained from the leaves and a fatty oil from the seeds. The flowers are used medicinally. The timber is used for internal consumption and a small quantity is exported to Middle East, Europe, Japan and Australia.

SHOREA ROBUSTA Gaertn.—Dipterocarpaceae

The Sal

Tall or medium sized tree, with resinous juice; subdeciduous; bark reddish borwn or grey, smooth or longitudnally fissured. Leaves simple, alternate, ovate-oblong, coriaceous, entire or subrepand, upto 30 cm. long and 18 cm. broad; stipules caducous. Inflorescence a lax axillary or terminal panicle. Flowers regular, hermaphrodite, small and inconspicuous. Calyx 5 - lobed, with a very short tube, adnate to the thalamus; lobes inbricate, persistent. Petals 5; stamens many. Ovary superior, 3 celled, with 2 ovules in each cell. Fruit nut — like, ovoid, 10-15 mm long and about 10 mm in diam. 1-seeded,enclosed by the persistent calyx, of which 3 outer lobes enlarged into 5-7 cm. long wings. Seed ovoid with fleshy unequal cotyledons; endosperm absent.

The Sal is indigenous to India. There is an unbroken Sal-belt in the Terai region from Ambala in Hariana running straight to the Darrang district of Assam. A patch of sal forest is also found in Kangra district of Himachal Pradesh to the West, while sal forests are also seen in Garo hills, Nowgong, Kamrup, Khasi and Jaintia hills, Tippera and in Mymensingh district of Bangladesh. Another large tract of Sal growing area comprises south western part of W. Bengal, Orissa, Andhra Pradesh, Madhya Pradesh and Chota Nagpur and Santal parganas of Bihar. From the foot hills of the Himalayas the sal climbs upto 1000 mtr. on the outer ranges and occasionally upto 1700 mtr.

Sal is a hardy tree as regards climate. It can stand frost to some extent and grows well in area with a maximum summer temparature of 44-47°C. If the soil is well drained an annual rainfall of about 450 cm. does no harm to sal. A moist deep sandy loam with good subsoil drainage appears to be best suited for sal growing, although bouldery or gravelly soils subtend extensive sal forests. An excess of clay in the subsoil produces trees of stunted growth. The tap root some times rot in clayey soil. Sal is light demanding but persists in moderate shade.

Sal comes to flower in March-April and fruits ripen in June. The seeds germinate soon after falling. For artificial germination fresh seeds should be collected and sown immediately, as the sal seeds do not keep their viability long. Line sowing is practised in the nurseries. Seedlings raised in nurseries are transplanted when 1-3 years old. Seedlings are planted with 1.5 mtr. spacing in between, and thinned out when 3-4 mtr. tall. Sal coppices well and regular coppicing is done where there is much demand for firewood and charcoal. For timber Sal tree may be felled when 30 years old but usually a tree matures after 50 years, and in a plantation a rotation is practised at an interval of a period of 80 years. Area under sal forests in India is about 10,083,000 h.a., i.e. about 13.3% of total forests in the country.

Sal is one of the best construction wood. As regards strength and durability it has perhaps no rival, the heart wood being extremely durable. But Sal does not season easily. It dries slowly, splits and warps and developes surface cracks. Sal seasoning is done in logs, under cover and is a slow process.

Timber of Sal is used in various ways. It is in great demand for sleeper wood, poles and posts, beams and rafters, floor-planks, pit props, bridges, dug out cauoes, carriages and wagons, wheels, agricultural implements, tent pegs, liquid storage vats, and also for fuel. Oleoresin is obtained by tapping the trunk. This is medicinal and is an incense and is used in various other ways. The resin on distillation gives "chua" oil.

Seeds are eaten after roasting. Seeds yield a fatty oil which is used for cooking and in lamps. The cake obtained after the extraction of the oil is used as cattle feed and poultry feed. Sal is a host of Tasar silkworm and a kind of lac-insect. The leaves of sal are made into platters and cups for serving food. Sal honey is of a very good quality.

MEDICINAL PLANTS

Scattered all over the country many important medicinal plants grow wild in the hills and the plains of India, e.g. SWERTIA CHIRAYITA Linn., PLANTAGO OVATA Forsk., HYDNOCARPUS KURZII (King) Warb., RAUVOLFIA SERPENTINA Benth. ex Kurz, STRYCHNOS NUX-VOMICA Linn. etc. A few foreign plants are also cultivated in India for their drug value and these are different species of CINCHONA, CEPHAELIS IPECACUANHA (Brot) A. Rich. (the Ipecac plant) and DIGITALIS PURPUREA Linn. Being important commercially RAUVOLFIA SERPENTINA, CEPHAELIS IPECACUANHA and CINCHONA species are grown in India.

CINCHONA — Rubiaceae

The Quinine Plants

Evergreen shrubs or trees with bitter bark. Leaves opposite, stipulate; stipules interpetiolar, caducous. Flowers in terminal panicles, hermaphrodite, regular, pentamerous, epigynous. Calyx 5 - toothed, pubescent, persistent. Corolla tubular, 5-lobed, pubescent outside, fringed with soft hairs on the margin, valvate; ovary 2-celled, inferior, with many ovules in each cell; style slender, bifid; stigma papillose. Capsule 2 valved, dehiscing septicidally from base. Seeds many, small, broadly winged, thin and compressed.

The genus consists of about 65 species growing in the forests of Andes Mts. of S. America. The bitter bark contains the alkaloid quinine which is a specific remedy in Malarial fever. Important species for the alkaloid content are C.OFFICINALIS Linn., C. SUCCIRUBRA Pav. ex Klotz, C. CALISAYA Wedd. and C. LEDGERIANA Moens. the genus is so named in honour of Countess Cinchon who introduced this important drug plant to the physicians of Europe and was instrumental for starting plantations of different species of the genus on commercial scale.

The diagnostic characters of the above 4 species are :-

C.OFFICINALIS — upto 10 m. high; leaves 10-12 cm. long, elliptic; flowers 2 cm. long.

C.SUCCIRUBRA — upto 12 m. high or taller; leaves 8-15 cm. long, ovate; fls. 1.5 - 2 cm long.

C.CALISAYA — 12 m. or more high; leaves 8 - 20 cm. oblong; flowers 1 - 2 cm.

C. LEDGERIANA — smaller plants; leaves 5 - 10 cm. lanceolate; flowers 1 cm. long.

The last species is considered by some to be a variety of C. calisaya.

Fig. 153. **Cinchona plant**

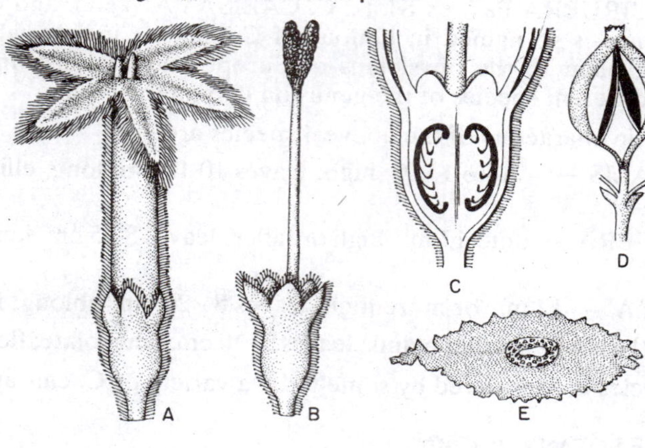

Fig. 154. Cinchona flower — (a) Flower (b) Same without perianth and androecium (c) L.S. through ovary (d) Splitting capsule (e) Winged seed.

CINCHONA plants thrive in a damp hot climate. Tropical and subtropical regions with a temperature ranging from 60° - 75° F and an annual rainfall of 250 - 325 mm (100 - 150 in.), well distributed throughout the year are well suited for growing CINCHONA. The soil should be well drained, rich in organic matters, acidic and with a Nitrogen level of 8%. The plants should be sheltered from wind. They are not frost-resistant.

Cinchona plants are propagated by seeds. Seeds have short viability. Fresh seeds are therefore sown in seed beds situated on sloping grounds. Size of seed beds are usually 3 × 1½ m. These are covered by thatched roofs. The seeds are thickly scattered on a layer of a mixture of leafmould and sand and covered by fine sand. The seed beds are lightly watered. Germination takes place in 3 - 6 weeks. Seedlings when about 3 cm. high and have 2 leaves are then transplanted in nursery beds with a thicker layer of leafmould and sand. No other organic or artificial manure is applied. Spacing of about 10 cm. is permitted in a row and between 2 rows. When the seedlings are of 14-18 months old these are transplanted in plantation-fields, usually in early monsoon. The sedlings are 50 - 70 cm. high at that time. The spacing in the plantation is 2 × 2 m. or less and shade trees are planted at intervals of 7 m. Stable-manure is applied as this increases the quinine content of the bark.

Harvesting starts from the 5th year onwards when annual thinning is necessary. The alkaloid content is maximum in trees of 10 years old or older. The bark is easily separated. Often tapping makes it more easy. Bark is collected from the basal part upto a height of 1 mtr. The root bark is also equally rich in alkaloid content and is collected when the tree is felled. Harvested bark is dried slowly in shade. In rainy season artificial heat may be applied but the bark should not be exposed to a temperature over 175°F.

For the manufacture of the drug the bark is ground to a fine powder. The powder is mixed with 1/3rd of its weight of sifted slaked lime and a 5% aquous solution of caustic soda. The mixture is extracted with high boiling kerosine. Extract is shaken with sufficient hot dilute sulphuric acid and precipitation of quinine sulphate is obtained.

In addition to quinine the bark also contains quinidine, cinchonine and cinchonidine. The quinine in addition to its antimalarial property is an insecticide. The bark can also be used in tanning.

The introduction of *Cinchona* into India has a history behind it. To meet the great demand from all over the world *Cinchona* forests were in the verge of extinction in their home and civilised world were thinking of starting plantations at suitable places in different countries. The Dutch Government introduced these plants in Java and were successful in cultivating *Cinchona* in that island. Dr. Royle suggested its introduction in India as early as 1852 and sent several reports to the secretary of State for India. T. Anderson, the then Superintendent of Botanic Garden in Sibpur also supported Royle and suggested several places for cultivation of *Cinchona*. Orders were received to that effect and cultivation was started in 1861 in Sikkim and the Nilgiri hills. In 1867 Cinchona — cultivation was started but later abandoned in the Khasi hills. In Kangra and different other parts of N.W. India plantations were started but later abandoned for various reasons. Plantation of Cinchona was started in Bhootan but was not found profitable. Several private plantations were started in S. India as early as 1862 but did not prove profitable. At present it is cultivated in the plantations at Mungpoo in the Darjeeling District and the plantation is maintained by the W. Bengal government.

RAUVOLFIA SERPENTINA (Linn.) Benth. ex Kurz. — Apocynaceae

Vernacular name — SARPAGANDHA

(See also under Pharmacognosy)

Glabrous undershrub, upto a mtr. high. Leaves ternately whorled, elliptic — laceolate, acuminate, entire, smooth and shinning, deep green above and pale beneath, 4 - 18 cm. long. Inflorescence terminal cymose umbelliform panicle, usually many flowered. Flowers bisexual, actinomorphic, hypogynous, bracteate with small subulate bracts. Calyx 5 - fid, glabrous, bright red; segments lanceolate, 2 mm. long, imbricate. Corolla tubular 1 - 1.5 cm. long, rose or pink; tube slender, swollen at middle, hairy at the throat, rarely curved; lobes 5, 3 - 4 mm. long, elliptic, rounded at apex, imbricate. Stamens 5, inserted in the dilated portion of the corolla-tube. A membranous cupular disc is present. Carpels 2, superior,style filiform; stigma with a broad calyptriform base, 2 - fid at the tip; ovules 2 in each carpel. Fruit a single or didymous drupe, 4 - 5 mm. in diam; purplish black when ripe.

The species is indigenous in India, Bangladesh, Burma, Ceylon and Malayasia. In India it is found in the mixed deciduous forests from the foot of the Himalayas to Kerala. It is no where abundant but grows scattered in the fringe of the forests, in open jungles and village shrubberies. It prefers a humid tropical climate but can stand a dry heat of about 110°F. for a short period. It grows well in gravelly or loamy soil with an annual rainfall of 1250 mm. to 3500 mm. provided the soil is well drained. The drug is collected from wild source but to meet the demand cultivation has been started on a small scale by the forest authorities in different states.

The plants are propagated from seeds which are swon direct in the plantation in rows with spacing of 70-80 cm. in the rows and about 1 mtr. between the rows. The plants are ready for harvesting after 2 years. In collecting wild plants those with a stem of 1 cm. or more in diam. are gathered. In *R. serpentina* the alkaloids are present in the root, more in the bark and less in the woody portions of the same. In other parts these are present in negligble quantities.

The alkaloids contained in the root of *R.serpentina* are several, the most important is the RESERPINE used to lower high blood pressure. Other alkaloids are : *Reserpinine, Serpentine, Serpentinine, Rauvolfinine,* etc. All are useful in different ways. The crude drug, i.e. the root is exported every year and the quantity is about 150,000 kg. and about 30,000 kg. is required for internal market.

Several other species of *Rauvolfia* grow wild in India and *R. tetraphylla* Linn. of the West Indies is naturalised in the coastal districts. *R. tetraphylla* contains similar alkaloids in the leaves and other parts but in less quantities. This differs from *R. serpentina* in having soft ,emareld green leaves, 4 in a whorl and smaller white flowers.

Other Indian species of the genus are :

R. beddomei Hk.f. — S. India, *R. decurva Hk.f.* — S.India, *R.densiflora* Benth — Khasi hills and S. India, and *R. micrantha Hk.f.* — Malabar. All these species contain reserpine in small quantities and segregation of the alkaloid from these plants is not commerclally profitable. Used as crude drug they do not yield the desired result.

RUBBER

Rubber is obtained from the latex of several species of plants the most important of which is Hevea brasiliensis (H.B.K.) M. Arg. and the rubber obtained from this tree is known as Para rubber. This tree is indigenous to Brazil but is cultivated in many tropical countries including India and forms the chief source of commercial rubber. Other rubber yielding plants are:—Manihot glaziovi M. Arg. Ficus elastica Roxb. and Taraxacum Koksaghyz Rodin.

HEVEA BRASILIENSIS M. Arg.

(Euphorbiaceae)

Para rubber

Tall trees, 25–35 mtr.; stem smooth, straight, unbranched up to a considerable height and then forming a leafy canopy; bark greyish with copious milky latex. Leaves trifoliolate, alternate or subopposite, at the end of the branchlets, long petioled; leaflets glabrous, elliptic-lanceolate, acuminate, entire, 10–15 cm. long; petiole 7—10 cm. long, glandular at apex. Flowers small sweet-scented, unisexual, in large, terminal, panicled cymes. Calyx 5-toothed or lobed. Corolla absent. Disc of 5 free or united glands. Stamens 5–10, filaments united to form a column; anthers sessile on the column. Ovary superior, 3-celled, with one ovule in each cell; stigma subsessile 2-lobed. Fruit a capsule, dehiscing into 3 one seeded cocci; seeds ellipsoid, 3–4 cm. long, mottled brown and shinning.

Hevea brasiliensis is indigenous to Brazil, Venezuella, Peru, Equador and Columbia. It is cultivated in India, Ceylon, Burma, Malay, Sumatra, Java, Borneo, Sarawak, Siam, Indo-china and in Equatorial Africa. In India rubber plantations were first started in Kerala in 1905 from seeds obtained from Ceylon. Ceylon was however the first country in Asia to start cultivating Hevea brasiliensis from seedlings sent from Royal Botanic Garden, Kew in 1876.

The latex of *H. brasiliensis* is obtained by tapping the bark of the trunk. The overflowing latex is collected in a plastic or enamel cup containing a small amount of preservative viz. Ammonia or Sodium sulphite or Formaldihyde to prevent coagulation As the latex stops flowing the cups are emptied into buckets which are carried to the factory. The liquid is strained first through a course sieve to remove the dirt and other impurities. It is then diluted and strained for second time through a fine sieve. The latex is an aquous serum with a colloidal suspension of rubber particles.

A warm, humid and equable climate is suitable for growing *H. brasiliensis.* It thrives well in tropical countries lying between latitudes 15°N and 10°S with a temperature ranging from 74°F and 95°F. A rainfall of 1750 mm. to 2500 mm. well distributed throughout the year is ideal for its healthy growth. Prolonged rainfall or prolonged drought are unfavourable while moderate showers alternating with sunny weather are much needed.

Deep well-drained loamy soil is best for *H. brasiliensis.* The pH value should range from 3.8 to 8.0. In alkaline soil the growth is stunted.

To start a rubber plantation a forest area is cleared of trees and undergrowths and these are left there for sometime. The tree trunks and the branches are then removed and the leaves that fall on the soil are allowed to rot. Arrangement is made for good drainage and terraces are prepared according to the sloping of the land. Square type of pits are dug in lines, 2/3 mtr. deep and of similar width. Pits are filled with surface soil and organic manure. Seedlings raised in the nursery or clones are transplanted in the pits during monsoon 200 per acre or more. Later the plants are thinned out and about 150 are left in a field of one acre.

Seeds are sown in seed beds in the nursery in winter and germinate in 1–3 weeks time. Seedlings attain a height of one mtr. or more in 6 months' time when they are ready for transplanting. In trees raised from seeds the yield of latex varies. In some the flow of latex is high while in others it is much less. So that in a plantation it is desirable to have all high yielding trees. So instead of transplanting seedlings, transplanting of budded clones are practised.

Such clones are prepared in the nurseries. Buds taken from high yielding trees are grafted near the base of vigorously growing seedlings about one year old. After a period of one month or a little more the budded stocks are stumped 15–20 cm. above the grafted bud. In another fortnight the budded stumps are ready for transplanting. After transplanting all other branches excepting the shoot developing from the grafted bud are pruned off.

Suitable cover crops are grown very close to check soil erosion and surface run off. For this purpose *Pueraria phaseoloides* Bth, *Centrosoma pubescens* Bth, species of *Crotalaria, Indigofera, Desmodium,* etc. are generally used. These enrich the soil also.

Sulphate of Ammonia and other nitrogenous fertilizers are used for manuring and this is important when cultivated lands are converted into rubber plantations. For grown up trees in a plantation, potash, phosphate and other fertilizers are used.. Small quantity of magnesium is often added.

The rubber trees are susceptible to fruit-rot disease and die-back disease. The former is controlled by spraying Bordeaux mixture and other by cutting off the affected portions and burning them. Black thread disease appear in the tapping cuts and this can be prevented by painting that portion with a 5% solution of Brunolium, Agriosol, Solignum or Jodelite. White ants often cause great damage to the trees. These are rubbed off and the tree trunks are painted with tar or kerosine.

Tapping is done on the base of the trunk up to a height of 1¾ mtr. from the ground. Cuts are made by removing a thin shaving of bark by special tapping knives. Usually the cut extends half way around the trunk but it may completely encircle it, i.e. half spiral system or full spiral system. It may also be a V-cut system or herring bone-cut system. The cut is made at 30–35° to the horizontal from upper to lower end of the cut and a vertical cut is made to conduct the latex to a cup placed below. In V-cut system two slanting incisions are made and at the base of their junction a cup is placed where the latex is collected. In herring bone system a vertical cut is made in the bark with 4–6 diagonal cuts on either sides. The cuts extend from one fourth to one half of the circumference of the trunk. A cup is placed bellow the vertical cut to receive the latex. The latex is collected through a small spout fixed into the bark.

Tapping is done early in the morning when the flow of latex is vigorous. The flow diminishes with the rise of temperature and ceases in about 3 hours. The latex is then transferred into large pails or buckets.

Tapping is done every alternate day. The yield increases with the repeated scrapings which is stopped before any injury is done to the cambial tissues. New tappings are done one below the other till it reaches almost the ground level on one side of the tree in a period of 5—6 years. After that tapping is done on the other side of the tree trunk and continued for another period of 5–6 years. Tapping commences when the tree is 7–8 years old.

Increase of flow of latex is effected by treating the bark below the tapping cut with hormones. Seedling trees respond better to such hormone treatment than the bud-grafts. Poor yielding trees are thus converted to high yielding ones.

Fresh latex is susceptible to enzymic and bacterial action leading to acid formation and coagulation. Preservatives and bactericide are added to the latex at the time of collection to inhibit acid development. Amonia (mainly) formaldehyde, Sodium hydroxide, soap and bactericides are used as preservatives. Usually a small quantity of ammoniated water is placed in the collection cup to prevent coagulation. Addition of 3 parts of 25% Ammonia solution to 100 parts of latex ensures the stabilisation of the latter for six months. Stabilised fresh latex free from sludge containing 30–40% of solids is called "Normal latex". By evaporation, creaming or centrifugation it is concentrated to give a product with higher solid contents. Concentration by eletro-decantation is popularly practised.

The latex is a colloidal suspension of rubber particles in an aqueous serum. Rubber content is richer in hard bark than in the soft bark. Other constituents in the latex are proteins, resins, sugar and glycosoids, tannins, alkaloids and mineral salts.

Raw rubber is obtained from the latex. There are two types of raw rubber, viz.

smoked sheet rubber and crepe rubber. To obtain the former type the latex is diluted with water and strained through a sieve to remove the impurities. This is them coagulated by adding Acetic acid or Formic acid. After adding the acid the latex is poured into aluminium pans or tanks and allowed to stand overnight. The rubber coagulates and floats on the surface as spongy slabs. As the slabs become firm these are taken out and washed in clean water. Washed slabs are pressed between smooth rollers to squeeze out the water and flatten them to a thickness of 3 mm. The sheets are passed through marking rolls to impart a ribbed pattern. The ribbed sheets are dried on racks or poles in shade for a few hours and then smoked in smoking rooms to make them immune to the attack of moulds. The dried sheets are translucent, amber coloured and elastic. These are then packed for the market.

For crepe rubber the diluted and cleaned latex is mixed with Sodium bisulphite and acid. The coagulated substance is cut into long pieces, squeezed, sheared and masticated through a series of differently geared corrugated rollers. It is then rolled into sheets with rough or corrugated rollers. It is finally rolled into sheets and dried by hanging on racks in well-ventilated drying rooms. Heat is often applied to hasten drying. The sheets are then packed in bales for the market.

In India about 70,000 acres of land are under rubber (H. brasiliensis) plantation. All plantations are located in the south, 91% being in Kerala, 7% in Tamil Nadu and 2% in Karnataka. Annual production is about 27,000 tons and is insufficient to meet the internal requirements of this country.

MANIHOT GLAZIOVI Muell-Arg.

(Euphorbiaceae)

Ceara rubber

This also is a native of Brazil. It is a small tree not exceeding 12 mtr in height, with a thick bark peeling off in horizontal strips. Leaves long petioled, palmipartite.

The tree is suitable for tapping when 5-years old. Continuous tapping is injurious and kills the tree in a few years time. The yield of latex as well as the quality is poor in comparison to that of *H. brasiliensis*.

FICUS ELASTICA Roxb.

(Moraceae)

India rubber

It is a large tree with prop roots. Leaves thick and glossy, 12–30 cm. long. Flowers minute, densly arranged in a hypanthodium. The hypanthodia occur in pairs in axils of fallen leaves.

The stem and the main branches as well as the thicker aerial roots are tapped for the latex. The latex coagulates readily. A part coagulates in the cut portion of the trunk while the rest flows down and is collected on mats where it coagulates. The coagulum from cut portion of the tree is pulled out and collected from the mats. The coagulum is then dried, cleaned and pressed into cubes.

The latex is acidic, slightly so when fresh but the acidity increases on keeping. The resin content in the latex is high and the rubber hardens on aging. It is inferior to para-or ceara—rubber.

The tree is indigenous to India and is common from Nepal tarai to Assam and extends to Burma.

TARAXACUM KOKSAGHYZ Rodin.

(Compositae)

Russian Rubber Plant

Small herbaceous plant growing as a weed in temperate countries. It is cultivated in Russia.

The leaves are basal, lyrate or pinnatifid. Capitulum terminates a hollow scape. Flowers all ligulate, yellow. The involucral bracts have prominent horn-like appendages.

The latex is obtained from the roots and the rubber is of good quality.

CHAPTER - XI

PHARMACOGNOSY

AIMS AND OBJECTS

Pharmacognosy is that branch of science that deals with the drugs, their identification, collection, uses, etc. The study of the action of the drug also comes under the perview of pharmacognosy. It has been a part of the Medial Science since the dawn of civilisation. The Babylonians were aware of the Medicinal effects of a number of plants. The ancient Egyptians possessed a sound knowledge of human anatomy as well as a knowledge of the medicinal uses of many plants and animals. In a treatise known as **Papyrys Ebers** – written in 1550 B.C. and discovered in a tomb of a mummy, much has been said about the skill and knowledge of those people in this field. In India also the study of the drugs was started about 5000 years ago at the time of the **Vedas.**

Hippocrates (460 — 370 B.C.) deals with anatomy and physiology in many of his treatises. He is referred to as the father of medicine. Aristotle (384 — 322 B.C.), the great philisopher wrote much about the animal kingdom and his writings were placed on scientific footing free from all superstitions. His disciple Theophrastus (370 — 287 B.C.) wrote about plants and like his master discarded superstitious beliefs while describing medicinal uses of plants. Dioscorides a Greek physician of the 1st Century A.D. was the writer of the first Materia Medica (78 A.D.) Here he described 600 medicinal plants, including Belladona, Colchicum, Opium, Hyoscyamus, etc. Galen, another Greek physician residing in Rome (131 — 200 A.D.) described the method of preparing drugs of vegetable and animal origin and laid down many formulas contained in a trearise of 20 volumes. Gradually the knowledge of medicine and pharmacy separated as distinct subjects of study and the physicians and pharmacists followed professions in separate lines. The term pharmacology was introduced by C.A. Seydler, a surgeon of Germany in 1815 to designate the applied science that deals with the biological, biochemical and economical features of natural drugs and their constituents.

A drug is an article of vegetable origin or derived from animal or mineral kingdom. It is used in the treatment of diseases, in curing, mitigation and prevention. A crude drug is available in small bits or slices, in powdered or shreded forms, or in the pressed specimens. The pharmacognostical study therefore teaches us the source of the drug, collection, drying, preservation and storage of the same, identification of the material, parts to be used and cleaning of the materials. The study included the extractions, separation and isolation of the component constituents of plant and animal drugs. It teaches us also to find out whether the drug is contaminated or not, and the substitutes. To classify the drugs morphologically and also according to their therapeutic properties comes also under the perview of pharmacognosy.

Collection and preparation of drugs

Medicinal plants are sometimes cultivated and drugs are collected from cultivated plants. But very often drugs are collected from wild plants growing in different parts of the world in various ecolocical conditions. Persons engaged in the collection of drugs should therefore be experts in their profession. Carelessness or ignorance on the part of the collector may result in gathering completely different material or mixed up articles. The proper time of harvesting the cultivated medicinal plants or gathering the drug from wild plant is to be taken into consideration as the nature and quantity of the constituents vary greatly in some species in different seasons. Drugs should therefore be collected when the active principle is at its highest in the plant. Different types of drugs, i.e. roots, leaves etc. should therefore be collected at different phases of the life of the plants and some general rules have been formulated for collection of the drugs. The rules generally followed are given below :

1. Roots and rhizomes should be collected when the vegetative growth of the plant is almost over, if collected earlier the roots shrink after some time.
2. Barks are collected in spring before the starting of annual growth.
3. Leaves and flowering tops are to be collected when photosynthetic action is going on very actively.
4. Flowers are usually collected just when they are fully open but in some cases these are collected when half open or even in bud condition.
5. Fruits are collected when full grown but still unripe in some cases, whereas in other cases fruits are collected when fully ripe.
6. Seeds are collected from fully ripe fruits. An expert collector knows which material is to be collected at what stage of maturity.

The mode of harvesting also varies in case of different types of drugs. Some are collected by engaging manual labour but mechanical devices are applied wherever suitable being much economical. Mechanical methods cannot replace manual labour when selected parts of the plant are only to be collected. Sometimes harvesting is therefore done by combined methods. For example plant materials required for distillation are harvested with a mower and hauled directly to dryers. When dry, the leaves are separated by hands. In case of small fruits or seeds e.g. caraway, flax seed etc. the fruits or fruiting tops are gathered with a combination of mower and binder. The fruits and seeds are later separated by threshing. Barks are collected striping by hand. Roots and other under ground parts are collected by hand as well as by mechanical devices. e.g. plough, potatodigger or shrubber-lifter.

Organoleptic studies

Organoleptic studies refer to evaluation of a drug by means of different organs of the human body or by sense, such as appearance of the drug material, its odour and taste. The sound or the 'snap' of its fracture and the touch of the drug are also helpful in the evaluation. Macroscopic characteristics are of 5 types, viz. (i) shape and size of the material, (2) colour and external markings, (3) fracture and internal colour (4) odour and (5) taste.

Crude drugs are available in markets in various farms. Leaves, flowers, fruits, seeds and some roots and rhizomes are brought as entire material. Wood, bark and some root and rhizome may come in cut, broken or sliced form. Sometimes they are matted together or in bales, may be pressed together or in powder. Often these are given different shapes. Sometimes roots, rhizomes and barks come to the market after removal of the periderm.

Drugs derived from the underground parts, e.g. rhizomes, roots, bulbs, corms and tubers are found in the market (1) as entire (2) in longitudinal slices (3) in oblique or transverse slices (4) cut in small cubical pieces or (5) broken into pieces. The shape may be cylindrical or subcylindrical, conical, fusiform, ovoid, terete or disc-shaped. The material may be simple or branched, straight or curved or twisted, the base and apex of the article are also to be determined i.e. the direction of growth is an important character. The size of the material is given in terms of length and diameter. If the material is conical in shape the diameter of the broader end as well as of the narrower end is to be noted.

The external colour of the material is to be given, and in case of bark material the colour of the outer surface and also of the inner surface should be noted. External markings are also noted. Such markings are classified as ridges and furrows, wrinkles, fissures, projection and scars.

The fracture or the nature of breaking may be (1) complete, (2) incomplete, (3) short, (4) fibrous, (5) splintery, (6) brittle, (7) tough and (8) weak. The nature of the fractured surface is also to be considered and it may be (1) even surface, (2) uneven surface, (3) granular surface, (4) hard surface, (5) horny surface, (6) mealy surface (7) resinous surface, (8) concoidal surface and (9) waxy surface. The colour of the fractured surface is known as the internal colour.

Exudates are products formed in the metabolic process of the plant or are pathologic products. They include gums, resins, mucilages, oleoresin, juices, latex, tar, extracts, etc. These occur in the form of tears, cylindrical pieces, rounded or flattened masses,angular masses and agglutinated masses.

Odour and taste of the durg-material are also considered important. The odour may be distinct or indistinct. The material may have a distinct taste or may be tasteless imsipid. The taste is distinct, may be acid, saline, saccharine or terpentine, and the material is classified accordingly.

GINGER

Botanical name : ZINGIBER OFFICINALE Roscoe

Family :-ZINGIBERAÇEAE

Description : Aromatic herb with an underground rhizome and an erect stem, upto 75 cm. in height,. Leaves simple, alternate, linear-lanceolate, sheathing at the base, sessile, acuminate at apex, glabrosus, upto 15 cm.long. Inflorescence a spike on a distinct scape; flowers densely arranged, bisexual, irregular, each subtended by a persistent scarious bract. Calyx tubular shortly 3-lobed; corolla bilabiate, tubular below, yellow with purplish spots stamens 3 in one whorl, one of which is perfect the other 2 united to form a labellum; filament of perfect stamen short, anther cells contiguous, connective produced into a beak, ovary of 3 carpels, syncarpous, 3-celled, inferior; ovules many on axile placentas; style filiform, lying in a groove of the anther; stigma subglobose. Fruit an oblong capsule, many seeded; seeds arillate, globose, with a small embryo and copious endosperm.

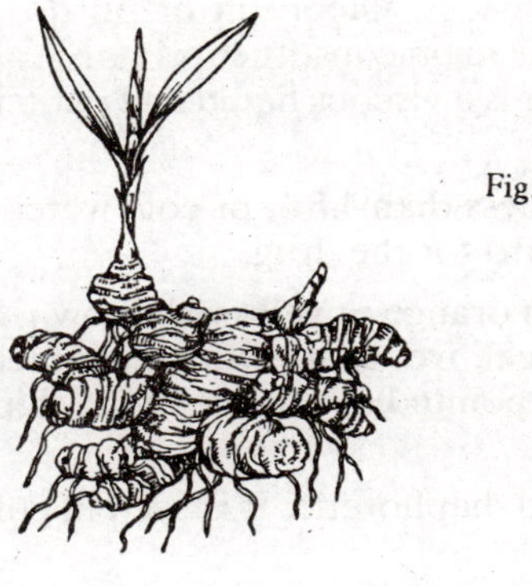

Fig. 155. **Zingiber officinale : Rhizome and an aerial shoot.**

Distribution : Ginger is indigenous to Indo-Malayan region and has been in cultivation in India since prehistoric times. It is now cultivated over a greater part of the tropical and temperate regions. The chief ginger growing countries of the world are India, China, Australia, East Indies, West Indies, Mexico, Jamaica, North Africa and West Africa.

Parts used : Rhizome.

The ginger rhizome is much branched, somewhat resembling the palm of a hand with fingers. It has circular scars representing the nodes with small scales. Fibrous roots are emitted from these nodes. Buds developing in the axil of these scales come up as aerial schoots with normal leaves. The rhizome continues to grow underground while the aerial shoots die out annually and the tail end of the rhizome also perishes when old.

Cultivation and Preparation : The plant is propogated from rhizome-cuttings. Small bits of rhizome, each containing a bud are planted in holes or trenches 10 - 15 cm. deep and about 30 cm. apart in Summer i.e. from March to May. The plants emit aerial shoots that dry up after flowering and fruiting in about 8-10 months time.

The rhizomes are then dug up and washed. During the growing season abundant rainfall is necessary but at no time water-logging should be permitted.

The rhizomes are then peeled and washed in clean water often containing lime-juice. The cleaned materials are then dried in sun for 5-6 days, taking care that they do not get damped or mouldy during the drying period. They are then bleached by washing and again dried for 2 days. This is how the Jamaica ginger is made.

In the case of Indian and African varieties the rhizome is peeled on the flat sides only. It is then treated with boiling water and then dried in sun. Some times the dug-up rhizomes are washed in clear water and peeled or scrapped and then coated with carbonate or sulphate of lime. This protects the rhizomes from insect attack.

The skin gathered from such peeled rhizomes often distilled and oil is obtained.

Commercial varieties : These are known from the place of origion, e.g. Indian ginger, African ginger, Chinese ginger and Jamican ginger. Indian ginger is again known as Cochin variety. Calicut variety and Calcutta variety from the ports wherefrom the material is exported. Two other varieties are known e.g. the Japanese ginger and Martinique ginger, the former being obtained from **Zingiber mioga** Roscoe and the other from **Z.zerumbet** Rosc ex Sm. This grows also in India and is locally called Karpoor haridra or Karpoor Kachuri.

Microscopical character : Below the epidermis the cortex is composed of parenchyma cells several layers thick with intercellular spaces. Oleoresin or oil drops are found scattered within the parenchymatous cells. The main constituent is starch and fibre. The oleoresin that gives pungent taste to the ginger is a viscous liquid and contains the active principle — the gingerol.

Standard : Ether soluble extraction of not less than 4.5%, or cold water extractive of not less than 12% has been fixed as the standard for the drug.

Powdered ginger : The powder is yellowish orange or yellowish brown. Starch grains are numerous, 5 - 40 μ in diam. nearly spherical, frequently with a characteristic beak, slightly lamellated; fibres long, with rounded, pointed or oblique ends, thin walled with oblique pits.

Uses : Ginger is stimulant, carminative and diaphoretic. It is used in cold and cough and as a febrifuge.

It is used to flavour food stuff, beer and other drinks. It is used as a condiment in curries.

Average dose : For medicinal use the dose recommended is 0.6 - 1.3 grm.

Adulterants : Ginger rhizome is often mixed with rhizome of **Z.casumunar** Roxb. The Martinique ginger (**Z.zerumbet**) and the Japanese ginger (**Z.mioga**) are also used as adulterants.

Powdered ginger is adulterated with various things, e.g. rice-powder, wheat-flour, powder of flax seed and ginger waste.

RAUVOLFIA

(See under Economic Botany.)

Botanical name : RAUVOLFIA SERPENTINA (L.) Bth. ex Kurz

Family : APOCYNACEAE

Description : Glabrous undershrubs, unbranched or with few branches, upto 1 m. high. Leaves whorled, 3 at each node, simple, elliptic lanceolate, acuminate, entire, upto 17 cm. long and 5.5 cm. broad. dark green and shinning above, pale beneath; petiole upto 1 cm. long. Inflorescence a terminal umbelliform cyme, often appearing as lateral due to the growth of the shoot. Flowers hermaphrodite, actinomarphic, short pedicelled, bracteate Calyx 5-fid, bright scarlet; segments 2 mm. long. Corolla salver-shaped, densely hairy inside, pink or rose; tube slender, slightly dilated at the middle, 1-1.5 cm. long; lobes 5; elliptic oblong, 3-4 mm. long, imbricate, stamens 5, inserted at the swollen portion of the corolla tube, included. Disc cupshaped, membranous; obscurely lobed. Carpels 2, connate; ovules 2 in each carpel, style filiform, stigma broad, calyptriform at base and 2-fid at the tip. Fruit a single drupe or didymous and connate, about 5 mm. in daim, purplish black when ripe.

Distribution : Indigenous to India occurring almost all over the country in the plains excepting the arid regions and climbing upto an elevation of 1200 mtr. in the hills. It is however, nowhere abundant. It is also found in the Andamans, Ceylon, Bangladesh, Burma, Malay, Thailand and Japan. It is also cultivated in a small scale in other tropical countries.

Parts used : Root of mature plant in dry state.

Description of the drug : The root is stout, upto 40 cm. long, some times branched, cylindrical to cylindrical-tapering, about 2 cm. in daim in the wider end, externally greyish yellow to brown, often with purplish blotches, slightly wrinkled, course and rough with longitudinal and irregular markings on the surface; fracture short, irregular, breaking with a snap and exhibiting some projecting strands of cork along periphery, wood yellowish white to pale yellow, of hard texture, indistinct odour and bitter taste.

Collection and preparation : Root should be collected with bark in tact in autumn from plants which are 3-4 years old.

Uses : The root is purgative, anthelnintic, a sedative and hypotensive and is an antidote for snake — and insect-bite; now mostly used in hypertension.

Constituents : The root contains many alkaloids the most important of which is **reserpine** which is a specific remedy in hypertension and certain neuropsychiatric disorders.

Dose : Reserpine — 0.5 mg. 1-4 times daily; or crude drug - 100 mg.

Trade : A small quantity is used in India by the pharmaceutical firms while 20600 kg. of roots and 600 kg. of the alkaloid are exported annually to other countries.

CHIRATA

Botanical name : SWERTIA CHIRAYITA (Roxb. ex Flem.) Karst

Family : GENTIANACEAE

Description : Erect annual herb, upto 1.5 mtr. high; stem cylindric below, 4-angled above and slightly winged, dark purple in colour; pith stout. Leaves alternate, subsessile broadly lanceolate, acute at both ends, 5-nerved, 3-6 cm. long; lower often larger and petioled. Racemes axillary in the upper part of the stem forming a leafy panicle. Flowers small,bisexual, tetramerous, in small fascicles on the racemes, about 1 cm. across. Sepals 4, lanceolate much smaller than petals. Petals 4, lanceolate, acute, greenish yellow, tinged with purple, each with 2 glandular depressions near base and hairy above the depressions. Stamens 4, filaments slender, free, Ovary superior, 1-celled, ovules many, parietal; style cylindric, filiform; stigma bilobed. Capsule 5-8 cm. seeds many-angled.

Distribution : Chirata grows wild in the Himalayas, from Kashmir to Bhutan at elevations between 1200 - 3000 mtr. and also in the Naga and Khasi hills.

Parts used : The dried plant.

Description of the drug : Available in market as dry entire plants or as broken pieces, dark brown in colour; wood of stem porous with easily separable pith; root conical; odour indistinct; taste very bitter.

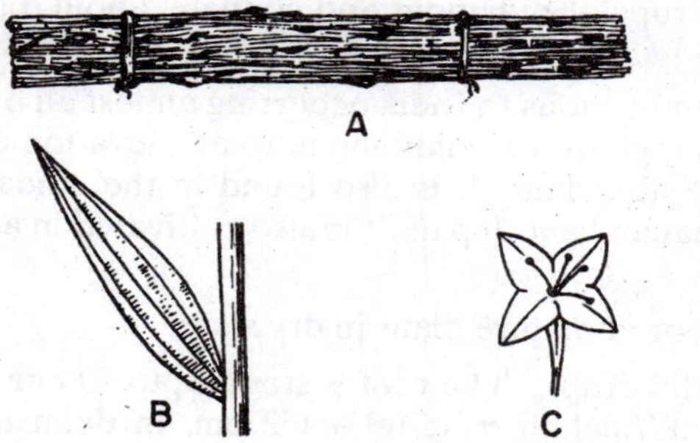

Fig. 156. Swertia chirayita :
(A) Bundle of dry stems; (B) Leaf
(C) Flower.

Preparation : The plants are uprooted and gathered in fruiting condition, carefully dried and tied in bundles with bamboo strips. These bundles are then packed into bales and exported.

Uses : It is used as a simple bitter and also as a medicine. It is a stomachic tonic and febrifuge and possesses antidiarhoetic properties.

Constituents : Amarogensin, Chiratin (a simple glucoside), Chiratogenin, ophelic acid, resin and tanin.

Average dose : 1 gram.

Adulterants : **S. angustifolia** Linn. **S. pulchella** Linn, **S. corymbosa** Benth. and **S decussata** Linn. are often mixed with **S. chirayita.** These are less bitter and have little or no pitch.

S. chinensis Franchet a smaller herb is a better substitute of S. chirayita.

Trade : After meeting the internal demand India exports 70000 kg to 80000 kg of Chirata to other countries, the major part going to West Asiatic countries.

VASAK OR ADHATODA

Botanical name : ADHATODA ZEYLANICA Medic.Syn. **A.vasica** Nees. **Justicea adhatoda** Linn

Family : ACANTHACEAE

Description : Tall shrubs, upto 2.5 mtr. high; younger parts tomentose. Leaves opposite, elliptic or elliptic-lanceolate, accuminate, obtuse or acute at base, entire, upto 18 cm long; petiole 1.5 - 2.5 cm. long; secondary veins 10 - 13 pairs; tomentose when young, glabrous afterwards. Inflorescence a dense terminal spike upto 7.5 cm. long on a peduncle upto 8 cm. long, or a fascicle at the axil of upper leaves, bracteate; bracts boradly elliptic, 5 - 7 — nerved from the base, longer than calyx, bacteoles oblong — lanceolate, 1-nerved, ciliate at the margin. Flowers subsessile, bisexual, zygomorphic, hypogynous. Calyx shortly campanulate with 5 lanceolate acute lobes, upto 1.2 cm long.

Fig. 157. Adhatoda – (A) A twigi
(B) One flower.

Corolla bilabiate, white with pinkish violet tinge at the throat upto 3 cm. long, minutely pubescent outside; tube upto 1.2 cm. long, narrow at base, much inflated above; upper lip ovate-oblong, notched at the middle, lower lip 3-lobed, recurved, oblong with rounded tip, the middle one broader; lips of corolla imbricate. Stamens 2, inserted at the throat of corolla; filaments hairy at base; anthers 2-celled; cells oblong, minutely apiculate, one cell little higher up than the other. A cup-like disc usually present. Ovary bicarpellary syncarpous, 2-celled, superior, tomentose; ovules 2 in each cell; style filiform, subclavate above; stigma entire. Fruit a clavate capsule upto 2 cm. long, contracted below into a solid stipe. Seeds 1 or 2, 5-6 mm. suborbicular, compressed, glabrous and rugose.

Distribution : This is found in the plains of India in wild condition and is cultivated in a small scale in village shrbberies. Outside India it is found in Bangladesh, Burma, Malaya and Sri Lanka.

Parts used : Leaves; fresh or dry.

Constituents : Alkaloid vasicine and adhatodic acid.

Uses : It is an expectorant and in asthama is antispamodic. It is used in the form of a liquid extract in alcohol or freshly expressed juice. Powder of dry leaves is also used.

Dose : Alcoholic extract — 1.3-4 ml; fresh juice — 4-15 ml.

Powder — 18 grains.

DITA BARK

Botanical name : ALSTONIA SCHOLARIS (L.-) R. Br.

Family : APOCYNACEAE

Description : A medium sized tree with milky latex, upto 45mtr. high, evergreen. Leaves whorled, oblanceolate, obtuse at apex, gradully tapering to base, margin entire; coriacious; petiole 7-10 mm. Inflorescence an umbellately branched cymose panicle, bracteate, terminal or subterminal. Flowers hermaphrodite, actinomorphic, small and inconspicuous, with rather an unpleasant smell. Calyx 3 mm.long, with 5 obtuse lobes pubescent and ciliate on the margin of lobes. Corolla salver-shaped, 5-lobed; tube 8 mm

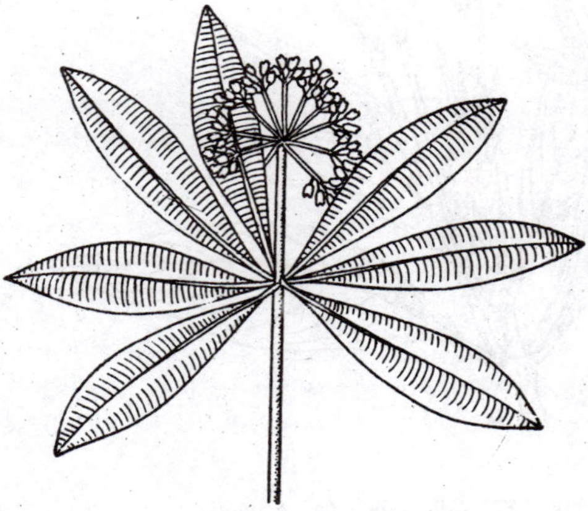

Fig. 158. Alstonia scholaris : A twig with leaves and flowers.

long, villous inside; lobes oblong, rounded at apex, 5 mm. long. Stamens 5, inserted near the top of and included within the tube; anthers subacute. Carpels 2, distinct at base, superior; style filiform, oblong at top with 2-fid stigma; ovules numerous in each cell, many seriate. Fruit a pair of linear follicles, 30-50 cm. long, cylindric and pendulous. Seeds 5-7 mm.long, linear oblong, flattened, with rounded ends and hairy at each end, peltately attached.

Distribution : **A.scholaris** is indigenous to a wide area in the Eastern Asia including India, Sri Lanka, etc. In India it grows in the plains and at lower altitudes in the hills and is planted as an avenue tree in the cities.

Parts used : The bark, known as DITA BARK is astrinengt and bitter.

Constituents : The alkaloid contents of the bark are mainly ditamine, echitamine and echitamidin.

Uses : Echitamine is beneficial in malarial fever.

Dose : The tincture contains 12% of the drug and the dose recommended is 2 - 4 ml.

IPECAC

CEPHAELIS IPECACUANHA (Brot) A. Rich

Family : RUBIACEAE

Small straggling shrub, 1 m. high with a slender rhizome bearing spreading gnarled roots 10-15 cm. long having thick brownish bark. Leaves opposite, elliptic, stipulate, 7-10 cm. long and 3-5 cm. broad; stipule intrapetiolar, Flowers regular, hermaphrodite, small and white in terminal involucrate cymes, Calyx tube short 5 toothed. Corolla tube short, 5 lobed. Stamens 5, inserted on the corolla tube. Ovary inferior, 2 celled, with basal erect ovule in each cell; style short with 2 stigmatic branches. Fruit small, globose or oblong, with two 1 seeded plano-convex pyrenes.

The plant is indigenous to Brazil and adjacent countries. It is cultivated on a commercial scale in Malaya and to a small extent in India, Burma and Sri Lanka.

In India it was first introduced in the Botanic Garden, Sibpur in 1866 and cultivation was started in Rungbi and other parts of Sikkim in 1868. From the Botanic Garden, Sibpur plants were distributed to Assam and Andamans, Burma, Malaya and Sri Lanka in 1877. It is now grown in India at Mangpoo in Darjeeling district, Bosego and Sinduhani in Jalpaigooree district of North Bengal, Jorhat and Srimangal in Assam, Bilaspur in Orissa and Kollar in the Nilgiries.

There are several commercial varieties, e.g. **Hio, Matto-grosso, Minas** and **Manaos.** These come from Brazil. The best quality of drug is obtained from Matto-grosso which grows wild. **Indian** and **Johore** varieties are cultivated in India and adjacent countries.

Ipecac plant is slow-growing. It thrives best in forest areas on sandy loam rich in humus, potash, magnesia and lime. Soil should be well drained. Annual rainfall of 2500 mm. to 3000 mm. well distributed throughout the year is ideal for successful cultivation. Maximum summer temperature should not excede 35°C while minimum winter temperature should be above 10°C in places where Ipecac is to be cultivated. The plant is not frost resistant and is grown under partial shade.

The plants are propagated from stem or root cuttings, planted in beds about 30 cm. apart. The beds are higher than the ground level and should have good drainage. The plants can be propagated from seeds but the growth is slow.

Roots are harvested when the plants are about 3 yrs. old. The alkaloid content in the roots is higher than 2% at that time.

The plants are dug up any time of the year. The roots are washed and dried in shade. A healthy plant produces 6-8 good roots.

Ipecac is emetic, diaphoratic and expectrorant. It is an excellent remedy in amoebic dysentry. It is an apitiser and digestive in small doses. Five alkaloids are obtained from the roots and of these emetine and cephaeline are very important. Emetine is non phenolic while cephaeline is phenolic and therefore toxic. This is converted to emetine by methylasion.

In India production of the roots is about 700 kg. per annum giving about 7 kg. of emetine, the annual requirement of the country being about 1000 kg. The roots obtained from Mangpoo are however considered of very good quality.

Cephaelis acuminata Karst of Central America is a good substitute of Ipecac and is called **Carthagena Ipecac.**

SANTONICA OR WORMSEED

Botanical name : (1) ARTEMISIA CINA Berg.
(2) ARTEMISIA MARITIMA Linn.

Family : COMPOSITAE (ASTERACEAE)

Description :

Small, aromatic, perennial undershrub with oblique, knotted rootstock from which arise many ascending leafy shoots; stems much branched. Leaves small, 2-3 cm. long, multipinnatifid; upper smaller with less segments. Inflorescence-branches terminal with numerous small floral heads or capitula; capitula 2 mm. across, 2-4 mm. long, obtuse, with 12-18 involucral scales, enclosing 3-5 tubular flowers.

Distribution :

A. cina is indigenous to W. Asia but is now cultivated in America. *A. maritima* occurs in Eurpoe and is distributed eastwards to Mongolia. It is also found in W. Asia, N. Pakistan and N. W. India.

Parts used:

Although commercially called wormseed, the material is actually the dried flower heads or the capitula.

Preparation:

The flower heads are collected in midsummer before the flowers open. The santonin content is highest at that time, 2.5-3.5% and decreases afterwards.

The flower heads are rapidly dried. These are then finely crushed and subjected to steam distilation. The volatile oil thus obtained is treated with milk of lime and the soluble salt calcium santoninate is formed. The filtered solution is converted to sodium santoninate by treating with sodium hydroxide. Carbon dioxide is passed in when calcium carbonate is precipitated and this is removed by filtration. The filtrate is warmed and santoninic acid separates out on cooling. The santoninic acid lactonises to santonin ($E_{15}H_{13}O_3$). The precipitate is filtered, dissolved in alcohol, decolorised by animal charcoal and purified by recrystalization.

Description of the drug :

Santonin is a neutral colourless crystalline powder. It is sparingly soluble in water and cold alcohol but readily dissolves in hot alcohol, chloroform and benzene. On exposure to sunlight it turns yellow. It is therefore preserved in coloured bottles. When 200 mg. of colourless santonin is heated with 2 ml. of alcoholic potassium hydroxide a red colour is produced. Santonica or sontonin powder is odourless and nearly tasteless at first but afterwards develops a bitter taste and camphor like odour.

Constituents :

In addition to santonin there is another volatile oil consisting of cineol with some dipentene and artemisin.

Use :

Santonin is effective in round worm, ascarids and oxyurids.

Dose :

The dose is more than 60 mg. for adults and less than 60 mg. for children. Each dose must be followed by a saline cathartic. This should be repeated for 2-3 consecutive days. Santonin should not be given to infants.

MYROBALAN

1. **Beleric myrobalan —Terminalia bellirica (Gaertn.) Roxb.**
2. **Chebulic myrobalan —Terminalia chebula Retz.**

Description :

T. bellirica—This is a large tree attaining a height of 30–40 mtrs. and a girth upto 3 mtrs., often buttressed at the base. Leaves broadly elliptic, acute at both ends, 10–18 cm. long, alternate and clustered near the end of the branches; petiole almost half the length of the blade. Spikes axillary, dense flowered. Flowers polygamous, very small, with a strong odour, bracteolate; bracteoles minute, caducous. Calyx campanulate, 5 lobed; lobes valvate, caducous. Corolla absent, stamens 10, inserted on the calyx tube with an epigynous disc in the hermaphrodite flowers. Ovary monocarpellary, inferior; ovules 2–3. Drupe ovoid, velvety outside, 1-seeded, 2–3 cm long.

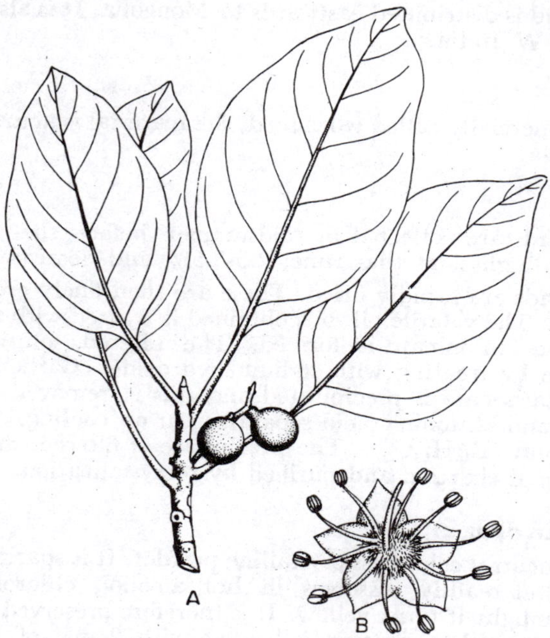

Fig. 159. Terminalia bellirica Roxb. A. Leafy twig with fruits (× 1/3)
B. Flower (enlarged.)

Distribution :

In the plains of India, excepting the arid region; nowhere abundant.

Parts used :

Pulp of the fruit.

Collection and preparation:

Half ripe fruits are collected and dried in shade. These are marketed as such.

Description of the drug :

The drug is sold in market as dry fruits, which are ovoid, 2-3 cm. long, dark greyish brown and velvety outside.

Constituents:

The fruit contains β-sitosterol, gallic acid, ellagic acid, ethyl gallate, galloyd glucose, chebulagic acid, mannitol, glucose, galactose, fruticose and rhamnose. Half ripe fruits contain an oil similar to castor oil.

Use :

The pulp is used as a laxative or purgative either alone or mixed with the pulp of the fruits of Terminalia chebula or Emblica officinolis. The fruits together form the "Trifala" of the Indian Kabirajas and it is a strong purgative.

Description :

T. chebula—Medium trees with more or less drooping branches; upto 25 mtr. high in moist region but dwarfish in drier area; bark dark brown, exfoliating in woody scales. Leaves alternate or subopposite, elliptic, with a pair of large glands at the top of the petiole, 7–18 cm. long, with a short petiole. Flowers very small, yellowish white, in terminal spikes, regular and hermaphrodite. Calyx campanulate, lobes 5, valvate. Corolla absent. Stamens 10, inserted on the calyx cup with an epigynous disc. Ovary monocarpellary, inferior, with 2–3 ovules. Drupe ellipsoid or obovoid or sometimes ovoid, 2–4 cm. long, yellow to orange-brown, sometimes tinged with red or black, hard when ripe, faintly 5-ribbed. Seed hard pale yellow.

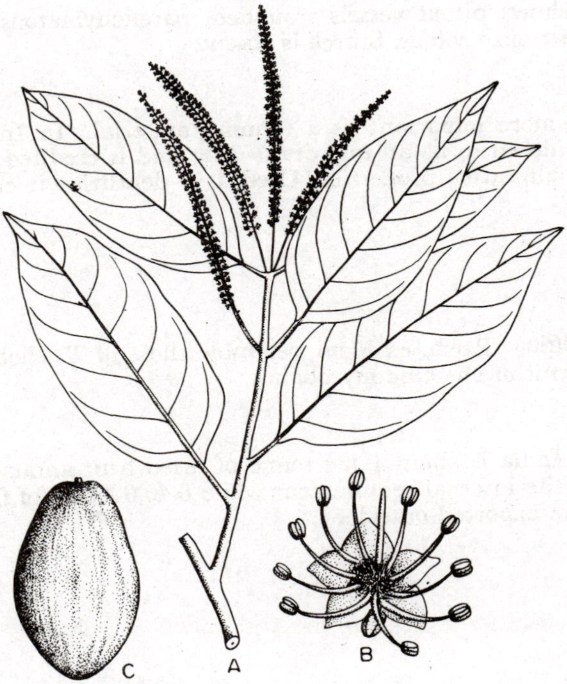

Fig. 160. Terminalia chebula Ritz. A. Leafy Twig with spikes (× 1/2); B. Flower (enlarged). C. Fruit.

Distribution :

All over India in the plains as well as on the hills at lower elevations.

Parts used:

Dried fruits, which are loosely called nuts although in reality they are drupes.

Myrobalans are marketed in the form of whole nuts or the dry pulp of the crushed nuts or solid and spray dried extracts.

Collection and Preparation :

Mature fruits are collected by shaking the trees during January to April. These are dried in thin layers in shade. For medicinal purpose green fruits are also picked up and these are dried, when they turn black. Very young fruits are also valued in medicine.

Description of the drug :

Mature fruits yellowish brown, 2-4 cm long, wrinkled and with 5 faint ribs, hard and stony; seed light yellow, rough, 15-25 mm. long; pulp 3-4 mm. thick, odourless, with an astringent but later sweetish taste.

Young fruits deep brown to black, elongated, tapering on both sides, often compressed, hard, with longitudinal wrinkles and ribs, odourless, astringent and bitter.

Microscopical character shows the epicarp of several layers of corky cells, often containing a few starch grains. Mesocarp formed of round parenchymatous cells having brownish cell contents. There are numerous stellate crystals of calcium oxalate. Starch is absent. Parenchymatous cells have cellulose walls. In semimature fruits isolated vascular strands of vessels are intermingled with parenchymatous tissues. Vessel walls have pitted thickening.

The powder shows pitted vessels rounded parenchymatous cells, containing resins and oils of brownish colour. Starch is absent.

Uses :

Myrobalan is more important as a tanning material. In India and adjacent countries it is considered to be an important drug and is credited with laxative, stomachic, toxic and alterative properties. Used as a dentifrice it cures bleeding gum.

Does :

30-60 gr.

Adulterant :

Fruits of T. citrina Roxb. ex Flem. resemble those of T. chebula and are often sold in market as fruit of chebulic myrobalan.

Trade :

Production in India is about 1 lac tonne of dried fruit annually. Major part of the produce meets the internal requirement while 6,40,000 kg. of fruits and 3,06,000 kg of the extract are exported outside.

PART V

TISSUE CULTURE

CHAPTER I

INTRODUCTION

Definition

Tissue culture is the method of 'in vitro' culture of plant or animal cells, tissue or organ on nutrient medium under aseptic conditions usually in a glass container.

Tissue culture is sometimes referred to as 'sterile culture' or 'in vitro' culture. By this technique living cells can be maintained outside the body of the organism for a considerable period.

According to Street ('77) tissue culture is referred to any multicellular culture with protoplasmic continuity between cells and growing on a solid medium or attached to a substratum and nourished by a liquid medium.

By plant tissue culture new plants may be raised in an artificial medium from very small parts of plants, such as, shoot tip, root tip, callus, seed, embryo, pollen grain, ovule or even a single cell, whether the cultured tissue develops into a plant or grows unorganized depends on the genetic potential of the tissue and the chemical and physical environment.

According to the parts used for culture the aseptic plant culture may be of following types.

(a) If a seedling is cultured it is called *plant culture*.

(b) When an embryo is cultured it is known as *embryo culture*.

(c) If plant organs, such as, shoot tips, root tips, leaf primordia, flower primordia or immature fruits are cultured, it is called *organ culture*.

(d) The culture of unorganized tissues from cell proliferations of segments of plant organs is called *callus culture*. Cell proliferations are formed in the explant due to injury caused by excision.

(e) When a single cell or small cell aggregate in a dispersed state is cultured, it is called *cell suspension culture*. It is also known as *cell culture*.

Culture of single cell is sometimes called *single cell cloning*.

The portion of the plant to start the culture is called an *explant*. Culture derived from a single explant is called a *clone*.

In order to maintain a culture for a comparatively longer period the culture medium is changed from time to time. This process will remove those harmful excretory substances which have accumulated due to metabolism.

By transferring a fragment of the parent culture to a new medium *subculture* is done. Such a fragment is called an *inoculum*.

HISTORY OF TISSUE CULTURE

In 1832 Theodor Schwann said that cells could be cultured outside the body of the organism if provided with proper external conditions. In 1835 Wilhelm Roux cultured embryonic cells of chicken in salt solution. Reichinger (1839) said that fragments thicker than 1.5 mm were capable of growth but fragments below this limit failed to grow. He did not used any nutrient in his experiment.

Arnold (1885) and Jolly (1903) observed growth and cell division of leucocyte cells of salamander in culture. In 1907 American zoologist Ross Granville Harrison successfully cultured nerve cells of frog in solidified lymph. Harrison is known as the father of tissue culture.

M. J. Burrows (1910) cultured embryonic tissue of chicken in plasma. Mammelian cells were first cultured by Alexis Carrel. By repeated subculturing he was able to culture the tissue for 34 years. Organ culture was first done by D.H. Fell (1929) in England. He used solidified plasma and embryonic extract as nutrient medium.

History of Plant Tissue Culture

German botanist Gottlieb Haberlandt first attempted to culture plant tissues 'in vitro'. He started his work in 1898. He used cells from palisade tissues of leaves, cells from pith, epidermis and epidermal hairs of various plants for culture in media containing Knop's solution, aspergine, peptone and sucrose. The cultured cells survived for several months but the cells failed to proliferate. This may be due to (a) use of very simple media, (b) culture of highly differentiated cells and (c) aseptic techniques were not used.

In similar experiments by some later workers (Winkler 1902, Thielmann '24, '25, Küster '28) cells remained alive for a long period but they failed to divide.

Culture of meristematic tissue was started in early 20th century. Isolated root tips were first cultured by Robbin in 1922. Working independently Kotte ('22) also made similar observations. Robbin and Maneval ('23) cultured roots and maintained the culture for 20 weeks by subculturing.

In 1934 White first successfully cultured isolated tomato roots in a medium containing sucrose, inorganic iron salts, thiamine, glycine, pyridoxine and nicotinic acid etc. Gautheret ('34) noted that cambium culture from *Salix capraea, Populus nigra* etc. continued to grow for few months under aseptic conditions. He later ('37, '38) used medium suplemented with B-vitamins and IAA.

In 1937 White recognised the importance of B-vitamins for growth of root cultures. Went and Thimann ('37) discovered the importance of auxin (IAA). Nobecourt ('37, '38) obtained some growth in culture of carrot root explants. He also noted root differentiation in tissue culture. In 1938 tumour tissues of tabacco hybrid were successfully cultured.

In 1939 working independently three scientists, White in USA and Nobecourt and Gautheret in France cultured successfully plant callus tissue on synthetic medium continuously.

Gautheret ('39) said that carrot culture required Knop's solution supplemented with Bertholots' salt mixture, glucose, gelatine, cysteine HCl and IAA.

White ('39a) in culture of procambial tissue from young stem of the hybrid *Nicotiana glauca* × *N. langsdorfii* noted unlimited and undifferentiated growth. He showed that this tissue could be repeatedly subcultured. White ('39b) recorded developement of leafy buds in tissue culture of the hybrid *N. glauca* × *N.langsdorfii* in nutrient medium.

Tissues from various plants were cultured subsequently. It was noted that older cultures show increasing degree of organization. The role of vitamins in plant growth was also recognized.

Wetmore and Wardlaw ('51) successfully cultured shoot tips of pteridophytes (*Selaginella, Equisetum* and ferns).

Tissues of *Sequoia semipervirens* were cultured by Ball ('55). Pollens of *Taxus* and *Ginkgo biloba* were cultured by Tulecke ('59). Conifer tissues were successfully cultured by Harvey and Grasham ('69).

From tissue culture studies important information about *root-shoot relationship* can be obtained (Street '57, '59, '66). Several scientists (Camus '49, Wetmore et al '55, '63, Jeffs and Northcote '67) reported about the factors controlling *vascular tissue differentiation* from tissue culture studies.

Van Oberbeck ('41) cultured embryos of *Datura* on a medium supplemented with coconut milk . Importance of *coconut milk* and 2-4D as nutrient was recognised (Steward, Caplin and Miller '52, Steward '58, Reinert '58, '59, Pulet '61). The stimulatory property of coconut milk is due to the presence of zeatin. The potent cell division factor was found to be kinetin (Miller '55), which is a 6 furfurylaminopurine. Cytokinin is

6-substituted amino-purine compound, which can stimulate cell division in culture of plant tissues. Monocot tissues were successfully cultured on a medium containing coconut milk (Morel '50).

Callus culture of *Tagetus erecta* and *Nicotiana tabacum* on liquid culture medium when agitated on a shaker produced suspension of single cells or cell aggregates (Muir '53). Such *cell suspension* could be subcultured. Studies on cell suspension culture were carried out by Muir, Hildebrandt and Riker ('54), Street, Shigomura ('57), Torrey and Reinert ('61), Reinert and Markel ('62). Muir ('53) developed *paper raft nurse* technique for single cell culture. In this method isolated single cells were put on a square filter paper, placed on a active nurse tissue, which supplies the required nutrients to the growing single cell. In another method cells were suspended on a hanging drop in a micro-chamber (Torrey '57, Jones et al '60). Bergman ('60) workin with suspension cultures of *Nicotiana tabacum* var. *sansum* and *Phaseolus vulgaris* var 'early golden rod' developed *agar plating* technique of single cell cloning. In this method single cell fraction was separated by filtration, mixed with warm agar and then plated in a petridish in thin layer.

Melchers and Bergmann ('59) noted that after several cultures of the haploid shoot of *Antirrhinum majus* there was increase in ploidy.

Ball ('46) noted the possibility of *regeneration of whole plant* in culture of shoot tip of angiospermic plants. Wetmore and Wardlaw ('51), Morel ('60) obtained whole plants from culture of shoot apices having 1 or 2 leaf primordia. Morel ('64) used this method for culture of orchids.

A cell which can develop into a whole organism by regeneration is called a *totipotent* cell. This term was coined by Morgan in 1901. According to White ('54) if all the cells of a multicellular organism is totipotent, then such cells in isolated condition regain their dividing power and can produce whole plants. In an organism this capacity remain suppressed.

It was noted that single cells are capable of producing new plants (Vasil and Hildebrandt '65). From *pollen* and *anther culture* haploid embryos were obtained (Guha and Maheswari '66, '67; Bourgin and Nitsch '67). A method of microspore culture of *Nicotiana* and *Datura* was developed by Nitsch ('74, '77). He was able to double the chromosome number and obtained homozygous diploid plants.

From anther culture of tobacco Bourgin and Nitsch ('67), Nakata and Tanaka ('68) obtained haploid tissues and haploid embryoids.

Cocking ('60) recorded release of protoplasts from root tip cells by using fungal cellulase in 0.6M sucrose. He was able to culture *isolated protoplasts,* which regenerate new cell walls and produce cell colonies and ultimately plantlets.

In many plant suspension cultures cell protoplasts had been successfully released (Eriksson and Jonasson '69).

Plant tissue culture technique is used for the study of *tumour physiology.* White and Brown ('42) were able to culture bacteria free crown gall tumour. In *Scorzonera hispanica* Gautheret ('46) noted that the callus culture which initially required auxin, produced some proliferations which can grow in auxin deficient medium. Such inherited changes occurring in the nutritional requirements (especially involving auxin) of cells of a culture is called *habituation.* An auxin habituated culture does not require the supply of exogenous auxin (Butcher '77). Butcher noted ('77) that when auxin and cytokinin habituated tissues are grafted into a healthy plant, tumours are produced.

Pathogen free plants can be obtained by culturing apical meristem.

By late 70's it was evident that plant tissue culture technique can be successfully used in various field of agriculture, such as, production of pathogen free culture, production of secondary products, clonal propagation, mutant culture, haploid breeding and genetic engineering.

By tissue culture, *pathogen free cultures* have been produced. This technique is important for plant pathological investigations. Protoplasts in culture are used for virus infection and biochemical studies.

From suspension culture secondary products can be synthesised in large amount. Some of these substances are enzymes, vitamins, food flavours, sweeteners, anti-tumour alkaloids and insecticides. In Japan 'in vitro' culture has been achieved (Misawa '77, '80) at industrial level.

Clonal propagation of orchids and several other ornamental and economic plants have been achieved by 'in vitro' culture. In potato clonal propagation has been achieved by culturing leaf cell protoplasts (Sephard '82).

By using mutagens in culture followed by selection disease resistant or stress resistant mutant plants have been regenerated.

By haploid breeding few cultivers were produced. Hybrids of related but sexually incompatible species have been produced by protoplast fusion. By this technique hybrid between potato and tomato has been produced (Melcher '78).

By cell fusion of isolated cells from two different species hybrid tobacco plants are produced.

Dormancy period of seeds can be shortened by excising the seeds and culturing its embryo on artificial medium (embryo culture). Abortive embryo can be grown successfully by embryo culture.

Foreign genes with desirable characters attached to a plasmid may be inserted into the naked protoplast usually by means of liposomes (Barton and Brill '83, Dodds and Bengochea '83). The expression of introduced gene in the mature plant is still doubtful.

IMPORTANCE OF TISSUE CULTURE

Tissue culture has great importance in studies of plant morphogenesis, physiology, biochemistry, pathology, embryology, cytology etc.

From tissue culture studies it is possible to know how simple cells differentiate and become specialized to perform special functions. Various changes taking place in a cell can be noted from clonal culture. Interrelationship between two cells can be studied in tissue culture. With the help of phase contrast cine-photomicrography a very clear understanding of mitosis and meiosis is possible in tissue culture.

Haberlandt noted the importance of tissue culture in studying plant morphogenesis. Relationship between growth and differentiation can be well understood from such a culture.

In vegetatively propagating plants many plantlets are formed very quickly from callus culture or culture of explants. Orchids, which normally propagate very slowly, can form many plantlets very rapidly in shoot tip culture. This is also noted in carnation.

By tissue culture method new plant variants can be obtained by isolating genetically unique cells. From callus cultures of tobacco, carrot, asparagus etc. new plants are formed. Such plants show genetic variability.

From studies of mutant cells, the biochemical and developmental process of an organism can be better understood. In tissue culture, mutation can be easily induced and from such mutant cells mutant plants may be produced.

In tobacco, paddy etc. from anther culture haploid plantlets are produced. By doubling the chromosome homozygous plants are obtained most rapidly. So, this process has imense importance in plant breeding.

Tissue culture technique has been successfully used in nutritional research. The effects of various mineral salts, vitamins etc. on growth may be studied in culture. Many important information about glucose metabolism, nitrogen metabolism and hormone production can be obtained from 'in vitro' culture.

Suspension culture under controlled conditions may be used to solve many physiological or biochemical problems and also provides a system for the production of important plant products, such as, plant alkaloids.

From cell and organ culture under controlled environmental conditions nutritional and metabolic processes can be studied. Some mutant cells cannot grow in a medium which does not contain a special nutrient. From this biochemical steps of a process can be determined.

Tissue culture has great significance in pathological studies. The effect of various medicine on cells infected by pathogens can be studied in tissue culture.

Culture of maize cells from plants susceptible to the race T of *Helminthosporium maydis* were treated with pathotoxin of the fungus (Gegebach and coworkers '77). Scientists were able to obtain cells resistant to this fungus. From such cells resistant plants were also produced.

Tissue culture technique is employed in the studies of plant tumour diseases and host parasite relationship. Disease free plants can be produced by tissue culture technique.

Tissue culture has great importance in vaccine production. In 1949 vaccine for poliomyelitis has been produced after observing that the poliomyelitis virus can attack human cells. Later vaccines for mumps, meseales, influenza have been produced.

The process of virus attack, effect of virus on host cells and how new viruses are produced etc. have been studied in tissue culture. The behaviour of substances, which can prevent virus attack has been studied on virus infected cells.

In tissue culture the behaviour of normal and cancer cells can be studied. It has been noted that some viruses and carcinogenic chemicals can produce cancer. Effect of radiation and chemicals on normal and cancer cells has been studied. From such studies it may be possible to know which chemical substances can destroy cancer cells.

From tissue culture studies information about some hereditary diseases of man has been obtained. Carriers of some diseases can also be identified through tissue culture technique. From leucocyte culture the cause of mongolism in man has been discovered. From such culture abnormal Philadelphia chromosome has been identified. This chromosome has some relation with chronic granulocytic leukomia.

When tissue transplant is done from one person to the other then sometimes there is tissue rejection. So it is necessary to match the tissue of donar and receiver before actual transplant. This can be done by culturing the mixed leucocytes of the donar and the receiver.

Distantly related species usually do not hybridize. This difficulty can be omitted by cell fusion and protoplast fusion technique.

Carlson in 1972 successfully produced hybrid plants by protoplast fusion between *Nicotiana glauca* × *N. langsdorfii*. Power ('76) obtained hybrids between *Petunia hybrida* and *P. parodii* by protoplast fusion. Kaw and Wetter ('77) produced hybrids between tobacco and soyabean by cell fusion. Thus cell fusion and protoplast fusion techniques have great importance in plant breeding. Tetraploid fertile *Lolium* and *Festuca* hybrids were obtained by somatic cell fusion.

Those embryos which fail to produce mature fruits normally can be cultured and from such embryo cultures plants are produced. Embryo culture also prevents seed dormancy. Cooper ('78) obtained hybrid plants between barley and rye by embryo culture.

Conservation of germplasm

By tissue culture plant germplasm can be stored. This method can be successfully used to solve various problems.

(a) Many seeds, such as, seeds of *Citrus* sp., *Coffea* sp., *Hevea brasiliensis* etc. retain their viability for a short period. These can be conserved by tissue culture.

(b) Vegetatively propagated plants (such as, banana, potato, sweet potato, yam) which do not produce seeds or which are highly heterozygous, are stored as cuttings or tubers. This requires much labour charge and are expensive to propagate. This problem can be solved by tissue culture.

Many fruit trees of Rosaceae are propagated by budding, grafting and layering. By tissue culture rapid propagation of such plants are possible.

(c) In many economic plants, such as, coconut, date plam etc. vegetative propagation normally does not occur. The germplasm of such plants can be conserved by tissue culture.

(d) Many trees reproduce very slowly. By tissue culture such palnts can be multiplied rapidly and many plants with parental genotypes are formed.

For conservation of germplasm the cells should be stored in such a condition which allows minimum cell division. One of the method attempted is storing of cells in liquid nitrogen having a temperature of −196°C.

For germplasm conservation shoot tips or plantlets can be stored. Such stored materials can be used as and when required.

In tissue culture cell division can be suppressed by various methods.

(i) To the medium growth retardant may be added. The substances used are absicic acid, mannitol, sorbitol, malic hydrazide, succinic acid etc. Potato shoots are successfully stored in a medium containing malic hydrizide.

(ii) Low temperature is helpful for storage of cells in culture. Cultures of potato, sweet potato, beet, grape, apple, etc. can by stored by this method. Temperate crops (e. g. potato) are stored usually at a temperature of 0—6°C. and tropical crops (e.g. sweet potato) at 15—20°C. By this method meristem culture of strawberry has been conserved for six years.

(iii) The concentration of nutrients of the culture medium may be changed. Some substances required for normal growth may be supplied at a lower concentration or may not be supplied at all.

(iv) The gas composition within the culture vessel may be changed. The atmospheric pressure or oxygen concentration may be lowered to conserve the cells.

Production of secondary metabolic products

Some plants produce secondary metabolic products, such as, alkaloid, antibiotic, glycoside, resin, tannin, saponin, volatile oil, etc., which are of considerable economic importance.

By cell culture various secondary metabolites (e.g. allergin) have been synthesised artificially (Nein '60, Puhan and Mwelin '70, Staba '77). Cultivation of plants producing secondary metabolites can be improved significantly by tissue culture.

There are certain disadvantages in the production of secondary metabolites by tissue culture. Some of these are: (i) In cell culture synthesis of secondary metabolites occur at a lower rate than in an entire plant. (ii) After prolonged culture 'in vitro' the production of secondary metabolites may decrease or even stop. (iii) The cost of large scale production of secondary metabolites in cell culture is high. So, only very rare and expensive secondary metabolites are produced by tissue culture.

Explants from stem, leaf (e.g. *Mentha*) or root (*Daucus carota*) are taken and cultured on suitable medium. After callus formation explants are subcultured on fresh medium. In early stages of callus formation and in first few subcultures secondary metabolites are formed. But in subsequent subcultures usually the amount of secondary metabolites decreases.

CHAPTER II

CONDITIONS REQUIRED FOR PLANT TISSUE CULTURE

There are some important aspects of tissue culture. These are : (A) aseptic condition, (B) aeration, (C) equipments, and (D) nutrient medium.

According to White ('63) a plant tissue culture laboratory should have following facilities : (i) preparation of media, (ii) storage and cleaning facilities, (iii) growth of the culture media under controlled and aseptic conditions ; (iv) examination of the culture and keeping records.

A. ASEPTIC CONDITION

Tissue culture should be done in completely aseptic condition. Care should be taken so that the tissues, equipments, culture media and the room should be completely free from microorganisms.

For sterilisation of plant materials, glass equipments, other instruments, culture media etc. several methods are used. These are dry heat, wet heat, ultrafiltration and chemicals. Dry heat is used to sterilise equipments in an incubator. Wet heat sterilization is done in an autoclave at 120°C at 15 lb pressure for 15 minutes. Liquid media, which are unstable at high temperature are sterilised by ultrafiltration. Chemicals, such as, alcohol is used to sterilise working area and instruments.

(i) Sterilisation of materials:

The tissue to be cultured may carry microorganisms. To prevent such contamination it is surface sterilised chemically.

The chemical agents to be used and the time of treatment depends on the material to be sterilised. The sterilising agent should be easily removable, because retention of such agents is harmful.

Some of the commonly used sterilising agents are : (a) 9—10% calcium hypochlorite ($Ca[OCl_2]$) is usually used for 5—30 minutes; (b) 2% sodium hypochlorite solution ($NaOCl$) is used for 5—30 minutes. Hypochlorite solutions (Na or Ca) are used at about pH6. After sterilising in these solutions the materials are thoroughly washed in double distilled water; (c) 10—12% hydrogen peroxide (H_2O_2) solution is used for 5—15 minutes; (d) 1—2% bromine water is used for 2—10 minutes. Some other sterilising agents are : 1% chlorine water, mercuric chloride, silver nitrate, antibiotics etc. If the tissue is sufficiently hard then it can be sterilised by washing in absolute alcohol.

The process of sterilisation differs according to the material to be sterilised. A short account of the method of sterilisation in various plant materials is discussed below:

(a) Seed:

The seeds are submerged in absolute alcohol for 10 minutes followed by washing in sterile distilled water. Then the seeds are submerged in 10% calcuim hypochlorite solution for 20—30 minutes or treated with 1% bromine water for 5 minutes. The time required depends upon the rigidity of the seed coat. After repeated (3—5 times) washing in sterile distilled water the seeds are allowed to germinate in sterile water or on sterile filter paper.

(b) Fruit:

Fruits are washed with absolute alcohol and then submerged in 2% hypochlorite solution for 10 minutes. Fruits are repeatedly washed in sterile distilled water. By dissecting such fruits seeds are obtained, from which sterile seedlings can be grown.

(c) Stem:

Pieces of stem are washed in running tap water, rinsed in absolute alcohol and then immersed in 2% sodium hypochlorite solution for 15—30 minutes. The end of the stem pieces are cut off. The stem piece is either planted vertically on solid agar medium or it is dissected out and the required tissue is taken for culture.

(d) **Leaf:**

Very young leaves are selected and their surfaces are wiped with absolute alcohol. The leaves are then immersed in 0.1% mercuric chloride for 1 minute. After repeated washing in sterile distilled water the leaves are dried with sterile tissue paper.

(e) **Storage organ:**

The material is washed in running tap water and then submerged in 2% sodium hypochlorite solution for 20—30 minutes. After repeated washing in distilled water it is dried with sterile tissue paper. The storage organ is dissected out and internal tissue is taken for culture.

For plant materials having cutin, suberin or epidermal appendages a small amount of detergent (0.05%), such as, teepol or tween 80 is added to the hypochlorite solution.

If the tissue is contaminated, as is evident from localized internal discoloration, then it should be discarded.

(ii) **Sterilisation of equipments:**

Glasswares (Pyrex or similar borosilicate glass) are generally cleaned with chromic acid-sulphuric acid mixture followed by thorough washing in running water for at least 5 minutes. This is followed by rinsing in distilled water and finally with double distilled water. Cleaned glasswares should be stored in a dust free place and washed with double distilled water before use.

Glasswares can also be cleaned with hydrochloric acid or nitric acid or detergent. Then the equipments are washed thoroughly with sterile distilled water.

Due to high corrosive nature of chromic acid-sulphuric acid mixture, in some laboratories detergents are used for cleaning glasswares. Glasswares are dipped overnight in strong detergent solution and then washed thoroughly with hot water followed by a wash with cold sterile distilled water.

Glass, metal or silicon rubber equipments can be sterilised in an incubator by keeping them at 180°C for one hour. The equipments are wrapped in aluminium foil before placing in an incubator. After sterilisation sufficient time is allowed for cooling. According to Collins and Lyre ('84) sterilisation can be done at 160°C for 45 mins., at 170°C for 18 mins., at 180°C for 7½ minutes and at 190°C for 1½ minutes.

All equipments can be sterilised in an autoclave at 15 lb pressure, at a temperature of 120°C for 20—30 minutes. For wrapping during autoclaving unwaxed papers are used. Aluminium foil is unsuitable as it is impermeable to steam (Hamilton '73). Paper products after autoclaving are kept in a drying oven at a temperature above 60°C to remove moisture. In an autoclave demineralized water is used.

All metal (stainless steel or nickel plated) instruments (such as, scalpel, scissor, forcep etc.) used for inoculation are dipped in alcohol, then flamed and cooled before use. The instruments may also be sterilised by exposing to UV light.

Culture apparatus and equipments should be wrapped in celophane paper or aluminium foil to keep the outer surfaces sterile during transport from the autoclave to the aseptic area.

Discarded and contaminated cultures are autoclaved for a short period to kill the contaminants and liquify the agar. Glasswares are then cleaned.

(iii) **Sterilisation of the culture medium:**

The culture medium may contain micro-organisms from the beginning. Sugar containing nutrient media favour rapid growth of various micro-organisms, which grow faster than the cultured tissue and ultimately destroy the tissue. Slow growing micro-organisms also interfere proper growth of the tissue by producing toxins or stimulants.

To prevent growth of the micro-organisms the medium can be sterilised in an autoclave at 15 lb pressure at 120°C for 15 minutes. Sterilisation time increases with increase in the liquid volume. 75 c.c. of liquid per vial requires a period of 20 minutes, 250—500 c.c./vial needs a period of 25 minutes and 1000 c.c./vial requires 30 minutes of autoclaving. The sterile medium should be used within 14 days of sterilisation.

Substances in pure aqueous solution may be stable when autoclaved; but they may be chemically modified in presence of some other substance of the medium during sterilisation. Such substances are separately autoclaved and after sterilisation added together.

Some of the chemicals used in tissue culture degrade at high temperature during autoclaving, e.g. gibberellins, vitamins, 1, 3 or 9 substituted purines. Sucrose on autoclaving is partially degraded to d-glucose and d-fructose, which may have some inhibitory effect. Such substances are sterilised by ultrafiltration, that is, by passing through a membrane filtration unit attached to a graduated syringe. The sterilised liquid is added directly to the autoclaved medium.

Ultrafilters may be of different types. These are: (a) durapore membrane filter consisting of fluorocarbon polymer, it is most suitable for membrane filtration; (b) nucleopore filter consisting of polyethelene film and having pores of definite diameter; (c) disposable filter of overlapping cellulose fibres; (d) fluoropore filter consisting of thin teflon is used to filter non-aqueous solution, such as, solvent dimethyl sulphoxide. Pores of a ultrafilter are usually 0.4 μm in diameter. A pore of 0.22 μm only can remove all micro-organisms.

Antibiotics, such as, penicillin, streptomycin etc. are sometimes added to the nutrient medium to prevent the growth of the micro-organisms. Potassium benzyl penicillin in 100 μg /ml concentration prevents the growth of gram positive bacteria. Streptomycin sulphate in 100 μg/ml concentration prevents the growth of gram negative bacteria. Gentamycin in 100 μg/ml concentration is supposed to prevent the growth of gram positive and gram negative bacteria. But, antibiotics are not very effective in plant tissue and cell culture. Antibiotics are not recommended for sterilisation of plant tissue culture because—(a) no antibiotic is effective against all contaminating micro-organisms; (b) degradation products of antibiotics might be metabolised by plant tissues causing unpredictable results; (c) antibiotics may inhibit growth as recorded in tobacco callus growth.

Large quantities of distilled water is needed for tissue culture. Distilled water should not be stored for a long time and the reservoir should be frequently cleaned. Water may be sterilised in an autoclave for an hour in a pyrex glass flask provided with a non-absorbent plug fitted to its mouth.

Mouths of the culture tubes and flasks are flamed during sterilisation. During combustion process ethylene is produced and this gas may enter in high concentration in the culture vials. Ethylene being a plant hormone may influence the growth and morphogenesis of plant tissue culture (Beasley and Eaks '79).

(iv) **Sterilisation of the environment:**

All sterilisation, inoculation etc. should be done under aseptic conditions in a clean room free from dust and convection current which may carry spores of micro-organisms.

Culture may be best done in an enclosed chamber (Fig. 1) under filtered air pressure in a well lighted, sterile and suitably ventillated condition.

The inoculation chamber is sterilised wtih ultraviolet ray before inoculation. The UV germicidal lamp is turned on about two hours before using the chamber and should be turned off before using the chamber. The chamber is kept free from micro-organisms by continuous flow of filter sterilised air.

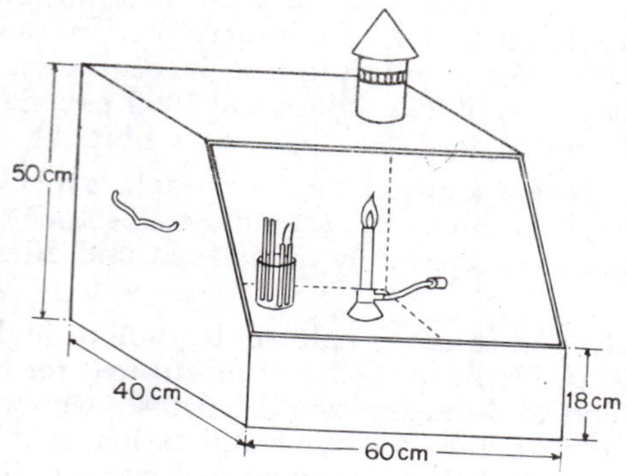

Fig. 1. Simple inoculating hood.

The table to be used for inoculation is wiped with ethyl alcohol or isopropanol (70% or 80%).

The neck of the culture vial is quickly flamed and its plug is rapidly removed. The tissue is inserted and the plug is immediately replaced.

Hands should be washed thoroughly with soap and hot water for several minutes and the skin is wiped with paper towels. Hands and fingers may be dipped in ethanol before certain operations, such as, removing seed coats by hands.

Discarded cultures should be immediately removed. All unnecessary glasswares, instruments, aluminium foils etc. which have been used should be removed.

B. AERATION

Proper aeration of the tissue in the culture medium is essential. Those tissues, which are cultured on semi-solid medium do not require any special method for aeration. But those tissues, which are cultured in liquid medium remain submerged and require special device for aeration.

(a) For proper aeration in liquid medium filter paper bridge may be used. The filter paper is placed in such a manner so that its two ends are dipped in a medium and the middle horizontal portion on which the tissue is placed remains above the level of the medium.

(b) By passing filter sterilised air through the medium and by stirring the medium proper aeration is possible.

Usually proper supply of oxygen is provided by keeping the culture vial with liquid medium on an automatic shaker. This method will also help in the separation of the tissue into individual cells or small groups of cells.

The mouths of the culture vials are closed with non-absorbent cotton covered in cheese cloth. This allows proper aeration but prevents the entry of micro-organisms.

C. EQUIPMENTS

Various equipments are necessary for tissue culture.

(i) Culture vessels—Glasswares used for tissue culture should be of borosilicate glass (pyrex glass), because soda glass may hamper the growth of the tissue. Pyrex glass containers can be easily sterilised and their mouths can be flamed during transfer processes.

For temporary cultures grooved glass slides are usually used.

Various types of culture vessels, such as, test tubes, conical flasks, bottles etc. are used. Usually 100 ml conical flask or large test tubes (25×150 mm) are used. Sometimes special flat tubes are used so that the culture is easily visible. Watch glasses were earlier used for organ culture.

(ii) In addition to culture vessels, different kinds of glasswares are required for preparing the nutrient media and culture tissue. These include measuring cylinders, beakers, funnels, petridishes, graduated pipette, conical flasks etc.

Petridishes made of pyrex glass or plastic are used for culturing or to hold the material during transferring.

Petridishes are sterilised in an autoclave for 30 minutes or more by placing them within metal containers or wrapped paper bags.

(iii) The mouth of the culture vial may be closed with non-absorbent cotton plug, screw cap backelite cover, metal or plastic cover, polyurethene foam or polypropylene plug.

The exposed part of the plug and the rim may be covered with aluminium foil. This will prevent the plug from becoming wet when autoclaved. Wet and contaminated plugs are immediately discarded.

The mouth of the culture vials may be directly covered with sterile square soft aluminium foil (0.25 mm thick). Sides of the foil are pressed neatly to the sides of of the test tubes or flasks by downward movement. These foils can be easily removed and replaced again and again. After one culture aluminium foils are discarded.

(iv) Alcohol lamps—Small spirit lamps can be used to sterilise and flame the instruments or the mouth of the culture vials.

(v) Sterilising agents—Various sterilising agents are used in tissue culture:

(a) Ethyl alcohol is used to wipe the surfaces of materials, working areas, to rinse hands or gloves, to dip instruments.

(b) Calcium or sodium hypochlorite is used to wipe surfaces of working areas and to sterilise equipments. It is very useful to disinfect surfaces of plant tissues and seeds without causing injury.

(c) Bromine or chlorine water is used to sterilise plant materials.

(d) Aqueous or alcoholic mercuric chloride (0.1%) is useful to disinfect working surfaces and materials.

(e) Sterile distilled water is used to rinse the surface of the material after disinfection. For preparing the media distilled, redistilled and deionized water is used.

(vi) Forceps, scalpels etc. are required for excising the explant and transferring the tissue to the culture vials.

(vii) Rubber gloves, aprons etc. are used to maintain aseptic conditions.

(viii) Incubator is required to sterilise equipments.

(ix) Autoclave—All nutrient media and equipments are sterilised in an autoclave.

(x) Inoculating chamber—All aseptic transfers should be done in an inoculation room under completely aseptic condition. If inoculation room is not available then a small inoculation chamber can be used. The inoculation chamber can be made from metal sheets and glass. Inner surface of the chamber is sterilised by wiping it with alcohol. Sterile air is allowed to pass through the chamber.

(xi) A refrigerator in the media room is required for storing chemicals and stock solutions.

(xii) A sensative balance is necessary for weighing the chemicals.

(xiii) A magnetic stirrer, a pH meter or pH indicator papers etc. are needed.

(xiv) A centrifuge is required.

(xv) Labels and marking pencils are needed.

(xvi) Hand lens, dissecting microscope, compound microscope with microphotographic accessories are required.

(xvii) Shelves are required to keep the media and reagents.

D. NUTRIENT MEDIA

Various nutrient media have been used for tissue culture. In the beginning different organic media, such as, plasma, tissue extract, coconut milk etc. were used. Later, various defined media were used.

Nutrient media required for culture vary with the kind of plant and the purpose of producing the culture. When starting the work specific medium for that tissue is worked out.

Most of the media contain some inorganic salts of major and minor elements, vitamins and sucrose. Such a medium is called a *basal medium.*

If required the medium is solidified with 0.5-1% agar. The pH of the culture medium is maintained between 5.6-5.8 (slightly acidic). The pH is adjusted by adding a drop of hydrochloric acid or by adding a few drops of caustic potash.

Various substances used in different culture media are—

I. Inorganic substances

Some inorganic ions used in culture media are sodium, potassium, calcium, magnesium, chloride, phosphate, sulphate, bicarbonate etc. Micronutrients, such as, manganese, boron, zinc, copper, molybdenum etc. are usually added to the culture media.

(i) Nitrogen is usually added in the form of nitrate or ammonium salt or a mixture of both.

(ii) Potassium is added as KCl or KNO_3 or KH_2PO_4. It is the most abundant cation. High concentration of potassium favours embryogenesis.

(iii) Calcium is added in the form of $CaCl_2$, $2H_2O$ or $Ca(NO_3)_2$, $4H_2O$ or anhydrous form of either.

(iv) Magnesium and sulpher are added in the form of magnesium sulphate ($MgSO_4.7H_2O$). Phosphorus is obtained from $NaH_2PO_4.H_2O$ or KH_2PO_4.

(v) Iron is essential and added to the medium as inorganic iron or chelated iron (such as, NaFeEDTA—i.e., ferric sodium ethylene diamine tatra-acetate). The presence of NaFeEDTA ensures that iron is available over a wide pH range in the medium.

Each inorganic material is made as stock solution having 10 or 100 times the concentration actually required. The solution is autoclaved and stored in a freeze.

II. Organic substances

(i) Sugar—2-4% sucrose (20,000-30,000 mg/l) is usually used in a medium. In some cases glucose is used. Sucrose is thermolabile, so it is good to sterilize glucose by filtration.

(ii) Vitamins and amino-acids—Vitamins are usually required in traces. Many scientists consider that thiamine (Vit B_1) is the only vitamin needed by all plant tissue cultures. Thiamine is added as thiamine hydrochloride. Nicotinic acid (0.5 mg/l), thiamine (0.1-1 mg/l) and pyrodoxine (0.5 mg/l) are usually added to the medium. Some other materials which may be benificial are inositol (100 mg/l), biotin (0.1 mg/l) and pantothenic acid (0.1 mg/l) or calcium pantothenate (1.0 mg/l) and folic acid (0.5 mg/l).

A stock solution of all these substances at 100 times the required concentration is prepared and stored in a freeze.

Vitamins are thermolabile and are filter sterilised and added with a syringe or pipette to warm unsolidified autoclaved medium.

Plants can prepare necessary nitrogenous substances from simple amino acids, such as, glycine and inorganic nitrogenous substances. But the presence of other amino acids is beneficial. Some of these amino acids are—arginine, aspergine, aspertic acid, glutamic acid, glutamine, methionine. In culture media containing complex nitrogenous substances growth is good. Sometimes organic nitrogen, such as, casein hydrolysate or casamino acid (0.05-0.1%) is added to the medium.

Addition of several amino acids to the medium may have an inhibitory effect probably due to competition among various amino acids.

(iii) Hormonés—Most callus cultures require a supply of auxin and cytokinin. Auxin stimulates shoot elongation and cytokinin promotes cell division. Auxin and cytokinin balance controls cell division, cell elongation, cell differentiation and organ formation.

Auxins are usually dissolved in a small amount of alcohol before preparing the stock solution. Indole acetic acid (IAA) at 1-50 mg/litre concentration, napthal acetic acid (NAA) at 0.1-10 mg /litre concentration and 2-4 dichloro-phenoxy acetic acid (2-4-D) at 0.05-0.5 mg/litre concentration are generally used. IAA and NAA are soluble in sodium hydroxide, 2-4-D is soluble in ethanol or dimethyl sulphoxide, which in higher concentration is toxic. For callus initiation 2-4-D is most suitable but it suppresses root and shoot initiation.

IAA is easily destroyed by light and enzyme, so IAA is added at a high concentration to the culture medium. NAA is not easily degraded, thus it is added at low concentration.

In culture cytokinins used are zeatin, kinetin and benzyl adenine. Kinetin at 0.01—10.0 mg/l concentration is used in culture. Kinetin at 0.1 mg/l concentration can induce callus formation. A stock solution is prepared by dissolving it in a small amount of hydrochloric acid and then water is added.

Gibberellin is not usually required, but it is needed for apical meristem culture.

Ethylene helps differentiation of tracheary elements (Muller and Roberts '84) and initiation of buds (Thorpe '82).

(iv) Other organic substances—Sometimes natural extracts are added to supplement the media especially when chemically defined media cannot produce desired results. Some such extracts are —coconut milk, yeast extract, casein hydrolysate, malt extract, fruit juice (such as, tomato juice).

10-15% (by volume) of coconut milk is usually added to the medium. Preparation of coconut milk—Fresh coconut milk is taken out through micropyler region of a ripe coconut. It is filtered and the filtrate is boiled for 10 minutes, the proteins precipitate out. This is cooled, decanted and filtered. This coconut milk is used in culture. Unused coconut milk is stored in a freeze.

In orchid seed culture banana extract is beneficial (Arditti '68). Explants of *Citrus* sp. is stimulated by orange extract (Einset '78).

(v) Charcoal—Activated charcoal is sometimes used in the culture medium. It has adsorbent property and may serve various purposes, such as: (a) removes contaminants from the medium, (b) absorbs secondary products secreted by the culture tissue, (c) controls the supply of endogenous growth hormone and (d) darkens the supporting matrix. According to Kolenbach and Wernicke ('78) presence of activated charcoal stimulates embryogenesis. But in some cases it may inhibit growth and morphogenesis.

Osmotica—The uptake of water by a cell depends upon the osmotic concentration of the cell sap and the external medium. Water availability of a culture medium, depends upon the concentration of agar, carbon source and any external non-metabolite added as an osmoticum. Sugar, such as, mannitol or sorbitol is used as an external osmoticum. In protoplast culture polyethylene glycol (PEG) is used as an osmoticum.

Water—Double distilled or demineralized water is used in culture media.

Media matrix—Solid and semisolid culture media usually contain 0.6—1.0% agar. Commercial agar contains various contaminants. Purified agar is available for tissue culture.

For different types of culture various types of culture media may be used. Some of the extensively used culture media are—White's medium, Murashige and Skoog's medium, Nitsch's medium, Nagata and Takebe's medium etc.

Knop's solution is sometimes used for embryo culture. It was first developed by Knop's in 1865, but later modified by different workers.

For callus culture of dicot Murashige and Skoog's medium is good. For monocot culture Schenk and Hildebrandt's ('72) medium may be used. It contains 2-4-D kinetin and 2 chlorophenoxy-acetic acid.

Composition of some nutrient media used in plant tissue culture is given in the table below:

Constituents	White's medium ('63) mg/l	Murashige and Skoog's high salt medium ('62) mg/l	Nitsch's medium ('69) mg/l	Nagata and Takebe's medium ('72) mg/l
INORGANIC				
(macronutrients)				
KCl	65	—	—	—
KNO_3	80	1,900	950	950
NH_4NO_3	—	1,650	720	825
$Ca(NO_3).4H_2O$	300	—	—	—
$CaCl_2.2H_2O$	—	440	166	220
$MgSO_4.7H_2O$	720	370	185	1233
Na_2SO_4	200	—	—	—
NaH_2PO_4	16.5	—	—	—
KH_2PO_4	—	170	68	680
(micronutrients)				
$MnSO_4.7H_2O$	7	22.3	25	22.3
H_3BO_3	1.5	6.2	10	6.2
KI	0.75	0.83	—	0.83
$CoCl_2.6H_2O$	—	0.025	—	—
$ZnSO_4.7H_2O$	3	8.6	10	8.6
$CuSO_4.5H_2O$	—	0.025	0.025	0.025
$CoSO_4$	—	—	—	0.03
$Na_2MoO_4.2H_2O$	—	0.25	0.25	0.25
Iron $Fe_2(SO_4)_3$	2.5	—	—	—
$FeSO_4.7H_2O$	—	27.8	27.8	27.8
Na_2EDTA	—	37.3	37.3	37.3

Table contd... to next page

Table contd.... from previous page

ORGANIC				
Sucrose	20,000	30,000	20,000	10,000
Glycine	3	2	2	—
Niacin	—	0.5	5	—
Pyridoxin HCl	0.1	0.5	0.25	—
Thiamine HCl	0.1	0.1	0.5	1
Cysteine	1.0	—	—	—
Nicotinic acid	0.5	0.5	—	—
Folic acid	—	—	0.5	—
Biotin	—	—	0.05	—
Calcium pantothenate	1.0	—	—	—
Myo-inositol	—	100	100	—
Meso-inositol	—	—	—	100
IAA	—	1.30	—	—
NAA	—	—	—	3
2-4-D	—	0.4—10	—	—
Benzyamino-purine	—	—	—	1

Preparation of the stock solution

Preparation of Murashige and Skoog's stock solution is described below:

(a) Micronutrient stock—To 400 c.c. of double distilled water each micronutrient salts are added. By adding double distilled water final volume of 1000 c.c. is obtained. This solution is stored in a freeze. 10 c.c. of this solution is added to 1000 c.c. of culture medium.

(b) Iron stock—To 80 c.c. of double distilled water iron salts are added. The final volume of 100 c.c. is made by adding double distilled water. This is stored at room temperature. 5 c.c. of this stock solution is added to 1 litre of the Murashige and Skoog's culture medium.

(c) Vitamin stock—To 50 c.c. of double distilled water required amount of each vitamin is added. By adding double distilled water final volume of 100 c.c. is obtained. Vitamin solution is sterilised by ultrafiltration and added to the sterilised culture medium while agar is still warm. To 1000 c.c. of MS culture medium 1 c.c. of vitamin stock solution is added. Unused vitamin solution is discarded after one month.

(d) Kinetin stock—Kinetin is weighed and dissolved in a few drops of hydrochloric acid. To it a few c.c. of distilled water is added. The final volume of 100 c.c. is made by adding double distilled water. To 1 litre of culture medium 1 c.c. of this stock solution is added.

Preparation of MS culture medium

Macronutrients are weighed, dissolved and added to 400 c.c. of double distilled water. To it 10 c.c. micronutrient stock, 5 c.c. of iron stock and 1.c.c. of kinetin stock are added with a pipette. To it 100 mg myo-inositol is added. To this medium a mixture of 10 mg of IAA dissolved in a few drops of sodium hydroxide is added. By adding double distilled water the volume of the culture mixture is made upto 800 c.c. The pH is adjusted to 5.7 by adding few drops of 1N NaOH or 1N HCl. The final volume is made upto 1000 c.c. by adding double distilled water. 3.0 gm sucrose, 0.8 gm of agar is added to 100 c.c. of MS medium in 250 c.c. flask. The mouth is closed with an aluminium foil. It is autoclaved and allowed to cool. 1 c.c. of vitiamin is added while the agar is still warm and the flask is gently swirled to mix the vitamin with the medium. About 10 c.c. of medium is poured in each culture vial.

The temperature of the medium should be maintained properly. Plant tissues are usually cultured at 25—27°C. In lily and *Gladiolus* if the tissues are kept at low temperature before culture then regeneration capacity increases.

In animal tissue culture the temperature of the medium should be similar to the body temperature in case of warm blooded animals. In case of cold-blooded animals the temperature of the medium is similar to the temperature of the environment, where the animals live.

The medium to be used for culture depends upon (a) the plant species, (b) the tissue to be cultured and (c) the purpose of culture. In different kinds of plant tissue culture various types of media are used.

(1) *Solid agar medium* is used for different tissue and organ culture. On agar medium tissue grows quickly and usually produces callus.

(2) *Static liquid medium* is mainly used for root culture.

(3) *Shaking liquid medium* is useful for the culture of cell population. Such a medium helps gaseous exchange. In a shaking liquid medium when a tissue is placed and agitated then a free cell culture is obtained.

(4) *One drop medium* is useful for culture of an isolated cell (clone).

CHAPTER III

METHODS OF TISSUE CULTURE

A. Hanging drop culture

The simplest method of tissue culture is hanging drop culture (Fig. 2).

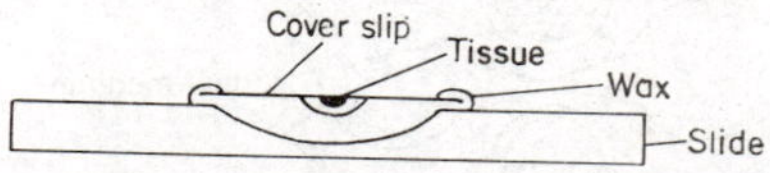

Fig. 2. Hanging drop culture of Harrison.

A portion of the tissue with 1 mm diameter is placed on a coverslip containing a drop of almost solidified medium. A 1″×3″ grooved slide is taken and the coverslip is placed over it. The rim region is sealed with wax. Harrison used this process for tissue culture. In such a culture the tissue remain viable only for few days. If the culture medium is changed from time to time the tissue remain viable for longer period. For subculture the tissue is divided into smaller parts and each part is subcultured in a new grooved slide with fresh medium. In 1955 de Ropp cultured single cells in hanging drop medium, but only few cells divided.

B. Double cover slip method

Maximov in 1928 first used this method. In this method (Fig. 3) a small round coverslip with the tissue and the medium is placed on a large square coverslip. A drop of water or salt solution attaches the small coverslip with the large coverslip. Double cover-slips are placed on a grooved slide and the rim of the coverslip is sealed with wax.

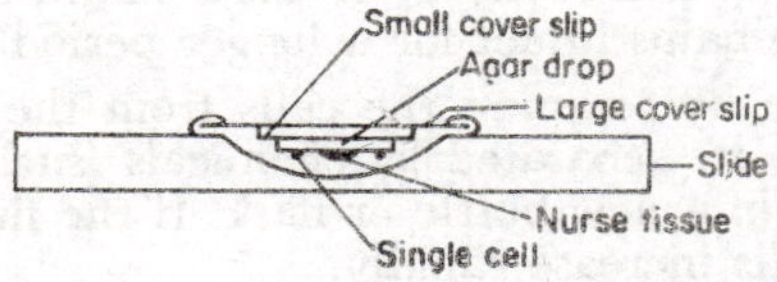

Fig. 3. Maximov's double cover slip method as used by Torrey.

When the culture medium has to be changed, then the small coverslip is carefully detached from the larger coverslip and washed with nutrient solution. The small coverslip is attached to a new larger coverslip and placed on a new grooved slide and the edge is sealed. Torrey ('57) used Maximov's double coverslip method for culture of pea root callus on agar medium.

C. Culture in Stewards auxophyton

Culture can be done in a tube (Fig. 4). The explant is placed in the culture tube and the nutrient medium is poured into it and the mouth of the tube is plugged. In 1952 Steward, Caplin and Miller designed a culture apparatus—called auxophyton for rapid proliferation of small explants (about 3 mg) from carrot root (conical tap root). They used a tube (12.5 cm long and 3.5 cm diameter) with a side neck at the middle. After introducing the explant and the medium (10 c.c.) the mouth is closed with a cotton plug, which helps gaseous exchange. About 24 such tubes can be mounted along the edge of a disc which is rotated at slight angle to the horizontal at a speed of 1-2 revolutions per minute. The tissues are thus alternately exposed to air and the liquid medium, which flows along the tube from end to end. The apparatus is kept in a temperature controlled room and with a fluorescent light the culture tubes are uniformly illuminated.

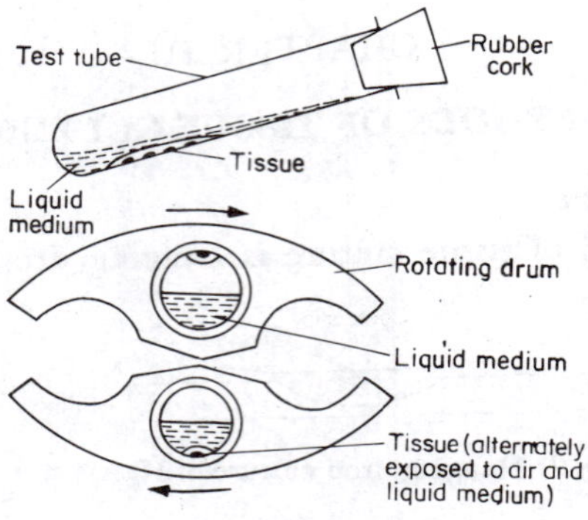

Fig. 4. Culture in a test tube.

In 1956 Steward and Shantz designed nipple flasks to culture several explants for biochemical investigations. 1000 c.c. nipple flask has ten nipples and 250 c.c. nipple flask has eight nipples. In these flasks explants are distributed in the nipples, and when placed in a auxophyton the explants are alternately exposed to air and culture medium. The medium generally becomes turbid due to the release of free cells and cell aggregates from the explants. This suspension itself may be used for subculture.

D. Culture in bottles, conical flasks etc.

When many cells are cultured together then culture is done in a conical flask, bottle or petridish.

In culture vessel containing liquid medium inoculation is given. Cells rapidly increase on the surface of the bottle or conical flask forming monolayer. When whole surface is utilised the cell growth is reduced. If the medium is changed at an interval of 3-4 days then the tissue remains intact for a longer period.

Subculture may be done by scraping the cells from the walls of the flasks or bottles or by shaking or cells are separated by chemicals (such as, trypsin). The cells are centrifuged and cultured in a new bottle or flask. If the flasks, tubes etc. are continuously shaked then the cells increase rapidly.

In spinning culture 10 litre culture bottles each containing 4.5 litres of medium are placed in an apparatus at 45° angle to the horizontal and rotated at 80—120 revolutions per minutes (Lamport '64, Short, Brown and Street '69). The mouth of the culture bottle is closed by cotton plug. Adequate gaseous exchange occurs and the cells grow very rapidly.

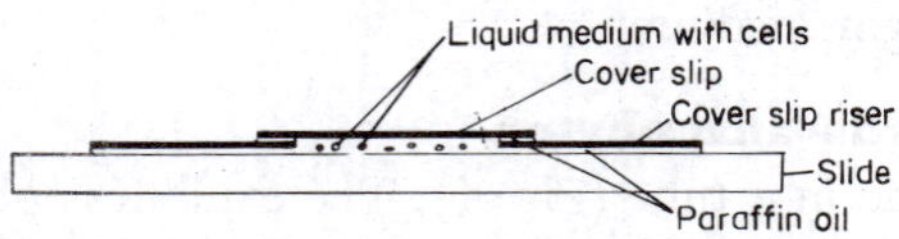

Fig. 5. Culture in a microchamber

E. Culture in a microchamber

Jones, Hildebrandt, Riker and Wu ('60) cultured cells from a callus of the hybrid *Nicotiana tabacum* × *N. glutinosa* in a microchamber, which was sealed with inert mineral oil (Fig. 5). Cells can be minutely observed in such a culture.

G.G.Rose ('54) used perfusion chamber for tissue culture of animal cells.

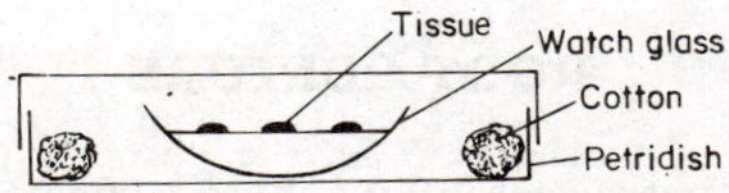

Fig. 6. Fehl's method of organ culture

F. Culture in petridish, watch glass etc.

Organ may be cultured in a petridish or watch glass (Fig. 6). The petridish may be incubated in a humified incubator. For culture of small number of cells petridish is recommended.

CHAPTER IV

ROOT CULTURE

Kotte and Robbins ('22) first successfully cultured wheat root tips for a short period. In 1934 White first successfully cultured tomato roots for an unlimited period in a medium containing mineral salts, sugar and yeast extract. After this several scientists attempted to culture roots of various plants. With roots of woody plants the success is comparatively less. But roots of some woody plants, such as, *Acacia* sp. (Bonner '42) and *Acer rubrum* L. (Bacheland and Stowe '63) were successfully cultured. Roots of some gymnosperms were also cultured with success (Bonner and Sommer '75).

Medium—Roots are usually grown in liquid medium. Murashige and Said ('79) observed in tomato root culture continuous and slow agitation, which helps gaseous exchange, resulted in doubling of root elongation and improved development of lateral roots. Medium supplemented with hormones helps root culture in certain cases. Inositol stimulates growth in isolated roots.

For root culture some modifications of the White's medium is found to be beneficial. Instead of $Fe(SO_4)_3$ as the source of iron use of chelated iron, in the form of NaFeEDTA (sodium-ferric-ethyl-diamine tetracetate) is preferable, because in prolonged culture use of ferric sulphate in the medium leads to iron deficiency. Sugar concentration of 1.5—2% is sufficient. Vitamin requirement varies according to the plant. Thiamine is needed by all species. Cereal roots require more auxin than dicot roots.

A medium supplemented with sugar, IAA, sometimes cytokinin and meso-inositol helps cambial development in excised roots.

Method—Roots are grown from young seedlings produced by the germination of aseptic seeds (Fig. 7). Tomato seeds are first surface sterilized with 80% alcohol for 1 minute in 100 ml conical flask. Then the seeds are treated with chlorine water for 10 minutes. The seeds are rinsed thoroughly in double distilled water. About 5 seeds

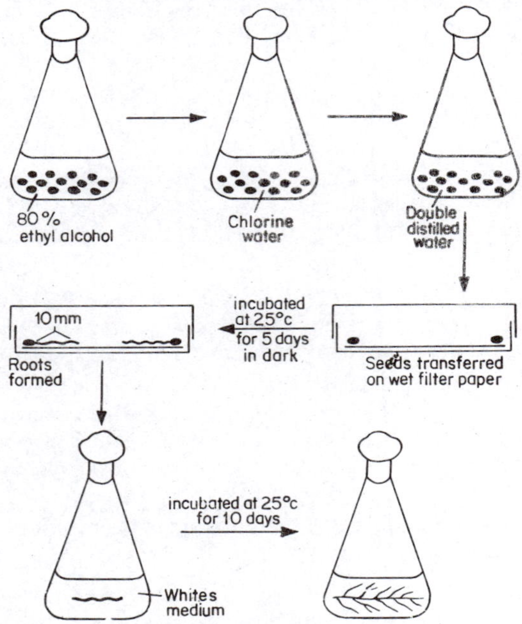

Fig. 7. Stages in root culture of tomato

are placed in a petridish lined with No. 1 filter paper and moistened with 8-10 c.c. of double distilled water. The petridish is wrapped with an aluminium foil and placed in an incubator at 25°C for about 5 days in dark. Sterile root tips obtained by germination of seeds are cultured on White's medium. About 10 mm long root tips are taken and transferred to flasks containing culture medium. The culture is incubated at 25°C for 10 days. The root has developed and produced many lateral roots. The main root is subdivided into sectors each of which contains a portion of the main root and several lateral roots. Each such sector is placed on a fresh medium. The lateral roots on their turn produce lateral roots. From such a culture a constant supply of root tips is available for experiments. At regular intervals subculture is done. In this way the culture can be maintained for several weeks.

Culture of roots of legumes

A technique has been developed for culturing legume roots with *Rhizobium*. The basal ends of the excised roots are inserted in a small vial containing organic nutrients. Apical parts of the roots are dipped in a petridish containing an inorganic medium inoculated with *Rhizobium*. Roots of *Glycine max* and *Phaseolus vulgaris* were grown in this way.

Nature of cultured roots

Biochemical composition of the cultured roots may be somewhat different from the normal roots, although they may be alike in several anatomical features and metabolic pathways.

According to the response of the roots in culture the plants are of three types.

(a) Roots continue to grow indefinitely in culture producing many lateral roots, e.g., *Datura, Lycopersicum.*

(b) Roots after a period show decrease in growth rate and produce weak lateral roots, e.g., *Pisum, Triticum, Linum* etc.

(c) Lateral roots do not develop at all. This may be because the nutrient medium does not contain the substance required for the growth of the lateral roots.

Significance of root culture

(1) From root culture many genetically uniform roots are produced within few days. These are called 'clones of isolated roots'. Such uniform root tips are available for further study.

(2) From continuous culture of isolated roots the nutritional requirements of the roots can be studied. Roots of some plants require a supply of vitamin thiamine for unlimited growth. Nutritional requirements of isolated tomato roots have been noted (Street '57).

(3) Root culture is also suitable for investigation on lateral root and bud formation, initiation of cambial activity and nodulation (Torrey '65).

(4) The influence of shoot on root growth can be studied from root culture.

(5) The factors controlling the development of secondary vascular tissues can be studied from root culture. In many plants the excised roots in culture failed to develop the secondary vascular tissues. This indicates that some substances are translocated from the shoot and influence the formation and development of vascular-cambium of roots.

(6) Root culture may be used for the commercial production of useful substances.

CHAPTER V

SHOOT TIP CULTURE AND LEAF CULTURE

CULTURE OF SHOOT APEX

White ('33) first attempted to culture the shoot apex of *Stellaria media*, but he was unsuccessful. Loo ('45) successfully cultured 5 mm long excised shoot tips of *Asparagus officinalis*. Cultured shoots produce cladophylls, which on subculture produce plantlets.

On agar medium containing inorganic salts and glucose Morel cultured the shoot tip of orchid *Cymbidium*, which produces callus (Fig. 8). This callus produces protocorms at certain regions. Protocorm formation increases when the shoot tips are cultured on agitated liquid medium. Protocorm on subculturing produce plantlets.

Shoot tips were successfully cultured in many other plants, such as, carnation, cauliflower and tobacco etc.

Isolated shoot tips of ferns produce plantlets on a simple medium. But shoot tips of angiosperms require a complicated medium.

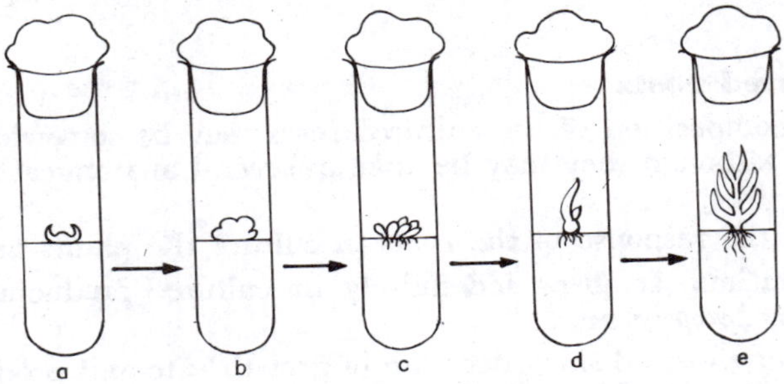

Fig. 8. Culture of shoot tip of orchid *Cymbidium*

a—Shoot tip placed on culture medium,
b—Callus is formed,
c—Several protocorms with buds and rhizoids are formed,
d—A protocorm is isolated and cultured on a fresh medium,
e—Plantlet is formed.

Materials—The size of the shoot tip selected for culture is important. According to Ball ('46) root initiation and plantlet formation can take place in culture of shoot tip containing at least three leaf primordia. But Smith and Murashige ('70) was able to get plantlets from explants containing only meristematic dome, without any leaf primordia in *Daucus carota*, *Coleus blumei*, *Nicotiana sp.* and *Tropeolum majus* etc.

Cutter ('65) distinguished apical meristem culture and shoot apex culture. Apical meristem includes apex distal to the young leaf primordia. Shoot apex includes apex and a few adjacent leaf primordia. In orchids sometimes 5-10 mm long shoot apex is used for culture. Smith and Murashige ('70) used 80 μm long apical meristem for culture, but such small explants are very difficult to survive in culture. Larger explants have greater chance of survival and they grow more rapidly (Hussey '83).

Shoot apex culture of woody plants have some problems. Buds from young growing shoots can be easily cultured, but buds from the mature shoots are difficult to culture. Buds from woody plants need an exogenous supply of cytokinin and gibberellin for growth. The explants are transferred to a medium without growth hormone. This favours shoot elongation. Then the explants are transferred to a medium supplemented with exogenous auxin, which helps root initiation.

Tissues with high phenolic content are difficult to culture. Due to injury polyphenol is oxidised to a dark brown coloured growth inhibiting substance. This has been observed in *Eucalyptus grandis*. This difficulty can be removed by—

(a) adding antiauxidents to the medium,

(b) presoaking the explants in antiauxidents,

(c) initial culture is grown in absence of light and

(d) immediate subculturing on a fresh medium when the tissue appears brown.

In *Eucalyptus* the explants are soaked in double distilled water for three hours. This removes the phenolic compounds. The explants are then incubated in darkness for several days.

Medium—Murashige and Skoog's medium is usually used for shoot tip culture. It is supplemented with vitamins, sucrose and suitable hormones. The culture is grown either on solid agar medium or on a filter paper bridge over a liquid medium.

In some plants the medium is supplemented with thiamine. Presence of napthalacetic acid (NAA) is required for root initiation in certain plants, such as, carnation. After root initiation the shoot is placed on a medium without IAA. Within 3-4 weeks roots develop and small leaves are formed. The plantlets produced can be transferred to soil.

Addition of malachite green or 2-4-D or thiouracil helps the growth of shoot tips.

For chlorophyll formation 1000 lux fluorescent lamp is used during initial stages and 3,000—10,000 lux lamp is used in later stages. The photoperiod is 16 hours.

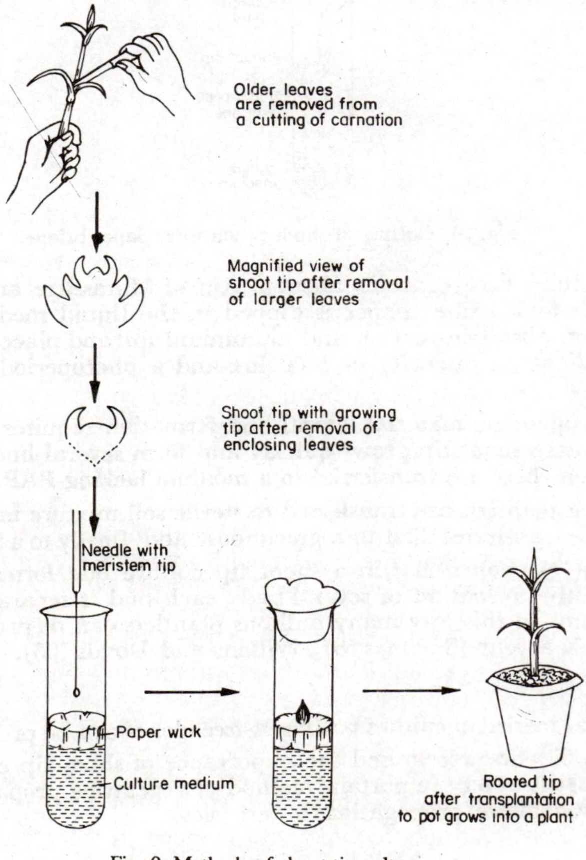

Fig. 9. Methods of shoot tip culture.

During initial stages cytokinin may be added in the form of kinetin or zeatin or benzyladenine. Auxin may be used as IAA, IBA (indole 3-butyric acid) or NAA. Gibberellin is required for certain plants, such as, *Chrysenthemum*, *Dianthus*, *Solanum tuberosum* etc.

During later stages IBA or NAA may be added in low concentration for a short time. This helps root initiation. Long period of auxin treatment may result in callus formation. In some plants root initiation can take place in auxin free medium.

Method—From healthy and actively growing shoot tip explant is selected for culture. In various plants, such as carnation, chrysenthemum etc. usually a larger portion of the shoot is cut from the plant and later the older leaves are removed with a sterile scalpel (Fig. 9). The dome-shaped apical meristem with 1 or 2 leaf primordia is suitable for culture.

Usually ten mm long shoot tips are removed from healthy plants and surface sterilised in hypochlorite solution for about 15 minutes. Explants are washed in double distilled water several times and placed on a petridish lined with filter paper for dissecting the shoot apex. The filter paper is moistened with double distilled water. Terminal 0.5 mm of the shoot apex is carefully excised and is placed in the depression (position V) of the filter paper bridge, which is folded in the form of letter M (Fig. 10). Shoot tips of various sizes may be cut and tested for optimal size of the explant for

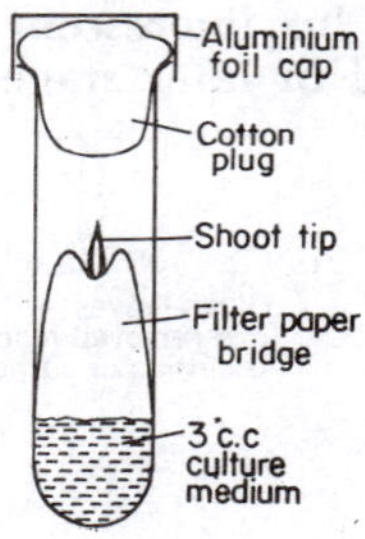

Fig. 10. Culture of shoot tip on filtre paper bridge.

culture. The culture tube contains about 3 c.c. of Murashige and Skoog's medium. The arms of the folded filter paper is dipped in the liquid medium. The tubes are plugged with non-absorbent cotton and aluminium foil and placed in a plant growth chamber at 27°C at an intensity of 1000 lux and a photoperiod of 16 hours at 70% relative humidity.

Depending upon the material lateral bud formation requires few weeks to several months time. Potato shoot tip grows quickly and form several buds within 5-6 weeks. For root initiation these are transferred to a medium lacking BAP.

After rooting plantlets are transferred to sterile soil mixture in a humid condition. The plantlets are transferred first to a greenhouse and finally to a field.

Murashige ('74) noted that in a shoot tip culture bud formation is induced by cytokinin. After the formation of several buds, each bud is separated and transferred to a fresh medium. In this way many millions plantlets can be produced from a single shoot apex within a year (Thomas '81, Wilkins and Dodds '83).

Significance

(1) By apical meristem culture pathogen-free clones can be produced very rapidly.

(2) Morel ('60) first recognised the importance of shoot tip culture for multiplication of clones. It is a very important method of vegetative propagation and used in orchids, where vegetative propagation is very slow.

CULTURE OF LEAVES

Sussex and coworkers successfully cultured very small (about 1.2 mm) excised leaf primordia from underground buds of *Osmunda* in simple culture medium containing mineral salts and sucrose. The leaves produced on such a culture are smaller than normal.

Steaves working with the fern *Osmunda cinnamomea* noted that very small leaf primordia (measuring about 300 μm or larger) on culture can produce shoots (Fig. 11). But larger the leaf primordia at excision there is a greater chance of leaf formation. Leaf primordia of 800 μm on culture always produce leaves. He also cultured young leaf primordia of *Nicotiana* and *Helianthus*.

Fig. 11. Culture of leaf primordia of *Osmunda cinnamomea* producing leaf.

Methods—Excised leaves are surface sterilized and then cultured on solidified agar medium. Such cultures can be maintained for a long period.

Growth of the leaves on the culture medium depends upon the stage of the leaves during excision. Explants from young leaves grow better than older leaves.

(See Page 469)

CHAPTER VI

CULTURE OF FLOWER, OVARY, OVULE ETC.

CULTURE OF FLOWER

Angiosperm flowers were first cultured by Larue ('42). He noted some growth of ovaries and rooting. Complete flowers of several dicots were successfully cultured by Nitsch ('51). Flower primordia of *Rananculus scleratus* were cultured by Konar and Nataraj ('64, '65). They obtained plantlets from such cultures.

Medium—Konar and Nataraj used White's medium containing sugar and ferric salt for culturing flower primordia of *R. scleratus*. On such culture floral primordia produce callus, from which many embryoids are formed. These embryoids on subculture produce plantlets.

In cucumber (*Cucumis sativus* Linn.) when young male flower buds were cultured on a medium containing inorganic salts, vitamin B, casein hydrolysate, coconut milk, then these buds tend to form ovaries. This tendency is increased by the addition of IAA to the medium.

Method—Nitsch ('51) selected flowers two days after pollination and surface sterilised the flower with 5% hypochlorite solution. These were then thoroughly washed with double distilled water and placed on culture medium containing inorganic salts and sucrose.

On culture such flowers produce fruits. Larger fruits were obtained on medium supplemented with hormones, such as, IAA, gibberellin, cytokinin. Flowers excised before pollination cannot produce fruits.

OVARY CULTURE

Horticulturist tried to improve the quality of the fruit by using various chemicals. In such studies, the culture of excised ovary supplied directly with the chemicals, has great importance.

Nitsch ('51) successfully cultured excised embryos of several plants, such as, *Lycopersicon esculentum* (Fig. 12), *Nicotiana tabacum*, *Phaseolus vulgaris*, *Cucumis anguria*, *Frageria* sp. etc. The excised ovaries of *Cucumis* and *Lycopersicon* produced fruits with viable seeds on culture. But these fruits are smaller than normal.

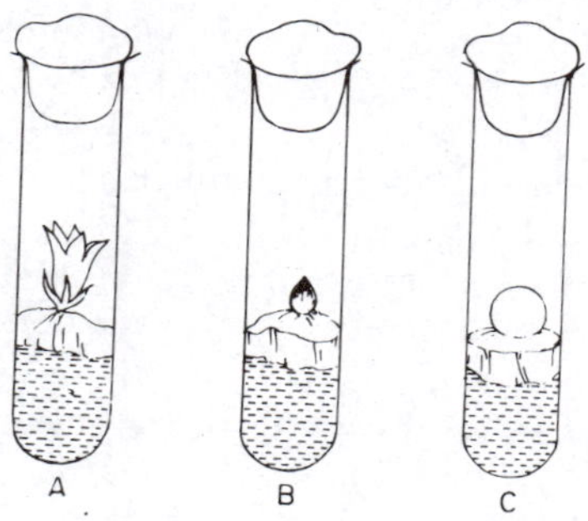

Fig. 12. Ovary culture of *Lycopersicon esculentum* on artificial medium.

A—Just excised flower,
B—Culture of excised ovary,
C—Small fruit produced on culture.

Maheswari ('58) successfully cultured ovaries of *Iberis amara* excised one day after pollination on a medium containing mineral salts and sugar. In such a medium smaller embryos are formed. But if the medium is supplemented with B-vitamins then healthy fruits of normal size develop. Addition of IAA to this vitamin containing medium further improves the size of the fruits (Maheswari and Lal '58). Ovaries excised at zygote stage develop normally in culture as seen in *Hyoscyamus niger* (Bajaj '66) and *Anethum graveolens* (Johri and Sehgal '66). If coconut milk is added to the medium then larger fruits are produced.

In several plants, such as, *Allium, Althea, Hordeum, Hyoscyamus, Iberis, Triticum* etc. it has been noted that the presence of sepals helps fruit development. In absence of sepals fruit development is poor. Guha and Johri ('66) demonstrated this in *Allium.*

Nitsch's medium supplemented with vitamin, glycine and yeast extract is most suitable for ovary culture. Ovaries of *Linaria moroccana* were grown on this medium. The fruits produced on this medium were usually smaller than the natural size (Sacher and Balder '58). In *Tropaeolum* also the fruits produced on culture were smaller (Sacher and Kanta '58).

Ovaries excised after pollination can produce fruits on simple medium containing mineral salts, sugar and, vitamin. Ovaries taken from unpollinated flowers fail to produce fruits on such a simple medium. Unpollinated flower may develop into seedless fruits on a medium supplemented with hormones. In *Lycopersicon* Nitsch ('51) obtained seedless fruits by culturing unpollinated ovaries on a medium supplemented with 2-4-D or 2-naphthoxyacetic acid. Chopra ('58) obtained parthenocarpic fruits of *Althea rosea* on a medium containing indole butyric acid.

Pollination stimulus is required for ovary and seed development even by most apomicts. Only female plants of *Aerva tomentosa* growing in Delhi is an apomict. Puri ('63) cultured excised spikes, flowers, ovaries. etc. of this plant and noted that on a medium supplemented with IAA and yeast extract portions of spike grow well and produce seeds, which are comparable to that growing in nature.

Fruits produced on ovary culture usually contain few seeds or poorly developed seeds or no seeds. Nitsch ('51) observed this in ovary culture of *Lycopersicon* and *Nicotiana.* But normal seed development was noted on ovary culture of *Iberis, Hyoscyamus* and *Linaria* on basal medium. *Anethum* requires a supply of coconut milk for normal seed development.

Significance

(1) By ovary culture the physiology of fruit development can be studied.

(2) By ovary culture haploids can be produced. Unfertilised ovaries of *Hordeum vulgare, Nicotiana tabacum* and *Triticum aestivum* develop into haploids.

Parthenogenetic haploids of *Mimulus luteus* cv. *tigrinus grandiflorus* were raised by Hess and Wagner ('75) by pollinating the exposed ovules in ovary culture.

(3) Dormancy period of seeds can be reduced by ovary culture. Achenes of *Ranunculus sceleratus* remain dormant for one year under normal conditions. But the achenes of this plant produced on ovary culture have no dormancy period (Sacher and Guha '62).

(4) Rare hybrids can also be produced on ovary culture.

OVULE CULTURE

White in 1932 first attempted to culture the ovules of *Antirrhinum majus.* The method of ovule culture was improved by Maheswari ('58, '61). He cultured ovules of *Papaver somniferum* excised 6 days after pollination in Nitsch's medium and obtained viable seeds. Initially the embryos grew slowly but after globular stage the growth was rapid.

Like *Papavar*, ovaries of orchids excised after pollination grew normally on a simple culture medium containing 10% sugar (Poddubnaya-Arnoldi '59, '60).

Culture of ovules excised at or after globular stage produced mature seeds easily. This has been noted in several plants, such as, *Allium cepa* (Guha and Johri '66), *Gynandropsis*, *Impatiens* (Chopra and Sabharwal '63) and *Nicotiana tabacum* (Dilieu '66) etc. Ovules excised soon after fertilization, before reaching globular stage, usually failed to produce mature seeds on culture. Such ovules require a special medium for proper growth.

Ovules from various plants excised at early stages, such as, zygote stage or 2-celled proembryo stage, show diverse growth requirements on culture. Thus, ovules of *Zephyranthus* required a medium supplemented with coconut milk and casamino acid for normal embryo development and formation of viable seeds (Kapoor '59). In *Trifolium repens* for proper growth of the ovule a medium containing fruit-juice of cucumber or watermelon was required (Nakajima '69). In *Petunia hybrida* ovules excised 2 days after pollination grew on a medium supplemented with fruit juice of cucumber (Wakizuko and Nakajima '74). It has been noted that the presence of placental tissue favours development of ovule in culture. This was observed in ovule culture of *Gynandropsis* by Chopra and Sabharwal ('63).

When excised ovules of *Gossypium hirsutum* was cultured on a medium supplemented with casein hydrolysate or its ovule extract then tannin accumulated on cotton fibre initials and the fibre initials colapsed (Johri '72). But when the ovule excised two days after anthesis was cultured on a medium containing gibberellin at 30°C then good fibre development was noted (Beasley and Ting '73).

In some interspecific crosses hybrid seedlings failed to develop even by embryo culture technique. By culturing ovules 3 days after pollination of *Gossypium arboreum* × *G. hirsutum* on Murashige and Skoog's medium Pundir ('67) was able to produce hybrid seedlings. Using similar method Steward and Hsu ('78) produced seedlings of different interspecific hybrids of *Gossypium*.

Significance

(1) Zygote or very young embryos which cannot be cultured easily can be grown by ovule culture.

(2) Developmental stages of zygote or young embryo can be studied in ovule culture.

(3) Nutritional requirements of young embryos can be studied.

(4) In some interspecific crosses where embryo culture fails to raise the seedlings, ovule culture may be the effective method to raise viable seedlings.

SEED CULTURE

Some plants produce unorganised embryos, which are not differentiated into radicle, plumule and cotyledons. This is observed in some species of Orchidaceae and Orobanchaceae. In these plants seedlings are formed by the globose embryo directly. In *Eranthis* sp. belonging to Ranunculaceae the seeds contain unorganised embryos during shedding. After the seeds have fallen to the ground, these by intraseminal growth form typical dicot embryos. In orchids during seed germination the plumular pole, that is the embryonal pole distal to the micropyle, forms a protocorm like structure, which later differentiates into roots and shoots (Advani '62). Such type of seedling formation only from one end is known as 'monopolar seedling formation'. In Orobanchaceae also monopolar seedling formation has been noted (Kardy and Tewfic '56). In *Orobanche crenata* the radicular pole (i.e. the pole proximal to the micropyle) produces the seedling.

In seed culture of *Orobanche aegyptica* both monopolar and bipolar seedling formation occurs depending upon the composition of the culture media (Usha '68).

In a medium containing coconut milk or yeast extract monopolar seedling formation occurs. If the medium is supplemented with IAA or gibberellin or kinetin bipolar seedling is formed.

In seed culture of some obligate root parasites such as *Orobanche*, *Striga*, the host stimulus can be replaced by some chemicals. The seeds cultured on a medium supplemented with gibberellin, cytokinin or strigøl can produce seedlings in absence of host stimulus.

Seed cultures of parasitic angiosperms in absence of host usually do not produce haustoria. But certain root-parasitic species of Scrophulariaceae on culture produce haustoria in absence of host when some chemically undefined substance, such as aqueous extract of gum tragacantha is present in the medium (Riopel and Musselman '79, Sahai and Shivanna '81). Some stem parasitic species of Loranthaceae (*Scurrula pulverulenta*) when cultured on White's medium supplemented with casein hydrolysate can produce haustoria (Johri and Bhojowani '77).

Rao ('63) successfully cultured seeds of some interspeoific hybrids of *Vanda* and obtained seedlings either directly or callus is formed from which seedling later differentiates.

NUCELLUS CULTURE

In various species of *Citrus* nucellar monoembryony and polyembryony occur. When nucellar tissue of polyembryonic species of *Citrus* excised after pollination is cultured on White's medium supplemented with casein hydrolysate then callus is formed. This callus produces several pseudobulbils, most of which form embryoids and ultimately produce seedlings (Rangaswamy '61, Sabharwal '62).

Nucellar tissue excised from unfertilized ovules having no adventitive embryoids if cultured on a medium containing malt extract and adenine then embryoids are formed but they are unable to germinate. When such embryoids are excised and cultured on a medium containing gibberellin, then plantlets may be formed which can be transplanted to soil (Button and Bornman '71).

Nucellus of monoembryonic species of *Citrus* (such as, *C. limon*, *C. reticulata*, *C. grandis* etc.) excised from post-fertilised ovules and cultured on White medium containing malt extract produce few embryoids directly without callus formation. From such embryoids healthy plantlets can develop within 6-7 weeks.

In nucellus cultures of *Malus domestica* (Eichholtz '79) and *Vitis vinifera* (Mullins and Srinivasan '76) polyembryony have been noted.

By nucellus culture disease free clones can be obtained.

CHAPTER VII

EMBRYO CULTURE

The method of culturing embryo excised from the seed on sterilised culture medium is called embryo culture.

Haning in 1904 working with *Raphanus* and *Cochlearia* (Brassicaceae) first successfully cultured embryos 'in vitro'. Later various workers cultured embryos of different plants. Dietrich ('25) used semi-solid medium containing some minerals, 2.5—5% sucrose, 1.5% agar for embryo culture. In such a medium mature embryos grew well, but immature embryos did not follow normal developmental stages. Such embryos skipped certain developmental stages and grew directly into seedlings.

Laibach ('25, '29) successfully applied embryo culture technique for raising plants from very light, greatly shrunken hybrid seeds, which normally fail to germinate. He worked with interspecific crosses of *Linum* (*Linum austriacum* × *L. perenne*). He cultured the excised embryos from hybrid seeds on moist blotting paper or cotton wadding containing 10—15% sugar or glucose and obtained fertile hybrid plants. This technique has been widely used to raise hybrid plants from abortive embryos of different interspecific crosses of various plants (such as, *Hordeum, Linum, Prunus* etc.) Jorgensen ('28) used this method to raise hybrids of *Solanum nigrum* × *S. luteum*. Beasley ('40) used it for raising hybrids of *Gossypium hirsutum* × *G. herbaceum*. Smith ('44) used this technique in crosses between *Lycopersicon esculentum* × *L. peruvianum*. In interspecific crosses of *Prunus, Lilium* (Skirm '45) and *Datura* (Sanders '48) this method was used. In interspecific crosses of *Prunus* (between species, such as, *Prunus avium, P. domestica, P. persica* etc.) if early varieties are used as female parents then the seeds abort. Takey ('44) cultured excised embryos of such seeds and obtained healthy, fertile plants.

Sapre ('63) cultured embryos of interspecific hybrids of *Oryza* on Nitsch's medium and obtained transplantable plants. Iyer and Govila ('64) cultured embryos of various interspecific hybrids of *Oryza* on semi-solid medium supplemented with 10% coconut milk, 0.1% malt extract and obtained seedlings which showed almost 100% survival.

Sometimes embryos of interspecific crosses may die at later stages of seed development due to failure of endosperm development or due to incompatibility between embryo and endosperm. Cooper ('78) obtained hybrid plants between barley and rye by embryo culture. Sometimes due to chromosome elemination haploid embryo is formed and endosperm degenerates. Such embryos may be excised and cultured successfully in vitro and from this haploid plantlets are obtained.

Methods—For culturing the embryos under aseptic conditions several measures are adopted. Working area is sterilised. Scalpels, needles, forceps etc. are dipped in 70% alcohol and then flamed. The selected fruit is surface sterilised for 15 minutes with alcohol or calcium hypochlorite or sodium hypochlorite solution and then washed thoroughly in double distilled water. The fruit is cut and ovule or seed is taken out with a sterile forcep and placed on a sterile petridish. The seed or ovule is cut open and the embryo is extracted. The excised embryo is immediately placed on the nutrient medium of a culture vial under aseptic conditions.

Planted embryos on tubes, flasks, bottles or other containers are kept at room temperature in diffused light. Seedlings are produced and these are transferred to a sterile growth stimulating medium before transfer to the field conditions.

Nutrient medium—The nutritional requirement of a growing embryo gradually decreases and its biosynthetic capacity gradually increases. So the composition of the culture medium will depend upon the stage of the embryo to be cultured.

For culturing young embryos (heteromorphic phase) inorganic medium only is not sufficient. Such a medium should be supplemented with organic substances, such as, yeast extract, malt extract, sugar etc. La Rue ('36) used IAA instead of yeast extract. In 1942 Van Overbeck used coconut milk in culture medium. In 1944 Blakeslee and Satina used malt extract. Sander ('48, '50) said that various plants have different nutritional requirements.

In jute many attempts to raise interspecific hybrids of *Corchorus olitorius* × *C. capsularis* failed due to post fertilization barriers. Islam ('64) used a medium supplemented with 0.1% yeast extract, 0.05 ppm kinetin, 0.05 ppm IIA for culturing the hybrid embryos of the cross between *C. capsularis* (♀) × *C. olitorius* (♂). In this medium the hybrid embryo grew into transplantable seedling.

It is easier to culture differentiated embryos. Such embryos can grow on culture medium containing some mineral salts and sucrose only, as they can synthesise most of the substances required for their growth. This stage is called autotrophic phase.

Factors influencing embryo culture

(1) **Stage of the embryo**—Globular or post-globular embryos are cultured on medium supplemented with coconut milk, yeast extract or casein hydrolysate or growth hormones (such as auxin, cytokinin, gibberellin etc.). Preglobular embryos usually fail to grow in culture or form unorganised callus tissue. This suggests that the mother tissue adjacent to the embryo not only supplies nourishment to the young embryo, but also helps the young embryos to pass through a predetermied course of embryogenesis.

Young embryo of *Cuscuta reflexa* and globular embryo of *Dendropthoe fulcata* (Johri and Bajaj '62) on culture produce callus tissue which later form many embryoids (Fig. 13). In barley Norstog ('65) observed that proembryos measuring 0.1 mm or less fail to grow normally. They produce callus tissue from which embryoids are formed. But he noted that larger embryos (0.15 mm) of barley can grow in normal culture medium.

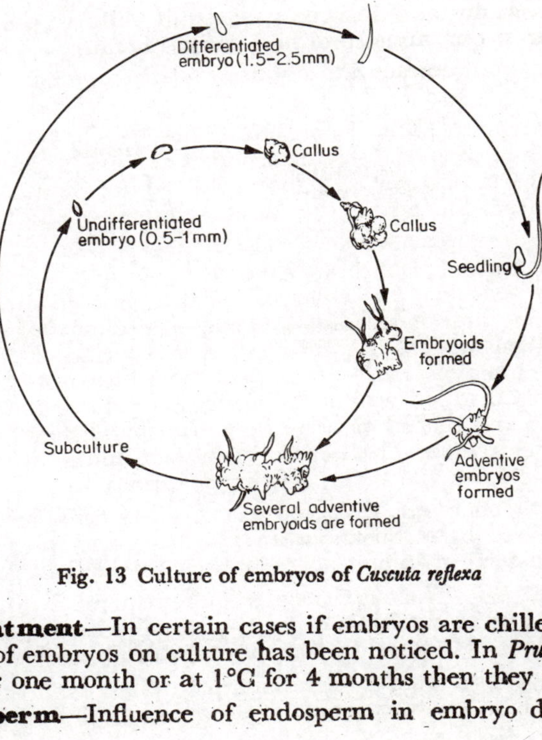

Fig. 13 Culture of embryos of *Cuscuta reflexa*

(2) **Pretreatment**—In certain cases if embryos are chilled before culture then better response of embryos on culture has been noticed. In *Prunus*, if the embryos are stored at 5°C for one month or at 1°C for 4 months then they grow better.

(3) **Endosperm**—Influence of endosperm in embryo development is signifi-

cant. Krause ('74) observed that hybrid embryos from a cross between *Hordeum* and *Secale* survive on culture only in 1% cases. But such an embryo on culture when placed on an endosperm, then the viability increases to 30—40%. This indicates that the young embryos in nature get their required growth substances from the endosperm and adjacent maternal tissue.

De Latour ('78), Williams ('78, '80) and Williams and De Latour ('80) developed methods of culturing young hybrid embryos in excised endosperm from normal ovules of either parent or of other species. Using this method they were able to raise several interspecific hybrids of *Trifolium*.

In *Colocasia esculenta* embryos fail to develop due to inadequate food supply from the endosperm. In 1960 Abraham and Ramachandaran excised the embryos and grew them on culture and obtained seedlings.

Regeneration potentiality of different parts of an embryo

Regeneration capacity of different parts of an embryo varies. Lee ('55) working with lupin noted that those segments which included the plumule can form seedlings. Bajaj ('66) observed similar behaviour of the embryo in *Dendropthoe fulcata*. Cotyledons play an important role in the development of the seedling. It has been observed in *Avena, Hordeum, Pennisetum* etc. that if part of the cotyledon is removed before culture then the development of the embryo is suppressed according to the size of the removed cotyledon. In *Cassythea* redicular halves of the cotyledon control shoot development. If the plumular halves of both cotyledons are removed then also healthy shoots can develop (Rangaswamy ano Rangan '71). (Fig. 14).

In 1981 Tilton observed in *Zea mays* that presence of scutellum is essential for growth and development of roots.

Culture of embryos of stem and root parasites in absence of hosts

In 1963 Rangaswamy and Rangan successfully cultured the embryos of *Cassytha filiformis*, a stem parasite in absence of host or its stimulus.

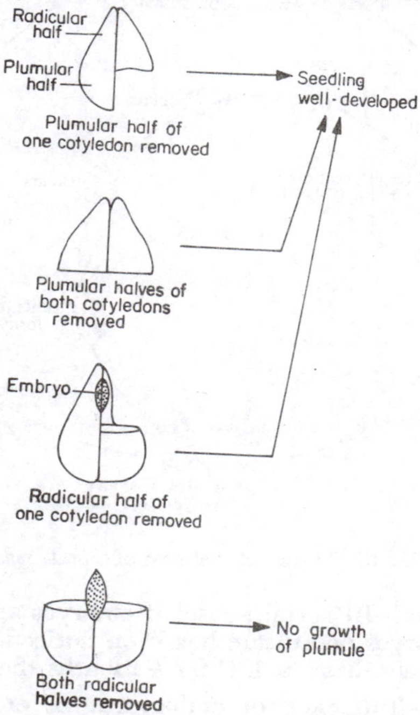

Fig. 14. Effect of cotyledon on seedling formation in *Cassythea filiformis*

In *Orobanche egyptica*, a root parasite culture of seeds with unorganised embryos produces callus tissue which later differentiates into shoot tips. Similar observations were made by Rangan in 1965 working with *Cistanche tubulosa.*

Significance of embryo culture

(1) We can study the nutritional requirements of the embryos at various developmental stages by embryo culture.

Differentiated embryos can grow in a simple medium containing sucrose and few mineral salts (autotrophic phase), whereas young embryos cannot grow on such a simple medium (heterotrophic phase).

(2) By embryo culture it is possible to know the factors controlling differentiation of embryos.

(3) Many interspecific hybrid plants can be produced by embryo culture. Utilising this technique wider range of hybridization can be done with success.

Many desirable crosses are not possible due to some pre-fertilization barriers or poor and abnormal endosperm development or endosperm-embryo incompatibility. In cross between *Hordeum vulgare* × *H. bulbosum* no endosperm is formed and the embryo aborts. Davis ('60) successfully cultured the embryos excised 14—28 days after pollination and raised the seedlings. In cross involving *Linum auratum* and *L. speciosum-album* due to embryo-endosperm incompatibility seedlings are not formed (Emsweller and Uhring '62). By culturing young embryos Bhatnagar and Bhojwani produced hybrid plants.

(4) **Shortening of dormancy period**—By embryo culture the dormancy period of seeds can be shortened. In *Iris* seeds remain dormant for 2-3 years, but by embryo culture such seeds can germinate in the same year. (Randolph and Cox '43, Randolph '45).

Nickel ('51) observed that *Malus* seeds take about 9 months to germinate. But the excised embryos on culture started germination within 48 hours and within 4 weeks produced transplantable seedlings which grew to a height of one meter approximately within five months.

(5) **Propagation of rare plants**—Some abnormal coconuts instead of producing endosperm form solid soft tissue (Mohan Ram '76), such nuts are rare and costly and are called 'makapuno'. The seeds of this variety failed to germinate normally. In 1969 de Guzman was successful in producing makapuno seedlings by using embryo culture technique.

(6) **Seed viability test**—According to Barton ('61) by embryo culture we can know about seed viability.

(7) **Production of haploids**—From haploid plants arising from crosses between distantly related plants viable plants can be produced by embryo culture.

(8) **Introduction of disease resistance character**—For introducing disease resistance character from wild tomato *Lycopersicon peruvianum* to cultivated tomato *L. esculentum* crosses were made but no seedling is obtained. Bhojowani and Bhatnagar cultured hybrid embryos excised thirty-five days after pollination and obtained callus followed by plantlet formation.

CHAPTER VIII

ANTHER AND POLLEN CULTURE

Shimakura first cultured anther 'in vitro' with a view to investigating the physiology of meiosis. Tulecke ('53) first noticed that the mature pollen grains of *Ginkgo biloba* could be induced to form a callus on suitable medium containing inorganic salts, sucrose, Vit. B and coconut milk. Guha and Maheswari ('66) cultured anthers of *Datura innoxia* on a medium supplemented with kinetin, coconut milk or grape juice and obtained haploid embryoids, which grew into plantlets. This method is now applied with success on various plant species, such as *Atropa, Brassica, Hordeum, Lycopersicon, Nicotiana, Oryza, Solanum, Triticum, Zea,* etc.

In *Taxus brevifolia* mature pollens can produce callus when cultured on a medium supplemented with synthetic auxin.

Nutrient Medium—Anthers or pollens can be cultured on a suitable medium containing sucrose (usually 2%), iron, vitamins, hormones etc. The hormonal component of the medium is important for initiation of growth. Usually to the culture medium auxin, cytokinin etc. are added either singly or in various combinations. Low concentration of auxin stimulates callus formation. In a medium supplemented with auxin embryoid formation usually occurs at a faster rate as observed in anther culture of *Datura* (Sopory '72). Anthers cultured on a medium containing coconut milk or kinetin develop embryoids which later form haploid plantlets. Callus is formed from pollen grains on a medium supplemented with yeast extract or casein hydrolysate.

In raising haploid plants from isolated pollen culture of *Nicotiana tabacum* and *Datura* Nitsch ('74) used a synthetic medium containing glutamine, l-serine, inositol.

In *N. tabacum* plantlet formation from pollen also depends on iron concentration. In culture of *Brassica* pollens on Nitsch's medium ('51) increased sucrose concentration is needed.

Factors affecting anther and pollen culture

(1) **Activated charcoal**—It has a stimulatory effect on embryogenesis and this has been observed in anther cultures of potato, rye, tobacco, etc. This may be due to removal of inhibitory substances from agar by activated charcoal. Charcoal may absorb the degradation product (5-2-furfural) of sucrose. Anther cultures of *Petunia* and *Nicotiana* indicate that activated charcoal removes both exogenous and endogenous growth hormones from culture medium.

(2) **Temperature**—Temperature has significant effect on pollen embryoid development. In *Datura* embryoids are not formed if cultures are maintained at 20°C or below (Sopory '72). In *Nicotiana tabacum* optimal temperature for embryoid growth is 25°C (Sunderland '72).

Pretreatment of anthers at 3—10°C for 2—30 days stimulates embryogenesis (Sunderland and Roberts '77). Wenzel ('77) observed that buds of *Secale cerale* pretreated at 6°C for 6—10 days develop embryoids. In *N. tabacum* if the buds are pretreated at 5°C for 72 hours then 58% anthers produce embryoids (Nitsch '74). Sometimes pretreatment at high temperature helps embryoid formation. In *Brassica campestris* pretreatment of anthers at 35°C for 24 hours helps embryoid formation.

Centrifugation of the anthers at 3—5°C for approximately 30 minutes helps embryoid formation.

(3) **Stage of the anther**—Particular stage of the anther at the time of culture is important. Usually anthers just before or immediately after pollen mitosis are most suitable for culture. Suitable stages of anthers for culture are pre-mitotic, mitotic and post-mitotic.

(a) Pre-mitotic stage—Anthers at this stage have microspores which have just completed the first meiotic division and the pollens are immature, uninucleate and starch-free. Anthers of *Hordeum vulgare* and *Hyocyamus* at this stage are suitable for culture. According to Nitsch ('72) and Sunderland ('71) anthers with uninucleate pollens are suitable for culture.

(b) Mitotic stage—In some plants, anthers at first pollen division stage are most suitable for culture, as observed in *Nicotiana tabacum* and *Datura innoxia*.

(c) Post-mitotic stage—Early bicellular stage of pollen development is most suitable for culture in *Atropa belladonna* and *Nicotiana* sp. etc.

Mature anthers are usually unsuitable for culture, but in *Brassica oleracea* mature anthers are the proper stage for anther culture.

Anthers of proper stage are choosen by selecting flower buds of definite length under fixed environmental conditions.

(4) **Photoperiod and light intensity**—Higher number of embryoids are formed when anthers are taken from plant grown under short days (Dunwell and Perry '73, Heberle-Boss and Reinert '80) and high light intensities.

(5) **Flowering time**—Anthers taken from flowers at the beginning of the flowering period of the plant are most suitable for culture.

(6) **Endogenous auxin**—Embryogenic pollens are found near the tapetum within the anthers. The tapetum may release some substance which initiates embryogenic development in pollens. This is observed in *Hyoscyamus niger* by Raghavan ('78).

(7) **Age of the plant**—Usually anthers from younger plants are more suitable for culture.

Methods of anther culture

(1) Selected plants are cultivated until they reach flower bud stage.

(2) In some cases flower buds are chilled few days prior to culture.

(3) Flower buds of proper size and developmental stage are taken and surfaces sterilised with alcohol or hypochlorite solution for 10—20 minutes. Buds are rinsed several times in sterile double distilled water.

(4) The anthers are carefully excised from flower buds using forcep and dissecting needle. Filaments must be removed prior to culture, otherwise callus may be formed at the cut ends.

(5) Anthers may be cultured either on agar-solidified culture medium (Sunderland and Wicks '71) or placed on a filter paper bridge over a liquid medium (Sunderland and Roberts '77).

(6) Anthers are cultured at 25°C in presence or absence of light. Light is essential after plantlets are formed. Continuous illumination from cool white fluorescent lamp of 300 lux is satisfactory.

(7) After a period of 4—5 weeks in culture plantlets are formed. From a single anther many plantlets are formed (Fig. 15).

(8) These plantlets are carefully separated quite early and cultured on a fresh root-inducing medium containing 0.5% agar and all other components in half-strength to that of the anther culture medium.

(9) After formation of proper root system they are transplanted to pots. These pots are preferably kept in humid condition for few days.

Nitsch ('72) cultured anthers of tobacco and obtained in 75% of the cultured anthers 1—100 plantlets per anther. Depending on the species and composition of the culture medium the plantlets may be formed directly from the pollens or a callus is formed, from which later plantlets are formed (Fig. 15). Plants arising from an anther are heterogenous.

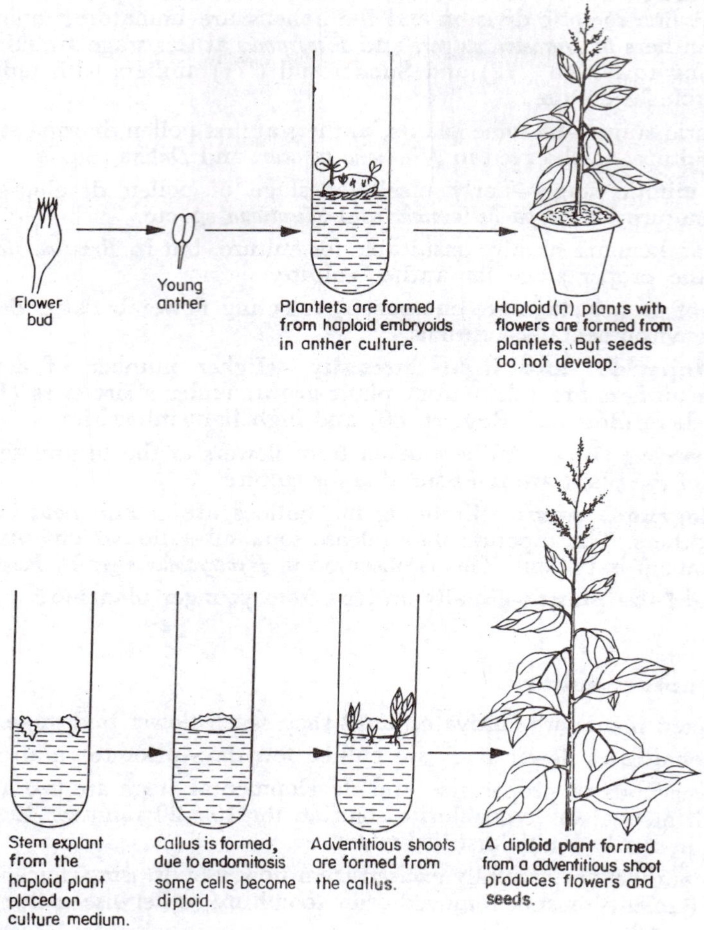

Fig. 15. Anther Culture : Haploid plants are formed on anther culture, from the stem explant of a haploid plant callus is formed. A diploid plant is produced from this callus.

Methods of pollen culture

Stages 1-4 are same as that of anther culture technique

(5) Anthers are placed in a 5 c.c. liquid medium in a petridish. Pollen grains are removed from the anthers either mechanically or by natural dehiscence. For removing pollen grains mechanically from the anthers a slight incision is made on the anther tissue with a scalpel and its contents are gently squeezed into the medium. To obtain pollen grains from the anthers Sunderland and Roberts developed 'float culture' technique. In this method whole anthers are taken from cold treated buds and are allowed to float on the surface of the liquid medium. Within few days the anthers dehisce and liberate pollen grains at various developmental stages.

(6) Petridishes containing the pollen grains in the culture media are sealed with parafilm and incubated at 28°C in dark for fourteen days.

(7) After 14 days the culture is kept in an illuminated chamber at 25°C and a day length of 12 hours.

(8) 3–8 weeks may be required to obtain haploid plantlets.

Nurse culture technique for pollen culture

Sharp ('73) working with tomato (*Lycopersicon esculentum*) developed nurse culture technique for the formation of haploid clones from isolated pollen grains (Fig. 16). This method in brief is as follows:

(1) An anther is placed horizontally on a semisolid nutrient medium. A filter paper disc is placed over it.

(2) From another anther pollen grain suspension is prepared in a liquid medium having about 10 pollens per 0.5 c.c. of the medium.

(3) Over each filter paper disc 10 pollen grains are transferred. This is incubated at 25°C in presence of light.

(4) Within a month several haploid clones are formed.

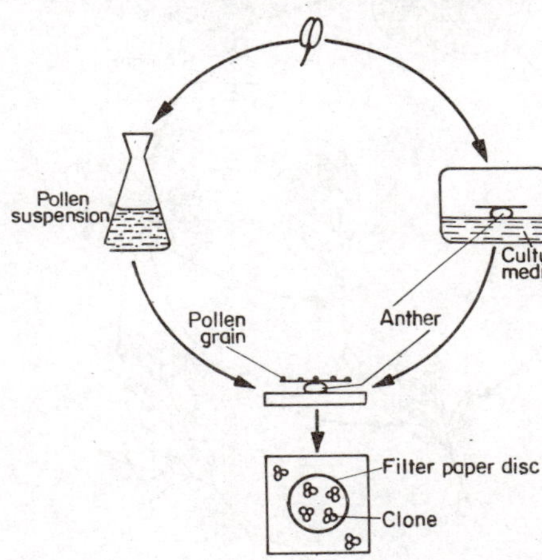

Fig. 16. Nurse culture technique for pollen culture in tomato.

Production of plantlets from pollen grains

Early pathway of pollen grain development differs in different plants. Uninucleate pollen grains divide in culture either equally or unequally into two cells (Fig. 17).

(a) If two equal cells are formed by division of pollen grain, then both cells participate in sporocyte formation as in *Datura innoxia*.

(b) Pollen grains divide unequally forming a small reproductive cell and a large vegetative cell. Sporocyte is formed from the vegetative cell, e.g. *Nicotiana tabacum*.

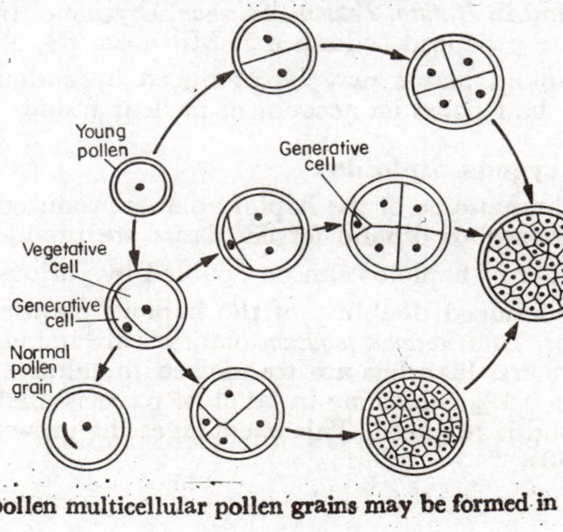

Fig. 17. From young pollen multicellular pollen grains may be formed in three different pathways.

(c) Small reproductive cell formed by unequal division of the pollen grain gives rise to the sporophyte, e.g. *Hyocyamus niger*.

(d) Pollen grain divides unequally and both cells participate in sporophyte formation.

Irrespective of the early pathway of division followed, the pollen grain gradually becomes multicellular. In *Atropa, Datura* and *Nicotiana* these cells gradually form a globular embryo which follows normal development. In this method one haploid plant is formed from one pollen grain. But in most cases the wall of the pollen grain bursts and the multicellular tissue is liberated, which by further divisions form callus. Many embryoids are formed from such a callus (Fig. 18).

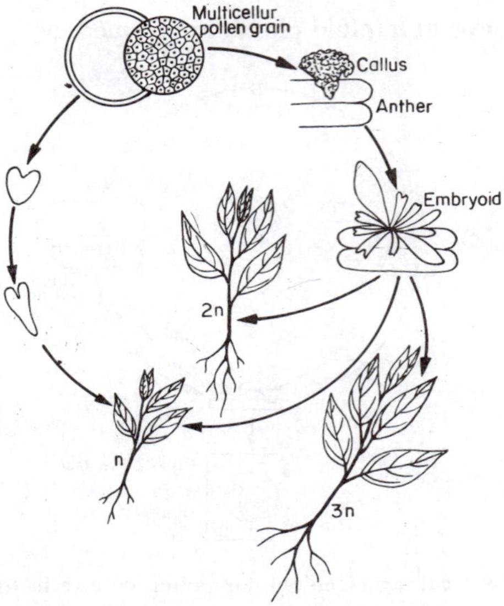

Fig. 18. From multicellular pollen embryoids may be formed directly, which produce haploid plants, or a callus is formed. From the callus in addition to haploid plants some diploid and triploid plants are formed.

Ploidy level of pollen plants

Embryoids formed directly from the pollen grains are haploid. But the sporophytic plants formed from the callus are mixoploid, because endopolyploidy usually occurs during callus culture. Plants derived from callus are usually diploids and triploids. Triploids are found in *Datura, Petunia, Solanum, Oryza* etc. In *Oryza sativa* haploid to pentaploid plants are produced (Nitsch and Mitsuoka '69, Nizeki and Oono '71).

Diploid and tetraploid plants may be produced by endomitosis. Triploid and pentaploid plants may be formed on account of nuclear fusion.

Production of homozygous diploids

By doubling the chromosome of the haploid plants produced by pollen or anther culture completely homozygous diploid fertile plants are produced.

Chromosome number of haploids can be doubled by various methods.

(1) In chemically induced doubling of the haploid plantlets, the plantlets are treated with colchicine. In *Nicotiana tabacum* plantlets are immersed in 0.4% solution of colchicine upto 96 hours. Plantlets are transferred to culture medium after treatment. In mature plants 0.4% colchicine in lanoline paste is used on the upper axillary buds. Terminal bud is removed. This encourages the growth of the lateral buds (Nakata and Taneka '70).

(2) In regeneration by tissue culture diploids may be produced due to endomitosis in callus.

Significance

(1) Pollen culture has great importance in mutagenic studies.

(2) By anther and pollen culture many haploid plants can be produced very rapidly.

(3) Homozygous diploid plants obtained by doubling the chromosomes of haploids have great importance in plant breeding and crop improvement.

CHAPTER IX

CALLUS CULTURE

Callus is formed by the proliferation of the parent tissue. The cells of a callus are parenchymatous, amorphous and unorganised. Generally callus is formed as a result of injury at the cut ends of a stem or a root. Localised centres of activity is recorded in a *callus*.

When tissues on culture produce unorganised mass of callus with no regular form then it is called *callus culture*.

Callus formation from isolated stem segments of *Populus* was first observed by Rechinger in 1893.

Working with cambial tissues of carrot and tobacco first prolonged callus culture were simultaneously reported by Gautheret in Paris, Nobecourt in England and White in Princeton, USA in 1930.

Gautheret cultured explants of carrot root on a medium containing inorganic salts, sugar (glucose), thiamine, cystine and IAA. On culture the explant grew forming undifferentiated tissue or callus. By repeated subculturing this callus was maintained for a prolonged period.

White ('39) cultured the stem procambium of hybrid *Nicotiana glauca* × *N. langsdorfii* on agar medium where callus was formed.

Materials—Callus may initiate from explants of any multicellular plant (Yeoman and Macleod '77). Explants from stem, root, leaf, flower, fruit or seed etc. may be taken for culture. Callus formation has been recorded from storage parenchyma, pericyclic cells of roots, cambial cells of vascular bundles, provascular cells, secondary phloem, pith cells, mesophyll cells and cotyledons.

Usually large pieces of tissue are selected for culture. Minimum size of the explant is generally determined by the average cell size of the tissue to be cultured. 3.8 mg carrot explant having about 25,000 cells is viable. But as the cells of Jerusalem artichoke is much larger, the minimum size of the explant is found to be 8 mg having about 20,000 cells. But Caplin ('63) successfully cultured much smaller explant of artichoke.

For subculturing the inoculum should not be very small, as very small inoculum fails to grow or shows little growth. According to Street ('69) the inoculum should be 0.5—1 cm and weighing about 20—100 mg.

Subculture—The callus is subcultured because (a) the nutrient may be exhausted, (b) agar may be dessicated, or (c) cell metabolites may accumulate and cause toxicity. Active growth can be maintained even after several subcultures. Repeated subculturing can be avoided by freeze preservation of the culture (Withers '79).

Nutrient medium

Some standard media, such as, Murashige and Skoog's medium can be successfully used for callus culture. For initiation and maintaining callus kinetin is widely used in the medium.

For callus initiation usually an exogenous supply of hormone is required. But explants having cambial cells do not require a supply of hormone. According to hormone requirements callus culture may be of five types. These are—(a) auxin requiring cultures, (b) cytokinin requiring cultures, (c) cultures requiring both auxin and cytokinin, (d) gibberellin requiring cultures. In some plants, such as tobacco, presence of gibberellin and N_6 2 isopentenyl adenine in the medium favours callus growth. But gibberellin inhibits growth of callus tissue in monocots, (e) cultures requiring other natural extracts, such as, yeast extract, coconut milk, casein hydrolysate or tomato juice etc.

Methods of culture

Usually explants from suitable materials (such as, carrot root, potato or sweet potato tuber, stem of tobacco, hypocotyl and cotyledon of soyabean etc.) are taken.

The explant is first surface sterilised with 1.6% sodium hypochlorite solution or 0.1% mercuric chloride solution or 1% aqueous solution of bromine. Then the inner uncontaminated tissue is excised.

If the excised tissue (such as, root, hypocotyl, cotyledon etc.) is taken from a seedling then the seed before germination is surface sterilised and allowed to germinate under aseptic conditions.

Carrot root culture

(1) Fresh and healthy carrot root is selected. It is thoroughly washed in running tap water.

(2) External 1-2 mm is scraped. Upper 1 cm of carrot root is discarded and then it is cut into 0.5 cm thick slices (Fig. 19).

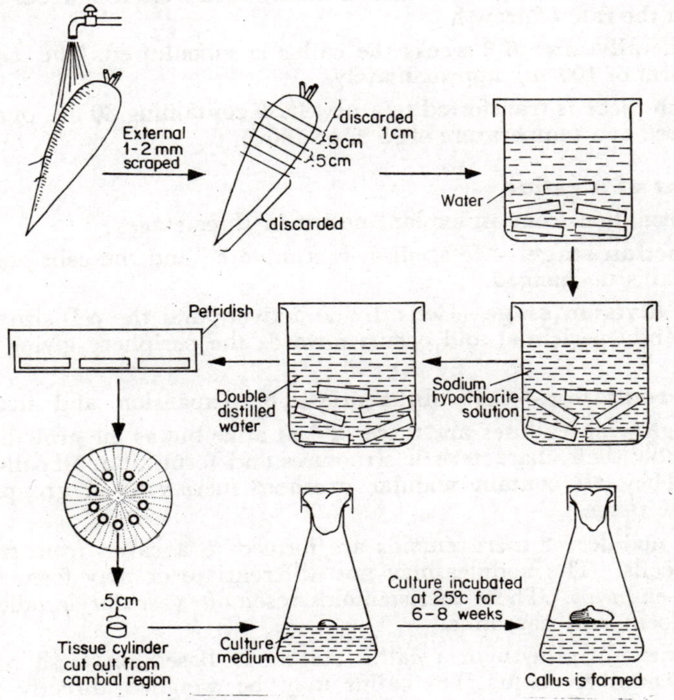

Fig. 19. Carrot root culture.

(3) These slices are placed immediately in a beaker containing water.

(4) These are then transferred to a beaker containing sodium hypochlorite solution and kept there for 10 minutes.

(5) Slices are taken out with a sterile forcep from the hypochlorite solution and washed successively in 3 beakers containing double distilled water keeping the slices for 20—30 seconds in each. The slices are kept in the third beaker.

(6) A carrot slice is taken and is placed on a petridish. Tissue cylinders are cut out from the cambial region by a sterilised cork borer. After cutting maximum number of tissue cylinders from the cambial region remaining portion of the slice is discarded.

(7) Tissue cylinders are placed in a petridish containing double distilled water.

(8) A tissue cylinder is transferred to a petridish and its two sides are trimmed with a sterile scalpel and discarded.

(9) Remaining cylinder is cut into explants measuring 5 mm diameter and 2 mm thickness.

(10) These explants are placed in a petridish containing double distilled water.

(11) Explants are then transferred with a sterile forcep on the surface of a sterile filter paper on a petridish. The upper and lower surfaces of each explant are blotted.

(12) One such explant is transferred to each culture tube containing the nutrient medium.

(13) Culture tubes are kept in a glass storage jar, wrapped in aluminium foil and placed in an incubator at 25°C.

(14) The surface of the explant after few days becomes somewhat rough, indicating initiation of the callus. Callus can be maintained from few weeks to three months depending on the rate of growth.

(15) Generally after 6-8 weeks the callus is subcultured. The callus is divided into small parts of 100 mg approximately.

(16) Each piece is transferred to a new flask containing 30 c.c. of culture medium and subcultured at a temperature of 25°C or above.

Development of a callus

Callus formation from an explant occurs in three stages:

(a) **Induction stage**—Metabolism is stimulated and the cells prepare to divide. Cell size remains unchanged.

(b) **Cell division stage**—Cells divide actively and the cell size decreases. Cell division is mainly periclinal and occurs towards the periphery giving rise to wound cambial cells.

(c) **Differentiation**—Cells differentiate by expansion and maturation.

Rapidly growing calluses are more or less alike but as the growth rate decreases the calluses show their characteristic structures and forms. But all calluses have some similarities. They all contain nodular or sheet meristems in groups or scattered throughout the tissue.

Vascular nodules or meristemoids are formed in a callus from small groups of meristematic cells. The nodules may not differentiate or may form root or shoot primordia or embryos. These meristemoids resemble vascular bundles and consist of xylem, phloem and cambium.

Measurement of growth in a callus culture is based on fresh weight or dry weight or cell number counts. The callus may be weighed directly under aseptic conditions.

Nature of callus tissue

Morphological nature of the callus tissue varies considerably. Some cultures are hard and anatomically consists of compactly arranged small cells without intercellular spaces. Such callus may be composed of lignified cells. Other callus may be *friable* and anatomically consists of large loosely arranged cells with intercellular spaces. Friable callus is fragile and easily breaks up. These are suitable for suspension culture, where the tissue can be dispersed by mechanical agitation.

Reinert and White ('56) working with *Picea glauca* noted that hard compact callus can easily give rise to friable callus but the friable type cannot form compact type. But Blakesly and Steward ('61) working with *Haplopappus gracilis* and Grant and Fuller ('68) working with *Vicia faba* showed that friable callus and hard callus are interconvertible.

The *colour* of the callus also varies and usually depends on the colour of the tissue from which it is taken. The callus may be colourless or green containing chlorophyll or yellow having carotenoids or flavonoids or it may be purple due to the presence of anthocyanin. Callus may be uniformly or partially coloured. Calluses derived from green explants are not always autotropic. Chlorophyll containing callus requires an exogenous supply of sugar (Hildebrandt and et al) and light. Carrot root explants cultured on a medium supplemented with IAA, inositol, kinetin in presence of light become autotropic. After repeated subculture the colour of the callus may change. Concentration of sugar, dextrose and soluble starch, deficiency of nitrogen, light, temperature and exogenous auxin etc. influence the colour of the callus.

Anatomically, a callus may be **homogenous,** consisting of uniform parenchyma cells or it may be **heterogenous,** having differentiation into tracheids, seive tubes, trichomes, secretory cells and suberised cells etc. Callus which grows actively may be composed of large vacuolated parenchyma cells and small closely arranged dividing cells. Such variations among the cells of the callus tissue is due to the origin and age of the callus and the composition of the culture medium.

Grant and Fuller ('68) noted that friable callus contains larger amount of cell wall polysaccharides than compact callus, but a lower amount of cellulose compared with hemicellulose and pectic substances.

In a callus culture phenotypic variations may occur due to *epigenetic* changes. Such changes are reversible and occur due to selective gene expression as in cytokinin habituation.

Callus on prolonged culture shows changes in the *nuclear cytology* of the cells. Changes both in chromosome structure and chromosome number have been noted. Chromosomal aberrations, nuclear fragmentation or endopolyploidy etc. are observed. With the age of the callus culture these nuclear abnormalities increase and certain aneuploid or polyploid cells divide more rapidly than normal cells and form the dominant cell line. Within few months of the callus culture nuclear changes may occur. But certain callus is comparatively stable. In *Crepis capillaris* and *Helianthus annus* callus remains stable for about two years.

Significance

(1) Yeoman and Mitchell ('70) described a method to determine the total amount of nucleic acids (i.e., DNA and RNA) rapidly from callus culture.

(2) By using tracer elements in callus culture the path of various metabolic processes has been determined. For determination of duration and extent of DNA tritiated thymidine was used (Harland '71). In rose callus culture Dougall ('65) used C_{14} amino acids to understand the pathway of protein synthesis. In callus culture of the Jerusalem artichoke Fraser ('68) used P_{32} phosphate to investigate the metabolism of RNA.

(3) Friable callus is suitable for cell suspension culture.

CHAPTER X

ORGANOGENESIS

From cells of tissue culture various organs, such as, roots, stems, leaves or flowers may be initiated. This is called *organogenesis*. Such organ development does not require any pre-existing initials. These new organs are formed in two stages. In the first phase (dedifferentiation) cells of the explant divide and form undifferentiated cells. In the second phase cell differentiation takes places.

Organ primordia are formed from single cells or small groups of differentiated cells. These cells form small meristem with cells containing dense cytoplasm and large nuclei.

According to Torrey ('66) meristemoids (i.e., meristematic zones) occur near the tissue medium interface.

Root formation in culture is called *rhizogenesis* and shoot initiation is called *caulogenesis*.

Root formation on culture has been noted in several cases. In culture of carrot cells root formation was first observed by Nobecourt ('39b). Explants taken from any part of a plant may produce roots. Like roots shoot buds are also formed frequently. Leaves develop less frequently than roots and shoots.

Root formation on culture of Jerusalem artichoke is influenced by mineral salts, auxin, sugar, temperature and light (Gautheret '69).

Root formation stops after several subcultures. These may be due to (a) some substances required for root initiation may be exhausted, (b) culture tissue is incapble of rhizogenesis or (c) epigenetic changes of some genes may occur (Meins '83).

Few layers of epidermal or subepidermal cells from various plants under regulated condition on culture can produce organs. (Tran Thanh Van '80). In *Begonia rex* explants from epidermal or subepidermal layers near the midveins of leaves can produce roots or shoots rapidly (Tran Thanh Van and Chlyah '75, Tran Thanh Van '80). Root initiation occurs in a medium supplemented with zeatin and NAA. Shoot initiation takes place in presence of zeatin but in absence of auxin.

In short term cultures organization of the new meristem bears a relationship with the original organization of the explant. In culture of tobacco stalk shoot primordium arises from the external phloem. In culture of *Convolvulus* roots shoot primordium originates near the protoxylem. In culture of carrot cells root primordium arises in association with the protoxylem strands and when this is transferred to an agar medium, it forms a complete plant.

In long term cultures shoot and bud primordia develop exogenously. But in some cases, as in *Convolvulus* callus shoot primordia develop either exogenously or endogenously (Bonnett and Torrey '66).

Culture of explants from lower internodes produce vegetative buds, whereas explants from young upper parts or from inflorescence produce flower buds. For flower formation high level of nitrogen, presence of cytokinin and various constituents of nucleic acid in the medium, are necessary. Presence of auxin, gibberellin and organic nitrogenous compounds have an inhibitory effect on flower formation.

Factors influencing organogenesis

(1) Age of culture

A young culture frequently produces organs. As the culture becomes older, this capacity decreases and ultimately disappears. But there are few exceptions. The culture of *Amorphophallus* retains its regeneration capacity indefinitely (Morel and Wetmore '51). Culture of carrot cells can produce roots for many years.

(2) **Ploidy level**

In culture there is instability of genome. Only a few weeks after isolation of a diploid callus various degrees of ploidy (mostly tetraploid) have been noticed in various plants (e.g. culture of medullary parenchyma of *Nicotiana tabacum*, *Haplopappus* shoots, pollens of *Ginkgo*). Only in a few cases the culture tissues maintain their normal diploid sets, as in culture of tubers of *Helianthus tuberosus*, leaves of *Crepis capillaris* and *Medicago sativa*.

In certain cases, as in culture of pea root callus with increase in ploidy there is decrease in organogenesis. But in some plants, under suitable conditions organs may develop with polyploid meristem.

Loss of capacity to organogenesis is reversible in some cases. This may be due to conditions of culture and other non-genetical factors.

(3) **Phytohormons**

Plant hormones have some effect on organogenesis. Gautheret ('45) noted that auxin at proper concentration can induce root primordia formation in carrot explants.

Skoog first said that organogenesis can be chemically controlled. Skoog and Miller ('57) observed in tobacco a high auxin cytokinin ratio favours root initiation and a low ratio favours shoot initiation. Other scientists also observed that under regulated auxin, cytokinin ratio and carbohydrate supply formation of roots and floral or vegetative buds occur (Tran Thanh Van, Chlyah and Chlyan '74, Tran Thanh Van and Trinh '78). In serveral dicots shoot formation occurs when the ratio between exogenous cytokinin and auxin is 100 : 10. But a ratio of 10 : 100 favours formation of root primordia.

In monocots shoot initiation occurs on a medium with high 2-4-D and kinetin ratio for four days and then transferred to a medium lacking hormone. In absence of auxin shoot initiation occurs in some cases. For bud initiation certain plants do not require an exogenous supply of cytokinin.

Endogenous gibberellin retards root and shoot initiation. In callus during shoot initiation starch accumulates. Gibberellin lowers the concentration of starch and thereby inhibits shoot initiation (Therpe '78, Maeda and Thorpe '79).

Endogenous ethylene retards organ initiation during early stages of culture, but in later stages it helps shoot initiation. This has been observed in culture of tobacco cotyledons (Everett '82) and *Lilium* bulb tissue (Aartrijük and Blom-Barnhoorn '83).

According to some scientists phenolic compounds in addition to auxin are more effective for root initiation than auxin alone (Welander and Hantrieser '81). On culture of *Helianthus tuberosus* explant in addition to the auxin the presence of sugar, light, temperature etc. play a major role in root initiation (Gautheret '66).

(4) **Phosphate concentration**

Increase in phosphate concentration favours shoot formation and suppresses or weakens root initiation.

(5) **Photoperiodism and Vernalization**

Flower formation on culture can be induced by photoperiodism in *Plumbago indica* (Nitsch '68) and by vernalization in *Cichorium intybus* and *Lunaria annua* (Nitsch and Nitsh '64, Pierik '67).

Plantlet formation form tomato leaves:

From surface sterilised young leaves rectangular explants (6 mm $\times$ 8 mm) are cut out. Each explant is placed on a tube containing 15 c.c. of Murashige and Skoog's medium, which is composed of mineral salts, thiamine (0.4 mg/l), myo-inositol (100 mg/l), sucrose (30,000 mg/l) and a growth regulator. For root initiation 2 mg/l IAA and 2 mg/l kinetin are needed at 12 hours photoperiod and a temperature of 25°C. After initiation of root the callus is transferred to a medium containing 4 mg/l kinetin and 4 mg/l IAA. In this medium shoot initiation occurs after four weeks. Culture is transferred to a medium without any hormone. Subculture can be done every 3-4 weeks.

CHAPTER XI

SOMATIC EMBRYOGENESIS

The formation of embryos (embryoids) in plant tissue culture was first reported by Steward ('59) in cell suspension culture of carrot. Formation of embryoids in callus culture of carrot on agar medium was reported by Reinert ('59). Vegetative embryoids have been noticed in tissue culture of various plants, such as, *Apium*, *Citrus*, *Cuscuta*, *Datura*, *Daucas* and *Nicotiana*. Embryogenesis has also been observed in several other angiospermic plants, such as, *Atropa belladonna* (Konar, Thomas, Street '72), *Bromus inermis* (Constabel, Miller and Gambarg '71), *Solanum melongena* (Yamada, Nakagawa and Sinobo '67), *Ranunculus scleratus* etc. and also in some gymnosperms, such as different species of *Cycas* (Norstog and Rhamstine '67).

Reinert ('59) observed that when undifferentiated callus was cultured on a medium supplemented with vitamins, amino-acids, the cells became granular. When such cells were transplanted on a medium having low auxin concentration, then many embryoids were formed. These embryoids later produced plantlets.

A suspension of cells from carrot roots when cultured on a medium containing coconut milk then many embryoids are formed. According to Steward coconut milk is required for initiation and development of embryoids. But other scientists do not support this view.

Somatic embryoids may be formed from (a) vegetative cells of a mature plant, (b) reproductive cells other than zygote or (c) cotyledons, hypocotyl or young plantlets.

According to Sharp ('80) embryoids are formed in two ways : (a) directly, without callus formation, from pre-embryonic cells, i.e., the cells that are destined to form the embryo, (b) after callus formation from induced embryogenic cells, as in carrot.

In carrot root culture it has been observed that single cell should produce a cell aggregate (proembryo) first, before embryo initiation (Reinert '71). During initiation embryogenic cells have protoplasmic connections with adjacent cells.

Embryogenic cells have certain characteristics. These cells have dense cytoplasm, prominent nucleolus, large nucleus, conspicuous starch grains, high concentration of protein and RNA and have dehydrogenase activity. These cells are distinguished by their staining behaviour.

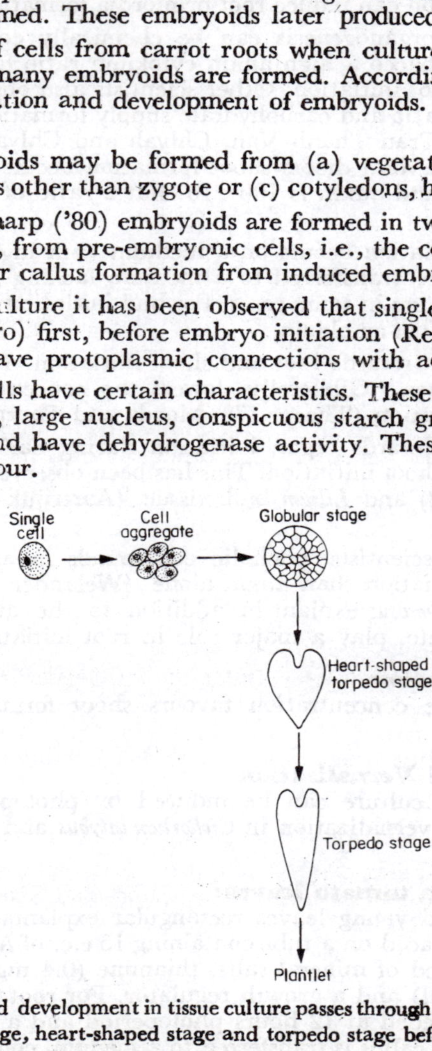

Fig. 20. Embryoid development in tissue culture passes through various stages, namely, globular stage, heart-shaped stage and torpedo stage before plantlet formation.

Embryoid development in tissue culture passes through three stages, namely, globular stage, heart-shaped stage and torpedo stage (Fig. 20).

During embryoid formation there is first cytodifferentiation of proembryoid cells followed by occurrence of various developmental stages.

Factors influencing somatic embryogenesis

(1) Auxin

In medium having relatively high concentration of auxin embryonal budding or embryonal clumps have been observed. For cell differentiation the medium should contain auxin and reduced nitrogen. Subsequent development takes place in medium with no auxin or low concentration of auxin and reduced nitrogen. In some plants first and second stages occur in the first medium and plantlet development takes place in the second medium (Ammirato '83).

(2) Nitrogen

As mentioned above, the ratio of nitrogen to auxin is an important factor controlling embryogenesis. Embryo development can be initiated on White's medium with low nitrogen content only in absence of auxin.

At low nitrogen concentration organic nitrogen is more suitable than inorganic nitrogen. Substances used as a source of nitrogen are potassium nitrate, ammonium chloride, glutamine, glutamic acid, alanine, urea etc.

Endogenous polyamines, such as, putrescine, sperdimine or spermine are required for induction of embryogenesis in wild carrot culture.

(3) Cytokinin

The role of cytokinin in embryogenesis is not clear. Embyogenesis in carrot cell suspension is stimulated by addition of zeatin in medium lacking auxin but inhibited by the addition of kinetin. Inhibitory effect of exogenous cytokinin may be due to an increase in endogenous cytokinin in growing embryoids.

(4) Activated charcoal

Presence of activated charcoal in the medium helps embryogenesis in several cases, as in *Daucas carota*, *Hedera helix* etc. Activated charcoal may adsorb the inhibitory substances present in the medium (Ammirato '83).

(5) Age of the culture

Embryogenesis usually occurs in short-term cultures. With older cultures this ability decreases and ultimately it is completely lost. This may be due to either the inability to synthesise some embryogenetic substances or changes in the ploidy level which may lead to loss of morphogenetic potential.

In carrot culture embryoid formation starts 4-6 weeks after isolation of the tissue. The optimal embryogenetic potential is reached after 15 weeks, then this potentiality gradually decreases and ultimately lost after 36 weeks. But carrot tissue may regain the embryogenetic potentiality when transferred to a medium containing proper nutrient substances.

Methods of embryogenesis from cell suspension culture of carrot root:

Carrot roots are cultured and callus is obtained. From an actively growing callus explants are taken for suspension culture on Murashige and Skoog's medium supplemented with sucrose, 0.2 mg/l zeatin and 1% agar. On this auxin free medium embryoids are formed. After the embryoids have reached the torpedo stage, they are transferred to filter paper bridges on tubes containing Murashige and Skoog's medium with 2% sucrose and 0.2 mg/l kinetin. Plantlets formed are later transferred to soil under humid condition.

Significance

By somatic embryogenesis many plants are produced very rapidly. By this method a desirable plant can be multiplied very quickly.

CHAPTER XII

CELL SUSPENSION CULTURE

Cell suspension culture is the culture of cells or cell aggregates dispersed in a moving liquid medium. Batcher and Ingram ('76) noted that all suspension cultures contain cell aggregates in addition to free cells (Fig. 21).

Cell suspension cultures were grown successfully in several plants, such as, *Nicotiana tabacum*, *Tagetes erecta* (Muir '53), *Daucus carota*, *Antirrhinum* and *Picea glauca*. Suspension cultures from various plants show different proportions of free cells and cell aggregates. In suspension culture of *Antirrhinum* cell aggregates are more frequent than free cells (Melcher and Bergmann '58). In suspension culture of Paul's Scarlet rose free cells occur at a very high frequency (Lian and Bull '70).

Cells of a suspension culture often possess large nuclei, dense cytoplasm and starch grains. Cells show hormone habituation, increase in ploidy level and loss in totipotency. Cell separation is high and cell doubling period is 24-78 hours (King '80). But cell suspensions from different sources vary considerably in the expression of these characteristics.

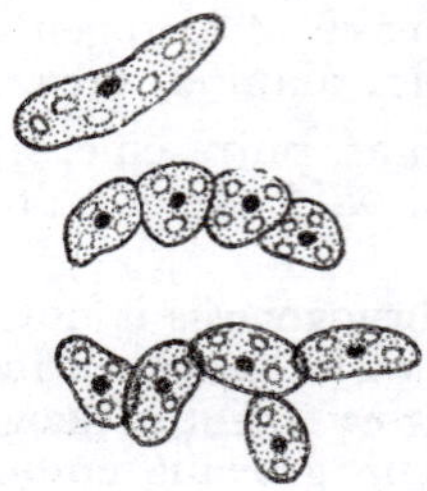

Fig. 21. Suspension culture of carrot showing single cell and cell aggregates.

Suspension cultures are mainly of two types—batch culture and continuous culture.

(a) In *batch culture* cells are grown in a fixed volume of medium. It is a closed system culture.

(b) In *continuous culture* by pumping a constant flow of the culture medium is maintained in the culture vessel, So there is replacement of equal volume of culture medium. New cell formation is more or less equal to the amount of old washed out cells. Thus the culture is maintained in a steady condition.

Continuous culture may be closed or open type. In an *open* system fresh medium is added and spent medium is withdrawn and the cells are also harvested.

In a *closed* culture all cells remain in the culture, thus the number of cells increases until the stationary phase is reached.

Initiation of culture

Cell suspension cultures can be initiated by transferring fragments of friable callus tissue to a liquid medium, which is constantly agitated. Cells of friable callus tissue readily dissociate. Highly friable callus is most suitable for suspension culture. Friability depends upon certain minerals, such as, the ratio of potassium and magnesium, amount of calcium etc. (Yashide and Watanabe '71).

Non-friable callus is sometimes used for suspension culture. As the cells do not separate easily, so auxin concentration of the liquid medium is increased or enzymes, such as, cellulase and pectinase are added to help dissociation. High auxin and cytokinin ratio sometimes favours formation of friable culture.

Besides callus, soft tissues from hypocotyl or cotyledon of sterile seedlings or embryos can be taken for suspension culture. This tissue is broken in a hand operated glass homogenizer and then the cells transferred to the medium. By subsequent subculture rasidual part of the inoculum can be excluded. The culture is sometimes allowed to settle for few seconds and then the cell suspension is taken only from the upper part of the culture.

Critical initial density or minimum effective density is the smallest inoculum from which a new suspension culture can be successfully grown.

Medium

The culture medium is composed of mineral salts, sucrose, vitamins and hormones. In some cases higher concentration of cytokinin and auxin is needed.

In liquid medium considerable pH change may occur with the addition of the inoculum because the medium is usually lightly buffered. To stabilize the pH of the medium, solid buffer, such as, sparingly soluble compounds of calcium dehydrogen orthophosphate, calcium phosphate and calcium carbonate are used.

Aeration

Cell suspension culture is constantly shaken by a platform shaker at a speed of 100-120 r.p.m. in a 250 c.c. Erlenmeyer flask. The volume of the flask and the amount of the culture medium are important. The amount of the culture liquid should be about 20% of the total volume of the flask. Other methods for aeration are magnetic stirrer, roller culture and Steward's auxophyton. In microculture no special method for aeration is necessary.

Growth of the cells in the liquid medium

After introducing the inoculum in the culture medium initially the cells fail to divide. This is the lag period. Then cell division starts and there is an increase in cell population. It reaches a maximum density per unit volume. Gradually the rate of cell division decreases (deceleration phase) due to exhaustion of the medium or accumulation of toxic substances. Ultimately the cells reach a stationary phase (Fig. 22). Then the cells are subcultured to maintain viability.

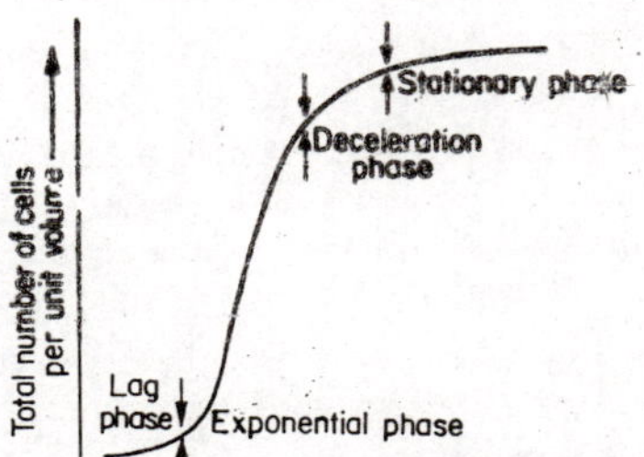

Fig. 22. Growth curve of a cell suspension culture

Subculture

Subculture should be done when the culture has reached the maximum cell density, otherwise the cells may die and lysis occurs. Subculture is usually done at early stationary phase or during progressive deceleration phase. Usually in a suspension culture maximum cell density is reached within 18-25 days. But in some cases maximum cell density is reached within 6-9 days. Before first subculture, the culture is passed through a stainless steel filter or nylon net to remove the cell aggregates and residual inoculum. By repeated subcultures a cell suspension culture can be maintained for a long time.

Cell suspension culture of carrot

Young and freshly growing carrot callus is taken and is placed on a petridish lined with filter paper. The sides of the callus are trimmed and an inoculum of about 0.5—0.75 gm callus is transferred to each flask containing the culture medium.

Usually Murashige and Skoog's basal medium supplemented with 1.0 mg/l 2-4D and sucrose is used. Presence of auxin in the medium increases the friability of the tissue.

The flask with the inoculum is kept in a shaker moving at a speed of 100 r.p.m. and at a temperature of 25-27°C.

After 7-10 days the culture is strained through a nylon mesh to remove cell aggregates and residual inoculum. Subculture is done on a fresh medium.

Cell counting can be done with a homocytometer or a Sedgwick-rafter slide.

Significances:

(1) Cell culture may be used in future for the whole or partial synthesis of secondary plant products, such as, alkaloids, glycosides etc.

(2) By cell culture many problems in applied botany can be solved.

CHAPTER XIII

SINGLE CELL CLONE

By culturing a single isolated cell single cell clone can be obtained.

Single cell clones derived from callus or suspension culture are heterogenous. They differ from one another in shape, texture, friability, colour, growth and morphogenetic potential etc.

Working with *Nicotiana tabacum* L. Winsconsin ('38), Murashige and Nakamo ('65) reported that single cell clones differ in their organ forming potential. Vasil and Hildebrandt ('65) working with hybrid tobacco also observed that single cell clones derived from a newly initiated culture differ in their capacity to produce plantlets by shoot-bud initiation. On continuing subculture single cell clones which were initially totipotent lost this capacity.

Single cell clones can be obtained usually by three methods. These are : (a) paper raft nurse technique, (b) petridish plating technique, (c) growth of isolated cells in a microchamber.

(a) Paper raft nurse technique

This technique was developed by Muir ('53). Isolated cells are placed on a filter paper raft placed over an actively growing nurse culture. This nurse culture supplies the cell clones all essential nutrients required for growth and also the factor needed to induce division through the paper barrier.

(b) Petridish plating technique

Bergman ('60) first plated out cell suspension on agar plates.

In this method the filtrate from suspension culture is subjected to cellular unit count. The counted suspension is adjusted either by diluting or concentrating by low speed centrifugation.

Sterile medium is prepared with 0.6% agar and cooled at 35°C. In this sterile medium 2 ml of suspension culture of known cellular density is mixed while the agar is still warm. Then the cells are immediately plated as a thin layer in a sterile petridish, which is sealed with parafilm. Cellular units can be counted with a sterio-binocular microscope. From this the number of cellular unit per square milimitre per plate can be calculated.

The plates are then incubated at 25°C for 21 days. The cells divide and form colonies. The rate of cell division depends upon the density of cells per plate. In a plated culture cell division first occurs at cell aggregate region and then in free cells.

Various factors influence the rate of cell division in culture. Increase in carbon dioxide concentration in the environment increases cell division. Ethylene at low concentration (2.5 mg/l) helps growth. A balance between auxin and cytokinin influences cell division.

The number of colonies per plate can be determined by shadow graph prints. The plating efficiency (PE) can be calculated from the following equation.

$$PE = \frac{\text{Number of colonies per plate} \times 100}{\text{Number of cellular units per plate}}$$

Plating efficiency can be increased by increasing the iron concentration or adjusting the pH.

In low density plate culture of *Convolvulus* cells presence of cytokinin, amino acids and proper concentration of auxin helps good growth. At low plating density sycamore cells need a medium containing cytokinin, gibberellin and amino acids. But these are not required for normal growth.

(c) Growth of isolated cells in a microchamber

De Ropp ('55) first attempted to culture single cells in hanging drop of a medium in a microchamber. Torrey ('57) used Maximov's double covership method for culturing single cells from pea root. He placed at the centre of the agar medium a piece of parent callus tissue and the cells were placed around the outer part of the agar medium. The parent callus tissue is supposed to nurse the isolated cells. After several weeks 8% cells show division.

Jones, Hildebrandt, Riker and Wu ('60) used microchamber sealed with inert mineral oil. They cultured callus cells from a hybrid of *Nicotiana tabacum* × *N. glutinosa.* Cell division was noted when there was at least thirty cells in the culture.

Significance

(1) By single cell clone culture resistant clones can be selected. By this method Carlson ('73) obtained cells resistant to methionine sulfoximine.

(2) By single cell clone culture we can obtain valuable information about cell physiology.

CHAPTER XIV

ISOLATION OF PROTOPLASTS AND PROTOPLAST CULTURE

Klerker (1892) made unsuccessful attempts to isolate protoplasts. In 1909 Kunster isolated protoplasts by mechanical method. Effective technique of protoplast isolation was evolved by Cocking ('60), Nagata and Takebe ('70) and Bhojwani and Cocking ('72). Enzymes used for isolation of protoplasts are cellulase, hemicellulase and pectinase.

Early works of protoplast isolation were done with spongy and palisade cells from the leaves of *Nicotiana* and *Petunia*. But later protoplasts from various tissues, such as, callus of *Gossypium hirsutum* and *Solanum tuberosum*, anthers of *Pelargonium* etc., were cultured.

P. S. Rao ('84) obtained a complete plant by culturing protoplasts isolated from the tissue of sandlewood tree (*Santalum album*) (Plate I and II).

This is the first report of successful development of a whole plant from the protoplast of a tree.

Method

Before removal of the cell wall the cells should be placed in an isotonic plasmolyticum, such as 13% mannitol or sorbitol. Some scientists used low osmotic potential with 0.2M sucrose or 2% polyvenylpyrrilodine. According to P.K. Evans and E. C. Cocking very low concentration may result in fusion of protoplasts producing multinucleate protoplasts.

Protoplasts can be isolated from the cells by two methods— (a) mechanical method, (b) enzymatic digestion of the cell wall.

(a) Mechanical method

The cell walls of plasmolysed cells are cut mechanically. During this condition the protplast remains in a contracted state. On subsequent deplasmolysis the protoplast swells and comes out of the cell wall. This method is not convenient and only a small percentage of protoplast remains viable. But this method is devoid of any harmful action caused by the enzymatic process.

(b) Enzymatic method

This method is used since early sixties. This method consists of: (i) surface sterilization of leaves, (ii) rinsed in proper osmoticum, (iii) lower epidermis is peeled off or the material is sliced to help entry of the enzymatic solution, (iv) treated with the enzymatic solution, (v) removal of cell debris or enzymes and purification of the protoplasts, (iv) protoplasts are transferred to a suitable culture medium.

The cell wall is mainly composed of cellulose, hemicellulose, pectin, some amount of lipid and protein. Cellulose is a polymer of glucose. Xylan is a kind of hemicellulose. Pectins are polysaccharides containing sugars, such as, galactose, arabinose, galactouronic acid—a derivative of galactose. Adjacent cells are attached to one another by the middle lamella, which is a pectic substance.

Enzymes used for cell wall degradation are cellulase, hemicellulase and pectinase. Enzyme treatment may be done in two ways: (a) In mixed-enzyme method cellulase, hemicellulase and pectinase mixture is used for cell wall degradation. (b) In sequential method first pectinase is used. This will separate the cells. Then cellulase, hemicellulase mixture is used for digestion of the cell wall.

Usually the enzymes extracted from the micro-organisms are used. But such an enzyme mixture generally contains various harmful substances and deleterious enzymes.

The time of treatment and the concentration of the enzymes to be used depend upon the nature of the culture tissue.

Isolation of protoplasts from the leaves

(1) Mature leaves of any suitable plant are taken and rinsed in tap water.

(2) The leaves are immersed in hypochlorite solution for about ten minutes.

(3) These are washed three times in double distilled water. A culture medium which is adjusted to the p*H* and osmolarity of the enzyme solution may be used for rinsing the leaves.

(4) With a fine forcep the lower epidermis is peeled off to help the entry of the enzyme solution (Fig. 23).

(5) The leaves are cut into small pieces.

(6) The leaf pieces are placed in a petridish containing the enzyme solution, having a composition of 0.5% macerozyme, 2% cellulase, 13% mannitol at pH 5.4.

(7) Petridishes are sealed with parafilm and wrapped with aluminium foils.

(8) These are incubated at 25°C for 12-18 hours. The mesophyll remains in the enzyme solution.

(9) By gentle agitation the protoplasts are released.

(10) The protoplast enzyme mixture is filtered through a nylon mesh. Filtration removes cell wall debris, cell clumps and undigested tissues.

(11) The filtrate is centrifuged. The supernatant fluid contains the debris and is removed by a pipette. The protoplasts remain at the base of the tube.

(12) Isolated protoplasts are resuspended in the culture medium and the process is repeated thrice.

The protoplasts are ready for culture.

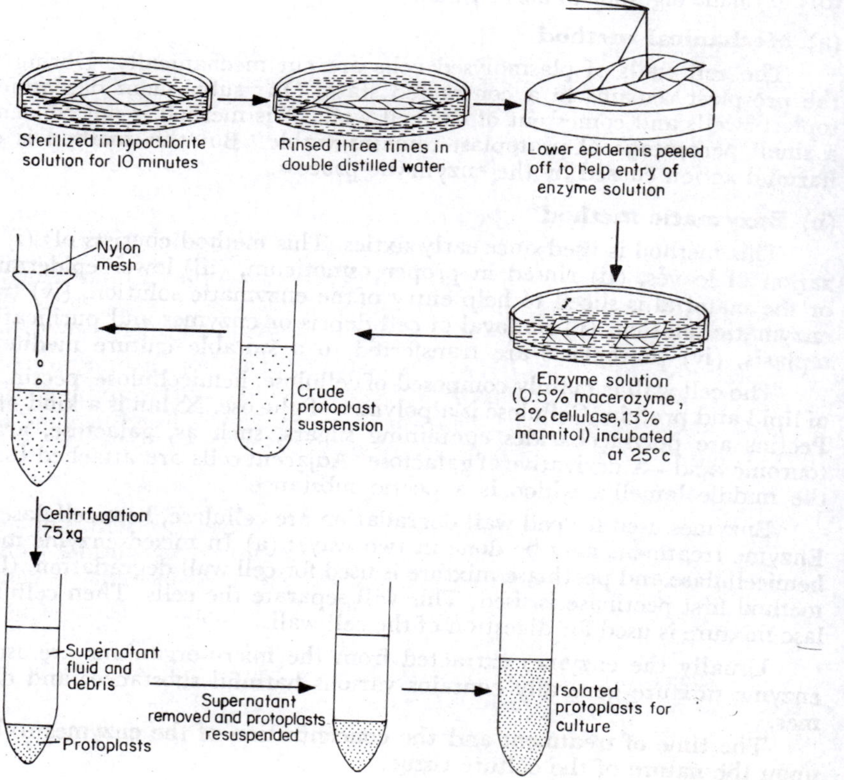

Isolation of protoplasts of tobacco leaf

Nagata and Takebe ('70) isolated protoplasts of the tobacco leaf. The method used by them is described here. The surface of a tobacco leaf is sterilised with 70% alcohol or 2% sodium hypochlorite solution. The epidermis is stripped and placed with its strippid surface facing downwards on a medium containing 10% mannitol for three hours. Leaves are cut into small segments. Segments are then placed on enzyme solution containing 0.5% macerozyme, 0.8% mannitol and 0.3% potassium dextran sulphate. It is incubated at 25°C for 2 hours. The medium is changed at an interval of every half an hour. Isolated cells are washed in 0.8 M mannitol. Cells are transferred to a medium containing 2% cellulase and 0.8 M mannitol for two hours at 36°C. Cell walls are destroyed. Protoplasts are filtered through wire gauge to separate them from the debris and are then collected by centrifugation. Isolated protoplasts are washed in 0.8 M mannitol.

Isolated protoplasts are fragile. So they are suspended in a medium containing sorbitol or mannitol of proper concentration, where protoplasts remain viable. On a medium of proper concentration isolated protoplasts appear rounded.

Isolation of protoplasts from pollen grains

Bhojowani and Cocking ('72) isolated proloplasts from pollen grain tetrads of several angiospermic plants by using 1% helicase. The stage of the tetrad is important for protoplast isolation. Early stage of tetrad formation when cell walls are very thin and made up of cellulose is suitable for protoplast isolation. Ito ('73) isolated protoplasts from pollen grains of plants belonging to Liliaceae by using cellulase and microzyme. Protoplast isolation from myocyte or tetrad in proper stage requires half an hour. In body cell the time required is 4-12 hours.

Protoplast culture

Proloplast just after isolation is more or less spherical.

Protoplasts can be cultured in a microchamber or in a soft agar medium or in hanging drop culture.

Murashige and Skoog's medium supplemented with auxin and cytokinin helps the growth of the protoplasts. Addition of 13% mannitol to the medium prevents osmotic lysis of isolated protoplasts. 1.5% agar may be added to the medium. Culture vials are incubated at 25°C in presence of dim white light. For wall formation in *Phaseolus* calcium chloride and ammonium nitrate are added to the medium.

Within 5-7 days cell wall is formed. The protoplasts divide forming cell aggregates and ultimately a callus. This callus when subcultured on a medium lacking auxin and mannitol form embryoids, which produce plantlets.

Takebe and coworkers ('71) obtained entire plant from hybrid protoplasts of tobacco. Nagata and Takebe ('72) cultured isolated protoplasts of tobacco on nutrient medium and obtained multicellular colony. It was then transferred to a fresh medium, where callus was formed. This callus produced buds and shoots.

Significance

(1) From isolated protoplasts hybrid plants can be produced by protoplast fusion. Even those hybrids, which cannot be produced by normal procedure due to sexual or physical incompatibilities, can be produced by somatic cell fusion.

(2) Isolated protoplasts are required for protoplast fusion experiments forming homokaryons and heterokaryons.

(3) In culture isolated protoplasts soon regenerate new walls. From this, the process of wall formation can be studied.

(4) From isolated protoplasts mutant cells can be selected and clonal propagation can be made.

(5) Isolated protoplasts can injest foreign materials into the cytoplasm by a process resembling endocytosis. The injested material may be a plasmid, bacterium, virus, DNA or mitochondria etc.

(6) It provides materials for plant cell modification experiments.

(7) It helps to solve many plant and cell physiological problems.

CHAPTER XV

PROTOPLAST FUSION AND SOMATIC HYBRIDIZATION

Plant breeders sometimes face difficulties due to sexual incompatibility. This difficulty can be removed by protoplast fusion. By this method wider crosses are possible. Even crosses between plants showing physical and chemical incompatibilities are possible by protoplast fusion.

In 1909 Kunster reported random fusion between mechanically isolated protoplasts. Method of fusion of naked protoplasts of somatic cells (Fig. 24) was developed in 1969. This is called '*parasexual hybridization*'. In 1972 Bhojowari and Cocking used isolated protoplasts from pollen grains for this purpose.

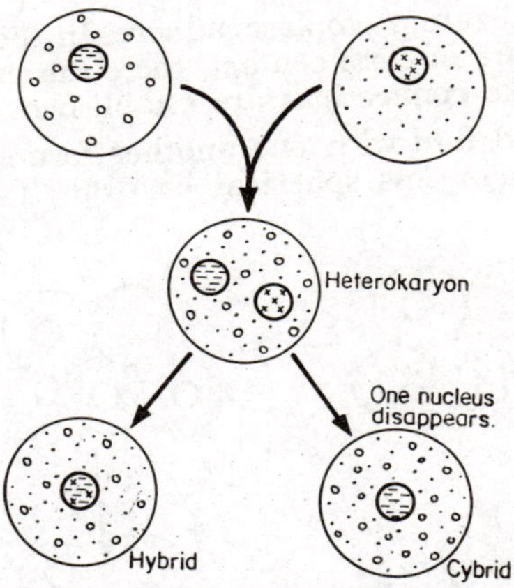

Fig. 24. Fusion products of two different protoplasts.

Some of the terms used in somatic hybridization are defined here. When two or more protoplasts fuse then their cytoplasm always fuse, but the nuclei may or may not fuse. A cell having similar nuclei is called a *homokaryon* and a cell having dissimilar nuclei is called a *heterokaryon* or *heterokaryocyte*. When two nuclei of a heterokaryon fuse then a true hybrid protoplast or *synkaryocyte* is formed. If in a binucleate heterokaryon one of the nuclei disappears then it is called a *cybrid* or a cytoplasmic hybrid or a *heteroplast*, as the cytoplasms remain in a fused state.

In animal cells cell fusion was first reported by G. Barki, S. Sorieul and F. Cornefert ('60). They mixed cancerous cells of two different mouse and after few months hybrid cells were formed. In the hybrid cell, chromosomes of both parents were present. During division of such hybrid cells some chromosomes were omitted.

Later hybridization of cells of different species was successfully done. Hybrid cells of mouse and rat were observed. Hybridization was also attempted between cells of man and rat (Weiss and Green '77). Such hybrid cells showed more similarities with rat cells, because during division of hybrid cells human chromosomes were generally omitted. Out of the 46 human chromosomes the hybrid cells contained only 2-15 human chromosomes.

Y. Okada of Osaka University reported that in presence of '*Sendai*' strain of parainfluenza virus cell fusion occurs at a higher frequency. Later H. Haris and J. F. Watkins ('65) of Oxford University used 'sendai virus' inactivated by UV ray for different types of cell fusion.

By using sendai virus, fusion of isolated protoplasts of animal cells was recorded. But this virus is ineffective for fusion of isolated protoplasts of plant cells.

During digestion of cell walls by enzymes two adjacent protoplasts may fuse. Such fusion of protoplasts of the same tissue is always intraspecific. But this type of fusion is very rare as negative charge exists on the surface of the protoplasts. Thus two protoplasts usually repel each other. Presence of *fusigenic agents* lower this charge. Molecular alteration in the bilayer structure of the plasma membrane is needed for protoplast fusion.

Power and coworkers ('70) reported successful protoplast fusion of higher plants (root protoplasts of oat) in presence of *sodium nitrate*—a fusigenic agent. Isolated protoplasts are placed on a medium containing sodium nitrate solution of proper osmotic concentration or a solution of sodium carbonate and proper osmoticum at 37°C for five minutes. The tubes are centrifuged at low speed and the protoplasts aggregate at the base of the tubes. The tubes are kept in darkness and left undisturbed at 37°C for 30 minutes.

By the action of sodium nitrate protoplasts adhere. In those regions where plasma membrane of the protoplasts are in close contact, there fusion of plasma membrane occurs and plasmodesmata like connections are established. These cytoplasmic connections gradually expand and fuse with one another forming broader connections. Fused protoplasts become more or less spherical or oval. Two or more protoplasts may fuse together (Fig. 25).

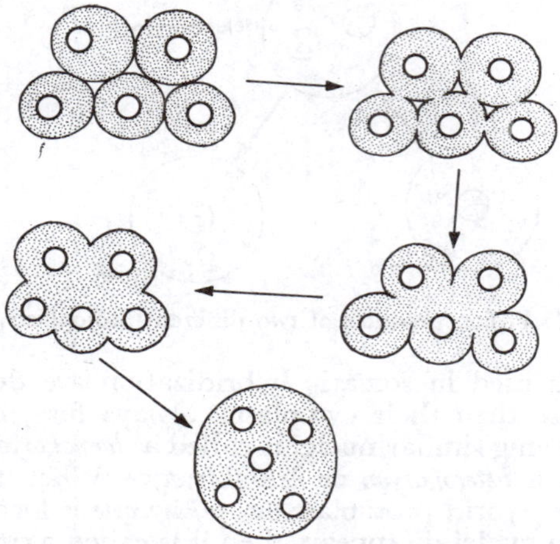

Fig. 25. Fusion of isolated protoplasts.

By using sodium nitrate only few heterokaryons are formed. To overcome this difficulty from 1974 onwards *polyethylene glycol* (PEG) is widely used instead of sodium nitrate. By using PEG heterokaryons occur in greater frequency. By its use fusion of protoplasts between two plant cells or two animal cells or between an animal cell and a plant cell was successful. Hybrid cells between soyabean-maize, soybean-pea and soyabean-barly were obtained by using PEG.

In this method at first concentrated suspensions of two types of protoplasts are mixed. Then to this 15% PEG solution is mixed in the ratio of 1 : 3 (protoplast suspension : PEG). Isolated protoplasts of two different plants are centrifuged at 75-100 ×g for ten minutes in presence of PEG. The protoplasts fuse readily. This results in various fusion products, such as, homokaryons, heterokaryons, multiple fusion products, cybrids.

Protoplasts of microspores or meiocytes may fuse in absence of any fusigenic substance. Ito ('73) used *grooved slides* for fusion of protoplasts of meiocytes of some plants of Liliaceae. Isolated protoplasts in enzymatic solution aggregate at the base of the groove. When the slide is gently tapped, the protoplasts fuse readily. Fused protoplasts are recognizable by their larger size. Fusion may occur between two or more protoplasts.

Fused or unfused protoplasts are resuspended, their viability and density are determined. The mixture is plated. This fusion product if forms callus then from this plantlets may be formed.

High pH (about 10.5), high temperature (37°C) and high concentration of calcium ions (50 mM $CaCl_2$, $2H_2O$) also help protoplast fusion.

Isolation of hybrids

Protoplasts with distinct pigments on fusion produce hybrids which can be isolated by visual method.

The hybrids can also be separated by a method of fluorescent cell sorting (Redenbaugh '82).

Another method of hybrid isolation is growing in a medium which helps selective growth (biochemical method).

Hybrid protoplasts formed by the fusion of protoplasts of *Nicotiana glauca* and *Nicotiana langsdorfii* can be isolated by biochemical method (Fig. 26). The parental protoplasts fail to grow in an auxin free medium, but in such a medium hybrid cells can grow. Thus, in an auxin free medium only hybrid cells can survive. These cells form callus, which on sub-culturing form hybrid plants (Carlson, Smith and Dearing '72).

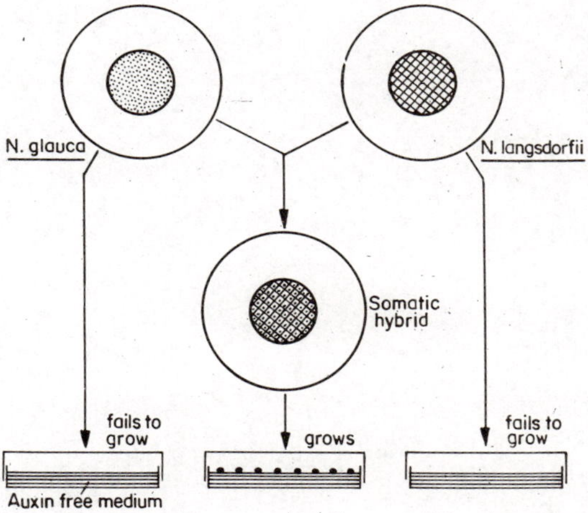

Fig. 26. Isolation of somatic hybrids formed by fusion of protoplasts of *N. glauca* and *N. langsdorfii* on a auxin free medium.

Hybrids can also be isolated by using biochemical mutants. *Petunia hybrida* cannot grow on a medium containing actinomycetes D. *P. parodii* can grow on such a medium, but its callus cells cannot produce entire plants. When hybrids are formed by protoplast fusion between these two species, then such hybrids can grow on actinomycetes D containing medium and are also capable of regenerating whole plants (Power '76).

Significance

(1) Protoplast fusion has great significance in somatic hybridization, plant breeding and virus infection studies.

Takebe and coworkers ('71) obtained entire plants from hybrid protoplasts of tobacco. Later entire plantlets were obtained by this method in *Citrus*, *Daucus*, *So-*

lanum and *Petunia*. Carlson and coworkers ('72) obtained hybrid plants of *Nicotiana glauca* and *N. langsdorfii* by protoplast fusion.

Hybrid cells of *Brassica campestris* and *Arabidopsis thaliana* were successfully cultured by Gleba and Boffmann ('78, '79). From such hybrid cells, they were able to produce hybrid plants.

(2) By protoplast fusion cytoplasmic male sterility can be transferred from one plant to another within a species or between two species. Medgyesy ('80) successfully transferred streptomycin resistance property from *Nicotiana tabacum* to *N. sylvestris*. This character is controlled by chloroplast DNA.

CHAPTER XVI

PLANT TUMOURS AND VIRUS ERADICATION

PLANT TUMOURS

Tumour means uncontrolled growth or proliferation of disorganised tissues. After its initiation the tumour can grow even in absence of the inciting agent, such as, virus, bacteria, chemical substances etc.

Braun ('42) studied plant tumours. Later various scientists induced tumours on susceptable plants by introducing *Agrobacterium tumefaciens* through wounds. The tumour inducing substance of this bacterium is a small T-DNA or Ti plasmid. It occurs only in the virulent strains of *A. tumefacians*.

Three types of tumours are usually studied in vitro. These are : (a) crown gall tumour of sunflower produced by *Agrobacterium tumefaciens*, (b) genetic tumours occurring in some tobacco hybrids and (c) wound tumours produced by *Aurogenus*.

All these tumours show some common features. These features are: (i) Host tissue must be damaged before tumour formation. (ii) Tumour tissue if grafted on healthy plant it continues to grow. (iii) Tumour free from inciting agent when placed on a simple hormone free medium it grows rapidly. This indicates that tumour tissue produces more hormone than normal tissue and thus causes abnormal growth and proliferations. Virus, bacteria and genetic instability may induce tumour formation.

Crown gall tumour (Fig. 27) is produced by *Agrobacterium tumefaciens*. Wounding and presence of inciting agent produce tumour. Working with *A. tumefaciens* Braun concluded that tumour formation takes place in two stages: (a) Inception phase—At this stage normal cells are transformed into tumour cells. (b) Developmental phase—Tumour cells continue to grow forming abnormal proliferation.

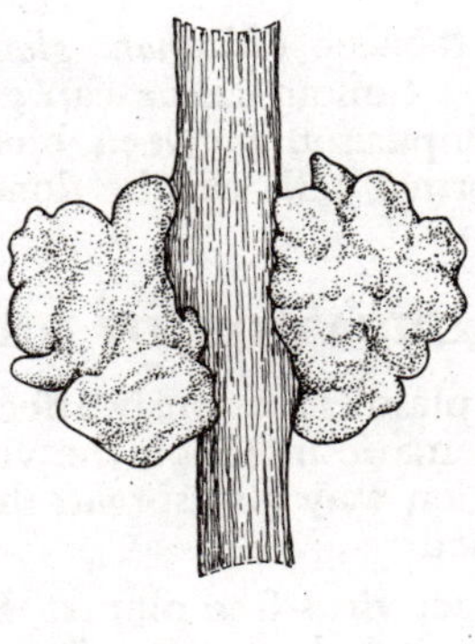

Fig. 27. Crown gall tumour

Studies on crown gall tissue suggest that the tumour forming substance is a small ring T-DNA or plasmid. The T-DNA is incorporated in the host genome and produces bacterial protein. This protein may be responsible for increased production of auxin and cytokinin which may lead to tumour-like growth.

T-DNA can act as a vector for the introduction of new genes into the host protoplasts. A desirable gene and marker genes are introduced into T-DNA or Ti plasmid (Fig. 28). The reconstructed Ti plasmid is inserted into an intact *Agrobacterium*. Now the selected plant is infected with this transformed bacterium, thereby introducing a new gene to the host plant.

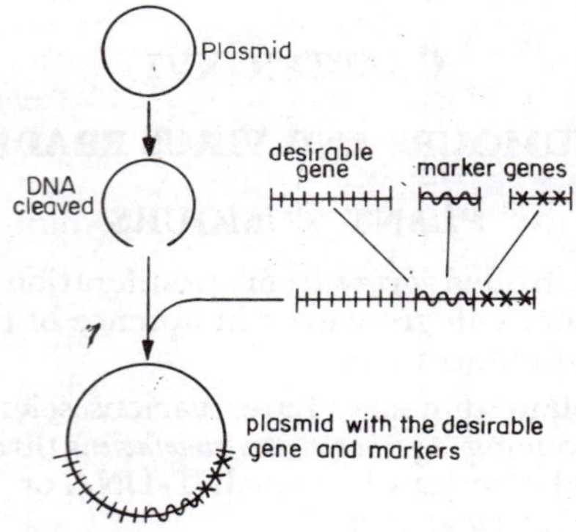

Fig. 28. Insertion of gene into a plasmid.

Indefinite growth of disorganized tumours has been noted on culture. Tumours can grow on simple culture medium and do not require a supply of hormones. In tumours both in vivo and in vitro the hormone concentration is high and this causes disorganised growth of tumours.

Gautheret ('46) noted that callus tissue of *Scorzonera hispanica* which initially grows in auxin containing medium, can grow on auxin free medium. This is also, noted in tobacco, carrot, sunflower etc. This phenomenon is known as habituation. Such tissues contain high concentration of hormones and low differentiating potentiality and are often friable. They can grow indefinitely on a simple auxin free medium. Thus habituation may be due to either increased auxin production or decreased auxin breakdown.

When habituated tobacco tissue is grafted on healthy plant it rapidly produces tumour (Gautheret '57).

Callus cultures of hybrid tobacco (*Nicotiana glauca* × *N. langsdorfii*) readily form tumours. It has been noted that tumour tissue can grow on a simple medium. From culture of tumour tissue a comparison between biochemical and physiological properties of tumour cells and normal cells can be done.

ERADICATION OF VIRUS

Yield of various economic plants is seriously affected by virus infection. In vegetatively growing plants with systematic infection the virus spreads rapidly from generation to generation. Virus infection may also spread through infected seeds. So production of virus free plant is needed.

Heat treatment is used to get virus free plants. But in many plants this method is not satisfactory. By meristem tip culture virus free plants and virus resistant plants can be produced most successfully.

In systematically virus infected plant viruses are not uniformly distributed. The root tip and shoot tip are usually free from virus. By culturing smallest shoot apex (0.5—1 mm. long) with few leaf primordia virus free plants can be obtained.

By meristem tip culture Morel and Martin ('52, '55) obtained virus free shoots in potato and *Dalhia*. These shoots failed to form roots and were grafted on healthy seedlings. But later, from meristem tip culture of various plants virus free plants with roots were obtained (Fig. 29).

In meristem tip culture small segment of stem or axillary bud tip is taken and is placed on a suitable culture medium. The size of the shoot tip to be cultured is important. In stem tip culture the meristem dome with first pair of leaves is usually taken. Depending on the plant the meristem tip taken for culture ranges from 0.5 mm to 1 mm. Very small shoot tips do not produce roots, whereas larger shoot tips may contain virus particles. The shoot tips may be cultured at 30-40°C to inactivate the virus.

Presence of virus in culture should be tested rigorously. Infected materials are immediately destroyed. Only one healthy explant from a diseased plant is cultured.

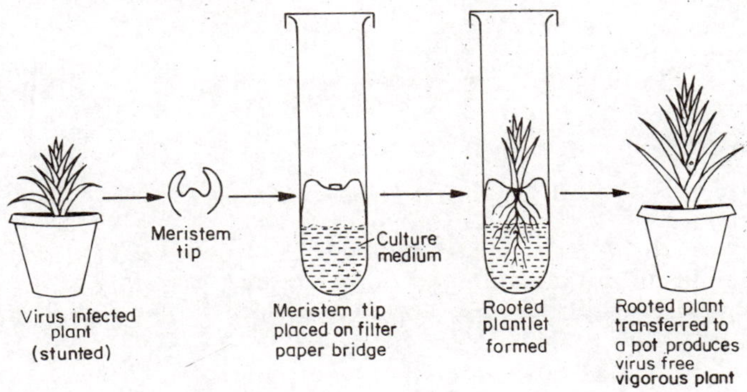

Fig. 29. By meristem tip culture a virus free plant is produced.

Stem tip to be cultured may be surface sterilised. According to Hollings ('65) it is not always required.

Liquid medium on culture tube with filter paper bridge is most satisfactory for meristem tip culture. The two ends of the filter paper bridge are immersed into the liquid medium. Agar medium is unsatisfactory for meristem tip culture. Hollings and Stone ('68) noted that a medium containing major and minor elements of Knops and Barthelots solution (without beryllium and titanium) and 40 g/l glucose, 10^{-3} g/l thiamine, 10^{-3} g/l mesoinositol having a pH 5.5 is the suitable medium for several plants. For root initiation 10^{-3} g/l NAA may be added. Cultures are then transferred to NAA free medium. Holling and Stone ('68) suggested to incubate the cultures below 20°C and illuminate for 22 hours/day. Formation of plantlets from meristem tip requires few weeks to several months.

Better results have been obtained when meristem tip for culture is taken from heat treated plants. In *Chrysenthemum* 5% of surviving meristem tips are free from leaf mottling virus, whereas 98% virus free tips are obtained when explants are taken after heat treatment.

On culture medium virus inhibiting substances, such as, malachite green, 2-4-D and thiouracil may be added to eliminate viruses. Once a virus free plant is produced it is well tested and then by clonal multiplication many healthy plants can be obtained from it.

Significance of tissue culture in plant pathogen studies :

By tissue culture virus free plants can be obtained.

Host parasite interaction can also be studied from tissue culture.

By tissue culture plants systematically infected by beneficial micro-organism, such as, nitrogen fixing bacteria can be obtained.

Tissue culture may be used to maintain stocks of contamination free special parasites, which may be required for various investigations.

Index

A

Abatia, 254
Abatieae, 255
Abelmoschus esculentus, 238
Abroma augusta, 236
Abrus precatorius, 195
Abuta rufescens, 163
Acacia catechu, 194
—dealbata, 194
—mearusii, 194
—melanoxylon, 194
—nilotica, 194
—pycnantha, 194
—senegal, 194
—stenocarpa, 194
—visco, 194
Acalypha indica, 215
Acalypheae, 216
Acanthaceae, 299, 322
Acanthineae, 299
Acanthoideae, 324
Acantholimon, 284
Acanthopanax, 276
Acanthosicyos, 331
Acanthus ilicifolius, 324
Acer carpinifolium, 227
—grandidentatum, 227
—nigrum, 227
—pseudoplatanus, 227
—rubrum, 227
—saccharum, 227
Aceraceae, 219, 226
Acetolysis, 10
Achariaceae, 243
Acharitea, 308
Achatocarpaceae, 141
Achlamydosporeae, 26
Achlys, 158
Achronychia, 206
Achyranthes aspera, 146
Acioa, 187
Aciphylla, 277
Acmantherea, 211
Acokanthera, 297
Aconitum, 160
—napellus, 161
Acorus, 85, 86, 87
Acotyledonae, 22
Acroglochin, 144
Acrotonae, 116
Acrotrema, 244
Actea, 160
Actinidiaceae, 243
Actinodaphne, 169
Adansonia digitata, 242
Adenandra, 205
Adenanthera pavonina, 194
Adenia globosa, 256
—keramanthus, 256
Adenium, 296
Adenostomateae, 189
Adhatoda vasica, 415
—zeysanica, 324, 415
Adina cordifolia, 327
Adinandra, 246
Adlumia, 170
Adoxaceae, 320
Adrianeae, 215
Aechmea, 97
Aegialitidaceae, 285
Aegialitis rotundifolia, 285
Aegiceras corniculatus, 282
Aegicerataceae, 281
Aeginetia, 320
Aegiphila, 306
Aegle, 205
—marmelos, 207
Aerva lanata, 146
Aesculus assamica, 224
—indica, 224
Aeschynomene aspera, 195
—indica, 195
Aexotoxiaceae, 216
Aganosma dichotoma, 296
Agapantheae, 105
Agapanthus, 101
Agatea, 252
Agavaceae, 31, 32, 82, 105
Agavales, 78
Agave americana, 389
—cantala, 389
—sisalana, 104, 389
—vera-curz, 389
Agavoideae, 104, 105
Agdestiaceae, 143
Agdestis, 148
Ageratum conyzoides, 338
Agrimonia, 187
Agrostis, 70
Ailanthus excelsa 207, 208
—integrifolia, 207
Aizoaceae, 141, 142, 148
Ajuga lobata, 308
Ajugoideae, 310
Ajwan, 274
Akariaceae, 196
Akec, 222

Alangium, 270
Alangiaceae, 261, 274
Albertia, 161
Albizzia lebbeck, 193
—procera, 193
Albert Magnus, 17
Alfred Gunderson, 33
—Wallace, 19
Alchemilla arvensis, 187
Aldrovandra vesiculosa 179
Aleurites, 201
—moluccana, 213
Alexandra, 143
Algae, 11, 23, 26
Alisma plantago, 63
Alismaceae, 59, 63
Alismataceae, 63
Alismatidae, 98
Alismatales, 32, 59
Alismidae, 33
Alkanna tinctoria, 304
Allamanda, 296
Alliaceae, 97, 105
Allieae, 32, 97, 105
Allioideae, 100
Allium cepa, 101
—porum, 101
—sativum, 101
Allspice, 266
Alnicida, 206
Alnus, 126
Alocasia indica, 84
Aloe vera, 101
Alphonsea lutea, 165
Alpinia allughas, 110
—galanga, 110
Alsineae, 152
Alsinoideae, 151, 152
Alsodeia, 252
Alstonia scholaris, 295, 416
Alstroemeria, 104
Alstroemeriaceae, 31, 105
Alstroemerioideae, 104, 105
Alternanthera versicolor, 146
Alternation of generations, 8
Alternifoliae, 29, 30
Althaea rosea, 234
Althenia, 60
Altingia excelsa, 185
Altingiaceae, 186
Amaranthaceae, 141, 145
Amaranthus caudatus, 146
—tricolor, 146
Amaryllidaceae, 31, 32, 97, 103
Amaryllidoideae, 104, 106
Amaryllis, 104
Amblyanthus, 282
Amborella, 153
Amentiferae, 32
American Code, 48
Amherstia nobilis, 46 193
Ammania baccifera, 263
—vesicatoria, 263
Amomum aromaticum, 110
—subulatum, 110
Amorphophalus, 84, 85
—campanulatus, 85
Ampelocissus latifolia, 227
Amyris, 208
Anacardiaceae, 216, 217
Anacardineae, 216
Anacardium occidentale, 221, 222, 379
Anagallis arvensis, 283, 284
Anamirta, 161
Ananta mool, 294
Ananus comosus, 96, 97
Anaphalis contorta, 339
Anaxogoria, 164
Anchietia, 252
—salutaris, 253
Ancistrocladaceae, 247
Andira, 191
Andrea Caesalpino, 17
Andrographis paniculata, 325
Andromeda, 280
Androecium, 6
Andropogon, 70
Androsaceae, 283
—saxifragifolia, 283
Androstachys, 215
Aneilema liniolatum, 91
—nudiflorum, 91
—scapiflorum, 92
Anemone pulsatilla, 160
Anemoneae, 160
Anethum graveolens, 278
Angiospermae, 11, 12, 26, 27, 29
Angiospermic plant, 5
Anhalonium, 260
Anisomcles indica, 309
Anisophyllea, 265
Anisophylleaceae, 265
Anneslea, 245
Annona cherimolia, 165
—muricata, 165
—reticulata, 165
—squamosa, 165
Annonaceae, 153, 164
Annonales, 153, 164
Annoneae, 166
Annonoideae, 166
Anogeissus acuminata, 167

—latifolia, 167
Anonophyles, 31
Anotis, 327
Ansphal, 222
Antena, 317
Anthelmideae, 339
Anther, 6
—culture, 459
Anthocarp, 146
Antholobus, 135
Anthocephalus, 326
—chinensis, 327, 328
Anthocerotae, 11
Anthophyta, 29, 30
Anthospermum, 327
Anthoxanthum, 70
Anthurium, 85, 86
Anthyllis, 191
Antiaris toxicaria, 130
Antiaxis, 161
Antidesma ghaesambilla, 211
Antigonon leptopus, 140, 141
Antipodal cell, 7
Antirrhinum, 316
Antirrhinioideae, 316
Anurosperma, 178
Apama wallichii, 138
Aperture, 9
Aphania, 221
Aphyllae, 23
Apiaceae, 276
Apioideae, 278
Apium graveolens, 278
Apocarpeae, 25, 26
Apocynaceae, 289, 295
Apocynales, 285, 293
Apolar, 9
Aponogetonaceae, 59
Aponogetonales, 59
Apostasia, 117
Apostasiaceae, 116, 117
Appanamixis, 206
Aquifoliaceae, 219, 223
Aquilegia, 159
Arachis hypogea, 193, 196, 392
Aralia nudicaulis, 274
Araliaceae, 261, 275
Araliales, 261, 274
Aralieae, 276
Araceae, 78, 82
Arales, 78
Arbores, 18
Arboretum, 43
Arbutoideae, 280
Arceuthobium minutissimum, 136
Archesporial cell, 6
Archichlamydeae, 27, 28, 32, 118
Arctopus, 273
Arctotideae, 339
Ardisia solanacea, 282, 283
Areca, 80, 82
—catechu, 81
Arecaceae, 75, 78
Arecales, 78
Arecideae, 33
Arecoideae, 83
Arenaria, 152
Arenga, 81
Argemone mexicana, 171
Argyreia speciosa, 302
Arisaema, 85
Arisarum, 86, 87
Aristolochia, 138
—acuminata, 138
—drurior, 138
—grandiflora, 138
—indica, 138
—Roxburghiana, 138
—saccata, 138
Aristolochiaceae, 137, 138
Aristolochiales, 28
Arka puspa, 294
Armen Takhtajan, 33
Armeria, 284
Arnebia, 304
Arnold Arboretum, 44
Aroideae, 87
Artedia squamata, 273
Artemesia cina, 340, 419
—nisagirica, 339
Arthur Cronquist, 34
Arthrocnemum indicum, 144
Artiplex crassifolia, 144
Artocarpoideae, 130
Artocarpus, 128
—chaplasa, 129
—heterophyllus, 129
—incisa 129
—infectoria, 129
—lakoocha, 129
Artorrhizae, 31
Arum Lily, 85
Arvi, 86
Asafoetida, 274
Asarum, 138
Asclepiadaceae, 289, 297
Ascyrum, 243
Asimina triloba, 165
Asparagaceae, 102
Asparagoideae, 100
Asparagus, 99
—adscendens, 101
—officinalis, 101
—racemosus, 101

Asphodiloideae, 100
Aspicarpa, 211
Aspidopteris rotundifolia, 208
Aster tripolium, 335
Asteraceae, 278, 334, 337
Asterad, 8
Asterales, 30, 329
Astereae, 339
Asteridae, 33
Asteropeia, 245
Astilbe, 183
Astragalus, 191
Astrania, 277
Astronioideae, 272
Ata, 165
Atalantia monophylla, 206
Atharva Veda, 18
Atragene, 159
Atriplex, 144
Atropa belladona, 312
Aubulia, 315
Augustin Pyrame de Candolle, 22
Autoniaceae, 287
Avena, sativa, 72
Averrhoa carambola, 198, 199
Averrhoaceae, 199
Avicennia, 306
Azadirachta, 206
—indica, 207
Azorella, 276

B

Baccauria, 212
Baccharis, 337
Bacopa monnieri, 316
Bacteria, 11
Bael tree, 206
Baer, 225
Bajra, 72
Balanitaceae, 207
Balanites, 207
—aegyptiaca, 207
Balanophora, 137
Balanophoraceae, 134, 136
Balanophorales, 28, 185
Balanophorineae, 134
Balanopsidales, 28
Balanostreblus, 128
Balkal, 130
Balsa Wood, 238
Balsaminaceae, 198, 200, 217
Balsaminae, 216
Bambusae, 70
Ban chichinga, 333
Banana, 377
Banera, 183
Baneroideae, 184
Banisteria, 208
Barbeuiaceae, 143
Barbeyaceae, 127
Barbeyales, 118
Barclaya, 155
Barclayaceae, 156
Barleria cristata, 323
—prionitis, 325
Barringtonia, 270
—acutangula, 271
Basanacantha, 327
Basella alba, 149
—rubra, 149
Basellaceae, 141, 143, 149
Basitonae, 116
Batabi Nimbu, 206
Bath sponge, 328
Batidaceae, 143
Batidales, 28
Bauhin Gaspard (Casper), 17
—Jean (Johna), 17
Bay oil tree, 266
Beaumontia, 296
Begonia rex, 259
—semperflorens, 259
—socotrana, 258
—tuberhybrida, 259
Begoniaceae, 243, 258
Begoniales, 243
Begoniella, 258
Begoniineae, 243
Beilschmedia, 168
Belamcanda chinensis, 106
Beli, 286
Beloperone, 323
Bembicia, 254
Bembicieae, 251
Benincasa hispida, 333
Bennettitales, 12, 27, 31
Bentham, George, 23
Berberidaceae, 137, 153, 157
Berberidales, 137, 153
Berberis lycium, 157
—vulgaris, 157
Berchemia scandens, 225
Bernard de Jussieu, 22
Berria cordifolia, 230
Bertolona, 271
Bessey Charles E, 29
Beta vulgaris, 144
Betula utilis, 126
Betulaceae, 124, 125, 127
Betuleae, 127
Beverages, 395

Bhabar, 383
Bhadali, 323
Bhang, 131
Bhela, 220
Bhilwa, 220
Bhui champa, 111
Bhurja patra, 127
Biarum, 89
Bicarpellatea, 24, 26
Biebersteinia, 197
Big Banyan tree, 46
Bigonnia caprialata, 320
—magnifica, 320
—speciosa, 320
Bignoniaceae, 299, 317
Bignoniales, 300, 319
Bignonieae, 319
Billbergia, 97
Biophytum sensitivum, 198
Biosystematics, 3
Bisboeclera, 76
Bischofia javanica, 210
Bisexual flower, 7
Bitter gourd, 328
Bixa orellana, 252
Bixaceae, 252
Bixales, 252
Blainvillea acmella, 338
Blastophaba, 129
Blepharis, 323
Blighia sapida, 222
Blumea, 338
Blyxa, 67
Bocagea laurifolia, 165
—virgata, 165
Bocconia arborea, 170
Boehmaria nivea, 132
Boenning housenia albiflora, 204
Boerhaavia repens, 147
Bombacacceae, 228, 234
Bombax ceiba, 236
Bonsai tree, 322
Boraginaceae, 299, 300, 303
Boraginales, 300, 305
Boraginineae, 299
Boraginoideae, 304
Borassieae, 83
Borassoideae, 83
Borassus, 78, 79, 80
—flabelifer, 82
Borneo camphor, 247
Borreria, 327
—articularis, 329
Bossiaea rufa, 191
Boswellia serrata, 208
—papyrifera, 208
—thurifera, 208
Botanic Garden, 41
Botanical Congress, International, 48
Botanical Survey of India, 47
Bottle brush tree, 266
—gourd, 328
Bouea, 218
Bougainvillea, 146
—spectabilis, 147
Boussingultia, 149
Brachiaria, 70
Brahmi, 312
Brasenia, 155
—schreberi, 156
Brassica campestris, 176, 390
—dichotoma, 390
—juncea, 177, 390
—nigra, 177, 390
—oleracea, 177
—rapa, 177
—sarson, 390
—toria, 390
Brassicaceae, 169, 173
Bread fruit tree, 129
Bretschneideraceae, 169
Breynia, 212
Brideleae, 215
Bridha-darak, 298
Brinjal plant, 308
Bromelia magdalenae, 97
—serra, 97
Bromeliaceae, 89, 95
Bromeliales, 89
Bromelioideae, 96
Brosimum galactodendron, 129
Broussonetia, 128
—papyrifera, 130
Browalia, 312
Brownea, 46, 195
Brucea antidysenteriea, 207
Bruguiera gymnorhiza, 265
—sexangula, 265
Bruneliaceae, 180
Brunfelsia latifolia, 312
Bruniaceae, 180
Brunoniaceae, 239
Bryanthus, 280
Bryonia, 332
Bryophyta, 11
Bryophytes, 11, 23
Buchanania lanzan, 220
Buckleya, 135
Buddleja asiatica, 292
Buddlejaceae, 289, 291, 292
Bulletin of Botanical Survey of India, 47
Bulnesia arborea, 203
—sarmientis, 203
Bundes garden, 44

Bupleurum, 276
Burmannia, 114
Burmanniaceae, 97, 113
Burmanniales, 113
Burseraceae, 197, 208
Bursera serrata, 208
Butea monosperma, 195
—superba, 195
Butomaceae, 59, 65
Butomales, 32, 59
Butomus, 65
Buxaceae, 219
Buxineae, 219
Buxus sempervirens, 219
—wallichiana Bail.

C

Cabomba, 155
Cabombaceae, 156
Cabomboideae, 155
Cactaceae, 142, 259
Cactales, 259
Cacteae, 260
Caesalpineae, 190
Caesalpinia crista, 193
—pulcherrima, 193
—sappan, 193
Caesalpiniaceae, 195
Caesalpinioideae, 190
Caesulia axillaris, 339
Cajanus cajan, 193
Cajuput oil, 266
Caladium, 85
Calamus, 83
—floribundus, 29, 83
Calceolaria, 316
Calendula officinalis, 340
Calenduleae, 339
Calla, 85
Calectaesieae, 101
Callicarpa, 306
Callistemon lanceolatus, 270
Callitrichaceae, 196, 257
Callitrichineae, 196
Callophylloideae, 247, 249
Callophyllum inophyllum, 248
Callus culture, 464
Calodendron, 204
Calothamnus, 268
Calotropis, 297
—gigantea, 298
—procera, 298
Calycanthaceae, 153
Calyceraceae, 329
Calycerales, 329
Calyciferae, 32
Calyciflorae, 22, 26
Calycineae, 135
Calyculus, 135
Caltha, 159
Camarea, 208
Camellia, 246
—assamica, 246
—japonica, 246
—kissi, 396
—sasanqua, 246
—sinensis, 246, 395
Campanula, 330, 332
Campanulaceae, 329, 330
Campanulales, 334
Campanulatae, 334
Campanuloideae, 330
Campsis radicans, 318
Cananga odorata, 165
Canarium commune, 208
Canavalia ensiformis, 193
Candolia, 225
Canna edulis, 111
—indica, 111
—orientalis, 111
Cannabis, 128
—sativa, 130, 131
Cannabaceae, 130
Cannabinaceae, 128, 130
Cannaboideae, 130
Cannaceae, 107, 111
Canscora, 293
—decussata, 294
—diffusa, 294
Canterberry bells, 332
Cape gooseberry, 308
Capparaceae, 169
Capparidaceae, 169, 172
Capparidales, 169
Capparidineae, 169
Capparis spinosa, 173
Capraria, 316
Caprifoliaceae, 325
Capsella, 174
Capsicum furticosum, 312
Caraipa, 247
Carameriana, 226
Carallia brachiata, 265, 329
Carapa, 206
Cardamine, 174
Cardiospermum halicacabum, 221
Carex, 76
—arenaria, 77
—indica, 77
Careya, 270
—arborea, 271
Carica lanceolata, 257

—papaya, 258
—pentagyana, 258
—quercifolia, 258
—cundinamarensis, 254
Caricaceae, 243, 257
Caricoideae, 77
Carissa carandus, 296
Carl von Linné, 18
Carmichaelia australis, 191
Carnegiea gigantea, 260
Carolus Linnaeus, 18
Carpodinus lanceolatus, 297
Carpolobia, 209
Carrot, 275
Carnegiea gigantea, 260
Carolus Linnaeus, 18
Carpodinus lanceolatus, 297
Carpolobia, 209
Carrot, 274
Carthagena Ipecae, 418
Carthamus tincotrius, 337, 341
Cartonemataceae, 92
Carum carvi, 278
Carvia callosa, 323
Carya pecan, 124
Caryocaraceae, 238
Caryophyllaceae, 141
Caryophyllad, 8
Caryophyllales, 141
Caryophylleae, 153
Caryophyllidae, 33
Caryophyllineae, 141
Caryophylloideae, 157, 153
Caryopsis, 69
Caryopterieae, 308
Caryopteris wallichiana, 806
Caryota, 46, 82
Cascara sagarda, 225
Casearia praecox, 254
—resinifera, 254
—tomentosa, 254
Cascarieae, 257
Cashew nut, 223, 379
Cassava, 213
Cassia, 46, 190
—acutifolia, 193
—angustifolia, 193
—fistula, 193
Cassiope, 280
Cassipourea, 265
Cassytha, 167, 168
Castanea, 125
Castilleja, 315, 316
Casuarina equisetifolia, 119
Casuarinaceae, 118
Casuarinales, 118
Catalpa, 318
—ovata, 320
Catha edulis, 224
Catharanthus, 295, 296
Catopherioideae, 310
Cattleya, 117
Cayratia pedata, 226, 227
—trifolium, 227
Ceanothus americanus, 225
Ceara rubber, 215, 407
Cedar oil, 207
Cedrela odorata, 207
Ceiba pentandra, 236
Celastraceae, 219, 224
Celastrales, 197, 220
Celastrineae, 219
Celery, 274
Cell suspension culture, 472
Cellulares, 22
Celosia cristata, 146
Celtis, 127
Centella asiatica, 278
Centrantherum anthelminticum, 335
Centranthus ruber, 331
Centrolepidaceae, 89
Centroplacus, 215
Centrospermae, 28, 141
Centunculus, 283
—tenellum, 283
Cephaelis ipecacuanha, 328, 401, 417
Cephalotaceae, 180, 182
Cephalotus follicularis, 183
Cerastium, 151
Ceratophyllaceae, 4, 154, 157
Ceratophyllales, 154
Ceratophyllum, 4
—demursum, 157
Cerbera odollam, 296
Cercidiphyllaceae, 153, 156
Cercidiphyllales, 153
Cereals, 72, 370
Cercocarpeae, 188
Cereus giganteus, 260
—grandiflorus, 260
—hexagonus, 260
Ceropegia, 294
Cersis siliquastrum, 195
Cestreae, 309
Cestrum nocfurnum, 312
Chalazal caecum, 135, 136
Chal Kumra, 328
Chalmoogra oil, 250
Chamaedora, 79
Chamaelaucieae, 268
Chamaerops humilis, 79, 83
Chameli, 285
Charles Darwin, 19
Charles B. Bessey, 29

CharlIs L'Ech... 17
Cheiranthus, 176
Cheli?onium, 170
Chemotaxonomy, 3
Chenopodiad, 8
Chenopodiaceae, 141, 143
Chenopodiales, 143
Chenopodinae, 141
Chenopodium album, 143
—ambrosioides, 144
—anthelminticum, 144
botiys, 144
—quino, 144
Chichinga, 333
Chickrasia tabularis, 207
Chikrasi, 207
Chin, 115
Chinese lantern, 308
Chiranjee, 220
Chironia, 293
Chirata, 396
Chalenaceae, 228, 229
Chlaeneae, 228
Chlamydospermae, 31
Chloantheae, 308
Chloanthes, 306
Chloranthaceae, 120, 122
Chloripetalae, 26, 29
Chloris barbata, 72
Chlorophyta, 11, 12
Chloroxylon, 205
—swietenia, 206
Chocho, 328
Choisenia, 123
Choisia, 205
Choc , 247
Chorisis, 148
Christisonia, 320
Chrozophora, 212
—Rottleri, 212
Chrysalidocarpus lutescens, 80,82
—madagascariensis, 82
Chrysanthemum cinerarifolium, 341
—coronarium, 339
Chrysobalanaceae, 188, 189
Chrysobalaneae, 188
Chrysobalanoideae, 187, 188
Chrysobalanus, 195
Chrysophyllum cainito, 287
Chrysophyta, 11,12
Chrysosplenium, 183
Chyota, 328
Cicer, 192
—arietinum, 194, 383
—kabulinum, 383
Cichorieae, 339
Cichorium, 337
—endivia, 341
—intybus, 341
Cimicifuga racemosa, 160
Cinchona, 327, 401
—calysaya, 327, 401
—Ledgeriana, 323, 327, 401
—officinalis, 323, 327, 401
—succirubra, 323, 327, 401
Cinchonoideae, 322
Cinnamomum, 168
—camphora, 168
—tamala, 168
—zeylanica, 168
Cipura paludosa, 106
Circaea, 274
Cirsium, 337
Cissampelos, 160
—pariera, 161
Cissus adnata, 226
—quadrangularis, 226, 227
—repens, 226, 227
Cistaceae, 238, 248
Cistineae, 238
Citharexylum, 302
Citronella, 72
Citrullus, 332
—colocynthus, 333
—lanatus, 333
Citrus, 204
—autantifolia, 206
—limettioides, 206
—maxima, 206
—paradisi, 206
—reticulata, 206
—sinensis, 206
Clarkia, 274
Class, 3
Claviceps purpurea, 72
Claytonia, 118
Clematis, 159
Cleome gynandra, 172, 173
—viscosa, 173
Clermontia, 335
Clerodendrum, 306
—fistulosum, 306
—fragrans, 306
—indicum, 306
—siphonanthus, 306
—viscosum, 306
Cleyara, 245
Clove plant, 266
Clusia, 247
—criuva, 247
Clusiaceae, 246
Clusioideae, 249
Clutieae, 214
Clyptostoma callistegioides, 320

Cneoraceae, 196
Cnesmone, 211
Cnicus, 337
Cob, 74
Cobaeaceae, 315
Coccinia grandis, 333
Coccoloba, 140
Cocculus, 161
—carolinus, 162
—hirsutus, 162
Cochlospermaceae, 239
Cochlospermineae, 239
Coconut, 391
—Double, 46
Cock's comb, 146
Cocos, 79, 82, 83
—nucifera, 79, 83, 391
Code, American, 48
—Paris, 48
—Rochester, 48
—Type-basis, 48
Codonopsis, 335
Coelogyne, 117
Coffea, 327, 397
—arabica, 328, 397
—liberica, 328, 398
—robusta, 398
—stenophylla, 398
Coffee plant, 397
Coffee powder, 328
Coir, 362
Coix lachrymajobi, 72
Cola acuminata, 232
Coldenia procumbens, 304
Coleanthus, 70
Coleoptile, 69
Coleorhiza, 69
Coleus, 309
Collar, 317
Colletia spinosa, 225
Colocasia Boryi, 84
—esculenta, 85
Colocasioideae, 87
Colpa, 9
Colpate, 9
Colporate, 9
Colquhounia, 308
Columelliaceae, 295
Column, 115
Colystegia sepium, 302
Combretum, 267
Combretaceae, 261, 266
Commelina bengalensis, 91
—nudiflora, 91
—obliqua, 91
Commelinaceae, 68, 89
Commelinales, 32, 89, 91, 107
Commelinidae, 33, 89, 107
Commelinieae, 91
Commiphora, 208
—wightii, 208
Compositae, 334, 337
Composite colporate, 9
Composition of Indian flora, 363
Coniferales, 12
Coniferophyta, 12
Conium maculatum, 278
Connaraceae, 180
Connaropsis, 198, 199
Conocarpus, 266
Conocephalus, 128
Conservation of germplasm, 429
Contortae, 289, 324
Convalaria majalis, 101
Conocephaloideae, 130
Convolvulaceae, 299, 300
Convolvulales, 300
Convolvulineae, 299
Convolvuloideae, 302
Copernicia cerifera, 83
Corallorhiza, 114
Corchorus capsularis, 234, 386,
—olitorius, 234, 386
Cordaitales, 12, 27
Cordia, 303
—dichotoma, 303
—sebestina, 304
Cordioideae, 303, 304
Coriandrum sativum, 278
Coriariaceae, 216
Coriarineae, 216
Coridaceae, 283
Corideae, 283
Coris, 283
Corispermum, 143
Cornaceae, 274
Cornales, 274
Corolliferae, 32
Coronopus, 174
Correa, 205
Corsicaceae, 113, 114
Corydalis, 170, 171
Corylaceae, 127
Corylea, 127
Corylops himalayana, 185
Corylus avellana, 126
—colurna, 126
—tabulosa, 126
Corynocarpaceae, 216
Corypha, 18, 46, 81, 82
Cosmos bipinnatus, 340
Costaceae, 107, 110
Costae, 272
Costoideae, 109, 110

Costus speciosus, 110
Cotoneastrum, 187
Cotton plant, 387
Cotylanthera, 293
Cotyloideae, 29
Couepea, 187, 189
Couroupita guianensis, 270, 271
Cow tree, 129
Cotynus coggygria, 218
Crassulaceae, 180, 181
Crataeva nurvala, 173
Cratoxylon, 248
Crepidospermum, 208
Crescentia, 318
—cujete, 319
Crescentieae, 319
Crinum latifolium, 104
Critica Botanica, 48
Crocus sativus, 106
Cronquist, Arthur, 34
Crosandra undulifolia, 325
Crossosomataceae, 180
Crotalaria juncea, 195
—sericea, 195
Croton Bonplandianum, 216
—oblongifolius, 211
Crotoneae, 214
Cruciales, 169
Cruciferae, 169, 173
Crypteroniaceae, 257
Cryptocarya, 168
Cryptocoryne, 86
Cryptostegia grandiflora, 298
Ctenolophon parviflorum, 202
Cucubalus, 151
Cucumerineae, 328
Cucumis melo, 333
—sativus, 333
Cucurbita, 332
—maxima, 333
—moschata, 333
—pepo, 332, 333
Cucurbitaceae, 331
Cucurbitales, 28, 331
Cucurbiteae, 333
Cudrania, 128
Cuminum cyminum, 278
Cunoniaceae, 180
Cunoniales, 184
Cuphia polycentra, 263
Cupule, 13, 125, 126
Curculigo orchioides, 92, 140
Curcuma amada, 110
—angustifolia, 110
—domestica, 110
—zedoaria, 110
Curry leaf, 206
Curvembryeae, 25, 26
Cuscuta, 301, 303
—reflexa, 303
Cuscutaceae, 300, 301, 303
Cuscutoideae, 302
Custard apple, 165
Cyanea, 335
Cyanastraceae, 89, 90, 102
Cyanophyta, 11, 12
Cyanotis cristata, 91
Cycadales, 12, 27
Cycadofilicales, 12, 27
Cycadophyta, 12
Cycadophytae, 12
Cyclamen, 283
—purpurascence, 284
Cyclamineae, 283
Cyclanthaceae, 78
Cyclanthales, 78
Cyclanthera, 332
Cyclanthereae, 328
Cyclea, 161
Cylicomorpha, 257
Cymaria, 309
Cymbidium, 117
Cymbopogon citratus, 72
—flexuosus, 72
—martini, 72
—nardus, 72
Cymodocea, 61
Cymodoceaceae, 61
Cymodoceae, 62
Cynanchoideae, 297, 298
Cynarea, 339
Cynocrambaceae, 143
Cynodon dactylon, 72
Cynoglossum, 303
Cynomoreaceae, 134, 261
Cynomorineae, 261
Cyperaceae, 67, 75
Cyperales, 68
Cyperus, 76
—corymbosa, 77
—esculentus, 77
—longus, 77
—papyrus, 77
—rotundus, 77
—stoloniferous, 77
—tegetum, 77
Cyphia, 335
Cyphioideae, 336
Cyphonandra betacea, 312
Cyrillaceae, 216
Cytinaceae, 138

D

Dacryodes hexandra, 208
Dactylocapnos, 170
—thalictrifolia, 171
Dactyloctenium aegypticum, 72
Dahlia, 337
—pinnata, 340
Dalbergia assamica, 194
—sisoo, 194
Dancing girl, 111
Daphnales, 25, 26
Daphniphyllaceae, 196
Darlingtonia, 177
Darwin, Charles, 19
Dasypogoneae, 101
Datiscaceae, 239
Datiscineae, 239
Datura metel, 312
—stramoneum, 312
Datureae, 313
Davidiaceae, 271
Davilla, 244
Daucus, 276
—carrota, 277, 278
Debdaru, 165
Decandria, 20
Deeringia amaranthoides, 146
Degeneria, 154
Degeneriaceae, 164
Dehu, 129
Deinbollia, 221
Delonix regia, 193
Delphinium, 159
—staphisagria, 160
Dendrarium, 43
Dendrobium, 117
Dendrocalamus, 72
Dendrosicyos, 331
Deophal, 129
Dentella, 326
De Plantes, 17
Derris elliptica, 194
Desfontainiaceae, 283
Desmodium motorium, 191
Desmos Dunali, 165
Deutzia, 183
De Vegetabilis, 17
Devil nettle, 132
Dhundul, 328
Diadelphia, 20
Diandrae, 116
Diandrea, 19
Dialypetalae, 31
Dialypetalanthaceae, 325
Dianthus, 151
—barbatus, 152
—caryophyllus, 152
—chinensis, 152
—plumarius, 152
Diapensiaceae, 279
Diapensiales, 28, 279
Diaperturate, 9
Diascia, 316
Dichroa febrifuga, 184
Dichapetalaceae, 196
Dichapetalineae, 196
Dicildantheraceae, 286
Dicotylae, 26
Dicotyledonae, 12, 22, 27, 28, 118, 279
Dicraea, 133
Dictamnus, 205
Didiereaceae, 216
Didiereineae, 216
Didiriadaceae, 142
Didymelales, 185
Didymoplexis, 114
Didynamea, 20
Diervilla, 329
Digitalis purpurea, 316
Digitaria sanguinalis, 72
Dillenia bracteata, 244
—indica, 244
Dilleniaceae, 242, 245
Dilleniales, 239
Dilleniidae, 33, 153, 239
Dilleniidae, 33, 153, 239
Dioecia, 21
Dioncophyllum, 254
Dioscoreaceae, 97
Dioscoreales, 97
Dioscorides, 17
Diosma, 204
Diospyrineae, 282
Diospyros cordifolia, 288
—discolor, 288
—ebenum, 288
—kaki, 288
—melanoxylon, 288
—peregrina, 288
—tomentosa, 288
—virginianum, 288
Dipelta, 329
Dipentodontaceae, 134
Diplacrum, 76
Diplochlamydeae, 22
Dipsacaceae, 320
Dipsacales, 320
Dipterix, 191
Dipterocarpaceae, 249
Dipterocarpoideae, 251
Dipterocarpus, 46, 250
Dirachma socotrana, 197
Dirachmaceae, 238

Disanthoideae, 185
Dischidia, 297, 298
Disciflorae, 24, 26
Distal, 9
Dita bark, 416
Division, 3, 4
Dobinaea, 220
Dodecandrea, 20
Dodecatheon, 283
Dodonaea, 221
Dodonaedeae, 222
Dog wood, 225
Dolichondrone, 319
Dolichos lablab, 194
Domatia, 267
Dombeya Mastersii, 232
Donatiaceae, 334
Donax arundiastrum, 112
Doona, 251
Dorstenia, 128
Dosh-bi-chandi, 106
Double coconut, 46
Double fertilisation, 7
Doum palm, 80
Dovyalis caffra, 250
Dracaena, 88, 99
Dracaenoideae, 99, 100, 101
Dracocephalum tanguticum, 309
Dracontium, 84, 85
Drimys, 154, 162
Drosera, 178, 179
—Burmanni, 179, 180
—indica, 179
—peltata, 179
Droseraceae, 176, 178
Drosophyllum, 178, 179
Dryadeae, 188
Dryas, 187
Drymaria, 151
--diandra, 151
Dryobalanops aromatica, 251
Drypetes, 212
Duguetia qutarensis, 165
Dumur, 129
Durandea, 202
Duranta repens, 306
Dunalia, 312
Durio zebethinus, 238
Durion, 238
Dutchman's pipe, 138
Dyad, 9
Dyschoriste, 323
Dyssaindaceae, 222

E

Eams, 32
Ebenaceae, 286, 288
Ebenales, 28, 286
Ecballium, 331
Ecbolium viride, 324
Eccremocarpeae, 319
Eccremocarpus, 318
Echinochloa, 68
Echinophora, 277
Echinops echinata, 339
Echitoideae,, 296
Echium, 303
Eclipta prostata, 339, 340
Economic Botany, 369
Egg apparatus, 7
Egg cell, 7
Ehretia, 303
—serrata, 304
Ehretiaceae, 300, 305
Ehretioideae, 303, 304
Eichler, 26
Eichhornia crassipes, 94
Ektexine, 9
Elaeagnaceae, 224, 257
Elaeagnus, 257
Elaeis, 80, 81
—guinensis, 83
Elaeocarpaceae, 228, 230
Elaeocarpineae, 228
Elaeocarpus ganitrus, 231
—serratus 231
Elatinaceae, 238, 239
Elatostemma, 132
Elattosis, 65
Eleocharis tuberosa, 77
Ellettaria cardamomum, 110
Elephantopus scaber, 339
Elephant's foot, 85
Elodea, 66
Elveria, 338
Elyna, 76
Elytraria, 323
Embelia, 282
—ribes, 283
Emblica officinalis, 212
Emblingia, 173
Embryo, 5, 7
—culture, 454
—sac, 7
Embryology, 8
Embryophyta, 11, 12
Embryostega, 90, 91
Embryotega, 90
Emilia sonchifolia, 339
Empeleurum, 205
Empetraceae, 216
Empetrineae, 216
Endexine, 9
Endive, 336

Endilcher, 23
Endodesmia, 247
Endodesmioideae, 249
Enantioblastae, 31
Endogene, 22
Endosperm, 7
Endospermum, 212
Engelhardtia, 124
Enhydra fluctuans, 341
Enneandria, 20
Ensatae, 31
Entada phaseoloides, 193
—pursaetha, 193
Fpacridineae, 279
Epaltes, 335
Ephedra, 118
Epigaea, 280
Epigaeoideae, 281
Epigynae, 25, 26
Epilobium, 274
Epimedium, 157
Epirrhizanthes, 209
Epithet—specific, 48
Equatorial, 9
Equisetineae, 12, 36
Eradication of virus, 486
Eargrostis, 71
Eranthis, 159
Eremostachys, 309
Eremosynaceae, 184
Ergot, 71
Erica, 276
Ericaceae, 279
Ericales, 28, 279
Ericineae, 279
Ericoideae, 281
Erigonium, 140
Eriobotrya japonica, 187
Eriocaulaceae, 89, 92
Eriocaulales, 89, 94
Eriocauloideae, 94
Eriocaulon, 93
—quinqueangulare, 93
—setaceum, 93
—sieboldianum, 93
—trilobum, 93
—truncatum, 93
Eriocaulonaceae, 92
Erioglossum, 221
Eriophorum, 76
—comosum, 77
Ervatamia divericata, 296
Eryeibe panciculata, 301
Eryngium bupleuroides, 276
—inaccessum, 276
—sarcophyllum, 276
Erythraea Roxburghii, 294
Erythrina variegata, 193
Erythrospermae, 255
Eucalyptus, 268
—citriodora, 269
—crebra, 269
—dealbata, 269
—elaeophora, 269
—globulus, 269
—leucoxylon, 269
—paniculata, 269
—punctata, 269
—sideroxylon, 269
Eucaridium, 274
Eucommiaceae, 127, 180
Eucryphiaceae, 238
Eugenia uniflora, 266
Euglenophyta, 11, 12
Eulaliopsis binata, 72
Eumonad, 9
Eumycophyta, 11, 12
Euonymus crenulatus, 224
—europaeus, 224
—indicus, 224
Eupatorieae, 339
Eupatorium ayapana, 340
—odoratum, 339
Euphorbia, 211
—antiquorum, 212
—dracunculoides, 212
—neriifolia, 212
—pilulifera, 212
Euphorbiaceae, 196, 210
Euphorbiales, 196
Euphoria longana, 241, 242
Euphrasia, 316
Eupomatiaceae, 165
Euptelea, 162
Eupteleaceae, 164
Eurya, 245, 246
Euryale, 155
—ferox, 156
Euterpe, 82
Everlasting flower, 335
Evodea, 205
Evolvulus nummularius, 302
Exacum tetragonum, 294
Exbucklandia, 185
Esbucklandioideae, 185
Excoecaria agallocha, 215
Exine, 9
Exocarpus, 134
Exogonium purga, 296
Exospermum, 164

F

Fabaceae, 195
Fabales, 195

Fagaceae, 124, 125
Fagales, 28, 118, 124
Fagara, 205
Fagopyrum esculentum, 141
Fagraea, 291
—auriculata, 291
—crenulata, 292
—elliptica, 292
—fragrans, 292
Fagus, 125
False Sandal wood, 125
Family, 3, 4
Fan palm, 78
Farinosae, 27, 89
Father of Botany, 17
—of Modern Botany, 18
Feather palm, 78
Feijoa sellowiana, 270
Fekhowa-fruit, 270
Female gametophyte, 7
Fertilisation, 7
—double, 7
Ferula asafoetida, 278
—foetida, 278
—galbaniflua, 278
—narthex, 278
—rubricaulis, 278
Festuca undata, 72
—valesiaca, 72
Fever nettele, 132
Fevilleae, 328
Fevillia, 331
Ficus, 128, 129
—benghalensis, 129
—carica, 129
—elastica, 129, 407
—glomerata, 129
—hispida, 129
—krishuae, 46
—racemosa, 129
—religiosa, 129
Field notebook, 38
Filament, 6
Filicineae, 12
Fimbristylis, 76
Finlaysonia maritiana, 298
Fishtail palm, 46
Flacourtia, 254
Flacourtiaceae, 243, 253
Flacourtieae, 258,
Flacourtiineae, 243
Flagellaria indica, 90
Flagellariaceae, 89,90
Flagellum, 80
Fleurya interrupta, 132
Floret, 68, 69
—disc, 332,
—ray, 332
Floscopa acandens, [illegible]1
Flower, 5, 6
—bisexual, 7
—culture, 450
—unisexual, 7
Foeniculum vulgare, 274
Foliaceae, 23, 295
Form, 4
Forskohlea, 132
Forsythia, 290
Fourcroya, 103, 104, 105
Four-o-clock plant, 147
Fouquieriaceae, 242, 252
Fouquierineae, 238
Fragaria vesca, 187
Francoaceae, 184
Francoideae, 184
Frangula alnus, 225
Frankeniaceae, 242, 252
Fraxinus, 290
—excelsior, 290
—floribunda, 290
Freesia, 106
Freycinetia, 57, 58
Fritillaria, 101
Fuchsia apetala, 274
Fumaria indica, 172
Fumariaceae, 169, 171
Fumarioideae, 170, 171
Fundamenta Botanica, 48
Fungi, 11, 23, 26
Funicle, 7
Fusion nucleus, 7

G

Gaertnera, 327
Gaillardia, 340
Galbanum, 274
Galcerea, 215
Galipea, 205
Galium, 326, 327
Gamber catechu, 323
Gamboge, 244
Gamete, 6
Gametophyte, 7, 8
Gamopetalae, 23, 24
Ganas, 18
Ganja, 131
Garcinia, 247
—cowa, 248
—mangostana, 248
—morella, 248
—xanthocyhmus, 248
Garden Nasturtium, 199

Gardenia, 326, 327
—jasminoides, 329
Garjan tree, 246
Garryaceae, 270
Garryales, 28
Garuga pinnata, 208
Gaspard Bauhin, 17
Gastridium, 70
Gastrodia, 114
Gaudichaudiana, 208
Gaultheria, 277
—fragrantissima, 280
Geissolomataceae, 257
Gelonieae, 215
Gelsemium, 291
—sempervirens, 292
Genera Plantarum, 23
Generative cell, 6
Generic name, 48
Genists, 191
—tinctoria, 194
Gentiana, 293
—acaulis, 294
—campestris, 294
—crassa, 293
—kurroo, 294
—lutea, 294
Gentianaceae, 289, 292
Gentianineae, 289
Gentianales, 289
Gentianoideae, 294
Genus, 3, 4
Genusia, 302
Geonoma, 78, 81
George Bentham, 23
—King, 45
Geosiridaceae, 97, 114
Geraniaceae, 197
Geraniales, 28, 196
Geraniineae, 196
Geranium oil, 198
—Wallichianum, 197
Germination, 5
Germ pore, 7
Gesneriaceae, 295
Gunderson, Alfred, 33
Ghia Toroi, 328
Ghuina, 85
Gillenieae, 188
Gilliesieae, 105
Ginger, 393
—Martinique, 394
Gingidia, 276
Ginkgoales, 12, 27
Ginseng, 272
Girardinia, 132
Githago, 150
Gladiolus, 106,
Glaucium, 170
Glaux, 283
Gliricidia maculata, 195
Globba, 110
Globe Amarnath, 146
Globulariaceae, 295
Glochidia, 255
Glochidion, 212
Gloriosa, 99
Glumaceae, 25, 26
Glumales, 68
Glumes, 68, 69, 73, 75
Glumiflorae, 27, 32, 67, 68, 71
Glycine max, 194
Glycosmis arborea, 205
Glycyrrhiza glabra, 194
Gmelina arborea, 306
Gnaphalium luteoalbum, 339
Gnetaceae, 25
Gnetales, 12, 27
Godoya splendida, 245
Gokshur, 203
Gomphostemma, 309
Gomphrena globosa, 146
Gomortegaceae, 153
Goniothalamus cardiopetalus, 165
Gonolobus cordurango, 299
Gonystylaceae, 257
Goodeniaceae, 334
Goodeniales, 335
Gooseberry, 184
Gordonia, 246
Gossypium, 237, 387
—arboreum, 238, 387
—barbadens, 288, 387
—herbaceum, 288, 387
—hirsutum, 387
Gouania, 225
Gourd, 328
Gram, 383
Graminae, 67, 68, 71
Grangea maderaspatana, 339
Grape-fruit 206
Grape vine 227
Gravesia 271
Grewia subinaequalis 230
Grossulariaceae 134
Ground nut, 196, 392
Ground tissue, 5
Grubbiaceae, 134
Guarea ropalocarpa, 206
Guazuma ulmifolia, 232
Guettardoideae, 327
Guiacum, 203
—officinale, 203
—sanctum, 203

Guizotia abyssinica, 341
Gular, 129
Gum-guiacum, 203
Gustavia augusta, 271
Guttiferae, 242, 246
Guttiferales, 245
Gymnema lactifera, 298
Gymnospermae, 11, 12, 25, 26, 27, 31
Gymnostachyas, 86
Gynandria, 21
Gymnosporia wallichiana, 224
Gynocardia odorata, 254
Gynoecium, 6
Gynotroches, 265
Gypsophila elegans, 152
—paniculata, 152
Gyrostemonaceae, 141, 143

H

Haemanthus coccineus, 104
Haematocarpus, 161
Haematoxylon campechianum, 193
Haemodoraceae, 97
Haemodorales, 89
Hair bells, 332
Haldu, 323
Halleria 316
Halocnemum, 143
Halophila, 90
Halophytes, 66
Haloragidaceae, 257
Haloxylon ammodendron, 143
Hamamelidaceae, 118, 180, 184
Hamamelidae, 118
Hamamelidales, 118
Hamamelididae, 33, 118, 153
Hamamelidoideae, 185
Hamamelis, 185
Hamelia patens, 329
Hamiltonia, 327
Hanguana, 90
Hanguanaceae, 90
Hans Hallier, 31
Haploclathra paniculata, 246
Haptera, 132
Hardwickia binata, 193
Harungana madagascariensis, 248
Harveya, 315
Hashish, 131
Hathishura, 299
Havetiopsis, 247
Hauya, 274
Hebe, 316
Hedera helix, 275
—nepalensis, 275
Hedwigia, 208
Hedychium, 110
—coccinium, 111
—coronarium, 110.
Hedyotis, 327
Heleniеae, 339
Heliantheae, 339
Helianthus, 337
—annuus, 340
—tuberosus, 341
Helichrysum, 340
Heliconia, 108
Heliconiaceae, 107
Helicteris isora, 232
Helinus, 225
Heliotropioideae, 303, 304
Heliotropium indicum, 303
—ovalifolium, 304
Heliptarum, 340
Helleboraceae, 160
Helleboreae, 160
Helleborus, 159
Helobieae, 27, 31, 59
Hemiangiosperm, 16
Hemicarpha, 76
Hemidesmus indicus, 298, 299
Hemigraphis, 323
Hemiophragma heterophylla, 316
Hemlock, 278
Hemp, 131
Henoonia, 312
Henriquezia, 327
Hepaticae, 11, 26
Heptandria, 20
Heracleum, 277
Herbaceae, 32
Herbae, 18
Herbarium, 37
—vivae Eiconis, 17
Heritiera fomes, 232
—littoralis, 232
Hernandiaceae, 153
Herniaria, 151
Herrerioideae, 100
Hesperella, 290
Hesperolinum, 202
—congestum, 202
Heteranthera, 94
Heteromerae, 24, 26
Heterophragma, 314
Heteropolar, 9
Heteropyxidaceae, 224, 225, 227
Heterosmilax, 100
Hevea, 213
—braziliensis, 215, 405
Hexandria, 20
Hibbertia, 244

Hibiscus cannabinus, 234
—matabilis, 234
—rosa-sinensis, 234
—schizopetalus, 234
—subdariffa, 234
—syreacus, 234
Hijal, 267
Hildebrandtia, 301
Hillebrandia, 258
Hilum, 7
Himatandraceae, 153
Hing, 274
Hingcha, 336
Hingul, 203
Hippocastanaceae, 216, 223
Hippocratiaceae, 216
Hippomaneae, 215
Hippuridaceae, 261
Hippuridineae, 261
Hiptage benghalensis, 208
—madoblata, 208
Historia naturalis, 17
—plantarum universalis, 17
Holargidium, 174
Holarrhena antidysenterica, 295, 296
Holigarna, 212
Hollyhock, 234
Holmskioldia, 306
Holodiscus, 188
Holoptelea, 127, 128
Holotype, 49
Homalieae, 255
Homonoia, 212
Hooker Joseph Dalton, 23
Hopea recopei, 250
Hoplestigmataceae, 286
Hoplophyllum, 337
Hoppea, 293
Hordeum vulgare, 72
Horto Botanico Calcuttensis, 45
Hottoina, 283
Houttuynia cordata, 122
Hovenia dulcis, 225
Hoya, 297, 298
Hugonia mystax, 202
Humiriaceae, 196, 202
Humulus, 130
—lupulus, 131
Hura, 212
Hutchinson, John, 31
Hybanthus enneaspermus, 259
Hydnocarpus venenatus, 254
Hydnophytum, 326
Hydrasticaceae, 160
Hydrastis 160
—canadens, 160
Hydrocaryaceae, 261, 272
Hydrocera, 200, 201
Hydrocotyle, 276
Hydrocotyloideae, 277
Hydrolythrum, 258
Hydrophyllaceae, 299
Hygrophila, 323
Hymenanthera, 252
Hymenantheriae, 253
Hymenocardia, 215
Hymenopogon, 326
Hyosciamus niger, 312
Hypericaceae, 246, 249
Hypericoideae, 249
Hypericum, 246
—japonicum, 248
Hypseocharis, 199
Hyptis, 308, 309

I

Iberis, 174, 176
Icacinaceae, 216
Icacinineae, 216
Ichnocarpus frutescens, 296
Icosandria, 20
Ilex, 224
—aquifolium, 224
—dipyrina, 224
—insignis, 224
—malabarica, 224
—paraguensis, 224
Illecebraceae, 139
Illicales, 153
Illiciaceae, 154
Illicium verum, 163
Imbricatae, 325
Impatiens, 200
—balasmina, 200
—fulva, 200
—noli-tangere, 200
—parviflora, 200
Imperata cylindrica, 72, 73
Imperfectae, 18
Imperial Botanical Conference, 48
Indigofera tinctoria, 194
Inferae, 24, 26, 31
Ingudi Briksha, 203
Integument, 6
International Botanical Congress, 47
International Code of Botanical Nomenclature, 4, 49
Intine, 9
Inuleae, 339
Ipecac, 400
—carthagena, 400

Ipomoea aquatica, 302
—arborescens, 301
—batatas, 301
—fistulosa, 302
—quamoclit, 302
—pulchella, 301, 302
—purpurea, 302
—wolcottiana, 301
Iridaceae, 97, 106
Iridales, 97, 107
Irideae, 107
Iris, 106
Isauxis lancaefolia, 251
Isoetes-Monocotyledon theory, 15
Isopyrum, 159
Isotoma longiflora, 337
Isotype, 49
Italian garden, 43
Ithaca congress, 48
Ivy, 271
Ixia, 106
Ixieae, 106
Ixora, 326
—arborea, 329
—coccinea, 329

J

Jaborandi, 195
Jaboticabo, 266
Jacaranda, 46, 318
—filicifolia, 319
—ovalifolia, 319
Jacaratia, 257
Jacquinia ruscifolia, 283
Jagnya Dumur, 129
Jamesia, 207
Jamoon, 266
Jamrool, 266
Japanese Garden, 43
Jasminoideae, 286
Jasminum, 290
—auriculatum, 290
—grandiflorum, 290
—nudiflorum, 290
—sambac, 290
Jatropheae, 214
Jatropha curcas, 212
—gossypifolia, 212
Jerome Bock, 17
John Gerard, 17
—Hutchinson, 31
—Ray, 18
Joseph Dalton Hooker, 23
—Pitton de Tournefort, 18
Judas tree, 195
Juglandaceae, 123, 124
Juglandales, 28, 118, 123
Juglans nigra, 124
—regia, 124
Julianiaceae, 124
Julianiales, 28, 124
Juncaginales, 59
Juncaceae, 97, 98
Juncales, 68, 71, 77, 89, 97
Juncellus inundatus, 77
Juncus, 98
—butonius, 98
—prismatocarpus, 98
—textiles, 98
Jussiaea repens, 274
—suffruticosa, 274
Jussieu, Bernard de, 22
—Antoine Laurent de, 22
Justicia betonica, 325
—gendarusa, 324
—procumbens, 324
Jute, 234, 386
Juthi, 290

K

Kachoo, 85
Kadamba tree, 328
Kadsura, 162
Kaempferia linearis, 111
—rotunda, 111
Kafir plum, 220
Kagzi nimbu, 206
Kakra shinga, 223
Kakrol, 333
Kalanchoe laciniata, 182
—pinnata, 182
Kali Toroi, 328
Kalmia, 280
Kalstroemia, 202
Kamala, 206
Kanthali champa, 166
Karela, 333
Karkata shringi, 223
Kebun Raya, 44
Kedrostis spinosa, 332
Kew Rule, 48
Kerosphaereae, 116
Kerrieae, 188
Key apple, 250
Kharbuz, 328
Khaya, 206
—senigalensis, 207
Khira, 328
Kickxia ramosissima, 316
Kielmeyera, 247

Kielmeyeroideae, 249
Kigelia, 318
King, Sir George, 45
Kingdom, Plant, 4
Kino, 269
Kleinhovia hospita, 232
Kmeria, 162
Kobresia, 76
Kochia indica, 143
—scoparia, 145
—trichophylla, 145
Koenigia, 140
Kool, 225
Kopsia, 296
Korthalsia scaphigera, 78
Krameria triandra, 210
Kudari, 328
Kudzu-vine, 194
Kumra, 328
Kuprianova, L.H., 33
Kustha, 335
Kuth, 335
Kyd, Colonel Robert, 45

L

Labiatae, 299, 308
Lacis monadelpha, 133
Lactoridaceae, 153
Lactuca sativa, 341
Lactucaceae, 30
Lafoensia, 262
Lagascea, 337, 339
—mollis, 334
Lagenandra, 86
Lagenaria, 331
—leucantha, 331
Lagerstroemia, 46
—indica, 263
—macrocarpa, 262
—parviflora, 262
—speciosa, 262, 263
Laguncalaria, 266
Lamiaceae, 308
Lamiales, 197, 198, 300
Laminar, 14, 15
Landolphia, 296
—Kirki, 297
Landscape garden, 43
Lannea, 218
Lantana aculeata, 306
Lapageria rosea, 101
Laplacea, 245
Lardizabalaceae, 138, 153, 162
Lasianthus, 327
Lasiocarpus, 208
Lasioideae, 86
Lasora, 300
Lathyrus macrorrhizus, 195
—sativus, 195
—odoratus, 195
Lata Palas, 195
Lauraceae, 153, 167
Lawrales 153
Laurentia longiflora, 336
Lauroideae, 168
Laurus, 168
—nobilis, 168
Lavandula, 310
Lavanduloideae, 310
Lowsonia inermis, 263
Leaf culture, 449
Leaf skin theory, 5
Leaf trace, 13
Lectotype, 49
Lecythidaceae, 261, 270
Lecythidales, 257
Lecythis zabucajo, 260
Ledothamuns, 280
Leea, 226
—crispa, 227
—macrophylla, 227
—robusta, 227
Leeaceae, 227
Leersia hexandra, 72
Leguminosae, 180, 189
Leiphaimos, 293
Leitneriales, 28, 185
Lemna, 69, 73, 74, 88
Lemnaceae, 78, 82, 88
Lemon grass, 72
Lennoaceae, 279, 299
Lennoineae, 299
Lens culinaris, 194
Lentibulariaceae, 299
Leonia, 258
Leonioideae, 249
Leonotis nepetifolia, 309
Leontochir, 103
Leonurus sibiricus, 309
Lepidium savitum, 174
Lepidobotrys, 198
Lepidocaryeae, 82
Lepidocaryoideae, 83
Leptospermoideae, 269
Leptospermum scoparianum, 270
Leptomeria, 135
Leucas biflora, 308
—cephalctes, 309, 310
—rosamarinifolia, 308
—ternifolia, 308
Leucocarpus, 316
Leucojam, 104
Leucomeris, 335

Leucosceptrum canum, 308, 309
Lichens, 23
Licuala, 81
—elegans, 83
—grandis, 83
—paludosa, 83
Lignosae, 32
Lignum—vitae, 203
Liguliflorae, 339
Ligustrales, 289
Ligustrum, 290
Lilaeopsis, 276
Liliaceae, 68, 97, 99, 101
Liliales, 32, 89, 97, 98, 101
Liliatae, 33
Liliflorae, 27, 31, 84, 97
Liliidae, 33, 78, 97
Lilioideae, 100
Liliopsida, 35
Lilium, 99
Limen, 252
Limnanthaceae, 298, 216
Limnanthineae, 216
Limnocharis, 65
Limnocharitaceae, 65, 66
Limnophila heterophylla, 316
Limnophyton obtusifolium, 63
Limonia acidissima, 207
Limoniaceae, 285
Linaceae, 196, 201
Linaria, 316
Lindenbergia indica, 315
Lindera, 168
Lindernia, 312
—indica, 312
—brachiata, 312
Linnaea, 329
Linnaeae, 330
Linnaean system, 19
Linnaeus, Carolus, 18
Linne, Carl von, 18
Linociera, 290
Linseed, 393
Linum usitatissimum, 203, 393
Lippia, 306
—geminata, 307
Liquidamber, 185
—orientalis, 185
—styraciflua, 185
Liquidambaroideae, 185
Liriodendron tulipifera, 163
Lissocarpaceae, 286
Litchi, 221
—chinensis, 222
Lithos, 148
Litsaea, 168
Livistona, 81
—chinensis, 83
Lloyd Botanic Garden, 46
Loasaceae, 239
Loasineae, 239
Lobelia, 336
—inflata, 337
—tupa, 337
Lobeliaceae, 334, 336
Lobelioideae, 336
Lodicules, 69, 73, 74
Lodoicea, 78, 81, 82
Loganiaceae, 289, 291
Loganiales, 285
Lois de la nomenclature botanique, 48
Lomandreae, 101
Longan, 222
Lonicerae, 350
Lopezia, 274
Lophira, 245
—alata, 245
Lophopetalum wightianum, 224
Lophophora, 260
Loranthaceae, 134, 135
Loranthineae, 134
Loranthoideae, 135
Louki, 328
Lowia, 109
Lowiaceae, 107
Lowioideae, 109
Luculia, 327
—gratissima, 324
Ludwigia adscendens, 273, 274
—octovalvis, 274
—palustris, 274
—parviflora, 274
—perennis, 274
Luffa, 331
—acutangula, 333
—cylindrica, 333
Lumnitzera littoria, 266
Luzula, 98
Luzuriageae, 32
Luzuriagoideae, 100, 101
Lyallia, 151, 152
Lycesteria, 325
Lycopersicon lycopersicum, 312
Lycopodineae, 12, 26
Lycopsida, 12, 32
Lycopsis, 303
Lycopus, 309
Lysiana, 136
Lysimachia, 283
—vulgaris, 284
Lysimachieae, 283
Lythraceae, 261
Lythrales, 196, 261
Lythrum salicaria, 262, 263

M

Maba, 288
Macassar oil, 165
Machadoa, 256
Macleya, 170
Madhabika, 208
Madhabilata, 208
Madhuca butyracea, 287
—indica, 287
Maeosopis emini, 225
Maesa, 282
Magnolia Campbelli, 163
—grandiflora, 163
Magnoliaceae, 30, 153, 162
Magnoliales, 12, 32, 153
Magnoliatae, 33, 118
Magnoliidae, 33, 120, 153
Magnoliophyta, 33
Magnoliopsida, 35
Mahonia, 157
Makal, 328
Malacca jamrool, 266
Malachra, 234
Malesherbiaceae, 239, 253
Mallotus philippinensis, 213
Maloideae, 188
Malope trifida, 234
Malpighia glabra, 208
Malpighiaceae, 196, 208
Malpighiales, 209
Malpighineae, 196
Malus sylvestris, 187
Malva, 234
Malvaceae, 228, 233
Malvinieae, 228
Malvales, 28, 228, 229
Malvastrum, 234
Mammea americana, 248
Mandar, 195
Mandarin, 206
Mandragora officinarum, 312
Mandrake, 308
Mangifera, 222
—indica, 222, 376
Manglietia, 163
Mango, 219, 376
Mangostene, 244
Manihot, 212
—esculenta, 82, 215
—glaziovii, 215, 407
Manilkara, 286
Manjistha, 328
Mankachoo, 85
Mankanda, 85
Mantisia saltatoria, 111
Manuka, 266
Maranta arundinacea, 112
Marantaceae, 107, 112
Maranteae, 113
Marking-nut tree, 220
Marquesia, 250
Marsippospermum, 92
Martyniaceae, 321
Martynia annua, 321
Masina, 202
Matelea, 299
Mathiasella, 277
Mathiola, 176
Mattias de L'Obel, 17
Maurandia, 315
Maurera, 133
Mauritia flexuosa, 82
Mayacaceae, 89
Mazus japonicus, 316
Meconopsis, 171
Medusandraceae, 134
Megacarpaea, 174
Megaphyll, 5
Megaspore, 7, 8
Megasporophyll, 6, 35
Mehendi, 258
Melaleuca, 268
—leucadendron, 270
Melamporum, 315
Melanorhoea, 218
Melanthioideae, 100
Melastoma, 271
—malabathricum, 272
Melastomoaceae, 261, 271
Melastomatoideae, 272
Melia, 206
—azedarach, 207
Meliaceae, 196
Meliales, 208
Melianthaceae, 216
Melianthineae, 216
Melica, 70
Melicocca bijuga, 222
Melodinus, 296
Melon, 328
Melothrieae, 328
Memecylaceae, 272
Memecyloideae, 272
Memecylon, 271
—edule, 272
—capitellatum, 272
Mendoncia, 323
Mendonceae, 324
Meni oil, 245
Menispermaceae, 161
Mentha arvensis, 309
—cablin, 310
—piperata, 310

—sylvestris, 309
Mentum, 115
Menyanthaceae, 289, 294
Menyanthoideae, 289
Merciera, 330
Mercurialis, 212
Mesembryanthemum, 149
Mesome, 5
Mesua, 247
—ferrea, 248
Metachlamydeae, 27, 28, 279
Metalasia, 338
Metroxylon, 78, 81
—rumphii, 82
—sagu, 82
Mez, C. 32
Michauxia, 335
Michelia champaca, 163
Micraria, 68
Microdesmis, 215
Microdracoides, 75
Microembryeae, 25, 26
Microlaena, 70
Microrhamuns, 225
Microspermae, 25, 26, 27, 113
Microsporangia, 6
Microspore, 6
Microtropis ramiflora, 224
Migration of plants, 346
Mikania, 337
Miliusa indica, 165
—tomentosa, 165
Millenia, 338
Milletia ovalifolia, 198
Millingtonia, 318
—hortensis, 319
Mimosa pudica, 193
Mimosaceae, 195
Mimosae, 189
Mimosideae, 189
Mimusopeae, 287
Mimusops elengi, 287
Mina lobata, 301
Mirabilis, 146
—jalapa, 147
Mitha Kadu, 328
—Kumra, 328
Mitha nimbu, 206
Mitragyna parvifolia, 327
Mitrasacme, 291
Mitrastemonaceae, 137
Mitreola, 291
Mocinna heterophylla, 257
Modeca triloba, 253
Molluginaceae, 142
Mollugo spergula, 149
Momordica, 332
—charantia, 333
—cochinchinensis, 333
Monadelphia, 20
Monandreae, 116
Monandria, 19
Mondoideae, 100
Monechma, 323
Monimiaceae 153
Monkey pot tree, 266
—puzzle tree, 266
Monoaperturate, 9
Monocarpic, 78
Monocharia hastata, 94
—vaginalis, 94
Monochlamydeae, 22,23,24,31,122
Monocotylae, 26
Monocotyledonae, 12, 27, 55
Monocotyledons, 31
Monodora, 46, 164
Monodoreae, 166
Monodoroideae, 166
Monolepis, 143
Monoporandra, 250
Monotoideae, 251
Monotropaceae, 275
Monotypic, 3
Monstera deliciosa 85
Monsteroideae, 86
Montrouziera, 248
Moraceae, 127, 128
Morinda, 22, 32
—tinctoria, 328
Moringa oleifera, 176
Moringineae, 169, 176
Moroideae, 129
Morus alba, 129
—australis, 129
—nigra, 129
Mounting paper, 40
Mouriria, 271
Muehlenbeckia platyclados, 140
Multiovulatae, 25, 26
Mung, 384
Muntingia calabura, 230
Murdannia nudiflora, 91
Murraya, 204
—koenigii, 205, 206
—paniculata, 205, 206
Musa, 108
—acuminata, 109, 378
—balbisiana, 378
—×paradisiaca, 109, 377
—textilis, 109
Musaceae, 107
Musali, 92, 104
Musambi, 206
Musci, 11, 26

Musk melon, 328
Musoideae, 109
Mussaenda glabra, 329
Mutisia, 337
Mutiseae, 339
Myoporineae, 295
Myosotis, 303, 304
—palustris, 303
Myricaceae, 123
Myricales, 28, 123, 185
Myricaira germanica, 251
Myriciaria cauliflora, 270
Myristica fragrans, 167
Myristicaceae, 153, 166
Myrmecodia, 326
Myrothamnaceae, 180, 185
Myrsinaceae, 281, 282
Myrsinales, 277
Myrtaceae, 261, 267
Myrtales, 261
Myrtiflorae, 28, 261
Myrtineae, 261
Myrtoideae, 269
Myrtus, 268
Myxomycophyta, 11, 12
Myzodendraceae, 134

N

Nageswai, 244
Nag Kesar, 244
Naglingam tree, 266
Naiades, 22
Najadaceae, 59, 62
Najadales, 59
Najas, 62, 71
—foveolata, 62
—graminea, 62
—marina, 62
—minor, 62
Nannorhops, 79
—ritchieana, 79
Napolea coccinelifera, 256
Naravelia, 159
—zeylanica, 160
Narcissus, 103
—pseudonarcissus, 103
Nardostachis jatamansi, 331
Nardus, 70
Nasturtium, 199
Natural Orders, 22,23
—Systems, 22
Nathanial Wallich, 45
Nauclea, 326
Navia, 96
Navioideae, 96
Nectandra, 168
Nectaropetalum, 202
Neea, 146
—theifera, 147
Neem, 207
Neillieae, 188
Nelsonia, 323
Nelsonieae, 324
Nelumbo nucifera, 155
Nelumboideae, 155
Nelumbonaceae, 156
Nelumbonales, 33, 153, 156
Nematostylis, 327
Nemopanthus, 223
Neoglaziovia variegata, 91
Neoleuderit ia, 203
Neottia nidus-avis, 114
Neotype, 49
Nepeta, 309
Nepenthaceae, 176, 177
Nepenthales, 177
Nepenthis, 178
—khasiana, 178
Nephelium lappaceum, 222
Nerium, 296
—indicum, 296
Neuradeae, 188
Neuradoideae, 187
Nexine, 9
Nicandreae, 313
Nicotiana plumbaginifolia, 312
—rustica, 312
—tabacum, 312
Nidularium, 97
Nigella, 159
—sativa, 160
Nitraria, 203, 209
Nitrariaceae, 209
Nolanaceae, 295, 310
Nolanoideae, 310
Nomenclatural type, 49
Nomenclature of plants, 48
Nopalea coccinellifera, 260
Nothofagus, 125
Notochaete hamosa, 309
Nucellus, 6
Nucleus, fi sion, 7
—, secondary, 7
—, tube, 7
Nue Kreuterbuch, 17
Nuytsia, 135
Nyctaginaceae, 141, 143, 146
Nyctanthaceae, 290
Nyctanthes, 290
—arbortristis, 290, 306
Nymphaea, 154, 155
—nouchali, 156
—stellata, 156

Nymphaeaceae, 153, 154
Nymphaeales, 33, 153
Nymphaeineae, 153
Nymphoideae, 155
Nymphoides, 293
—cristata, 293, 294
Nypa, 79, 81, 82, 83
—fruticans, 79
Nyssaceae, 261

O

Oaks, 125
Obturator, 210
Ochlandra, 70
Ochna squarrosa, 245
Ochnaceae, 242, 244
Ochnales, 245
Ochnigenes, 31
Ochrocarpus, 247
—longifolius, 248
Ochroma, 238
Ocimum americanum, 310
—basilicum, 310
—Kilimandscharicum, 310
—sanctum, 309
Ocimoideae, 310
Octandria, 20
Octoknemataceae, 134
Odontostemoneae, 101
Oenanthe benghalensis, 277
Oenothera lamarckiana, 274
Oil yielding plants, 390
Ol, 85
Olacaceae, 134
Olacales, 134
Oldenlandia, 327
—corymbosa, 328
Olea europaea, 290
Oleaceae, 289
Olealis, 289
Oleineae, 289
Oleoideae, 290
Oliniaceae, 257
Olive tree, 290
Omniaperturate, 9
Onagraceae, 261, 273
Onagrad, 8
Oncoba, 254
Oncobeae, 255
Ononis, 191
Oolong tea, 367
Operculina turpethum, 302
Operculum, 252
Ophiopogonoideae, 160
Ophrydoideae, 116
Opiliaceae, 134
Oppositifoliae, 29
Opuntia dillenii, 260
—elatior, 260
—ficus-indica, 260
—tuna, 260
—vulgaris, 260
Opuntiales, 28, 259
Opuntieae, 260
Ora, 9
Orange, 206
Orchidaceae, 113, 114
Orchidales, 113
Orchidaria, 46
Order, 3, 4
Oreobolus, 76
Organogenesis, 469
Organoleptic studies, 392
Origin of Angiosperms, 15
Ormosia, 191, 195
Orobanchaceae, 299, 320
Orobanche, 320
Oroxylon indicum, 318
Orthoploceae, 174
Orthospermae, 328
Oryza, 70
—sativa, 72, 370
Osbeckia, 271
—crinita, 272
—nepalensis, 272
Osmaronieae, 188
Ostenia, 65
Oswald Tippo, 32
Osyris pyrularia, 135
Otostegia, 309
Ottelia, 66
—alismoides, 67
Otto Brunfels, 17
Ouratea, 245
Oxalidaceae, 196, 198
Oxalis corniculata, 198
—tetraphylla, 198
Oxyria, 140
Oxyspora, 271
—paniculata, 278

P

Pachycentria, 271
Pachylarnax 162
Pachynema 244
Pachyrhizus angulatus, 194
Paederia foetida, 328
Paeonia, 159
Paeoniaceae, 160, 161
Paeoniales, 153
Paeonieae, 160
Paepalanthoideae, 94

Paepalanthus, 93
Pagamea, 327
Pajanelia, 318
Palaquium, 286
—gutta, 288
Palaquiaeae, 287
Palas, 195
Pali, 252
Paliurus, 225
Palmae, 75, 78
Palmales, 78
Palm, 79, 80
—Date, 82
—Doum, 80
Palwal, 333
Palynology, 9
Panax ginseng, 276
Pandanaceae, 57, 82
Pandanales, 27, 28, 55, 78
Pandanus, 57, 58
—fascicularis, 58
—tectorius, 58
Pangieae, 255
Pangium, 254
Panicoideae, 74
Panicum, 72
—miliaceum, 72
Pantoaperturate, 9
Papaver rhoeas, 171
—somniferum 71
Papaveraceae, 169
Papaveroideae, 171
Papaynieae, 239
Paphiopedilium, 117
Papilionaceae, 190, 195
Papilionatae, 190
Papilionoideae, 190
Parabaena, 161
Paracorola, 103
Para rubber, 215, 405
Parasara, 18
Paraspipul, 234
Paratype, 49
Pariana, 70
Parideae, 101
Parietales, 28, 242, 249
Parietaria, 132
Paris Code, 48
—Convension, 48
Parmentiera, 314
Parnasia, 183
Parnasiaceae, 184
Paropsia, 250
Paropsieae, 255
Paropsiopsis, 250
Parrottia, 185
Parley, 274
Parsnip, 274
Parsnychia, 157
Parthenium argentatum, 341
Parul, 315
Pasania, 125
Passiflora caerulea, 256, 257
—edulis, 257
—foetida, 257
—holosericea, 257
—incarnata, 257
—ligularis, 257
—racemosa, 257
—suberosa, 257
Passifloraceae, 255
Passiflorales, 239, 253
Pastinaca sativa, 278
Patala, 315
Patinimbu, 206
Paullinia, 221
Paulownia, 315
Pavetta, 326
Pavonia, 234
Paypayrola, 252
Pea, 193, 382
Pearl glands, 226
Pedaliaceae, 321
Padalium murex, 321
Pedicularis, 315, 316
Pedilanthes, 211
Peganum harmala, 203
Pelargonium, capitatum, 198
—graveolens, 198
—nodule, 198
—odoratissimus, 198
—zonale, 197, 198
Pelican flower, 138
Pelletiera, 283
Penaceaceae, 257
Penine, 9
Pennisetum typhoides, 72
Pentacycliae, 31
Pentalacunar, 15
Pentandesma butyracea, 248
Pentandria, 20
Pentaphyllaceae, 216
Pentstemon, 316
Pentstemonacanthus, 323
Peperomia, 121
Pera, 215
Pereskia, 260
Pereskieae, 260
Pereskiopsis, 260
Perfectae, 18
Pergularia daemia, 298, 299
Periplocaceae, 294
Periplocoideae, 297, 298

Perowskia, 209
Persea americana, 168
Perseoides, 169
Persimon, 284
Personales, 296, 310
Petagnia, 273
Petha, 328
Petiveriaceae, 143
Petrea volubilis, 306
Petrosavia, 100
Petrosavieae, 101
Petroselinum crispum, 278
Petunia, 313
Phaeophyta, 11
Phanerogamae, 22, 26
Phanerogams, 18
Pharmacognosy, 409
Phaseolus lunatus, 195
—radiatus, 384
—vulgaris, 195
Phellie, 224
Phellinaceae, 224
Phenology, 37
Philadelphaceae, 184
Philadelphus, 183
—coronarius, 184
Philesiaceae, 32
Philodendroideae, 8, 87
Philosophia Botanica, 18, 48
Philydraceae, 89
Phlogacanthus, 323
—thyrsiflorus, 320, 325
Phlomis, 310
Phoebe, 168
Phoeniceae, 83
Phoenix, 78, 80
—dactylifera, 80, 82
—paludosa, 79
—sylvestris, 80, 82
Phunti, 328
Phyla nodiflora, 302
Phylica, 225
Phylla, 306
Phyllantheae, 214, 215
Phyllanthus, 211
—flutians, 211
—niruri, 212, 214
simplex, 212
Phyllobotryeae, 255
Phyllobotrium, 254
Phyllochlamis, 128
Phyllospadix, 60
Phyllospermae-Stachyospermae, 16, 321
Phylogenetic system, 26
Phyrma leptostachya, 306
Phyrmaceae, 299
Phyrmineae, 295
Physalis, 312
—alkekengi, 312
—peruviana, 312
Physopsis, 306
Phytelephantoideae, 83
Phytelephas macrocarpa, 83
Phyteuma, 335
Phytochoria, 348
Phytogeographic divisions, 348
—of India, 352
Phytogeography, 375
Phytolacca decandra, 148
Phytolaccaceae, 141, 147
Phytolaccineae, 141
Phytonic theory, 5
Phytons, 5
Picrasma excelsa, 207
Picrodendraceae, 123
Pieris, 276
Pilocarpus pennatifolius, 205
Pimenta dioica, 270
—racemosa, 270
Pimpinella anisum, 278
—Heyniana, 278
Pinanga, 79, 81
Pinax theatri Botanic, 17
Pinguicula, 322
Pinus excelsa, 136
Piper, 120
—betle, 120
—chaba, 120
—cubebe, 120
—longum, 120
—nigrum, 120
Piperaceae, 120, 121
Piperad, 8
Piperales, 28, 84, 120, 121
Pisonia, 146
Pistacia integerrima, 219
—lentiscus, 220
—terebinthes, 220
—vera, 220
Pistacio nut, 220
Pistia, 84, 86
—stratiotis, 86
Pisum arvens, 382
—exiphiens, 382
—sativum, 193, 382
——var speciosum, 352
Pitcairnia felicina, 96
Pitcarnioideae, 96
Pittosporaceae, 180
Piyal, 220
Plagianthus, 234
Planera abelica, 128
Planitorae, 209
Plant Press, 38

—tumors, 485
Plantaginales, 28
Platanaceae, 180, 186
Platanus orientalis, 186
Platonia insignis, 248
Platylobae, 216
Platylobeae, 176
Platystemon, 170
Plectocomia himalayana, 79
Plectranthus ternifolius, 308
Pleuroplocaceae, 175
Pliny, 17
Plumbaginaceae, 284
Plumbaginales, 28, 284
Plumbagineae, 285
Plumbago, 284
—auriculata, 284
—capensis, 284
—indica, 286
—rosea, 284
—scandens, 284
—zeylanica, 285
Plumeria, 296, 297
—rubra, 294
Plumieroideae, 297
Poaceae, 72
Podandrogynae, 173
Podophyllaceae, 160
Podophyllum, 157
Podostemaceae, 133
Podostemales, 133
Podostemon, 133
Podostemonaceae, 132
Podostemonales, 132
Pogostemon plectranthoides, 309
Polar, 9
Polemoniaceae, 299
Polemoniales, 300
Pollen, 6
—chamber, 6
—culture, 459
—sac, 6
—slide, 9
——tube, 7
Pollination, 7
Pollinium, 115
Polyad, 9
Polyadelphia, 21
Polyalthia longifolia, 160
Polyandria, 20
Polyanthes tuberosa, 104, 105
Polycarpaea, 151
—corymbosa, 152
Polycarpeae, 153
Polycarpicae, 29, 33
Polycarpon, 151
—loeflingiae, 152
Polychondraea, 116
Polygala, 212
—crotalarioides, 212
—senega, 212
—tinctoria, 212
—venenosa, 212
Polygalaceae, 211
Polygalales, 197
Polygalineae, 197
Polygamia, 21
Polygonaceae, 139
Polygonum, 140
—barbatum, 141
—chinensis, 141
—molle, 141
—orientale, 141
—plebeium, 141
—runcinatum, 141
Polypetalae, 23, 24
Polyscias fruticosus, 276
Pomaderris, 225
Pomeae, 188
Pomoideae, 187, 188
Pontederiaceae, 89, 92, 94, 97
Pooideae, 74
Populus, 123
Porantheroideae, 215
Porate, 9
Pornychieae, 153
Pororate, 9
Portia tree, 234
Portulaca garndiflora, 148, 149
—oleracea, 149
—quadrifida, 149
Portulaccaceae, 141, 148
Portulacineae, 141
Posidonia, 60
Posidoniaceae, 62
Posidonieae, 61
Posoqueria, 327
Posta dana, 171
Potaliaceae, 287
Potamogeton, 60, 61
—crispus, 61
—indicus, 61
—natans, 61
Potamogetonaceae, 59
Potamogetonales, 59
Potamogetoneae, 61
Potentilla, 187
Potentillae, 188
Poterieae, 188
Poterium, 187
Pothoideae, 86
Pothos, 84, 86
Pouteria, 282
Pouzolzia, 132

Prasioideae, 310
Pratia, 335
Premna, 306
—barbata, 306
—latifolia, 306
Primrose, 284
Primula, 283
—sinensis, 284
—vulgaris, 284
Primulaceae, 281, 283
Primulales, 28, 281
Primuleae, 283
Principes, 78
Prionium, 98
Pritchardia, 83
Proangiospermae, 31, 32, 33
Prodromus systematis naturalis regni vegitabilis, 23
Prosopanche, 139
Prosopis juliflora, 193
Prostantheroideae, 310
Protangiospermae, 16
Protangiosperm theory, 15
Proteales, 28, 257
Proteragenes, 31
Protoanthophyta, 33
Protolirion, 100
Protoplast culture, 477
—Fusion, 489
—Isolation of, 477
Proximal, 9
Pruneae, 188
Prunoideae, 188
Prunus armeniaca, 187
—domestica, 187
—dulcis, 187
—persica, 187
Pseudosolanioideae, 316
Pseudowolffia, 89
Psidium, 268
—cattleianum, 268
—guajava, 264, 268
Psilophytales, 12
Psilophytinae, 12
Psilopsida, 12, 32
Psilotales, 12
Psilotrichum, 146
Psoralea corylifolia, 264
Pterandra, 208
Pterantheae, 153
Pteranthus, 151
Pterocarpus marsupium, 194
—santalinus, 194
Pteropetalum, 173
Pterospermum acerifolium, 232
Pterostemonoideae, 184
Ptychosperma macartheri, 83
Pueraria mirifica, 194
—Thunbergiana, 194
—tuberosa, 194
Pulmonaria, 303
Pulses, 352
Pumpkin, 328
Punarnaba, 147
Punica granatum, 264
—protopunica, 264
Punicaceae, 261, 263
Pupalia atropurpurea, 146
Putranjiva, 211
—Roxburghii, 212
Puya, 95, 97
Pycnarrhena, 161
Pycnophyllum, 150
Pyramidotorae, 209
Pyrenaria diospyricarpa, 246
Pyrethrum, 336
Pyroideae, 188
Pyrolaceae, 275
Pyrostegia venusta, 320
Pyrrophyta, 11
Pyrularia, 135
Pyrus communis, 187

Q

Quassia amara, 267
Quercus, 125
—suber, 125
Quiabentia, 260
Quiinaceae, 242
Quillaja saponaria, 187
Quillajeae, 188
Quinidine, 373
Quinine, 323, 371, 373
—plant, 371
Quisqualis indica, 267

R

Rabdosia ternifolia, 308
Rachis, 69, 74
Rachilla, 69, 74
Radii, 252
Radiola, 202
Rafflesia Arnoldi, 139
Rafflesiaceae, 135, 137
Rafflesiales, 137
Rajanigandha, 104
Rambutan, 222
Ramie, 132
Ranales, 28, 30, 32, 153
Ranalisma, 63, 64
—rostrata, 64
—humilis, 64

Randia, 326
Ranunculaceae, 153, 158
Ranunculales, 153
Ranunculineae, 153
Ranunculoideae, 33, 120, 153
Ranunculus ficaria, 160
—sceleratus, 158, 160
Rapataceae, 89
Raphanus sativus, 176
Raphidophora, 85
Raphis flabelliformis, 83
—humilis, 83
Rauvolfia, 296, 413
—beddomei, 404
—decurva, 404
—densiflora, 404
—micrantha, 404
—serpentina, 297, 404, 413
—tetraphylla, 297, 404
Rauvolfinine, 374
Ravenala, 108
—madagascariensis, 109
Reinwardtia tetragyna, 202
—trigyna, 202
Reissekia, 225
Resedaceae, 169
Resedales, 169
Resedineae, 169
Reserpine, 374
Reserpinine, 374
Restionaceae, 71, 72, 89
Restionales, 90
Rhabdodenadron, 327
Rhamnaceae, 224
Rhamnales, 28, 224
Rhamnus, 225
—cathartica, 225
—chlorophora, 225
—infectoria, 225
—nepalensis, 225
—purshiana, 225
—virgata, 225
Rheum, 141
Rhinanthoideae, 316
Rhinacanthus, 323
Rhipsalis, 260
Rhiziocarya, 161
Rhizophora mucronata, 264
Rhizophoracdae, 261, 264
Rhodochiton, 315
Rhododendroideae, 280
Rhododendron, 280
—arboreum, 280
—campanulatum, 280
—cinnabarinum, 280
—dalhousie, 280
—falconeri, 280
—Leschenaultianum, 280
Rhodoleiaceae, 186
Rhodoleioideae, 185
Rhodophyta, 11, 12
Rhodophytes, 31
Rhoeadales, 169
Rhoeadineae, 169
Rhoeo discolor, 91
Rhoipteliaceae, 123
Rhopalochnemis phalloides, 137
Rhus, 218
—coriaria, 220
—cotinus, 218
—glabra, 220
—khasiana, 219, 220
—punjabensis, 219
—styphina, 220
—succedanea, 220
—toxicodendron, 220
—venenata, 218, 220
—vernicifera, 220
Rhynchospora, 76
Rhynchosporoideae, 77
Ribes alpina, 183
—grossularia, 184
Ribesioideae, 184
Rice, 341
Richard von Wettstein, 29
Ricineae, 215
Ricinocarpoideae, 215
Ricinodendron, 213
Ricinus communis, 212
Rinorea, 252
Rinoreae, 253
Rivina humilis, 148
Rochester Code, 48
Romulea, 106
Root culture, 444
Roridulaceae, 180
Rorippa, 174
Rosa centifolia, 187
—damascena, 187
Rosales, 28, 180
Rosamarinus officinalis, 310
Roscheria, 81
Rose apple, 266
Roseae, 188
Roselle, 234
Rosideae, 33
Rosineae, 180
Rosoideae, 188
Rostellum, 115
Rotala, 262
Roxburgh, William, 21, 45
Roxburghiaceae, 97
Roystonia, 80
—regia, 83

Royllea calycina, 310
Rubia, 326
—cordifolia, 328
—tinctoria, 328
Rubiaceae, 278, 325
Rubiales, 28, 325
Rubieae, 189
Rubioideae, 327
Rubiteueris palmata, 309
Rubus caesius, 187
Rudbekia, 337
Ruellia, 323
Rules of Nomenclature, 49
Rumex, 140
—vescicarius, 141
Ruppia, 60, 61
—rostellata, 61
Rungia repens, 324
Ruscaceae, 32, 97, 101, 102
Ruscineae, 101
Ruscus, 99, 100
Ruta, 204
—graveolens, 205
Rutaceae, 196
Rutales, 196
Rye, 72

S

Sabai grass, 73
Sabal, 79
Sabalae, 83
Sabiaceae, 216
Sabineae, 216
Saccharum arundinaceum, 73
—munja, 73
—officinarum, 72, 380
—robustum, 381
—sinense, 381
—spontaneum, 73
Safed, Kadu, 328
Safra Kumra, 328
Sageretia theezans, 225
Sagina apetala, 151
Sagittaria humilis, 64
—sinensis, 63, 64
Sal, 246, 370
Salicaceae, 122, 123
Salicales, 28, 122
Salicornia herbacea, 141
Salix tetrasperma, 123
Salomonia, 209, 210
Salpiglossidaceae, 310
Salpiglossideae, 313
Salpiglossis, 312
Salvadoraceae, 216, 285
Salvia, hydrangea, 308
—plectranthoides, 309
—plebeia, 309
Salviacanthus 323
Samadera indica, 207
Samaruba amara, 207
Sambucineae, 330
Sambucus, 329
—javanicus, 330
Samoleae, 283
Samolus, 283
Samyda, 250
Sandal wood tree, 135
Sanicula, 277
Saniculoideae, 278
Sansevieria, 105
Santalaceae, 134
Santalales, 28, 134
Santalinae, 134
Santalum album, 135
Santara, 206
Sapindaceae, 216, 220
Sapindales, 28, 196, 216
Sapindinicae, 216
Sapindoideae, 222
Sapindus, 221
—mukorossi, 222
—saponaria, 222
—trifoliatus, 222
Sapium sebiferum, 213
Saponaria vaccaria, 152
Sapotaceae, 286
Sapotales, 287
Sapotineae, 286
Sapria himalayana, 139
Saraca asoka, 193
Sarangadhara, 19
Sararanga, 57, 58
Sarcandra, 120, 122
Sarcobatus, 143
—maximiliani, 143
Sarcocaulon, 197
Sarcocephalus, 326, 327
Sarcococca pruniformis, 219
Sarcolaenaceae, 229
Sarcophyte, 137
Sarcosperma, 286
Saritaea magnifica, 320
Sarracenia, 177
Sarraceniaceae, 176, 177
Sarraceniales, 28, 132, 176
Sarsaparila, 101, 272, 294
Saruma, 137, 138
Saussurea, 338
—candicans, 339
—lappa, 340
Sauvagesia, 241

Savannah, 383
Saxifraga, 183
Saxifragaceae, 180, 183
Saxifragales, 132, 181
Saxifragineae, 180
Saxifragoideae, 184
Schefflera, 276
—elata, 276
Scheuchzeriaceae, 59
Schima wallichii, 246
Schizandra, 162
Schizandraceae, 153
Schizanthus, 312
Schizeilema, 276
Schizomycophyta, 11, 12
Schizopepon, 331
Schleichera, 221
—oleosa, 222
Shoot apex culture, 446
Schoenia. 337
Schrebera, 290
—swietenioides, 290
Schweinfurth, 41
Scidotonia, 161
Scilla, 101
Scindapsus, 85
Scirpoideae, 77
Scirpus articulatus, 76
—grossus, 77
Scitaminae, 27, 107
Sclerantheae, 153
Sclerotesta, 153
Scolopieae, 254
Scolynus hispanicus, 341
Scoparia dulcis, 316
Scrophularia, 315
Scrophulariaceae, 299, 315
Scrophulariales, 300
Scutellaria, 309
Scutellarioideae, 310
Scutellum, 69
Scytopetalaceae, 228
Scytopetalineae, 228
Secale cereale, 72, 73
Secamone, 297
Sechium edule, 333
Secondary nucleus, 7
—metabolic products, 430
Section, 4
—, Sub, 4
Securidaca, 209, 210
Sedum, 182
Seetzenia, 195, 203
Semecarpeae, 220
Semecarpus, 218
—anacardium, 220
Senecianeae, 339
Senecio, 338
Series, 4
—, Sub, 4
Serjania, 221
Sesbania grandiflora, 195
Sesamum angustifolium, 321
. —indicum, 321
Seseli indicum, 278
Sesuvium portulacastrum, 149
Setaria glauca, 70
Setcreasia purpurea, 91
Sharbati nimbu, 206
Shefali, 286
Shephalika, 302
Shorea, 246
—aptera, 247
—Koordarsii, 251
—robusta, 250, 251, 400
Sicyoideae, 328
Sicyos, 332
Siddhi, 131
Sideroxylon, 286
Siegesbeckia orientalis, 339
Silybium, 335
Simarubaceae, 197, 207
Simaruba amara 207
Single cell culture 475
Siphocampylos, 337
Sisal hemp, 389
Sisyrhinchieae, 106,
Sisyrhinchium, 106
Skimmia laureola, 205
Sladenia, 245
Smilacaceae, 32, 97, 101, 102
Smilacoideae, 101
Smitax, 99
—macrophylla, 101
—sarsa-parila,.101
Smith Gilbert, 32
Smyrna fig, 379
Snake gourd, 328
Solanaceae, 299, 311
Solanad, 8
Solanales, 300
Solaneae, 313
Solanineae, 299, 314
Solanum jasminoides, 312
—melongena, 312
—surattense, 312
—torvum, 311
—trilobatum, 312
—tuberosum, 312
—Wenlandii,, 312
Soldanella, 283
Somatic embryogenesis, 470
—hybridization, 481
Someraj, 335

Sonerila, 271
So oneratiaceae, 257
Sophora, 191, 195
Sopubia, 315
Sorghum vulgare var. saccharum, 72
Sorosis, 128
Sosha, 328
Sowa, 274
Soya bean, 194
Soyauxia, 250
Soymida, 206
—febrifuga, 207
Spadiciflorae, 31
Spanish gourd, 328
Sparganiaceae, 57
Spathela, 133
Spathelia, 205
Spathicarpa, 87
Spathiflorae, 27, 78
Spathiphyllum, 86
Spathodea, 318
—campanulata, 319
Species, 3, 4
—plantarum, 18
Specific epithet, 48
Specularia, 332
Spergula, 151
—avensis, 152
Spergulae, 153
Spermacoce, 326
Spermatophyta, 11, 12, 31
Sphaeranthus indicus, 334
Sphagnum, 18
Sphenoclea zeylanica, 336
Sphenocleaceae, 334, 336
Sphenodesma, 306
Sphenopsida, 12, 32
Spigeliaceae, 287
Spikelet, 68, 69
Spilanthes, 337
Spinacea, 143
—oleracea, 144
Spinifex littoralis, 72
Spiraea, 187
Spiraeeae, 188
Spiraeoideae, 187, 188
Spirodela, 88
Spondias, 218
—mombin, 220
—pinnata, 220
—purpurea, 220
Spondieae, 220
Sporobolus, 71
Sporoderm, 9
—morphology, 9
Sporogenous cells, 6
Sporophylls, 6
Sporophyte, 8
Sporopollinin, 9
Squamulae intravaginalis, 59
Stachydoideae, 306
Stachys, 310
Stachytarpheta indica, 306
Stachyuraceae, 243, 253
Stackhousiaceae, 216
Stapelia, 297
Staphyliaceae, 216
Staticeae, 285
Stavesacree, 160
Stele, 5
Stelechocarpus, 164
Stellaria media, 152
Stemonaceae, 97
Stemotria, 316
Stenolobeae, 212, 215
Stephania, 161
—japonica, 162
—oynantha, 162
Stephen Endlicher, 25
Sterculiaceae, 228, 229, 231
Stereospermum, 318
—personatum, 319
—suvacolens, 319
Stewartia, 242
Stigmatophyllon, 208
Stilbe, 306
Stilbeae, 308
Streblus, 128
—asper, 129
Strelitzia, 108, 109
Strelitziaceae, 107, 108, 109
Strelitzioideae, 109
Streptolirion cordifolium, 92
Streptothamnus, 254
Striga, 315
Strobilanthus, 323
Strobyloideae, 29
Strychnaceae, 291
Strychnos, 291
—nux-vomica, 292
—potatorum, 292
—toxifera, 292
Styracaceae, 286
Stylidiaceae, 334
Suaeda, 143
—fruticosa, 144
—maritima, 144
Sugarcane, 72, 380
Sugar maple, 227
Sulpha, 274
Sumatra camphor, 247
Sundari tree 232
Sun flower, 335
Superae, 31

Suran, 85
Suregada, 212
Suregadeae, 216
Surinam Cherry, 266
Suritonia, 218
Susruta Samhita, 18
Susum, 90
Swartzieae, 195
Swertia, 293
—angustifolia, 415
—chirayita, 294, 401, 414
—corymbosa, 415
—decussata, 415
—pulchella, 415
Swintonia, 218
—floribunda, 220
Swietenia, 206
—macrophylla, 207
—mahagony, 207
Symbegonia, 258, 259
Sympetalae, 26, 279
Symplectochilus, 323
Symplocaceae, 286
Symphorema, 306
Symphoremeae, 308
Symphoricarpus, 329
Synanthae, 27, 28
Synaptantha, 327
Synergids, 7
Syringa, 290
Systematics, 3
Syzygium aromaticum, 270
—cumini, 270
—jambos, 269, 270
—malaccense, 270
—samarangense, 270

T

Tabashir, 73
Tabebuia, 46, 318
—chrysantha, 320
—donnel-smithii, 320
—rosea, 320
Taccaceae, 97
Tagetis erecta, 340
—patula, 340
Takhtajan, Armen, 33
Talauma, 162
Talinum, 149
Tallow tree, 213
Talmuli, 92, 104
Tamal tree, 168
Tamaricaceae, 242, 251
Tamericales, 243, 252
Tamaricineae, 242
Tamarindus indica, 193
Tamarix articulata, 251
—gallica, 251
——var, mannifera, 251
—Troupii, 251
Tanacetum cinerariefolium, 341
Tapiary, 43
Tapioca, 213
Taraxacum Koksaghyz, 407
Tarbuz, 333
Taxodium distichum, 46
Taxon, 3
Taxonomy, 3
—alpha, 3
—classical, 3
—experimental, 3
—numerical, 3
—omega, 3
—orthodox, 3
Taxotropis, 128
Tea, Black, 367
—, Brick, 367
—, Green, 367
—oil, 242
—, Oolong, 367
—plant, 242, 365
—tree, 266,
Teak tree, 309, 349
Tecklea, 205
Tecoma stans, 320
Tecomaria capensis, 320
Tecomeae, 319
Tecophilaeaceae, 32, 97, 101, 102
Tetona grandis, 304, 399
Teesdalia, 174
Tejpatra, 168
Telakucha, 328
Telome, 5
Tenagocharis, 65
—lanceolatus, 66
Terebinthaceae, 206
Terebinthales, 206
Terebinthenae, 206
Terminalia Arjuna, 267
—bellirica, 267, 420
—catappa, 267
—chebula, 267, 421
—ivorensis, 267
—sericea, 267
—superba, 267
—tomentosa, 267
Terniola, 134
Ternstroemia, 245
Tessarandra, 290
Tetra-aperturate, 9
Tetracentraceae, 164
Tetracentron, 152
Tetracera empedoclea, 244

Tetracycliae, 31
Tetrad, 9
Tetradynamia, 20
Tetragonia expansa, 149
Tetramerantheae, 166
Tetrandria, 20
Tetrapoma, 174
Tetrastigma, 227
Teucrium, 309
Thalamiflorea, 22, 24, 26
Thalictrum, 159
Thallophyta, 11, 26, 32
Theaceae, 238, 239, 241
Theales, 229, 239
Theineae, 238, 239
Thelygonaceae, 257
Theobroma cacao, 232
Theophrastaceae, 277
Theophrastus, 17
Theorie elementaire de la botanique, 48
Thespesia populnea, 234
Thevetia, 296
—peruviana, 297
Thismiaceae, 113
Thladiantha, 332
Thunberg, 21
Thunbergia, 323
—coccinea, 324
—grandiflora, 320, 325
Thunbergieae, 324
Thunbergioideae, 324
Thurniaceae, 89
Thymelaeaceae, 261
Thymelaeales, 143
Thymelaeineae, 261
Thymus serpyllum, 309
—vulgaris, 10
Tibouchina semidecandra, 272
Ticorea, 205
Tigellum, 6
Tilia europia, 230
Tiliaceae, 228, 229
Tiliacora, 161
Tiliales, 229
Tillandsia, 95
—usnioides, 97
Tillandsioideae, 96
Tinospora cordifolia, 162, 202
Tippo, Oswald, 32
Tisi, 202
Tissue culture, 425
—ground, 5
—vascular, 5
Tiwrea febrifuga, 205
Tobacco, Central Asian, 308
—Virginian, 308
Toddalia, 205
Toona, 206
Torenia cordata, 316
Tournefort, Jesoph Pitt, 18
Tovariaceae, 169
Tovomita, 247
Toxicodendron, 213
Tracheophyta, 11, 32
Trachycarpus martiana, 79
Trachyspermum ammi, 273
Tradescantieae, 91
Tragia, 211
—involucrata, 212
Tragopogon gracile, 339
Trapaceae, 261, 272
Trapa bispinosa, 273
—natans, 272
Trapella, 321
Trema, 127
Tremandaceae, 196, 209
Trewia, 210
—nudiflora, 212
Triandra, 19
Trianthema portulacastrum, 149
Triaperturate, 9
Tribe, 4
—sub, 4
Tribulus terrestris, 203
Tribonanthes, 103
Trichosanthes anguina, 333
—bracteata, 333
—cucumerina, 333
—dioica, 333
Trichostephaneae, 255
Trichostephanus, 254
Tricoceae, 196, 213
Tricyrites, 100
Tridax procumbens, 338, 339
Trientalis, 283
Trifolium subterraneum, 192
Trigonella foenum-graecum, 195
Trigoniaceae, 196, 209
Trigoniastrum, 209
Trilacunar, 15
Trilliaceae, 32, 97, 101, 102
Triosteum, 330
Triphasia, 204
Triplaris, 140
Tristicha, 133
Triticum aestivum, 72, 372
—dicoccum, 72, 373
—durum, 72, 373
—monococcum, 72, 373
—polonicum, 73, 373
—spelta, 73, 373
—sphaerococcum, 73, 373
—turgidum, 373
Triuridales, 26, 68, 71

Trochlea, 253
Trochodendraceae, 153
Trochodendrales, 33, 153
Trochodendrineae, 153
Tropaeolaceae, 196, 199
Tropaeolum majus, 199, 200
Tryphostemma, 256
Tube rose, 104
Tubiflorae, 28, 299
Tubuliflorae, 334
Tulip tree, 163
Tulipa, 99
Tunicate, 17
Turgenia latifolia, 274
Turion, 66
Turneraceae, 239, 253
Turpinia, 221
Type, Nomenclatural, 49
—basis Code, 48
—concept, 48
Typha angustata, 56
—elephantina, 56
Typhaceae, 55
Typhales, 32, 55, 78
Typhonium, 86

U

Ullucus tuberosus, 149
Ulmaceae, 127
Ulmarieae, 188
Ulmus, 127, 128
Umbellales, 274
Unmebelliferae, 275, 276
Umbelliflorea, 28, 274
Uncaria, 326
— gambier, 328
Uncinia, 76
Unilacunar, 15
Unisexuales, 25, 26
Upaban Vinoda, 19
Upaca, 215
Upas tree, 130
Urena, 234
Urginea, 101
Urtica, 132
Urticaceae, 127, 131
Urticaeflorae, 127
Urticales, 28, 127
Usteria, 291
Utricularia, 322
Uvaria hamiltoni, 165
Uvarieae, 166

V

Vacciniaceae, 279
Vaccinioideae, 281
Vaccinium, 280
Vahlia oldenlandioides, 184
—viscosa, 184
Vahliaceae, 184
Valecullae, 272
Valerian root, 331
Valariana officinalis, 331
—olitoria, 331
Valarianaceae, 325, 330
Valerianales, 325
Valerius Cordus, 17
Vallaris, 296
Vallisneria, 66
—spiralis, 66, 67
Valve, 69
Valvule, 69
Vangueria, 327
—edulis, 329
Vanilla planifolia, 116
Variety, 4
—sub, 4
Vascular plants, 6
Vasculares, 22
Vasculum, 38
Vateria, 250
—indica, 251
Vatica, 250
Vegetation of India, 356
Vegetative cell, 6
Velamen, 114
Velloziaceae, 97, 105
Ventilago, 225
—maderaspatana, 225
Veratrum album, 101
Verbascum, 315
Verbena, 306
Verbenaceae, 299, 305
Verbenales, 300
Verbeneae, 308
Verbenineae, 299
Vernonia arborea, 335
Vernonieae, 339
Veronica, 316
Verticillatae, 28, 118
Vetiveria zizanioides, 72
Viburneae, 330
Viburnum, 329
—opulus, 329
Vicariads, 377
Vicia amphicarpa, 192
—faba, 194
Victoria, 156
—amazonica, 46
—regia, 157
Vigna mungo, 194
—radiata, 194, 384
— —var. aurea, 384

— —var. brunga, 384
— —var. glabra, 384
— —var. grandis, 384
— —var. radiatus, 384
— —var. sublobatus, 384
Viliceae, 308
Vinca, 296
Viola, 252
—odorata, 253
—tricolor, 253
Violaceae, 243, 252
Violales, 243, 252, 253
Violeae, 253
Violoideae, 253
Viscum, 135
—album, 136
—articulatum, 136
—monoicum, 136
—orientale, 136
Vitaceae, 224, 225, 226
Vitex, 302
—negundo, 306
—peduncularis, 306
Vitidaceae, 228
Vitis aestivalis, 227
—labrusca, 227
—vinifera, 226, 227
Vittae, 272
Vittelaria mamosa, 287
Vivania, 197
Vochysiaceae, 196
Voyria, 293
Vriesia, 97

W

Wahlenbergia gracilis, 335
—marginata, 335
Wallace, 19
Wallich, Nathaniel, 45
Wallichia, 81
Wallichian Catalogue, 45
Walsura, 207
Wax gourd, 333
Wedelia calendulacea, 340
Wellstedioideae, 304
Wettstein, Richard von, 29
Wilkesia, 337
William Roxburgh, 21, 45
Winteraceae, 153, 164, 239
Withania somnifera, 312
Wolffia, 88
—arrhiza, 89
Wolffiela, 88
Wolfiopsis, 89
Woodfordia, 262
—fruticosa, 263
Wrightia coccinia, 296
—tinctoria, 297

X—Y

Xanthium strumarium, 339
Xanthophyllum, 209, 210
Xanthosoma maximiliani, 84, 85
Xanthoxylum, 205
Xerophytes, 43
Xylia dolabriformis, 193
Xylocarpus, 206, 207
Xylopia, 164
Xylosma, 254
—longifolium, 254
Xyridaceae, 89
Xyridales, 89
Yesterday, today & tomorrow plant, 308
Yucca, 82, 101, 105
—filamentosa, 101

Z

Zamiae, 23
Zamin Kanda, 85
Zannichellia, 60, 61
—palustris, 61
Zannichelliaceae, 62
Zannichellieae, 61
Zanonia, 332
Zanonieae, 333
Zantedeschia, 85
Zea mays, 70, 72, 74, 374
Zebrina pendula, 91
Zehneria umbellata, 333
Zelkova cretica, 128
Zephyranthes roseus, 104
Ziegenspeck, H. 35
Zingiber casumunar, 413
—mioga, 412, 413
—officinalis, 110, 411
—zerumbet, 110, 412, 413
Zingiberaceae, 107, 109
Zingiberales, 107
Zingiberoideae, 110
Zinnia elegans, 340
—pauciflora, 340
Ziziphora, 309
Zizyphus jujuba, 225
—mauritiana, 225
—oenoplia, 225
—vulgaris, 225
Zostera, 60, 61
Zostereae, 61
Zoysia, 70
Zygogynum, 162
Zygophyllaceae, 196, 202, 203